UNIX®
the textbook   second edition

Syed Mansoor Sarwar
Lahore University of Management Sciences

Robert Koretsky
University of Portland

Syed Aqeel Sarwar
GE Capital IT Solutions

PEARSON

Addison
Wesley

Boston San Francisco New York
London Toronto Sydney Tokyo Singapore Madrid
Mexico City Munich Paris Cape Town Hong Kong Montreal

Senior Acquisitions Editor	Michael Hirsch
Project Editor	Katherine Harutunian
Production Supervisor	Marilyn Lloyd
Project Management	Keith Henry/Dartmouth Publishing, Inc.
Marketing Manager	Michelle Brown
Composition and Art	Dartmouth Publishing, Inc.
Text Design	Alisa Andreola/Dartmouth Publishing, Inc.
Cover Design	Joyce Cosentino Wells
Cover Image	© 2004 PhotoDisc
Prepress and Manufacturing	Caroline Fell

Access the latest information about Addison-Wesley titles from our World Wide Web site: http://www.aw-bc.com/computing

Many of the designations used by manufacturers and sellers to distinguish their products are claimed as trademarks. Where those designations appear in this book, and Addison-Wesley was aware of a trademark claim, the designations have been printed in initial caps or all caps.

The programs and applications presented in this book have been included for their instructional value. They have been tested with care, but are not guaranteed for any particular purpose. The publisher does not offer any warranties or representations, nor does it accept any liabilities with respect to the programs or applications.

UNIX® is a registered trademark of The Open Group in the United States and other countries.

Library of Congress Cataloging-in-Publication Data

Sarwar, Syed Mansoor.
 Unix : the textbook / Syed Mansoor Sarwar, Robert Koretsky, Syed Aqeel [sic] Sarwar.-- 2nd ed.
  p. cm.
 Includes bibliographical references and index.
 ISBN 0-321-22731-X
 1. UNIX (Computer file) 2. Operating systems (Computers) I. Koretsky, Robert. II. Sarwar, Syed Aqeel. III. Title.

 QA76.76.O63S3555 2004
 005.2'82--dc22

                                    2004008954

ISBN 0-321-22731-X

1 2 3 4 5 6 7 8 9 10–PH–07 06 05 04

Dedications

To my teachers	S.M.S.
To my family	R.M.K.
To my parents	S.A.S.

Preface

The Matured Subject

Since the first edition of this book, very little has been introduced in the world of business, scientific, or engineering computing and computer science that was either patently expected or blatantly announced in advance, and perhaps this is a mark of just how developed these disciplines have become. Still, the disciplines remain pervasive, and are notoriously segregated into the "open source" and proprietary camps. But the entrenched powers—whether legitimate or licentious—that dominate the business of computing continue to grow, and now reach an incredible level of influence on the distribution, consumption, and assimilation of information in the transnational marketplace. Commensurate with this growth, UNIX and its clones now almost exclusively control the service of information globally, and from all indications, this control will not be relinquished in the near future.

Changes in the Second Edition of This Book

Because UNIX has some important functional additions to the application user's interface since the first edition came out, and because UNIX is an even more widely dispersed system in the marketplace than it previously was, the authors felt that the book needed new instructional material to cover these additions, to include:

- Implementations of UNIX in a broader context rather than just demonstrating the surviving variants of the system
- A complete tutorial section on the XFree86 KDE GUI
- A description of Mac UNIX as seen in the Aqua GUI
- A "Quick Start Guide to UNIX" as Chapter Zero, to allow new users to get hands-on experience
- Many new diagrams, tables, interactive shell sessions, in-chapter tutorials, in-chapter exercises, and end-of-chapter problems
- Enhanced coverage in the chapter on networking by adding a section on RFCs, revising the coverage of domain name hierarchy, and describing the various organizations that set Internet standards and plan for its growth
- Coverage of new commands such as `ssh`, `scp`, `sftp`, `host`, and `dig`, and enhanced coverage of existing commands such as `telnet` and `finger`
- URLs of important Web resources about the history of UNIX and various commands and programming tools
- Supplemental materials, including an online Lab Manual with additional problem sets, and a test bank for each chapter
- A redesign of the text layout to provide a more usable reference to programmers

When you look at these additions, the sequence and presentation of all the material in the book, keep in mind that the authors have a cumulative total of almost 40 years in practical teaching experience at the college level. As educators, the authors retain an unwillingness to use either the large, intractable UNIX reference sources, or the short, "nutshell" guides in order to teach meaningful, complete, and relevant introductory classes on the subject. The authors still feel very strongly that a textbook approach, with pedagogy incorporating in-chapter tutorials and exercises, as well as useful problem sets at the end of each chapter, allows a presentation of all the important UNIX topics for a classroom lecture-laboratory-homework presentation. The fine-tuned second edition of this textbook achieves a consistent manner of optimal learning outcomes (i.e., a well thought-out sequence of old and new topics, well-developed and timely lessons, online laboratory problems, and homework exercises/problems synchronized with the progression of the chapters in the book). As in the earlier edition, the in-depth coverage of the topics presented in this textbook will provide anyone interested in furthering their professional knowledge of the subject matter with useful information.

The Purposes of the Second Edition

The primary purpose remains a didactic description of the UNIX application user's interface (AUI), and the authors try to provide this in a way that gives the reader insight into the inner workings of the system, along with explanations of some important UNIX concepts, data structures, and algorithms. Notable examples of the inner workings of the system as revealed in this edition are the in-depth descriptions of the UNIX file, process, and I/O redirection concepts. The secondary purpose of this textbook is to describe some of the most important UNIX software engineering tools for developers of C/C++ software and shell scripts. As in the first edition, the authors do not describe the UNIX application's programmer's interface (API) in terms of C/C++ libraries and UNIX system calls. In writing this second edition, the authors assumed no previous knowledge of UNIX or programming on the part of the reader.

The Presentation Format

The didactic structure of each chapter in this new edition follows one of two similar formats: the shell session format, or the tutorial format. In the shell session format, (used in all chapters except 5, 6, and 21), the following outline is employed:

1. Learning objectives
2. Introduction
3. Topic discussion and background organized in sections and sub-sections
4. Illustrative commands or topic illustrations presented as actual shell sessions, where the user types in commands shown and results are displayed
5. In-Chapter Exercises that reinforce what was discussed on a topic or done interactively in a shell session
6. Summary
7. End-of-Chapter Problems keyed to topics presented

In the Tutorial Format, (used in Chapters 5, 6, and 21), the following outline is used:

1. Learning objectives
2. Introduction
3. Topic discussions and background organized in sections and sub-sections
4. One Example Session and several Practice Session tutorials that illustrate the commands and topics of interest in any particular section or sub-section
5. Illustrative commands or topic illustrations presented as shell sessions, where the user types in commands shown and results are displayed
6. In-Chapter Exercises that reinforce what was discussed on a topic or done interactively in a shell session
7. Summary
8. End-of-Chapter Problems keyed to topics presented

This edition adds new diagrams and tables, and includes many in-chapter tutorials, interactive shell sessions, in-chapter exercises, and end-of-chapter problems. More syntax boxes appear whenever the authors introduce a new command or utility. These syntax boxes provide exact usage of the command (and any other pertinent variants of the basic syntax), its purpose, the output produced by the command, and its useful options and features. In addition, every chapter contains a summary of the material covered in the chapter.

Pathways through the Text

If this book is to be used as the main text for an introductory course in UNIX, all the chapters should be covered, with the possible exception of Chapter 20. If the book is to be used as a companion to another, main text on operating systems concepts and principles course, the coverage of chapters would be dictated by the order in which the main topics of the course are covered but should include Chapters 7, 12, and 13. For use in a C/C++ or Shell programming course, Chapters 0, 7–20 and relevant sections of Chapters 3–6 would be a great help to students. The extent of coverage of Chapter 20 would depend on the nature of the course-partial coverage in an introductory and full coverage in an advanced course.

The Design of Fonts

The following typefaces have been used in the book for various types of text items.

Typeface	Text Type
Boldface Roman	Keywords
`Boldface Monospace`	Any character or string typed at the keyboard (commands, shell variables, and user input)
`Monospace`	Commands, tools, applications, and their options in the text
Italic	A word being used as a word and text being emphasized
Roman	Everything else, including file pathnames

The keyboard presses are enclosed in angle brackets (e.g., <Enter> and <Ctrl-D>). The instruction "press <Ctrl-D>" means to hold the <Ctrl> key down while pressing the <D> key. This instruction is also denoted <Ctrl-D>.

Supplements

A variety of supplemental materials are available to support this textbook.

Materials Available to All Users of This Textbook

To access these materials, go to http://www.aw.com/cssupport

- **Online Lab Workbook** that includes a variety of keystroke-oriented, structured, and open-ended problems for use in a two- to three-hour lab environment
- **Answers** to In-Chapter Exercises
- **Source Code** for C programs and long shell scripts
- Links to other UNIX resources on the Web

Resources Available to Qualified Instructors Only

Please contact your Addison-Wesley representative, or send an e-mail to aw.cse@aw.com, for information on how to access these resources.

- **Test Bank**
- **Powerpoint** slides
- **Solutions** to the problems at the end of each chapter
- **Solutions** to Online Lab Manual Workbook problems

The authors take full responsibility for any errors in this book. Please send error reports and comments to msarwar@lums.edu.pk and bobk@egr.up.edu (or koretsky@up.edu). The authors will incorporate your feedback and fix any errors in subsequent printings.

Acknowledgments

We started writing this second edition during summer 2003 and finished in early summer 2004. The completion of such a large revision would not have been possible without the help of many participants. First and foremost, we sincerely thank the editor of the book, Michael Hirsch, for his support, guidance, reassurance, professionalism, and understanding throughout this project. He is the top of the line. Thanks are extended to Marilyn Lloyd of AWL for her many excellent suggestions and outstanding work in the production phase of this book. We are also grateful to Joyce Wells for designing a beautiful cover for the book. Thanks also to Katherine Harutunian at AWL for her many valuable suggestions and support. The work of the whole Addison Wesley team was superb! Special thanks to Keith Henry, Misty Horten and Alisa Andreola at Dartmouth Publishing for their excellent project management and interior design, and to Lydia Horton for her first-rate copyediting.

We convey our sincere thanks to the following reviewers of this edition, who gave valuable feedback and numerous accurate and insightful comments. We are particularly grateful to Professor Robert Albright, who meticulously read the manuscript and gave many useful suggestions that greatly enhanced the final product.

- Robert Albright   University of Delaware
- Hussein Abdel-Wahab   Old Dominion University
- Dunren Che   Southern Illinois University
- C. Michael Costanzo   University of California, Santa Barbara
- Robert M. Cubert   University of Florida
- James P. Durbano   University of Delaware
- Nisar Hundewale   Georgia State University
- Mark Hutchenreuther   California Polytechnic State University
- Stephen P. Leach   Florida State University
- Susan Lincke-Salecker   University of Wisconsin Parkside
- Mike Qualls   Grossmont Community College
- Daniel Tomasevich   San Francisco State University
- Paul Tymann   Rochester Institute of Technology
- Troy Vasiga   University of Waterloo

We would like to acknowledge Ronald E. Bass, Thomas A. Burns, Chuck Lesko, Toshimi Minoura, Selmer Moen, Gregory B. Newby, Dr. Marianne Vakalis, and Dr. G. Jan Wilms for their insightful comments after reviewing the first edition of this book.

Thanks go to Kent Thompson, Senior System Administrator, University of Portland School of Engineering Computer Network (UPSECN), for kindly contributing the .Xdefaults file found in Chapter 21. Thanks also go to Sheila Smith, Computer Operator, also of UPSECN, for her support in various capacities.

Personal Acknowledgments

Syed Mansoor Sarwar I thank my parents, children, wife, and siblings for their love, support, and trust. They all have been a positive influence in my life and helped me in many ways. My son Hassaan and daughter Maham have been particularly patient and supportive during this project. Thank you for your understanding, guys! The "snug bug" Ibraheem, who has already developed a love for learning and is an avid reader of picture books, is just a joy to have around. *Ibraheem, gidha kidhr hai? Truck aina wadda aiy.* Special thanks to my brother Nadeem and sisters Farhana and Rizwana for their continued encouragement. *Buggie, hun bichian paindian nay?*

I thank my colleagues at the Lahore University of Management Sciences (LUMS) who encouraged and helped me as I wrote this book: Haroon Babri, Mohammad Ali Maud, Syed Zahoor Hassan, Anwar Khurshid, Aamer Mahmood, Sohaib Khan, Shahid Masud,

Tariq Jadoon, Salim Tariq, Zartash Uzmi, Asim Loan, Wasif Khan, Jamshed Khan, Mohammad Ali Khan (MAK), and Nuzhat Kamran. I also thank the many students at the University of Portland, Portland Community College, and LUMS who helped me as I developed the material for the book. Special thanks to my students, Sana Naveed Khawaja and Qudsia Khan, for their help in preparing the Powerpoint slides, and to Mohammad Zia-ur-Rahman for pointing out typos and errors in the first edition of the book, and for helping me with the test bank.

I convey my sincere thanks to my teachers—to whom this book is dedicated—for their devotion to their profession and for motivating me to pursue a teaching career. The teachers who inspired me the most are: Mrs. Haq, Ms. Mir, Mrs. Farooqi, Mrs. Hashim (elementary school); Aslam Nasir, Chishty Sahib, Sabir Sahib, and Akram Akhtar (middle and high school teachers); R. A. Khan, Mohammad Ishaq, and Ghulam us Saqlain Naqvi (college professors); and Shahid Bokhari, Ashraf Iqbal, Noor Sheikh, Sufi Rasheed, Hafiz Mohammad Saeed, Mohammad Ali Maud, Norman Scott, Janice Jenkins, Art Pohm, James Davis, Arthur Oldehoeft, Thomas Piatkowski, Douglas Jacobson, James "Jolly" Triska, Charlie Wright, and David Schmidt (professors at UET Lahore; University of Michigan, Ann Arbor; and Iowa State University). Shahid Bokhari, Art Pohm, James Davis, Arthur Oldehoeft, and David Schmidt played a key role in enhancing my interest in computers, in general, and operating systems and programming languages, in particular. By their inspirational example, Art Pohm and Jim Davis showed me how to advise and mentor my students. Ashraf Iqbal's art of teaching impressed me the most. And, Mohammad Ali Maud taught me what commitment to students really means.

I also thank my co-authors, Bob Koretsky and Aqeel Sarwar, for their help, encouragement, and trust. Bob, I could not have done it without you!

Robert M. Koretsky I thank my wife Kathe, daughter Tara, and son Cody, for all of their love and continued support during this project. I also thank Mansoor Sarwar, for his inspiration and friendship.

Syed Aqeel Sarwar I thank my parents for their personal sacrifices, support, and lasting love. I also thank my elder brother, Syed Mansoor Sarwar, for his continued encouragement and guidance. My special love to *putree*, Mohammad.

Table of Contents

UNIX®

the textbook   *second edition*

A "Quick-Start" into the UNIX Operating System

Objectives

- ■ To introduce the UNIX Text User Interface and show the generic structure of UNIX commands
- ■ To describe how to connect and log on to a computer running UNIX operating system
- ■ To explain how to manage and maintain files and directories
- ■ To show where to get online help for UNIX commands
- ■ To demonstrate the use of a beginner's set of utility commands
- ■ To cover the basic commands and operators `alias`, `biff`, `cal`, `cat`, `cd`, `cp`, `exit`, `hostname`, `login`, `lp`, `lpr`, `ls`, `man`, `mesg`, `mkdir`, `more`, `mv`, `passwd`, `pg`, `pwd`, `rm`, `rmdir`, `talk`, `telnet`, `unalias`, `uname`, `whatis`, `whereis`, `who`, `whoami`, `write`

0.1   Introduction

To commence operating in UNIX, the beginner needs to know five sequential topics, in the order presented here.

1. How to type a syntactically correct command on the UNIX command line, because the predominant mode of interaction with the UNIX system is text-based.

2. How to log in to and log out of a computer running UNIX using one of the standard methods. UNIX allows users to enter the operating system autonomously, construct code by keystrokes, and exit gracefully.

3. How to maintain and organize files. Creating a tree-like structure of folders (also called "directories"), and storing files in a logical fashion in these folders, is a critical role to working efficiently in UNIX.

4. How to get help on commands and their usage. In a command-based environment, being able to find out, in a quick and easy way, how to use a command correctly is imperative to working efficiently.

5. How to execute a small set of essential utility commands to set up or customize your working environment. Once a beginner is familiar with the right way to construct file maintenance commands, adding a set of utility commands makes each session more productive.

To use this chapter successfully as a springboard into the remainder of the book, you should read and follow the instructions in the order presented. Each chapter builds on the information that precedes it and will give you the concepts, command tools, and methods to program in UNIX operating system. In this chapter, the major commands are defined in a "Syntax Box" and will clarify general components for the remainder of the textbook.

SYNTAX

The exact syntax of how a command, its options, and its arguments are typed on the command line

Purpose: The specific purpose of the command

Output: A short description of the results of executing the command

Commonly used option/features:

                   A listing of popular and most useful options and option arguments

---

0.2   The Structure of a UNIX Command

Because UNIX is unique for being a text-based interface, correctly typed syntax is critical to ensure subsequent execution of commands.

After a user successfully logs on to a UNIX computer, a shell prompt, such as the $ character, appears on the screen. The shell prompt is simply a message from the computer system to say that it is ready to accept keystrokes in the command line that directly follows the prompt. The general syntax, or structure, of a *single* command (as opposed to a command line that may have *multiple* commands typed on the same line separated with input and output redirection characters) as it is typed on the command line is as follows:

```
$ command [[-]option(s)] [option argument(s)] [command argument(s)]
```

where:

`$` is the command line or **shell prompt** from the computer and anything enclosed in [ ] is not always needed,

`command` is the name of the valid UNIX command for that shell in lowercase letters,

`[-option(s)]` is one or more modifiers that change the behavior of `command`,

`[option argument(s)]` is one or more modifiers that change the behavior of `[-option(s)]`, and

`[command argument(s)]` is one or more objects that are affected by `command`.

Note the following four essentials.

1. A space separates commands, options, option arguments, and command arguments, but no space is necessary between multiple option(s) or multiple option arguments.
2. The order of multiple options or option arguments is irrelevant.
3. A space character is optional between the option and the option argument.
4. Always press the `<Enter>` key to submit the command for interpretation and execution.

The following are examples of commands typed on the UNIX command line after the `$` prompt. These examples illustrate some of the variations of the correct syntax for a single command that may have options and arguments.

```
$ ls
$ ls -la
$ ls -la m*
$ lpr -Pspr -n 3 proposal.ps
```

The first example contains only the command. The second contains the command `ls` and two options, `l` and `a`. The third contains the command `ls`; two options, `l` and `a`; and a command argument, `m*`. The fourth contains the command `lpr`; two options, `P` and `n`; two option arguments, `spr` and `3`; and a command argument, `proposal.ps`. (Note that these items are case-specific.)

You must also use the following rule of thumb: If the command executes properly, then you are returned to the shell prompt; if it does not execute properly, then you get an error message displayed on the command line, and you are returned to the shell prompt. For example, if you type xy on the command line and then press <Enter>, usually you will get an error message saying that no such command can be found, and you are returned to the shell prompt so that you can keystroke a valid command. This rule of thumb does not ensure that what you wanted to achieve by typing the syntactically correct command on the command line will be achieved; that is, you could execute a command and get no error messages, but the command may not have done the things you wanted it to do, simply because you used it with the wrong options or command arguments.

0.3   Logging On and Logging Off

There are three steps of a typical UNIX session: getting access to a UNIX system properly in an autonomous way, doing your work, and then leaving in a graceful manner. The first step is done using one of three general categories for connecting and logging in to a UNIX system, which we define and explain in more detail in Chapter 3, Section 3.4. These general categories are:

1. *Local Area Network (LAN) Connection.* When you use this method, you sit at a computer that acts like a "terminal." It is connected by a high-speed communications link to another single computer or multiple computers that are all interconnected with a Local Area Network. At the terminal, and the console or command window that appears on its screen, your interface with the operating system runs on a single or multiple computer(s). This method could also be called intranet log-in. This is a shared resource method, where several users on many different terminals can share a single UNIX system.

2. *Internet Connection.* You sit at a remote, stand-alone computer, and via software such as PuTTY or Windows Telnet, you connect to another system over a moderately high-speed telecommunications link. The PuTTY or telnet software then becomes your graphical server, allowing you to log on and use a remote computer or system that is running UNIX. This method can also be called Internet log-in. This is a shared resource method, where several users on many different remote computers can share a single UNIX system.

3. *Stand-Alone Connection.* This method, probably the most rare case, involves sitting at a computer that is not hooked up to a LAN, intranet, or Internet. Rather, the connection is dedicated to a single user who is at the computer and is logging on to use UNIX on that hardware platform only. The first two methods, described in this list, open the console or terminal windows that look and feel exactly like your interaction with UNIX in this third method.

In the following section, we detail three popular ways of connecting and logging on and logging off a computer running the UNIX system. These methods, and their associated general connection categories from the preceding list, are:

1.   Connecting via a UNIX terminal–intranet or LAN Connection.

2.   Connecting via the PuTTY program using a computer running Microsoft Windows–Internet Connection.

3.   Connecting via a telnet client using a computer running Microsoft Windows–Internet Connection.

What is common to all three of these methods is that your first task is to identify yourself correctly as a valid and autonomous user to the UNIX system. Doing so involves typing in a valid **username**, or **log-in name**, consisting of a string of valid characters. You then have to type in a valid **password** for that **username**.

   NOTE CAREFULLY: Before proceeding with the remainder of this chapter, you should determine which one of the preceding three methods you will use to connect and log in to a UNIX system, and then select from the three following sections that give the details for how to use that method correctly. If you cannot determine this on your own, get help from your instructor or the system administrator at your site. Or, on your own, try each of the methods in succession until you determine which one is applicable to your site and situation.

0.3.1 Connecting via a UNIX Terminal

In this section, it is assumed that you are logging on to a computer running UNIX using the Local Area Network Connection and are typing commands into a console window or terminal screen displayed on-screen. What you type in is shown as follows in **bold** text and is always followed by pressing the <Enter> key on the keyboard. As previously stated, when you log in, identifying yourself to the UNIX system is your first task. Doing so involves typing in a valid username, or log-in name, consisting of a string of valid characters. Then you type in a valid password for that username. If you don't know the valid characters to input your username and password, ask your system administrator or instructor. Depending on the way your system administrator has set up your particular installation, the log-in prompt appears in different formats on your screen. Also, an optional message from the system administrator might appear on your screen announcing news or important information. The following is a typical log-in procedure.

```
login: your_username <Enter>

password: your_password <Enter>

NOTICE:   1. This machine is rebooted at 4:15 AM daily.

          2. Please keep accounts below 100 MB. (du)

          3. Limit TOTAL modem connect times to ONE hour from the hours of
             5:00 PM to midnight.

You have new mail.

DISPLAY = (upsun17.egr.up.edu:0.0) <Enter>

TERM = (FreeBSD) <Enter>

upibm7.egr.up.edu:~ 1$
```

   In the preceding log-in procedure, in response to the log-in prompt, you should keystroke your_username, and then press <Enter> on the keyboard. Be aware that when typing code, UNIX is case-sensitive. When the password prompt appears, type in your_password, and then press <Enter> on the keyboard. In the preceding typical log-in procedure, the NOTICE and prompt declaring that you have new mail is part of the system administrator's log-in message. The DISPLAY and TERM prompts, and their defaults enclosed in parentheses, allow you to designate what computers will manage the output and input of your command line session.

Finally, the command line prompt appears on-screen, prefaced with the name of the computer you are logged into, and the pathname to the current working directory or folder in the file structure of this computer. In the preceding log-in procedure, this appears as `upibm7.egr.up.edu:~ 1$.`

To terminate your connection with the computer running UNIX, you type `logout` on the command line, and then press `<Enter>` on the keyboard, or on a blank line press and hold down the `<Ctrl-D>` on the keyboard. You will then be logged off the system for the current session with the computer, and the log-in prompt will usually reappear. Logging out is system-dependent, and it is an operation that can be tailored to a specific installation of UNIX by the local system administrator. Because we used the C Shell in the session and example, the `logout` command is the default way of leaving the system. If you use the Bourne shell or Korn shell, pressing `<Ctrl-D>` on the keyboard or typing the command `exit` will accomplish the same thing.

If you started a new shell during your session and didn't exit that shell before logging off, UNIX will prompt **Not login shell**, and you will not be able to log off immediately. *See* Chapter 4 for a more detailed description of what a UNIX shell is. In this case, press `<Ctrl-D>`, and the new shell will terminate. Also, if you started more than one shell and haven't exited from those shells before you log off, you will have to use the `<Ctrl-D>` as many times for each shell before you can log off. On some systems, you type `exit` on the command line to terminate a shell process. In either case, you will then be able to use the log-off procedure described here to leave the system correctly.

0.3.2 Connecting via PuTTY on a Microsoft Windows Machine

In this section, we make these basic assumptions:

1. That you are sitting at a computer running Microsoft Windows, and you are trying to connect and log on to a UNIX operating system using the Internet Connection method.

2. On your Microsoft Windows computer, you first have to connect to the Internet.

3. You have downloaded and installed the PuTTY program on your Microsoft Windows computer, or the system administrator has done so for you. The details of downloading this software and installing it are not given here. The most current download site for the PuTTY program is: http://www.chiark.greenend.org.uk/~sgtatham/putty/download.html

4. You are using PuTTY to make a telnet connection to a UNIX computer, and you know the host name or Internet Protocol (IP) address of the UNIX computer you want to use for this connection.

5. You know a valid username and password pair that will allow you to log in to the UNIX computer.

6. Once you execute the PuTTY program, you use the valid username/password pair, and then you can type commands into a console window or terminal screen. What you type in is shown as follows in **bold** text and is always followed by pressing the `<Enter>` key on the keyboard.

To begin, oîn the Microsoft Windows computer, double click on the PuTTY program icon, or from the Sctart Menu → Programs submenu, and choose PuTTY. When the PuTTY program first launches, the PuTTY Configuration Dialog Window opens on-screen, similar to Figure 0.1.

From the PuTTY Configuration Window, you can modify several of the parameters that control your interactive session with a UNIX system. Almost all of these parameters can be left at their defaults. The only two things that most users will need to do in this Configuration window is type the host name (or IP address) of the UNIX computer they are trying to connect and log in to, and click the protocol button for telnet, as seen in Figure 0.1. If you don't know what the host name or IP address of the UNIX computer is, ask your instructor or the system administrator at your site. Then click on the Open button, and a console window will open on-screen, as seen in Figure 0.2, thus allowing you to log in to the UNIX computer.

As previously stated, in the process of logging in, identifying yourself to the UNIX system is your first task. Doing so involves typing in a valid username, or log-in name, consisting of a string of valid characters. You then type a valid password for that username. There are both valid and invalid characters that you can use in both your username and password. See your system administrator or instructor to find out what these characters are on the UNIX system you want to log in to, if they have not already told you what they are.

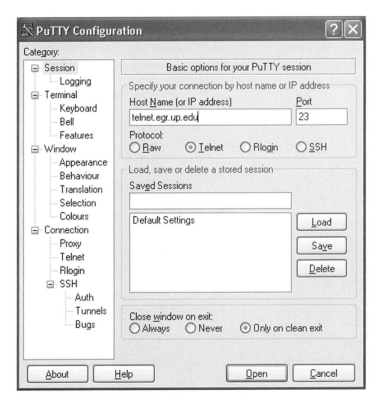

Figure 0.1 PuTTY Configuration Dialog Window

As shown in Figure 0.2, in response to the `login:` prompt, you type in your username on the UNIX system, and then press `<Enter>` on the keyboard. In our case, the username is bobk, as seen in Figure 0.2. Remember that UNIX is case-sensitive. When the `Password:` prompt appears, type your `password` on the UNIX system, and then press `<Enter>` on the keyboard. In Figure 0.2, the DISPLAY and TERM prompts, and their defaults enclosed in parentheses, allow you to designate which computers will manage the output and input of your command line session. To accept the defaults, press `<Enter>` on the keyboard. Finally, the command line prompt appears on-screen, as seen in Figure 0.2, at 51%.

To terminate your connection, type `logout` on the command line, and then press `<Enter>` on the keyboard, or on a blank line press `<Ctrl−D>`. Logging out is somewhat system-dependent, as well as an operation that can be tailored to a specific installation of UNIX by the local system administrator. Because we used the C shell in this session, the `logout` command is the default way of leaving the system gracefully. If you use the Bourne shell or Korn shell, holding down `<Ctrl−D>` or typing `exit` will accomplish the same thing. You will then be logged off the system and the current PuTTY session will end, and all PuTTY windows will close.

If you started a new shell during your session and didn't exit that shell before logging off, UNIX will prompt `Not login shell`, and you will not be able to log off immediately. See Chapter 4 for a more detailed description of what a UNIX shell is. In this case, press `<Ctrl−D>`, and the new shell will terminate. Also, if you started more than one shell and haven't exited from those shells before you log off, you will have to use the `<Ctrl−D>` to terminate each shell individually. On some systems, you type `exit` on the command line to terminate a shell process. In either case, you will then be able to use the previously described log-off procedure to leave the system.

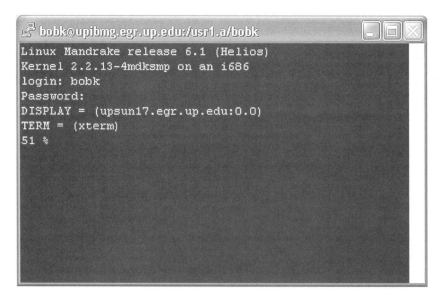

Figure 0.2 PuTTY Log-in Window

0.3.3 Connecting via a Telnet Client on a Microsoft Windows Machine

In this section, we make these basic assumptions:

1. That you are using Windows, and you want to connect and log on to a computer that is running UNIX by using the Internet Connection method.

2. On your Microsoft Windows computer, you connect to the Internet by a standard method through an Internet Service Provider (ISP) or at some locations simply by logging on to the Microsoft Windows computer itself, which then automatically connects you to the Internet.

3. You want to make a telnet connection by running the telnet Client program on a Microsoft Windows computer attached to a UNIX computer, and you know the host name or IP address of the UNIX computer system.

4. You know a valid username and password that will allow you to log in to the UNIX computer. You can use your own username and password.

5. Once you make the telnet connection, you use the valid username/password, and you can now type commands into a console window or terminal screen. What you type in is shown as follows in **bold** text and is always followed by pressing the <Enter> key on the keyboard.

To begin, using a Microsoft Windows computer, pull up the Start menu and choose Run. The Run dialogue box opens. *See* Figure 0.3.

In the Open: field, type the command `telnet telnet_client`, where telnet_client is the host name or IP address of the UNIX telnet machine you use. Then click on the OK.

On your Microsoft Windows computer, a telnet console window opens on-screen, as seen in Figure 0.4.

As previously stated, in the process of logging in, identifying yourself to the UNIX system is your first task. To do this, type a valid username, or log-in name, consisting of a string of

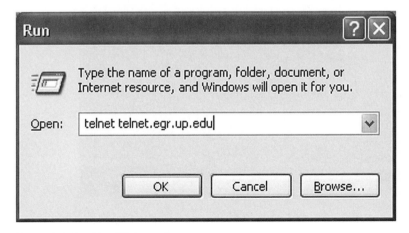

Figure 0.3 The Run Dialogue Box

valid characters. You then type a valid password for that username. There are both valid and invalid characters that you can use in both your username and password. See your system administrator or instructor to find out what these characters are on the UNIX system you want to log in to, if they have not already told you what they are.

As shown in Figure 0.4, in response to the `login:` prompt, you type your username on the UNIX system, and then press `<Enter>` on the keyboard. In our case, the username is bobk, as seen in Figure 0.4. Again, remember to use upper- or lowercase letters, as appropriate. When the `Password:` prompt appears, type your `password` on the UNIX system, and then press `<Enter>` on the keyboard. Optionally, a Last login system message will appear on-screen, as seen in Figure 0.4. Also, in Figure 0.4, the DISPLAY and TERM prompts, and their defaults enclosed in parentheses, allow you to designate what computers will manage the output and input of your command line session. To accept the defaults, press `<Enter>` on the keyboard. Finally, the command line prompt appears on-screen, prefaced with the name of the computer you are logged in to and the pathname to the current working directory or folder in the file structure of this computer. In the previous log-in procedure, this appears as `upibmg.egr.up.edu:~ 51$`.

The best way to terminate your telnet connection with the UNIX computer system is to type `logout` on the command line, and then press `<Enter>` on the keyboard, or on a blank line press `<Ctrl-D>`. Because we used the C shell in this session, the log-out command is the default way of leaving the system. If you used the Bourne shell or Korn shell, hold down `<Ctrl-D>` on the keyboard or type `exit`. You will then be logged off the system for the current telnet session, and all telnet windows will close.

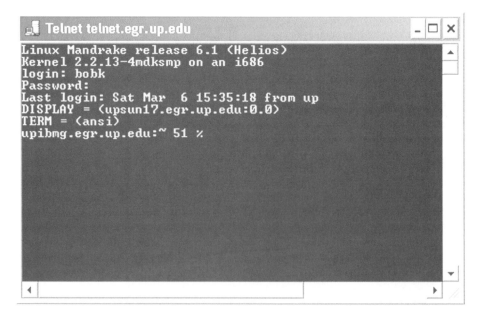

Figure 0.4 telnet Console Window

If you started a new shell during your session and didn't exit that shell before logging off, UNIX will prompt `Not login shell`, and you will not be able to log off immediately. See Chapter 4 for a more detailed description of what a UNIX shell is. In this case, press `<Ctrl-D>`, and the new shell will terminate. Also, if you started more than one shell and haven't exited from those shells before you log off, you will have to use the `<Ctrl-D>` individually for each shell before you can log off. On some systems, you have to type `exit` on the command line to terminate a shell process.

0.4   File Maintenance Commands and Help on UNIX Command Usage

After you have logged on to a UNIX system using one of the three methods we described, your first action is to construct and organize your work space and the files contained in it. The operation of organizing your files according to some logical scheme is known as **file maintenance**. A logical scheme used to organize your files might consist of creating "bins" for storing files according to the subject matter of the contents of the files, or according to the dates of their creation. In the following sections, you will type file creation and maintenance commands that produce a structure as shown in Figure 0.5. Complete the operations shown in the next sections in the order they are presented to get a better overview of what file maintenance really is. Also, it is critical that you review what was presented in Section 0.2

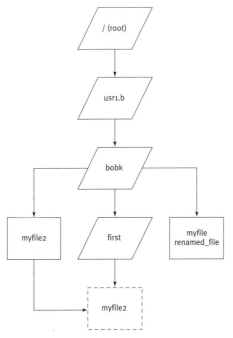

Figure 0.5 Example of a File and Directory Structure

regarding the structure of a UNIX command so that when you begin to type commands for file maintenance, you understand how the syntax of what you are typing conforms to the general syntax of any UNIX command.

0.4.1 File and Directory Structure

When you first log in, you are working in the **home directory**, or folder, of the autonomous user associated with the username and password you used to log in. Whatever directory you are presently in is known as the **current working directory**, and there is only one current working directory active at any given time. It is helpful to visualize the structure of your files and directories using a diagram. Figure 0.5 is an example of a home directory and file structure for a user named bobk. In this figure, directories are represented as parallelograms, and plain files (e.g., files that contain text or binary instructions) are represented as rectangles. A pathname, or path, is simply a textual way of designating the location of a directory or file in the complete file structure of the UNIX system you are working on. For example, the path to the file myfile2 in Figure 0.5 is /usr1.b/bobk/myfile2. The designation of the path begins at the root(/) of the entire file system, descends to the folder named usr1.b, and then descends again to the home directory named bobk.

   As shown in Figure 0.5, the files named myfile, myfile2, and renamed_file are stored under, or in, the directory named bobk. Beneath the directory bobk is a "subdirectory" of bobk named first. In the next sections, you will create these files and the subdirectory structure in the home directory of the username that you have logged in to your UNIX system.

0.4.2 Viewing the Contents of Files

To begin working with files, you create a new file by using the `cat` command. The syntax of the `cat` command is as follows:

cat [options] [file-list]

Purpose:	Join one or more files sequentially or display them in the console window
Output:	Contents of the files in 'file-list' displayed on the screen, one file at a time

Commonly used options/features:

`+E`	Display $ at the end of each line
`-n`	Put line numbers on the displayed lines
`--help`	Display the purpose of the command and a brief explanation of each option

The `cat` command, short for concatenate, allows you to join files. In the example, you will join what you type on the keyboard to a new file being created in the current working directory. This is achieved by the redirect character, >, which takes what you type at the standard input (in this case the keyboard) and directs it into the file named myfile. As stated in Section 0.2, this usage involves the command cat, but no options, option arguments, or command arguments. It simply employs the command; a redirect character; and a target, or destination, named myfile, where the redirection will go. This is an example of a multiple command typed on the command line.

```
$ cat > myfile
This is an example of how to use the cat command to add plain text to a file
<Ctrl-D>
$
```

You can type as many lines of text as you want, pressing <Enter> on the keyboard to distinguish between lines in the file. Then, on a new line, when you hold down the <Ctrl-D>, the file is created in the current working directory, using the command you typed. You can view the contents of this file, since it is a plain text file that was created using the keyboard, by doing the following:

```
$ more myfile
This is an example of how to use the cat command to add plain text to a file
$
```

The general syntax of the more command is as follows:

more [options] [file-list]	
Purpose:	Concatenate/display the files in 'file-list' on the screen, one screen at a time
Output:	Contents of the files in 'file-list' displayed on the screen, one page at a time
Commonly used options/features:	
+E/str	Start two lines before the first line containing str
−nN	Display N lines per screen/page
+N	Start displaying the contents of the file at line number N

The more command shows one screen of a file at a time. If the file is several pages long, you can proceed to view subsequent pages by pressing the <Space> key on the keyboard or by pressing the <Q> key to quit. System V UNIX has a command named pg that accomplishes the same thing as the more command.

0.4.3 Creating, Deleting, and Managing Files

To copy the contents of one file into another file, use the cp command. The general syntax of the cp command is as follows:

cp [options] file1 file2

Purpose:	Copy 'file1' to 'file2'; if 'file2' is a directory, make a copy of 'file1' in this directory
Output:	Copied files

Commonly used options/features:

−i	If destination exists, prompt before overwriting
−p	Preserve file access modes and modification times on copied files
−r	Recursively copy files and subdirectories

For example, to make an exact duplicate of the file named myfile with the new name myfile2, type the following:

```
$ cp myfile myfile2
$
```

This usage of the cp command has two required command arguments. The first argument is the source file that already exists, and that you want to copy. The second argument is the destination file, or the name of the file that will be the copy. Be aware that many UNIX commands can take plain, ordinary or regular files as arguments, or they can take directory files as arguments. This can change the basic task accomplished by the command. It is also worth noting that not only can file names be arguments, but pathnames can be arguments as well. This changes the site or location of operation of the command in the path structure of the file system.

In order to change the name of a file or directory, you can use the mv command. The general syntax of the mv command is as follows:

mv [options] file1 file2
mv [options] file-list directory

Purpose:	First Syntax: Rename 'file1' to 'file2' Second Syntax: Move all the files in 'file-list' to 'directory'
Output:	Renamed or relocated files

Commonly used options/features:

−f	Force the move regardless of the file access modes of the destination file
−i	Prompt the user before overwriting the destination

In the following usage, the first argument to the mv command is the source file name, and the second argument is the destination name.

```
$ mv myfile2 renamed_file
$
```

It is important at this point to notice the use of spaces in UNIX commands. What if you obtain a file from an MS-DOS or Windows 98/2000/XP system that has one or more spaces in one of the file names? How can you work with this file in UNIX? The answer is simple. Whenever you need to use that file name in a command as an argument, enclose the file name in double quotes (i.e., "double quotes"). For example, you might obtain a file that you have detached from an e-mail message from someone on an MS-DOS or Windows 98/2000/XP system, such as 'latest revisions october.txt'. In order to work with this file on a UNIX system—that is, to use the file name as an argument in a UNIX command—enclose the whole name in double quotes, such as "latest revisions october.txt". The correct command to rename that file to something shorter would be:

```
$ mv "latest revisions october.txt" laterevs.txt
$
```

In order to delete a file, you can use the rm command. The general syntax of the rm command is as follows:

rm [options] file-list	
Purpose:	Removes files in 'file-list' from the file structure (and disk)
Output:	Deleted files
Commonly used options/features:	
−f	Remove regardless of the file access modes of 'file-list'
−i	Prompt the user before removing files in 'file-list'
−r	Recursively remove the files in 'file-list' if 'file-list' is a directory; use with caution!

To delete the file renamed_file from the current working directory, type:

```
$ rm renamed_file
$
```

The most important command you will execute to do file maintenance is the ls command. The general syntax for the ls command is as follows:

ls [options] [pathname-list]	
Purpose:	Sends the names of the files and directories in the directory specified by 'pathname-list' to the display screen *(continued)*

---

ls [options] [pathname-list] (continued)

Output: Names of the files and directories in the directory specified by 'pathname-list', or the names only if 'pathname-list' contains file names only

Commonly used options/features:

−F   Display a / character after directory names, an * (asterisk) after binary „< executables, and an @ character after symbolic links

−a   Display names of all the files, including hidden files

−i   Display inode numbers

−l   Display long list that includes file access modes, link count, owner, group, file size (in bytes), and modification time

---

ls will list the names of files or folders in your current working directory or folder. In addition, as with the other commands we have used so far, if you include a complete pathname specification for the pathname-list argument to the command, then you can list the names of files and folders along that pathname list. To see the names of the files now in your current working directory, type the following:

```
$ ls
Desktop
Mail
XF86Config.new
kdeinit.core
order.asp.html
order.asp_files
myfile myfile2
$
```

Please note that you will probably not get a listing of the same file names as we did here, because your system will have placed some files automatically in your home directory, as in the example we used, aside from the ones we created together named myfile and myfile2. Also note that this file name listing does not include the name renamed_file–because we deleted that file.

The next command you will execute is actually just an alternate or modified way of executing the ls command, one that includes the command name and options. As shown in Section 0.2, a UNIX command has options that can be typed on the command line along with the command to change the behavior of the basic command. In the case of the ls command, the options l and a produce a longer listing of all ordinary and system (dot) files, as well as provide other attendant information about the files. Don't forget to put the space character between the s and the dash. Remember again from Section 0.2 that spaces delimit, or partition, the components of a UNIX command as it is typed on the command line.

Now type the following command:

```
$ ls -la
```

```
drwxr-xr-x   10    bobk     wheel     1024 Oct 11 13:42.
drwxr-xr-x   17    bobk     wheel     512 Sep 20 16:30 ..
lrwxr-xr-x   1     bobk     wheel     32 Oct 11 13:13
-rw- - - -   1     bobk     wheel     197 Oct 11 13:13 .ICEauthority
-rw- - - -   1     bobk     wheel     105 Oct 11 13:13 .Xauthority
-rw-r-r—     2     bobk     wheel     797 Jan 16   2004 .cshrc
-rw-r-r—     2     bobk     wheel     251 Jan 16   2004 .profile
drwxr-xr-x   2     bobk     wheel     512 Apr 15 15:11 .qt
-rwxr-xr-x   1     bobk     wheel     14 Apr 15 08:06 .xinitrc
-rwxr-xr-x   1     bobk     wheel     14 Apr 15 08:06 .xsession
drwx- - —    3     bobk     wheel     512 Sep 20 16:29 Desktop
drwx- - —    7     bobk     wheel     512 Apr 15 16:40 Mail
-rw-r-r—     1     bobk     wheel     2798 Apr 17 16:07 XF86Config.new
-rw- - - -   1     bobk     wheel     7360512 Sep 20 16:29 kdeinit.core
-rw-r-r—     1     bobk     wheel     35394 Apr 17 15:23 order.asp.html
drwxr-xr-x   2     bobk     wheel     1024 Apr 17 15:23 order.asp_files
-rw-r-r—     2     bobk     wheel     797 Jan 16   2004 myfile
-rw-r-r—     2     bobk     wheel     797 Jan 16   2004 myfile2
$
```

As you see in this screen display (that shows the listing of files in our home directory, and will not be the same as the listing of files in your home directory), the information about each file in the current working directory is displayed in eight columns. The first column shows the type of file, where d stands for directory, l stands for symbolic link, and — stands for ordinary or regular file. Also in the first column, the access modes to that file for user, group, and others is shown as r, w, or x. In the second column, the number of links to that file is displayed. In the third column, the username of the owner of that file is displayed. In the fourth column, the name of the group for that file is displayed. In the fifth column, the number of bytes that the file occupies on disk is displayed. In the sixth column, the date that the file was last modified is displayed. In the seventh column, the time that the file was last modified is displayed. In the eighth and final column, the name of the file is displayed. This way of executing the command is a good way to list more complete information about the file. Examples of using the more complete information are (1) so that you can know the byte size and be able to fit the file on some portable storage medium, or (2) to display the access modes so that you can alter the access modes to a particular file or directory. Access modes are discussed in Chapter 8.

You can also get a file listing for a single file in the current working directory by using another variation of the ls command, as follows:

```
$ ls -la myfile
-rw-r--r-- 1 bobk wheel 797 Jan 16 2004 myfile
$
```

This variation shows you a long listing with attendant information for the specific file named myfile. A breakdown of what you typed on the command line is (1) ls, the command name; (2) —la, the options; and (3) the command argument, myfile.

What if you make a mistake in your typing and misspell a command name, or one of the other parts of a command? Type the following on the command line:

```
$ lx —la myfile
lx: not found
$
```

The lx: not found reply from UNIX is an error message. There is no lx command in the UNIX operating system, so an error message is displayed. If you had typed an option that did not exist, you would also get an error message. If you supplied a file name that was not in the current working directory, you would get an error message, too. This makes an important point about the execution of UNIX commands. If no error message is displayed, then the command executed correctly, and the results might or might not appear on-screen, depending on what the command actually does. If you get an error message displayed, you must correct the error before UNIX will execute the command as you type it. Typographic mistakes account for about 98% of the errors that beginners make.

0.4.4 Creating, Deleting, and Managing Directories

Another critical aspect of file maintenance is the set of procedures and the related UNIX commands you use to create, delete, and organize directories in your UNIX account on a computer. When moving through the file system, you are either ascending or descending to reach the directory you want to use. The directory directly above the current working directory is referred to as the **parent** of the current working directory. The directory or directories immediately under the current working directory are referred to as the **children** of the current working directory. For more information on file system structure, see Chapter 7. The most common mistake for beginners is misplacing files. They cannot find the file names listed with the ls command because they have placed or created the files in a directory either above or below the current working directory in the file structure. When you create a file, if you have also created a logically organized set of directories beneath your own home directory, you will know where to store the file. In the following set of commands, we create a directory beneath the home directory and use that new directory to store a file.

To create a new directory beneath the current working directory, you use the mkdir command. The general syntax for the mkdir command is as follows:

SYNTAX	**mkdir [options] dirnames**	
	Purpose:	Creates directory or directories specified in 'dirnames'
	Output:	New directory or directories
	Commonly used options/features:	*(continued)*

> **_mkdir [options] dirnames_** *(continued)*
>
> **−m** MODE   Create a directory with given access modes (*see* Chapter 8)
>
> **−p**   Create parent directories that don't exist in the pathnames specified in 'dirnames'

To create a child, or subdirectory named first under the current working directory, type the following:

```
$ mkdir first
$
```

This command has now created a new subdirectory named first under, or as a child of, the current working directory. Refer back to Figure 0.5 for a graphical description of the directory location of this new subdirectory.

In order to change the current working directory to this new subdirectory, you use the cd command. The general syntax for the cd command is as follows:

> **cd [directory]**
>
> **Purpose:**   Change the current working directory to 'directory', or return to the home directory when 'directory' is omitted
>
> **Output:**   New current working directory
>
> **Commonly used options/features:**
>
>   None

To change the current working directory to first by descending down the path structure to the specified directory named first, type the following:

```
$ cd first
$
```

You can always verify what the current working directory is by using the pwd command. The general syntax of the pwd command is as follows:

> **pwd**
>
> **Purpose:**   Displays the current working directory on-screen
>
> **Output:**   Pathname of current working directory
>
> **Commonly used options/features:**
>
>   None

You can verify that first is now the current working directory by typing the following:

```
$ pwd
/usr1.b/bobk/first
$
```

The output from UNIX on the command line shows the pathname to the current working directory or folder. As previously stated, this path is a textual route through the complete file structure of the computer that UNIX is running on, ending in the current working directory. In this example of the output, the path starts at /, the root of the file system. Then it descends to the directory usr1.b, a major branch of the file system on the computer running UNIX. Then it descends to the directory bobk, another branch, which is the home directory name for the user. Finally, it descends to the branch named first, the current working directory.

On some systems, depending on the default settings, another way of determining what the current working directory is can be done by simply looking at the command line prompt. This prompt may be prefaced with the complete path to the current working directory, ending in the current working directory.

You can ascend back up to the home directory, or the parent of the subdirectory first, by typing the following:

```
$ cd
$
```

An alternate way of doing this is to type the following, where the ~ character resolves to, or is a substitute for, the specification of the complete path to the home directory:

```
$ cd ~
$
```

To verify that you have now ascended up to the home directory, type the following:

```
$ pwd
/usr1.b/bobk
$
```

You can also ascend to a directory above your home directory, sometimes called the parent of your current working directory, by typing the following:

```
$ cd ..
$
```

In this command, the two periods (..) represent the parent, or branch above the current working directory. Don't forget to type a space character between the d and the first period. To verify that you have ascended to the parent of your home directory, type the following:

```
$ pwd
/usr1.b
$
```

To descend to your home directory and re-create the file myfile2, type the following:

```
$ cd
$ cp myfile myfile2
$
```

To verify that there are two files in the home directory that begin with the letters my, type the following command:

```
$ ls my*
myfile myfile2
$
```

The asterisk following the y on the command line is known as a **metacharacter**, or a character that represents a pattern; in this case, the pattern is any set of characters. When UNIX interprets the command after you press the <Enter> key on the keyboard, it searches for all files in the current working directory that begin with the letters my and end in anything else.

Another aspect of organizing your directories is movement of files between directories, or changing the location of files in your directories. For example, you now have the file myfile2 in your home directory, but you would like to move it into the subdirectory named first. See Figure 0.5 for a graphic description to change the organization of your files at this point. To accomplish this, you can use the second syntax method illustrated above for the mv command to move the file myfile2 down into the subdirectory named first. To achieve this, type the following:

```
$ mv myfile2 first
$
```

To verify that myfile2 is indeed in the subdirectory named first, type the following:

```
$ cd first
$ ls
myfile2
$
```

You will now ascend to the home directory and attempt to remove or delete a file with the rm command. **Caution**: You should be very careful when using this command, because once a file has been deleted, the only way to recover it is from archival backups of the file system that you or the system administrator have made.

```
$ cd
$ rm myfile2
rm: myfile2: No such file or directory
$
```

You get the error message because in the home directory, the file named myfile2 does not exist. It was moved down into the subdirectory named first.

Directory organization also includes the ability to delete empty or nonempty directories. The command that accomplishes the removal of empty directories is `rmdir`. The general syntax of the `rmdir` command is as follows:

S Y N T A X

rmdir [options] dirnames

Purpose: Removes the empty directories specified in 'dirnames'

Output: Removes directories

Commonly used options/features:

    −p   Remove empty parent directories as well

To delete an entire directory below the current working directory, type the following:

```
$ rmdir first
rmdir: first: Directory not empty
$
```

Since the file myfile2 is still in the subdirectory named first, first is not an empty directory, and you get the error message that the `rmdir` command will not delete the directory. If the directory was empty, `rmdir` would have accomplished the deletion. One way to delete a non-empty directory is by using the rm command with the −r option. The −r option recursively descends down into the subdirectory and deletes any files in it before actually deleting the directory itself. Be cautious when using this command, since you may inadvertently delete directories and files with it. To see how this command deletes a nonempty directory, type the following:

```
$ rm -r first
$
```

The directory first and the file myfile2 are now removed from the file structure.

0.4.5 Obtaining Help with the man Command

A very convenient utility available on UNIX systems is the online help feature, achieved via the use of the man command. The general syntax of the man command is as follows:

S Y N T A X

man [options][-s section] command-list
man –k keyword-list

Purpose: First Syntax: Display UNIX Reference Manual Pages for commands in 'command-list' one screenful at a time   *(continued)*

man [options][-s section] command-list, man –k keyword-list (continued)

S Y N T A X

	Second Syntax: Display summaries of commands related to keywords in 'keyword-list'
Output:	Manual pages one screen at a time

Commonly used options/features:

–k keyword-list	Search for summaries of keywords in 'keyword-list' in a database and display them
–s sec-num	Search section number 'sec-num' for manual pages and display them

To get help by using the man command on usage and options of the ls command, for example, type the following:

```
$ man ls
LS(1)                         FreeBSD General Commands Manual                  LS(1)
NAME
     ls - list directory contents
SYNOPSIS
     ls [-ABCFGHLPRTWZabcdfghiklmnopqrstuwx1] [file ...]
DESCRIPTION
```

For each operand that names a file of a type other than directory, ls displays its name as well as any requested, associated information. For each operand that names a file of type directory, ls displays the names of files contained within that directory, as well as any requested, associated information.

If no operands are given, the contents of the current directory are displayed. If more than one operand is given, nondirectory operands are displayed first; directory and nondirectory operands are sorted separately and in lexicographical order.

```
The following options are available:
Press <SPACE> to continue, or q to quit q
$
```

This output from UNIX is one manual page, or man page, that gives a synopsis of the command usage showing the options and a brief description that helps you understand how the command should be used. Pressing <q> after one pageful has been displayed, as seen above, returns you to the command line prompt. Pressing the <space> key on the keyboard would have shown you more manual pages, one screen at a time, related to the ls command.

To get help in using all the UNIX commands and their options, use the man command to go to the UNIX Reference Manual Pages.

■ **TABLE 0.1** Sections of the UNIX Manual

Section	Describes
1	User commands
2	System calls
3	Language library calls (C, FORTRAN, etc.)
4	Devices and network interfaces
5	File formats
6	Games and demonstrations
7	Environments, tables, and macros for troff
8	System maintenance-related commands

The pages themselves are organized into eight sections, depending on the topic described and the topics that are applicable to the particular system. Table 0.1 lists the sections of the manual and what they contain. Most users find the pages they need in Section 1. Software developers mostly use library and system calls and thus find the pages they need in Sections 2 and 3. Users who work on document preparation get the most help from Section 7. Administrators mostly need to refer to pages in Sections 1, 4, 5, and 8.

The manual pages comprise multipage, specially formatted, descriptive documentation for every command, system call, and library call in UNIX. This format consists of seven general parts: name, synopsis, description, list of files, related information, errors, warnings, and known bugs. You can use the man command to view the manual page for a command. Because of the name of this command, the manual pages are normally referred to as UNIX man pages. When you display a manual page on the screen, the top left corner of the page has the command name with the section it belongs to in parentheses, as in LS (1) seen at the top of the above output manual page.

On some systems, such as AIX, you specify the section number without the -s option. The command used to display the manual page for the passwd command is:

```
$ man passwd
```

The manual page for the passwd command now appears on the screen, but we do not show it. Because they are multipage text documents, the manual pages for each topic take more than one screenful of text to display their entire contents. To see one screen of the manual page at a time, press the space bar on the keyboard. To quit viewing the manual page, press the <Q> key.

Now type this command:

```
$ man pwd
```

If more than one section of the man pages has information on the same word and you are interested in the man page for a particular section, you can use the -s option. The following command line therefore displays the man page for the read system call and not the man page for the shell command read:

```
$ man -s2 read
```

As we mentioned before, on some systems, such as IBM's AIX, you specify the section number without the `-s` option. On such systems, `man 2 read` displays the manual page for the read system call. The command `man -s3 fopen, fread strcmp` displays man pages for three C library calls: `fopen`, `fread`, and `strcmp`.

Another example of using the man command includes typing the command with the `-k` option, thereby specifying a keyword that limits the search. The search then yields man page headers from all the man pages that contain just the keyword reference. For example, typing `man -k passwd` yields the following onscreen output on our system:

```
chpasswd(8)     -     update password file in batch
gpasswd(1)      -     administrate the /etc/group file
mkpasswd(8)     -     update passwd and group database files
nwpasswd(8)     -     change password for a Netware user
passwd(5)       -     password file
yppasswd(1)     -     NIS password update clients
```

0.4.6 Other Methods of Obtaining Help

To get a short description of what any particular UNIX command does, you can use the `whatis` command. This is similar to the command `man -f`. The general syntax of the `whatis` command is as follows:

---

whatis keywords

Purpose: Search the **whatis** database for abbreviated descriptions of each 'keyword'

Output: Print a one-line description of each 'keyword' to the screen

Commonly used options/features:
     None

SYNTAX

The following is an illustration of how to use `whatis`.

```
$ whatis man
man(1)-format and display the online manual pages
$
```

You can also obtain short descriptions of more than one command by entering multiple arguments to the `whatis` command on the same command line, with spaces between each argument. The following is an illustration of this method. The output on your UNIX system may be different.

```
$ whatis login set setenv
login(1)        -sign on
set(1)          -set runtime parameters for session
setenv (1)      -change or add an environment variable
$
```

The In-Chapter Exercises ask you to use the man command and the whatis command to find information about the passwd command. After doing the exercises, you can use what you have learned to change your log-in password on the UNIX system that you use.

IN-CHAPTER EXERCISES

0.1   Use the man command with the -k option to display abbreviated help on the passwd command. Doing so will give you a screen display similar to that obtained with the whatis command, but it will show all apropos command names that contain the characters man. Note the list of commands, their names, and their brief descriptions.

0.2   Use the whatis command to find brief descriptions of the commands shown in Exercise 0.1 and note the differences. Then use the man command with no options to view the manual pages for the same commands, and again note the essential differences in them.

0.5   Utility Commands

There are several major commands that allow the beginner to be more productive when using the UNIX system. A sampling of these kinds of utility commands is given in the next sections and is organized as system setups, general utilities, and communications commands.

0.5.1 Examining System Setups

The whereis command allows you to search along certain prescribed paths to locate utility programs and commands, such as shell programs. The general syntax of the whereis command is as follows:

whereis [options] filename

Purpose: Locate the binary, source, and man page files for a command

Output: The supplied names are first stripped of leading pathname components and extensions, then <pathnames are displayed on-screen

Commonly used options/features:

-b   Search only for binaries

-s   Search only for source code

For example, if you type the command `whereis csh` on the command line, you will see a list of the paths to the C shell program files themselves. Note that the paths to a built-in, or internal, command cannot be found with the `whereis` command. We provide more information about internal and external shell commands in Chapter 13.

When you first log on, it is useful to be able to view a display of information about your userid, the computer or system you have logged on to, and the operating system on that computer. These tasks can be accomplished with the `whoami` command, which displays your userid on the screen. The general syntax of the `whoami` command is as follows:

---

whoami _____

Purpose: Displays the effective user id

Output: Displays your effective user id as a name on standard

Commonly used options/features:

    None

S Y N T A X

The following shows how our system responded to this command when we typed it on the command line.

```
$ whoami
bobk
$
```

The following In-Chapter Exercises give you the chance to use `whereis`, `whoami`, and two other important utility commands, `who` and `hostname`, to obtain important information about your system.

IN-CHAPTER EXERCISES _____

0.3 Use the `whereis` command to locate binary files for the Korn shell, the Bourne shell, the Bourne Again shell, and the Z shell. Verify the pathname locations using Chapter 4, Table 4.1. Are any of these shell programs not available on your system?

0.4 Use the `whoami` command to find your username on the system that you're using. Then use the `who` command to see how your username is listed, along with other users of the same system. What is the onscreen format of each user's listing that you obtained with the `who` command? Try to identify the information in each field on the same line as your username.

0.5 Use the `hostname` command to find out what host computer you are logged on to. Can you determine from this list whether you are using a stand-alone computer or a networked computer system? Explain how you can know the difference from the list that the `hostname` command gives you.

0.5.2 Printing and General Utility Commands

A very useful and common task performed by every user of a computer system is the printing of text files at a printer. The command to perform printing is lpr. The general syntax of the lpr command is as follows:

lpr [options] filename

Purpose:	Send files to the printer
Output:	Files sent to the printer queue as print jobs

Commonly used options/features:

−P printer	Send output to the named printer
−# copies	Produce the number of copies indicated for each named file

The following lpr command, used when working under a BSD-compliant system such as FreeBSD or SunOS, accomplishes the printing of the file named order.eps at the printer designated on our system as spr. Remember from Section 0.2 that no space is necessary between the option (in this case −P) and the option argument (in this case spr).

```
$ lpr -Pspr order.eps
$
```

The following lpr command, used when working under a BSD-compliant system such as FreeBSD or SunOS, accomplishes the printing of the file named memo1 at the default printer.

```
$ lpr memo1
$
```

The following multiple command combines the man command and the lpr command, and ties them together with the UNIX pipe (|) redirection character to print the man pages describing the ls command at the printer named hp1. This will work under a BSD-compliant system such as FreeBSD or SunOS.

```
$ man ls | lpr -Php1
$
```

The following shows how to perform similar printing tasks on a System V-based UNIX system using the lp command. In the first command, the file to be printed is named file1. In the second command, the files to be printed are named sample and phones. Note that the −d option is used to specify which printer to use. The option to specify the number of copies is −n for the lp command. These commands were run on a LINUX system compliant with System V.

```
$ lp -d spr file1
request id is spr-983 (1 file(s))
```

```
$ lp -d spr -n 3 sample phones
request id is spr-984 (2 file(s))
$
```

Among the most useful of the general purpose, personal productivity utility commands, the `cal` command displays a calendar for a year or a month. The general syntax of the `cal` command is as follows:

---

cal [[month]year]

Purpose: Displays calendar on-screen as text

Output: Displays a calendar of the month or year

Commonly used options/features:
    None

The optional parameter 'month' can be between 1 and 12, and 'year' can be 0 to 9999. Just like the UNIX system, the `cal` command is Y2K compliant. If no argument is specified, the command displays the calendar for the current month of the current year. If only one parameter is specified, it is taken as the year. Thus the `cal 3 2005` command displays the calendar for March 2005. The command `cal 1969` displays the calendar for the year 1969, the year the UNIX operating system was born.

0.5.3 Communications Commands

The `write` command is used to send a message to another user who is currently logged on to the system. The syntax and a brief description of the command is as follows.

---

write username [terminal]

Purpose: Write on the terminal screen or console window of the user with log-in
                      name **username**; the user must be logged on to the system, and the user's
                      terminal must have write access privilege given by the `mesg` command.

Output: Message on another user's console window

Commonly used options/features:
    None

The example shown in Figure 0.6 illustrates the use of this command. The prerequisite for executing the `write` command is execution of the `mesg y` command by both sender (in anticipation of a reply) and receiver to allow writing to their respective terminal screen or console windows. The `who` command is used to determine whether the person to whom you want to write is logged on. In this case, both sender (sarwar) and receiver (bobk) are logged on to the computer (upibm7), sarwar at terminal ttyp0 and bobk at terminal ttyC2. The receiver's screen is garbled with the message, but no harm is caused to any work that the user is doing. Under the shell, pressing <Enter> does the trick of resetting the screen, and inside the vi editor (discussed in Chapter 5), the screen can be reset by pressing <Ctrl–R> (^R).

In Figure 0.6, the mesg command enables or disables real-time one-way messages and chat requests from other users with the write and talk commands, respectively (*see* Chapter 14). The mesg y command permits others to initiate communication with you by using the write or talk command. If you think that you are bothered too often with write or talk, you can turn off the permission by executing the mesg n command. When you do so, a user who runs a write or talk command sees the message Permission denied. When the mesg command is used without an argument, it returns the current value of permission, n or y.

The biff command lets the system know whether you want to be notified immediately of an incoming e-mail message. The system notifies you by sounding a beep on your terminal. You can use the command biff y to enable notification and biff n to disable notification. When the biff command is used without an argument, it displays the current setting, n or y.

```
$ mesg y
$ who
bobk           upibm7:ttyC2      Oct  12      13:47:34
sarwar         upibm7:ttyp0      Oct  12      14:20:15
$ write bobk ttyC2
Bob,
How are the new chapter revisions coming along?
Take care,
Mansoor
^d
$
```

```
$ mesg y
$
Message from sarwar@upibm7.egr.up. edu on ttyp0 at 14:26
Bob,
How are the new chapter revisions coming along?
Take care,
Mansoor
EOF
```

Figure 0.6 Illustration of the Write Command

0.6   Command Aliases

The `alias` command can be used to create pseudonyms (nicknames) for commands. The `alias` command has one syntax in the Bourne, Korn, and Bash shells, and another in the C shell, all of which are illustrated here. The general syntax for the `alias` command is as follows:

alias [name [=string] ...]	**Bourne, Korn, Bash shells**
alias [name [string]]	**C shell**

Purpose: Create pseudonym 'string' for the command 'name'

Output: Pseudonyms that can be used for commands

Commonly used options/features:

   None

SYNTAX

When you use the `alias` command to create pseudonyms, you have created aliases. Pseudonyms are usually created for commands, but they can also be used for other items, such as naming e-mail groups (*see* Chapter 6). The C shell allows you to create aliases from the command line, but the Bourne, Korn, and Bash shells don't.

Command aliases can be placed in the .profile file (System V) or the .login file (BSD), but they are typically placed in the .bashrc file (Bash) and the .cshrc file (C) shell. The term profile or .login file executes when you log on, and the .cshrc or .bashrc file executes every time you start a C or Bash shell. Table 0.2 lists some useful aliases to put in one of these files. If set in your environment, these aliases allow you to use the names `dir`, `rename`, `spr`, `ls`, `ll`, and `more` as commands, substituting them for the actual commands given in quotes. The `\!*` string is substituted by the actual parameter passed to the `dir` command. For example, when you use the `dir` command, the shell actually executes the `ls -la` command. Thus for the `dir unixbook` command, the shell executes the `ls -la unixbook` command.

▬ TABLE 0.2 Some Useful Aliases for Various Shells

Bourne, Korn, and Bash Shells	C Shell
alias dir='ls –la \!*' alias dir 'ls –la \!*'	
alias rename='mv \!*' alias rename 'mv \!*'	
alias spr='lpr –Pspr \!*'	alias spr 'lpr –Pspr \!*'
alias ls='ls –C'	alias ls 'ls –C'
alias ll='ls –ltr' alias ll 'ls –ltr'	
alias more='pg'	alias more 'pg'

When you use the `alias` command without any argument, it lists all the aliases currently set by default. The following session illustrates the use of this command with a Bourne, Korn, or Bash shell.

```
$ alias
dir='ls -la \!*'
rename='mv \!*'
spr='lpr -Pspr \!*'
ls='ls -C'
ll='ls -ltr'
more='pg'
$
```

Running the same command with the C shell produces the following output.

```
% alias
dir        ls -la \!*
rename     mv \!*
spr        lpr -Pspr \!*
ls         ls -C
ll         ls -ltr
more       pg
%
```

You can use the `unalias` command to remove one or more aliases from the alias list. You can use the `-a` option to remove all aliases from the alias list. The first of the two `unalias` commands in the following session removes the alias for `ls`, and the second removes all of the aliases from the alias list. Note that the output of the first `alias` command does not contain an alias for the `ls` command after the `unalias ls` command has been executed. Use of the second `alias` command produces no output because the `unalias -a` command removes all the aliases from the alias list.

```
$ unalias ls
$ alias
dir='ls -la \!*'
rename='mv \!*'
spr='lpr -Pspr \!*'
ll='ls -ltr'
more='pg'
$ unalias -a
$ alias
$
```

In the following In-Chapter Exercises, you will use the `write`, `alias`, `uptime`, and `cat` (or `more`) commands to practice their syntax and gain more insight into their utility. Table 0.3 shows useful commands for beginners.

IN-CHAPTER EXERCISES

0.6   Use the `write` command to communicate with a friend who is logged on to the system.

0.7   Use the `alias` command to display the nicknames (aliases) of commands in your system.

0.8   Display the contents of the /etc/passwd file on your system to determine how many users can log on to the system.

■ **TABLE 0.3** Useful Commands for the Beginner

Command	What It Does
`<Ctrl-D>` or `(^D)`	Terminates a process or command.
`alias`	Allows you to create pseudonyms for commands.
`biff`	Notifies you of new e-mail.
`cal`	Displays a calendar on screen.
`cat`	Allows joining of files.
`cd`	Allows you to change the current working directory.
`cp`	Allows you to copy files.
`exit`	Ends a shell that you have started.
`hostname`	Displays the name of the host computer that you are logged on to.
`login`	Allows you to log on to the computer with a valid username/ password pair.
`lpr` or `lp`	Allows printing of text files.
`ls`	Allows you to display names of files and directories in the current working directory.
`man`	Allows you to view a manual page for a command or topic.
`mesg`	Allows or disallows writing messages to the screen.
`mkdir`	Allows you to create a new directory.
`more`	Allows viewing of the contents of a file one screenful at a time.
`mv`	Allows you to move the path location of or rename files.
`passwd`	Allows you to change your password on the computer.
`pg`	System V command that displays one screenful of a file at a time.
`pwd`	Allows you to see the name of the current working directory.
`rm`	Allows you to delete a file from the file structure.

(continued)

TABLE 0.3 *(continued)*

`rmdir`	Allows deletion of directories.
`talk`	Allows you to send real-time messages to other users.
`telnet`	Allows you to log on to a computer on a network or the Internet.
`unalias`	Allows you to undefine pseudonyms for commands.
`uname`	Displays information about the operating system running the computer.
`whatis`	Allows you to view a brief description of a command.
`whereis`	Displays the path(s) to commands and utilities in certain key directories.
`who`	Allows you to find out log-in names of users currently on the system.
`whoami`	Displays your username.
`write`	Allows real-time messaging between users on the system.

▬ Summary

The UNIX Operating System is most famous for its text-based command execution. This chapter serves to familiarize you with the basic structure of a UNIX command. It also shows you how to log in via three popular and typical log-in methods, and how to gracefully log off. A beginner must be able to do basic file maintenance, and a core set of file maintenance commands and their options are introduced in this chapter, which will be useful throughout the rest of this book. Finally, you can see some basic utility commands—most important, the commands and their options that allow you to print files.

Problems

1. Create a directory called UNIX in your home directory. What command line did you use?

2. Give a command line for displaying the files lab1, lab2, lab3, and lab4. Can you give two more command lines that do the same thing? What is the command line for displaying the files lab1.c, lab2.c, lab3.c, and lab4.c? (*Hint:* Use shell metacharacters.)

3. Give a command line for printing all the files in your home directory that start with the string memo and end with .ps on a printer called 'upmpr'. What command line did you use?

4. Give the command line for nicknaming the command who -H as w. Give both Bourne and C shell versions. Where would you put this command line so that it executes every time you log on? Where would you put it if you want it to execute every time you start a new shell?

5. Type the command man ls > ~/unix/ls.man on your system. This command will put the man page for the ls command in the ls.man file in your ~/unix directory. Give the command for printing two copies of this file on a printer in your lab. What command line did you use?

6. What is the mesg value set to for your environment? If it is on, how would you turn off your current session? How would you set it permanently?

7. What does the command lpr -Pqpr [0-9]*.jpg do? Explain your answer.

8. Use the passwd command to change your password. If you are on a network, be aware that you might have to use the yppasswd command to modify your network log-in password. Also, make sure you abide by the rules made by your system administrator for coming up with good passwords.

9. Using the correct terminology (e.g., command, option, option argument, and command argument), identify the constituent parts of the following UNIX single commands.

    ```
    ls -la *.exe

    lpr -Pwpr

    chmod g+rwx *.*
    ```

10. View the man pages for each of the useful commands listed in Table 0.3. Which part of the man pages is most descriptive for you? Which of the options shown on each of the man pages is most useful for beginners? Explain.

11. How many users are logged onto your system at this time? What command did you use to discover this?

12. Determine the name of the operating system that your computer runs. What command did you use to discover this?

13. Give the command line for displaying manual pages for the socket, read, and connect system calls. What will be the command line for an AIX-based computer?

Overview of Operating Systems

Objectives

- To explain what an operating system is
- To describe briefly operating system services
- To describe character and graphical user interfaces
- To discuss different types of operating systems
- To briefly describe the UNIX operating system

1.1 Introduction

Many operating systems are available today, some general enough to run on any type of computer (from a **personal computer**, or **PC**, to a **mainframe**), and some specifically designed to run on a particular type of computer system, such as a **real-time computer system** used to control the movement of a robot. In this chapter, we describe the purpose of an operating system and different classes of operating systems. Before describing different types of operating systems and where UNIX fits in this categorization, we present a layered diagram of a contemporary computer system and discuss the basic purpose of an operating system. We then describe different types of operating systems and the parameters used to classify them. Finally, we identify the class that UNIX belongs to and briefly discuss the different members of the UNIX family.

1.2 What Is an Operating System?

A computer system consists of various hardware and software resources, as shown in a layered fashion in Figure 1.1. The primary purpose of an operating system is to facilitate easy, efficient, fair, orderly, and secure use of these resources. It allows the users to employ **application software**—spreadsheets, word processors, Web browsers, e-mail software, and other programs. Programmers use **language libraries**, **system calls**, and **program generation tools** (e.g., text editors, compilers, and version control systems) to develop software. Fairness is obviously not an issue if only one user at a time is allowed to use the computer system. However, if multiple users are allowed to use the computer system, fairness and security are two main issues to be tackled by the operating system designers.

Hardware resources include keyboard, display screen, main memory (commonly known as **random access memory**, or **RAM**), disk drive, modem, and **central processing unit (CPU)**. Software resources include applications such as word processors, spreadsheets, games, graphing tools, picture processing tools, and Internet-related tools such as Web browsers. These applications, which reside at the topmost layer in the diagram, form the **application user's interface (AUI)**. The AUI is glued to the operating system **kernel** via the language libraries and the system call interface. The system call interface comprises a set of functions that can be used by the applications and library routines to start execution of the kernel code for a particular service, such as reading a file. The language libraries and the system call interface comprise what is commonly known as the **application programmer's interface (API)**. The kernel is the part of an operating system where the real work is done. The layers in the diagram are shown in an expanded form for the UNIX operating system in Chapter 3, where we also describe them briefly.

There are two ways to view an operating system: top-down and bottom-up. In the bottom-up view, an operating system can be viewed as a piece of software that allocates and de-allocates system resources (hardware and software) in an efficient, fair, orderly, and secure manner. For example, the operating system decides how much RAM space is to be allocated to a program before it is loaded and executed. The operating system ensures that only one file is printed on a particular printer at a time. The operating system also prevents an existing file on the disk from being accidentally overwritten by another file. The operating system further guarantees that, when execution of a program given to the CPU for processing has been completed, the program relinquishes the CPU so that other programs can be executed. Thus the operating system can be viewed as a **resource manager**.

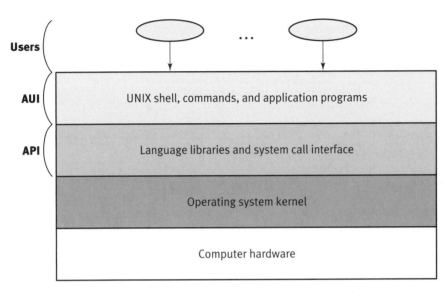

Figure 1.1 A layered view of a contemporary computer system

In the top-down view, which we espouse in this textbook, an operating system can be viewed as a piece of software that isolates you from the complications of hardware resources. You therefore do not have to deal with the extremely difficult (and sometimes impossible for most users) task of interacting with these resources. For example, as a user of a computer system, you don't have to write the software that allows you to save your work as a file on a hard disk, to use a mouse as a point-and-click device, or to print on a particular printer. Also, you do not have to write new software for a new device (e.g., mouse, disk drive, or DVD) that you buy and install in your system. The operating system performs the task of dealing with complicated hardware resources and gives you a comprehensive and simple machine, ready to use. This machine allows you to use simple commands to retrieve and save files on a disk, print files on a printer, and play movies on a DVD. In a sense, the operating system provides a **virtual machine** that is much easier to deal with than the physical machine. You can, for example, use a command such as `cp memo letter` to copy the memo file to the letter file on the hard disk in your computer without having to worry about the location of the memo and letter files on the disk, the structure and size of the disk, the brand of the disk drive, and the number or name of the various drives (floppy, CD-ROM, and one or more hard drives) on your system.

1.3   Operating System Services

An operating system provides many ready-made services for users. Most of these services are designed to allow you to execute your software, both application programs and program development tools, efficiently and securely. Some services are designed for housekeeping tasks, such as keeping track of the amount of time that you have used the system. The major operating system services therefore provide mechanisms for following secure and efficient operations and processes:

❖ Execution of a program
❖ Input and output operations performed by programs
❖ Communication between processes
❖ Error detection and reporting
❖ Manipulation of all types of files
❖ Management of users and security

A detailed discussion of these services is outside the scope of this textbook, but we discuss them briefly when they are relevant to the topic being presented.

1.4 Character Versus Graphical User Interfaces

In order to use a computer system, you have to give commands to its operating system. An input device, such as a keyboard, is used to issue a command. If you use the keyboard to issue commands to the operating system, the operating system has a **character user interface (CUI)**, commonly known as the **commandline interface**. If the primary input device for issuing commands to the operating system is a **point-and-click device** such as a mouse, the operating system has a **graphical user interface (GUI)**. Some operating systems have both character and graphical user interfaces, and you can use either. Some have a CUI as their primary interface but allow you to run software that provides a GUI. Operating systems such as DOS and UNIX have character user interfaces, whereas MacOS, OS/2, and Microsoft Windows primarily offer graphical user interfaces but have the capability to allow a user to enter a DOS- or UNIX-like commandline-based screen. Although UNIX comes with a CUI as its basic interface, it can run software based on the X Window System (Project Athena, MIT) that provides a GUI interface. Moreover, most UNIX systems now have an X-based GUI. We discuss the UNIX GUI in Chapter 21.

Although a GUI makes a computer easier to use, it gives you an automated setup with minimal flexibility. A GUI also presents an extra layer of software between you and the task that you want to perform on the computer, thereby making the task slower. In contrast, a CUI gives you ultimate control of your computer system and allows you to run application programs any way you want. A CUI is also more efficient because a minimal layer of software is needed between you and your task on the computer, thereby making doing the task faster. It is also malleable and gives the user more control. Because many people are accustomed to the graphical interfaces of popular gizmos and applications such as Nintendo and Web browsers, the character interface presents an unfamiliar and sometimes difficult style of communicating commands to the computer system. However, computer science students are usually able to meet this challenge after a few hands-on sessions.

1.5 Types of Operating Systems

Operating systems can be categorized by the number of users who can use a system at the same time and the number of **processes** (executing programs) that an operating system can run simultaneously. These criteria lead to three types of operating systems.

❖ *Single-user, single-process system:* These operating systems allow only one user at a time to use the computer system, and the user can run only one process at a time. Such operating systems are commonly used for PCs. Examples of these operating systems are MacOS, DOS, and Windows 3.1.

❖ *Single-user, multiprocess system:* As the name indicates, these operating systems allow a single user to use the computer system, but the user can run multiple processes simultaneously. These operating systems are also used on PCs. Examples of such operating systems are OS/2 and Windows XP Workstation.

❖ *Multiuser, multiprocess system:* These operating systems allow multiple users to use the computer system simultaneously, and every user can run multiple processes at the same time. These operating systems are commonly used on computers that support multiple users in organizations such as universities and large businesses. Examples of these operating systems are UNIX, LINUX, WindowsNT Server, MVS, and VM/CMS.

Multiuser, multiprocess systems are used to increase **resource utilization** in the computer system by multiplexing expensive resources such as the CPU. This capability leads to increased system **throughput** (the number of processes finished in unit time). Resource utilization increases because, in a system with several processes, when one process is performing input or output (e.g., reading input from the keyboard, capturing a mouse click, or writing to file on the hard disk), the CPU can be taken away from this process and given to another process—effectively running both processes simultaneously by allowing them both to make progress (one is doing I/O and the other is using the CPU). The mechanism of assigning the CPU to another process when the current process is performing input/output (I/O) is known as **multiprogramming**. Multiprogramming is the key to all contemporary multiuser, multiprocess operating systems. In a single-process system, when the process using the CPU performs I/O, the CPU sits idle because there is no other process that can use the CPU at the same time.

Operating systems that allow users to interact with their executing programs are known as **interactive operating systems**, and the ones that do not are called **batch operating systems**. Batch systems are useful when programs are run without the need for human intervention, such as systems that run payroll programs. The VMS operating system has both interactive and batch interfaces. Almost all well-known contemporary operating systems (UNIX, LINUX, DOS, Windows, etc.) are interactive. UNIX and LINUX also allow programs to be executed in batch mode, with programs running in the background (*see* Chapter 13 for details of "background process execution" in UNIX). The multiuser, multiprocess, and interactive operating systems are known as **time-sharing systems**. In time-sharing systems, the CPU is switched from one process to another in quick succession. This method of operation allows all the processes in the system to make progress, giving each user the impression of sole use of the system. Examples of time-sharing operating systems are UNIX, LINUX, and WindowsNT Server.

1.6 The UNIX Family

Years ago the name UNIX referred to a single operating system, but it is now used to refer to a family of operating systems that are offshoots of the original in terms of their user interfaces. Some of the members of this family are AIX, BSD, DYNIX, FreeBSD, HP-UX, LINUX, MINIX, NetBSD, SCO, Solaris2, SunOS, System V, XENIX, and XINU. In Chapter 2, we give a brief history of some of the most popular and developmentally influential UNIX systems.

Summary

An operating system (OS) is software that runs on the hardware of a computer system to manage the system's hardware and software resources. It also gives the user of the computer system a simple, virtual machine that is easy to interact with. The basic services provided by an operating system offer efficient and secure program execution. These services include program execution, I/O operations, communication between processes, error detection and reporting, and file manipulation.

Operating systems are categorized by the number of users that can use a system at the same time and by the number of processes that can execute on a system simultaneously: single-user single-process, single-user multiprocess, and multiuser multiprocess operating systems. Furthermore, operating systems that allow users to interact with their executing programs (processes) are known as interactive systems, and those that do not are called batch systems. Multiuser, multiprocess, interactive systems are known as time-sharing systems, of which UNIX is a prime example. The purpose of multiuser, multiprocess systems is to increase the utilization of system resources by switching them among concurrently executing processes. This capability leads to higher system throughput, or the number of processes finishing in unit time.

In order to use a computer system, the user issues commands to the operating system. If an operating system accepts commands via the keyboard, it has a character user interface (CUI). If an operating system allows users to issue commands via a point-and-click device such as a mouse, it has a graphical user interface (GUI). Although UNIX comes with a CUI as its basic interface, it can run software based on the X Window System (Project Athena, MIT) that provides a GUI. Most UNIX systems now have both interfaces.

Problems

1. What is an operating system?

2. What are the three types of operating systems? How do they differ from each other?

3. What is a time-sharing system? Be precise.

4. What are the main services provided by a typical contemporary operating system? What is the basic purpose of these services?

5. List one advantage and one disadvantage each for the commandline interface and the graphical user interface.

6. What is the difference between the character and graphical user interfaces? What is the most popular graphical user interface for UNIX systems? Where was it developed?

7. What comprises the application programmer's interface (API) and the application user's interface (AUI)?

8. Name five popular members of the UNIX family. What is the name of your UNIX system?

9. In the late '60s and early '70s, Digital Equipment Corporation (DEC) was a key player in the development of time-sharing systems. Browse the Web and find an article on RSTS, an operating system developed at DEC. What was its full name? What machines did it run on? What were its key features?

Brief History of the UNIX Operating System

Objectives

- To describe briefly the history of the UNIX operating system
- To provide an overview of the different types of UNIX systems

2.1 Introduction

The people who use the UNIX operating system comprise application developers, systems analysts, programmers, administrators, business managers, academicians, and people who just wish to read their e-mail. From its earliest inception in 1969 as a laboratory research tool, it was further developed in the academic community, and then endorsed for commercial uses. In its version today, UNIX has an underlying functionality that is complex but easy to learn, and extensible yet easily customized to suit a user's style of computing. The key to understanding its longevity and its heterogeneous appeal is to study the history of its evolution.

2.2 The Development of the UNIX Operating System

Before we describe the evolution of UNIX, first we have to ask, Why is this operating system so "friendly" and accommodating? Part of the answer is: This ever-evolving operating system that is accepted and used throughout the world, was developed in response to the needs and activities of a very heterogeneous community of computer users. It grew, changed, and improved because of the work and cooperation of many diverse, and sometimes opposing, individuals and groups.

UNIX continuously grew, changed, and improved alongside the development of computer hardware, software applications, networking, and other components of the "computer revolution." The UNIX project started as a personal and subjective endeavor but exploded into a universal and generic technical tool. Thus its various audiences must have found some basic advantages in this tool–particularly the largest audience of common users. Separating the influences of these various user groups in the development of UNIX is difficult. Moreover, because the system is fundamentally an **open software system**–that is, the source code is freely distributed among the community of users–its evolution has been shaped to some extent by a populist mindset. And it will continue to be in the future, with the pervasive use of the Internet.

It is the underlying core functionality of UNIX that brings together its diverse audiences into a community not so much in the sociological sense, but more in an independent, intellectual sense. As you delve into the subject matter of this textbook, you might wonder where you fit into the UNIX community and how its functionality might be adapted for your uses. Essentially, it is the *style* of your interaction with the computer that will be the most important, invigorating, and critical aspect of your work with the UNIX operating system.

The development of other contemporary operating systems is motivated and informed by completely different forces and bases (primarily commercialization) than those that motivated the inception and development of UNIX (primarily a user-friendly, text-based operating system). The history of UNIX is a record of how a system should be developed, regardless of how you believe that system should be structured, how you think it should function (whatever your user perspective), and whom you believe should control that development.

2.2.1 Beginnings

Figure 2.1 describes the three main branches of UNIX systems as they were developed from 1969 to the present. The approximate dates of the development of milestone versions in each of the branches are shown on the left. The UNIX Support Group (USG), UNIX System

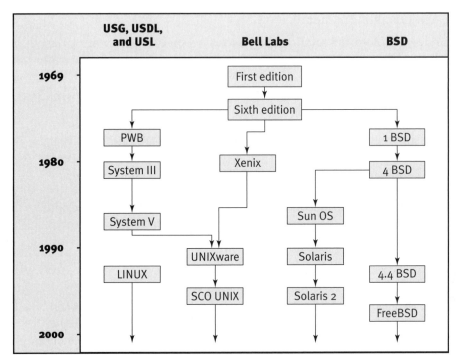

Figure 2.1 Schematic UNIX time line

Development Laboratory (USDL), and UNIX System Laboratories (USL) were commercial spin-offs of AT&T. The UNIX Programmer's Work Bench (PWB) was distributed initially through the USG.

In the mid-1960s, Bell Laboratories began a collaborative effort to develop a multiuser operating system known as MULTICS. One of the biggest drawbacks inherent in the functionality of this new operating system was the complexity of the software and hardware required to accomplish simple tasks for multiple users. Following the failure of the MULTICS project, Ken Thompson, Dennis Ritchie, and others at Bell Laboratories developed a multiuser operating system called UNIX, which first ran on a DEC PDP-7 computer and later was ported to a PDP-11 computer [Ritchie, 1978]. One of the features of UNIX that distinguished it from MULTICS was that it allowed a process to be created easily by a single user, a feature we cover in depth in Chapter 13.

The most important historical development in the early 1970s was the recoding of most of the operating system in a **high-level programming language**, C. At that time, most operating system programs were written in a **low-level programming language**, known as an **assembly language**, which was specifically tailored to the architecture of the processor that a particular make of computer used. Thus the operating system written in a low-level language was not *portable* between computers with different processors made by different manufacturers. Written in C, UNIX was very portable. Also, C, as well as other high-level languages, is much easier to program than an assembly language, which is characteristically difficult to program.

2.2.2 Research Operating System

Bell Laboratories controlled the research systems versions of UNIX, known as Versions 1 through 6. These versions had three important characteristics.

1. The UNIX system was continually developed and written in C, with only a small subset of the code tailored to a target processor.

2. Releases were distributed as C **source code**, which could be easily modified and improved upon to add functionality by those who obtained any of the research versions of the system.

3. The design of the system allowed users to run multiple processes concurrently and to connect these processes with **streams**. For example, multiple commands performing input/processing/output functions could be connected with redirection mechanisms. We present the implementation of this design aspect in Chapter 12.

2.2.3 AT&T System V

In response to a changing business environment in the early 1980s, Bell Laboratories/AT&T licensed further releases of UNIX as System III and finally as System V, starting in 1983. This main branch of UNIX continued to be developed, as shown in Figure 2.1, through System V, Release 4, when it again diverged and evolved to survive as SCO UNIX in the mid- to late-1990s.

2.2.4 Berkeley Software Distributions

The University of California at Berkeley initiated and maintained the development of UNIX along its second main branch throughout the 1980s and into the 1990s. Contractual agreements made the operating system freely available to universities, so these releases contributed in large part to the popularization of UNIX. These versions were released as Berkeley Software Distributions, 3BSD, and 4BSD-4.4BSD. Most recently, BSD UNIX survives as FreeBSD and NetBSD.

2.2.5 The History of Shells

Development of the **shell** as a UNIX utility parallels development of the system itself. The first commercially available shell, the Bourne shell, was written by Steven R. Bourne. Available in the Seventh edition in 1979, it is the default shell on many System V versions. The C shell, written in the late 1970s primarily by Bill Joy, was made available soon after in 2.0 BSD. When introduced, it provided a C–program-like programming interface for writing shell scripts. Following the development of the C shell, the Korn shell was introduced officially in System V, Release 4, in 1986. Written by David Korn of Bell Laboratories, it included a superset of Bourne shell commands but had more functionality. It also included some useful features of the C shell. (*See* Figure 4.1 for further illustrations of shell history development.)

The three major shells have slightly different features and command sets. In this textbook, we discuss common features and command sets for all UNIX shells and versions. Whenever we discuss a feature or command that is particular to a shell or version, we state that specifically.

2.2.6 Current and Future Developments–LINUX

Probably the most exciting and challenging current UNIX development focuses on the UNIX-based system known as LINUX. The LINUX system was developed initially by Linus Torvalds, but through a concerted Internet-based effort on the part of many programmers, it grew into the logical successor of both System V and BSD. It contains features of both of these branches, as well as features of MIT's X Window System and other operating systems. As the primary market for computers in the world today is the networked personal computer and workstation, on which LINUX runs comfortably, significant advances in functionality and user-interface and personal productivity applications are anticipated in the near future.

2.3   Variations in UNIX Systems

As shown in Figure 2.1, the development of the UNIX systems proceeded along three main branches from a single core. Many of the branches' divergences and similarities were caused by the Bell Laboratories and AT&T legal licensing arrangements during the 1970s and 1980s. The primary advantage of the divergences was a command- and function-rich operating system in each of the branches. The early Bell Labs' releases were copied and distributed as source code, which academic and commercial users could easily modify to suit their hardware and software. Such adaptations led to a proliferation of ways in which various aspects of the operating system evolved. Even the later releases of System V and BSD could be modified easily via accommodations provided by the vendor of the operating system version, even if source code was not available. Many of the later releases were **compatibility releases** meant to provide uniformity between any particular implementation and its perceived competitors. The important contribution of these compatibility releases and their offshoots is a certain amount of homogeneity that is helpful, regardless of whether you use a modern derivative of System V, Release 4, BSD 4.4, XENIX, or LINUX.

Divergence has the drawback that programs and even commands that work on one version fail to work on another version, thus defeating the inherent strength of user-friendliness of the system itself. Attempts have been made to standardize UNIX–for example, via the IEEE Portable Operating System Interface (POSIX). This software standard not only covers UNIX, but also in particular specifies program operation and user interfaces, leaving their implementations to the developer. Several standards have been adopted, and more have been proposed. For example, adopted standard POSIX.2 specifies shell and utility standardization.

2.4   Web Resources

Table 2.1 lists useful Web sites for UNIX history.

■ **TABLE 2.1** Web Resources for UNIX History Reference

URL	Description
`www.bell-labs.com/history/unix/`	A Web page at Bell Labs, the birthplace of UNIX, describes the history of UNIX and biographies of its two primary creators, Dennis Ritchie and Ken Thompson. This page also gives a brief overview of UNIX.
`www.levenez.com/unix/`	This Web page has a wealth of interesting resources, including a detailed time line of UNIX history—an amazing diagram—and pictures of UNIX creators and other computer scientists who made major contributions toward its development and proliferation, including that of Linus Torvalds, the creator of LINUX Operating System. Also listed on this page are links for the histories of many popular UNIX systems such as BSD, HP-UX, SunOS, and FreeBSD. In addition, the page has links to the history of Windows operating systems, the history of non-UNIX operating systems, and the history of programming languages.
`http://www.unix-systems.org/ what_ is_unix/history_timeline.html`	The Web page contains a compact history of UNIX, with short descriptions of the new features added to the previous version.

Summary

The historical development of UNIX is characterized by an open systems approach, whereby the source code is freely distributed among users. Development of many versions of UNIX progressed along three main branches. Two of these branches, System V and BSD, can best be characterized as commercial and academic. Compatibility releases of various versions have been aimed at standardizing the system. The Portable Operating System Interface (POSIX) is one standardization effort.

Problems

1. How can you tell which variant from the main branches of UNIX (*see* Figure 2.1) is being used on the computer system that you log on to?

2. If you were designing a POSIX standard, what would you include in it? You might want to research the already adopted and proposed standards before answering this question.

3. What system was the immediate predecessor of UNIX? Where was this predecessor and UNIX itself initially developed, and by whom?

4. Name the major versions and the three main branches of UNIX development. Which was the commercial branch? Which was the academic branch?

5. What three important characteristics of UNIX during its early development helped popularize it? Explain how these characteristics apply to you as a UNIX user, whatever your perspective.

6. Name the two most popular UNIX systems that are the basis of most UNIX systems. Where were they developed?

7. Trace the history of UNIX by browsing the Web. How many UNIX systems have been developed so far? How many non-UNIX systems have been developed? What is the most popular UNIX system for PCs? Why do you think it is so popular?

Getting Started

Objectives

- To give an overview of the structure of a contemporary system
- To describe briefly the structure of the UNIX operating system
- To detail some important system setups

3.1   Introduction

As we mentioned previously, a computer system consists of several hardware and software components (also called *resources*). In this chapter, we describe the structure of a contemporary computer system and its most important and visible components. We also describe briefly the structure of the UNIX operating system, including the purpose of each component and the operations performed by the main part of the UNIX operating system, called the UNIX *kernel*. We then explain the log-in and log-out procedures and introduce some simple but important UNIX commands. One useful feature of the UNIX operating system is its online manual, which you can search to view the description of any command, utility, tool, or application. One of the commands described in this chapter allows you to browse the online UNIX manual.

3.2   Computer System Hardware

The hardware of a contemporary computer system consists of several subsystems, including main/primary memory, one or more CPUs, secondary storage devices (floppy and hard disk drives), and input/output (I/O) devices (CD-ROM drive, keyboard, scanner, printer, and mouse). Figure 3.1 shows schematically how these subsystems are connected. A brief description of each subsystem follows.

3.2.1   Main/Primary Storage

The main memory is a storage place that comprises a number of storage locations, with each location having an address. The size of a location is typically 1 byte. A **byte** (abbreviated B) is made up of 8 bits, and a **bit** is the smallest unit of storage that can store a 1 or a 0. The address of a location is a positive integer, with the first location having an address of 0. Each location can be randomly accessed by specifying its address. Figure 3.2 shows the logical view of a RAM with 2^N locations. If N is 10, the RAM size is $2^{10} = 1024$, also known as 1K (K for kilo), locations. If N is 20, the RAM size is $2^{20} = 1024*1024$, also known as 1M (M for mega), locations. If N is 30, the RAM size is $2^{30} = 1024*1024*1024$, also known as 1G (G for giga, or billion), locations. (Note the use of the asterisk for the multiplication symbol.)

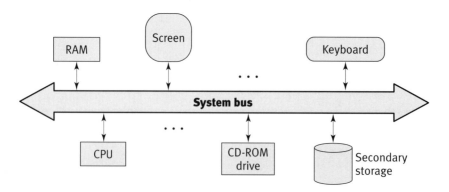

Figure 3.1 Diagram of a typical computer system

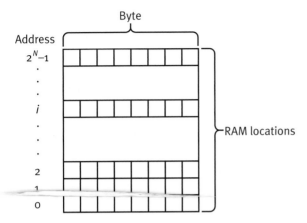

Figure 3.2 Logical structure of RAM with 2^N locations

The purpose of main storage is to store executing programs, or processes. This storage place is also called the *volatile* storage place because, when the power to the computer system is turned off, it loses whatever is stored in it. Typical personal computer systems today contain 128MB of RAM, and typical multiuser time-sharing systems contain about 512MB to 1GB of RAM. The speed at which a memory location can be accessed is known as the RAM **access time**. Today, typical RAMs have access times of 10 to 60 nanoseconds. A **nanosecond** is 10^{-9} sec.

3.2.2 Central Processing Unit (CPU)

The CPU is the brain of a computer system. This subsystem executes your programs by fetching them from the RAM, one instruction at a time. Most of the CPUs in today's computers can execute only one program at a time. The speed at which a CPU can execute instructions is dictated by its clock speed. Today's CPUs typically operate at 500M or more cycles per second. By the time this textbook is available, CPUs with clock speeds of 1.5G to 2G cycles per second will be available. One cycle per second is also known as 1 Hertz (Hz).

Every CPU has its own language, called its **instruction set**. A CPU can understand instructions only in its own instruction set, which is usually a superset of its predecessors made by the same company. Thus, most CPUs made by the same company can also execute programs written for their predecessors.

A CPU is functionally divided into two parts: a **control unit** and an **execution unit** (also called the *arithmetic and logic unit*, or *ALU*). The purpose of the control unit is to interact with the devices in the computer system (memory, keyboard, disk, display monitor, etc.) via the **controllers** (electronic circuitry) in these devices. The control unit also fetches a program instruction from the main memory and decodes it to determine whether the instruction is valid. If the instruction is valid, the control unit orchestrates execution of the instruction by the execution unit by delivering the appropriate sequence of control signals. Therefore, the purpose of the CPU is to fetch, decode, and execute program instructions. A CPU contains a number of storage locations that it uses as scratch pads. These storage locations are called the CPU **registers**. The number of registers in a CPU varies from a few to a few hundred. Each register has the same size–typically 32 or 64 bits for contemporary CPUs.

3.2.3 Disk

A disk is a storage place that contains all the computer system's programs and applications. It is a nonvolatile storage place that retains its contents even if the power to the computer is turned off. Disks are read and written in terms of **sectors** or **blocks**. Typical disks have a sector size (or blocksize) of 512B. Today's PCs use disk drives with storage capacities of 10 to 20GB. Typical multiuser network-based systems use 512GB hard disk storage space. The speed of a disk drive is dictated by its latency and seek times. The **latency time** for a disk is dictated by the speed at which the drive can spin (the unit used is rotations per minute, or rpm), and the **seek time** is governed by the speed at which the head can move (laterally). A typical disk drive has a latency time of a few milliseconds and a seek time of 8 milliseconds. A **millisecond** is 10^{-3} sec.

3.2.4 Bus

A *bus* is a set of parallel wires used to carry information in the form of bits from one subsystem in a computer to another. Each wire carries a single bit. The bus size, therefore, is measured in bits. A **system bus** consists of three types of buses: data bus, address bus, and control bus. The **data bus** is used to carry data from one subsystem to another. For example, it carries instructions for an executing program from the main memory to the CPU and the results of some computation from the CPU to the main memory. The **address bus** carries the address of a main memory location that has to be written to or read from. The **control bus** carries the control information, such as read or write instructions from the CPU to the main memory. The sizes of these buses in a computer system are dictated by the type of CPU. Typical data and address bus sizes today are 32 to 64 bits.

Before a command (application/program/tool/utility) starts execution, it resides on disk in the form of an executable program (a *binary* program or a *shell script*). When the user types a command line and hits the `<Enter>` (or `<Return>`) key (or points and clicks the application icon in a graphical user interface) to run the application, the **loader program** reads the application from the disk and loads it into the main memory. It then sets the internal state of the CPU so that it knows the location of the program's first instruction. The control unit of the CPU then fetches the first program instruction and decodes it to determine whether the instruction is a valid instruction for the CPU. If the control unit finds that the instruction is valid, it gives it to the execution unit, which executes the instruction. The fetch, decode, and execute operations form a **machine cycle**, as shown in Figure 3.3. The CPU remains in this cycle until either the program finishes and terminates normally or produces an error (exception) and

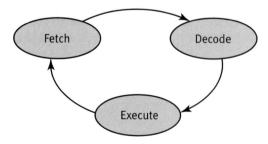

Figure 3.3 The machine cycle

terminates abnormally. The CPU then becomes idle and stays in this state until it starts execution of another user or system program or an I/O device needs the CPU's service.

3.2.5 I/O Devices

A contemporary computer system also has several input and output (I/O) devices that allow the user to run commands and applications, supply inputs, and capture outputs. Commonly used I/O devices are the keyboard, mouse, display monitor, printer, plotter, scanner, tape drive, DVD, and CD-ROM drive.

3.3   UNIX Software Architecture

Figure 3.4 shows a layered diagram for a UNIX-based computer system, identifying the system's software components and their logical proximity to the user and hardware. We briefly describe each software layer from the bottom up.

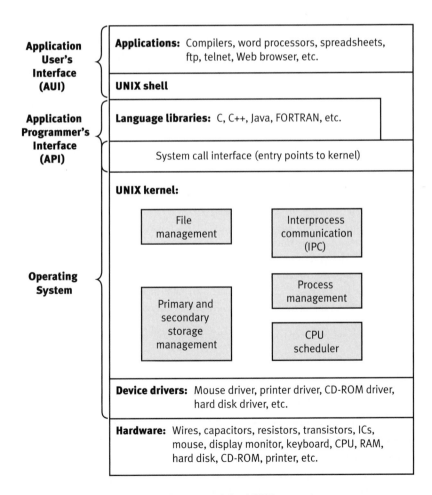

Figure 3.4 The software architecture of the UNIX operating system

3.3.1 Device Driver Layer

The purpose of the device driver layer is to interact with various hardware devices. It contains a separate program for interacting with each device, such as the hard disk driver, floppy disk driver, CD-ROM driver, keyboard driver, mouse driver, and display driver. These programs execute on behalf of the UNIX kernel when a user command or application needs to perform a hardware-related operation such as a file read (which translates to one or more disk reads). The user doesn't have direct access to these programs and therefore can't execute them as commands.

3.3.2 The UNIX Kernel

The UNIX kernel layer contains the actual operating system. Some of the main functions of the UNIX kernel are listed in Figure 3.4.

Process Management

The kernel manages processes in terms of creating, suspending, and terminating them, and maintaining their states. It also provides various mechanisms for processes to communicate with each other and schedules the CPU to execute multiple processes simultaneously in a time-sharing system. Interprocess communication (IPC) is the key to today's client-server–based software that is the foundation for Internet applications such as Netscape Navigator. The UNIX system provides three primary IPC mechanisms/channels.

- ❖ *Pipe:* A pipe can be used as an IPC channel by two or more related processes running on the same computer. Typically, these processes have a parent-child or sibling relationship. A pipe is a temporary channel that resides in the main memory and is created by the kernel usually on behalf of the parent process.
- ❖ *Named Pipe:* A named pipe (also known as *FIFO*) is a permanent communication channel that resides on the disk and can be used for IPC by two or more related or unrelated processes that are *running on the same computer.*
- ❖ *BSD Socket:* A BSD socket is also a temporary channel that allows two or more processes in a network (or on the Internet) to communicate, although they can also be used by processes on the same computer. Sockets were originally a part of the BSD UNIX only, but they are now available on almost every UNIX system. Internet software such as Web browsers, ftp, telnet, and electronic mailers are implemented by using sockets. AT&T UNIX has a similar mechanism called the *Transport Layer Interface (TLI).*

A detailed description of these mechanisms is beyond the scope of this textbook.

File Management

The kernel also manages files and directories (also known as folders). It performs all file-related tasks, such as file creation and removal, directory creation and removal, and file and directory attribute maintenance. A file operation usually requires manipulation of a disk. In a multiuser system, a user must never be allowed to manipulate a disk directly because it contains files belonging to other users, and user access to a disk poses a security threat. Only the kernel must perform all file-related operations, such as file removal. Also, only the kernel must decide where and how much space to allocate to a file.

Main Memory Management

This part of the kernel allocates and deallocates RAM in an orderly manner so that each process gets enough space to execute properly. It also ensures that part or all of the space allocated to a process does not belong to some other process. The space allocated to a process in the memory for its execution is known as its **process address space**. The kernel maintains areas in the main memory that are free to be used so that, when a program is to be loaded in the main memory, adequate space can be allocated. It also records where all the processes reside in the memory so that, when a process tries to access main memory space that does not belong to it, the kernel can terminate the process and give a meaningful message to the user. When a process terminates, the kernel deallocates the space allocated to the process and puts this space back in the free space pool so that it can be reused.

Disk Management

The kernel is also responsible for maintaining free and used disk space and for the orderly and fair allocation and deallocation of disk space. It decides where and how much space to allocate to a newly created file. Also, the kernel performs **disk scheduling**, deciding which request to serve next when multiple requests (for file read, write, etc.) arrive for the same disk.

In addition, the kernel performs several other tasks for fair, orderly, and safe use of the computer system. These tasks include managing the CPU, printers, and other I/O devices. The kernel ensures that no user process takes over the CPU forever, that multiple files are not printed on a printer simultaneously, and that a user cannot terminate another user's process.

3.3.3 The System Call Interface

The system call interface layer contains *entry points* into the kernel code. Because all system resources are managed by the kernel, any user or application request that involves access to any system resource must be handled by the kernel code. But user processes must not be given open access to the kernel code for security reasons. So that user processes can invoke (start) the execution of kernel code, UNIX provides several gates, or function calls, known as *system calls*. Tens of system calls allow the user to manipulate processes, files, and other system resources. These calls are well tested, and most of them have been used for several years, so their use poses much less of a security risk than if any user code were allowed to perform the task.

3.3.4 Language Libraries

A **library** is a set of prewritten and pretested functions available to programmers for use with the software that they develop. The availability and use of libraries saves time because programmers do not have to write these functions from scratch. This layer contains libraries for several languages, such as C, C++, Java, and FORTRAN. For the C language, for example, there are several libraries, including a string library (that contains functions for processing strings, such as a function for comparing two strings) and a math library (that contains functions for mathematical operations, such as a finding the cosine of an angle).

As we mentioned in Chapter 1, the libraries and system call interface what is commonly known as the application programmer's interface (API). In other words, programmers who write software in a language such as C can use library and system calls in their codes.

3.3.5 UNIX Shell

The UNIX shell is a program that starts running when you log on and interprets the commands that you enter. We discuss this topic in detail later in this chapter and in Chapters 4 and 13.

3.3.6 Applications

The applications layer contains all the applications (tools, commands, and utilities) that are available for your use. A typical UNIX system contains hundreds of applications; we discuss the most useful and commonly used applications throughout this textbook. When an application that you're using needs to manipulate a system resource (e.g., reading a file), it needs to invoke some kernel code that performs the task. An application can get the appropriate kernel code to execute in one of two ways: (1) by using a proper library function and (2) by using a system call. Library calls constitute a higher level interface to the kernel than system calls, which makes library calls a bit easier to use. However, all library calls eventually use system calls to start execution of appropriate kernel code. Therefore, the use of library calls results in slightly slower execution. A detailed discussion of library and system calls is beyond the scope of this textbook, but we briefly describe a few library and system calls in later chapters.

The user can use any command or application that is available on the system. As we mentioned in Chapter 1, this layer is commonly known as the application user's interface (AUI).

3.4   Logging On and Logging Off

The UNIX system is a multiprocess, multiuser, and interactive computing environment. That is, a user can start and run several computational processes or programs at once, and many users can be using the system at the same time. One of the most important differences between UNIX and other operating systems is that UNIX was originally designed for a multiuser computing environment, where many people share the same computer system by hooking up to it with terminals, or *consoles*. But UNIX can be run on a stand-alone computer, such as a PC, just as well. The hallmark of UNIX is its **portability**, or the ability to move the source code for the system easily and without major modifications from one hardware platform to the next.

You can connect to a UNIX operating system in three basic ways. However, there are variations of all three methods that can be combinations of two or more of them. Also, any variations are affected by the system setup of any single component.

1. *Local area network connection.* Loosely stated, this method is a modern variation of the traditional terminals connected to a mainframe, such as VT-100 connected to VAX 11/780, using RS-232. That is true because, even in the modern method, the "terminal" has little or no local compute power, it acts as a dumb graphical server, and a single computer (the component that does have local compute power) can serve many such terminals. When you use this method, you sit at a terminal that is connected by a very high-speed communications link to a single computer or multiple computers that are all interconnected with a **Local Area Network (LAN)**. That terminal is your interface with the operating system running on a single or multiple computer(s). This method can also be called **intranet login**. We present more information on the concept of graphical servers in Chapter 21.

2. *Internet connection.* This method is similar to LAN login, but the network is a federation of LANs and **Wide Area Networks (WANs)**, usually the Internet. You sit at a remote, stand-alone computer, and via some software, such as Windows Telnet for the PC or NCSA Telnet for Macintosh, you connect to another system over a moderately high-speed telecommunications link. The telnet software then becomes your graphical server, allowing you to log on to and use a remote computer or system that is running UNIX. This method can also be called **Internet login**. We present more information on the UNIX telnet command in Chapter 14.

   3. *Stand-alone connection.* This method involves sitting at a computer that is *not* hooked up to a LAN, intranet, or Internet. Rather, the connection is dedicated to a single user sitting in front of the computer and logging on to use UNIX on that hardware platform only. The first two methods described here eventually look and feel exactly like your interaction with UNIX in this method.

   For example, a combination of the three methods can work as follows. You sit at a stand-alone computer and turn the power button to On; the computer boots up and shows you the UNIX **login prompt**. You log in to this stand-alone machine, and you enable the LAN connection on this stand-alone computer. You then use the UNIX telnet command to log on to a remote host on your intranet, which is also running UNIX, and work with the operating system there. Finally, you use telnet to go from your LAN to a remote site on the Internet, log on to a computer in a remote location–perhaps Pakistan–and work with UNIX on that computer. We've simplified the example by assuming that most of the computers in this combination scheme are running UNIX. If you use telnet or ssh to connect to a UNIX system and you are a beginner, you should write down the exact steps involved in making the telnet connection. Be sure to include all the details of the connection procedure, including any preference changes, and be as explicit as possible.

   If you use any of the three methods or a combination of them to connect to a UNIX system, identifying yourself to the system is your first task. Doing so involves typing in a valid **username**, or **login name**, consisting of a string of valid characters associated with a **userid** given to you by your system administrator. For our purposes, we use the words *username*, *login name*, and *userid* interchangeably. You then type in a valid **password** for that username. See Section 3.7.1 to find out how to change your password. Depending on the way that your system administrator has set up your particular installation, the login prompt appears on the screen of the terminal or computer that you sit in front of, similar to Figure 3.5. Items enclosed in brackets [ ] are system-dependent and may or may not appear during your log-in procedure.

```
login: your username  ↵

password: your password  ↵

[display=default]  ↵

[terminal=default]  ↵

[message from the file /etc/motd]

$
```

Figure 3.5 Login screen display for a typical UNIX computer

Note: In this chapter, we use <Enter> or <↵> to indicate either the <Enter> or <Return> key. In the remainder of the book, when we ask you to type or use a command, we assume that you will press the <Enter> key because the shell does not start interpreting your command until you do so. But we will no longer show either <Enter> or <↵>.

At the login: prompt, you type in your username and press the <Enter> key. Next, a password: prompt appears, and you type in your assigned password, followed by pressing the <Enter> key. Optionally, depending on your system setup, you may be asked to type in both the kind of display that you are sitting in front of and the kind of terminal that you want to use during this session. Both may have defaults assigned, for which you can signify acceptance by pressing the <Enter> key after the display and terminal prompts. Also, an optional message may appear on your screen from the system administrator, announcing news or important information.

Note: Write down your username and password on paper, and keep them in a secure place, in case you forget them.

After successfully logging on to your UNIX computer, a **shell prompt**, such as the $ character, appears on the screen. The shell prompt is simply a message from the computer system telling you that it is ready to accept typed input on the **command line** that directly follows the prompt. The general syntax, or structure of a single command as it is typed on the command line, is as follows:

```
$ command [[-]option(s)] [option argument(s)] [command argument(s)]
```

where:

> $ is the shell prompt from the computer,
> anything enclosed in [   ] is *not* always needed,
> command is the name of the valid UNIX command for that shell in lowercase letters,
>
> [-option(s)] is one or more modifiers that change the behavior of command,
>
> [option argument(s)] is one or more modifiers that change the behavior of -option(s), and
>
> [command argument(s)] is one or more objects that are affected by command.

Note that a space separates command, option, option argument, and command argument, but *no* space is necessary between multiple option(s) or multiple option arguments. Note that the order of multiple options or option arguments is irrelevant. Also, a space character is optional between the option and the option argument. *Always press the* <Enter> *key to submit the command to the shell for interpretation.*

The following items illustrate some of the ways that a single command can be typed, along with options and arguments, on the command line.

```
$ ls
$ ls -la
$ ls -la m*
$ lpr -Pspr -n 3 proposal.ps
```

The first item contains only the command. The second contains the command `ls` and two options, `l` and `a`. The third contains the command `ls`; two options; `l` and `a`; and a command argument, `m*`. The fourth contains the command `lpr`; two options, `P` and `n`; two option arguments; `spr` and `3`; and a command argument, `proposal.ps`. (Note that these items are case-specific.)

Thus you are able to type commands on the command line displayed in the console window. UNIX systems use this **text-based form of interaction** between each user and the computer system, where each user can concurrently type commands using the correct syntax. Then the operating system interprets the command line contents and takes actions based on the content of the command. We discuss the details of shells and how commands are interpreted in Chapters 4 and 13.

The procedure for logging off the computer, or leaving the system correctly, is as important as the procedure for logging on. To log off, at the shell prompt on a blank line, press and hold down the `<Ctrl>` key while pressing the `<D>` key on the keyboard. You will then be logged off the system for the current session with the computer, and the login prompt shown in Figure 3.5 will reappear on-screen, allowing you to log on for another session. If you initiated your connection with the UNIX system via the `telnet` command, your telnet connection closes at this point. We refer to pressing and holding down the `<Ctrl>` key while pressing the `<D>` key as `<Ctrl-D>` or `<^D>` in this textbook. We use text type with brackets for the keyboard keys to indicate that you are to press (type) them, and we use boldface monospace type for commands and strings of characters that you type on the keyboard.

If you started a new shell during your session and didn't exit that shell before logging off, UNIX will prompt `Not login shell`, and you will *not* be able to log off immediately. In this case, press `<Ctrl-D>`, and the new shell will terminate. Also, if you started more than one shell and haven't exited from those shells before you log off, you will have to use the `<Ctrl-D>` as many times as you have nonterminated shells before you can log off. On some systems, you must type `exit` on the command line to terminate a shell process. In either case, you will then be able to use the logoff procedure described to leave the system properly. To practice logging on and logging off, do Problem 9 at the end of this chapter.

3.5 Correcting Mistakes

While you are using a UNIX system, you may need to correct typos before you press `<Enter>`. Table 3.1 lists some important keys or key combinations that you can use to correct your typing mistakes. Also listed are some key combinations that you can use to stop and restart output of a program on the screen. For each key combination, as with `<Ctrl-D>`, press and hold down the `<Ctrl>` key while pressing the second key.

■■ **TABLE 3.1** Important Control Key Combinations

Key Combination	Purpose
`<Back Space>` or `<Ctrl-H>`	Erase the previous character and move the cursor to the previous character position

(continued)

TABLE 3.1 (continued)

`<Ctrl-U>`	Erase the entire current line and move the cursor to the beginning of the current line
`<Ctrl-C>`	Terminate the current command and move the cursor to the beginning of the next line
`<Ctrl-S>`	Stop scrolling of output on the screen (or console window); this keystroke is no longer commonly used because the output shown on the screen scrolls very fast on today's high-speed computers
`<Ctrl-Q>`	Restart scrolling of output on the screen (or console window); this key combination is used in tandem with `<Ctrl-S>`

3.6   Some Important System Setups

The properties and appearance of the console window itself—and the environment within which the commands are interpreted—have been established by your system administrator for a typical computer user. The environmental settings are controlled by **environment variables**, which obtain or are set to their default when you log on. The environment controls which shell, or command line interpreter, you use when you type commands and other important processes. In this textbook, we assume that you are running one of the popular shells—the Bourne shell (abbreviated **sh**), the Bourne Again shell (abbreviated **bash**), the Korn shell (abbreviated **ksh**), or the C shell (abbreviated **csh**).

To find the default setting of an individual environment variable (e.g., the environment variable that controls the shell you are running), type `echo $SHELL` and then press `<Enter>`. The system replies by showing on the screen the path to the shell that you are running by default.

To view a list of the default environment variable settings if you are running sh, bash, or ksh, type `set` and then press `<Enter>`. The settings of the sh, bash, or ksh environment variables will appear on the screen.

To see a list of the default environment variable settings if you are running csh, type `setenv` or `printenv` at the shell prompt and then press `<Enter>`. The settings of the csh environment variables will be displayed on the screen.

You can easily change these environment variable settings for the duration of one session or for every subsequent session. However, you should *not* change several of the environment variables, particularly if you are a beginner with UNIX. For a list of environment variables that you can safely change, *see* Table 4.3.

To set an environment variable for the current session if you are running sh, bash, or ksh, type `Variable=Setting` and then press `<Enter>`. `Variable` is a valid environment variable, and `Setting` is a valid setting for that environment variable.

To set an environment variable for the current session if you are running the csh, type
`setenv Variable Setting` and then press `<Enter>`. `Variable` is a valid environment
variable, and `Setting` is a valid setting for that environment variable.

To set an environment variable for all subsequent sessions, you must edit the **configuration file** for the shell you are running by using a text editor, change the environment variable
setting of interest, and then save the changes you make in that configuration file in the editor. Table 3.2 contains a list of UNIX shells and the names of the primary and/or secondary
configuration files for those shells in your home directory; the tilde (~) is a shorthand way
of representing your home directory on most contemporary UNIX systems. *Note:* Do *not*
attempt to edit that file.

■ **TABLE 3.2** Shell Configuration Files

UNIX Shell	Name of the Configuration File(s)
Bourne (sh), Korn (ksh)	/etc/profile*, ~/.profile
Korn (ksh)	~/.kshrc
C (csh)	~/.login, ~/.cshrc
Bash (bash)	~/.bashrc, ~/.bash_profile
Z (zsh)	~/.zshrc
TC (tcsh)	~/.tcshrc

Always make copies of your default configuration files with the `cp` command *before*
attempting to edit them to change environment variables. For example, to make a backup
copy of your .cshrc file, type `cp .cshrc .cshrc_bak_20Mar04` and then press `<Enter>`.
After this command executes, you will have two identical files, one named .cshrc and another
named .cshrc_bak_20Mar04. That way, if you make a mistake while editing .cshrc, you can
revert to the .bak version of the file using the `mv` command, as follows: Leave the text editor,
type `rm .cshrc` and then press `<Enter>`. Type `cp .cshrc_bak_20Mar04 .cshrc` and
then press `<Enter>`. Your old .cshrc file has now been reinstalled. If you need to correct both
the original and the backup(s), you can get a new .cshrc file from the system administrator.

These changes in your environment variables will take effect the next time you log on
and will remain in effect for every subsequent session. See Chapter 4 for a further description of how to change your environment variables in the appropriate configuration file for
a shell.

The following In-Chapter Exercises ask you to change one of your environmental variables
and see the effects of the change. We assume that you are running the Bourne shell. If you
are running another shell, substitute the syntax for that shell for the syntax shown.

IN-CHAPTER EXERCISES

3.1 At the shell prompt, type echo $LINES and then press <Enter>. The system gives you a message that shows the number of lines visible in the console window. How many are visible in your console window? If your system shows a blank line, run the following commands.

```
LINES=25

export LINES
```

Run the echo $LINES command again, and you will see 25 as the output of the command.

3.2 At the shell prompt, type set | more and then press <Enter>. The system displays a list of environment variables and their current settings. What is the setting for each of the variables shown in Table 3.1? How many lines at a time are displayed by the more command?

3.3 At the shell prompt, type LINES=half and press <Enter>, and then type export LINES and press <Enter>. Here, half is a number half the size of that which the system showed you in Exercise 3.1. Run the echo $LINES and set | more commands again. How does your screen display differ from the screen display obtained in Exercise 3.1?

3.4 At the shell prompt, type LINES=full and press <Enter>, and then type export LINES and press <Enter>. Here, full is a number equal to the one the system showed you in Exercise 3.1. How does your screen display differ from the screen displays obtained in Exercises 3.1 and 3.3?

For further practice in setting environment variables, do Problem 10 at the end of this chapter.

Summary

A computer system consists of several hardware and software components. The primary hardware components of a typical computer system include a central processing unit (CPU), main memory (commonly known as RAM), disk drive(s), a keyboard, a mouse, a display screen, a bus, and several other input/output (I/O) devices. The software components of a typical UNIX system consist of several layers: applications, shell, language libraries, system call interface, UNIX kernel, and device drivers. The kernel is the main part of the UNIX operating system and performs all the tasks that deal with allocation and deallocation of system resources. The shell and applications layers contain what is commonly known as the application user's interface (AUI). The language libraries and the system call interface contain the application programmer's interface (API).

A computer using the UNIX operating system can run many programs for the same user at the same time (multiprocess and multitasking). It can also support many different users at once (multiuser and time-sharing). To operate in a multiuser environment, a user must log on and log off the system in order to maintain the security of the system and the integrity of the files of all the users.

Problems

1. What is the purpose of main memory?

2. What do *bit* and *byte* represent? What do the storage units *kilo*, *mega*, and *giga* signify?

3. What is the purpose of the central processing unit? What comprises a machine cycle?

4. What is a bus, and what is its purpose in a computer system? What are the sizes of the data, address, and control buses in your computer? (*Hint:* Read the user's manual for the CPU in your computer or visit the home page of the CPU manufacturer on the Internet.)

5. What is an operating system kernel? What are the primary tasks performed by the UNIX kernel?

6. What is a system call? What is the purpose of the system call interface?

7. What comprises AUI and API?

8. Give the sequence of events that take place when you type a command line and press <Enter> before the command executes. Be precise.

9. If you access a UNIX system with the `telnet` command, write down the exact step-by-step procedure you go through to log on and log off. Include as many descriptive details as possible in this procedure so that if you forget how to log on, you can always refer back to this written procedure.

10. Log on to your UNIX computer system and note the shell prompt being used. Most important, which shell is it for? How can you identify a particular shell by the prompt displayed on-screen? How can you change the shell prompt? Experiment with changing the shell prompt to some other character, such as > or + .

11. What is your initial username/password pair? What is the name of the computer system that you are logging on to? What command did you use?

12. Give several examples of bad passwords, that is, passwords that you should *not* use, and explain why they are bad.

UNIX Shells

Objectives

- To describe what a UNIX shell is
- To describe briefly some commonly used shells

4.1 Introduction

When you log on, the UNIX system starts running a program that acts as an interface between you and the UNIX kernel. This program, called the UNIX *shell*, executes the commands that you have typed on the keyboard. When a shell starts running, it gives you a prompt and waits for your commands. When you type a command and press <Enter>, the shell interprets your command and executes it. If you type a nonexistent command, the shell tells you this, then redisplays the prompt and waits for you to type the next command. Because the primary purpose of the shell is to interpret your commands, it is also known as the UNIX **command interpreter**.

A shell command can be *internal/built-in* or *external*. The code to execute an internal command is part of the shell process, but the code to process an external command resides in a file in the form of a binary executable program file or a shell script. (We describe in detail how a shell executes commands in Chapter 13.) Because the shell executes commands entered from the keyboard, it terminates when it finds out that it cannot read anything else from the keyboard. You can inform your shell of this by pressing <Ctrl-D> at the beginning of a new line. As soon as the shell receives <Ctrl-D>, it terminates and logs you off the system. The system then displays the login: prompt again, informing you that you need to log on again in order to use it.

The shell interprets your commands by assuming that the first word in a command line is the name of the command that you want to execute. It assumes that any of the remaining words starting with a hyphen (-) are options and that the rest of them are the command arguments. After reading your command line, it determines whether the command is an internal or external command. It processes all internal commands by using the corresponding code segments that are within its own code. To execute an external command, it searches several directories in the **file system structure** (*see* Chapter 7), looking for a file that has the name of the command. It then assumes that the file contains the code to be executed and runs the code. The names of the directories that a shell searches to find the file corresponding to an external command are stored in the shell variable *PATH* (or *path* in the C shell). Directory names are separated by colons in the Bourne, Korn, and Bash shells and by spaces in the C shell. The directory names stored in the *PATH* variable form what is known as the **search path** for the shell. You can view the search path for your variable by using the echo $PATH command in the Bourne, Korn, and Bash shells and the echo $PATH command in the C shell. The following is a sample run of this command under the Bourne (Korn and Bash) and C shells, respectively. Note that in the Bourne shell the search path contains the directory names separated by colons and that in the C shell the directory names are separated by spaces.

```
$ echo $PATH
/usr/sbin:/usr/X11/include/X11:.:/users/faculty/sarwar/bin:/usr/ucb
:/bin:/usr/bin:/usr/include:/usr/X11/lib:/usr/lib:/etc:/usr/etc:/usr
/local/bin:/usr/local/lib:/usr/local/games:/usr/X11/bin
$
% echo $path
/usr/sbin /usr/X11/include/X11 . /users/faculty/sarwar/bin /usr/ucb /bin
```

```
/usr/bin /usr/include /usr/X11/lib /usr/lib /etc /usr/etc /usr
/local/bin /usr/local/lib /usr/local/games /usr/X11/bin
%
```

The *PATH* (or *path*) variable is defined in a **hidden file** (also known as a **dot file**) called .profile (System V) or .login (BSD). If you can't find this variable in one of those files, it is in the **start-up file** (also a dot file) specific to the shell that you're using. (*See* Section 4.2.4 for more details.) You can change the search path for your shell by changing the value of this variable. To change the search path temporarily for your current session only, you can change the value of *PATH* at the command line. For a permanent change, you need to change the value of this variable in the corresponding dot file. In the following example, the search path was augmented by two directories, ~/bin and . (current directory). Moreover, the search starts with ~/bin and ends with the current directory. But, be careful when editing or changing the *PATH* variable so that you don't lose any component of the default research path set by the system administrator for all users of the system.

```
$ PATH=~/bin:$PATH:.
$
```

You can determine your login shell by using the echo $SHELL command, as described in Chapter 3. Each shell has several other environment variables set up in a hidden file associated with it. We describe these files in Section 4.2 and present a detailed discussion of UNIX files in Chapter 7.

4.2   Various UNIX Shells

Every UNIX system comes with a variety of shells, with the Bourne, C, and Korn shells being the most common. The Bash, TC, and Z shells are relatively new and are more popular with LINUX systems. When you log on, one particular type of shell starts execution. This shell is known as your **login shell**, and it is determined by the system administrator of your computer system. If you want to use a different shell, you can do so by running a corresponding command available on your system. For example, if your login shell is Bourne but you want to use the C shell, you can do so by using the csh command.

4.2.1   Shell Programs

As we mentioned in Section 4.1, essentially a shell is an **interpreted program**, which might give you a hint about why there are so many different shells. Programs have a tendency to evolve and grow with time, depending on the needs of users, and shell programs are typical of this evolution. Table 4.1 contains a list of the most common shells, their location on the system, and the program names of those shells. *Note:* The locations shown here are typical for most systems; consult your instructor or system administrator if you can't find the location shown for a shell on your system, or if you can't use the whereis command, as shown in Chapter 3.

Figure 4.1 traces the development of various shell families and indicates the increasing functionality of each family as it appears higher in the hierarchy. The Bourne shell (sh) is the "grandmother" of the main shell families and has nearly the least level of functionality. Near

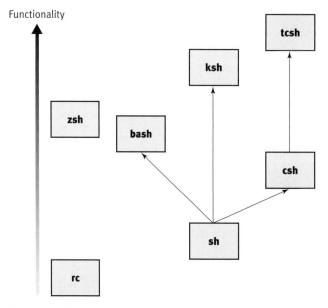

Figure 4.1 Shell families and their relative functionalities

the top of the hierarchy is the Korn shell (ksh), which includes all the functionality of the Bourne shell and much more. The rc and zsh shells are outliers that cannot be readily associated with any of the primary shell families.

4.2.2 Which Shell Suits Your Needs?

Most shells perform some similar functions, and knowing the details of how they do so is important in deciding which shell to use for a particular task. Also, using more than one shell during a session is a common practice, especially among shell programmers. For example, you might use the Bourne or Korn shell for their programming capabilities and use the C shell to execute individual commands. We discuss this example further in Section 4.2.3. The similarities of major shell functions are summarized in Table 4.2.

■■ **TABLE 4.1** Shell Locations and Program Names

Shell	Location on System	Program (Command) Name
rc	/usr/bin/rc	rc
Bourne shell	/usr/bin/sh	sh
C shell	/usr/bin/csh	csh
Bourne Again shell	/bin/bash	bash
Z shell	/usr/local/bin/zsh	zsh
Korn shell	/usr/bin/ksh	ksh
TC shell	/usr/bin/tcsh	tcsh

■■ **TABLE 4.2** Shell Similarities

Function	Description
Execution	The ability to execute programs and commands
I/O Handling	The control of program and command input and output
Programming	The ability to execute sequences of programs and commands

4.2.3 Ways to Change Your Shell

As we mentioned in Section 4.1, you can easily determine what your default shell is by typing echo $SHELL on the command line when you first log on to your computer system. The question is: Why would you want to change your default shell, or for that matter, even use an additional shell? The answer is that you want the greater functionality of another shell. For example, your default shell might be the C shell (csh). A friend of yours offers you a neat and useful Bourne shell script that allows you to take advantage of the Bourne shell programming capabilities, a script that wouldn't work if it ran under the C shell. You can use this script by running the Bourne shell at the same time you are running the default C shell. Because UNIX is a multiprocess operating system, more than one command line interpreter at a time can be active. That doesn't mean that a single command will be interpreted multiply; it simply means that input, output, and errors are "hooked" into whatever shell process has control over them currently. (*See* Chapter 13 for more information about process and shell command input/output.)

You can change your shell in one of two ways: (1) changing to a new default for every subsequent login session on your system; and (2) creating additional shell sessions running on top of, or concurrently with, the default shell. The premise of both methods is that the shell you want to change to is available on your system, as described in Section 4.2.1.

To change your default shell, after you have logged on, type chsh and then press <Enter>. Depending on your system, you will be prompted for the name of the shell you want to change to. Type the location of the shell you want to change to–for example, /usr/bin/sh to change to the Bourne shell. If this method doesn't work on your system, consult your instructor or system administrator for more help.

To create or run additional shells on top of your default shell, simply type the name of the shell program (*see* Table 4.1) on the command line whenever you want to run that shell. The following session illustrates the use of this method to change a default Bourne shell, which uses the $ as the shell prompt, to a C shell, which shows the % as the shell prompt.

```
$ echo $SHELL
/usr/bin/sh
$ csh
%
```

The first command line allows you to determine your default shell. In this case, the system shows you that the default setting is the Bourne shell. The second command line allows you to run the C shell. The fourth line shows that you have been successful, because the default

C shell prompt appears on your display. If the C shell was not available on your system or was inaccessible to you, you would get an error message after the third line. If your search path does not include /usr/bin, you either have to type `/usr/bin/csh` in place of csh or include /usr/bin in your shell's search path and then use the `csh` command.

To terminate or leave this new, temporary shell and return to your default login shell, press `<Ctrl-D>` on a blank line. If this way of terminating the new shell doesn't work, type `exit` on the command line and then press `<Enter>`. By doing so, you halt the running of the new shell, and the default shell prompt appears on your display.

The following In-Chapter Exercises ask you to determine whether various shells are available on your system by using the `whereis` command and, for those that are available, to read the *Manual Pages* for them by using the `man` command.

IN-CHAPTER EXERCISES

> **4.1**   Using the `whereis` command illustrated in Chapter 3, verify the locations of the various shells listed in Table 4.1. Are all these shells available on your system? Where are they located if you do not find them at the locations shown in Table 4.1?
>
> **4.2**   Using the `man` command illustrated in Chapter 3, read the *Manual Pages* for each shell listed in Table 4.1 that is on your system.

4.2.4 Shell Start-up Files and Environment Variables

The actions of each shell, the mechanics of how it executes commands and programs, how it handles the command and program I/O, and how it is programmed, are affected by the setting of certain environment variables, which we mentioned briefly in Section 3.6. Each UNIX system has an initial system start-up file, usually named .profile in System V and .login in BSD. This file contains the initial settings of important environment variables for the shell and some other utilities. In addition, hidden files for specific shells are executed when you start a particular shell. Known as the shell start-up files, they are .cshrc for C shell and .bashrc for Bash. These hidden files are initially configured by the system administrator for secure use by all users. Table 4.3 lists some important environment variables common to Bourne, Korn, and C shells; the C shell variable name, where applicable, is in lowercase following the Bourne and Korn shell variable name. Note that your system administrator may not have set some of these variables, such as *ENV*.

■■ TABLE 4.3 Shell Environment Variables

Environment Variable	What It Affects
CDPATH, cdpath	The alias names for directories accessed with the `cd` command
EDITOR	The default editor used in programs such as the e-mail program `pine`

(continued)

TABLE 4.3 (continued)

ENV	The path along which UNIX looks to find configuration files
HOME, home	The name of the user's home directory when the user first logs on
MAIL, mail	The name of the system mailbox file
PATH, path	The directories that a shell searches to find a command or program
PS1, prompt	The shell prompt that appears on the command line
PWD, cwd	The name of the current working directory
TERM	The type of console terminal being used

The following In-Chapter Exercises let you view the settings of your environment variables. They assume that you are initially running the Bourne or Korn shells. If you aren't, run either of those shells as described in Section 4.2.3 and then do the exercises.

IN-CHAPTER EXERCISES

4.3 At the shell prompt, type set | more and then press <Enter>. What is displayed on your screen? Identify and list the settings for all the environment variables shown in Table 4.3.

4.4 At the shell prompt, type csh and then press <Enter>. Next, type setenv | more and then press <Enter>. Identify and list the settings for all the environment variables shown in Table 4.3.

In addition to the shells, several other programs have their own hidden files. These files are used to set up and configure the operating environment within which these programs execute. We discuss some of these hidden files in Chapters 5 and 6. They are called hidden files because when you list the names of files contained in your home directory—for example, with the ls -l command and option (*see* Chapter 7)—these files do not appear on the list. The hidden file names always start with a dot (.), such as .login.

4.3   Shell Metacharacters

Most of the characters other than letters and digits have special meaning to the shell. These characters are called **shell metacharacters** and therefore cannot be used in shell commands as literal characters without specifying them in a particular way. Thus, try not to use them in naming your files. Also, when these characters are used in commands, no space is required before or after a character. However, you can use spaces before and after a shell metacharacter for clarity. Table 4.4 contains a list of the shell metacharacters and their purpose.

The shell metacharacters allow you to specify multiple files in multiple directories in one command line. We describe the use of these characters in subsequent chapters, but we give some simple examples here to explain the meanings of some commonly used metacharacters:

*, ?, ~, and [ ]. The ?.txt string can be used for all the files that have a single character before .txt, such as a.txt, G.txt, @.txt, and 7.txt. The [0-9].c string can be used for all the files in a directory that have a single digit before .c, such as 3.c and 8.c. The lab1\/c string stands for lab1/c. Note the use of backslash (\ ) to quote (escape) the slash character (/). The following command prints the names of all the files in your current directory that have two-character file names and an .html extension, with the first character being a digit and the second being an uppercase or lowercase letter. The printer on which these files are printed is spr.

■ **TABLE 4.4** Shell Metacharacters

Metacharacter	Purpose	Example
New Line	To end a command line	
Space	To separate elements on a command line	`ls /etc`
Tab	To separate elements on a command line	`ls /etc`
#	To start a comment	`# This is a comment line`
"	To quote multiple characters but allow substitution	`"$file" bak`
$	To end line and dereference a shell variable	`$PATH`
&	To provide background execution of a command	`command &`
'	To quote multiple characters	`'$100,000'`
( )	To execute a command list in a subshell	`(command1; command2)`
*	To match zero or more characters	`chap*.ps`
[ ]	To insert wild cards	`[a-s]` or `[1,5-9]`
^	To begin a line and negation symbol	`[^3-8]`
`	To substitute a command	`` PS1=`command` ``
{ }	To execute a command list in the current shell	`{command1; command2}`
|	To create a pipe between commands	`command1 | command2`
;	To separate commands in sequential execution	`command1; command2`
<	To redirect input for a command	`command < file`
>	To redirect output for a command	`command > file`

(continued)

TABLE 4.4 *(continued)*

?	To substitute a wild card for exactly one character	`lab.?`
/	To be used as the root directory and as a component separator in a pathname	`/usr/bin`

\	To escape/quote a single character; used to quote <New Line> character to allow continuation of a shell command on the following line	`command arg1 \`
		`arg2 arg3`
		`\?`

C and Korn Shells Only

!	To start an event specification in the history list and the current event	`!!, !$, !4`
%	The C shell prompt, or the starting character for specifying a job number	`% or %3`
~	To name home directory	`~/.profile`

```
$ lpr -Pspr [0-9][a-zA-Z].html
$
```

Note that `[0-9]` means any digits from 0 through 9 and `[a-zA-Z]` means any lowercase or uppercase letter. The following command displays the names of all six-character–long files with .c extension in your current directory, with the first three characters being 'lab', the fourth being a digit, and the remaining being any two characters.

```
$ ls lab[0-9]??.c
lab11a.c lab1a1.c lab123.c lab4ab.c
$
```

Summary

When you log on to a UNIX computer, the system runs a program called a shell that gives you a prompt and waits for you to type commands, one per line. When you type a command and hit <Enter>, the shell tries to execute the command, assuming that the first word in the command line is the name of the command. A `shell` command can be built-in or external. The shell has the code for executing a built-in command, but the code for an external command is in a file. To execute an external command, the shell searches several directories, one by one, to locate the file that contains the code for the command. If the file is found, it is executed if it contains code (binary or shell script). The names of the directories that the shell searches to locate the file for an external command form what is known as the search path. The search path is stored in a shell variable called *PATH* (for the Bourne, Korn, and Bash shells) or *path* (for the C shell). You can change the search path for your shell by adding new directory names in *PATH* or by deleting some existing directory names from it.

Several shells are available for you to use. These shells differ in terms of convenience of use at the command line level and features available in their programming languages. The most commonly used shells in a UNIX-based system are the Bourne, Korn, and C Shells. The Bourne shell is the oldest and has a good programming language. The C shell has a more convenient and rich command-level interface. The Korn shell has some good features of both and is a superset of the Bourne shell.

Certain characters, called shell metacharacters, have special meaning to the shell. Because the shell treats them in special ways, they should not be used in file names. If you must use them in commands, you need to quote them for the shell to treat them literally.

Problems ▬▬▬▬▬▬▬▬▬▬▬▬▬▬▬▬▬▬▬▬▬▬▬▬

1. What is a shell? What is its purpose?

2. What are the two types of shell commands? What are the differences between them?

3. Give names of five UNIX shells. Which are the most popular? What is a login shell?

4. What do you type in to terminate the execution of a shell? How do you terminate the execution of your login shell?

5. What shells do you think are "supersets" of other shells? In other words, which shells have other shells' complete command sets plus their own? Can you find any commands in a subset shell that are not in a superset shell? Refer to Figure 4.1.

6. What is the search path for a shell? What is the name of a shell variable that is used to maintain it for the Bourne, C, and Korn shells? Where (in which file) is this variable typically located?

7. What is the search path set to in your environment? How did you find out? Set your search path so that your shell searches your current and your ~/bin directories while looking for a command that you type. In what order does your shell search the directories in your search path? Why?

8. What are hidden files? What are the names of the hidden files that are executed when you log on to System V and BSD UNIX systems?

9. What is a shell start-up file? What is the name of this file for the C shell? Where (in which directory) is this file stored?

10. What important features of each shell, as discussed on the manual pages for that shell, seem to be most important for you as a new, intermediate, or advanced user of UNIX? Explain the importance of these features to you in comparison to the other shells available and their features.

11. Suppose that your login shell is a C shell. You received a shell script that runs with the Bourne shell. How would you execute it? Clearly write down all the steps that you would use.

12. What are the outputs of the following commands?

      a. `ls prog[0-9].java`

      b. `ls memo.*`

      c. `ls [0-9][a-zA-Z]*.c`

      d. `ls [0-9][a-zA-Z]?.C`

Editing Text Files

Objectives

- To explain the utility of editing text files
- To show that `pico` is the editor of choice to create short, simple files
- To show how `vi` has the capabilities of a word processor
- To learn maximum control using the `emacs` editor
- To cover the commands and primitives `cp`, `emacs`, `ls`, `pico`, `pwd`, `sh`, `vi`, `who`

5.1 Introduction

By now, it should be clear that UNIX is a **text-driven operating system**. Therefore, to do useful things such as execute multiple commands from within a script file, or write e-mail messages, or create C language programs, you must be familiar with one or perhaps many ways of entering text into a file. In addition, you must also be familiar with how to edit existing files efficiently, that is, to change their contents or otherwise modify them in some way. Text editors also allow you simply to view a file's contents, similar to the more command (see Chapter 3), so that you can perhaps identify the key features of the file. For example, a file without any extension, such as foo (rather than foo.eps) might be an Encapsulated PostScript file that you can identify with a valid PostScript header at the start of the file. That header can be viewed with a text editor.

The editors that we consider here are all considered **full screen display editors**. That is, in the console window or terminal screen that you are using to view the file, you are able to see a portion of the file, which fills most or all of the screen display. You are also able to move the **cursor**, or point, to any of the text you see in this full-screen display. That material is usually held in a temporary storage area in computer memory called the **editor buffer**. If your file is larger than one screen, the buffer contents change as you move the cursor through the file. The difference between a file, which you edit, and a buffer is crucial. For text editing purposes, a file is stored on disk as a sequence of data. When you edit that file, you edit a copy that the editor creates, which is in the editor buffer. You make changes to the contents of the buffer—and can even manipulate several buffers at once—but when you save the buffer, you write a new sequence of data to the disk, thereby saving the file.

Another important operational feature of all the editors discussed in this chapter is that their actions are based on **keystroke commands**, whether they are a single keystroke or combinations of keys pressed simultaneously or sequentially. Because the primary input device in UNIX is the keyboard, the correct syntax of keystroke commands is mandatory. But this method of input, once you have become accustomed to it, is as efficient or even more efficient than mouse/GUI input. Keystrokes also are more flexible, giving you more complete and customizable control over editing actions. Generally, you should choose the editor you are most comfortable with, in terms of the way you prefer to work with the computer. However, your choice of editor also depends on the complexity and quantity of text creation and manipulation that you want to do. Practically speaking, the more powerful editors such as vi and emacs are capable of handling complex editing tasks. But to take advantage of that power, you have to learn the commands that are needed to perform those tasks and how they are implemented—and retain that knowledge. The text editing functions common to the text editors that we cover here are listed in Table 5.1, along with a short description of each function.

■ **TABLE 5.1** Common Functions of UNIX Text Editors

Function	Description
Cursor movement	Moving the location of the insertion point or current position in the buffer
Cut or copy, paste	"Ripping out" text blocks or duplicating text blocks, reinserting ripped or duplicated blocks *(continued)*

TABLE 5.1 *(continued)*

Deleting text	Deleting text at a specified location or in a specified range
Inserting text	Placing text at a specified location
Opening, starting	Opening an existing file for modification, beginning a new file
Quitting	Leaving the text editor, with or without saving the work done
Saving	Retaining the buffer as a disk file
Search, replace	Finding instances of text strings, replacing them with new strings

5.2   How to Do Short and Simple Edits by Using the `pico` Editor

The `pico` UNIX text editor allows you to do simple editing on small text files efficiently. Its user interface is friendly and simple compared to the editors that we cover later in this chapter. The `pico` editor is distributed free with the pine e-mail system, so if you cannot access the program by typing `pico` at the shell prompt, ask your system administrator where your shell can locate it. Then set your search path to include that location, as described in Chapter 4.

5.2.1   Creating the Text of an E-mail Message with the `pico` Text Editor

Example: `pico` Text Editor shows how to create and save a small e-mail message with the `pico` text editor.

Example: pico Text Editor

Step 1:   At the shell prompt, type `pico` and then press `<Enter>`.

Step 2:   The pico screen display appears similar to Figure 5.1 (on page 84).

Step 3:   On the first blank line in the text area, type `Subject: My first file` and then press `<Enter>`.

Step 4:   Type `Dear Me: This is what the first file I created with pico looks like.`

Step 5:   Hold down the `<Ctrl>` and `<O>` keys on the keyboard at the same time, and when prompted to enter a filename, type `first.txt`, and then press `<Enter>` on the keyboard.

Step 6:   Hold down the `<Ctrl>` and `<X>` keys on the keyboard at the same time, and you will exit from `pico`.

5.2.2 How to Start, Save a File, and Exit

For small text files, such as short e-mail messages or shell scripts, the `pico` editor is easily and quickly learned. As apparent in Figure 5.1, it has a straightforward screen display that has two main parts: a text area, where you can enter and change text by typing, and a keystroke command area at the bottom of the screen, which shows valid keystroke commands. The general methods of starting `pico` from the command line are as follows.

---

pico [options] [file]

Purpose: Allows you to edit a new or existing text file

Output: With no options or file(s) specified, you are placed in the `pico` program and can begin to edit a new buffer

Commonly used options/features:

    -h   List valid command line options

    -m   Enable mouse functionality under the X Window System

    -o dir   Set the operating directory; only files within *dir* are accessible

---

To edit a new buffer, type `pico` at the shell prompt and press `<Enter>`. The program begins, and you will see a screen display similar to that shown in Figure 5.1. You are immediately in text-entry mode, and whatever you type will appear in the text area of the `pico` screen display. Note that, to the left of each keystroke command listed at the bottom of the screen, there are two

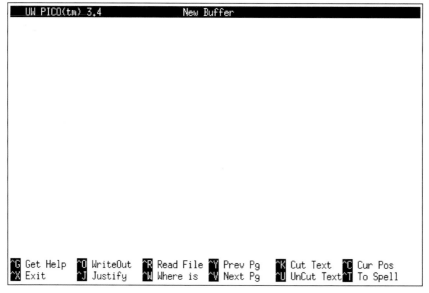

Figure 5.1 First `pico` screen display

characters (e.g., `<Ctrl-O>` next to `WriteOut` and `<Ctrl-X>` next to `Exit`). Recall that the first character (the caret) tells you to hold down the `<Ctrl>` key on your keyboard while holding down the next character (the letter key) to execute the command (i.e., writeOut a file [save the file] or eXit from `pico`).

To save at any point, hold down the `<Ctrl>` and `<O>` keys at the same time. A prompt appears near the bottom of the screen asking you to type in a filename to which the current text body will be saved. Type in a name, as shown in Figure 5.2. When you want to save the text that you have entered, use `<Ctrl-O>` to confirm the filename that the text will be saved to. Then press `<Enter>`, and the current text will be saved to the filename that you specify. You should save your file at least once every 15 to 20 minutes so that you do not lose more than that amount of work if the system crashes.

To exit `pico`, hold down the `<Ctrl>` and `<X>` keys at the same time. If you have made any changes in the text since the last time you saved the file, you can type `<Y>` to save the changes.

Practice Session 5.1 gives you the chance to use these commands to enter and save text and exit from `pico`.

Practice Session 5.1

Step 1:　At the shell prompt, type `pico` and then press `<Enter>`.

Step 2:　In the text area of the `pico` screen, place the cursor on the first line and type

`This is text that I have entered on a line in the pico editor.`

Use the `<Delete>` and `<arrow>` keys to correct any typing errors you make.

Step 3:　Press `<Enter>` three times.

Step 4:　Type `This is a line of text three lines down from the first line.`

Step 5:　Hold down the `<Ctrl>` and `<O>` keys at the same time (`<Ctrl-O>` or `<^O>`).

Step 6:　At the prompt `File Name to Write:` type `linespaced` and then press `<Enter>`.

Step 7:　Hold down the `<Ctrl>` and `<X>` keys at the same time (`<Ctrl-X>` or `<^X>`) to return to the shell prompt.

Step 8:　At the shell prompt, type `more linespaced` and then press `<Enter>`.

5.2.3　General Keystroke Commands and Cursor Movement

In addition to the `WriteOut` and `Exit` commands mentioned in Section 5.2.2, `pico` has some general basic text editing features, as summarized in Table 5.2.

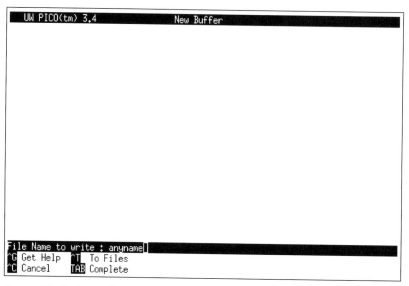

```
 UW PICO(tm) 3.4                    New Buffer
```

```
File Name to write : anyname
^G Get Help    ^T To Files
^C Cancel      TAB Complete
```

Figure 5.2 Saving a file with a name in `pico`

For example, to read the Help pages while in `pico`, hold down the `<Ctrl>` and `<G>` keys at the same time. Then move down through the Help pages by holding down the `<Ctrl>` and `<V>` keys at the same time. To move up through the pages, hold down the `<Ctrl>` and `<Y>` keys at the same time. Although `pico` is a basic text editor, fortunately it has useful features such as search and cut and paste. Advanced text editing options that you might be familiar with from a word processor are not available in it, though. The `vi` and `emacs` text editors, which we discuss shortly, have those capabilities.

■ **TABLE 5.2** Keystroke Commands and Their Actions in `pico`

Keystroke Command	Action
`<Ctrl-Shift 6>`	Begins to mark a section of text for cutting out text
`<Ctrl-C>`	Reports the current cursor position as line # and character #
`<Ctrl-G>`	Allows access to `pico` Help text
`<Ctrl-J>`	Justifies the selected text, similar to word wrap in a word processor
`<Ctrl-K>`	Cuts the selected text
`<Ctrl-O>`	Writes out, or saves, the current text to a file
`<Ctrl-R>`	Reads in text from a file and pastes the text at the current cursor position
`<Ctrl-T>`	Checks spelling
`<Ctrl-U>`	Pastes the current line of text

(continued)

TABLE 5.2 *(continued)*

`<Ctrl-V>`	Scrolls one page down in the Help pages
`<Ctrl-W>`	Whereis (allows you to search for a string of characters)
`<Ctrl-X>`	Exit (pico allows you to save any changes before exiting)
`<Ctrl-Y>`	Scrolls one page up in the Help pages

Table 5.3 shows how to move the cursor to different positions in the file quickly and easily. Along with using the `<arrow>` keys on the keyboard, these keystroke commands are quick and efficient ways of positioning text.

TABLE 5.3   Important Cursor Movement Keystroke Commands in pico

Keystroke Command	Action
`<Ctrl-F>`	Moves the cursor forward a character
`<Ctrl-B>`	Moves the cursor backward a character
`<Ctrl-P>`	Moves the cursor to the previous line
`<Ctrl-N>`	Moves the cursor to the next line
`<Ctrl-A>`	Moves the cursor to the start of the current line
`<Ctrl-E>`	Moves the cursor to the end of the current line
`<Ctrl-V>`	Moves the cursor to the next page of text
`<Ctrl-Y>`	Moves the cursor to the previous page of text

The following In-Chapter Exercise asks you to evaluate some of the results obtained in Practice Session 5.1.

IN-CHAPTER EXERCISE

5.1   After finishing Step 8 in Practice Session 5.1, what did you see on the screen?

Edit the file named linespaced that you created in Practice Session 5.1, and use the appropriate keystroke commands to position the cursor at the beginning and ending character of each line of text. Use the `<Ctrl-C>` command to locate each character position as you use the cursor movement commands. How many characters are in the file? The beginning of each line is what percent of the total file?

5.2.4   Cutting/Pasting and Searching

A useful function to have in even a basic text editor is the ability to cut and paste sections of text. In pico, to cut out a section of text and paste it back in at another location, do the following.

1. Mark the beginning of the text section that you want to cut out by holding down the <Ctrl> key and *both* the <Shift> and <6> keys at the same time. Note that the boundary of the selected text will start at the left edge of the current character under the cursor.

2. Then move the cursor (using the <arrow> keys on the keyboard) to a point *one character beyond* the end of the text you want to cut out. Note that the selected text will end at the left edge of the current character under the cursor, thus leaving that character out of the selection.

3. Hold down the <Ctrl> and <K> keys at the same time to cut out the marked text.

4. Use the <arrow> keys to move the cursor to where you want to insert the text that you just cut. Hold down the <Ctrl> and <U> keys at the same time to paste in the text after the cursor location.

Practice Session 5.2 lets you edit the file that you created in Practice Session 5.1 by using the commands presented in the preceding list.

Practice Session 5.2

Step 1: At the shell prompt, type pico linespaced and then press <Enter>. The linespaced file you created in Practice Session 5.1 appears in the pico screen.

Step 2: Position the cursor at the beginning of the fourth line, at the character T in the word This, using the <arrow> keys on the keyboard.

Step 3: Hold down the <Ctrl> and both the <Shift> and <6> keys at the same time.

Step 4: Move the cursor with the <right arrow> key on the keyboard until you have highlighted the entire fourth line, including the period. The cursor should be one character to the right of the period at the end of the line.

Step 5: Hold down the <Ctrl> and <K> keys at the same time. This action cuts the line of text out of the current "buffer," or file that you are working on.

Step 6: Position the cursor with the <arrow> keys at the beginning of the second line of the file, directly under the line that reads This is text that I have entered on a line in the pico editor.

Step 7: Hold down the <Ctrl> and <U> keys at the same time. This action pastes the former fourth line into the second line of the file.

Step 8: Use the <arrow> keys on the keyboard to position the cursor at the third line of the file.

Step 9: Hold down the <Ctrl> and <U> keys on the keyboard at the same time. This action pastes the former fourth line into the third line of the file.

(continued)

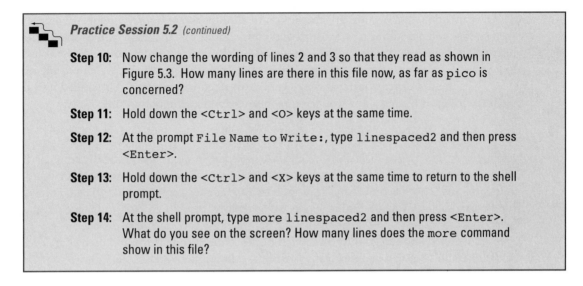

Practice Session 5.2 (continued)

Step 10:   Now change the wording of lines 2 and 3 so that they read as shown in Figure 5.3. How many lines are there in this file now, as far as pico is concerned?

Step 11:   Hold down the <Ctrl> and <O> keys at the same time.

Step 12:   At the prompt File Name to Write:, type linespaced2 and then press <Enter>.

Step 13:   Hold down the <Ctrl> and <X> keys at the same time to return to the shell prompt.

Step 14:   At the shell prompt, type more linespaced2 and then press <Enter>. What do you see on the screen? How many lines does the more command show in this file?

To get some further practice with pico, do Problems 5–7 at the end of this chapter.

5.3   Obtaining More Control by Using the **vi** Editor

The vi UNIX text editor has almost all the features of a word processor and tremendous flexibility in creating text files. It is significantly more complex than pico, but it gives you the ability to work on much larger files.

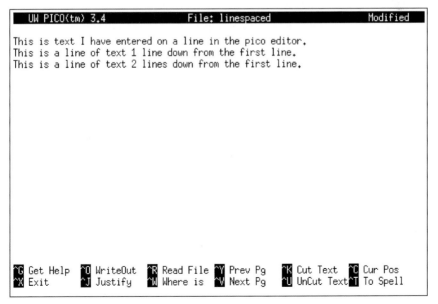

Figure 5.3 Cut and pasted **linespaced** text in pico

As we mentioned in Section 5.1, the notion of a buffer as a temporary storage facility for the text that you are editing is very useful and important in vi. The **main buffer**, sometimes referred to as the *editing buffer*, or the *work buffer*, is the main repository for the body of text that you are trying to create or to modify from some previous permanently archived file on disk. The **general purpose buffer** is where your most recent "ripped-out" (cut/copied text) is retained. **Indexed buffers** allow you to store more than one temporary string of text.

5.3.1 Shell Script File

Example: vi Text Editor shows how to create a *script* file, or collection of UNIX commands that are executed in sequence, and then execute the script. We present more about shell programming and script files in Chapters 15–18. For this example, we assume that you are running the Bourne shell. If you are running some other shell by default, go back to Chapter 4 and review how to identify and change shells. And do not worry too much if you make an error in Steps 2, 3, and 4; you can go through the rest of the script file discussion and then come back to this example after you have learned some of the editing commands.

Example: vi Text Editor

Step 1: At the shell prompt, start vi by typing vi firscrip and then pressing <Enter>. The vi screen appears on your display.

Step 2: Type A, type ls -la, and then press <Enter>.

Step 3: Type who and then press <Enter>.

Step 4: Type pwd and then press the <Esc> key. At this point, your screen should look like that shown in Figure 5.4.

Step 5: Type :wq and then press <Enter>.

Step 6: At the shell prompt, type sh firscrip and then press <Enter>.

Step 7: Note the results. How many files do you have in your present working directory? What are their names and sizes? Who else is using your computer system? What is your present working directory?

5.3.2 How to Start, Save a File, and Exit

When you need to do UNIX text editing that gives you as much functionality as a typical word processor, you can use the vi text editor. To start vi from the command line, use the following general syntax.

---

vi [options] [file(s)]

Purpose: Allows you to edit a new or existing text file(s)

Output: With no options or file(s) specified, you are placed in the vi program and can begin to edit a new buffer

Commonly used options/features:

  +n Begin to edit file(s) starting at line # *n*

  +/exp Begin to edit at the first line in the file matching string *exp*

SYNTAX

The operations that you perform in vi fall into two general categories: **Command mode operations**, which consist of key sequences that are commands to the editor to take certain actions, and **Insert mode operations**, which allow you to input text. The general organization of the vi text editor and how to switch modes are illustrated in Figure 5.5. For example, to change from the command mode, which you are in when you first enter the editor, to the insert mode, type a valid command, such as <A>, to append text at the end of the current line. Certain commands that are prefixed with the :, /, ?, or :! characters are echoed or shown to you on the last line on the screen and must be terminated by pressing <Enter>. To change from Insert Mode to Command Mode, press the <Esc> key. The keystroke commands that you execute in vi are case-sensitive—for example, uppercase <A> appends new text after the last character at the end of the current line, whereas lowercase <a> appends new text after the character the cursor is on.

```
ls -la
who
pwd
~
~
~
~
~
~
~
~
~
~
~
~
~
~
~
~
~
~
~
~
~
~
~
```

Figure 5.4 UNIX vi screen with example script file

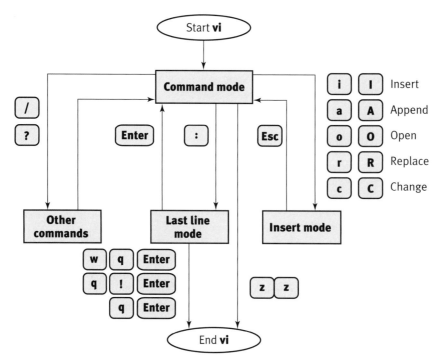

Figure 5.5 Operating modes of the vi text editor

In Example: vi Text Editor, at Step 2, typing <A> took vi out of Command Mode (which is what vi starts in by default) and placed it in one of the forms of Insert Mode. In other words, anything that you typed at the keyboard was appended as text on the first line in the text area of the editor. When you pressed the <Esc> key in Step 4, vi was taken out of the Insert Mode and was put back into Command Mode. When you typed the : in Step 5, it was a valid Command Mode prefix character for the two commands that followed. When you typed wq after the :, vi interpreted those commands as write out or save the file, and quit the editor.

To start vi, at the shell prompt, type vi and then press <Enter>. The vi display appears on your screen, as shown in Figure 5.6. You are now in the Command Mode. To enter Insert Mode, type <A>, and you are now able to insert text on the first line of the file. After entering text, you can press the <Esc> key to enter Command Mode. From Command Mode, you can save the text that you just inserted to a file on disk by typing :w filename and pressing <Enter>, where filename is the name of the file you want to save the text to. To quit the editor, type :q.

5.3.3 The Format of a vi Command and the Modes of Operation

In either the Command or the Insert Mode, the generic syntax of keystrokes is,

```
[#1] operation [#2] target
```

where,

anything enclosed in [ ] is optional;

Figure 5.6 The vi start-up screen

#1 is an optional number, such as 5, specifying how many operations are to be done; **operation** is what you want to accomplish, such as deleting lines of text; **#2** is an optional number, such as 5, specifying how many targets are affected by the operation; and target is the text that you want to do the operation on, such as an entire line of text.

Note that, if the current line is the target of the operation, the syntax for specifying the target is the same as the syntax of the operation—for example, dd deletes the current line. Also, a variation on this generic syntax are cursor movement commands, whereby you can omit the numbers and operation and simply move the cursor by word, sentence, paragraph, or section. Table 5.4 lists some specific examples of this generic syntax and variations used in both Command and Insert Modes.

■ TABLE 5.4 Examples of vi Command Syntax

Command	Action
5dw	Deletes five words, starting at the current cursor position
7dd	Deletes seven lines, starting at the current line
7o	Opens seven blank lines after the current line
7O	Opens seven blank lines before the current line
c2b	Changes back two words
d7,14	Deletes lines seven through fourteen in the buffer
1G	Puts the cursor on the first line of the file
10yy	Yanks (copies) the next (starting with the current line) ten lines into a temporary buffer

As previously stated, you enter vi in Command Mode. When you want to use Insert Mode instead of Command Mode, press a valid key to accomplish the change. Some of these keys are shown in Table 5.5.

■ **TABLE 5.5** Important Keys for the Insert Mode

Key	Action
<a>	Appends text after the character the cursor is on
<A>	Appends text after the last character of the current line
<c>	Begins a change operation, allowing you to modify text
<C>	Changes from the cursor position to the end of the current line
<i>	Inserts text before the character the cursor is on
<I>	Inserts text at the beginning of the current line
<o>	Opens a blank line below the current line and puts the cursor on that line
<O>	Opens a blank line above the current line and puts the cursor on that line
<R>	Begins overwriting text
<s>	Substitutes single characters
<S>	Substitutes whole lines

After inserting text, you can edit the text, move the cursor to a new position in the buffer, and save the buffer and exit the editor—all from within Command Mode. When you want to change from Insert Mode to Command Mode, press the <Esc> key. The general commands that are useful in Command Mode are shown in Table 5.6, with those executed from the status line prefaced with a : character.

■ **TABLE 5.6** Important Commands for the Command Mode

Command	Action
d	Deletes words, lines, etc.
u	Undoes the last edit
p	Pastes (inserts) the yanked or deleted line(s) after the current line
P	Pastes (inserts) the yanked or deleted line(s) before the current line
:r filename	Reads and inserts the contents of the file filename at the current cursor position
:q!	Quits vi without saving the buffer
:wq	Saves the buffer and quits
:w filename	Saves the current buffer to filename
:w! filename	Overwrites filename with the current text
ZZ	Quits vi, saving the file only if changes were made since the last save

Practice Session 5.3 lets you continue editing the file you created in Practice Session 5.1 by using the commands presented in Tables 5.5 and 5.6.

Practice Session 5.3

Step 1: At the shell prompt, type vi firstvi and then press <Enter>.

Step 2: Type <A>, type This is the first line of a vi file, and then press <Enter>.

Step 3: Type This is the line of a vi file and then press <Enter>.

Step 4: Type is the 3r line of a vi.

Step 5: Press the <Esc> key.

Step 6: Type :w and then press <Enter>. Your screen display should look similar to Figure 5.7.

Step 7: Use the <arrow> keys to position the cursor on the character l in the word line on the second line of the file.

Step 8: Type i and then 2nd_ .

Step 9: Press the <Esc> key.

Step 10: Use the <arrow> keys to position the cursor anywhere on the third line of the file.

Step 11: Type <I> and then This_ .

Step 12: Press the <Esc> key.

Step 13: Use the <arrow> keys to position the cursor on the character r in 3r on this line.

Step 14: Type <a> and then <d>.

Step 15: Press the <Esc> key.

Step 16: Type <A> and then _file.

Step 17: Press the <Esc> key on the keyboard. Your screen display should look similar to Figure 5.8.

Step 18: Type :wq. You will be back at the shell prompt.

```
This is the first line of a vi file.
This is the line of a vi file.
is the 3r line of a vi
~
~
~
~
~
~
~
~
~
~
~
~
~
~
~
~
~
~
~
~
~
~
~
"firstvi" 3 lines, 91 characters written
```

Figure 5.7 Saved file firstvi

```
This is the first line of a vi file.
This is the 2nd line of a vi file.
This is the 3rd line of a vi file.
~
~
~
~
~
~
~
~
~
~
~
~
~
~
~
~
~
~
~
~
~
~
~
```

Figure 5.8 Final form of file firstvi

The following In-Chapter Exercise asks you to apply some of the operations you learned about in the previous Practice Sessions.

IN-CHAPTER EXERCISE

5.3 With vi you begin editing a file that you created yesterday. You want to save a copy of it with a different filename while still in vi, but you don't want to quit this editing session. How do you accomplish this result in vi?

What happens if you accomplish five operations in vi and then type 5u when in Command Mode?

5.3.4 Cursor Movement and Editing Commands

In Command Mode, several commands accomplish cursor movement and text editing tasks. Table 5.7 lists important cursor movement and keyboard editing commands. As we have already shown, character-at-a-time or line-at-a-time moves of the cursor can be accomplished easily with the <arrow> keys.

■ **TABLE 5.7** Cursor Movement and Keyboard Editing Commands

Command	Action
<1G>	Moves the cursor to the first line of the file
<G>	Moves the cursor to the last line of the file
<0> (zero)	Moves the cursor to the first character of the current line
<Ctrl-G>	Reports the position of the cursor in terms of line # and column #
<$>	Moves the cursor to the last character of the current line
<w>	Moves the cursor forward one word at a time
<b>	Moves the cursor backward one word at a time
<x>	Deletes the character at the cursor position
<dd>	Deletes the line at the current cursor position
<u>	Undoes the most recent change
<r>	Replaces the character at the current cursor location with what is typed next

Practice Session 5.4 lets you continue editing the file you created in Practice Session 5.1 by using commands presented in Table 5.7.

Practice Session 5.4

Step 1: At the shell prompt, type vi firstvi, and then press <Enter>.

Step 2: Type <G>. The cursor moves to the last line of the file.

(continued)

Practice Session 5.4 *(continued)*

Step 3: Hold down the `<Ctrl>` and `<G>` keys at the same time. On the last line of the screen display, `vi` reports the following: "`firstvi`" line 3 of 3 `– –` `100%` `– – col 1`. This is a report of the buffer that you are editing, the current line number, the total number of lines in the buffer, the percentage of the buffer that this line represents, and the current column position of the cursor.

Step 4: Type `<o>`. A new line opens below the third line of the file.

Step 5: Type `This is the 5th line of a vi file`. Type `<esc>`.

Step 6: Type `<0>` (zero). The cursor moves to the first character of the line you just typed in.

Step 7: Type `<$>`. The cursor moves to the last character of the current line.

Step 8: Type `<O>`. A new line opens above the current fourth line.

Step 9: Type `This is the 44th line of a va file`. Type `<esc>`.

Step 10: Use the `<arrow>` keys to position the cursor over the first 4 in `44` on this line.

Step 11: Type `<x>`.

Step 12: Use the `<arrow>` keys to position the cursor over the a in `va` on this line.

Step 13: Type `<r>` and then type `<i>`.

Step 14: Type `dd`.

Step 15: Type `:wq` to go back to the shell prompt.

Step 16: At the shell prompt, type `more firstvi` and then press `<Enter>`. How many lines with text on them does `more` show in this file?

5.3.5 Yank and Put (Copy and Paste) and Substitute (Search and Replace)

Every word processor is capable of copying and pasting text and also of searching for old text and replacing it with new text. Copying and pasting are accomplished with the `vi` commands yank and put. In general, you use yank and put in sequence and move the cursor (with any of the cursor movement commands) only between yanking and putting. Some examples of the syntax for yank and put are given in Table 5.8.

■ **TABLE 5.8** Examples of the Syntax for the yank and put Commands

Command Syntax	What It Accomplishes
`y2w`	Yanks two words, starting at the current cursor position, going to the right
`4yb`	Yanks four words, starting at the current cursor position, going to the left
`yy or Y`	Yanks the current line

(continued)

Table 5.8 *(continued)*

p	Puts the yanked text after the current cursor position
P	Puts the yanked text before the current cursor position
5p	Puts the yanked text in the buffer five times after the current cursor position

The simple vi forms of search and replace are accomplished using the substitute command. This command is executed from the last line of the screen display, where you preface the command with the : character and terminate the command by pressing <Enter>. The format of the substitute command as it is typed on the status line is,

`:[range]s/old_string/new_string[/option]`

where,

anything enclosed in [   ] is not mandatory;

: is the colon prefix for the status line command;

range is a valid specification of lines in the buffer (if omitted, the current line is the range);

s is the syntax of the substitute command;

/ is a delimiter for searching;

old_string is the text you want to replace;

/ is a delimiter for replacement;

new_string is the new text;

and

/ option is a modifier, usually g for global, to the command.

Note that the grammar of old_string and new_string can be extremely explicit and complex and takes the form of a **regular expression**. (We present more information on the formation of regular expressions in Chapter 10.) Some examples of the syntax for the substitute command are given in Table 5.9.

■ **TABLE 5.9** Examples of the Syntax for the substitute Command

Command Syntax	What It Accomplishes
`:s/john/jane/`	Substitutes the word *jane* for the word *john* on the current line, only once
`:s/john/jane/g`	Substitutes the word *jane* for every word *john* on the current line
`:1,10s/big/small/g`	Substitutes the word *small* for every word *big* on lines 1–10
`:1,$s/men/women/g`	Substitutes the word *women* for every word *men* in the entire file

Practice Session 5.5 shows you how to use the vi commands yank and put to copy and paste. It also allows you to do individual and multiple searches and replace text with the vi substitute command.

Practice Session 5.5

Step 1: At the shell prompt, type vi multiline and then press <Enter>.

Step 2: Type A and then type Windows is the operating system of choice for everyone.

Step 3: Press the <Esc> key. You have left the Insert Mode and are now in the Command Mode.

Step 4: Press the <0> (zero) key. The cursor moves to the first character of the first line.

Step 5: Type yy. This action yanks, or copies, the first line to a special buffer.

Step 6: Type 7p. This action puts, or pastes, the first line seven times, creating seven new lines of text containing the same text as the first line. The cursor should now be on the first character of the eighth line.

Step 7: Type 1G. This action puts the cursor on the first character of the first line in the buffer.

Step 8: Hold down the <Shift> and <;> keys at the same time. Doing so places a : in the status line at the bottom of the vi screen display, allowing you to type a command.

Step 9: Type s/everyone/students/ and then press <Enter>. The word everyone at the end of the first line is replaced with the word students.

Step 10: Use the <arrow> -# keys to position the cursor on the first character of the second line.

Step 11: Type :s/everyone/computer scientists/ and then press <Enter>.

Step 12: Repeat Steps 8–10 on the third through eighth lines of the buffer, substituting the words engineers, system administrators, web servers, scientists, networking, and mathematicians for the word everyone on each of those six lines.

Step 13: Type :1,$s/Windows/UNIX/g and then press <Enter>. You have globally replaced the word Windows on all eight lines of the file with the word UNIX. Correct?

Step 14: Type :wq. You have now saved the changes and exited from vi.

To get some further practice with vi, do Problems 8–11 at the end of this chapter.

5.3.6 Setting the vi Environment

You can use any of several environment options to customize the behavior of the vi editor. These options include specifying maximum line length and automatically wrapping the cursor to the next line, displaying line numbers as you edit a file, and displaying the mode that vi is in at any time. You can use full or abbreviated names for most of the options. Some of the most important and useful options are summarized in Table 5.10.

You can set these options by using the the :set command (i.e., using the set command in the Last Line Mode). Thus, after the :set shomode command has been executed, vi displays the current mode at the bottom right of the screen. Similarly, after the :set nu command has been executed, vi displays the line numbers for all the lines in the file. When the :set ai command has been executed, the next line is aligned with the beginning of the previous line. This useful feature allows you to easily indent source codes that you compose with vi. Pressing <Ctrl-D> on a new line moves the cursor to the previous indentation level.

When you set the environment options within a vi session, the options are set for that session only. If you want to customize your environment permanently, you need to put your options in the .exrc file in your home directory. You can use the set command to set one or more options in the .exrc file, as in,

```
$ cat .exrc
set wm=5 shm nu ic
$
```

The wm=5 option sets the wrap margin to 5. That is, each line will be up to 75 characters long. The ic option allows you to search for strings without regard to the case of a character. Thus, after this option has been set, the /Hello/ command searches for strings hello and Hello.

■ **TABLE 5.10** Important Environment Options for vi

Option	Abbreviation	Purpose
autoindent	**ai**	Aligns the new line with the beginning of the previous line
ignorecase	**ic**	Ignores the case of a letter during the search process (with a/ or the ? command)
number	**nu**	Displays line numbers when a file is being edited; line numbers are not saved as part of the file
scroll		Sets the number of lines to scroll when the <Ctrl-D> command is used to scroll the vi screen up
showmode	**smd**	Displays the current vi mode in the bottom right corner of the screen
wrapmargin	**wm**	Sets the wrap margin in terms of the number of characters from the end of the line, assuming a line length of 80 characters

5.3.7 Executing Shell Commands from Within `vi`

At times you will want to execute a shell command without quitting `vi` and then restarting it. You can do so in Command Mode by preceding the command with `:!`. Thus, for example, `:! pwd` would display the pathname of your current directory, and `:! ls` would display the names of all the files in your current directory. After executing a shell command, `vi` returns to its Command Mode.

5.4   Getting Maximum Control Using the `emacs` Editor

The `emacs` editor is the most complex and customizable of the UNIX text editors, and it gives you the most freedom, flexibility, and control over the way you edit text files. It can format text for very specific technical applications, such as program source code development, more effectively than a word processor. Its use in that application makes the process of program development more efficient. In addition, from within the `emacs` program, in multiple windows, you can accomplish a wide variety of personal productivity and operating system tasks, such as sending e-mail and executing shell commands and scripts. But along with more control, specificity, and capabilities comes some additional learning in terms of a more complex keystroke command structure. This complexity can be offset in part for some users, and totally for others, by using the graphical forms of input and command execution that we will emphasize in the sections that follow.

It is important to realize before you begin that there are some common terms used in `vi`, the editor from the previous section, and `emacs` that describe the facilities of each editor–but the terms do not have the same meaning in each editor. For example, `emacs` has major modes of operation, such as Lisp mode and C mode, but they are for special formatting of text in that operation, rather than for allowing you to switch between actions in the editor, as the `vi` Command and Insert Modes do, as seen in the previous section. The keystroke command syntax itself in `emacs` is different and more complex than in `vi`, involving use of the `<Ctrl>` and `<Esc>` prefix characters. The `emacs` concepts of `point` and cursor location are also more refined and specific than in `vi`. In `emacs`, the point is the location in the buffer where you are currently doing your editing; the point is assumed to be at the left edge of the cursor, or always between characters or white space (what you enter into a text file when you press the space bar). This difference becomes an important issue when you want to use the cut/copy/paste operations. In `vi`, yanking removes text from the main buffer, or cutting/copying, whereas in `emacs` yanking is more like pasting into the main buffer. The concept of a buffer is very important in `emacs`, as described in Section 5.4.1, and is very much the same in `emacs` as it is in `vi`.

Currently, there are two major "brands" of `emacs` for UNIX: GNU `Emacs` and `Xemacs`. Their functionality is very similar, and we use the graphical form of GNU `Emacs` version 21.2.1 running in its own frame in the following illustrations, Exercises, Practice Sessions, and Problems. If you cannot run a graphical `emacs` because of the remote possibility that you are working in a text-only console or terminal, you can still gain access to the Menu Bar at the top of the `emacs` screen by pressing `<Esc>` on the keyboard and then pressing the single backquote `<`>` key. You can then descend through the menu bar choices by pressing the letter key of the menu choice you want to make. For example, pressing the `<F>` key gives you access to the File pull-down menu choices, and then pressing the `<S>` key allows you to save the current buffer. Unfortunately, you cannot access the speed button bar menu choices from within a text-only display of `emacs`.

5.4.1 emacs Screen Display, General emacs Concepts and Features

You run the emacs program by either typing the command emacs in a terminal window or, if you are using a GUI, by making the emacs program menu choice. When the program launches, a new window appears on-screen, and if you click the left mouse button in that window, your screen display will look similar to Figure 5.9.

emacs *Screen Display Components*

A brief description of the major components of the emacs screen display labeled in Figure 5.9 is as follows. (*Note:* Items J, A, B, D, and C are found on what is called the "Mode line").

A. Name of the current buffer–This is the name of the entity or "file" you are editing in this window. In Figure 5.9, the name of the buffer is "alien."

B. Major and minor mode–Different major modes are used to edit different kinds of files, like C programs, Lisp, or HTML; and special configurations of the major modes define the minor modes. In Figure 5.9, only the major mode "Fundamental" is shown, with no minor mode set.

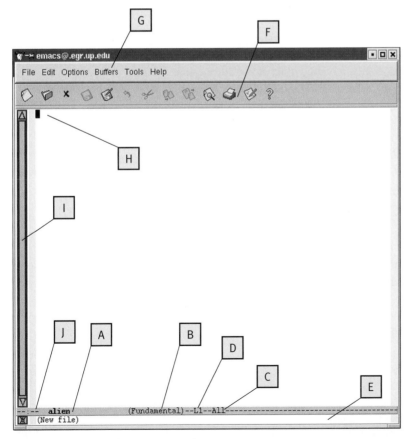

Figure 5.9 First emacs screen display

C. Percentage of the text shown on-screen—This shows how much of the text in the buffer is seen on-screen. In Figure 5.9, "All" of the text in the current buffer is shown on-screen.

D. Current line number—The line location of the cursor in the current buffer is displayed here.

E. Minibuffer—Information and questions/prompts from emacs appear here. In Figure 5.9, "(New file)" is shown on-screen.

F. Speed button bar—This allows you to do quick, common operations graphically.

G. Menu bar—This gives you pull-down menus that contain all of the important emacs operations.

H. Text—The actual text you are editing appears here.

I. Scroll bar—The scroll bar allows you to graphically scroll or move through the text.

J. Status Indicator—Two-character codes are used to tell you about your file. In Figure 5.9, two hyphens (--) indicate that the file has changed in emacs and is the same as the version saved to disk, and you can work on the file.

Graphical Features

The most useful graphical features of emacs are the menu bar and speed button bar seen in the above diagram as F and G. These features incorporate all of emacs' functionality into a graphical style of interaction. When a menu choice is grayed-out, that means it is not available at the current level you are operating at. Following is a brief description of what tasks each menu bar item accomplishes.

File—Facilities for opening, saving, and closing buffers, files, windows, and frames

Edit—Means to modify text in buffers

Options—Facilities to make configuration changes

Buffers—A pull-down menu listing of the currently open buffers

Tools—File and application functions

Help—Extensive documentation and on-line manual for emacs

The speed button bar contains single-button presses for (1) file and buffer operations; (2) common text editing operations, such as cut, paste; and (3) printing, searching, and changing preferences.

Buffers, File, Windows, and Frames

The most important concept in emacs is that of a *buffer*, or text object that is currently being edited by emacs. This is different from a file, which is a text object stored on disk. The differentiation is made, in simple terms, because (1) the object currently being modified and viewed in emacs cannot be the same object stored on disk because you have not saved your edits yet, and (2) emacs can work on text objects that are not files and never will be, such as the output from commands typed on the UNIX command line. When you first launch emacs and specify a file to edit, you are looking into the buffer created by emacs for that file in what is generally known as an emacs *frame*, with a single *window* open to allow you to see the buffer contents. A frame consists of one window, or possibly many windows, tiled in it, the pull-down and speed button bar menus, the Mode line, and a minibuffer. In the In-Chapter Exercises 5.6, 5.9, and 5.10, you will work with multiple buffers viewed in emacs using multiple windows in one frame only.

Point, Mark, and Region

The second most important concept in emacs is that of the *point* and *mark*, and the *region* of text they demarcate. The point is located in the white space before the character the cursor is highlighting. The mark, set by placing the cursor over a character and then holding down <Ctrl>+<space> or <Ctrl>+<@>, is also in the white space before the character the cursor is highlighting. The region, or area of text you want to manipulate in operations such as cutting and copying, is all text between the point and the mark.

For example, in the line of text Now is the time for all good men, if the cursor is on or highlighting the N in the word Now (the point is in the white space before the N), and the mark has been set before the character i in the word time by placing the cursor on the letter i and holding down <Ctrl>+<space>, then the region is defined as Now is the t.

5.4.2 DOS Aliases Example

The following example shows how to create a file to define aliases, or command name substitutes, that allow you to type DOS command names at the UNIX shell prompt to execute some of the common UNIX file maintenance operations you learned in Chapter 3. DOS commands are similar to UNIX commands but are used in the Windows Operating System environment. As you will see in the example, you can use an efficient combination of keyboard typing and graphical interaction to work with emacs. In this section, we assume that you are running the C shell; if you are running another shell, review Chapter 4 to find out how to change shells. In Practice Session 5.6, we ask you to insert the file you create in the following Example into your .cshrc file, so that, upon login, these DOS-aliased commands will be available. (*See* Chapters 3 and 4 to review how you examine your shell environment and shell setups, and how you change your shell to the C shell.)

Example: emacs **Text Editor**

Step 1:   At the shell prompt, type emacs alien and then press <Enter>.
The emacs screen appears in your display, as in Figure 5.9.

Step 2:   Type # DOS aliases and then press <Enter>.

Step 3:   Type alias del = "rm" and then press <Enter>.

Step 4:   Type alias dir = "ls -la" and then press <Enter>.

(continued)

> **Example:** emacs **Text Editor** (continued)
>
> **Step 5:** Type alias type = "more" and then press <Enter>.
>
> **Step 6:** Hold down the <Ctrl> and <X> keys at the same time, and then hold down the <Ctrl> and <S> keys at the same time to save your file with the name alien.
>
> **Step 7:** Hold down the <Ctrl> and <X> keys on the keyboard at the same time, and then hold down the <Ctrl> and <C> keys at the same time to return to the shell prompt.

5.4.3 How to Start, Save a File, and Exit

As previously stated, emacs has the most functions and features and is the most customizable of the UNIX text editors. To start emacs from the command line, use the following general syntax.

Syntax: emacs [options][file(s)]

Purpose:	Allows you to edit a new or existing test file(s)
Output:	With no options or file(s) specified, emacs runs and begins or opens on the *scratch* buffer
Commonly used options/features:	
–n	Begin to edit file(s) starting at line # n
+nw	Run emacs without opening a window, useful in an elementary GUI environment

It is a full-screen display editor with which you can use keystroke commands prefixed with either the <Ctrl> key or a "META" key (which in most cases is the <Esc> key), or you can use the GUI menus and graphical input methods.

The most important keystroke commands in emacs are listed in Table 5.11.

■ **TABLE 5.11** Important emacs commands

Command	Action
<Ctrl-X>+<Ctrl-C>	Exits emacs
<Ctrl-G>	Cancels the current command or command operations
<Ctrl-X>+<Ctrl-W>	Saves a buffer that has never been saved before
<Ctrl-X>+<Ctrl-S>	Saves the current buffer
<Ctrl-X>+<U>	Undoes the last edit and can be used multiple times if necessary

(continued)

TABLE 5.11 (continued)

`<Ctrl-H>`	Gets Help documentation
`<Ctrl-X I>`	Inserts text from a file at the current cursor position
`<Ctrl-X 1>`	Deletes all windows but this one (useful in Help documentation)

5.4.4 Cursor Movement and Editing Commands

In addition to general purpose commands, emacs has some important cursor movement and editing commands that allow you to move quickly and easily around the text and make changes. These commands are listed in Table 5.12.

■ **TABLE 5.12** Important emacs Cursor Movement and Editing Commands

Command	Action
`<Esc-<>`	Moves cursor to the beginning of the buffer
`<Esc->>`	Moves cursor to the end of the buffer
`<Ctrl-A>`	Moves cursor to the beginning of the current line
`<Ctrl-E>`	Moves cursor to the end of the current line
`<Esc-F>`	Moves cursor forward one word at a time
`<Esc-B>`	Moves cursor backward one word at a time
`<Ctrl-D>`	Deletes the character at the cursor
`<Esc-D>`	Deletes the word at the cursor
`<Esc-Delete>`	Deletes the word before the cursor
`<Ctrl-K>`	Deletes from the cursor to the end of the current line
`<Ctrl>+<space>`	Places the mark before the cursor
`<Ctrl-Y>`	Puts back into the buffer what had been deleted

Practice Session 5.6 lets you edit the file alien that you created in Example: DOS Aliases so that it may be used as aliases for the C shell. You will also modify an existing file, .cshrc, in your home directory so that when you log in and are using the C shell, you have the aliased commands in the file alien2 that will be available to you. Before you begin Practice Session 5.6, do the following:

1. *Use the 1s −1a command to find out if you have a .cshrc file in your home directory.* If you have no .cshrc file in your home directory, then use emacs to create a new file named .cshrc with *nothing* in it.

2. *Find out which shell you are currently using by typing echo $SHELL.* If you are already using the C shell, the system will respond with /bin/csh. If you are using the Bourne shell, the system will respond /bin/sh.

3. *If you are not using the C shell as determined in Step 2, switch to the C shell by using the* **chsh** *command.* On our system, FreeBSD 5.0, when we typed chsh, we were able to edit a file that allowed the shell to change upon login.

Practice Session 5.6

Step 1: At the shell prompt, type emacs alien and then press <Enter>. The file you created in the example at the beginning of this section is loaded into the buffer, and your screen display should look similar to the one shown in Figure 5.10.

Step 2: Using the <arrow> keys, position the cursor to the right of the " character at the end of the third line.

Step 3: Press <Enter>.

Step 4: Type alice dir/w= "ls".

Step 5: Hold down the <Ctrl> and <A> keys at the same time. The cursor moves to the beginning of the line.

Step 6: Hold down the <Esc> and <D> keys at the same time. The word alice has been cut from the buffer.

Step 7: Type alias.

Step 8: Hold down the <Esc> and <B> keys at the same time. The cursor moves to the beginning of the word alias.

Step 9: Position the cursor with the arrow keys on the keyboard at the beginning of the first blank line, below the line that reads alias type ="more".

Step 10: Hold down the <Ctrl> and <Y> keys at the same time. The cut word alice has been put back into the buffer at the start of the line.

Step 11: Use the <arrow> keys to position the cursor at the end of the word alice if it is not there already.

Step 12: Use the <Delete> or <Back Space> key to delete the letters c and e from the word alice.

Step 13: Type as copy ="cp".

Step 14: Hold down the <Ctrl> and <X> keys at the same time and then hold down the <Ctrl> and <W> keys at the same time.

Step 15: At the Write file: prompt, erase anything on the line with the <Back Space> key, type ~/alien2, and then press <Enter>. Your screen display should now look similar to the one shown in Figure 5.11.

(continued)

Practice Session 5.6 (continued)

Step 16: Hold down the <Ctrl> and <H> keys at the same time and then press the <A> key. The minibuffer area shows a prompt for you to obtain Help. Hold down the <Ctrl> and <G> keys at the same time. Doing so cancels your Help request.

Step 17: Hold down the <Ctrl> and <X> keys at the same time and then hold down the <Ctrl> and <C> keys at the same time to quit emacs and return to the shell prompt.

Step 18: In the minibuffer, type ~/alien2. The lines of text from alien2's DOS aliases should now be inserted into the file .cshrc.

Step 19: From the pull-down menu File, make the choice File> Save (current buffer).

Step 20: Hold down the <Ctrl> and <X> keys at the same time and then hold down the <Ctrl> and <C>. keys at the same time to quit emacs and return to the shell prompt.

Step 21: To test your new .cshrc file, log out and then log in to your UNIX system again. Then in a terminal or console window, at the shell prompt, type one of the aliased commands and note the results.

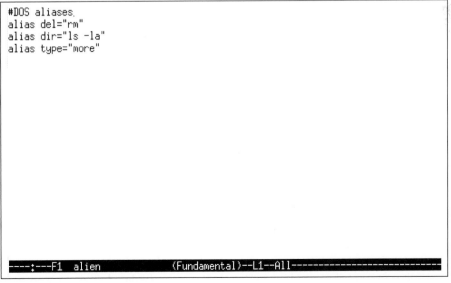

Figure 5.10 The emacs display of the file alien

```
#DOS aliases
alias del="rm"
alias dir="ls -la"
alias dir/w="ls"
alias type="more"
alias copy="cp".




----;**-F1  alien2          (Fundamental)--L6--All--------------------------
```

Figure 5.11 The file alien2 after the buffer contents have been saved

5.4.5 Keyboard Macros

The emacs text editor contains a simple function that allows you to define keyboard macros, or collections of keystrokes that can be recorded and then accessed at any time. This capability allows you to define repetitive multiple keystroke operations as a single command and then execute that command at any time—as many times as you want. The keystrokes can include emacs commands and other keyboard keys. A macro can also be saved with a name, or even be saved to a file, for use during subsequent emacs editing sessions. Table 5.13 shows a list of some of the most important keyboard macro commands.

■ **TABLE 5.13** Important Keyboard Macro Commands

Keystrokes	Action
<Ctrl-X>(>	Begins the macro definition
<Ctrl-X)>	Ends the macro definition
<Ctrl-X E>	Executes the last keyboard macro defined
<Esc-X name-last-kyd-macro Enter>	Names the last macro created
<Esc-X name>	Repeats the named macro name

Practice Session 5.7 lets you create a new text file using the commands presented in Table 5.13.

Practice Session 5.7

Step 1: At the shell prompt, type emacs datafile and then press <Enter>. The emacs screen appears on your display.

Step 2: Hold down the <Ctrl> and <X> keys on the keyboard at the same time, and then hold down the <Shift> and <9> keys at the same time. These actions begin your keyboard macro definition. If you make a mistake anywhere in subsequent steps, simply hold down the <Ctrl> and <G> keys at the same time to cancel the current macro definition.

Step 3: Type 1 2 3 4 5 6 7 8 9 10 and then press <Enter>.

Step 4: Hold down the <Ctrl> and <X> keys at the same time and then hold down the <Shift> and <0> (zero) keys at the same time. These actions end your macro definition.

Step 5: Hold down the <Ctrl> and <X> keys at the same time and then press the <E> key. Doing so replays the macro that you just defined, placing another line of the numbers 1–10 in the buffer.

Step 6: Repeat Step 5 eight more times so that your display looks similar to that shown in Figure 5.12.

Step 7: Hold down the <Ctrl> and <X> keys at the same time and then hold down the <Ctrl> and <S> keys at the same time. These actions save the buffer to the file datafile.

Step 8: Hold down the <Ctrl> and <X> keys at the same time and then hold down the <Ctrl> and <C> keys at the same time to exit from emacs.

```
1 2 3 4 5 6 7 8 9 10
1 2 3 4 5 6 7 8 9 10
1 2 3 4 5 6 7 8 9 10
1 2 3 4 5 6 7 8 9 10
1 2 3 4 5 6 7 8 9 10
1 2 3 4 5 6 7 8 9 10
1 2 3 4 5 6 7 8 9 10
1 2 3 4 5 6 7 8 9 10
1 2 3 4 5 6 7 8 9 10
1 2 3 4 5 6 7 8 9 10




---:---F1  datafile        (Fundamental)--L1--All------------------------
```

Figure 5.12 The file datafile with 10 rows of data

5.4.6 Cut or Copy and Paste and Search and Replace

As we mentioned previously, every word processor has the capability to cut or copy text and then paste that text back into the document and to search for old text and replace it with new text. Because emacs operations can be totally text-activated, whereby you use sequences of keystrokes to execute commands, cutting or copying and pasting are fairly complex operations. They are accomplished with the **Kill Ring**, whereby text is held in a buffer by killing it and is then restored to the document at the desired position by yanking it. Global search and replace are somewhat less complex and are accomplished by either an unconditional replacement or an interactive replacement.

The Mark is simply a place holder in the buffer. For example, to cut three words from a document and then paste them back at another position, move Point before the first word you want to cut and press <Esc-D> three times. The three words are then cut to the Kill Ring. Because the Kill Ring is a **FIFO** buffer, you can now move Point to where you want to restore the three words and press <Ctrl-Y>. The three words are yanked into the document in the same order, left-to-right, that they were cut from the document.

To copy three words of text and then paste them back at another position, set **Mark** by positioning Point after the three words, and then press <Ctrl-@> at that position. Then reposition Point before the three words; you have now defined a Region between Point and Mark. There is only one Mark in the document. Press <Esc-W> to send the text between Point and Mark to the Kill Ring; the text is sent, but it is not blanked from the screen display. To restore the three words at another position, move Point there and press <Ctrl-Y>. The three words are restored at the new position. Table 5.14 gives the important **kill** and **yank** commands for emacs.

■ **TABLE 5.14** Important emacs Kill and Yank Commands

Command	Action
`<Ctrl-Delete>`	Kills the character at the cursor
`<Esc-D>`	Kills characters from the cursor to the end of the current word
`<Ctrl- U 1> <Ctrl-K>`	Kills characters from the cursor forward to the end of the line
`<Esc-W>`	Copies the Region to the Kill Ring, but does not blank the text from the document
`<Ctrl-W>`	Kills the Region
`<Ctrl-Y>`	Pastes the most recent text in the Kill Ring into the document at Point

Global search and replace can be either unconditional, where every occurrence of old text you want to replace with new text is replaced without prompting, or it can be interactive, where you are prompted by emacs before each occurrence of old text is replaced with new text. Also, the grammar of replacement can include regular expressions, which we do not cover here (*see* Chapter 10).

For example, to replace the word men unconditionally with the word women from the current position of Point to the end of the document, press <Esc-x>, type `replace-string`, and then press <Enter>. You are then prompted for the old string. Type men and then press <Enter>. You are then prompted for the new string. Type women and then press <Enter> on the keyboard. All occurrences are replaced with no further prompts.

To accomplish an interactive replacement, simply press <Esc-x>, type `query-replace`, and then press <Enter>. You can then input old and new strings, but you are given an opportunity at each occurrence of the old string to replace it or not to replace it with the new string. Table 5.15 shows the actions that you can take while in the midst of an interactive search and replace. Practice Session 5.8 contains further examples of copying and pasting and global search and replace, both unconditional and interactive. Your objective will be to type in one line of text, copy it into the Kill Ring, and then paste it into the document seven times. Then modify the contents of the original line and each pasted line by using both interactive search and replace and unconditional search and replace.

■■ TABLE 5.15 Interactive Search and Replace Actions

Key	Search and Replace Action
`Delete`	Do not make this replacement; keep searching
`Enter (or Return)`	Do not continue replacements; quit now
`space bar`	Do this replacement and then continue searching
`, (comma)`	Make this replacement, display the replacement, and prompt for another command
`. (period)`	Make this replacement and then end searching
`! (exclamation mark)`	Replace this and all the remaining occurrences unconditionally

Practice Session 5.8

Step 1: At the shell prompt, type emacs `osfile` and then press <Enter>.

Step 2: Type `Windows is the operating system of choice for everyone.`

Step 3: Press <Ctrl-@>. The Mark is now set at the end of the line you typed in Step 2. Highlight the whole first line with the cursor.

Step 4: Press the <Esc> key and then the <W> key. This action copies the Region to the Kill Ring.

Step 5: Position the cursor at the beginning of the second line in the buffer, which should be blank.

(continued)

Practice Session 5.8 *(continued)*

Step 6:   Press <Ctrl-Y>. The first line of text is now pasted into the second blank line.

Step 7:   Repeat Steps 5 and 6 six more times so that you now have eight lines of text in the buffer, all containing the text Windows is the operating system of choice for everyone.

Step 8:   Position the cursor on the W in Windows on the first line of the buffer.

Step 9:   Save the buffer at this point with <Ctrl-X Ctrl-S>.

Step 10:   Press the <Esc> key and then the <X> key. Then type query-replace and press <Enter>. These actions begin an interactive search and replace. The prompt Query replace: appears.

Step 11:   Type everyone and then press <Enter>. The prompt with: appears.

Step 12:   Type students and then press <Enter>. The prompt Query replacing everyone with students: (? for help) appears.

Step 13:   Pressing the <space bar> on the keyboard replaces the word everyone on the first line with the word students, and the prompt Query replacing everyone with students: (? for help) appears again.

Step 14:   Press <Enter>. The prompt Replaced 1 occurrence appears.

Step 15:   Position the cursor over the e in the word everyone on the second line of the buffer.

Step 16:   Repeat Steps 10–14, interactively replacing the word everyone each time it appears with the words computer scientists, engineers, system administrators, web servers, scientists, networking, and mathematicians on lines 2–8 of the buffer.

Step 17:   Position the cursor on the W in Windows on the first line of the buffer.

Step 18:   Press the <Esc> key and then the <X> key. Then type replace-string and press <Enter>. These actions begin an unconditional search and replace. The prompt replace string: appears.

Step 19:   Type Windows and then press <Enter>. The prompt Replace string Windows with: appears.

Step 20:   Type UNIX and then press <Enter>. The prompt Replaced 8 occurrences appears. Correct?

Step 21:   Save the buffer with <Ctrl-X Ctrl-S>, and then print it using the facilities available on your computer system.

The following In-Chapter Exercises ask you to apply some of the operations you learned about in the previous Practice Sessions.

IN-CHAPTER EXERCISES

5.5   Run emacs and define keyboard macro commands that automatically delete

❖ every other word in a line of unspecified length,

❖ every other line in a file of unspecified length,

❖ every other word and every other line in a file of unspecified length with lines of unspecified length.

5.6   Write a keyboard macro, as shown in Section 5.4.4, to do everything shown in Steps 10–14 of Practice Session 5.8.

To get some further practice with emacs, do Problems 12–14 at the end of this chapter.

5.4.7 How to Do Purely Graphical Editing with GNU emacs

Up to this point in our work, it was possible to use emacs in a single text-based terminal window and obtain the results shown. If you connect to UNIX by using one of the methods described in Chapter 2, you are likely interfacing with the operating system via an intermediary known as the **X Window System**, which would allow you to do all of your emacs work in a graphical environment. We present more information on the X Window System and some of its facilities (e.g., the particular features of the GUI) in Chapter 21. For the purposes of learning emacs–if you are using UNIX and the X Window System–you may be able to run emacs in its own frame on your screen display, or possibly in several frames on your screen display simultaneously.

5.4.8 Editing Data Files

The following example demonstrates the use of emacs in an X Window System environment to do some further editing of the datafile created in Section 5.4.4. The look and feel of emacs running under the X Window System are very similar to a word processor application or program running under any other operating system that has a GUI, such as Windows 2000 or XP. In the Example: Graphical emacs and the Practice Sessions that follow, we used GNU emacs 21.2.1.

 Example: Graphical emacs

Step 1:   While running the X Window system—in an xterm window—at the shell prompt, type emacs datafile and then press <Enter>. Your screen display should look similar to the one shown in Figure 5.13.

Step 2:   Use the mouse to position the cursor over the character 1 at the beginning of the tenth line in the buffer, and then click the left-most mouse button. The cursor is now positioned over the character 1.

(continued)

Example: Graphical emacs (continued)

Step 3: Click and hold down the left-most mouse button over the character 1, and then drag the mouse so that the entire tenth line is highlighted, including one character to the right of the 0 in the number 10 at the end of the line. Release the left-most mouse button.

Step 4: Position the cursor with the mouse so that the arrow points to the menu choice Edit at the top of the emacs screen. Click the left-most mouse button. A set of pull-down menu choices appears, similar to that shown in Figure 5.14.

Step 5: Move the mouse so that the pointer arrow is over Copy and click the left-most mouse button. The text that you highlighted (selected) in Step 3 is now held in a temporary buffer.

Step 6: Move the mouse so that the cursor is over the first character position on the eleventh line, and click the left-most mouse button. The cursor is now in that position in the buffer.

Step 7: Make the pull-down menu choice Edit>Paste. You have now pasted the 10 characters from the tenth line in the buffer into the eleventh line in the buffer. Your screen display should now look similar to Figure 5.15.

Step 8: Make the pull-down menu choice File>Save (current buffer) and then the pull-down menu choice File>Exit Emacs.

Figure 5.13 The emacs screen display showing datafile

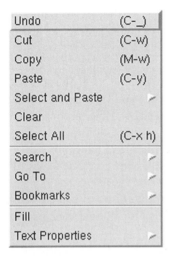

Figure 5.14 The emacs Edit pull-down menu

Figure 5.15 Datafile after editing and adding an 11th line

5.4.9 How to Start, Save a File, and Exit

As illustrated in the Example: Graphical emacs, this text editor gives you exclusive mouse/GUI expediency. This method of working on a text file is most efficient for beginners as well as experienced users. In doing Practice Session 5.9, which simply repeats Practice Session 5.6, you will be able to compare the speed and ease of operations using keystroke commands to those of mouse/GUI interaction. Note that, on the pull-down menu shown in Figure 5.14, keystroke commands also are shown for some of the menu choices. Clicking the menu choice button or pressing the keyboard keys would accomplish the same thing. This flexibility adds to the ease of your use of the editor.

Practice Session 5.9 lets you edit the file alien that you created at the start of this section in Example: DOS Aliases, so that it can be used as aliases for the Bourne shell. You will also modify an existing file, .profile, in your home directory so that when you log in and are using the Bourne shell, you have the aliased commands in the file alien3 available to you. Before you begin Practice Session 5.9, do the following:

(1) Use the `ls —la` command to find out if you have a .profile file in your home directory. If you have no .profile file in your home directory, then use `emacs` to create a new file named .profile with *nothing* in it.

(2) Find out which shell you are currently using by typing `echo $SHELL`. If you are using the C shell, the system will respond with /bin/csh. If you are using the Bourne shell, the system will respond /bin/sh.

If you are not using the Bourne shell as determined in Step 2, switch to the Bourne shell by using the `chsh` command. On our system, FreeBSD 5.0, when we typed `chsh`, we were able to edit a file that allowed change of shell when we logged in again.

Practice Session 5.9

Step 1: At the shell prompt, type `emacs alien` and then press `<Enter>`. The file that you created in Example: emacs Text Editor is loaded into the buffer, and the contents of the emacs buffer looks like the one shown in Figure 5.10.

Step 2: Position the cursor, using the mouse and left-most mouse button, to the right of the character a at the end of the third line.

Step 3: Press `<Enter>` to open a blank line and put the cursor at the beginning of the line.

Step 4: Type `alice dir/w='ls'`

Step 5: Position the cursor, using the mouse and left-most mouse button, at character a in `alice`.

Step 6: Hold down the left-most mouse button and move the mouse so that the word `alice` and the following space are highlighted. Press the `<Delete>` key to cut the word `alice` from the buffer.

Step 7: Type `alias`.

Step 8: Move the mouse so that the cursor is over the second a character in the word `alias`. Click the left-most mouse button.

Step 9: Press the down `<arrow>` key on the keyboard twice. The cursor should now be at the beginning of the blank line below the line that reads `alias type more`.

(continued)

Practice Session 5.9 *(continued)*

Step 10: From the Edit pulldown menu, choose Paste. The cut word alice has been put back into the buffer at the start of the line.

Step 11: Use the mouse and left-most mouse button to position the cursor at the end of the word alice, after the character e.

Step 12: Use the <Delete> or <Back Space> key to delete the letters c and e from the word alice.

Step 13: Type as copy='cp'.

Step 14: Continue moving the cursor to the proper positions and add the necessary character so that your screen display looks like the one shown in Figure 5.16.

Step 15: From the pulldown menu Files, choose Save Buffer As... .

Step 16: At the Write file: prompt, erase anything on the line with the <Back Space> key, type ~/alien3, and then press <Enter>.

Step 17: From the File pull-down menu, make the choice File>Open File. In the minibuffer, after the prompt Find file: ~/ type .profile. A new buffer opens on-screen containing the contents of the .profile file.
Position the cursor anywhere on a blank line in the file .profile.

Step 18: From the File pull-down menu, make the choice File>Insert file... In the minibuffer, type ~/alien3. The lines of text from alien3's DOS aliases should now be inserted into the file .profile.

Step 19: From the pull-down menu File, make the choice File>Save (current buffer).

Step 20: Make the pull-down menu choice File>Exit Emacs to quit emacs and return to the shell prompt.

Step 21: To test your new .profile file, log out and then log in to your UNIX system again. Then in a terminal or console window, at the shell prompt, type one of the aliased commands and note the results. For example, if you type dir, you should get the results of the ls −la command.

```
#DOS aliases
alias del='rm'
alias dir='ls -la'
alias dir/w='ls'
alias type='more'
alias copy='cp'
```

Figure 5.16 Emacs display of the contents of file alien$_3$

5.4.10 `emacs` Graphical Menus

Figure 5.17 shows the contents of another two of the most important pull-down menus in a graphical `emacs`: Files and Tools. To the right of each pull-down choice is the keystroke command equivalent, if there is one.

To get some further practice with a graphical `emacs`, do Problems 15 and 16 at the end of this chapter.

5.4.11 Creating and Editing C Programs

Besides being a powerful text editor/word processor, `emacs` can do multiple chores that are useful to a computer user from within the `emacs` program itself, such as composing e-mail, executing shell scripts, Internet work, and program development in C, HTML, and Java. Since the text for anything more than a trivial program must be generated in a text editor of some sort, it stands to reason that this editor should also be able to compile, link, debug, and keep a record of source code revisions, as well as execute the program itself. This is easily done in `emacs` using some of its built-in capabilities. These kinds of all-in-one capabilities are present because in the days of character-only terminals and consoles, instead of leaving the editor to accomplish a chore outside

Figure 5.17 emacs Files and Tools menu choices

of it, you could accomplish common tasks from within the editor. In modern UNIX, we can now simply switch between windows and never leave the editor. But it is still very useful to be able to harness some of the multiple capabilities of the program, mainly for the sake of efficiency.

Practice Session 5.10 allows you to type in the source code of a C program and use the special facilities of the editor to properly indent the text, compile and link the source code, and implement revisions according to compile-time errors. You can then execute the program in a terminal window to test it. The purpose of the program is to allow the user to type in an integer, and then another integer, and the first integer will be raised to the power indicated by the second integer. A note about paths: If the path for the shell you are executing includes the working directory where the compiled and linked executable program is saved by emacs, then you can run the program. Otherwise, you will have to include the path to this directory. For example, emacs saved the source code and executable files in the current working directory /root on our system when we did Practice Session 5.10. Before running the program, since we knew we were running under the C shell, we checked the *path* variable by typing echo $PATH. The path display included the current working directory where emacs was saving our files. See Chapter 4, Section 4.1 Introduction, for information on how to view the *path* and set the *path* variable. Also see Chapter 20 for more about the program development process. The source code for the program is as follows.

```c
#include <math.h>
main()
{
  float x,y;
  printf("This program takes x and y values from stdin and displaysx^y.\n");
  printf("Enter integer x: ");
  scanf("%f", &x);
  printf("Enter integer y: ");
  scanf("%f", &y);
  printf("x^y is: %6.3f\n", pow((double)x,(double)y));
}
```

 Practice Session 5.10

Step 1:   At the shell prompt, type emacs power.c. Notice that the Major mode for this new buffer is set to C mode.

Step 2:   Type in the above program source code exactly as shown. Emacs will automatically indent the code according to the standard style used in structured programming. Your emacs screen display should look similar to Figure 5.18.

Step 3:   From the pull-down menus, make the choice File>Save (current buffer).

(continued)

Practice Session 5.10 *(continued)*

Step 4: From the pull-down menus, make the choice Tools>Compile... . In the minibuffer, the prompt Compile command: make −k appears. Use the backspace key to erase the make −k, and then type cc power.c −lm −o power. A new window appears in the emacs frame, showing the progress of the compilation/linking process. An error in compilation will appear, as seen in Figure 5.19, since you made the syntax mistake of not including the last curly brace. If you get other errors, they are probably generated by other typos you made, and you will have to correct them.

Step 5: Edit the text of power.c and add the last curly brace and correct any other typos indicated in the compilation window. Then save the current buffer with the pull-down menu choice File>Save(current buffer).

Step 6: From the pull-down menus, make the choice Tools>Compile... . In the minibuffer, the prompt Compile command: cc power.c −lm −o power should appear. Press <Enter> to accept this compile/link command.

Step 7: If all syntax errors have been removed from the power.c source code, you should get a screen display similar to Figure 5.20, which indicates that you have successfully compiled and linked power.c.

Step 8: You can now exit emacs, and in a terminal window test the program by typing power on the command line. Remember that the path must be set for the current shell so that executable programs in the directory the file power is in will run.

```
emacs@.egr.up.edu

File  Edit  Options  Buffers  Tools  C  Help

#include <math.h>

main()
{
    float x,y;
    printf("This program takes x and y values from stdin and displaysx^y.\n");
    printf("Enter integer x: ");
    scanf("%f", &x);
    printf("Enter integer y: ");
    scanf("%f", &y);
    printf("x^y is: %6.3f\n", pow((double)x,(double)y));







--:**  power.c         (C Abbrev)--L11--All------------------------------------
```

Figure 5.18 Source code in emacs

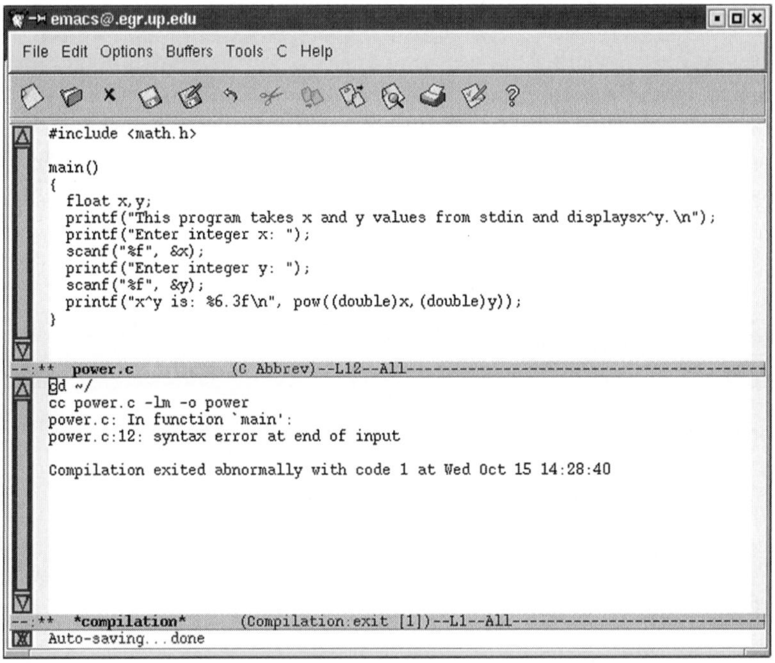

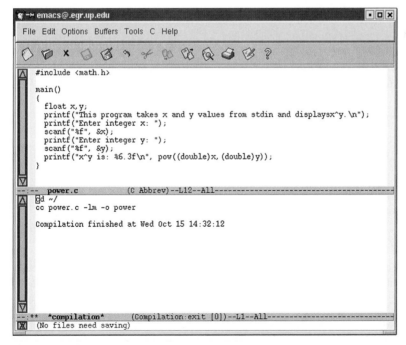

Figure 5.19 Compilation in an error syntax window

Figure 5.20 Correct completed compile/link window

5.4.12 Working in Multiple Buffers

As seen in previous exercises, it is possible to insert one buffer or file contents into another and to open windows into different buffers, some that may not even contain text you want to edit, at the same time. This capability is important when you want to compose the contents of a buffer or file from perhaps many other buffers or files that you have previously created. The following Practice Session shows you how to create, move between, and copy and paste between several buffers open within one emacs frame.

Practice Session 5.11

Step 1:   Create a subdirectory under your home directory named multi, and make that subdirectory the current working directory.

Step 2:   At the shell prompt, type emacs newfile. You should now be editing the buffer newfile with a single window.

Step 3:   In emacs, make the pull-down menu choice File>Split Window. The frame should now be split horizontally, so that you have two windows, one above the other, both showing the contents of newfile.

Step 4:   Click with the mouse in the upper window, and then hold down the <Ctrl>+<X> keys on the keyboard at the same time. Then press the <3> key on the keyboard. The upper window from Step 3 should now be split vertically into two windows, showing you a total of three windows into the buffer newfile.

Step 5:   Repeat Step 4 in the lower window of the frame. You should now have four windows showing the contents of the buffer newfile. Your screen display should look similar to Figure 5.21. If you did the above steps incorrectly, you can always use the File>Unsplit Window pull-down menu choice to return you to a single window display, and then try again.

Step 6:   Click the mouse in the upper-left window and type 1 2 3 4 5. Then make the pull-down menu choice File>Save buffer as. In the minibuffer, type firstrow. A new file named firstrow is created on disk in the current working directory named multi, and you are still seeing four windows into that buffer.

Step 7:   Click the mouse in the upper-right window, position the cursor at the right after the 5, and use the backspace key to erase the numbers 1, 2, 3, 4, and 5. Then type 6 7 8 9 10. Then make the pull-down menu choice File>Save buffer as. In the minibuffer, type secondrow.

Step 8:   Click the mouse in the upper-left window. Make the pull-down menu choice File>Open File. In the minibuffer, type firstrow. You now should have a screen display similar to Figure 5.22, with the upper left window showing the contents of firstrow, and the remaining three windows showing the contents of secondrow.

(continued)

Practice Session 5.11 *(continued)*

Step 9: Click the mouse in the lower-left window, position the cursor to the right of the 0, erase the 6, 7, 8, 9, and 10, and type 11 12 13 14 15. Then make the pull-down menu choice File>Save buffer as. In the minibuffer, type `thirdrow`. A new file is created in the current working directory named thirdrow.

Step 10: Click in the upper-right window, and make the pull-down menu choice File>Open File. In the minibuffer, type `secondrow`.

Step 11: Click in the lower-left window, and make the pull-down menu choice File>Open File. In the minibuffer, type `thirdrow`. Your screen display should now look similar to Figure 5.23.

Step 12: Click the mouse in the lower-right window, and make the pull-down menu choice File>Save buffer as. In the minibuffer, type `four` . Click in the lower-left window, and make the pull-down menu choice File>Open File. In the minibuffer, type `thirdrow`.

Step 13: Click the mouse in the lower-right window, and use the backspace key to erase the 11, 12, 13, 14, and 15. Then use the pull-down menu choices Edit>Copy and Edit>Paste to copy the 1 2 3 4 5, 6 7 8 9 10, and 11 12 13 14 15 onto the first three rows of the lower-right window. Your screen display should look similar to Figure 5.24.

Step 14: Finally, with the lower-right window the current window, make the pull-down menu choice File>Save (current buffer), and type `four`. Then quit emacs without saving any of the buffers.

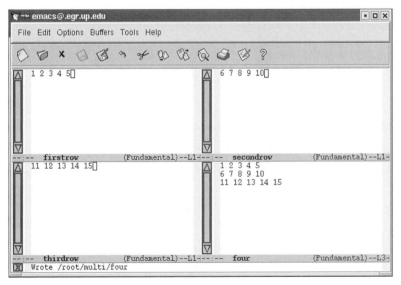

Figure 5.21 Four tiled windows in a frame display

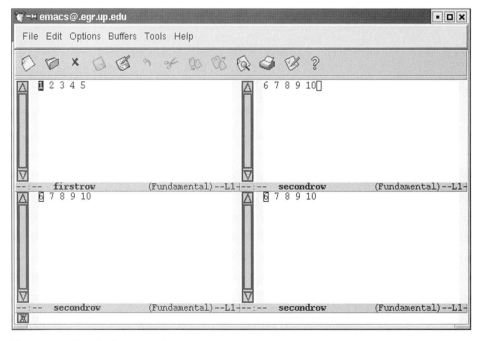

Figure 5.22 Two buffers saved

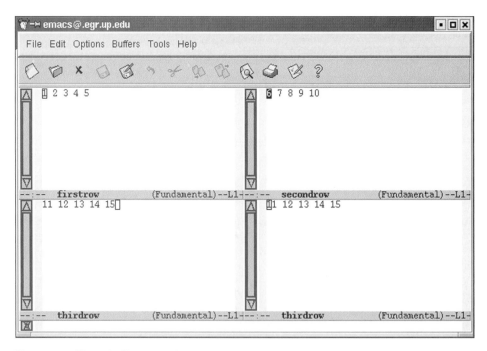

Figure 5.23 Three buffers saved

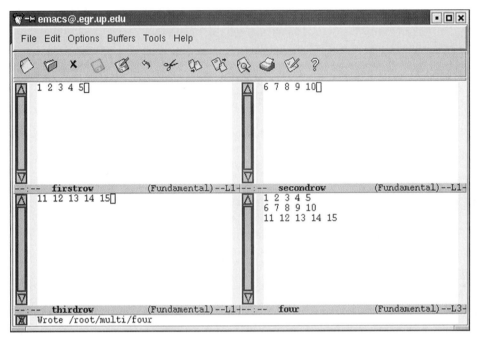

Figure 5.24 File four with three pasted rows in it

Summary

In this chapter, we covered the three most useful text editors that UNIX offers. They are useful because UNIX is a text-driven operating system. Useful operations, such as editing script files, writing e-mail messages, or creating C language programs, are done with text editors. A full-screen display editor shows a portion of a file that fills most or all of the screen display. The cursor, or point, can be moved to any of the text shown in the screen display. Editing a file involves editing a copy that the editor creates, called a buffer. Keystroke commands are the primary way of interacting with these editors. The editor(s) used should fit the user's personal criteria. The most important functions that are common to these UNIX text editors are cursor movement, cut/copy–paste, deleting text, inserting text, opening an existing file, starting a new file, quitting, saving, and search and replace.

Problems

1. Despite the availability of fancy and powerful word processors, why is text editing still important?

2. List 10 commonly used text editing operations.

3. What are the three most popular text editors in UNIX? Which one is your favorite? Why?

4. What is an editor buffer?

5. Run `pico` on your system. Create and edit a block of text that you want to be the body of an e-mail message explaining the basic capabilities of the `pico` editor. For example, part of your message might describe the three most important keystroke commands in `pico`, devoting one line of description to each command. Try not to type more than 15 to 20 lines of text into the file. Then save the file with <Ctrl-O> as first.txt. Use the `mail` command in Chapter 6 to send this message to yourself.

6. Run `pico` and create a file with three lines of text in it. Then use the cut and paste features of `pico` to duplicate the three lines so that the file contains nine lines of text. How do you copy a line of text from one place to another in `pico`? Save this file as prob6.

7. Run `pico` and use the keystroke commands <Ctrl-G>, <Ctrl-V>, and <Ctrl-Y> to find out how to position the cursor *without* using the <arrow> keys. Then use the <Ctrl-R> command to read the text from the file prob6 that you created in Problem 6. Position the cursor within this new file, using only the keystroke commands that you learned from the Help text.

8. Run `vi` on your system and create a Bourne shell script file that contains the lines

```
echo $SHELL

cat /etc/shells

ls /usr/local/bin *.sh
```

Then save the file as sheller and quit `vi`. At the shell prompt, type `bash sheller` and then press <Enter>. You get a listing on the screen of the current shell and the contents of two common UNIX directories that contain other shells that are available on your system. Review Chapter 4 on the various shells and their uses (if necessary).

9. Run `vi` on your system. Create and edit a block of text that you want to be the body of an e-mail message explaining the basic capabilities of the `vi` editor. For example, part of your message might describe the difference between the Insert and Command Modes. This file can be at least one page, or 45 to 50 lines of text, long. Then save the file as vi_doc.txt. Use the `mail` command in Chapter 6, insert the body of text in an e-mail message, and send it to yourself.

10. Run `vi` on your system and write definitions in your own words, without looking at the textbook, for
    a. full-screen display editor,
    b. file versus buffer,
    c. keystroke commands, and
    d. text file versus binary file.

    Then refer back to the relevant sections of this chapter to check your definitions. Make any necessary corrections or additions. Re-edit the file to incorporate any corrections or additions that you made, and then print out the file using the print commands available on your system.

11. Edit the file you created in Problem 10, and change the order of the text of your definitions to (d), (a), (c), and (b), using the `yank`, `put`, and `D` or `dd` commands. Print out the file using the print commands available on your system.

12. This problem assumes that you can interactively start up a new shell, the Bourne Again shell, or bash. If you type `bash` at the command line and you get an error message `bash: not found`, then check with your system administrator or teacher to find out how to enable this shell. Before you begin, be sure to back up your .bashrc file by using the `cp` command described in Chapter 3. To do so, type

```
cp .bashrc .bashrc_bak
```

and then press `<Enter>`. If for any reason you destroy the contents of the .bashrc file while doing this problem, you can restore the original by typing

```
cp .bashrc_bak .bashrc
```

and then pressing `<Enter>`. If there is no .bashrc file in your home directory, use emacs to create one, and make it an empty file with nothing in it. Use emacs to edit the .bashrc file in your home directory, and then use the `<Ctrl-X I>` command to insert the file alien3 that you created in Practice Session 5.9 at the bottom of the buffer. Save the buffer, exit emacs, and log off your computer system. Log on to your computer system again, start up a new bash shell interactively by typing `bash` at the command line (so that the new .bashrc is in effect), and test each of the DOS aliases that are in alien3 by typing them at the shell prompt, with their proper arguments (if necessary). They should give you the same results as when you ran the Bourne shell aliases after Practice Session 5.9.

13. As you saw in the Practice Sessions, you can be editing more than one file at a time in emacs, where each of the files' contents are being held in different buffers. Experiment by first using the `cp` command at the shell prompt to make a copy of the file datafile that you created in Practice Session 5.7. Name this copy datafile2. Use emacs to open both files with the command `<Ctrl-X>+<Ctrl-F>` and switch between buffers with `<Ctrl-X B>`. Then edit both of them at the same time and cut and paste three or four lines of each between the two, using `<Ctrl-@>`, `<Ctrl-W>`, and `<Ctrl-Y>`. Don't save your changes to the file datafile.

14. Write a keyboard macro, as described in Section 5.4.4, to do everything shown in Steps 10–16 of Practice Session 5.8.

15. Try working with emacs in a text-only window, and use only keystroke commands.

To do this, you will have to launch emacs from a console or terminal window by typing `emacs–nw newfile`. The `–nw` option specifies that emacs will run in a nongraphical mode. Then, in the console or terminal window, a nongraphical emacs will open on the buffer newfile. As stated in the introduction to Section 5.4, you can still gain access to the Menu Bar menus at the top of the emacs screen by pressing the escape `<Esc>` key on the keyboard and then pressing the single backquote `<`>` key. You can then descend through the menu bar choices by pressing the letter key of the menu choice you want to make. For example, pressing the `<F>` key gives you access to the File pull-down menu choices, and then pressing the `<S>` key allows you to save the current buffer.

16. To compare keystroke to graphical emacs, repeat Problem 13, using purely graphical emacs—that is, with no keystroke commands allowed. This time, make two copies of datafile named datafilex and datafilexx at the UNIX shell prompt with the cp command. Open all three files and, using the multiple-buffer and multiple window capability of an X Window emacs, cut and paste among the files using only the mouse. Again, as in Problem 13, don't save your changes to the file datafile.

17. Use emacs' capability of sending e-mail while you're in emacs. Send an e-mail message to one of your friends, composing the message body and sending from within emacs.

Electronic Mail

Objectives

- To describe basic e-mail concepts and their specific implementations on a UNIX system

- To illustrate the effective use of a line display e-mail system—the UNIX `mail` command

- To show how `KMail`, a graphic e-mail system, is more advantageous than a line display e-mail system

- To show further capabilities of a full-screen display text-based e-mail system with `pine`

- To cover the commands and primitives `cd`, `mail`, `mkdir`, `pine`, `rm`

6.1 Introduction

This section describes what is common to the electronic mail (e-mail) systems on UNIX. The fundamental purpose of e-mail is to give you the ability to communicate via some permanent record medium on your own computer system with other users, or with users on other systems over an intranet or the Internet. Other forms of communication can also be facilitated by the computer: audio, video, and data that are fundamentally transitory, real-time media that may be archived for permanent record purposes. However, because UNIX systems are text-based, they accommodate the e-mail permanent record medium most successfully.

6.1.1 E-mail Protocols

There are basically two kinds of e-mail programs: the e-mail user agent program you use to compose and read messages and the e-mail transfer agent program, which transfers messages between your computer and host computers on the Internet for delivery and disposition.

All e-mail user agents, or e-mail programs such as `pine`, Eudora, or KMail, as well as those illustrated in Figure 6.1, use a standard protocol for the form of an e-mail message known as the **Simple Mail Transfer Protocol (SMTP)**. This dictates the format of the message in terms of an envelope, a header, and a body, and facilitates the movement of the message between the components of a typical e-mail transfer as seen in Figure 6.1.

The e-mail transfer agent, such as sendmail, Exim, etc., and those illustrated in Figure 6.1, can use two common protocols for transferring e-mail messages between computers, either

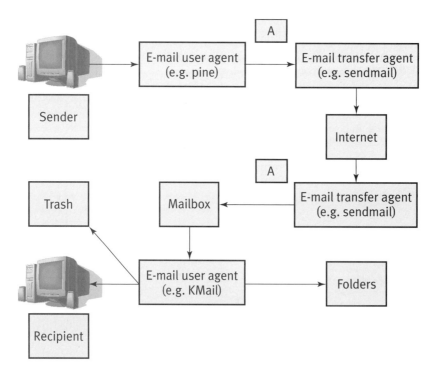

Figure 6.1 Typical e-mail transfer dialog

the **Post Office Protocol (POP)** or the **Internet Message Access Protocol (IMAP)**. The basic difference is that the POP protocol works best for offline e-mail reading from a single host computer that contains your e-mail. The IMAP protocol works best when you have access from several computers to a single e-mail host computer that you want to read and send messages from. In Figure 6.1, the point A in the diagram would be where the IMAP protocol is implemented. In that case, the e-mail user agent is not on the same computer as the e-mail transfer agent, because you want to use the transfer agent on a remote e-mail host from possibly many different computers running different e-mail user agents. A good example of this is when you dial up your **Internet Service Provider (ISP)** from home, school, or work and use different computers at those locations, and their e-mail user agent programs, to access the transfer agent on the ISP's IMAP e-mail server. Part of the configuration you will do to the KMail system below in the In-Chapter Exercises for Section 6.3 asks you to specify the protocol your e-mail server uses, and this information should be available through your system administrator. More than likely, if you use `pine` on your UNIX system, the protocol configuration has already been done by the system administrator.

Another important standard that applies to e-mail is the attachment standard **Multimedia Internet Mail Standard (MIME)**. This dictates the format of multimedia files used as attachments to an e-mail message. Finally, the Internet **Domain Name System** dictates the exact form of an e-mail address. Figure 6.1 shows schematically the components of the e-mail transfer dialog, wherein a sender's message is composed by an e-mail user agent mail program, and then the e-mail transfer agents handle the transfer of the message, on the same computer or over a network, to a recipient. On the recipient side, the system mailbox contains incoming messages, the recipient's e-mail user agent mail program handles the incoming message, and it is disposed of either in the recipient's collection of folders or is deleted.

6.1.2 E-mail Features

One of the most important structural parts of an e-mail message that you see on-screen is the message header. It usually appears at the top of the message text, called the message body, and contains some standard or universal blank fields that you fill in as you write a message. The purpose of the message header is to help in the automated delivery of e-mail by your local e-mail program and by the various mail handling programs on your system or on the network(s) to which your system is linked. The most important of these fields are,

- the To: field, which contains the e-mail address(es) of the recipient(s);
- the From: field, which contains the e-mail address of the originator of the message;
- the Cc: field, which contains the address(es) of any additional recipient(s);
- the Attch: field, which lists any attachments that might accompany the message, usually in the form of external files; and
- the Subject: field, which indicates the subject or purpose of the message.

Basically, two kinds of attachments can accompany an e-mail message. The simplest kind is a text file, which contains only ASCII text. It can be part of the message body or in a separate file along with the message. Of course, a binary, nonhuman readable file can be converted with the UNIX uuencode utility into an ASCII text file for attachment to an e-mail message. Then, at the recipient's end, the uudecode utility will translate the ASCII text back into binary. We present more information about this method in Chapter 10. The more prevalent kind of attachment in contemporary e-mail is supported by **Multimedia Internet Mail Standard (MIME)**, which defines various multimedia content types and subtypes for attachments. In particular, digital images (.jpeg), audio files (.mp3), and movie files (.mpeg) can be transported via e-mail attachment, even on dissimilar e-mail systems, if the systems are MIME compliant. All the e-mail systems that we examine here are capable of attaching text, and both KMail and `pine` are capable of attaching multimedia files easily. Going hand-in-hand with the basic concept of e-mail as a permanent record is the notion of a folder, or subdirectory, into which you can place that record in some organized and logical fashion. You can create a variety of folders based on whom you send e-mail to (the recipients) or whom you get e-mail from (the sender). Similar to paper mail, an e-mail correspondent is someone with whom you have a dialog by exchanging e-mail messages. The messages themselves are simply files stored archivally in those folders or awaiting further disposition. The most common form of disposition of e-mail messages is deletion. In fact, a very contemporary issue regarding the disposition of e-mail is junk e-mail, or "spam." How to delete or filter this spam before it reaches individual users is important to the success of the Internet in the future. Further disposition might be forwarding a message, or passing it along for its information content. Another form of disposition might be replying to the sender and giving a response to the message. Forwarding and replying can also be a multiple operation, with more than one destination for retransmission. The process of sending a message to one recipient but at the same time sending copies of this original message to others is called sending carbon copies (abbreviated cc). Finally, e-mail can be disposed of by printing it on paper, using the printing facilities of your system.

The proper form of an e-mail address underpins the entire system of electronic mail. On the UNIX local host computer system (*see* Chapter 14) that you are logged on to–and on which you have a username–your e-mail address is your username. When you send mail and specify a username as the recipient, either on the command line or in the To: field of the e-mail message header, that username can be resolved to a valid local host e-mail address with the aid of the UNIX system. When you want to send e-mail over the Internet, the e-mail address relies on the Internet Domain Name System for its basic form.

Being able to maintain a list of frequent correspondents is also a fundamental part of any e-mail system. That way, as in a paper address book, you can quickly route e-mail messages by looking up recipients' addresses automatically in an electronic address book functionally attached to your e-mail program.

An important basic feature of e-mail on a UNIX system is a system mailbox file, usually in the directory /usr/mail or /usr/spool/mail; messages that people send you are stored in that file. When you log on to the system and have messages in that system mailbox, you are notified on the screen that you have mail. When you read your mail, with the `mail` command, for example, the `mail` program reads your system mailbox and informs you of the individual messages in it. You may then dispose of the messages that you have already read, or they are saved for further disposition in a folder (e.g., mbox).

For our purposes, there are three categories of e-mail systems for UNIX. The `mail` program in Section 6.2 is a line display e-mail system, which means that you can only edit one line at a time when you are composing an e-mail message. The `pine` program is a text-based full-screen display e-mail system, which means that you can edit any text you see on a single screen display, as you would on a word processor. Finally, the KMail program runs under an integrated desktop environment known as KDE and is fully graphical.

Table 6.1 lists and briefly describes the common e-mail functions found in the UNIX e-mail systems that we cover in this chapter.

■ **TABLE 6.1** E-mail Functions Common to UNIX E-mail Systems

Function	Description
aliases (addressbook)	Allows the user to define a list of frequent correspondents' e-mail addresses
attachments	Allows the sender to attach either text or multimedia files to a message
cc	Allows the sender to specify recipients of copies of a message
deleting	Allows the sender to dispose of messages by deleting them from the system mailbox
forwarding	Allows the sender to pass a received message to a new recipient quickly
reading	Allows the recipient to read incoming messages
replying	Allows the recipient to reply immediately to a current or disposed message
saving in folders	Allows the recipient to dispose of messages in a logical directory structure for e-mail
sending	Allows the user to send messages

6.2   How to Use the UNIX `mail` Command Effectively

The easiest and quickest e-mail system to use on UNIX systems is the `mail` program. On System V, the `mail` program is named `mailx`, and on BSD systems it is named `Mail`. The `mail` command usually invokes BSD `Mail`. We chose to use the `mail` command to illustrate the following discussion. The general syntax of the `mail` command is as follows.

`mail` **[options] [recipient(s)]**

Purpose:	Allows you to send and receive e-mail
Output:	With no options or recipients specified, you are placed in the `mail` program, and a list of message headers appears on your screen display

Commonly used options/features:

For sending mail

−s	A `Subject:` line is included in the message header for all recipients
−c add	A carbon copy is sent to address add
−b add	A blind carbon copy is sent to address add

(continued)

> `mail [options] [recipient(s)]` (continued)
>
> **For reading mail**
>
> **-h**   A screen display of message headers is shown first
>
> **-P**   All messages are displayed with full headers

The `mail` program commonly runs at the command line in one of two ways. In the first way, you are sending e-mail; type `mail` at the shell prompt, followed by options and option arguments if necessary, and then type an e-mail address or addresses. Then type in the body of the e-mail message, one line at a time. When you press `<Ctrl-D>` at the beginning of a blank line, the e-mail message is sent. In the second way, you are reading `mail`; type `mail` at the shell prompt and then press `<Enter>`. If you have undisposed or new e-mail messages in the system mailbox, a list of message headers appears on-screen, showing you some information about each undisposed message. You may then type in commands to read and dispose of your messages. If you have no e-mail in the system mailbox, you get a reply from UNIX: `No mail for user-name`, where `username` is your username on the computer system you are logged on to.

You may also send e-mail on a UNIX system in one of two ways when using the `mail` command. If you want to use the `mail` command to send an e-mail message to someone on your system, you can type the `mail` command and then type one or more usernames of the recipients to whom you want to send the e-mail message. Recall from Chapter 3 that your username identifies you on your UNIX computer system. Users on your system have system mailboxes in /var/spool/mail or /usr/spool/mail. When you include a recipient on the command line, that recipient's username is resolved to an "address," or location in the file structure of the computer system that your mail message will be sent to. (For more information on the UNIX file system structure, *see* Chapter 7.)

If you want to use the `mail` command to send an e-mail message to someone not on your system, presuming that your system is connected to the Internet, you must know the valid Internet address of the recipient, which usually takes the form,

`username@hostname.domain_name... ,`

where,

> `username` is the name that identifies that recipient on the system he or she is on,
>
> `hostname` is the computer on which the recipient has a username, and
>
> `domain_name...` are valid Internet domain names.

Of course, you can also specify the complete Internet address of someone who is on your computer system. This brings up the question of how to find a person's Internet address. The simplest way is to ask that person, but if this is not feasible, there are mechanisms available on the Internet for finding a person's e-mail address, and we explore them in Chapter 14.

For more information on the `mail` command, see section entitled "e-mail with the UNIX `mail` command" on the book Web site.

6.3   Graphical E-mail with KMail

What really differentiates KMail as a UNIX e-mail system from the other e-mail systems we have used so far in this chapter is that almost everything that was done previously by using text-based commands and operations can be accomplished graphically in KMail. KMail is very similar to the Netscape Messenger used to send and receive e-mail within Netscape Communicator.

The common functions found in Table 6.1 are all accomplished in KMail via mouse "point and click" operations. The only typing on the keyboard that might be done is for the message body itself, and also for the entry of necessary parameter changes or text specifications in the input fields of various menus or command windows in the KMail graphical environment. As was mentioned in the introduction to Chapter 5, a combination of keyboard entry of text and graphical operations, suited to the needs of the individual user, is the best approach to take with both text editing and with e-mail.

6.3.1 Starting Out with KMail

Example: Setting your identity and testing KMail assumes that you are connected to a network, that you know your e-mail address, and that your instructor or system administrator can provide you with e-mail server information. Also, it assumes that you are running the KDE window management system as the "front-end" to your UNIX Operating System. All the examples, Exercises, and Problems for this section were done using KMail 1.4.3 running with KDE 3.0.5 under the FreeBSD 5.0 UNIX Operating System. More information on KDE is found in Chapter 21.

 Example: Setting Your Identity and Testing KMail

Step 1:   Create a "signature" file in your home directory with your favorite text editor, such as GNU emacs, as shown in Chapter 5. A "signature" file contains informational text that you want to include as part of any e-mail message you send. Save this file as ksig.sig, and include in it text that you would want to appear at the bottom of an e-mail message you send.

Step 2:   Launch the KMail Mail client by left-clicking on the KMail button or by making the launcher pop-up menu choice Internet→KMail (Mail Client).

Note: When you run KMail for the first time, it creates a Mail directory containing the files (inbox, outbox, sent-mail, and trash) in your home directory. Also, either a Settings Window appears, where you must enter some initial information so KMail will be able to properly retrieve and send your messages, or you can make the KMail pull-down menu choice Settings>Configure KMail... and enter the same initial information. In either case, to begin sending and receiving e-mail, you will only have to change the settings in the Identity and Network tabs.

(continued)

Example: Setting Your Identity and Testing KMail *(continued)*

Step 3: If it is *not* already the current icon, click on the Identity icon in the Settings Window, and be sure the General tab is selected. Fill in your name, Organization, and e-mail address. Click on the Advanced tab, and fill in your Reply-To Address. Click on the Signature tab, and click on Enable Signature. Then make the pull-down choice Obtain signature text from file. Specify the path to your signature file, ksig.sig, in the Signature File field, by clicking on the Browse for File button if necessary. See Figure 6.2, where the path to the signature file is seen as /root/ksig.sig.

Step 4: Next, click on the Network icon in the Settings Window, and with the Sending tab selected, click on the Add... button. In the Add Transport dialog box that opens, make the SMTP choice. Then fill in the Name, Host, and Port of your e-mail server. This is information you will have to get from your instructor or system administrator at the site where you log in. Click OK in the Add Transport dialog box. An outgoing account has been added.

Step 5: To set up an account so you can receive mail, click the Receiving tab. Then click the Add... button.

Step 6: In the Add Account dialog box, select either POP3 or IMAP, depending on the information supplied by your teacher or system administrator, and then click OK.

Step 7: In the Add Account Window, fill in the Name field to name your account. The Login, Password, and Host fields should be filled in with the login name, password, and hostname that you need to use to log in to the e-mail server. This is information you will have to get from your instructor or system administrator at the site where you log in. You should also select Automatically compact folders (expunges deleted messages) to not leave your `mail` on the server. Finally, make the OK choice in the Add Account Window. A new account should now appear in the Incoming accounts block.

Note: If at this point you get error messages, you have not configured the Network settings properly. Go back and readjust the settings starting in Step 4 above. Get help from your instructor or system administrator.

Step 8: Close the Settings Window by clicking on the OK choice. The Message reader window should now be displayed on the screen, similar to Figure 6.3.

Step 9: From the pull-down menus in the Message Reader Window, make the choice Message>New Message. Alternatively, you can use the left-most speed bar button New Message to accomplish the same thing. A Composer Window will appear, allowing you to compose a new e-mail message.

Step 10: In the To: field, type your e-mail address.

Step 11: In the subject field, type `My first KMail e-mail message!` and then press `Enter`. Notice that in the title bar of the Composer Window, that subject is now

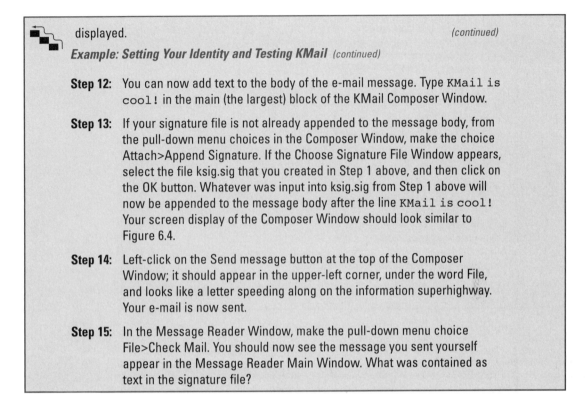

displayed.   *(continued)*

Example: Setting Your Identity and Testing KMail *(continued)*

Step 12: You can now add text to the body of the e-mail message. Type `KMail is cool!` in the main (the largest) block of the KMail Composer Window.

Step 13: If your signature file is not already appended to the message body, from the pull-down menu choices in the Composer Window, make the choice Attach>Append Signature. If the Choose Signature File Window appears, select the file ksig.sig that you created in Step 1 above, and then click on the OK button. Whatever was input into ksig.sig from Step 1 above will now be appended to the message body after the line `KMail is cool!` Your screen display of the Composer Window should look similar to Figure 6.4.

Step 14: Left-click on the Send message button at the top of the Composer Window; it should appear in the upper-left corner, under the word File, and looks like a letter speeding along on the information superhighway. Your e-mail is now sent.

Step 15: In the Message Reader Window, make the pull-down menu choice File>Check Mail. You should now see the message you sent yourself appear in the Message Reader Main Window. What was contained as text in the signature file?

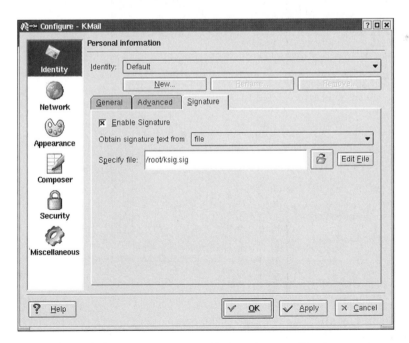

Figure 6.2 Configure KMail signature file location specification

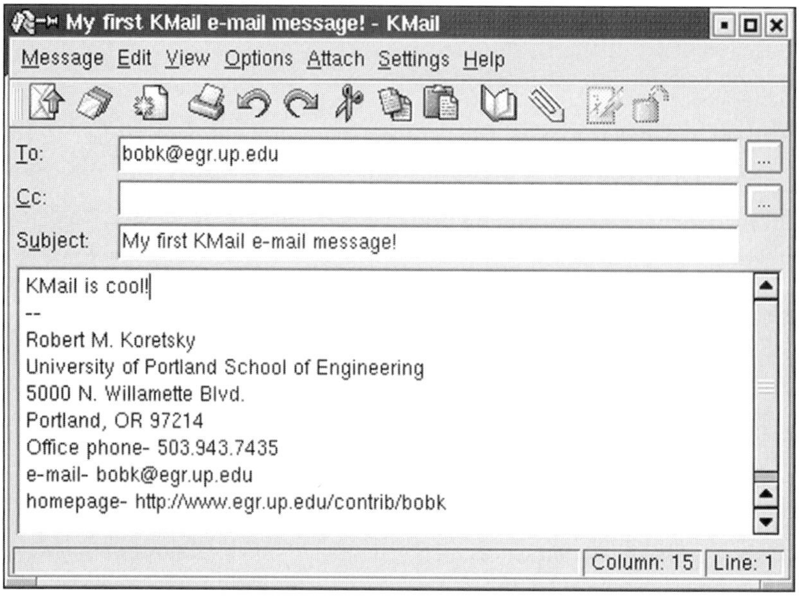

Figure 6.3 Message Reader Window in Kmail

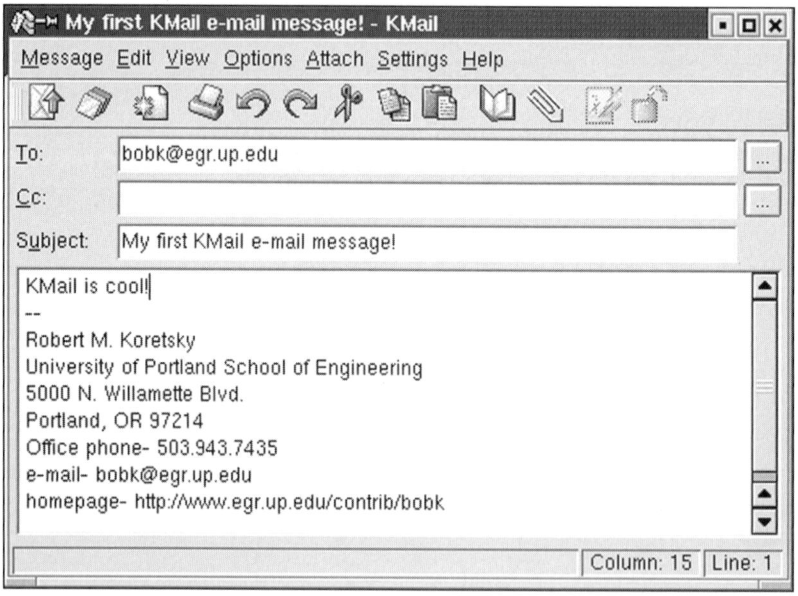

Figure 6.4 First KMail e-mail message

6.3.2 Reading E-mail in KMail

When you launch the KMail program, the Mail Reader window is the first window that opens, and it has three major "panes." These are:

1. The Folders Pane (in the upper left of the message reader window) that shows your available message folders. This pane contains a list of your message folders. To view the contents of a folder, simply click on it.

2. The Header Pane (in the upper right of the message reader window). This pane lists e-mail message "header" information (message Status Flags [the column headed by an F], Sender, Subject, and the Date the message was sent) for the messages in the currently selected folder. Clicking on a header will select that message and display it in the Message Pane. See Table 6.2 for a list of the meaning of the message status flags. You can also select a series of messages by clicking on one message, holding down the <Shift> key, and clicking on another message. The two messages you just clicked on will be selected, along with all the messages in between. You can sort the messages by clicking on the column that you want to sort.

3. The Message Pane (the main area of the window). To scroll through the message, use the scroll bar at the right of the Message Pane.

■■ TABLE 6.2 Message Status Flags in the Header Pane

Status Flag (Appearance)	What It Means
New: (red dot, message colored red)	The message has been received for the first time and is unread
Unread: (green dot, message colored blue)	The message has already been retrieved off the server at least once but has not been read yet
Read: (dash)	The message has been read
Replied: (blue u-turn arrow)	A reply has been composed to this message
Queued: (envelope)	The message has been queued in the outbox to be sent later
Sent: (angled envelope)	The message has been sent

The following Practice Session gives you further practice in reading e-mail with KMail and disposing of e-mail messages. It assumes you are still in KMail after doing Example: Setting Your Identity and Testing KMail and the two In-Chapter Exercises 6.1 and 6.2. If you are not running KMail, launch it now.

IN-CHAPTER EXERCISES

6.1   Launch KMail now, and examine the Header Pane. What appears in it? What is (are) the status of message(s) shown?

6.2   In the Folders Pane, click on the sent-mail folder. What appears in the Headers Pane? What is (are) the status of the message(s) shown? What appears in the Message Pane?

Practice Session 6.1

Step 1:   In the Message Reader Window, in the Folders Pane, click on sent-mail folder icon, then click on the message with Subject My first KMail e-mail message!

Step 2:   Press the <D> key on the keyboard. The message is deleted from the sent-mail folder.

Step 3:   In the Message Reader Window, in the Folders Pane, click on the trash folder icon, then click on the message with Subject My first KMail e-mail message!

Step 4:   Press the <D> key on the keyboard. The message is deleted from the trash folder.

Step 5:   In the Message Reader Window, in the Folders Pane, click on the in box folder icon, and then click on the message with Subject My first KMail e-mail message!

Step 6:   Left-click on the Forward button in the row of button bars at the top of the Message Pane. It looks like a blue arrow over a white page. The Composer Window opens on-screen, with Fwd: My first KMail e-mail message! listed in the title bar of that window, as well as in the subject line. The message body of that message is also shown in the Message Pane of the Composer Window.

Step 7:   In the To: field, type your e-mail address. Click on the Subject: field, erase whatever is in there using the backspace key, and type `Forwarded first KMail message`.

Step 8:   Left-click on the send button at the upper left of the Composer Window. You are returned to the Message Reader Window, and at the extreme bottom-left corner, a line of text appears telling you that KMail is done sending messages. In the Header Pane, what is the status flag showing for the message My first KMail e-mail message!? Refer back to Table 6.2.

Step 9:   Depending on the speed of your system, a new message header appears in the Header Pane. The Subject of this message should be Forwarded first KMail message. What is the status flag showing for this message? Refer back to Table 6.2.

Step 10:   Click on the new message in the Header Pane. Notice that the status flag changes from a red button to a dash, meaning it is now a read message. Delete both messages, My first KMail e-mail message! and Forwarded first KMail message. How did you accomplish this deletion? Also, delete these messages from the trash folder and the sent-mail folder. Exit KMail by making the File>Quit choice from the pull-down menus at the top of the Message Reader Window.

6.3.3   Sending E-mail in KMail

In order to send new e-mail messages in KMail, you use the Composer Window. You open the Composer Window by clicking on the Compose new message button in the upper-left corner of the Mail Reader Window, or by making the pull-down menu choice Message>New Message (keyboard shortcut <Ctrl-N>).

If you have not indicated the location of your signature file and you have **Automatically Append Signature** checked in the **Composer** tab of the **Settings** dialog, you will be prompted for the location of your signature file before the Composer Window opens.

Refer to Figure 6.5 in the following discussion of the Composer Window.

Notice the components of this window: Pull-down menus at the top, speed button bar, header fields for the message, and a large pane to contain the body of the e-mail message. To send a new message, fill in the blank header fields correctly in the Composer Window. Following are some useful operations you can perform to compose a new message.

1. *To use the Addressbook:* The buttons to the right of the `To:` and `Cc:` field boxes (the ones with ellipses in them) allow you to use Addressbook entries to help fill in these fields, if indeed you have any Addressbook entries. You can easily add, edit, or delete entries in your Addressbook by clicking on the Addressbook button at the top of the Composer Window (the tenth icon from the left in the speed button bar, the one that looks like an open book) or by making the pull-down menu choice Message>Addressbook... from the top of the Composer Window. An Addressbook Manager Window opens on-screen, allowing you to add, edit, or delete entries to your Addressbook.

2. *Bcc: If you want to add a Bcc:* field (send Blind Carbon Copies) to the display, make the pull-down menu choice View>Bcc, and make sure there is a check next to the box in this pull-down menu next to Bcc.

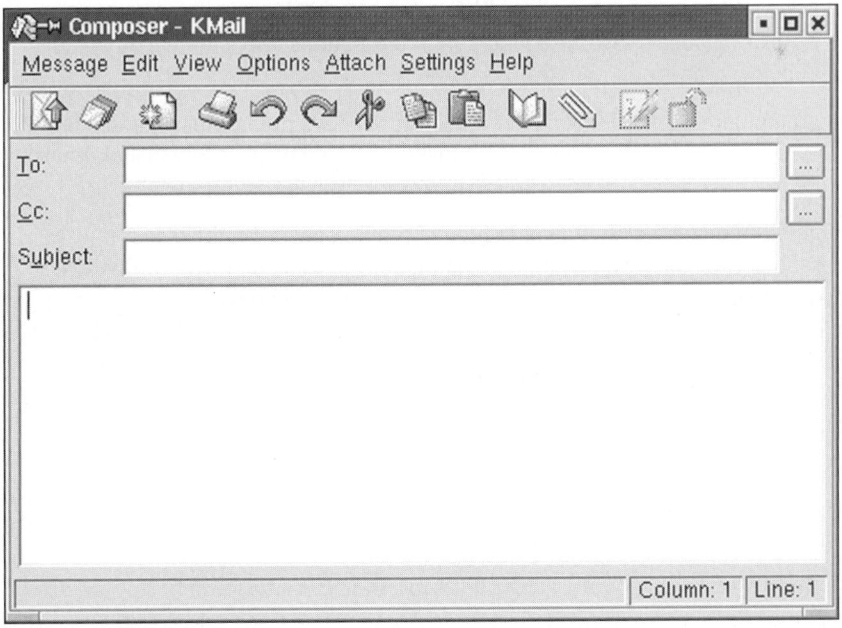

Figure 6.5 The KMail Composer Window

3. *Attachments:* To include files as attachments, use the Attach pull-down menu and choose File, or click on the Attach file button (it looks like a large paper clip) in the speed button bar. Once you specify the file, either graphically or by typing a pathname, it is attached to the current message you are composing, and you see a new pane open below the main message pane.

4. *Spellchecking:* You can use the Edit>Spellchecking pull-down menu choice to verify that your message uses proper spelling.

5. *Help with KMail:* Make the Help pull-down menu choice, and help documentation on KMail opens in its own window on-screen.

6. ***Including text from another file directly in the message body:*** You can use the pull-down menu choice Message>Insert File to insert text from a file in one of your directories directly into the message body at the cursor location in the message body. Also, if you have copied text onto the KDesktop "clipboard" in another window by highlighting the text, the Paste button in the speed button bar (ninth from the left; looks like a clipboard) will paste whatever is on the clipboard into your message wherever the cursor is positioned in the message body.

To get practice with these facilities when composing a new e-mail message, do Practice Session 6.2.

Practice Session 6.2

Step 1: Use your favorite text editor, such as GNU emacs, to compose a short description of the KMail Composer Window speed button bar buttons. Save the file as buttons in your home directory.

Step 2: If you are not already in KMail, launch the program now. In the Message Reader Window, click on the New Message button. Your screen display should look similar to Figure 6.5.

Step 3: Click on the Addressbook button at the top of the Composer Window. In the Addressbook Browser Window that opens-on screen, click on the New Contact speed button bar button. The Address Book Entry Editor window opens on-screen. Fill in as many details as you think are appropriate when each of the the three tabs is active. Then click on the OK button at the bottom of the Address Book Entry Editor Window. You have added your own e-mail address to your Addressbook. Make the pull-down menu choice File>Quit in the Addressbook Browser window.

Step 4: To the right of the To: field, click on the button with the ellipses (. . .) in it. The Addressbook Window opens on-screen. Click on your e-mail address, then click on OK. Your e-mail address is added into the To: field of this new message.

Step 5: In the Subject: field, type My second KMail e-mail message!

(continued)

Practice Session 6.2 *(continued)*

Step 6: If you have created the signature file from Example: Setting Your Identity and Testing KMail, and it was not automatically appended to this message, make the pull-down menu choice Attach>Append Signature. Whatever is in your file ksig.sig will be appended into the body of the e-mail message, leaving just one blank line at the top of the message body. Otherwise, go on to Step 7.

Step 7: Click on the Attach file button at the top of the Composer Window. In the Attach File Window that opens on-screen, click on the file named buttons shown in your home directory, the one you created in Step 1 above. Then click on OK in the Attach File Window. Notice that a new pane opens below the main message body pane, showing you some information about the attachment you just made to this message.

Step 8: In the main message body pane, type `Find attached a plain text file describing the buttons found at the top of the KMail Composer Window`. Then press <Enter> on the keyboard.

Step 9: Click on the Send message button. The Composer Window closes. The e-mail message is delivered to you, in an amount of time dependent on your system's speed.

Step 10: In the Message Reader Window, make the pull-down menu choice File>Check Mail. In the Header Pane, a new message is shown, and the body of the message is shown in the Message Pane.

Step 11: If necessary, scroll to the bottom of the message body. Click on the icon that is named buttons. In a short time, the text editor window opens on-screen, showing you the contents of the buttons file. On our system, the text editor by default was kwrite. From within this text editor window, you could save or print this file if you desire. Quit the text editor by making the File>Quit pull-down menu choice.

Step 12: Leave all messages in all folders in preparation for the next In-Chapter Exercises.

Step 13: Quit KMail by making the File>Quit pull-down menu choice in the Message Reader Window.

6.3.4 Simple Filtering of E-mail into Folders

As seen in previous sections of this chapter, it is very useful to be able to "sort" your e-mail into folders for reading and disposition. This is particularly true if you receive many messages in a day and want to be able to organize them on the basis of certain personal criteria. KMail has a facility, known as filtering, that allows you to apply criteria to e-mail messages and sort them automatically into folders that you specifically create for such purposes. For example, suppose that you are getting a lot of mail from a particular sender, and you wish to have that sender's e-mail automatically stored in a folder all by itself as soon as it comes in. This can be accomplished in two easy steps.

1. Create a folder for storage of the messages, using the Message Reader Window pull-down menu choice Folder>Create. In the Create Folder Window that opens on-screen, type a name that you want the new folder to have into the Name: field, then click OK to close this window. Notice that a new folder icon has appeared in the Folders Pane.

2. Design a "Filter" using the Message Reader Window pull-down menu choice Message>Create Filter>Filter on From... . In the Filter Rules Window that opens on-screen, select the criteria for filtering and the action(s) to be taken when e-mail from this particular sender arrives in your KMail inbox folder.

Now everything sent from that sender will automatically go to the designated folder whenever you check your e-mail with File>Check Mail... . Of course, designing the criteria for sorting can be a complex operation if you have several logically dependent criteria, but the simple, two-step model shows you how you can achieve the automated process. To get some experience in designing a simple filter criteria, do the following Practice Session.

 Practice Session 6.3

Step 1:   Launch KMail if you are not already running the program.

Step 2:   In the Message Reader Window, make the pull-down menu choice Folder>Create. The Create Folder Window appears on-screen.

Step 3:   In the Name: field of the New Folder Window, type fromme, and then click OK. This creates a new empty folder under your Mail directory named me. In fact, you can now see this folder name appear in the Folders Pane on your screen (scroll down to it if necessary).

Step 4:   In the Message Reader Window, click on one of the folders in the Folders Pane that has messages in it from the previous work you have done in KMail, like trash or sent-mail, and also click on one of the messages to highlight it in that folder. This should be a message from yourself that you sent in the previous In-Chapter Exercises. This is the e-mail message you will build the filter rules around, or the criteria that determine how to put incoming messages into the folder.

Step 5:   Make the pull-down menu choice Message>Create Filter>Filter on From... . The Filter Rules window opens on-screen.

Step 6:   In the left-most pane of the Filter Rules Window, in the Available Filters Pane, a highlighted filter appears as <from e-mail address>, where e-mail address is

(continued)

Practice Session 6.3 *(continued)*

your e-mail address as specified in the message you selected in Step 4 above. Use the scroll bar at the bottom of the Available Filters Pane to view the entire e-mail address to verify it is correct, the one you want to do the sorting based upon. It should be highlighted as shown in Figure 6.6; if it is not, click on it.

Step 7: The three fields at the top of the Filter Criteria Pane (*Note*: These are the matching criteria fields, i.e., they allow you to design criteria for sorting the messages) should be filled in as follows, going from left to right: From for the first field, contains choice in the second field, and in the third field your complete e-mail address.

Step 8: In the Filter Actions Pane, make sure the fields read move to folder and fromme.

Step 9: In the Advanced Options Pane, make sure that the box is checked for Applying this filter to incoming messages, on manual filtering; and if this filter matches, stop processing here. Your screen display of the Filter Rules Window should look similar to Figure 6.6.

Step 10: Click on the OK button at the bottom of the Filter Rules Window. You have now designed a new filter for use on sorting, or disposing of, new e-mail that arrives in your inbox that originates from yourself.

Step 11: To test this filter, open a new Composer Window by clicking on the New Message button at the upper right of the Message Reader Window.

Step 12: Send an e-mail message to yourself as you did in Practice Session 6.2, but this time make the subject Automatic Sort 1. Contents of the message are up to you.

Step 13: Send the message from the Composer Window.

Step 14: In the Message Reader Window, make the pull-down menu choice File>Check Mail... . The e-mail message that you sent to yourself in Step 13 is now in the folder fromme, not in the inbox. Where else can you see this new message? How do you see in what other folders the message has been retained? To complete this Practice Session, delete the new e-mail message from the three locations it occupies, as well as the folder me.

In conclusion, KMail gives you the capability to graphically accomplish all of the important e-mail functions. The above Practice Session showed you how to start KMail, how to send and read messages, how to dispose of messages, how to attach files to outgoing messages, and how to perform simple filtering operations to sort incoming messages into folders. To follow up on the Practice Sessions above, you should go on to the Problems at the end of this chapter that deal with KMail.

Figure 6.6 KMail Filter Rules Window components

6.4 `pine`–Another Full-Screen Display E-mail System

The `pine` system is probably the most extensive and friendly e-mail program available for UNIX. It has a complete set of functions, extensive help options online, and handles the common functions of e-mail optimally.

6.4.1 Sending an E-mail Message by Using `pine` with an Attachment Created in `vi`

Example: `pine` System shows how to send an e-mail message and an attached text file with `pine`. We have assumed that you did Problem 9 at the end of Chapter 5, creating the file vi_doc.txt with the vi text editor. If you have *not* done so, before you start this example, create a text file using the vi text editor–or a text editor of your choice–that contains a short explanation (100–150 words) of the capabilities of vi or the text editor you chose. Then, save the text as vi_doc.txt in your main directory, exit vi or other text editor, and proceed with the example.

Example: `pine` System

Step 1: At the shell prompt, type `pine` and then press `<Enter>`.

Step 2: The `pine` Main Menu screen, similar to the one shown in Figure 6.7, appears. The highlighted menu choice is `L Folder List - Select a folder to view`.

Step 3: Type `<C>` to compose a message. The `pine` Compose Message screen, similar to the one shown in Figure 6.8, appears.

Step 4: In the `To:` field, type your login name and then press `<Enter>`.

Step 5: Use the `<down arrow>` key to move the cursor to the `Attchmnt:` field.

Step 6: Type `vi_doc.txt` and then press `<Enter>`. This file should be in your main directory.

Step 7: Use the `<down arrow>` to move the cursor to the `Subject:` field. *(continued)*

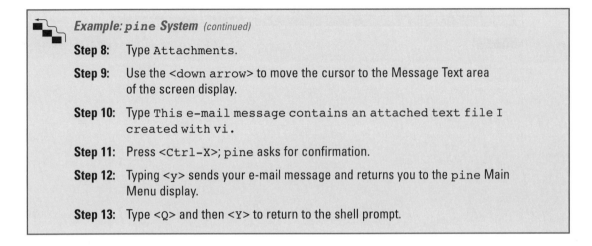

Example: pine System *(continued)*

Step 8: Type Attachments.

Step 9: Use the <down arrow> to move the cursor to the Message Text area of the screen display.

Step 10: Type This e-mail message contains an attached text file I created with vi.

Step 11: Press <Ctrl-X>; pine asks for confirmation.

Step 12: Typing <y> sends your e-mail message and returns you to the pine Main Menu display.

Step 13: Type <Q> and then <Y> to return to the shell prompt.

IN-CHAPTER EXERCISES

6.3 In the Example: pine System, how would you have specified the name of the attachment if you had wanted to attach a file from a subdirectory under your home directory instead of a file from your home directory?

6.4 In that same example, what would have happened if you had specified a non-existent e-mail address in the To: field? Although it might be difficult for pine running on your system to check the validity of an Internet e-mail address, do you think that it could do so? How should it respond before you send that message?

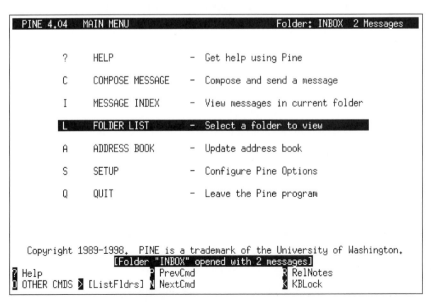

Figure 6.7 The pine Main Menu screen

Figure 6.8 The pine Compose Message screen

6.4.2 Sending E-mail with pine

The pine program is an Internet e-mail and news-reading program that is freely distributed for UNIX systems by the University of Washington. It is a screen display e-mail system that allows you to use keystroke combinations, similar to emacs and vi, to execute commands. It presents a menu of available commands at all times at the bottom of the screen and also has extensive online help. Figures 6.7 and 6.8 show pine's typical user interface format. The following is a brief description of the command to run the pine program.

---

pine [options] [recipient(s)]

Purpose:	Allows you to send and receive e-mail
Output:	With no options or recipients specified, you are placed in the pine program and the pine Main Menu appears on-screen

Commonly used options/features:

To send mail:

signature-file=file	Set new signature file to *file*
recipient	Go directly to Compose Message screen with To: field set to recipient

To receive mail:

-i Inbox	Go directly to Inbox, bypassing Main Menu

The quickest way to send an e-mail message to someone with `pine` is to type `pine recipient`, where recipient is a valid username of someone on your UNIX system, or a valid Internet address, and then press `<Enter>`. When you run `pine` this way, the Compose Message screen appears immediately on your display, with the `To:` field already filled in with the recipient's address. The following is a general step-by-step procedure for sending `mail` with `pine`, starting from the Compose Message screen.

1. Press `<Enter>`, as the recipient's address has already been entered in the To: field. Unfortunately, the only way of verifying that the recipient's address is correct is to send the e-mail message, and then, if you get a returned-to-sender response, you can try again.

2. Type in entries for the `Cc:`, `Attchmnt:`, and `Subject:` fields, pressing `<Enter>` after typing each entry. If you change your mind or make a mistake in any of these fields, simply use the `<up>` or `<down arrow>` key to reposition the cursor in a field and then correct or redo the entry. You can also use the `<arrow>` keys and reposition the cursor to change the entries in any of these fields at any time before you send the message.

3. When the cursor is in the `Message Text` field, type the message body. You can cancel sending this message by pressing `<Ctrl-C>` at the same time. Then `pine` will prompt you to confirm your cancellation. If you type `<y>`, you will exit `pine` and return to the shell prompt. A file dead.letter will be created, which you can then delete with the `rm` command.

4. When you have finished composing the message body, press `<Ctrl-X>`. Then `pine` will prompt you to confirm sending the message. If you type `<y>`, the message is sent and you exit `pine`.

Practice Session 6.4 lets you send e-mail with `pine`.

Practice Session 6.4

Step 1:   At the shell prompt, type `pine recipient`, where recipient is a valid user-name on your UNIX system, or a valid Internet address, and then press `<Enter>`. The pine Compose Message screen appears on your display, with the To: field already filled in.

Step 2:   Use the `<down arrow>` key to place the cursor in the `Cc:` field.

Step 3:   Type `your_username`, where `your_username` is your username on the UNIX system you are now logged on to, and then press `<Enter>`.

Step 4:   Use the `<down arrow>` key to place the cursor in the `Subject:` field.

Step 5:   Type `My 2nd pine e-mail!1` and then press `<Enter>`. The cursor is now in the Message Text area of the Compose Message screen.

(continued)

Practice Session 6.4 *(continued)*

Step 6: Type `Pine is a really neat and easy-to-use e-mail program.` and then press <Enter>. Your screen display should now look something like that shown in Figure 6.9.

Step 7: Press <Ctrl-X>. The prompt `Send message?` appears.

Step 8: Type <y> to send your message, exit `pine`, and return to the shell prompt.

6.4.3 Reading E-mail with `pine`

The `pine` program features an extensive set of facilities for message reading and disposal. In Practice Session 6.4, you sent a copy of the e-mail message to yourself. To read that message, you can use the following general step-by-step procedure for reading mail with `pine`.

1. At the shell prompt, type `pine` and then press <Enter>. The `pine` Main Menu screen appears on your display, as shown in Figure 6.7, with the Folder List menu option highlighted.

2. Press <Enter> or press L. The Folder List screen appears on your display, with the Inbox folder highlighted. If the Inbox folder is *not* highlighted, use the <arrow> keys on the keyboard to highlight the Inbox folder.

3. Press <Enter>. The Message Index screen appears on your display, with a list of messages displayed. To view the contents of one of these messages, use the <down> or <up arrow> key to highlight that message.

Figure 6.9 Compose Message screen showing My 2nd `pine` e-mail

4. Press <Enter> to display the header and body of that message on-screen.

5. At this point, you can dispose of the message, read other messages by returning to the Message Index screen, or return to the **pine** Main Menu screen and quit.

Practice Session 6.5 gives you the opportunity to read e-mail with **pine**.

 Practice Session 6.5

Step 1: At the shell prompt, type **pine** and then press <Enter>. The **pine** Main Menu screen appears on your display, similar to the one shown in Figure 6.7, with the Folder List menu choice highlighted.

Step 2: Press <Enter>. The Folder List screen appears on your display, with the Inbox folder highlighted.

Step 3: Press <Enter>. The Message Index screen appears on your display.

Step 4: If the message from Practice Session 6.4 is *not* highlighted, use the <up> or <down arrow> key to highlight that message in this list. If it is *not* in the list, go back to Practice Session 6.4 and redo those steps.

Step 5: Press <Enter> when the Practice Session 6.4 message is highlighted. The Message Text screen appears on your display.

Step 6: When you have read the message text, press the <O> key on the keyboard, which gives you access to other commands. Another menu of keystroke commands appears at the bottom of the Message Text screen.

Step 7: Type <M>. The **pine** Main Menu screen appears on your display.

Step 8: Type <Q> and pine prompts Really quit pine?

Step 9: Type <Y> to exit **pine** and go back to the shell prompt.

6.4.4 Disposing of E-mail in Folders in **pine**

As you become a frequent user of e-mail on a UNIX system, you will soon need to organize the e-mail you receive and send, in some logical structure. As we discussed with regard to the mail command earlier in this chapter, this structure will be implemented in UNIX as directories, subdirectories, and files. In fact, directories, subdirectories, and the messages they contain are all simply files in the file structure of the UNIX system. A subdirectory, or folder, useful for storing e-mail messages handled by pine is just a special kind of file that enables pine to separate easily the messages stored in it. This capability is similar to the concept that your system mailbox is just a larger file that a mail program reads and then separates into messages, or smaller files, that can be read and disposed of individually.

The pine program has a facility for organizing your messages in groups of folders, similar to the folders you worked with in mail. When you first run pine, it creates three folders in one collection for you: an Inbox folder, for storing your most recently received messages; a Sent Mail folder, for storing messages that you send to other recipients; and a Saved Mail folder, for storing messages that you save. The name of this collection in terms of your directory structure depends on your system and pine configuration, but they are generally created by pine initially as ~/mail. By default, when you take some action to dispose of a message, it goes into this collection.

You can create any number of folder collections in which you can dispose of messages. In addition, you can add, delete, or change folders and their contents in each collection. Of course, within the default collection, you can add, delete, or change folders—which is probably what most users of pine will do in managing their messages. Then you can save messages to specific folders. Practice Session 6.6 allows you to add a folder and then move a message from your Inbox folder to the newly created folder.

Practice Session 6.6

Step 1:   At the shell prompt, type pine -i and then press <Enter>. The Message Index screen for your Inbox folder appears on your display immediately because you have specified the i option on the command line.

Step 2:   Press <Shift-,>. This action yields the < character, telling pine to go to the Folder List screen, where all the folders in your default collection are displayed. These folders should include Inbox, Sent Mail, and Saved Mail. Inbox will be highlighted.

Step 3:   Press the <A> key. A prompt Folder name to add: appears.

Step 4:   Type myown and then press <Enter>. On the Folder List screen, a new folder name, myown, appears.

Step 5:   Using the <arrow> keys, highlight Inbox on the Folder List screen. Then press <Enter>. The Folder Index screen for the Inbox folder appears on your display.

Step 6:   Use the <arrow> keys to highlight one of the messages in the list, perhaps Subject: My first pine message.

Step 7:   Press the <O> key to get access to Other commands.

Step 8:   Press the <S> key to Save this message. The prompt SAVE #1 to folder [saved-messages]: appears.

Step 9:   Type myown and then press <Enter>. The prompt [Message 1 copied to folder "myown" and deleted] appears. Note that, in the status field of the Message Index screen for the Inbox folder, a D now appears to the left of the message that you just saved in the new folder myown, signifying that this message has been deleted.

(continued)

Practice Session 6.6 *(continued)*

Step 10: Press the `<Shift-,>` key. Doing so yields the `<character`, telling `pine` to go to the Folder List screen.

Step 11: Use the `<arrow>` keys to highlight the folder name myown. Then press `<Enter>`.

Step 12: The Message Index screen for the folder myown appears on your display. It contains a list of the files that you saved to this folder in Steps 6–9.

Step 13: Press the `<M>` key to return to the `pine` Main Menu screen.

Step 14: Press the `<Q>` key. The prompt `Expunge the 1 deleted message from "Inbox"?` appears.

Step 15: Press the `<Y>` key to confirm the deletion of this file from your Inbox folder.

6.4.5 Using the `pine` Address Book

If you frequently correspond with one person or several people via e-mail, having a list of their e-mail addresses stored in the `mail` program is very useful. That way, whenever you want to send e-mail to one or more of these people, you can use the internal address list rather than having to retrieve them from some external source. For example, you might frequently send e-mail to a person who has a long e-mail address that is difficult to memorize. So, instead of trying to remember that address whenever you want to compose a new e-mail message and send it to that person, you can simply store the address in the `mail` program and recall it whenever you want to insert the address in the message header. If you frequently send messages to the same group of people but do not want to type each recipient's e-mail address, you can send a message to the group. To do so, compile a list of e-mail addresses of the group and give it a name. Then, simply insert that name in the `To:` or `Cc:` field of a message and have the group name converted automatically to the individuals' e-mail addresses. This method is very efficient if the group has a large number of members—say, 50 or 100.

The `pine` program includes a feature that handles such tasks—and many more similar tasks—known as the Address Book. Address Book entries can be of two general types: aliases, which associate a nickname with a single e-mail address; or distribution lists, which associate a single nickname with a group of e-mail addresses. With the `pine` Address Book, you can use aliases or distribution lists for automatic insertion in the `To:` field of the Compose Message screen. You can also compose a message with the `To:` field of the message header being automatically filled in with an alias or distribution list's e-mail address(es). Finally, you can have more than one Address Book.

You can activate the Address Book by selecting Address Book on the `pine` Main Menu screen. When you make this menu choice, the Address Book screen appears on your display, as shown in Figure 6.10. This screen in `pine` allows you to add, delete, and edit entries in your Address Book. Table 6.3 contains a summary of the actions of each menu choice on the Address Book screen.

■ **TABLE 6.3** The pine Address Book Menu Choices

Menu Choice	Action
? Help	Gives screen displays of Help on the Address Book
< Main Menu	Returns the user to the Main Menu screen
P PrevEntry	Goes to the previous entry in the Address Book
– PrevPage	Goes to the previous page of the Address Book
@ AddNew	Adds a new Address Book entry
C ComposeTo	Composes a new e-mail message supplying the current Address Book entry in To: field
O Other CMDS	Allows the user to apply additional mail commands, such as Index, Print, Save, Forward, List Folders, and Quit pine
> [View/Update]	Edits a selected entry in the Address Book (e.g., to change e-mail addresses)
N NextEntry	Goes to the next entry in the Address Book
SpaceBar NextPage	Goes to the next page of the Address Book
D Delete	Deletes an entry in the Address Book
W Whereis	Searches for a word or name in the Address Book

Practice Session 6.7 shows you how to add a new entry (a distribution list) to your pine Address Book for a group of your friends to whom you would frequently like to send e-mail. We have assumed that you are currently running the pine program.

Practice Session 6.7

Step 1:   From the pine Main Menu screen, select Address Book. Your screen display will look similar to the one shown in Figure 6.10.

Step 2:   Type @. Your screen display will now look similar to the one shown in Figure 6.10. The cursor should be in the Nickname field of this screen, allowing you to start a new entry by adding a nickname for the new distribution list entry. Note that, any time during the next five steps you want to edit any of the entries that you have made in any of the fields, you can simply use the <arrow> keys to reposition the cursor over the entry and change the entry (or delete it).

Step 3:   Type buds and then press <Enter>.

(continued)

Practice Session 6.7 *(continued)*

Step 4: In the `Fullname:` field, type `My friends` and then press `<Enter>`. This entry will be included in the message header if you put the distribution list nickname in the `To:` or `Cc:` field when you are composing a message.

Step 5: In the `Fcc:` field, type `""` (two double-quotes) and then press `<Enter>` to signify that you don't want any file copies associated with this entry.

Step 6: In the `Comment:` field, type `My best buddies` and then press `<Enter>`.

Step 7: In the Addresses: field, type in the e-mail addresses of some of your friends, being sure to separate the addresses with commas—for example, `bobk@ucsd.edu, sarwar@umich.edu`, etc. You have now finished making a distribution list entry. If necessary, go back over the field entries and check them to see that they are correct, particularly the e-mail addresses!

Step 8: Press `<Ctrl-X>`. At the prompt `Exit and Save changes?` type `Y`. This action causes you to save the entry, leave the Address Book Add screen, and return to the Address Book screen. Note that the Address Book screen now shows one highlighted, or selected, entry with three fields. The first field is the nickname, the second is the full name, and the third contains the e-mail addresses.

Step 9: If you do not want to compose a message at this time, return to the `pine` Main Menu screen by typing `<` and then quitting `pine`. You can then use this entry at any time in the future by typing the nicknames into the `To:` field of the Compose Message screen when you are ready to send a message to them. If for some reason you forget this particular distribution list's nickname, when you begin to compose a message, press `<Ctrl-T>` to open the Address Book. Then you can examine the entries to find this one. Use the `S` (select) command to have `pine` automatically use this entry in the `To:` field.

Step 10: To use this selected distribution list entry immediately, type `C`. The `pine` Compose Message screen appears, with the `To:` field automatically filled in with the full name of the distribution list entry, and the e-mail addresses of your friends. You can then proceed to send a message and test the correctness of the entries in the distribution list.

To get more practice with the Address Book, and with `pine`, do Problems 10 and 11 at the end of this chapter.

6.4.6 A Summary of **pine** Commands

The following tables present summaries of the important operations of `pine`. Table 6.4 contains operations that may be executed while you are reading and disposing of messages. Table 6.5 contains operations that you may execute while composing a message. Table 6.6 contains general `pine` operations. Table 6.7 contains Folder Index screen commands. Table 6.8 contains Address Book commands.

```
  PINE 4.04   ADDRESS BOOK (Add)               Folder: INBOX   2 Messages

 Nickname :
 Fullname :
 Fcc      :
 Comment  :
 Addresses :


   Fill in the fields just like you would in the composer.
   To form a list, just enter multiple comma-separated addresses.
   It is ok to leave fields blank. Press "^X" to save the entry, "^C" to cancel.
   If you want to use quotation marks inside the Fullname field, it is best
   to use single quotation marks; for example: George 'Husky' Washington.







 ^G Get Help  ^X eXit/Save ^R RichView  ^Y PrvPg/Top ^K Cut Line
 ^C Cancel    ^D Del Char              ^V NxtPg/End ^U UnDel Line^T To AddrBk
```

Figure 6.10 The pine Address Book screen display

■■ **TABLE 6.4** Message Disposition Commands

Command	Description
\<D\>	Deletes the current message
\<E\>	Saves the current message as a plain text file in the default folder
\<F\>	Forwards the current message
\<R\>	Replies to the current message
\<S\>	Saves the current message in a folder
\<U\>	Undeletes the current message
\<Y\>	Prints the current message with a default print command

■■ **TABLE 6.5** General Message Composition Commands

Command	Description
\<Ctrl-C\>	Cancels the message being composed and writes it to dead.letter
\<Ctrl-G\>	Gets online help that is context-sensitive
\<Ctrl-L\>	Refreshes the screen contents
\<Ctrl-O\>	Postpones sending the message being composed
\<Ctrl-T\>	Invokes the spell checker
\<Ctrl-X\>	Sends the message being composed

■■■ **TABLE 6.6** General pine Commands

Command	Description
<?>	Shows the Help screen for this screen menu
<C>	Composes a new message using the Compose Message screen display
<L>	Goes to the Folder List screen display
<M>	Returns to the Main Menu screen display
<O>	Shows all other available commands for this screen menu
<Q>	Quits pine, allowing disposal of deleted messages

■■■ **TABLE 6.7** Folder Index Screen Commands

Command	Description
<F>	Forward the currently selected message
<J>	Jump to a specific message addressbook
<N>	Move to the next message
<P>	Move to the previous message
<Space>	Show the next screen full of messages
<W>	Whereis – search for a specific folder

■■■ **TABLE 6.8** Addressbook Commands

Command	Description
<->	Move to the previous page of the current addressbook
<A>	Add a new entry into the current entry in this addressbook
<C>	Compose a message to the current entry in this addressbook
<D>	Delete selected entry in the current addressbook
<N>	Move to the next address
<P>	Move to the previous address
<Space>	Move to the next page of the current addressbook
<T>	Take address to another addressbook
<V>	View/edit the selected entry in the current addressbook
<X>	Export the current entry to a file
<Y>	Print the current addressbook

— Summary

The fundamental concept of e-mail is to give you the ability to communicate via some permanent record medium on your own computer system with other users or with users on other systems over an intranet or the Internet. Because UNIX systems are text-based, they accommodate the e-mail medium successfully. Similar to paper mail, an e-mail correspondent is someone with whom you have a dialog by sending and receiving e-mail messages. If you initiate the e-mail message, you are the sender; the recipient is the person to whom you addressed the e-mail message.

The proper form of an e-mail address underpins the entire system. When you want to send e-mail over the Internet, the e-mail address relies on the Internet Domain Name System for its basic form. The System Mailbox file, usually in the directory /usr/spool/mail, is where messages you receive are held. There are two categories of e-mail system for UNIX systems: line display e-mail systems, which means that you can only edit one line at a time when you are composing an e-mail message; and full screen display e-mail systems, which means that you can edit any text you see on a single screen display.

The most important functions common to the UNIX e-mail programs described in this chapter are aliases (address book), attachments, carbon copy, deleting, forwarding, reading, replying, saving in folders, and sending.

Problems

1. What is the purpose of electronic mail (e-mail)? Name the three most commonly used UNIX utilities for e-mail.

2. What is the difference between an e-mail message body and attachment?

3. List five operations that can be performed while you are using an e-mail utility.

4. What is local host?

5. On a UNIX system, where (which directory) are your incoming e-mail messages saved?

6. Using the editor of your choice from Chapter 5, compose an e-mail message addressed to a friend on your UNIX system, and then send it by using the `mail` command. In addition, edit your .mailrc file and add an alias for this recipient so that you can use this alias every time you want to e-mail that friend.

7. The KMail GUI is most similar to what other e-mail user agent interface that you are familiar with?

8. If the K desktop is not installed on your UNIX system, what other GUI e-mail programs can you use with the desktop you have installed? Are they as easy to use as what is described in KMail in this chapter? Can you list any important differences between KMail as shown here and e-mail user agent programs like Eudora, Mozilla Mail, Netscape Messenger, or other graphical e-mail programs you are familiar with?

9. After completing the Practice Sessions and In-Chapter Exercises found in Chapter 21, XFree86, how does the `KMail` interface change when you change the style of the window manager?

10. Compose an e-mail message addressed to another user on your system and then send it by using `pine`.

11. The `pine` program allows you to reconfigure the way that you interact with it, via the Setup Menu. Run `pine`, and at the Main Menu screen type S. The Setup Menu appears at the bottom of the Main Menu screen. Type C to access the Configuration Setup Menu. You can review the pages of the Configuration Menu by pressing the – (hyphen) key to go to a previous page and the <space bar> to go to the next page. When features need to be set or unset, using the <X> key activates or deactivates the feature of interest. When options need to be typed, type in valid options. Use the information given in Table 6.9 to reconfigure your `pine` program to take advantage of these useful operating characteristics.

    Exit `pine` Setup, being sure to retain the changes. Then run `pine` and note the differences in its operation. If you don't like the new operating parameter settings, return to the original `pine` program configuration.

■ **TABLE 6.9** Addressbook Commands

Parameter	What you enter, either a string of characters or place an X or *
fcc-name-rule	Place an X in the by recipient box to save an fcc to folder with recipient's name
personal-name	Your own personal first and last name, like Jill Stevens
quit-without-confirm	Place an X in this box so that pine does not ask for confirmation on exit
user-domain	Your Internet domain name, like egr.up.edu

12. What is a blind e-mail copy? Why is it needed? How do you send a blind e-mail message in `pine`?

13. Can you read e-mail messages composed in `pine` using KMail? How?

Files and File System Structure

Objectives

- To explain the UNIX file concept
- To discuss various types of files supported by UNIX
- To describe attributes of a file
- To explain the notion of pathnames
- To explain the user view of the UNIX file system
- To describe the user's interface to the UNIX file system—browsing the file system
- To discuss representation of a file inside the UNIX system
- To describe how a UNIX file is stored on the disk
- To explain the concept of standard files in UNIX
- To cover the commands and primitives
  `~, ., .., /, PATH, cd, echo, file, ls, mkdir, pwd, rmdir`

7.1 Introduction

Most computer system users work mostly with the file system structure. While using a computer system, a user is constantly performing file-related operations: creating, reading, writing/modifying, or executing files. Therefore, the user needs to understand what a file is in UNIX, how files can be organized and managed, how they are represented inside the operating system, and how they are stored on the disk. In this chapter, the description of file representation and storage is simplified, due to the scope of this textbook. More details on these topics are available in books on operating system concepts and principles and in books on UNIX internals. All references to a file system in this textbook are to the **local file system**. The description of the UNIX network file system (NFS) is beyond the scope of this textbook, but it is briefly mentioned in Chapter 14.

7.2 The UNIX File Concept

One of the many remarkable features of the UNIX operating system is the concept of files used in it. This concept is simple, yet powerful—and results in a uniform view of all system resources. In UNIX, a file is a sequence of bytes. Period. Thus everything, including a network interface card, a disk drive, a keyboard, a printer, a simple/ordinary (text, executable, etc.) file, or a directory, is treated as a file. As a result, all input and output devices are treated as files in UNIX, as described under file types and file system structure.

7.3 Types of Files

UNIX supports seven types of files:

- ❖ simple/ordinary file
- ❖ directory
- ❖ symbolic (soft) link
- ❖ special (device) files—block special files and character special files
- ❖ named pipe (FIFO)
- ❖ socket

7.3.1 Simple/Ordinary File

Simple/ordinary (or ordinary for short) files are used to store information and data on a secondary storage device, typically a disk. An ordinary file can contain a source program (in C, C++, Java, etc.), an executable program (applications such as compilers, database tools, desktop publishing tools, graphing software, etc.), PostScript code, pictures, audio, graphics, and so on. UNIX does not treat any one of these files any differently from another. It does not give a structure or attach a meaning to a file's contents because every file is simply a sequence of bytes. Meanings are attached to a file's contents by the application that uses/processes the file. For example, a C program file is no different to UNIX than an HTML file for a Web page or a file for a video clip. However, these files are treated differently by a C compiler (e.g., cc), a Web browser (e.g., Netscape Navigator), and a video player (e.g., RealPlayer).

You can name files by following any convention that you choose to use; UNIX does not impose any naming conventions on files of any type. File names can have as many as 14 letters in System V and 255 letters in BSD. Most contemporary UNIX systems comply with the BSD naming scheme. Although you can use any characters for file names, we strongly recommend that nonprintable characters, white spaces (spaces and tabs), and shell metacharacters (described in Chapter 4) not be used because they are difficult to deal with as part of a file name. You can give file names any of your own or application-defined extensions, but the extensions mean nothing to the UNIX system. For example, you can give an .exe extension to a document and a .doc extension to an executable program. Some applications require extensions, but others do not. For example, all C compilers require that C source program files have a .c extension, but not all Web browsers require an .html extension for files for Web pages. Some commonly used extensions are given in Table 7.1.

Even so, extensions should be used—it helps keep track of which files are for what purposes.

■■ **TABLE 7.1** Commonly Used Extensions for Some Applications

Extension	Contents of File
.bmp, .jpg, jpeg, .gif	Graphics
.c	C Source code
.C, .cpp, .cc	C++ Source code
.java	Java source code
.html, .htm	File for a Web page
.o	Object code
.ps	Postscript code
.Z, .gz	Compressed

7.3.2 Directory

A directory contains the names of other files and/or directories (the terms directory and sub-directory are used interchangeably). In some systems, terms such as *folder, drawer,* or *cabinet* are used for a directory. A directory file in any operating system consists of an array of directory entries, although contents of a directory entry vary from one system to another. In UNIX, a directory entry has the structure shown in Figure 7.1.

The **inode number** is 4 bytes long and is an index value for an array on the disk. An element of this array, known as an **index node** (more commonly called an **inode**) contains file

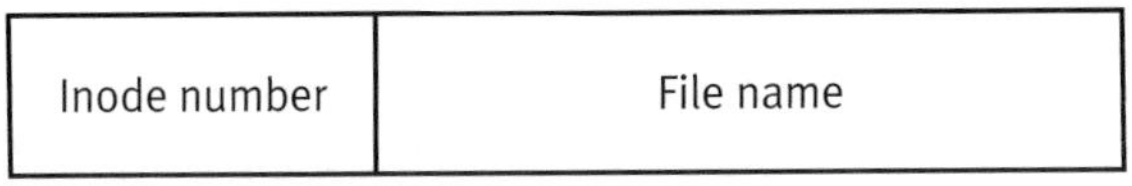

Inode number	File name

Figure 7.1 Structure of a directory entry

attributes such as file size (in bytes). The UNIX kernel allocates an inode whenever a new file is created. Thus, every unique file in UNIX has a unique inode number. The details of an inode and how it is used by the kernel to access file contents (on the disk) are discussed later in this chapter.

7.3.3 Link File

The concept of a **link** in UNIX under file sharing is fully discussed in Chapter 11. But for now, a **link file** is created by the system when a symbolic link is created to an existing file. The link file points to the existing file, which allows you to rename an existing file and share it without duplicating its contents. Symbolic links are a creation of BSD UNIX but are presently available on almost all versions of UNIX.

7.3.4 Special (Device) File

A **special file** is a means of accessing hardware devices, including the keyboard, hard disk, CD-ROM drive, tape drive, and printer. Each hardware device is associated with at least one special file—and a command or an application accesses a special file in order to access the corresponding device. Special files are divided into two types: **character special files** and **block special files**. Character special files correspond to **character-oriented devices**, such as a keyboard, and block special files correspond to **block-oriented devices**, such as a disk.

Special files are typically placed in the /dev directory (*see* Section 7.4). This directory contains at least one file for every device connected to the computer. Applications and commands read and write peripheral device files in the same way that they read or write an ordinary file. That capability is the main reason that input and output in UNIX is said to be *device-independent*. Some special files are fd0 (for floppy drive 0), hda (for hard drive a), lp0 (line printer 0), and tty (for teletype–terminal). Various special devices simulate physical devices and are therefore known as **pseudo devices**. These devices allow you to interact with a UNIX system without using the devices that are physically connected to the system. These devices are becoming more and more important because they allow use of a UNIX system via a network or modem or with virtual terminals in a window system such as the X Window System (*see* Chapter 21).

7.3.5 Named Pipe (FIFO)

UNIX has several tools that enable processes to communicate with each other. These tools, which are the key to the ubiquitous client-server software paradigm, are called **interprocess communication (IPC) mechanisms** (commonly known as *IPC primitives*). These primitives are called **pipes**, **named pipes** (also called *FIFOs*), and **sockets** (systems that are strictly System V–compliant have a mechanism called **Transport Layer Interface**, or **TLI**). A detailed description of these primitives is beyond the scope of this textbook, but we briefly mention the purpose of each so that you can appreciate the need for each mechanism and understand the need for FIFOs.

A pipe is an area in the kernel memory (a kernel buffer) that allows two processes to communicate with each other, provided the processes are running on the same computer system and are related to each other; typically, the relationship is parent-child. A **FIFO** is a file (of named pipe type) that allows two processes to communicate with each other if the processes are on the same computer; but the processes do not have to be related to each other. We illustrate the use of pipes and FIFOs at the command level in Chapter 12. Discussion of UNIX IPC primitives at the application development level is beyond the scope of this textbook, but you can learn about them from any book on UNIX TCP/IP network programming.

7.3.6 Socket

A **socket** can be used by processes on the same computer or on different computers to communicate with each other; the computers can be on a network (intranet) or on the Internet. Sockets can belong to different address families, each specifying the protocol suite to be used by processes to communicate. For example, a socket of address family AF_INET is used for communication by using the transport level protocols in the TCP/IP protocol suite (e.g., TCP—*see* Chapter 14). A socket with AF_INET address family is also known as the **Internet domain socket.** A socket with address family AF_UNIX can be used for communication between processes that run on the same machine under a UNIX operating system; this kind of a socket is also known as a **UNIX domain socket.** On System V UNIX systems, a socket file type means a UNIX domain socket.

7.4   File System Structure

Three issues are related to the file system structure of an operating system. The first is how files in the system are organized from a user's point of view. The second is how files are stored on the secondary storage (usually, a hard disk). The third is how files are manipulated (read, written, etc.).

7.4.1 File System Organization

The UNIX file system is structured hierarchically (upside-down and treelike). Thus, the file system structure starts with one main directory, called the **root directory,** and can have any number of files and subdirectories under it, organized in any way desired. This structure leads to a parent-child relationship between a directory and its subdirectories/files. A typical UNIX system contains hundreds of files and directories, organized as shown in Figure 7.2.

7.4.2 Home and Present Working Directories

When you log on, the UNIX system puts you in a specific directory, called your **home/login directory.** For example, the directory called sarwar in Figure 7.2 is the home directory for the user with login sarwar. As mentioned in Chapter 4, while using the C, tcsh, bash, or Korn shell, you can specify your home directory by using the tilde (~) character. The directory that you are in at any particular time is called your **present working directory** (also known as *your current directory*). The present working directory is also denoted **.** (pronounced "dot"). The parent of the present working directory is denoted **. .** (pronounced "dot dot").

Later in this chapter, we describe commands you can use to determine your home and present working directories. We also identify commands you can use to interact with the UNIX file system in general.

7.4.3 Pathnames: Absolute and Relative

A file or directory in a hierarchical file system is specified by a **pathname**. Pathnames can be specified in three ways: (1) starting with the root directory, (2) starting with the present working directory, and (3) starting with the user's home directory. When a pathname is specified starting with the root directory, it is called an **absolute pathname** because it can be used by any user from anywhere in the file system structure. For example, /users/faculty/sarwar/courses/ee446 is the absolute pathname for the ee446 directory under sarwar's home directory. The absolute pathname for the file called mid1 under sarwar's home directory is /users/faculty/sarwar/courses/ee446/exams/mid1.

Pathnames starting with the present working directory or a user's home directory are called relative pathnames. When the user sarwar logs on, the system puts him into his home directory, /users/faculty/sarwar. While in his home directory, sarwar can specify the file mid1 (*see* Figure 7.2) by using a relative pathname ./courses/ee446/exams/mid1 or courses/ee446/exams/mid1. Sarwar (or anyone else) in the directory ee446 can specify the same file with the relative pathname exams/mid1. The owner (or anyone logged on as the owner) of the mid1 file can also specify it from anywhere in the file structure by using the pathname ~/courses/ee446/exams/mid1 or $PATH/courses/ee446/exams/mid1. Or, you could specify ee446 from personal directory as ../courses/ee446.

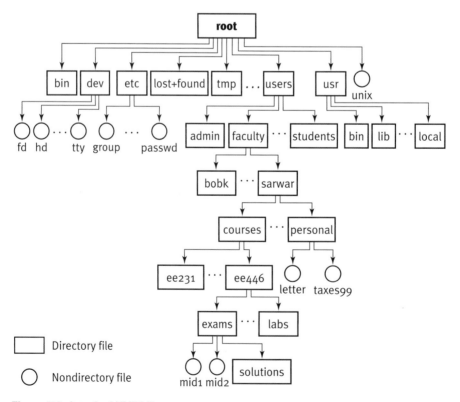

Figure 7.2 A typical UNIX file structure

A typical UNIX system has several disk drives that contain user and system files, but as a user, you don't have to worry about which disk drive contains the file that you need to access. In UNIX, multiple disk drives and/or disk partitions can be mounted on the same file system structure, allowing their access as directories and not as named drives A:, B:, C:, etc., as in MS-DOS and Microsoft Windows. Files and directories on these disks and/or partitions can be accessed by specifying their pathnames as if they are part of the file structure on one disk/partition. Doing so gives a unified view of all the files and directories in the system, and you don't have to worry about remembering the names of drives and files (and directories) they contain.

7.4.4 Some Standard Directories and Files

Every UNIX system contains a set of standard files and directories. The standard directories contain some specific files.

Root directory (/)

The root directory is at the top of the file system hierarchy and is denoted as a slash (/). It contains some standard files and directories and, in a sense, is the master cabinet that contains all drawers, folders, and files.

/bin

Also known as the binary directory, the /bin directory contains binary (executable) images of most UNIX commands, including `cat`, `chmod`, `cp`, `csh`, `date`, `echo`, `kill`, `ksh`, `ln`, `ls`, `mail`, `mkdir`, `more`, `mv`, `ping`, `ps`, `pwd`, `rm`, `rmdir`, `sh`, `stty`, `tar`, `vi`, and `zcat`. All the files in this directory are either executable files or symbolic links to executable files in some other directories. This directory is usually a symbolic link to the /usr/bin directory.

/dev

The /dev directory, which is also known as the device directory, contains files corresponding to the devices (terminals, disk drives, CD-ROM drive, tape drive, modem, printer, etc.) connected to the computer. These files are the special files described in Section 7.3.4. Files in this directory include cdrom (CD-ROM drive), console (the console), fd (floppy drive), hd (hard disk or a partition on a hard disk), isdn (an ISDN connection), lp (line printer), midi (a midi interface), pty (pseudo terminal), ram (RAM disk), and tty (a terminal). A system may have several devices of each type—for example, 10 hard disks or partitions, 20 terminals, 100 pseudo terminals, and two RAM disks. The network-based system that two authors of this book use at work contain a total of 1,006 files in the /dev directory, including 68 for disk drives/partitions and 6 for RAM disks.

/etc

The /etc directory contains commands and files for system administration. A typical user is generally not allowed to use the commands and files in this directory. Files in this directory include inetd.conf, login, passwd, printcap, profile, rc.d, services, and termcap. Discussion of most of the files in this directory is beyond the scope of this textbook. However, we do mention the /etc/login (BSD) and /etc/profile (System V) files in the chapters on shell programming. We briefly discuss the /etc/passwd file toward the end of this section.

/lib

The library, or /lib, directory contains a collection of related files for a given language in a single file called an **archive**. A typical UNIX system contains libraries for C, C++, and FORTRAN. The archive file for one of these languages can be used by applications developed in that language. Some libraries are also stored in the /usr/lib directory, but /lib contains all essential libraries. This directory is usually a symbolic link to the /usr/lib directory.

/lost+found

The /lost+found directory contains all the files not connected to any directory. These files are found by a UNIX tool, `fsck` (file system check), which system administrators use to check a file system. System administrators decide the fate of the files in this directory.

/tmp

Used by several commands and applications, the /tmp directory contains temporary files. You can use this directory for your own temporary files as well. All the files in this directory are deleted periodically so that the disk (or a partition of disk) doesn't get filled with temporary files. The life of a file in the /tmp directory is set by the system administrator and varies from system to system, but it is usually only a few minutes.

/users

Organized in some fashion, the /users directory is normally used to hold the home directories of all the users of the system. For example, the system administrator can create subdirectories under this directory that contain home directories for certain users. For example, the diagram in Figure 7.2, which shows a university-like setup, has one subdirectory each for the home directories of members of the administration, faculty, staff, students, and so on. These subdirectories are labeled admin, faculty, and students. Users' home directories can be located in various places in the file system structure. A system administrator might decide to put the subdirectories containing the home directories of the users directly under the root directory or under a directory called /home. The two places where one author of this book has a UNIX account presently use these two structures. On the University of Portland system that two of the authors use, 43 subdirectories contain the users' home directories, each holding home directories for administration, staff, students, and faculty belonging to various departments.

/usr

The /usr directory contains subdirectories that hold, among other things, the UNIX utilities, tools, language libraries, and manual pages. Two of the most important subdirectories in this directory are bin and lib, which contain binary images of most UNIX commands (utilities, tools, etc.) and the language libraries, respectively.

/var

The /var file contains, among several other directories, the /var/spool/mail directory that receives and holds incoming e-mail messages. When you read your new e-mail, it comes from a file in this directory. Once you have read the `mail`, it is put in a file in your home directory called mbox.

/etc/passwd

The /etc/passwd file contains one line for every user on the system and describes that user. Each line has seven fields, separated by colons. The following is the format of the line.

```
login_name:password:user_ID:group_ID:user_info:home_directory:login_shell
```

The `login_name` is the login name by which the user is known to the system and is what the user types to log in. The `password` field contains the dummy password x or * in newer systems (starting with System VR4) and the encrypted version of the password in older systems. The newer versions store encrypted passwords in /etc/shadow. The `user_ID` is an integer between 0 to 65535 assigned to the user; 0 is assigned to the superuser and 1–99 are reserved. The `group_ID` identifies the group that the user belongs to, and it also is an integer between 0 and 65535, with 0–99 reserved. The `user_info` field contains information about the user, typically the user's full name. The `home_directory` field contains the absolute pathname for the user's home directory. The last field, `login_shell`, contains the absolute pathname for the user's login shell. The command corresponding to the pathname specified in this field is executed by the system when the user logs on. Back-to-back colons mean that the field value is missing, which is sometimes done with the user_info field. The following line from the /etc/passwd file on this system is for the user sarwar.

```
sarwar:x:134:105:Mansoor Sarwar:/users/faculty/sarwar:/usr/bin/sh
```

In this line, the login name is sarwar, the password field contains x, the user ID is 134, the group ID is 105, the personal information is the user's full name (Mansoor Sarwar), the home directory is /users/faculty/sarwar, and the login shell is /usr/bin/sh, or the Bourne shell.

/unix

The /unix file contains the binary image of the UNIX kernel to be loaded into memory at system bootup time. The BSD UNIX has its binary image in /vmunix. However, not all systems put this binary under the root directory. For example, IBM's AIX system has the binary in the /unix file, but Sun's Solaris system has it in /kernel/unix. The name of the file could also be something other than unix, reflecting a particular brand of UNIX.

The following In-Chapter Exercises give you practice in browsing the file system on your UNIX machine and help you understand the format of the /etc/passwd file.

IN-CHAPTER EXERCISES ━━━━━━━━━━━━━━━━━━━━━━━━

7.1   Go to the /dev directory on your system and identify one character special file and one block special file.

7.2   View the /etc/passwd file on your system to determine your user ID.

7.5   Navigating the File Structure

Now we describe some useful commands for browsing the UNIX file system, creating files and directories, determining file attributes, determining the absolute pathname for your home directory, determining the pathname for the present working directory, and determining the type of a file. The discussion is based on the file structure shown in Figure 7.2 and the user name sarwar.

7.5.1 Determining the Absolute Pathname for Your Home Directory

When you log on, the system puts you in your home directory. You can find the full pathname for your home directory by using the echo and pwd commands. The following is a brief description of the echo command.

echo [string]	
Purpose:	Send 'string' to the display screen; 'string' can contain white spaces and terminates with newline
Output:	'string'
Commonly used options/features:	
\c	Send line without newline
\t	Tab character
\\	Backslash

With no argument, the command displays a blank line on the screen. You can determine the absolute pathname of your home directory by using the echo command, as in,

```
$ echo $HOME
/users/faculty/sarwar
$
```

HOME is a shell variable (a placeholder) which that shell uses to keep track of your home directory. We discuss shell variables and the echo command in detail in Chapters 15–18.

Another way to display the absolute pathname of your home directory is to use the pwd command. You use this command to determine the absolute pathname of the directory you are currently in; it doesn't require any arguments. When you log on, the UNIX system puts you in your home directory. You can use the pwd command right after logging on to determine the absolute pathname of your home directory. The command doesn't take any parameter, as in,

```
$ pwd
/users/faculty/sarwar
$
```

7.5.2 Browsing the File System

You can browse the file system by going from your home directory to other directories in the file system structure and displaying a directory's contents (files and subdirectories in the directory), provided that you have the *permissions* to do so. (We cover file security and permissions in detail in Chapter 8.) For now, we show how you can browse your own files and directories by using the `cd` (change directory) and `ls` (list directory) commands. The following is a brief description of the `cd` command.

---

cd [directory]

Purpose:	Change the present working directory to 'directory', or to the home directory if no argument is specified

SYNTAX

The shell variable *PWD* is set after each execution of the `cd` command. The `pwd` command uses the value of this variable to display the present working directory. After getting into a directory, you can view its contents (the names of files or subdirectories in it) by using the `ls` command. The following is a brief description of this command. The `cd` and `ls` commands are two of the most heavily used UNIX commands.

---

ls [options] [pathname-list]

Purpose:	Send the names of the files in the directories and files specified in 'pathname-list' to the display screen
Output:	Names of the files and directories in the directory specified by 'pathname-list', or the names only if 'pathname-list' contains file names only

Commonly used options/features:

−F	Display / after directories, * after binary executables, and @ after symbolic links
−a	Display name of all the files, including hidden files ., .., etc.
−i	Display inode number
−l	Display long list that includes access permissions, link count, owner, group, file size (in bytes), and modification time

SYNTAX

If the command is used without any argument, it displays the names of files and directories in the present working directory. The following session illustrates how the `ls` and `cd` commands work with and without parameters. The `pwd` command displays the absolute pathname of the current directory. With the exception of hidden files, the `ls` command displays the name of all the files and directories in the current directory. The `cd courses` command is used to make the courses directory the current directory. The `cd ee446/exams` command makes the ee446/ exams the current directory. The `ls ~` and `ls $HOME` commands display the names of the files and directories in the home directory. The `cd` command (without any argument) takes you back to your home directory. In other words, it makes your home directory your current directory.

```
$ pwd
/users/faculty/sarwar
$ ls
courses    personal
$ cd courses
$ ls
ee231     ee446
$ cd ee446/exams
$ pwd
/users/faculty/sarwar/courses/ee446/exams
$ ls
mid1   mid2
$ ls ~
courses    personal
$ ls $HOME
courses    personal
$ cd
$ ls
courses    personal
$
```

We demonstrate the use of the `ls` command with various flags in the remainder of this chapter and other chapters of the book.

In a typical UNIX system, you are not allowed to access all the files and directories in the system. In particular, you typically are not allowed to access many important files and directories related to system administration and to other users' files and directories. However, you have permissions to read a number of directories and files. The following session illustrates that we have permissions to go to and list the contents of, among many other directories, the / and /usr directories.

```
$ cd /usr
$ ls
bin  lib   local
$ cd /
$ ls
bin  dev  etc  install   lost+found  tmp  users  usr  unix
```

```
$ cd
$ ls /usr
bin   lib   local
$
```

Without any flag, the `ls` command does not show all the files and directories; in particular, it does not display the names of hidden files. Examples of these files include `.`, `..`, `.addressbook`, `.bashrc`, `.cshrc`, `.exrc`, `.login`, `.mailrc`, and `.profile`. We have already discussed the `.` and `..` directories. The purposes of some of the more important hidden files are summarized in Table 7.2.

TABLE 7.2 Some Important Hidden Files and Their Purposes

File Name	Purpose
.	Present working directory
..	Parent of the present working directory
.addressbook	Address book for `pine`
.bashrc	Setup for Bash shell
.cshrc	Setup for C shell
.exrc	Setup for vi
.login	Setup for shell if `C` or `TC` shells are the login shells; executed at login time
.mailrc	Setup and address book for `mail` and `mailx`
.profile	Setup for shell if Bourne or Korn shell is the login shell; executed at login time

You can also display the names of the hidden files by using the `ls` command with the `-a` option. The following command line is an example.

```
$ ls -a
.   ..   .cshrc   .exrc   .pinerc   courses   personal
$
```

You can use shell metacharacters in specifying multiple files or directory parameters to the `ls` command. For example, the command **`ls /usr/*`** displays the names of all the files in the /usr directory and in the directories in /usr.

7.5.3 Creating Files

While working on a computer system, you need to create files and directories: files to store your work and directories to organize your files more efficiently. You can create files by using various tools and applications, such as editors, and directories by using the `mkdir` command. In Chapter 5 we discussed various editors (`pico`, `vi`, and `emacs`) that you can use to create files containing plain text. You can create nontext files by using various applications and tools, such as a compiler, that translates source code in a high-level language (e.g., C) and generates a file that contains the corresponding executable code.

7.5.4 Creating and Removing Directories

We briefly discussed the `mkdir` and `rmdir` commands in Chapter 4. Here, we cover these commands fully. You can create a directory by using the `mkdir` command. The following is a brief description of this command.

SYNTAX

mkdir [options] dirnames

Purpose: Create directories specified in 'dirnames'

Commonly used options/features:

   −m MODE   Create a directory with the given access permissions (*see* Chapter 8)

   −p   Create parent directories that don't exist in the pathnames specified in 'dirnames'

Here, 'dirnames' are the pathnames of the directories to be created. When you log on, you can use the following command to create a subdirectory, called memos, in your home directory. You can confirm the creation of this directory by using the `ls` command, as in,

```
$ mkdir memos
$ ls
courses    memos   personal
$
```

Similarly, you can create a directory called test_example in the /tmp directory by using,

```
$ mkdir /tmp/test_example
$
```

While in your home directory, you can create the directory professional and a subdirectory letters under it by using the `mkdir` command with the −p option, as in,

```
$ mkdir -p professional/letters
$
```

You can use the `rmdir` command to remove an empty directory. If a directory is not empty, you must remove the files and subdirectories in it before removing it. For removing nonempty directories, you need to use the `rm` command with the −r option (*see* Chapter 9). The following is a brief description of the `rmdir` command.

rmdir [options] dirnames

Purpose: Remove the empty directories specified in 'dirnames'

Commonly used options/features:

   −p   Remove empty parent directories as well

The following command removes the letters directory from the present working directory. If letters is not empty, the rmdir command displays the error message rmdir: letter: Directory not empty on the screen. If letters is a file, the command displays the error message rmdir: letters: Path component not a directory.

```
$ rmdir letters
$
```

The following command removes the directories letters from your present working directory and memos from your home directory.

```
$ rmdir letters ~/memos
$
```

If the ~/personal directory contains only one subdirectory, called **diary**, and it is empty, you can use the following command to remove both directories.

```
$ rmdir -p ~/personal/diary
$
```

7.5.5 Determining File Attributes

You can determine the attributes of files by using the ls command with various options. The options can be used together, and their order doesn't matter. For example, you can use the -l option to get a long list of a directory that gives the attributes of files, such as the owner of the file, as in,

```
$ ls -l
drwxr-x---    2   sarwar   faculty   512   Apr 23 09:37   courses
drwxr-----    1   sarwar   faculty   12    May 01 13:22   memos
drwx------    1   sarwar   faculty   163   May 05 23:13   personal
$ ls -l ~/courses/ee446/exams
-rwxr--r--    1   sarwar   faculty   163   Mar 16 11:10   mid1
-rwxr--r--    1   sarwar   faculty   163   Apr 11 14:34   mid22
drwxrwxrwx    1   sarwar   faculty   163   May 12 23:44   solutions
$
```

The information displayed by the ls -l command is summarized in Table 7.3.

■ **TABLE 7.3** Summary of the Output of the ls -l Command
(fields are listed left to right)

Field	Meaning
First letter of first field	File type: − ordinary file **b** block special file **c** character special file **d** directory **l** link **p** named pipe (FIFO) **s** socket
Remaining letters of first field	Access permissions for owner, group, and others
Second field	Number of links
Third field	Owner's login name
Fourth field	Owner's group name (can also be a number)
Fifth field	File size in bytes
Sixth, seventh, and eighth field	Date and time of last modification
Ninth field	File name

In the preceding two uses of ls F -l, courses, memos, personal, and solutions are directories, and mid1 and mid2 are ordinary files. (We discuss access permissions and user types in Chapter 8.) The owner of the files is sarwar, who belongs to the group faculty. The values of the remaining fields are self-explanatory.

You can use the ls command with the -i option to determine the inode numbers of files. The following example of its use shows that the inode numbers for courses, memos, and personal are 12329, 22876, and 12487, respectively.

```
$ ls -i
12329 courses 22876 memos 12487 personal
$
```

The ls -al command displays the long list of all the files in a directory, as in,

```
$ ls -al ~/courses/ee446/exams
drwxr-x--   1   sarwar   faculty    512   Mar 16 08:24   .
drwxr-x--   1   sarwar   faculty    512   Jan 29 13:27   ..
-rwxr--r--  1   sarwar   faculty   1863   Mar 16 11:10   mid1
-rwxr--r--  1   sarwar   faculty    459   Apr 11 14:34   mid22
drwxrwxrwx  1   sarwar   faculty    512   May 12 23:44   solutions
$
```

You can use the -F option to identify directories, executable files, and symbolic links. The ls -F command displays an asterisk (*) after an executable file, a slash (/) after a directory, and an "at" symbol (@) after a symbolic link (discussed in Chapter 11), as in,

```
$ ls -F /
bin/   dev/   etc/   install@   lost+found/   tmp/   usr/   unix*
$
```

You are encouraged to read the online man pages for the ls command on your system, or *see* Appendix A for a concise description of the command.

By using the shell metacharacters, you can specify a particular set of files and directories. For example, the following command can be used in C shell to display the long lists for all the files in the ~/courses/ee446 directory that have the .c extension and start with the string lab followed by zero or more characters, with the condition that the first of these characters cannot be 5. Under the Bourne shell, replace the ^ character with the !^ character.

```
$ ls -l ~/courses/ee446/lab[^5]*.c
...
$
```

Similarly, the following command can be used to display the inode numbers and names of all the files in your current directory that have four-character names and an .html extension. The file names must start with a letter, followed by any two characters, and end with a digit from 1 through 5.

```
$ ls -i [a-zA-Z]??[1-5].html
...
$
```

The following command under C shell displays the names of all the files in the your home directory that do not start with a digit and that end with .c or .C. In other words, the command displays the names of all the C and C++ source program files that do not start with a digit. Again, under the Bourne shell, replace the ^ character with the ! character.

```
$ ls ~/[^0-9]*.[c,C]
...
$
```

7.5.6 Determining the Type of a File's Contents

Because UNIX does not support types of ordinary files and extensions, you cannot determine what a file contains by simply looking at its name. However, you can find the type of a file's contents by using the file command. Mostly, this command is used to determine whether a file contains text or binary data. Doing so is important because text files can be displayed on the screen, whereas displaying binary files can freeze your terminal, as it may interpret some of the binary values as control codes. The command has the following syntax.

SYNTAX

file [options] file-list

Purpose: Attempt to classify files in 'file-list'

Commonly used options/features:

   −f FILE   Use FILE as a file of 'file-list'

The following session shows a sample run of the command. In this case, types of the contents of all the files in the root directory are displayed.

```
$ file /*
all.backup:    POSIX tar archive
bin:           directory
dev:           directory
etc:           directory
install:       symbolic link to var/lib/LST
lost+found:    directory
tmp:           directory
usr:           directory
unix:          ELF 32-bit LSB executable
$
```

Some more classifications that the `file` command displays are English text, C program text, Bourne shell script text, empty, nroff/troff, perl command text, PostScript, `sccs`, `setuid executable`, and `setgid` executable.

The following In-Chapter Exercises familiarize you with the `echo`, `cd`, `ls`, and `file` commands and the formats of their output.

IN-CHAPTER EXERCISES

7.3   Right after you log on, run `echo ~` to determine the full pathname of your home directory.

7.4   Use the `cd` command to go to the /usr/bin directory on your system and run the `ls −F` command. Identify two symbolic links and five binary files.

7.5   Run the `ls −l` command in the same directory and write down sizes (in bytes) of the `find` and `sort` commands.

7.6   Run the `file /etc/*` command to identify types of all the files in this directory.

7.6 File Representation and Storage in UNIX

As we mentioned before, the attributes of a file are stored in a data structure on the disk, called *inode*. At the time of its creation, every file is allocated a unique inode from a list (array) of inodes on the disk, called the **i-list.** The UNIX kernel also maintains a table of inodes, called the **inode table,** in the main memory for all open files. When an application opens a file, an inode is allocated from the inode table. The i-list and inode table are indexed by a file's inode number. The inode number is used to index the inode table, allowing access to the attributes of an open file. When a file's attributes (e.g., file size) change, the inode in the main memory is updated; disk copies of the inodes are updated at fixed intervals. For files that are not open, their inodes reside on the disk. Some of the contents of an inode are shown in Figure 7.3.

The 'link count' field specifies the number of different names the file has within the system. The 'file mode' field specifies what the file was opened for (read, write, etc.). The 'user ID' is the ID of the owner of the file. The 'access permissions' field specifies who can access the file for what type of operation (discussed in more detail in Chapter 8). The 'file's location on disk' is specified by a number of *direct* and *indirect* pointers to **disk blocks** containing file data.

A typical computer system has several disk drives. Each drive consists of a number of platters with top and bottom *surfaces*; each surface is logically divided into concentric circles called *tracks*, and each track is subdivided into fixed size portions called **sectors.** Tracks at the same position on both surfaces of all platters comprise a cylinder. Disk I/O takes place in terms of one sector, also called a disk block. The address of a sector is a four-dimensional address comprising <disk #, cylinder #, track # (surface #), sector #>. This four-dimensional address is translated to a *linear* (one-dimensional) block number, and most of the software in UNIX deals with block addresses because they are relatively easy to deal with. These blocks are numbered with sector 0 of the outermost cylinder at the topmost surface (i.e., the topmost track of the outermost cylinder) assigned block number 0. The block numbers increase through the rest of the tracks in that cylinder, through the rest of the cylinders on the disk, and then through the rest of the disks. The diagram shown in Figure 7.4 is a logical view of a disk system consisting of an array of disk blocks. File space is allocated in *clusters* of two, four, or eight 512-byte disk blocks.

```
┌─────────────────────────────┐
│        Link Count           │
│        File Mode            │
│        User ID              │
│        Time Created         │
│      Time Last Updated      │
│     Access Permissions      │
│                             │
│            .                │
│            .                │
│            .                │
│                             │
│  File's Location on Disk    │
└─────────────────────────────┘
```

Figure 7.3 Contents of an inode

Disk drive

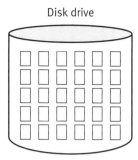

Figure 7.4 Logical view of a disk drive—an array of disk blocks

Figure 7.5 shows how an inode number for an open file can be used to access a file's attributes, including the file's contents, from the disk. It also shows contents of the directory ~/courses/ee446/labs and how the UNIX kernel maps the inode of the file lab1.c to its contents on disk. As previously discussed, and as shown in the diagram, a directory consists of an array of entries <inode #, filename>. Accessing (reading or writing) the contents of lab1.c requires use of its inode number to index the in-memory inode table to get to the file's inode. The inode, previously stated, contains, among other things, the location of lab1.c on the disk.

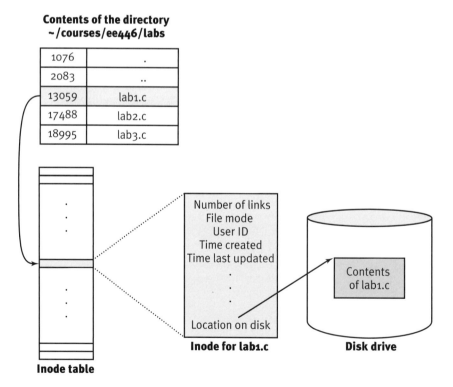

Figure 7.5 Relationship between the file labl.c in a directory and its contents on a disk

The inode contains the location of lab1.c on the disk in terms of the numbers of the disk blocks that contain the contents of the file. The details of how exactly a UNIX file's location is specified in its inode and how it is stored on the disk are beyond the scope of this textbook. These details are available in any book on UNIX internals.

7.7   Standard Files and File Descriptors

When an application needs to perform an I/O operation on a file, it must first open the file and then issue the file operation (read, write, seek, etc.). UNIX automatically opens three files for every command it executes. The command reads input from one of these files and sends its output and error messages to the other two files. These files are called *standard files:* **standard input (stdin) files, standard output (stdout) files,** and **standard error (stderr) files.** By default, these files are attached to the terminal on which the command is executed. That is, the shell makes the command input come from the terminal keyboard and its output and error messages go to the monitor screen (or the console window in case of a telnet session or an xterm in a UNIX system running the X Window System, as discussed in detail in Chapter 21). These default files can be changed to other files by using the **redirection operators:** < for input redirection and > for output and error redirection.

A small integer, called a **file descriptor,** is associated with every open file in UNIX. The integer values 0, 1, and 2 are the file descriptors for stdin, stdout, and stderr, respectively, and are also known as *standard file descriptors.* The kernel uses file descriptors to perform file operations (e.g., file read), as illustrated in Figure 7.6. The kernel uses a file descriptor to index the per-process **file descriptor table** to get a pointer to the systemwide file table. The **file table,** among other things, contains a pointer to the file's inode in the inode table. Once the inode for the file has been accessed, the required file operation is performed by accessing appropriate disk block(s) for the file by using the direct and indirect pointers, as described in Section 7.6.

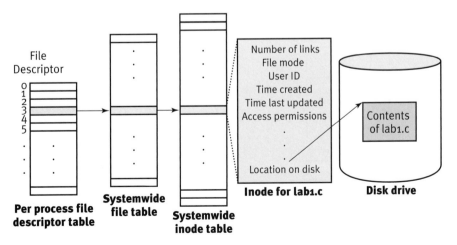

Figure 7.6 Relationship between a title descriptors and contents of the file on disk

Recall that every device, including a terminal, is represented by a file in UNIX. The diagram shown in Figure 7.7 depicts the relationship between a file and its file descriptor. Here, we assume that files lab1.c and lab2.c are open for some file operations (say, file read) and have descriptors 3 and 4, respectively, that the kernel associated with the files when they were opened. We have described the details of this relationship in the preceding paragraph and in Section 7.6, in terms of a file table, inode table, and storage of the file on disk; also see Figures 7.5 and 7.6.

The UNIX system allows standard files to be changed to alternate files for a single execution of a command, including a shell script. This concept of changing standard files to alternate files is called input, output, and error redirection.

We address input, output, and error redirection in detail in Chapter 12. We have briefly mentioned the standard files and file descriptors here because most UNIX commands that take input get it from standard input, unless it comes from a file (or list of files) that is passed to the command as a command line argument. Similarly, most UNIX commands that produce output send it to standard output. This information is important for proper understanding and use of commands in the remaining chapters.

7.8 End-of-File (eof) Marker

Every UNIX file has an **end-of-file (eof) marker.** The commands that read their input from files read the eof marker when they reach the end of a file. For files that can be stored, the value of the eof marker is not a character; it is usually a small negative integer such as −1. The <Ctrl-D> on a new line is the UNIX eof marker when the input file is a keyboard. That is why commands such as cat while reading input from the keyboard (*see* Chapter 9) terminate when you press <Ctrl-D> on a new line.

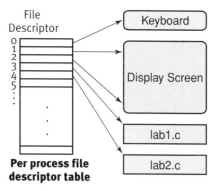

Figure 7.7 Logical view of the relationship of a file descriptors and the corresponding file

Summary

In UNIX, a file is a sequence of bytes. This simple, yet powerful, concept and its implementation lead to everything in the system being a file. UNIX supports six types of files: ordinary file, directory, symbolic link, special file (device), named pipe (also known as FIFO), and socket. No file extensions are supported for files of any type, but applications running on a UNIX system can require their own extensions.

Every file in UNIX has several attributes associated with it, including file name, owner's name, date last modified, link count, and the file's location on disk. These attributes are stored in an area on the disk called an inode. When files are opened, their inodes are copied to a kernel area called the inode table for faster access of their attributes. Every file in a directory has an entry associated with it that comprises the file's name and its inode number. The kernel accesses an open file's attributes, including its contents, by reading the file's inode number from its directory entry and indexing the inode table with the inode number.

The UNIX file structure is hierarchical with a root directory and all the files and directories in the system under it. Every user has a directory, called the user's home directory, that he or she enters when logging on to the system. Multiple disk drives and/or disk partitions can be mounted on the same file system structure allowing their access as directories, and not as named drives A:, B:, C:, etc., as in MS-DOS and Microsoft Windows. This approach gives a unified view of all the files and directories in the system, and users don't have to worry about remembering the names of drives and the files (and directories) that they contain.

Directories (primarily) can be created and removed under the user's home directory. The file structure can be navigated by using various commands (mkdir, rmdir, cd, ls, etc.). The name of a file in the system can be specified by using its absolute or relative pathname. An absolute pathname starts with the root directory, and a relative pathname starts with a user's home directory or present working directory.

UNIX automatically opens three files for every command for it to read input from and send its output and error messages to. These files are called standard input (stdin), standard output (stdout), and standard error (stderr). By default, these files are attached to the terminal on which the command is executed; that is, the command input comes from the terminal keyboard, and the command output and error messages go to the terminal's screen display. The default files can be changed to other files by using redirection primitives: < for input redirection, and > for output and error redirection.

The kernel associates a small integer with every open file. This integer is called the file descriptor. The kernel uses file descriptors to perform operations (e.g., read) on the file. The file descriptors for stdin, stdout, and stderr are 0, 1, and 2, respectively.

Every UNIX file has an end-of-file (eof) marker, which is a small negative integer such as 21. The eof marker is <Ctrl-D> if a command reads input from the keyboard.

Problems

1. What is a file in UNIX?

2. Does UNIX support any file types? If so, name them. Does UNIX support file extensions?

3. What is a directory entry? What does it consists of?

4. What are special files in UNIX? What are character special and block special files? Run the `ls /dev | wc -w` command to find the number of special files your system has.

5. What is meant by interprocess communication? Name three tools that UNIX provides for interprocess communication.

6. Draw the hierarchical file structure, similar to the one shown in Figure 7.2, for your UNIX machine. Show files and directories at the first two levels. Also show where your home directory is, along with files and directories under your home directory.

7. Give three commands that you can use to list the absolute pathname of your home directory.

8. Write down the line in the /etc/passwd file on your system that contains information about your login. What are your login shell, user ID, home directory, and group ID? Does your system contain the encrypted password in the /etc/passwd or /etc/shadow file?

9. What would happen if the last field of the line in the /etc/passwd file were replaced with /usr/bin/date? Why?

10. What are the inode numbers of the root and your home directories on your machine? Give the commands that you used to find these inode numbers.

11. Create a directory, called memos, in your home directory. Go into this directory and create a file memo.james by using one of the editors discussed in Chapter 5. Give three pathnames for this file.

12. Give a command line for creating a subdirectory personal under the memos directory that you created in Problem 11.

13. Make a copy of the file memo.james and put it in your home directory. Name the copied file temp.memo. Give two commands for accomplishing this task.

14. Draw a diagram like that shown in Figure 7.5 for your memos directory. Clearly show all directory entries, including inode numbers for all the and directories in it.

15. Give the command for deleting the memos directory. How do you know that the directory has been deleted?

16. Why does a shell process terminate when you press <Ctrl-D> at the beginning of a new line?

17. Give a command line to display the types of all the files in your ~/unix directory that start with the word chapter, are followed by a digit 1, 2, 6, 8, or 9, and end with .eps or .prn.

18. Give a command line to display the types of all the files in the personal directory in your home directory that do not start with letters a, k, G, or Q and the third letter in the name is not a digit and not a letter (uppercase or lowercase).

19. Use the `ls -i` command to display inode numbers for the /, /usr, and ~ directories on your system. Show outputs of your commands and identify the inodes numbers for these directories.

File Security

Objectives

- To show the three protection and security mechanisms that UNIX provides
- To describe the types of users of a UNIX file
- To discuss the basic operations that can be performed on a UNIX file
- To explain the concept of file access permissions/privileges in UNIX
- To discuss how a user can determine access privileges for a file
- To describe how a user can set and change permissions for a file
- To cover the commands and primitives `?`, `~`, `*`, `chmod`, `groups`, `ls -l`, `ls -ld`, `umask`

8.1 Introduction

As we pointed out earlier, a time-sharing system offers great benefits. However, it poses the main challenge of protecting the hardware and software resources in it. These resources include the I/O devices, CPU, main memory, and the secondary storage devices that store user files. We limited this chapter to a discussion of the protection of a user's files from unauthorized access by other users. UNIX provides three mechanisms to protect your files.

The most fundamental scheme for protecting user files is to give every user a login name and a password, allowing a user to use a system (*see* Chapter 3). To prevent others from accessing your files, keep the password for your computer account strictly confidential. The second scheme protects individual files by converting them to a form that is completely different from the original version by means of encryption. This technique is used to protect your most important files so that the contents of these files cannot be understood even if someone somehow gains access to them on the system. The third file protection scheme allows you to protect your files by associating **access privileges** with them so that only a subset of users can access these files for a subset of file operations. In other words, the owner of the files can decide to whom to grant access to these files. All three mechanisms are described in this chapter, with emphasis on the third scheme.

8.2 Password-Based Protection

The first mechanism that allows you to protect your files from other users is the login password scheme. Every user of a UNIX-based computer system is assigned a login name (a name by which the user is known to the UNIX system) and a password. Both the login name and password are assigned by the system administrator and are required for a user to enter a UNIX system. All login names are public knowledge and can be found in the /etc/passwd file. A user's password, however, is given to that user only. This scheme prevents users from accessing each other's files. Users are encouraged to change their passwords frequently by using the passwd command (*see* Chapter 3). On some networked systems, you may have to use the yppasswd or nispasswd command to change your password on all the network's computer systems. Consult your instructor about the command that you need to use on your particular system. Usually login names can be changed by the system administrator only. Under some UNIX installations, users are allowed to change their usernames.

The effectiveness of this protection scheme depends on how well protected a user's password is. If someone knows your password, that person can log on to the system and access your files. There are primarily three ways of discovering a user's password:

1. you, as the owner of an account, inform others of your password;
2. a password can be guessed by another user; and
3. a user's password can be extracted by "brute force."

Never let anyone else know your password under any circumstances; as a safety measure, you should change your password regularly. Always choose passwords that would be difficult for others to guess. A good password is one that is a mixture of letters, digits, and punctuation marks—but it must be easy for you to memorize. Never write your password on a piece of paper, and never use birthdays or the names of relatives, friends, or favorite movie actors. Also, avoid using words as passwords.

By using "brute force," someone tries to learn your password by trying all possible passwords until the right one is found. Guessing someone's password is a time-consuming process and is commonly used by hackers. The brute force method can be made more time-consuming for an infiltrator if the password is long and consists of letters, digits, and punctuation marks. To illustrate the significance of using a more complex password, consider a system that requires an eight-character password consisting of decimal digits only. It would allow a maximum of 10^8 (100 million) passwords that the brute force method would have to go through, in the worst-case analysis. If the same system requires passwords to consist of a mixture of digits and uppercase letters (a total 36 symbols: 10 digits and 26 uppercase letters), the password space would comprise 36^8 (about 2.8 trillion) passwords. If the system requires passwords that consist of a mixture of digits, uppercase letters, and lowercase letters, the password space would comprise 62^8 (about 218 trillion) passwords.

Many systems force a short (e.g., five-second) delay after an invalid password is entered before the next login prompt to make the infiltrator's job even harder.

The following In-Chapter Exercise asks you to figure out how to change your password on your system.

IN-CHAPTER EXERCISE

8.1   In some UNIX systems you are not allowed to change your password. Does your system allow you to change your password? If so, change your password. What command did you use?

Note: Be sure to memorize your new password, because if you forget it you will have to request your system administrator to reset your password to a new value, unless your system allows you to change your password back to the previous password.

8.3   Encryption-Based Protection

In the second protection scheme, a software tool is used to convert a file to a form that is completely different from its original version. The transformed file is called an **encrypted file**, and the process of converting a file to an encrypted file is called **encryption**. The same tool is used to perform the reverse process of transforming the encrypted file to its original form, called **decryption**. You can use this technique to protect your most important files so that their contents cannot be understood even if someone else gains access to them. Figure 8.1 illustrates these processes.

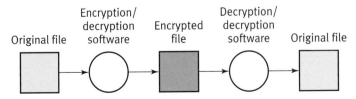

Figure 8.1 The process of encryption and decryption

The UNIX command `crypt` can be used to encrypt and decrypt your files. You can learn more about this command by running the `man crypt` command. This command is discussed in detail in Chapter 10.

8.4   Protection Based on Access Permission

The third type of file protection mechanism prevents users from accessing each others' files when they are not logged on as a file's owner. As file owner, you can attach certain **access rights** to your files that dictate who can and cannot access them for various types of file operations. This scheme is based on the types of users, the types of access permissions, and the types of operations allowed on a file under UNIX. Without this protection scheme, users can access each others' files because the UNIX file system structure (*see* Figure 7.2) has a single root from which all the files in the system hang.

8.4.1 Types of Users

Each user in a UNIX system belongs to a group of users, as assigned by the system administrator when a user is allocated an account on the system. A user can belong to multiple groups, but a typical UNIX user belongs to a single group. All the groups in the system and their memberships are listed in the file /etc/group (*see* Figure 7.2). This file contains one line per group, with the last field of the line containing the login names of the group members. A user of a file can be the owner of the file (known as the **user** in UNIX terminology); someone who belongs to the same **group** as the owner; or users known as **others**–everyone else who has an account on the system. These comprise the three types of users of a UNIX file. As the owner of a file, you can specify who can access it.

Every UNIX system has one special user who has access to all of the files on the system, regardless of the access privileges on the files. This user, commonly known as the **superuser**, is the administrator of the computer system. The login name for the superuser is **root**, and the user ID is 0.

A typical UNIX user belongs to one group, but a user can be part of multiple groups. You can see the list of all user groups on your system by displaying the /etc/group file, shown as follows.

```
$ more /etc/group
root::0:root,davis
other::1:
bin::2:root,bin,daemon
sys::3:root,bin,sys,adm
adm::4:root,daemon,adm
uucp::5:root,uucp
mail::6:root
tty::7:root,tty,adm
lp::8:root,lp,adm
nuucp::9:root,nuucp
staff::10:
```

```
daemon::12:root,daemon
sysadmin::14:davis
nobody::60001:
noaccess::60002:
nogroup::65534:
utadmin::100:
faculty::101:
ra::102:
courses::103:zartash
student::104:ank
...
$
```

There is one line in this file for every group on the system, each line having four colon-separated fields. The first field specifies the group name, the second specifies some information about the group, the third specifies the group ID, and the last specifies a comma-separated list of users who are members of the group. For example, the bin group has group ID 2 and its members are users root, bin, and daemon. If the membership list in a line is missing (e.g., the faculty group), it means that its membership is specified in the /etc/passwd file. The default group membership of a user is specified in the user's entry in the /etc/passwd file. The system administrator can make a user part of another group (in addition to his/her default group) by placing his/her username in the comma-separated list of members for the group. You can use the groups command to display which groups on your system a user is a member of. The following session shows that msarwar is a member of the faculty group only; zartash belongs to the groups faculty and courses; davis is a member of three groups: faculty, root, and sysadmin; and root is a member of 11 groups: other, root, bin, sys, adm, uucp, mail, tty, lp, nuucp, and daemon.

```
$ groups msarwar
faculty
$ groups zartash
faculty courses
$ groups davis
faculty root sysadmin
$ groups root
other root bin sys adm uucp mail tty lp nuucp daemon
$
```

8.4.2 Types of File Operations/Access Permissions

In UNIX, three types of access permissions/privileges can be associated with a file: read (r), write (w), and execute (x). The **read permission** allows you to read the file, the **write permission** allows you to write to or remove the file, and the **execute permission** allows you to execute (run) the file. The execute permission should be set for executable files only (files containing binary codes or shell scripts), as setting it for any other type of file doesn't make any sense.

With three types of file users and three types of permissions, a UNIX file has nine types of permissions associated with it, as shown in Table 8.1. Note that bits are read across row by row. As stated in Chapter 7, access privileges are stored in a file's inode.

■ TABLE 8.1 Summary of File Permissions in UNIX

User Type	Permission Type		
	Read (r)	Write (w)	Execute (x)
User (u)	X	X	X
Group (g)	X	X	X
Others (o)	X	X	X

The value of X can be 1 (for permission allowed) or 0 (permission not allowed). Therefore 1 bit is needed to represent a permission type, and a total of 3 bits are needed to indicate file permissions for one type of user (user, group, or others). In other words, a user of a file can have one of the eight possible types of permissions for a file. These eight 3-bit values can be represented by octal numbers from 0 through 7, as shown in Table 8.2; 0 means no permissions, and 7 means all (read, write, and execute) permissions.

■ TABLE 8.2 Possible Access Permission Values for a File for a User, Their Octal Equivalents, and Their Meanings

r	w	x	Octal Digit for Permission	Meaning
0	0	0	0	No permission
0	0	1	1	Execute-only permission
0	1	0	2	Write-only permission
0	1	1	3	Write and execute permissions
1	0	0	4	Read-only permission
1	0	1	5	Read and execute permissions
1	1	0	6	Read and write permissions
1	1	1	7	Read, write, and execute permissions

The total of 9 bits needed to express permissions for all three types of file users results in possible access permission values of 000 through 777 (as octal numbers) for file permissions. The first octal digit specifies permissions for the owner of the file, the second digit specifies permissions for the group that the owner of the file belongs to, and the third digit specifies permissions for everyone else. A bit value of 0 for a permission is also denoted dash (-), and a value of 1 is also denoted r, w, or x, depending on the position of the bit according to the table. Thus a permission value of 0 in octal (no permissions allowed) for a user of a file can be written as — — — and a permission of 7 (all three permissions allowed) can be denoted rwx. The outputs of the `ls −l` commands in the following session show that the /etc/passwd file is read-only for everyone on the system and the ~/courses/cs475/programs/client.c file has read and write permissions for the owner (`msarwar`), and read-only permission for everybody else.

```
$ ls -l /etc/passwd
-r--r--r-- 1 root sys 33020 Mar 10 15:47 /etc/passwd
$ ls -l ~/courses/cs475/programs/client.c
-rw--r--r-- 1 msarwar faculty 1277 Dec 19 07:30 courses/cs475/programs/client.c
$
```

8.4.3 Access Permissions for Directories

Next, we will look at what the read, write, and execute permissions mean for directories. The read permission for a directory allows you to read the contents of the directory; recall that the contents of a directory are the names of files and directories in it. Thus the `ls` command can be used to list its contents. The write permission for a directory allows you to create a new directory or file in it or to remove an existing entry from it. The execute permission for a directory is permission for searching the directory but not to read from or write to it. Thus, if you do not have execute permission for a directory, you cannot use the `ls-l` command to list its contents or use the `cd` command to make it your current directory. The same is true if any component in a directory's pathname does not contain execute permission. We demonstrate these aspects of the search permission on directories in Section 8.5.2.

8.5   Determining and Changing File Access Privileges

The following describes how you can determine the access privileges for files and directories and how you can change them to enhance or limit someone's access to your files.

8.5.1 Determining File Access Privileges

You can use the `ls` command with the `-l` or `-ld` option to display access permissions for a list of files and/or directories. The following is a brief description of the `ls` command with the two options.

ls -l [file-list]	
ls -ld [directory-list]	
Purpose:	First syntax: Display long list of files/directories in 'file-list' on the display screen; in case 'file-list' contains directories, display long list of all the files in these directories
	Second syntax: Display long list of directories in 'directory-list' on the display screen.
Output:	Long list of the files/directories in 'file-list'

SYNTAX

If no 'file-list' is specified, the command gives long lists for all the files (except hidden files) in the present working directory. Add the `-a` option to the command line to include the hidden files in the display. Consider the following session.

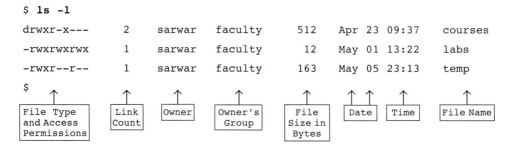

The left-most character in the first field of the output indicates the file type (d for directory and – for ordinary file). The remaining nine characters in the first field show file access privileges for user, group, and others, respectively. The second field indicates the number of hard links (discussed in Chapter 11) to the file. The third field gives the owner's login name. The fourth field gives the owner's group name. The fifth field gives the file's size (in bytes). The sixth, seventh, and eighth fields give date and time of the file's creation (or last update). The last field gives the file's name. Table 8.3 shows who has what type of access privileges for the three files in this session: courses, labs, and temp.

■ **TABLE 8.3** Permissions for Access to the courses, labs, and temp files for the Three Types of Users

| | **Access Permissions** | | |
File Name	User	Group	Other
courses	Read, write, and search	Read and search	No permission
labs	Read, write, and execute	Read, write, and execute	Read, write, and execute
temp	Read, write, and execute	Read	Read

If an argument of the `ls -l` command is a directory, the command displays the long lists of all the files and directories in it. You can use the `ls -ld` command to display long lists of directories only. When executed without an argument, this command displays the long list for the current directory, as shown in the first command in the following session. The second and third commands show that when the `ls -ld` command is executed with a list of directories as its arguments, it displays the long lists for those directories only. If an argument to the `ls -ld` command is a file, the command displays the long list for the file. The fourth command, `ls -ld pvm/*`, displays the long lists for all the files and directories in the pvm directory.

```
$ ls -ld
drwx--x--x  2  sarwar  faculty  11264  Jul 8 22:21 .
$ ls -ld ABET
drwx------  2  sarwar  faculty    512  Dec 18 1997 ABET
$ ls -ld ~/myweb/Images courses/ee446
drwx------  3  sarwar  faculty    512  Apr 30 09:52 courses/ee446
drwx--x--x  2  sarwar  faculty   2048  Dec 18 1997
/users/faculty/sarwar/myweb/Images
$ ls -ld pvm/*
drwx------  3  sarwar  faculty    512  Dec 18 1997 pvm/examples
drwx------  2  sarwar  faculty   1024  Oct 27 1998 pvm/qsort
-rw-------  1  sarwar  faculty   1606  Jun 19 1995 pvm/Book_PVM
-rw-------  1  sarwar  faculty   7639  Sep 11 1998 pvm/Jim_Davis
$
```

8.5.2 Changing File Access Privileges

You can use the chmod command to change access privileges for your files. The following is a brief description of the command.

---

chmod [options] octal-mode file-list
chmod [options] symbolic-mode file-list

Purpose: Change/set permissions for files in 'file-list'

Commonly used options/features:

   -R   Recursively descend through directories changing/setting permissions for all of the files and subdirectories under each directory

   -f   Force specified access permissions; no error messages are produced if you are the file's owner

---

The *symbolic mode*, also known as *mode control word*, has the form <who><operator> <privilege>, with possible values for 'who', 'operator', and 'privilege' shown in Table 8.4.

Note that u, g, or o can be used as a privilege with the = operator only. Multiple values can be used for 'who' and 'privilege', such as ug for the 'who' field and rx for the 'privilege' field. Some useful examples of the chmod command and their purposes are listed in Table 8.5.

■■■ **TABLE 8.4** Values for Symbolic Mode Components

Who	Operator	Privilege
u User	+ Add privilege	r Read bit
g Group	− Remove privilege	w Write bit
o Other	= Set privilege	x Execute/search bit
a All		u User's current privileges
ugo All		g Group's current privileges
		o Others' current privileges
		l Locking privilege bit
		s Sets user or group ID mode bit
		t Sticky bit

■■■ **TABLE 8.5** Examples of the chmod Commands and Their Purposes

Command	Purpose
`chmod 700 *`	Sets access privileges for all the files (including directories) in the current directory to read, write, and execute for the owner, and provides no access privilege to anyone else
`chmod 740 courses`	Sets access privileges for courses to read, write, and execute for the owner and read-only for the group, and provides no access for others
`chmod 751 ~/courses`	Sets access privileges for ~/courses to read, write, and execute for the owner, read and search for the group, and search-only permission for others
`chmod 700 ~`	Sets access privileges for the home directory to read, write, and execute for the owner, and no privileges for anyone else
`chmod u=rwx courses`	Sets owner's access privileges to read, write, and execute for courses and keeps the group's and others' privileges to their present values
`chmod ugo-rw sample` or `chmod a-rw sample`	Does not let anyone read or write sample
`chmod a+x sample`	Lets everyone execute sample
`chmod g=u sample`	Makes sample's group privileges match its user (owner) privileges
`chmod go= sample`	Removes all access privileges for the group and others for sample

The following session illustrates how access privileges for files can be determined and set. The chmod commands are used to change (or set) access privileges, and the ls -l (or ls -ld) commands are used to show the effect of the chmod commands. After the chmod 700 courses command has been executed, the owner of the courses file has all three access privileges for it, and nobody else has any privileges. The chmod g+rx courses command adds the read and execute access privileges to the courses file for the group. The chmod o+r courses command adds the read access privilege to the courses file for others. The chmod a-w * command takes away the write access privilege from all users for all the files in the current directory. The chmod 700 [l-t]* command sets the access permissions 700 for all the files that start with letters l through t, as illustrated by the output of the last ls -l command, which shows access privileges for the files labs and temp changed to 700.

```
$ cd
$ ls -l
drwxr-x---   2   sarwar   faculty   512   Apr 23 09:37   courses
-rwxrwxrwx   1   sarwar   faculty    12   May 01 13:22   labs
-rwxr--r--   1   sarwar   faculty   163   May 05 23:13   temp
$ chmod 700 courses
$ ls -ld courses
drwx------   2   sarwar   faculty   512   Apr 23 09:37   courses
$ chmod g+rx courses
$ ls -ld courses
drwxr-x---   2   sarwar   faculty   512   Apr 23 09:37   courses
$
$ chmod o+r courses
$ ls -ld courses
drwxr-xr--   2   sarwar   faculty   512   Apr 23 09:37   courses
$ chmod a-w *
$ ls -l
dr-xr-x---   2   sarwar   faculty   512   Apr 23 09:37   courses
-r-xr-xr-x   1   sarwar   faculty    12   May 01 13:22   labs
-r-xr-r---   1   sarwar   faculty   163   May 05 23:13   temp
$ chmod 700 [l-t]*
$ ls -l
dr-xr-x---   2   sarwar   faculty   512   Apr 23 09:37   courses
-rwx------   1   sarwar   faculty    12   May 01 13:22   labs
-rwx------   1   sarwar   faculty   163   May 05 23:13   temp
$
```

The access permissions for all the files and directories under one or more directories can be set by using the chmod command with the -R option. In the following session, the first command sets access permissions for all the files and directories under the directory called courses to 711 recursively. The second command sets access permissions for all the files and directories under ~/personal/letters to 700.

```
$ chmod -R 711 courses
$ chmod -R 700 ~/personal/letters
$
```

If you specify access privileges with a single octal digit in a chmod command, it is used by the command to set the access privileges for 'others'; the access privileges for 'user' and 'group' are both set to 0 (no access privileges). If you specify two octal digits in a chmod command, the command uses them to set access privileges for 'group' and 'others'; the access privileges for 'user' are set to 0 (no privileges). In the following session, the first chmod command sets 'others' access privileges for the courses directory to 7 (rwx). The second chmod command sets 'group' and 'others' access privileges for the personal directory to 7 (rwx) and 0 (---), respectively. The ls -l command shows the results of these commands.

```
$ chmod 7 courses
$ chmod 70 personal
$ ls -l
d------rwx   2 sarwar   faculty   512 Nov 10 09:43 courses
d---rwx---   2 sarwar   faculty   512 Nov 10 09:43 personal
drw-------   2 sarwar   faculty   512 Nov 10 09:43 sample
$
```

8.5.3 Access Privileges for Directories

As previously stated, the read permission on a directory allows you to read the directory's contents (recall that the contents of a directory are the names of files and directories in it), the write permission allows you to create a file in the directory or remove an existing file or directory from it, and the execute permission for a directory is permission for searching the directory. It is important to note that read and write permissions on directories are not meaningful without the search permission. So, you must have both read and execute permissions on a directory to be able to list its contents. Similarly, you must have both write and execute permissions on a directory to be able to create a file in it.

In the following session, write permission for the courses directory has been turned off. Thus, you cannot create a subdirectory ee345 in this directory by using the mkdir command or copy a file foo into it. Similarly, as you do not have search permission for the personal directory, you cannot use the cd command to get into (change directory to) this directory. If the sample directory had a subdirectory for which the execute permission was turned on, you still could not change the directory to it because search permission for sample is turned off. Finally, as read permission for the personal directory is turned off, you cannot display the names of files and directories in it by using the `ls` command, even though search permission on it is turned on.

```
$ chmod 600 sample
$ chmod 500 courses
$ chmod 300 personal
$ ls -l
dr-x------   2   sarwar   faculty   512 Nov 10 09:43 courses
d-wx------   2   sarwar   faculty   512 Nov 10 09:43 personal
drw-------   2   sarwar   faculty   512 Nov 10 09:43 sample
$ mkdir courses/ee345
mkdir: Failed to make directory "courses/ee345"; Permission denied
$ cp foo courses
cp: cannot create courses/foo: Permission denied
$ cd sample
sample: Permission denied
$ ls -l personal
personal unreadable
$
```

The next session shows that simply having the read or write permission on a directory is not sufficient to read its contents (e.g., display them with the `ls` command) or create a file or directory in it. For example, the dir1 directory has the write permission turned on, but you cannot copy the prog1.cpp file into it because search permission on it is turned off. Similarly, you cannot remove the f1 file from dir2. After you turn on its search permission with the `chmod u+x dir2` command, you can remove the f1 file.

```
$ ls -ld dir1
d-w-------   2   msarwar faculty   512 Oct 22 12:13 dir1
$ cp prog1.cpp dir1
cp: cannot create dir2/prog1.cpp: Permission denied
$ rm dir2/f1
dir2/f1: Permission denied
$ chmod u+x dir2
$ ls -ld dir2
d-wx------   2   msarwar faculty   512 Oct 22 12:13 dir2
$ rm dir2/f1
$
```

The following In-Chapter Exercises ask you to use the `chmod` and `ls -ld` commands to see how they work, and to enhance your understanding of UNIX file access privileges.

IN-CHAPTER EXERCISES

8.2   Create three directories called courses, sample, and personal by using the `mkdir` command. Set access permissions for the sample directory so that you have all three privileges, users in your group have read access only, and the other users of your system have no access privileges. What command did you use?

8.3   Use the `chmod o+r sample` command to allow others read access to the sample directory. Use the `ls -ld sample` command to confirm that 'others' have read permission for the directory.

8.4   Use the session preceding these exercises to understand fully how the read, write, and execute permissions work for directories.

8.5.4 Default File Access Privileges

When a new file or directory is created, UNIX sets its access privileges based on the argument of the umask command. The default access privileges are 777 for executable files and directories and 666 for text files. The following is a brief description of the command.

---

umask mask

Purpose: Set access permission bits on newly created files and directories to 1, except for those bits that are set to 1 in the 'mask'

The argument of umask is a **bit mask**, specified in octal, that identifies the protection bits that are to be turned *off* when a new file is created. Thus, the access permission value an executable file or directory is computed by the expression,

```
file access permission = 777 - mask
```

where 'mask' is the argument of the umask command. Therefore, if the umask 013 command is executed, file access privileges for the newly created files are set to (777 − 013) = 764. Thus, every new executable file or directory has its access privileges set to rwxrw-r--. The execution of the following umask command therefore disallows any access to newly created executable files and directories because all the bits in the 'mask' (777) are set. In other words, the access privileges for the newly created executable files and directories are set to (777 − 777) = 000.

```
umask 777
```

A commonly used mask value is 022, which sets the default access privileges for executable files and directories to (777 − 022) = 755 and for text files to (666 − 022) = 644. The authors prefer a mask value of 077 so that their new files are always created with full protection in place, that is, files have full access permissions for the owner and no permissions for anyone else. Recall that you can change access privileges for files on an as-needed basis by using the chmod command. Another common 'umask' value is 027, which gives default privileges to group members and no permissions to others.

The umask command is normally placed in the system startup file ~/.profile file (in System V UNIX) or the ~/.login file (in BSD UNIX) so that it executes every time you log on to the system. When the command is executed without an argument, it displays the current value of the bit mask, as in,

```
$ umask
777
$
```

The following In-Chapter Exercise asks you to use the umask command to determine the current file protection mask.

IN-CHAPTER EXERCISE

8.5   Run the umask command without any argument to display the current value of the bit mask.

8.6   Special Access Bits

In addition to the nine commonly used access permissions bits described in this chapter (read, write, and execute for user, group, and others), three additional bits are of special significance. These bits are known as the **set-user-ID (SUID) bit, set-group-ID (SGID) bit,** and **sticky bit.**

8.6.1 The Set-User-ID (SUID) Bit

We've previously shown that the external shell commands have corresponding files that contain binary executable codes or shell scripts. The programs contained in these files are not special in any way in terms of their ability to perform their tasks. Normally, when a command executes, it does so under the access privileges of the user who issues the command, which is how the access privileges system described in this chapter works. However, a number of UNIX commands need to write to files that are otherwise protected from users who normally run these commands. An example of this file is /etc/passwd, the file that contains a user's login information (*see* Chapter 7). Only the superuser is allowed to write to this file to perform tasks such as adding a new login and changing a user's group ID. However, UNIX users normally are allowed to execute the passwd command to change their passwords. Thus, when a user executes the passwd command, the command changes the user password in the /etc/passwd file on behalf of the user who runs this command. The problem is that we want users to be able to change their passwords, but at the same time they must not have write access to the /etc/passwd file to keep information about other users in this file from being compromised.

As previously stated, when a command is executed, it runs with the privileges of the user running the command. Another way of stating the same thing is that, when a command runs, it executes with the "effective user ID" of the user running the command. UNIX has an elegant mechanism that solves the problem stated in the preceding paragraph—and many other similar security problems—by allowing commands to change their "effective user ID" and become privileged in some way. This mechanism allows commands such as passwd to perform their work, yet not compromise the integrity of the system. Every UNIX file has an additional protection bit, called the SUID bit, associated with it. If this bit is set for a file containing an executable program for a command, the command takes on the privileges of the owner of the file when it executes. Thus, if a file is owned by 'root' and has its SUID bit set, it runs with superuser privileges, and this bit is set for the passwd command. So when you run the passwd command, it can write to the /etc/passwd file (replacing your existing password with the new password), even though you do not have access privileges to write to the file.

Several other UNIX commands require 'root' ownership and SUID bit set because they access and update operating system resources (files, data structures, etc.) that an average user must not have permissions for some of these commands are lp, mail, mkdir, mv, and ps. Another use of the SUID bit can be made by the authors of a game software that maintains a scores file. When the SUID bit is set for such software, it can update the scores file when a user plays the game, although the same user cannot update the scores file by explicitly writing to it.

The SUID bit can be set by the chmod command by using octal or symbolic mode, according to the following syntaxes.

SYNTAX

chmod 4xxx file-list
chmod u+s file-list

Here, 'xxx' is the octal number that specifies the read, write, and execute permissions, and the octal digit 4 (binary 100) is used to set the SUID bit. When the SUID bit is set, the execute bit for the user is set to 's' if the execute permission is already set for the user; otherwise, it is set to 'S'. The following session illustrates use of these command syntaxes. The first ls -l cp.new command is used to show that the execute permission for the cp.new file is set. The chmod 4710 cp.new command is used to set the SUID bit. The second ls -l cp.new command shows that the x bit value has changed to s (lowercase). The following two chmod commands are used to set the SUID and execute bits to 0. The ls -l cp.new command is used to show that execute permission has been taken away from the owner. The chmod u+s cp.new command is used to set the SUID bit again, and the last ls -l cp.new command shows that the bit value is S (uppercase) because the execute bit was not set prior to setting the SUID bit.

```
$ ls -l cp.new
-rwx--x---   1   sarwar   faculty   12   May 08 20:00    cp.new
$ chmod 4710 cp.new
$ ls -l cp.new
-rws--x---   1   sarwar   faculty   12   May 08 20:00    cp.new
$ chmod u-s cp.new
$ chmod u-x cp.new
```

```
$ ls -l cp.new
-rw--x---     1   sarwar   faculty   12   May 08 20:00     cp.new
$ chmod u+s cp.new
$ ls -l cp.new
-rwS--x---    1   sarwar   faculty   12   May 08 20:00     cp.new
$
```

Although the idea of the SUID bit is sound, it can compromise the security of the system if not implemented correctly. For example, if the permissions of any Set-UID program are set to allow write privileges to others, you can change the program in this file or overwrite the existing program with another program. Doing so would allow you to execute your (new) program with superuser privileges.

8.6.2 The Set-Group-ID (SGID) Bit

The SGID bit works in the same manner that SUID bit does, but it causes the access permissions of the process to take the group identity of the group to which the owner of the file belongs. This feature is not as dangerous as the SGID feature because most privileged operations require superuser identity regardless of the current group ID. The SGID bit can be set by using either of the following two command syntaxes.

---

chmod 2xxx file-list
chmod g+s file-list

S Y N T A X

Here, 'xxx' is the octal number specifying the read, write, and execute permissions, and the octal digit 2 (binary 010) specifies that the SGID bit is to be set. When the SGID bit is set, the execute bit for the group is set to 's' if the group already has the 'execute' permission; otherwise, it is set to 'S'. The following session illustrates the use of these command syntaxes. The command chmod 2751 cp.new sets the SGID bit for the cp.new file and sets its access privileges to 751 (rwxr-x--x). The rest of the commands are similar to those in Section 8.6.1.

```
$ ls -l cp.new
-rwxr-x--x    1   sarwar   faculty   12   May 08 20:00     cp.new
$ chmod 2751 cp.new
$ ls -l cp.new
-rwxr-s--x    1   sarwar   faculty   12   May 08 20:00     cp.new
$ chmod g-s cp.new
$ chmod g-x cp.new
$ ls -l cp.new
-rwxr----x    1   sarwar   faculty   12   May 08 20:00     cp.new
$ chmod g+s cp.new
```

```
$ ls -l cp.new
-rwxr-S--x   1   sarwar   faculty   12   May 08 20:00    cp.new
$
```

You can set or reset the SUID and SGID bits by using a single chmod command. Thus, the command chmod ug+s cp.new can be used to perform this task on the cp.new file. You can also set the SUID and SGID bits along with the access permissions bits (read, write, and execute) by preceding the octal number for access privileges by 6 because the left-most octal digit 6 (110) specifies that both the SUID and SGID bits be set. Thus, the command chmod 6754 cp.new sets the SUID and SGID bits for the cp.new file and its access privileges to 750.

8.6.3 The Sticky Bit

The last of the 12 access bits, the sticky bit, can be set for a directory to ensure that an unprivileged user cannot remove or rename files of other users in that directory. You must be the owner of a directory or have appropriate permissions to set the sticky bit for it. It is commonly set for shared directories that contain files owned by several users. Some systems do not allow non-superusers to set the sticky bit.

Originally, this bit was designed to inform the kernel that the code segment of a program is to be shared or kept in the main memory or the swap space owing to frequent use of the program. Thus, when this bit is set for a program, the system tries to keep the executable code for the program (process) in memory after it finishes execution—the processes literally "stick around" in the memory. If, for some reason, memory space occupied by this program is needed by the system for loading another program, the program with the sticky bit on is saved in the **swap space** (a special area on the disk used to save processes temporarily). That is, if the sticky bit is set for a program, the program is either kept in memory or on the swap space after it finishes its execution. When this program is executed again, with the program code in memory, program execution starts right away. If the program code is on the swap space, the time needed for loading it is much shorter than if it were stored on disk as a UNIX file. The advantage of this scheme, therefore, is that, if a program with the sticky bit on is executed frequently, it is executed much faster.

This facility is useful for programs such as compilers, assemblers, and editors and commands such as ls and cat, which are frequently used in a typical computer system environment. However, care must be taken that not too many programs have this bit set. Otherwise, system performance will suffer because of lack of free space, with more and more space being used by the programs whose sticky bit is set. This historical use of the sticky bit is no longer needed in newer UNIX systems (starting with 4.4BSD) because virtual memory systems use page replacement algorithms that do not remove recently used program pages/segments.

The sticky bit can be set by using either of the following command syntaxes.

SYNTAX

chmod 1xxx file-list
chmod +t file-list

Here, 'xxx' is the octal number specifying the read, write, and execute permissions, and the octal digit 1 (binary 001) specifies that the sticky bit is to be set. When the sticky bit is set, the execute bit for 'others' is set to 't' if 'others' already has execute permission; otherwise, it is set to 'T'. The following session illustrates the use of these command syntaxes. The chmod 1751 cp.new command sets the sticky bit for the cp.new file and sets its access privileges to 751. The rest of the command lines are similar to those explained in Sections 8.6.1 and 8.6.2 and need not be explained in more detail here.

```
$ chmod 1751 cp.new
$ ls -l cp.new
-rwxr-x--t   1   sarwar   faculty   12   May 08 20:00   cp.new
$ chmod -t cp.new
$ ls -l cp.new
-rwxr-x--x   1   sarwar   faculty   12   May 08 20:00   cp.new
$ chmod 750 cp.new
$ chmod +t cp.new
$ ls -l cp.new
-rwsr-x--T   1   sarwar   faculty   12   May 08 20:00   cp.new
$
```

Summary

A time-sharing system has to ensure protection of one user's files from unauthorized (accidental or malicious) access by other users of the system. UNIX provides several mechanisms for this purpose, including one based on access permissions. Files can be protected by informing the system what type of operations (read, write, and execute) are permitted on the file by the owner, group (the users who are in the same group as the owner), and others (everyone else on the system). UNIX allows a user to be part of multiple groups. Only the system administrator (also known as the superuser in UNIX jargon) can add you to a group or take you off a group. You can display the groups you (or any user) are a member of by using the groups command. These nine commonly used access permissions are represented by bits. This information is stored in the inode of the file. When a user tries to access a file, the system allows or disallows access based on the file's access privileges stored in the inode.

Access permissions for files can be viewed by using the ls -l command. When used with directories, this command displays attributes for all the files in the directories. The ls -ld command can be used to view access permissions for directories. The owner of a file can change access privileges on it by using the chmod command. The umask command, which is usually placed in the ~/.profile file (for System V) or the ~/.login file (for BSD), allows the user to specify a bit mask that informs the system of access permissions that are disabled for the user, group, and others. When a file is created by the UNIX system, it sets access

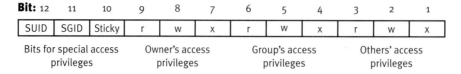

Figure 8.2 Position of access privilege bits for UNIX files as specified in the chmod command

permissions for the file according to the specification given in the umask command. In a typical system, the access permissions for a new file are set to (777 2 mask).

UNIX also allows three additional bits—the set-user-ID (SUID), set-group-ID (SGID), and sticky bits—to be set. The SUID and SGID bits allow the user to execute commands such as passwd, ls, mkdir, and ps that access important system resources to which access is not allowed otherwise. The sticky bit can be set for a directory to ensure that an unprivileged user cannot remove or rename files of other users in that directory. Only the owner of a directory, or someone else having appropriate permissions, can set the sticky bit for the directory. It is commonly set for shared directories that contain files owned by several users. Historically, the sticky bit has served another purpose. It can be set for frequently used utilities so that UNIX keeps them in the main memory or on a fixed area on the disk, called the swap space, after their use. This feature makes subsequent access to these files much faster than if they were to be loaded from the disk as normal files.

The final format of the 12 access permissions bits, as used in the chmod command, is shown in Figure 8.2.

Problems

1. What are the three basic file protection schemes available in UNIX?

2. List all possible two-letter passwords comprising digits and punctuation letters.

3. If a computer system allows six-character passwords comprising a random combination of decimal digits and punctuation marks, what is the maximum number of passwords that a user will have to try with the brute force method of breaking into a user's account? Why?

4. What is the maximum number of passwords that can be formed if a system allows digits, uppercase and lowercase letters, and punctuation marks to be used? Assume that passwords must be 12 characters long.

5. Suppose that a hacker is trying to guess a password—consisting of eight characters—using uppercase, lowercase, and digits. Further, suppose that the system forces a five-second delay after each password guess. How long will it take the hacker to guess the password in the worst-case analysis? Why? Show all your work.

6. How does file protection based on access permissions work? Base your answer on various types of users of a file and the types of operations they can perform. How many permission bits are needed to implement this scheme? Why?

7. How do the read, write, and execute permissions work in UNIX? Illustrate your answer with some examples.

8. How many user groups exist on your system? How did you get your answer? What groups are you a member of and what is your default group? How many groups is root a member of, on your system? How did you obtain your answer? If used any commands, show the commands and their outputs.

9. Create a file test1 in your present working directory and set its access privileges to read and write for yourself, read for the users in your group, and none to everyone else. What command did you use to set privileges? Give another command that would accomplish the same thing.

10. The user 'sarwar' sets access permissions to his home directory by using the command chmod 700 $HOME. If the file cp.new in his home directory has read permissions to 777, can anyone read this file? Why or why not? Explain your answer.

11. What is the effect of each command? Explain your answers.

    a. chmod 776 ~/lab5

    b. chmod 751 ~/lab?

    c. chmod 511 *.c

    d. chmod 711 ~/*

    e. ls -l

    f. ls -ld

    g. ls -l ~/personal

    h. ls -ld ~/personal

12. What does the execute permission mean for a directory, a file type for which the execute operation makes no sense?

13. Create a file dir1 in your home directory and use cp /etc/passwd dir1/mypasswd command to copy the /etc/passwd file in it. Use the chmod command to have only the search permission on for it and execute the following commands. What is the results of executing these commands? Do the results make sense to you? Explain.

    a. cd dir1

    b. ls

    c. rm dir1/mypasswd

    d. cp /etc/passwd dir1

14. What umask command should be executed to set the permissions bit mask to 037? With this mask, what default access privileges are associated with any new file that you create on the system? Why? Where would you put this command so that every time you log on to the system this mask is effective?

15. Give a command line for setting the default access mode so that you have read, write, and execute privileges, your group has read and execute permissions, and all others have no permission for a newly created executable file or directory. How would you test it to be sure that it works correctly?

16. Give `chmod` command lines that perform the same tasks that the `mesg n` and `mesg y` commands do. (*Hint:* Every hardware device, including your terminal, has an associated file in the /dev directory.)

17. What are the purposes of the set-user-ID (SUID), set-group-ID (SGID), and sticky bits?

18. Give one command line for setting all three special access bits (SUID, SGID, and sticky) for the file `cp.new`. (*Hint:* Use the octal mode.)

19. In a UNIX system, the `cat` command is owned by root and has its SUID bit set. Do you see any problems with this setup? Explain your answer.

20. Some UNIX systems do not allow users to change their passwords with the `passwd` command. How is this restriction enforced? Is it a good or bad practice? Why?

Basic File Processing

Objectives

- To discuss how to display contents of a file
- To explain copying, appending, moving/renaming, and removing/deleting files
- To describe how to determine the size of a file
- To discuss commands for comparing files
- To describe how to combine files
- To discuss printer control commands
- To cover the commands and primitives
  `>`, `>>`, `^`, `~`, `[ ]`, `*`, `?`, `cancel`, `cat`,
  `cp`, `diff`, `head`, `lp`, `lpc`, `lpq`, `lpr`,
  `lprm`, `lpstat`, `lptest`, `less`, `ls`, `more`,
  `mv`, `nl`, `pg`, `pr`, `rm`, `tail`, `uniq`, `wc`

9.1   Introduction

This chapter describes how some basic file operations can be performed in UNIX. These operations are primarily for nondirectory files, although some are applicable to directories as well. (We previously discussed the most commonly used directory operations in Chapter 7.) When discussing these operations, we also describe related commands and give examples to illustrate how these commands can be used to perform the needed operations. Remember, complete information on a particular command is available via the man command.

9.2   Viewing Contents of Text Files

Files are viewed to identify their contents. Several UNIX commands can be used to view contents of text files on the display screen. These commands differ from each other in terms of the amount of the file displayed, the portion of file contents displayed (initial, middle, or last part of the file), and whether the file's contents are displayed one screen or one page at a time. Recall that you can view only those files for which you have read permission. In addition, you must have search (execute) permissions for all the directories involved in the pathname of the file to be displayed. Viewing does not mean edit, write, or update—just view.

9.2.1 Viewing Complete Files

You can display the complete contents of one or more files on-screen by using the cat command. However, because the command does not display file contents a screen or page at a time, you see only the last page of a file that is larger than one page in size. The following is a brief description of the cat command.

---

cat [options] [file-list]

Purpose:	Concatenate/display the files in 'file-list' on standard output (screen by default)
Output:	Contents of the files in 'file-list' displayed on the screen, one file at a time

Commonly used options/features:

−e	Display $ at the end of each line; works in conjunction with the −v option
−n	Put line numbers with the displayed lines
−t	Display tabs as ^I's and formfeeds as ^L's
−v	Display nonprintable characters, except for the tab, formfeed, and newline characters

(margin label: SYNTAX)

Here, 'file-list' is an optional argument that consists of pathnames for one or more files, separated by spaces. For example, the following command displays the contents of the student _records file in the present working directory. If the file is larger than one page, the file contents quickly scroll off the display screen.

```
$ cat student_records
```

John	Doe	ECE	3.54
Pam	Meyer	CS	3.61
Jim	Davis	CS	2.71
Jason	Kim	ECE	3.97
Amy	Nash	ECE	2.38

```
$
```

The following command displays the contents of files lab1 and lab2 in the directory ~/courses/ee446/labs. The command does not pause after displaying the contents of lab1.

```
$ cat ~/courses/ee446/labs/lab1 ~/courses/ee446/labs/lab2
[ contents of lab1 and lab2 ]
$
```

As discussed in Chapter 4, shell metacharacters can be used to specify file names. The contents of all the files in the current directory can be displayed by using the `cat *` command. The `cat exam?` command displays all the files in the current directory starting with the string exam and followed by one character. The contents of all the files in the current directory starting with the string lab can be displayed by using the `cat lab*` command.

As indicated by the command syntax, the file-list is an optional argument. Thus, when the `cat` command is used without any arguments, it takes input from standard input one line at a time and sends it to standard output. Recall that, by default, standard input for a command is the keyboard, and standard output is the display screen. Therefore, when the `cat` command is executed without an argument, it takes input from the keyboard and displays it on the screen one line at a time. The command terminates when the user presses <Ctrl-D> or <^D>, the UNIX eof, on a new line. Again, the boldface text is typed by the user.

```
$ cat
This is a test.
This is a test.
In this example, the cat command will take input from stdin (keyboard)
In this example, the cat command will take input from stdin (keyboard)
stdout (screen). So, this is not how this command is normally used.
stdout (screen). So, this is not how this command is normally used.
It is commonly used to display the one line at a time and send it to
It is commonly used to display the one line at a time and send it to
contents of a user file on the screen.
contents of a user file on the screen.
<Ctrl-D>
$
```

At times, you will need to view a file that has line numbers. You typically need to do so when, during the software development phase, a compilation of your source code results in compiler errors having line numbers associated with them. The UNIX utility `nl` allows you to display files having line numbers. Thus, the `nl student_records` command displays the lines in the student_records file with line numbers, as shown in the following session. The same task can also be performed by using the `cat -n student_records` command.

```
$ nl student_records
     1    John      Doe       ECE     3.54
     2    Pam       Meyer     CS      3.61
     3    Jim       Davis     CS      2.71
     4    Jason     Kim       ECE     3.97
     5    Amy       Nash      ECE     2.38
$
```

Also, if you need to display files with a time stamp and page numbers, you can use the `pr` utility. It displays file contents as the `cat` command does, but it also partitions the file into pages and inserts a header for each page. The page header contains today's date, current time, file name, and page number. The `pr` command, like the `cat` command, can display multiple files, one after the other. The following session illustrates a simple use of the `pr` command.

```
$ pr student_records
May 26 12:34 1999    student_records Page 1
John         Doe         ECE        3.54
Pam          Meyer       CS         3.61
Jim          Davis       CS         2.71
Jason        Kim         ECE        3.97
Amy          Nash        ECE        2.38
$
```

You can print files with line numbers and a page header by connecting the `nl`, `pr`, and `lp` (or `lpr`) commands. This method is discussed in Chapter 12.

9.2.2 Viewing Files One Page at a Time

If the file to be viewed is larger than one page, you can use the `more` command, also known as the UNIX pager, to display the file a screenful at a time. The following is a brief description of the command.

SYNTAX

more [options] [file-list]

Purpose: Concatenate/display the files in 'file-list' on standard output a screenful at a time

(continued)

> **_more [options] [file-list]_** _(continued)_
>
> **Output:**   Contents of the files in 'file-list' displayed on the screen one page at a time
>
> **Commonly used options/features:**
>
>   **+ /** _str_   Start two lines before the first line containing _str_
>
>   **−n**N   Display _N_ lines per screen/page
>
>   **+N**   Start displaying the contents of the file at line number _N_

When run without 'file-list', the `more` command, like the `cat` command, takes input from the keyboard one line at a time and sends it to the display screen. If a 'file-list' is given as an argument, the command displays the contents of the files in 'file-list' one screen at a time. To display the next screen, press the `<space bar>`. To display the next line in the file, press `<Enter>`. At the bottom left of a screen, the command displays the percentage of the file that has been displayed up to that point. To return to the shell, press the `<Q>` key.

The following command displays the sample file in the present working directory a screenful at a time. Running this command is equivalent to running the `cat sample | more` command. We discuss the | operator, known as the pipe operator, in detail in Chapter 12.

```
$ more sample
[contents of sample]
$
```

The following command displays contents of the files sample, letter, and memo in the present working directory a screenful at a time. The files are displayed in the order they occur in the command.

```
$ more sample letter memo
[contents of sample, letter, and memo]
$
```

The following command displays the contents of the file param.h in the directory /usr/include/sys one page at a time with 20 lines per page.

```
$ more -n20 /usr/include/sys/param.h
[contents of /usr/include/sys/param.h]
$
```

The following command displays, one page at a time, the contents of all the files in the present working directory that have the .c extension (files containing C source codes).

```
$ more ./*.c
[contents of all .c files in the current directory]
$
```

The less command can also be used to view a file page by page. It is similar to the more command but is more efficient and has many features that are not available in more. It has support for many of the vi command mode commands. For example, it allows forward and backward movement of file contents one or more lines at a time, redisplaying the screen, and forward and backward string search. It also starts displaying a file without reading all of the file, which makes it more efficient than the more command or the vi editor for large files.

9.2.3 Viewing the Head or Tail of a File

Having the ability to view the head (some lines from the beginning) or tail (some lines from the end) of a file is useful in identifying the type of data stored in the file. For example, the head operation can be used to identify a PostScript file or a uuencoded file, which have special headers, and the tail information could be used to inspect status information at the end of a log file or error file. (We discuss encoding and decoding of files in Chapter 10.) The UNIX commands for displaying the beginning lines or ending lines of a file are head and tail. The following is a brief description of the head command.

S Y N T A X	**head [option] [file-list]**
	Purpose: Display the beginning portions (head) of files in 'file-list'; the default head size is 10 lines
	Output: Heads of the files in 'file-list' displayed on the display screen
	Commonly used options/features:
	−N Display first *N* lines

Without any option and the 'file-list' argument, the command takes input from standard input (the keyboard by default). The following session illustrates use of the head command. The cat sample command is used to display the contents of the sample file. The head sample command displays the first 10 lines of the sample file. The head −5 sample command displays the first 5 lines of sample.

```
$ cat sample
Ann
Ben
Chen
David
Eto
Fahim
George
Hamid
Ira
```

```
Jamal
Ken
Lisa
Mike
Nadeem
Oram
Paul
Queen
Rashid
Srini
Tang
Ursula
Vinny
Wang
X Window System
Yen
Zen
$ head sample
Ann
Ben
Chen
David
Erik
Fahim
George
Hamid
Ira
Jamal
$ head -5 sample
Ann
Ben
Chen
David
Erik
$
```

You can display heads of multiple files by specifying them as arguments of the head command. For example, the `head sample memo1 phones` command displays the first 10 lines each of the sample, memo1, and phones files.

The following command, which displays the first 10 lines of the file otto, shows that the file is a PostScript file. The output of the command gives additional information about the file, including the name of the software used to create it, the total number of pages in the file, and the page orientation. All of this information is important to know before the file is printed.

```
$ head otto
%!PS-Adobe-3.0
%%BoundingBox: 54 72 558 720
%%Creator: Mozilla (NetScape) HTML->PS
%%DocumentData: Clean7Bit
%%Orientation: Portrait
%%Pages: 1
%%PageOrder: Ascend
%%Title: Otto Doggie
%%EndComments
%%BeginProlog
$
```

Similarly, the following command shows that data is a **uuencoded file** and that, when uudecoded (see Chapter 10), the original file will be stored in the file data.99.

```
$ head -4 data
begin 600 data.99
M.0I$3T4L($3IO092!#.B`@,#%`P.3`3H@00T4Z("``@("`"!!34C8@9&]E,4!S
M;;6EEL92YC;VT;(#44,RX,,,R,H@R,M,3(`S+C,`.@@0@ST-C,MC-S,SMS
M4WEE93"!-.C`P,,,`33455442.Z(Z<V\=V%R0'5P+F=D=3=:3##,/7,,3%A#$R
$
```

The tail command is used to display the last portion (tail) of one or more files. It is useful to ascertain, for example, that a PostScript file has a proper end or that a uuencoded file has the required end on the last line. The following is a brief description of the command.

---

tail [options] [file-list]

Purpose:	Display the last portions (heads) of the files in 'file-list'; the default tail size is 10 lines
Output:	Tails of the files in 'file-list' displayed on the monitor screen

Commonly used options/features:

−f	Follow growth of the file after displaying the last line of a file, and display lines as they are appended to the file—this option is terminated by pressing <Ctrl-C>

(continued)

tail [options] [file-list] (continued)	
±n	Start *n* lines from the beginning of the file for +*n*, and n lines before the end of file or *n* units before the end of file for −*n*; by default, −*n* is −10
−r	Display lines in reverse order (last line first)

Like the head command, the `tail` command takes input from standard input if no 'file-list' is given as argument. The following session illustrates how the `tail` command can be used with and without options. We use the same sample file that we used for the head command. The `tail sample` command displays the last 10 lines (the default tail size) of the sample file, and the `tail -5 sample` displays the last five lines of the sample file. The `tail +12 sample` command displays the tail of the file starting with line number 12. Finally, the `tail -5r sample` command displays the last five lines of the sample file in reverse order.

```
$ tail sample
Queen
Rashid
Srini
Tang
Ursula
Vinny
Wang
X-Window-System
Yen
Zen
$ tail -5 sample
Vinny
Wang
X-Window-System
Yen
Zen
$ tail +12 sample
Lisa
Mike
Nadeem
Oram
Paul
Queen
Rashid
Srini
```

```
Tang
Ursula
Vinny
Wang
X Window System
Yen
Zen
$ tail -5r sample
Zen
Yen
X Window System
Wang
Vinny
$
```

The first command displays the last 10 lines of sample, and the second command displays the last five lines of sample. The third command displays all the lines in the sample file, starting with the eighth line. The last command displays the last five lines in reverse order (the last line of the file is the first displayed).

The following commands show that files otto and data have proper PostScript and uuencoded tails.

```
$ tail -5 otto
8 f3
( ) show
pagelevel restore
showpage
%%EOF
$
$ tail data
M;W4@:&%V9OIN;WO@=')I960@;W5T(&9O<B!L;;VYG('1I;64N("!(;;W=E=F5R
M+"!T;R!B92!S=6-C97-S9G5L+"!Y;;W4@;75S="!T<@I(96QL;;RP@5V]R;&0A
"(OH`
`
end
$
```

The -f option of the tail command is very useful if you need to see the tail of a file that is growing. This situation occurs quite often when you run a simulation program that takes a long time to finish (several minutes, hours, or days) and you want to see the data produced by the program as it is generated. It is convenient to do so if your UNIX system runs X Window System (see Chapter 21). In an X environment, you can run the `tail` command in an xterm (a console window) to monitor the newly generated data as it is generated and keep doing your other work concurrently. The following command displays the last 10 lines of the sim.data file and displays new lines as they are appended to the file. The command can be terminated by pressing `<Ctrl-C>`.

```
$ tail -f sim.data
... last 10 lines of sim.data ...
... more data as it is appended to sim.data ...
```

In the following In-Chapter Exercises, you are asked to use the `cat`, `head`, `more`, `pr`, and `tail` commands for displaying different parts of text files, with and without page titles and numbers.

IN-CHAPTER EXERCISES

9.1   Insert the student_records file used in Section 9.2.1 in your current directory. Add to it 10 more students' records. Display the contents of this file by using the `cat student_records` and `cat -n student_records` commands. What is the difference between the outputs of the two commands?

9.2   Display the student_records file by using the `more` and `pr` commands. What command lines did you use?

9.3   Display the /etc/passwd file two lines before the line that contains your login name. What command line did you use?

9.4   Give commands for displaying the first and last seven lines of the student_records file.

9.3   Copying, Moving, and Removing Files

In this section, we describe commands for performing copy, as well as move/rename and remove/delete operations on files in a file structure. The commands discussed are `cp`, `mv`, and `rm`.

9.3.1 Copying Files

The UNIX command for copying files is `cp`. The following is a brief description of the command.

cp [options] file1 file2	
Purpose:	Copy 'file1' to 'file2'; if 'file2' is a directory, make a copy of 'file1' in this directory

(continued)

SYNTAX

---

cp [options] file1 file2 *(continued)*

Commonly used options/features:

−f	Force copying if there is no write permission on the destination file
−i	If the destination exists, prompt before overwriting
−p	Preserve file attributes such owner ID, group ID, permissions, and modification times
−r	Recursively copy files and subdirectories

You must have permission to read the source file ('file1') and permission to execute (search) the directories that contain 'file1' and 'file2'. In addition, you must have write permission for the directory that contains 'file2' if it does not already exist. If 'file2' exists, you don't need the write permission to the directory that contains it, but you must have the write permission to 'file2'. If the destination file ('file2') exists by default, it will be overwritten without informing you if you have permission to write to the file. To be prompted before an existing file is overwritten, you need to use the −i option. If you do not have permission to write to the destination file, you will be informed of this. If you do not have permission to read the source file, an error message will appear on your screen.

The following command line makes a copy of temp in temp.bak. The ls commands show the state of the current directory before and after execution of the cp command. Figure 9.1 shows the same information in pictorial form.

```
$ ls
memo    sample   temp
$ cp temp temp.bak
$ ls
memo    sample   temp    temp.bak
$
```

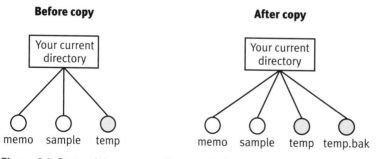

Figure 9.1 State of the current directory before and after the temp file is copied into temp.bak

The command returns an error message if temp does not exist or if it exists but you do not have permission to read from it. The command also returns an error message if temp.bak exists and you do not have permission to write to it. The following session illustrates these points. The first error message is reported because the letter file does not exist in the current directory. The second error message is reported because you do not have permission to read the sample file. The last command reports an error message because temp.bak exists and you do not have write permission for it. You can override the absence of write permission and force copying by using the –f option, as shown in the next command. The ls –l memo temp.bak command is used to show that the copying has actually taken place (i.e., the data has been copied), but access privileges for the file have not changed and the time stamp for the file is the current time. If you want to copy both the data and attributes of the source file, you need to use the cp command with –f and –p options, as in the last cp command that follows. The last ls –l memo temp.bak command is used to show that both data and file attributes such as the time stamp have been copied.

```
$ ls -l
-rwxr-----  1  sarwar  faculty  371  Nov  17  21:57 memo
--wxr-----  1  sarwar  faculty  164  Nov  17  22:22 sample
-r-xr-----  1  sarwar  faculty  792  Nov  17  10:57 temp
-r-xr-----  1  sarwar  faculty  792  Nov  17  23:01 temp.bak
$ cp letter letter.bak
cp: cannot access letter
$ cp sample sample.new
cp: cannot open sample: Permission denied
$ cp memo temp.bak
cp: cannot create temp.bak: Permission denied
$ cp -f memo temp.bak
$ ls -l memo temp.bak
-rwxr-----  1  sarwar  faculty  371  Nov  17  21:57 memo
-r-xr-----  1  sarwar  faculty  371  Dec  14  12:33 temp.bak
$ cp -fp memo temp.bak
$ ls -l memo temp.bak
-rwxr-----  1  sarwar  faculty  371  Nov  17  21:57 memo
-rwxr-----  1  sarwar  faculty  371  Nov  17  21:57 temp.bak
$
```

The following command makes a copy of the .profile file in your home directory and puts it in the .profile.old file in the sys.backups subdirectory (also in your home directory). This command works regardless of the directory you are in when you run the command because the pathname starts with your home directory. You should execute this command before changing your run-time environment (as specified in the ~/.profile file) so that you have a backup copy of the previous working environment in case something goes wrong when you set up the new environment. The command produces an error message if ~/.profile does not exist, if you do not have permission to read it, if the ~/sys.backups directory does not exist or you do not have execute (search) and write permissions for it, or if .profile.back exists but you do not have permission to read it.

```
$ cp ~/.profile ~/sys.backups/.profile.bak
$
```

The following command copies all the files in the current directory, starting with the string lab to the directory ~/courses/ee446/backups. The command also prompts you for overwriting if any of the source files already exist in the backups directory. In this case (in which multiple files are being copied), if backups is not a directory, or if it does not exist, an error message is displayed on the screen informing you that the target must be a directory.

```
$ cp -i lab* ~/courses/ee446/backups
$
```

If you want to copy a complete directory to another directory, you need to use the cp command with the -r option. This option recursively copies files and subdirectories from the source directory to the destination directory. It is a useful option that you can use to create backups of important directories periodically. Thus, the following command recursively copies the ~/courses directory to the ~/backups directory.

```
$ cp -r ~/courses ~/backups
$
```

9.3.2 Moving Files

Files can be moved from one directory in a file structure to another. This operation in UNIX can result in simply renaming a file if it is on the same file system. The renaming operation is equivalent to creating a hard link (*see* Chapter 11) to the file, followed by removing/deleting (*see* Section 9.3.3) the original file. If the source and destination files are on different file systems, the move operation results in a physical copy of the source file to the destination, followed by removal of the source file. A **filesystem** is a directory hierarchy with its own root stored on a disk or disk partition, mounted under (glued to) a directory. The files and directories in the filesystem are accessed through the directory under which they are mounted. The command for moving files is mv. The following is a brief description of the command.

SYNTAX

mv [options] file1 file2
mv [options] file-list directory

Purpose: First syntax: Move 'file1' to 'file2' or rename 'file1' as 'file2'

Second syntax: Move all the files in 'file-list' to 'directory'

(continued)

mv [options] file1 file2, mv [options] file-list directory (continued)

Commonly used options/features:

    −f   Force move regardless of the permissions of the destination file

    −i   Prompt the users before overwriting the destination

You must have write and execute access permissions to the directory that contains the existing file ('file1' in the description), but you do not need read, write, or execute permission to the file itself. Similarly, you must have write and execute access permissions to the directory that contains the target file ('file2' in the description), execute permission for every directory in the pathname for 'file2', and write permission to the file if it already exists. If the destination file exists, by default it is overwritten without informing you. If you used the −i option, you are prompted before the destination file is overwritten.

The following command moves temp to temp.moved. In this case, the temp file is renamed temp.moved. The mv command returns an error message if temp does not exist, or if you do not have write or execute permission for the directory it is in. The command prompts you for moving the file if temp.bak already exists, but you do not have write permission for it.

```
$ mv temp temp.moved
$
```

The following command moves temp to the backups directory as the temp.old file. Figure 9.2 shows the state of your current directory before and after the temp file is moved.

```
$ mv temp backups/temp.old
$
```

The following command is a sure move; you can use it to force the move, regardless of the permissions for the target file–temp.moved in this case.

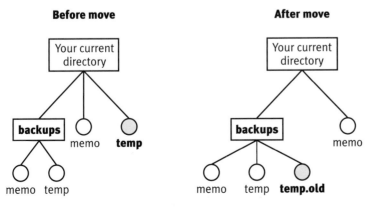

Figure 9.2 Current directory before and after the mv temp backups/temp.old command

```
$ mv -f temp temp.moved
$
```

The following command moves all the files and directories (excluding hidden files) in dir1 to the dir2 directory. The command fails, and an error message appears on your screen if dir2 is not a directory, if it does not exist, or if you do not have write and execute permissions for it.

```
$ mv dir1/* dir2
$
```

After the command is executed, dir1 contains hidden files only; the ls -a command can be used to confirm this status.

9.3.3 Removing/Deleting Files

When files are not needed anymore, they should be removed from a file structure to free up some disk space to be reused for new files and directories. The UNIX command for removing (deleting) files is rm. The following is a brief description of the command.

---

rm [options] file-list

Purpose: Remove files in 'file-list' from the file structure (and disk)

Commonly used options/features:

   −f   Force remove regardless of the permissions for 'file-list'

   −i   Prompt the user before removing the files in 'file-list'

   −r   Recursively remove the files in the directory, which is passed as an argument; this removes everything under the directory, so be sure you want to do so before using this option

---

If files in 'file-list' are pathnames, you need the execute permission for all the directory components in the pathnames and write and execute permissions for the last directory (that contains the file or files to be deleted), but you do not need to have read or write permission to the files themselves. If you run the command from a terminal and do not have the write permission for the file to be removed, the command displays your access permissions for the file and prompts you for an action.

The following command lines illustrate use of the rm command to remove one or more files from various directories.

```
$ rm temp
$ rm temp backups/temp.old
$ rm -f phones grades ~/letters/letter.john
$ rm ~/dir1/*
$
```

The first command removes temp from the current directory. The second command removes the temp file from the current directory and the temp.old file from the backups directory. Figure 9.3 shows the semantics of this command. The third command removes the files phones grades and ~/letters/letter.john regardless, of their access permissions. The fourth command removes all the files from ~/dir1 directory; the directories are not removed.

Now, consider the following commands that use some shell metacharacter features.

```
$ rm [kK]*.prn
$ rm [a-kA-Z]*.prn
$
```

The first command removes all the files in current directory that have the .prn extension and names starting with k or K. The second command removes all the files in the current directory that have the .prn extension and names starting with a lowercase letter from a through k or an uppercase letter.

In Chapter 7, we talked about removing directories and showed that the `rmdir` command can be used to remove only the empty directories. The rm command with the **-r** option can be used to remove nonempty directories recursively. Thus, the following command recursively removes the OldDirectory in your home directory. This command prompts you if you do not have the permission to remove a file. If you do not want the system to prompt you and you want to force remove the ~/OldDirectory recursively, then use the `rm -rf ~/Old-Directory` command. This command is one of the commands that you must never execute unless you really know its potentially catastrophic consequences–the loss of all the files and directories in a complete directory hierarchy. But the command is quite useful if you want to free up some disk space.

```
$ rm -r ~/OldDirectory
$
```

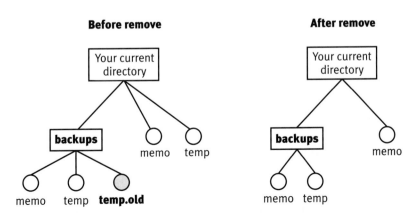

Figure 9.3 Current directory before and after execution of `rm temp backups/temp.old`

You should generally combine the -i and -r options to remove a directory (~/OldDirectory in this case) recursively, as shown in the following command. The -i option is for interactive removal, and when you use this option, the rm command prompts you before removing a file. This way you can ensure that you do not remove an important file by mistake.

```
$ rm -ir ~/OldDirectory
rm: examine files in directory /home/sarwar/OldDirectory (y/n)? y
rm: remove /home/sarwar/OldDirectory/John.11.14.2002 (y/n)? y
rm: remove /home/sarwar/OldDirectory/Tom.2.24.2001 (y/n)?
...
$
```

9.3.4 Determining File Size

You can determine the size of a file by using one of several UNIX commands. The two commands commonly used for this purpose (and are available in all UNIX versions) are ls -l and wc. We described the ls -l command in Chapter 8, where we used it to determine the access permissions for files. We revisit this command here in the context of determining file size.

As we mentioned before, the ls -l command displays a long list of the files and directories in the directory (or directories) specified as its argument. You must have read and execute permissions for a directory to be able to run the ls command on it successfully; no permissions are needed on the files in the directory to be able to see the list. The command gives output for the current directory if none is specified as an argument. The output of this command has nine fields, and the fifth field gives file sizes in bytes (*see* Section 8.5). In the following command, the size of the lab2 file is 163 bytes.

```
$ ls -l lab2
-r-xr--r--  1   sarwar    faculty    163   May 16 23:46  lab2
$
```

This command also displays the size of directory files. You can also use it to get the sizes of multiple files by specifying them in the command line and separating them by spaces. For example, the following command displays long lists for files lab1 and lab2.

```
$ ls -l lab1 lab2
-r-xr--r--  1   sarwar    faculty    163   May 16 23:46  lab1
-r-xr--r--  1   sarwar    faculty    709   Apr 23 11:15  lab2
$
```

The following command uses the shell metacharacter * to display long lists for all the files in the ~/courses/ee446 directory.

```
$ ls -l ~/courses/ee446/*
... output of the command ...
$
```

Whereas `ls -l` is a general purpose command that can be used to determine most of the attributes of one or more files, including their sizes in bytes/characters, `wc` is a special purpose command that displays only file sizes. The following is a brief description of the `wc` command.

wc [options] file-list

Purpose: Display sizes of the files in 'file-list' as number lines, words, and characters

Commonly used options/features:

−c	Display only the number of characters
−1	Display only the number of lines
−w	Display only the number of words

The output of the command for every file is a line with four fields: line count, word count, character count, and file name. The command does not work with directories on all UNIX systems. On systems where it does work, its output is based on the `cat` command with the directory as the argument. The following session illustrates use of this command.

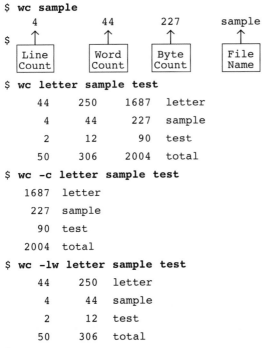

```
$ wc sample
      4        44       227     sample
$
```

```
$ wc letter sample test
     44       250      1687    letter
      4        44       227    sample
      2        12        90    test
     50       306      2004    total
$ wc -c letter sample test
   1687    letter
    227    sample
     90    test
   2004    total
$ wc -lw letter sample test
     44       250    letter
      4        44    sample
      2        12    test
     50       306    total
$
```

The first command displays the number of lines, words, and characters in the file sample in the present working directory. The size of sample is 4 lines, 44 words, and 227 bytes. The second command displays the same information for the files letter, sample, and test in the present working directory. The last line in the output of this command also displays the total for all three files. The third command displays the number of characters in letter, sample, and test. The last command shows that multiple options can be used in a single command; in this case, the output is the number of words and letters for the three files in the command line.

As previously stated, on some systems the wc command cannot be used to display the size of a directory and returns an error message when used with a directory argument, as in,

```
$ wc /etc/uucp
wc: /etc/uucp: Is a directory
            0    0       0 /etc/uucp
$
```

On some UNIX systems, such as SunOS 5.8, it does show nonzero output without the error message, as shown in the following session. The output of the wc /etc command, as shown in the second command that follows, is the size of the output of the cat /etc command and does not mean much. (UNIX pipes are discussed in detail in Chapter 12.)

```
$ wc /etc
          15    187     4096 /etc
$ cat /etc | wc
          15    187     4096
$
```

The wc command can be used with shell metacharacters such as * and ?. The following command displays sizes of all the files in the directory /usr/include/sys.

```
$ wc /usr/include/sys/*
97 420 2641 /usr/include/sys/acct.h
93 341 2181 /usr/include/sys/acctctl.h
97 394 2616 /usr/include/sys/acl.h
...
$
```

9.4 Appending to Files

Appending to a file means putting new data at the end of the contents of the file. If the file does not exist, it is created to contain the new data. The append operation is useful when an application or a user needs to augment a file by adding data to it. The following command syntax is used to append one or more files, or keyboard input, at the end of a file.

SYNTAX

cat [file-list] >> destination-file

Purpose:　　　Append the contents of the files in 'file-list' at the end of 'destination-file'

The >> operator is the UNIX append operator. We discuss the >>, <, and > operators in detail in Chapter 12. That chapter describes how input of your commands can be read as input from a file instead of the keyboard and how output and error messages of your commands can be redirected from the terminal (or console widow) to files. In this chapter, we use these operators only to describe how you can append new data at the end of the current contents of a file and how you can combine the contents of multiple files and put them in one file.

The following session illustrates how the append operation works. The `cat sample >> temp` command appends the contents of sample at the end of temp. The `cat` commands before and after this command show the contents of the files involved. The command syntax can be used to append multiple files to a file, as shown in the command `cat memo1 memo2 memo3 >> memos.record`. This command appends the contents of the memo1, memo2, and memo3 files at the end of the memos.record file.

```
$ cat temp
This is a simple file used to illustrate the working of append operation.
The new data will be appended right below this line.
$ cat sample
These are the new data that will be appended at the end of the test file.
$ cat sample >> temp
$ cat temp
This is a simple file used to illustrate the working of append operation.
The new data will be appended right below this line.
These are the new data that will be appended at the end of the test file.
$ cat memo1 memo2 memo3 >> memos.record
$
```

Without the optional 'file-list' argument (*see* the command description), the command can be used to append keyboard input at the end of 'destination-file'. The following command takes input from the keyboard and appends it to a file called test.letter. The command terminates when you press <Ctrl-D> on a new line.

```
$ cat test.letter
John Doe
12345 First Lane
Second City, State 98765
$ cat >> test.letter
November 14, 1999
Dear John:
This is to inform you ...
...
<Ctrl-D>
$ cat test.letter
```

```
John Doe
12345 First Lane
Second City, State 98765
November 14, 1999
Dear John:
This is to inform you ...
...
$
```

9.5 Combining Files

The following command syntax can be used to combine multiple files into one file.

SYNTAX

cat [file-list] > destination-file

Purpose: Combine the files in 'file-list' and put them in 'destination-file'

The 'destination-file' is overwritten if it already exists. If you do not have write permission for the 'destination-file', the command displays an error message informing you that you do not have permission to write to the file. Without the optional 'file-list' argument, you can use the command to put keyboard input in 'destination-file'. Thus, this command syntax can be used to create a new file whose contents are what you enter from the keyboard until you press <Ctrl-D> on a new line, as is the case with the `cat >> test.letter` command in the previous session.

The following session illustrates how this command works with arguments. The `ls -l` command is used to view permissions for the files. The `wc memo?` command displays the sizes of all the files in the current directory that start with the string memo and have one or more letters after this string. The third command combines the contents of the memo1, memo2, and memo3 files and puts them in the memos.y2k file in the order they appear in the command. The `wc memos.y2k` command is used to confirm that the memos.y2k file has the same number of lines, words, and characters as the three memo files combined. Execution of the `cat memo1 memo2 memo3 > memos.2005` command shows that you do not have permission to write to memos.2005.

```
$ ls -l
-r-xr--r--   1   sarwar   faculty   1687   Jan 10 11:26   memo1
-r-xr--r--   1   sarwar   faculty   1227   Feb 19 14:37   memo2
-r-xr--r--   1   sarwar   faculty   790    Apr 23 15:46   memo3
-r--------   1   sarwar   faculty   9765   Jan 15 22:11   memos.2005
$ wc memo?
```

```
        44        250       1687 memo1
        34        244       1227 memo2
        12        112        790 memo3
        90        606       3704 total
$ cat memo1 memo2 memo3 > memos.y2k
$ wc memos.y2k
                  90       606      3704 memos.y2k
$ cat memo1 memo2 memo3 > memos.2005
memos.2005: Permission denied.
$
```

You can also do the task of the `cat memo1 memo2 memo3 > memos.y2k` by using the following command sequence.

```
$ cat memo1 > memos.y2k
$ cat memo2 >> memos.y2k
$ cat memo3 >> memos.y2k
$
```

The following In-Chapter Exercises ask you to practice using the `cp`, `mv`, `ls -l`, `wc`, and `cat` commands and the operator for appending to a file.

IN-CHAPTER EXERCISES

9.5   Copy the .profile (or .login in a BSD UNIX based system) file in your home directory to a file .profile.old (or .login.old) in a directory called backups, also in your home directory. Assume that you are in your home directory. What command did you use?

9.7   Create a directory called new.backups in your home directory and move all the files in the backups directory to new.backups. What commands did you use?

9.8   Display the size in bytes of a file lab3 in the ~/ece345 directory. What command did you use?

9.9   Give a command for appending all the files in the ~/courses/ece446 directory to a file called BigBackup.ece446 in the ~/courses directory.

9.6 Comparing Files

At times, you will need to compare two versions of a program code or some other document to find out where they differ from each other. You can use the `diff` command to perform this task. The command compares two files and displays differences between them in terms of commands that can be used to convert one file to the other. The following is a brief description of the command.

SYNTAX

diff [options] [file1] [file2]

Purpose: Compare 'file1' with 'file2' line-by-line and display differences between them as a series of commands that can be used to convert 'file1' to 'file2' or vice versa; read from standard input if — is used for 'file1' or 'file2'

Commonly used options/features:

   −b   Ignore trailing (at the end of lines) white spaces (blanks and tabs), and consider other strings of white spaces equal

   −e   Generate and display a script for the ed editor that can be executed to change 'file1' to 'file2'

   −h   Do fast comparison (the −e option cannot be used)

The 'file1' and 'file2' arguments can be directories. If 'file1' is a directory, diff searches it to locate a file named 'file2' and compares it with 'file2' (the second argument). If 'file2' is a directory, diff searches it to locate a file named 'file1' and compares it with 'file1' (the first argument). If both arguments are directories, the command compares all pairs of files in these directories that have the same names.

The diff command does not produce any output if the files being compared are the same. When used without any options, the diff command produces a series of instructions for you to convert 'file1' to 'file2' if the files are different. The instructions are a (add), c (change), and d (delete) and are described in Table 9.1.

■ TABLE 9.1   File Conversion Instructions Produced by diff

Instruction	Description for Changing 'file1' to 'file2'
L1aL2, L3 > lines L2 through L3	Append lines L2 through L3 from 'file2' after line L1 in 'file1'
L1, L2cL3, L4 < lines L1 through L2 in file1 - - - > lines L3 through L4 in file2	Change lines L1 through L2 in 'file1' to lines L3 through L4 in file2
L1, L2dL3 < lines L1 through L2 in 'file1'	Delete lines L1 through L2 from 'file1'

The following session illustrates a simple use of the diff command.

```
$ cat Fall_OH
Office Hours for Fall 2003
Monday
    9:00 - 10:00 A.M.
    3:00 - 4:00 P.M.
```

```
Tuesday
    10:00 - 11:00 A.M.
Wednesday
    9:00 - 10:00 A.M.
    3:00 - 4:00 P.M.
Thursday
    11:00 A.M. - 12:00 P.M.
    2:00 - 3:00 P.M.
    4:00 - 4:30 P.M.
$ cat Spring_OH
Office Hours for Spring 2004
Monday
    9:00 - 10:00 A.M.
    3:00 - 4:00 P.M.
Tuesday
    10:00 - 11:00 A.M.
    1:00 - 2:00 P.M.
Wednesday
    9:00 - 10:00 A.M.
Thursday
    11:00 A.M. - 12:00 P.M.
$ diff Fall_OH Spring_OH
1c1
< Office Hours for Fall 2003
---
> Office Hours for Spring 2004
8a9
>   1:00 - 2:00 P.M.
12c13
<   3:00 - 4:00 P.M.
---
>
15d15
<   2:00 - 3:00 P.M.
<   4:00 - 4:30 P.M.
$
```

The instruction 1c1 asks you to change the first line in the Fall_OH file (Office Hours for Fall 2003) to the first line in the Spring_OH file (Office Hours for Spring 2004).

Similarly, the instruction `12c13` asks you to change line 12 in Fall_OH (`3:00–4:00` P.M.) to a blank line (note that nothing is given after the `>` symbol). The `8a9` instruction asks you to append line 9 in Spring_OH after line 8 in Fall_OH. The `15,16d15` instruction asks you to delete lines `15` and `16` from Fall_OH.

The following session illustrates use of the `-e` option with the `diff` command and how the output of this command can be given to the `ed` editor in order to make Fall_OH the same as Spring_OH. The command is used to show you what the output of the command looks like. The second command (with `> diff.script`) is used to save the command output (the ed script) in the diff.script file. The `cat` command is used to convert the `diff.script` file into a complete working script for the `ed` editor by adding two lines containing `w` and `q`. As previously stated, this command terminates with `<Ctrl-D>`. Finally, the `ed` command is run to change the contents of Fall_OH, according to the script produced by the `diff -e` command, and make it the same as Spring_OH. The last command, `diff Fall_OH Spring_OH`, is run to confirm that the two files are the same.

```
$ diff -e Fall_OH Spring_OH
15,16d
12c
.
8a
    1:00 - 2:00 P.M.
.
1c
Office Hours for Spring 2004
.
$
$ diff -e Fall_OH Spring_OH > diff.script
$ cat > diff.script
w
q
<Ctrl-D>
$ ed Fall_OH < diff.script
216
183
$ diff Fall_OH Spring_OH
$
```

Most systems have a command called `diff3` that can be used to do a three-way comparison—that is, three files can be composed.

9.7 Removing Repeated Lines

You can use the uniq command to remove all but one copy of successive repeated lines in a file. In other words, the command is designed to work on sorted files. (Sorting is discussed in Chapter 10.) The following is a brief summary of the command.

---

uniq [options] [+N] [input-file] [output-file]

Purpose: Remove repetitious lines from the sorted 'input-file' and send unique (non-repeated) lines to 'output-file'. The 'input-file' does not change. If no 'output-file' is specified, the output of the command is sent to standard output. If no 'input-file' is specified, the command takes input from standard input.

Commonly used options/features:

−c	Precede each output line by the number of times it occurs
−d	Display the repeated lines
−u	Display the lines that are not repeated

(SYNTAX)

The following session illustrates how the uniq command works. The cat command is used to show the contents of the sample file. The uniq sample command shows that only consecutive duplicate lines are considered duplicate. The uniq −c sample command shows the line count for every line in the file. The uniq −d sample command is used to output repeated lines only. Finally, the uniq −d sample outfile sends output of the command to the outfile file. The cat command is used to show contents of outfile. Note that the uniq command only works for unsorted files if repeated lines are adjacent.

```
$ cat sample
This is a test file for the uniq command.
It contains some repeated and some nonrepeated lines.
Some of the repeated lines are consecutive, like this.
Some of the repeated lines are consecutive, like this.
Some of the repeated lines are consecutive, like this.
And, some are not consecutive, like the following.
Some of the repeated lines are consecutive, like this.
The above line, therefore, will not be considered a repeated
line by the uniq command, but this will be considered repeated!
line by the uniq command, but this will be considered repeated!
$ uniq sample
This is a test file for the uniq command.
It contains some repeated and some nonrepeated lines.
Some of the repeated lines are consecutive, like this.
```

```
And, some are not consecutive, like the following.
Some of the repeated lines are consecutive, like this.
The above line, therefore, will not be considered a repeated
line by the uniq command, but this will be considered repeated!
$ uniq -c sample
1 This is a test file for the uniq command.
1 It contains some repeated and some nonrepeated lines.
3 Some of the repeated lines are consecutive, like this.
1 And, some are not consecutive, like the following.
1 Some of the repeated lines are consecutive, like this.
1 The above line, therefore, will not be considered a repeated
2 line by the uniq command, but this will be considered repeated!
$ uniq -d sample
Some of the repeated lines are consecutive, like this.
line by the uniq command, but this will be considered repeated!
$ uniq -d sample out
$ cat out
Some of the repeated lines are consecutive, like this.
line by the uniq command, but this will be considered repeated!
$
```

In the following In-Chapter Exercises, you will use the `diff` and `uniq` commands to appreciate the tasks they perform.

IN-CHAPTER EXERCISES

    9.9   Duplicate the interactive sessions given in Section 9.6 to appreciate how the `diff` command works.

    9.10   Give a command to remove all but one occurrence of the consecutive duplicate lines in a file called Phones in the ~/personal directory. Assume that you are not in your home directory.

9.8   Printing Files and Controlling Print Jobs

We briefly discussed the UNIX commands for printing files in Chapter 4. In this section, we cover file printing fully, including commands related to printing and printer control. These commands include commands for printing files, checking the status of print requests/jobs on a printer, and canceling print jobs. We describe commands for both the BSD and the SV versions of UNIX.

9.8.1 UNIX Mechanism for Printing Files

The process of printing files is similar to the process of displaying files; in both cases the contents of one or more files are sent to an output device. In the case, of displaying output, the output device is a display screen, whereas in the case of printing output, the output device is a printer. Another key difference results primarily from the fact that every user has an individual display screen but that many users share a single printer on a typical UNIX (or any time-sharing) system. Thus, when you use the cat or more command to display a file, the contents of the file are immediately sent to the display screen by UNIX. However, when you print a file, its contents are not immediately sent to the printer because the printer might be busy printing some other file (yours or some other user's). To handle multiple requests, a **first-come, first-served (FCFS) mechanism** places a print request in a queue and processes the request in its turn when the printer is available.

UNIX maintains a queue of print requests, called the **print queue**, associated with every printer in the system. Each request, also called a **job**, is assigned a number, called **job ID**. When you use a command to print a file, the system makes a temporary copy of your file, assigns a job ID to your request, and puts the job in the print queue associated with the printer specified in the command line. When the printer finishes its current job, it is given the next job from the front of the print queue. Thus, your job is processed when the printer is available and your job is at the head of the print queue.

The work of maintaining the print queue and directing print jobs to the right printer is performed by a UNIX process called the **printer spooler,** or **printer daemon.** This process, called **lpd,** starts execution in the background when the system boots up, and waits for your print requests. We discuss daemons in Chapter 13, but for now, you can think of a daemon as a process that runs but you are not aware of its presence while it interacts with your terminal.

System V and BSD have different command sets for printing and controlling print jobs. Because many of the contemporary UNIX systems are compatible with both System V and BSD, they contain both sets of commands. Table 9.2 contains a list of the printing-related commands for both systems. The last two commands (lpc and lptest) are normally used by the superuser–the system administrator.

■■ **TABLE 9.2** List of Commands Related to Printing

System V Compatible UNIX	BSD Compatible UNIX	Purpose
lp	lpr	Submits a file for printing
lpstat	lpq	Shows the status of print jobs for one or more printers
cancel	lprm	Removes/purges one or more jobs from the print queue
	lpc	Activates the printer control program
	lptest	Generates ripple pattern for testing the printer

9.8.2 Printing Files

As shown in Table 9.2, you can print files by using the lp command on a System V–compatible UNIX system and the lpr command on a BSD-compliant UNIX system. It is very important to note that you should never try printing nontext files with the lp or lpr command, especially files with control characters (e.g., executable files such as a.out). Doing so will not print what you want printed and will waste many printer pages. Do not even try testing it. If by accident you do send a print request for a nontext file, turn off the printer immediately and alert your system administrator that you need immediate assistance.

The following is a brief description of the lp command.

---

lp [options] file-list

Purpose: Submit a print request to print the files in 'file-list'

Commonly used options/features:

−P page-list	Print the pages specified in 'page-list'
−d ptr	Submit the print request for the 'ptr' printer
−m	Send mail after printing is complete
−n N	Print 'N' copies of the file(s) in 'file-list'; default is one copy
−t title	Print 'title' on a banner page
−w	Write to user's terminal after printing is complete

The following session shows how to use the lp command with and without options. The first command prints the sample file on the default printer. The job ID for the first print request is cpr-981, which tells you that the name of the printer is cpr. The second command uses the -d option to specify that the sample file should be printed on the spr printer. The third command is for printing three copies each of the sample and phones files on the qpr printer. These commands were run on a LINUX system; LINUX systems have compatible print commands.

```
$ lp sample
request id is cpr-981 (1 file(s))
$ lp -d spr sample
request id is spr-983 (1 file(s))
$ lp -d qpr -n 3 sample phones
request id is qpr-984 (2 file(s))
$
```

As mentioned before, the BSD counterpart of the lp command is the lpr command. The following is a brief description of this command.

lpr [options] file-list	
Purpose:	Submit a print request to print the files in 'file-list'
Commonly used options/features:	
—# N	Print 'N' copies of the file(s) in 'file-list'; default is one copy
—P ptr	Submit the print request for the 'ptr' printer
—T title	Print 'title' on a banner page
—m	Send mail after printing is complete
—p	Format the output by using the pr command

The following session shows the BSD versions of the commands that perform the same print tasks as the lp command. Thus, the first lpr command sends the print request for printing the sample file on the default printer. The second command sends the request for printing the sample file on the spr printer. The third command prints three copies of the sample and phones files on the qpr printer. We used the following commands on a Sun workstation running Solaris2.

```
% lpr sample
% lpr -P spr sample
% lpr -P qpr -# 3 sample
%
```

You can use the following command to print the sample file with the header information on every page produced by the pr command. The vertical bar (|) is called the pipe symbol, which we discuss in detail in Chapter 12.

```
% pr sample | lpr
%
```

You can perform the same task with the lpr -p sample command. You can print the sample file with line numbers and a pr header on each page by using the following command. You can also perform the same task with the nl sample | lpr -p command.

```
% nl sample | pr | lpr
%
```

You can enable the lpr command to print a nonstandard text file, such as a TEX file, by specifying an appropriate flag. For example, you can use the -t option to print a troff file and the -n option to print an nroff file.

9.8.3 Finding the Status of Your Print Requests

In a System V–compatible system, the lpstat command can be used to display the status of print jobs on a printer. The following is a brief description of the lpstat command.

lpstat [options]

Purpose:	Display the status of print jobs on a printer
Commonly used options/features:	
−d	Display the status of print jobs on the default printer for the lp command
−o job-ID-list	Display the status of the print jobs in 'job-ID-list'; separate the job-IDs with spaces and enclose the requests in double quotes for more than one job
−p printer-list	Display the status of print jobs on the printers specified in 'printer-list'
−u user-list	Display the status of print jobs from the users in 'user-list'

Without any option, the lpstat command displays the status of all your print jobs that are printing or waiting in the print queue. The commands in the following session show some typical uses of the command. The lpstat -p command shows the status of all printers on the network. The lpstat -p qpr displays the status of print jobs on the qpr printer. The lpstat -u sarwar displays all print jobs for the user sarwar. The output of the command shows that there are three print jobs that sarwar submitted–two to qpr (job IDs qpr-3998 and qpr-3999) and one to tpr (job ID tpr-203). Finally, the lpstat -a command displays all the printers that are up and accepting print jobs.

```
$ lpstat -p
printer cpr is idle. enabled since Tue Nov 16 10:43:48 GMT 2003. available.
printer mpr faulted. enabled since Mon Oct 25 10:48:29 GMT 2003. available.
printer qpr now printing qpr-53. enabled since Mon Oct 25 10:48:29 GMT 2003. available.
printer spr is idle. enabled since Mon Oct 25 10:48:29 GMT 2003. available.
$ lpstat -p qpr
printer qpr now printing qpr-53. enabled since Mon Oct 25 10:48:29 GMT 2003. available.
$ lpstat -u sarwar
qpr-3998 sarwar     93874 Nov 16 22:05 on qpr
qpr-3999 sarwar     93874 Nov 16 22:05
tpr-203  sarwar     93874 Nov 16 22:05 on tpr
$ lpstat -a
cpr accepting requests since Tue Nov 16 10:43:48 GMT 2003
spr accepting requests since Mon Oct 25 10:48:29 GMT 2003
$
```

The following is a brief description of the BSD counterpart of the lpstat command, the lpq command.

lpq [options]

Purpose:	Display the status of print jobs on a printer

Commonly used options/features:

−**P** printer-list	Display the status of print jobs on the printers specified in 'printer-list'
−**1**	Display the status of print jobs on the default printer for the lpr command in a long format

The most commonly used option is −P. In the following session, the first command is used to display the status of print jobs on the mpr printer. The output of the command shows that four jobs are in the printer queue: jobs 3991, 3992, 3993, and 3994. The active job is at the head of print queue. When the printer is ready for printing, it will print the active job first. The second command shows that the qpr printer does not have any job to print.

```
$ lpq -Pmpr
mpr is ready and printing
Rank       Owner      Job     Files            Total Size
active     sarwar     3991    mail.bob         1056 bytes
1st        sarwar     3992    csh.man          93874 bytes
2nd        davis      3993    proposal1.nsa    2708921 bytes
3rd        tom        3994    memo             8920 bytes
$ lpq -Pqpr
no entries
$
```

9.8.4 Canceling Your Print Jobs

If you realize that you have submitted the wrong file(s) for printing, you will want to cancel your print request(s). The System V command for performing this task is cancel. The following is a brief description of the command.

cancel [options] [printer]

Purpose:	Cancel print requests made by using the lp command—that is, remove these jobs from the print queue

Commonly used options/features:

−**jobID-list**	Cancel print jobs specified in the 'jobID-list'
−**u**login	Cancel all print jobs that were issued by the user 'login'

The following commands show how to cancel a print job. The first command cancels print job mpr-3991. The second command cancels all print requests by the user sarwar on all printers. You can cancel your own print jobs only. The last command therefore works only when run by sarwar or the superuser.

```
$ cancel mpr-3991
request "mpr-3991" canceled
$ cancel -u sarwar mpr
request "mpr-3992" canceled
request "mpr-3995" canceled
$
```

The BSD counterpart of the cancel command is lprm. The following is a brief description of the command.

SYNTAX

lprm [options] [jobID-list] [user(s)]

Purpose: Cancel print requests made by using the lprm commands, that is, remove these jobs from the print queue; the jobs IDs in 'jobID-list' are taken from the output of the lpq command

Commonly used options/features:

−	Remove all the jobs owned by 'user'
−P ptr	Specify the print queue for the 'ptr' printer

The following lprm commands perform the same tasks as the cancel commands.

```
% lprm -Pmpr 3991
mpr-3996 dequeued
% lprm -Pmpr sarwar
mpr-3997 dequeued
mpr-3998 dequeued
%
```

When run without an argument, the lprm command removes the job that is currently active, provided it is one of your jobs.

The following In-Chapter Exercises will give you practice on using the printing-related commands.

IN-CHAPTER EXERCISES

9.11 How would you print five copies of the file memo on the printer ece_hp1? Give commands for both System V and BSD UNIX.

9.12 After submitting the two requests, you realize that you really wanted to print five copies of the file letter. How would you remove the print jobs from the print queue? Again, give commands for both System V and BSD UNIX.

Summary

The basic file operations involve displaying (all or part of) a file's contents, renaming a file, moving a file to another file, removing a file, determining a file's size, comparing files, combining files and storing them in another file, appending new contents (which can come from another disk file, keyboard, or output of a command) at the end of a file, and printing files. UNIX provides several utilities that can be used to perform these operations.

The cat and more commands can be used to display all the contents of a file on the display screen. The > symbol can be used to send outputs of these commands to other files, and the >> operator can be used to append new contents at the end of a file. The cat command sends file contents as continuous text, whereas the more command sends them in the form of pages. Furthermore, the more command has several useful features, such as the ability to display a page that contains a particular string. The less command supports even more features than the more command, including vi style forward and backward searching. The pg command is similar to the more command but is available on System V UNIX only.

The head and tail commands can be used to display the initial or end portions (head or tail) of a file. These helpful commands are usually used to find out the type of data contained in a file, without using the file command (*see* Chapter 7). In addition, the file command cannot decipher contents of all the files.

A copy of a file can be made in another file or directory by using the cp command. Along with the > operator, the cat command can also be used to make a file copy, although there are differences between using the cp and cat > commands for copying files (see Chapter 12). A file can be moved to another file by using the mv command. However, depending on whether the source and destination files are on the same file system, its use might or might not result in actual movement of file data from one location to another. If the source and destination files are on the same file system, the file data is not moved and the source file is simply linked to the new place (destination). If the two files are on different file systems, an actual copy of the source file is made at the new location and the source file is removed (unlinked) from the current directory. Files can be removed from a file structure by using the rm command. This command can also be used to remove directories recursively.

The size of a file can be determined by using the `ls -l` or `wc` command; both give file size in bytes. In addition, the `wc` command gives number of lines and words in the file. Both commands can be used to display the sizes of multiple files by using the shell metacharacters `*`, `?`, `[ ]`, and `^`.

The `diff` command can be used to display differences between two files. The command, in addition to displaying the differences between the files, displays useful information in the form of a sequence of commands for the `ed` editor that can be used to make the two files the same. The `uniq` command can be used to remove all but one occurrence of successive repeated lines. With the `-d` option, the command can be used to display the repeated lines.

The `lp` (System V) or `lpr` (BSD) command can be used for printing files on a printer. The `lpstat` (System V) or `lpq` (BSD) command can be used for checking the status of all print jobs (requests) on a printer (waiting, printing, etc.). The `cancel` (System V) or `lprm` (BSD) command can be used to remove a print job from a printer queue so that the requested file is not printed.

Problems

1. List 10 operations that you can perform on UNIX files.

2. Give a command line for viewing the sizes (in lines and bytes) of all the files in your present working directory.

3. What does the `tail -10r ../letter.John` command do?

4. Give a command for viewing the size of your home directory. Give a command for displaying the sizes of all the files in your home directory.

5. Give a command for displaying all the lines in the Students file, starting with line 25.

6. Give a command for copying all the files and directories under a directory courses in your home directory. Assume that you are in your home directory. Give another command to accomplish the same task, assuming that you are not in your home directory.

7. Repeat Problem 6, but give the command that preserves the modification times and permissions for the file.

8. Give an option for the `rm` command that could protect you from accidently removing a file, especially when you are using wild cards such as `*` and `?` in the command.

9. What do the following commands do?

    a. `cp -f sample sample.bak`

    b. `cp -fp sample sample.bak`

    c. `rm -i ~/personal/memo*.doc`

    d. `rm -i ~/unixbook/final/ch??.prn`

    e. `rm -f ~/unixbook/final/*.o`

    f. `rm -f ~/courses/ece446/lab[1-6].[cC]`

    g. `rm -r ~/NotNeededDirectory`

    h. `rm -rf ~/NotNeededDirectory`

    i. `rm -ri ~/NotNeededDirectory`

10. Give a command line for moving files lab1, lab2, and lab3 from the ~/courses/ ece345 directory to a newlabs.ece345 directory in your home directory. If a file already exists in the destination directory, the command should prompt the user for confirmation.

11. Give a command to display the lines in the ~/personal/Phones file that are not repeated.

12. Refer to In-Chapter Exercise 9. Give a sequence of commands to save the sequence of commands for the ed editor and use them to make sample and example the same files.

13. You have a file in your home directory called tryit&. Rename this file. What command did you use?

14. Give a command for displaying attributes of all the files starting with a string prog, followed by zero or more characters and ending with a string .c in the courses/ece345 directory in your home directory.

15. Refer to Problem 13. Give a command line if file names have two English letters between prog and .c. Can you give another command line to accomplish the same task?

16. Give a command line for displaying files gotlcha and M*A*S*H one screenful at a time.

17. Give a command line for displaying the sizes of files that have the .jpg extension and names ending with a digit.

18. What does the `rm *[a-zA-Z]??[1,5,8].[^p]*` command do?

19. Give a command to compare the files sample and example in your present working directory. The output should generate a series of commands for the ed editor?

20. Give a command for producing 10 copies of the report file on the ece_hp3 printer. Each page should contain a page header produced by the `pr` command. Give commands for both System V and BSD UNIX.

21. Give the command line to print the nroff file Chapter1 by using the `lpr` command. What command line would you use to print the troff file Sample with the `lpr` command?

22. Give a command for checking the status of a print job with job ID ece_hp3-8971. Is this command for System V or BSD? How would you remove this print job from the print queue? Give commands for both System V and BSD UNIX.

Advanced File Processing

Objectives

- To discuss the formation and use of regular expressions
- To explain file compression and how it can be performed
- To explain the sorting process and how files can be sorted
- To discuss searching for commands and files in the UNIX file structure
- To describe searching files for expressions, strings, and patterns
- To describe how database-type operations of cutting and pasting fields in a file can be performed
- To discuss encoding and decoding of files
- To explain file encryption and decryption
- To cover the commands and primitives
  ```
  >, ~, compress, crypt, .cut, egrep, fgrep, find,
  grep, pack, paste, pcat, sort, uncompress, unpack,
  uuencode, uudecode, whereis, which, zcat
  ```

10.1   Introduction

In this chapter, we describe some of the more advanced file processing operations and show how they can be performed in UNIX. But before describing these operations, we discuss the important topic of **regular expressions**, which are a set of rules that can be used to specify one or more items in a single character string (sequence of characters). While discussing the operations, we also describe their related commands and give examples to illustrate how these commands can be used to perform the needed operations.

10.2   Regular Expressions

While using some of the UNIX commands and tools, you will need to be able to specify a set of items by using a single character string, similar to the use of shell metacharacters. Regular expressions allow you to do just that; that is, they are a set of rules that you can use to specify one or more items, such as words in a file, by using a single character string. Some of the commonly used tools that allow the use of regular expressions are awk, ed, egrep, grep, sed, and vi, but the level of support for regular expressions isn't the same for all these tools. Whereas awk and egrep have the best support for regular expressions, grep has the weakest.

Table 10.1 lists the regular expression operators, their names, example of usage, meanings, and tools that support them. The regular expression operators overlap with shell metacharacters, but you can use single quotes around them to prevent the shell from interpreting them. The word *All* in the last column means that all the tools mentioned support the corresponding operator.

■ **TABLE 10.1** Regular Expression Operators and Their Support by UNIX Tools

Name/Function	Operator	Example Usage	Meaning	Supported By
Alternation	|	x|y|z	x, y, or z	awk, egrep
Any Character	.	.com	Acom, acom, Bcom, bcom, Ccom, ccom, ...	All
Beginning of Line	^	^x	A line starting with an x	All
Concatenation		xyz	Xyz	All
End of Line	$	x$	A line ending with an x	All
Escape Sequence: Cancels the special meaning of the metacharacter that follows it	\	*	*	ed, sed, vi
Delimiter: Marks the beginning or end of a regular expression	/	/L..e/	Love, Live, Lose, Lase, ...	ed, sed, vi

(continued)

TABLE 10.1 *(continued)*

Grouping	( ) or \ (\ )	(xy)+	xy, xyxy, xyxyxy, ...	All
Optional	?	xy?	x, xy	awk, egrep
Repetition (0 or more times)	*	xy*	x, xy, xyy, xyyy, ...	All
Repetition (1 or more times)	+	xy+	xy, xyy, xyyy, ...	awk, egrep
Set: Matches any character enclosed in brackets.	[ ]	/[Hh]ello/	Hello, hello	All
Matches any character not enclosed in brackets.	[^]	/[^A-KM-Z]ove/	Love	

Table 10.2 lists some commonly used regular expressions in the vi editor and their meanings. Needless to say, regular expressions are used in the vi commands. We discuss examples for grep and egrep in Section 10.6.

■ TABLE 10.2 Examples of Regular Expressions for vi and Their Meaning

Regular Expression	Meaning	Examples
/^Yes/	A line starting with the string **Yes**	**Yes** ... **Yes**teryear ... **Yes**terday ... etc.
/th/	Occurrence of the string **th** anywhere in a word	the, there, path, bathing ...
/:$/	A line ending with a colon	... the following: ... below: etc.
/[0-9]/	A single digit	0, 1, ..., 9/
[a-z][0-9]	A single lowercase English letter followed by a single digit	a0, a1, ..., b0, b1, ..., z0, z1, ..., z9
/\.c/	Any word that ends with .c (all C source code files)	lab1.c, program1.c, client.c, server.c, ...
/[a-zA-Z]*/	Any string composed of letters (uppercase or lowercase) and spaces; no numbers and punctuation marks	1) All strings without numbers and punctuation marks such as 767-N

Table 10.3 lists some examples of the `vi` commands that use regular expressions and their meaning. Note that these commands are used when you are in `vi`'s command mode.

■ **TABLE 10.3** Some Commonly Used `vi` Commands Illustrating
the Use of Regular Expressions

Command	Meaning
`/ [0-9] /`	Do forward search for a single stand-alone digit character in the current file; digits that are part of strings are not identified
`?\.c[1-7] ?`	Do backward search for words or strings in words that end with .c followed by a single digit between 1 and 7
`:1,$s/:$/./`	Search the whole file and substitute colon (:) at the end of a line with a period (.)
`:.,$s/^[Hh]ello /Greetings /`	From the current line to the end of file, substitute the words **Hello** and **hello** starting a line with the word **Greetings**
`:1,$s/^ *//`	Eliminate one or more spaces at the beginning of all the lines in the file

In the following In-Chapter Exercises, you will use regular expressions in the `vi` editor to appreciate their power.

IN-CHAPTER EXERCISES

10.1 Create a file that contains the words UNIX, LINUX, Windows, and DOS. Be sure that some of the lines in this file end with those words. Replace the string Windows NT with UNIX in the whole document as you edit it with the `vi` editor. What command(s) did you use?

10.2 As you edit the document in Exercise 10.1, in `vi`, run the command `:1,$s/DOS\./LINUX\./gp`. What did the command do to the document?

10.3   Compressing Files

Reduction in the size of a file is known as **file compression**, which has both space and time advantages. A compressed file takes less disk space, less time to transmit from one computer to another in a network or internet environment, and less time to copy. Compression takes time, but if a file is to be copied or transmitted several times, the time spent compressing the file could be just a fraction of the total time saved. In addition, if the compressed file is to be stored on a secondary storage device (e.g., disk) for a long time, the savings in disk space is considerable. Another consequence of compression is that the compressed file is not readable.

However, this condition is not a problem because the process is fully reversible, and a compressed file can be converted back to its original form.

The UNIX operating system has many commands for compressing and decompressing files and for performing various operations on compressed files. These commands include the traditional UNIX commands for compressing and decompressing files, `compress` and `uncompress`, and the GNU tools `gzexe` (compress executable files), `gzip` (for compressing files), `gunzip` (for uncompressing files that were compressed with `gzip`), `zcat` (for displaying compressed files; `gzcat` does the same), `gzcmp` (for comparing compressed files), `gzforce` (for forcing '.gz' extension on compressed files so that `gzip` will not compress them twice), `gzmore` (for displaying compressed files one page at a time), and `gzgrep` (the `grep` command for compressed files—it searches possibly compressed files for a regular expression). This section will primarily discuss file compression and decompression. Although the GNU tools (`gzip` and `gunzip`) are better than `compress` and `uncompress` commands, we discuss both sets of commands for completion.

10.3.1 The `compress` Command

The `compress` command reads contents of files that are passed to it as parameters, analyzes their contents for repeated patterns, and then substitutes a smaller number of characters for these patterns by using **adaptive Lempel–Ziv coding**. A compressed file's contents are altogether different from the original file. The compressed file contains nonprintable characters, so displaying a compressed file on the screen shows a bunch of control characters, or garbage. The `compress` command saves the compressed file in a file that has the same name as the original file, with an extension .Z appended to it. The file has the same access permissions and modification date as the original file. The original file is removed from the file structure.

The following is a brief description of the `compress` command; the syntax of and options used in the `uncompress` command are exactly the same.

---

compress [options] [file-list]

Purpose: Compress files in 'file-list'

Output: The compressed .Z file or standard output if input is from standard input

Commonly used options/features:

    `-c`   Write compressed file to the display screen instead of a .Z file

    `-f`   Force compression (no prompts)

    `-v`   Display compression percentage and the names of compressed files

SYNTAX

With no file argument or – as an argument, the `compress` command takes input from standard input (keyboard by default), which allows you to use the command in a pipeline (*see* Chapter 12). We normally use the command with one or more files as its arguments. In the following session, we use the command with one file, t2, as its argument. The compressed file is stored in the t2.Z file, and the t2 file is removed from the file system.

```
$ cat t2
This file is being used to test various
commands and tools. Long live UNIX!
UNIX rules the networking world!!
$ compress t2
$ cat t2.Z
¨6e@
     !_L¨7g@ÔS
                :o.C
                   0rÒ_¨`ÎÂ¸!CP¥EoØÌq7A°Ic'a'I°
                    P_3)uÎ 1
$
```

The following session illustrates the use of compress with the –v (verbose) option and multiple files. Note that the use of the shell metacharacter ? denotes a single character and that the output of the compress command with the –v option shows the percentage of compression performed on the source files.

```
$ ls -l t?
-rw-rw-rw-   1   sarwar    faculty    227   May    17   21:59   t1
-rwx------   1   sarwar    faculty     90   May     7   1998    t2
-rwx------   1   sarwar    faculty    150   Nov    21   1996    t3
-rwx------   1   sarwar    faculty   7119   Nov    12   1996    t4
$ compress -v t1 t2 t3 t4
t1: -- replaced with t1.Z Compression: 14.53%
t2: -- replaced with t2.Z Compression: 26.66%
t3: -- replaced with t3.Z Compression: 10.00%
t4: -- replaced with t4.Z Compression: 77.80%
$ ls -l t?.Z
-rw-rw-rw-   1   sarwar    faculty    194   May    17   21:59   t1.Z
-rwx------   1   sarwar    faculty     66   May     7   1998    t2.Z
-rwx------   1   sarwar    faculty    135   Nov    21   1996    t3.Z
-rwx------   1   sarwar    faculty   1580   Nov    12   1996    t4.Z
$
```

10.3.2 The uncompress Command

You can use the uncompress command to uncompress the compressed files and put them in the corresponding original files (i.e., names of the compressed files without .Z extensions). The following session shows the use of the uncompress command with the –v option.

```
$ uncompress -v t1.Z t2.Z t3.Z t4.Z
t1.Z: -- replaced with t1
```

```
t2.Z: -- replaced with t2
t3.Z: -- replaced with t3
t4.Z: -- replaced with t4
$
```

The uncompress -v t?.Z command performs the same task. Note that the output of the uncompress command goes into a file (the original file).

As given in the command description, multiple files can be displayed by the zcat command. For example, the command zcat t1.Z t2.Z t3.Z displays uncompressed forms of the three files t1.Z, t2.Z, and t3.Z.

10.3.3 The `gzip` Command

The gzip command is the GNU tool for compressing files. The compressed file is saved in a file that has the same name as the original file, with an extension .gz appended to it. As is the case with the compress command, the compressed files retain the access/modification times, ownership, and access privileges of the original files. The original file is removed from the file structure. With no file argument or with – as an argument, the gzip command takes input from standard input (keyboard by default), which allows you to use the command in a pipeline (*see* Chapter 12). We normally use the command with one or more files as its arguments. Here is a brief description of the command.

gzip [options] [file-list]	
Purpose:	Compress each file in 'file-list' and store it in filename.gz, where 'filename' is the name of the original file; if no file is specified in the command line or if—is specified, take input from standard input
Output:	The compressed .gz file or standard output if input is from standard input
Commonly used options/features:	
−N	Control compression speed (and compression ratio) according to the value of N, with 1 being fastest and 9 being slowest; slow compression compresses more
−c	Send output to standard output; input files remain unchanged
−d	Uncompress a compressed (.gz) file
−f	Force compression of a file when its .gz version exists, or it has multiple links, or input file is stdin
−1	Send For compressed files given as arguments, display sizes of uncompressed and compressed versions, compression ratio, and uncompressed name
−r	Recursively compress files in the directory specified as arguments
−t	Test integrity of the compressed files specified as arguments
−v	Display compression percentage and the names of the compressed files

10.3.4 The `gunzip` Command

The `gunzip` command can be used to perform the reverse operation and bring compressed files back to their original forms. The `gzip -d` command can also perform this task. With the `gunzip` command, the -N, -c, -f, -l, and -r options work just like they do with the `gzip` command.

The following session shows the use of the two commands with and without arguments. We use the `man bash > bash.man` and `man tcsh > tcsh.man` commands to save the manual page for the Bourne Again and TC shells in the `bash.man` and `tcsh.man` files, respectively. The `gzip bash.man` command is used to compress the bash.man file, and the `gzip -l bash.man.gz tcsh.man.gz` command is used to display some information about the compressed and uncompressed versions of the bash.man and tcsh.man files. The output of the command shows, among other things, the percentage compression achieved: 74.4% for bash.man and 71.7% for tcsh.man. The `gzip bash.man.gz` command is used to show that gzip does not compress an already compressed file that has a .gz extension. If a compressed file does not have the .gz extension, gzip will try to compress it again. The `gunzip bash.man.gz` command is used to decompress the compressed file bash.man.gz file. The `gzip -d bash.man.gz` command can be used to perform the same task. The `ls -l` commands have been used to show that the modification time, ownership, and access privileges of the original file are retained for the compressed file.

```
$ man bash > bash.man
$ ls -l bash.man
-rw-------    1   sarwar   faculty   284064   Nov 20 12:24 bash.man
$ gzip bash.man
$ ls -l bash.man.gz
-rw-------    1   sarwar   faculty   72501    Nov 20 12:24 bash.man.gz
$ gzip bash.man tcsh.man
$ gzip -l bash.man.gz tcsh.man.gz
compressed        uncompr.        ratio     uncompressed_name
72501             284064          74.4%     bash.man
73790             261316          71.7%     tcsh.man
146291            545380          73.1%     (totals)
$ gzip bash.man.gz
gzip: bash.man.gz already has .gz suffix — unchanged
$ gunzip bash.man.gz
$ ls -l bash.man
-rw-------    1   sarwar   faculty   284064   Nov 20 12:24 bash.man
$
```

10.3.5 The `gzexe` Command

The `gzexe` command can be used to compress executable files. An executable file compressed with the `gzexe` command remains an executable file and can be executed by using the name of the executable file. This is not the case if an executable file is compressed with the gzip command. Therefore, an executable file is compressed with the gzexe command in order to save disk space and network bandwidth if the file is to be transmitted from one computer to another, for example, via e-mail over the Internet. The following is a brief description of this command.

---

gzexe [options] [file-list]

Purpose: Compress the executable files given in 'file-list'; backup files are created in filename~ and should be removed after the compressed files have been successfully created

Commonly used options/features:

   -d   Decompress compressed files

SYNTAX

The following session illustrates the use of the gzexe command. Note that when the executable file banner is compressed with the gzexe command, a backup of the original file is created in banner~. After the banner file has been compressed, it can be executed as an ordinary executable file. The gzexe -d banner command is used to decompress the compressed file banner. The backup of the compressed version is saved in the banner~ file.

```
$ file banner
banner: ELF 32-bit LSB executable, Intel 80386, version 1, dynamically
linked (uses shared libs), not stripped
$ banner datafile 10
[ output of the banner command ]
$ gzexe banner
banner:  58.0%
$ ls -l banner*
-rwx------  1  sarwar  faculty  5239   Nov 19  11:45  banner
-rwx------  1  sarwar  faculty  10881  Nov 19  11:44  banner~
$ banner datafile 10
[ output of the banner command ]
$ gzexe -d banner
$ ls -l banner*
-rwx------  1  sarwar  faculty  10881  Nov 19  11:48  banner
-rwx------  1  sarwar  faculty  5239   Nov 19  11:45  banner~
$
```

10.3.6 The zcat Command

Converting the compressed file back to the original and then displaying it is a time-consuming process because file creation requires disk I/O. If you only want to view the contents of the original file, you can use the LINUX command zcat (the cat command for compressed files) that displays the contents of files compressed with compress or gzip. The command uncompresses a file before displaying it. The original file remains unchanged. The zmore command can be used to display the compressed files one screenful at a time. When no file or – is given as a parameter, these commands read input from stdin. Both commands allow you to specify one or more files as parameters. Here is a brief description of the zcat command.

zcat [options] [file-list]

Purpose: Concatenate compressed files in their original form and send them to standard

Output: If no file is specified, take input from standard input

Commonly used options/features:

  -h   Display help information

  -r   Operate recursively on subdirectories

  -t   Test integrity of compressed files

In the following session, the gzip command is used to compress the bash.man file and store it in the bash.man.gz file. When the more command is used to display the compressed file, garbage is displayed on the screen. The zmore command is used to display the contents of the original file. We did not use the zcat command because bash.man is a large, multipage file.

```
$ gzip bash.man
$ more bash.man.gz
:bash.manÔ´y{µ?ÿ;3/4i)Ä2{  'li      a
MJá´9ÉXÙÓH¡âÛkö}¯}YI´Yç÷<újË3ûºöÛëújo1/2õÖïî?k´y´Y£;¯Pü1/4úüê·_¯Pzë3ê3ûÕ´y
O«OVß?5ÃÅ´Yú1kä3¯êßõ»Íª=1kt«úñïÛÅâ-·WÿV´y
Oëoæ´Y¢}úÖ[ªü.´6eõ%1/4kIõÉï«ß?©h#¿AÔ´YP?è3Wîüb[=8®
üê¿urçW¿úU}vUo/ÚúãMÛÖûùö2ÙÀo´ynu¢-
ÎìuR?ZMOßzë£ê#″úæ.¡{è-¡Àd¬âêw6z@3ªùi¿\Cg¶ÍjV/Õù®9oënµm7ëM
      ÿãj¶ÚZûªî¶ÍPë+DÓ{mfõ|Ó/iÃ3/4m63hb1/2Ûõ´yÿÔh
5¿ùn·Ív·Áo¨ìB[zV´yñYÕ?«6ÏªU£V=¨           ¸d§É°ÅaÃóÓ~3î7
      Øó¡>zQ1/2aÆá/ÓjÊ¿ÃÒWç1/4µ3zÛ3gm´YÀWó~3ÜÖ´Yr1/2h
jKP÷s?G>¬¿øüñ£¿Ö±{ê2-Ò÷0zX·Ón¯PMùÅú®¿î7/ºÕ1¶DÉ{ß-ë;·oÿìô._©Éo§£ÇGDL3uÜ
^L3[´′ÓfÓLqÑH®¸aèÎWLFøXïíªî¶1/4Ê/ûíìÛê¶6oxVmi7;ØagÕy´yhÎSÕG¸5lú`üó*″m5|yæ]
!
>¢Ãakèç;\Ø·fsÊ[£ñä
$ zmore bash.man.gz
------> bash.man.gz <------
BASH2(1)
```

```
NAME
        bash2 - GNU Bourne-Again SHell
SYNOPSIS
        bash2 [options] [file]
COPYRIGHT
        -Bash is Copyright (C) 1989-1999 by the Free Software Foundation, Inc.
DESCRIPTION
        -Bash is an sh-compatible command language interpreter that exe-
cutes commands read from the standard input or from a file. Bash also
incorporates useful features from the Korn and C shells (ksh and csh).
$
```

The following command decompresses the t2.Z file (compressed with the compress command in Section 10.3.1) and sends its output to standard output (the display screen in this case). The file t2.Z remains intact.

```
$ zcat t2.Z
This file is being used to test various
commands and tools. Long live UNIX!
UNIX rules the networking world!!
$
```

As given in this command description, multiple files can be displayed by the xtra zcat command. For example, the command zcat t1.z t2.z t3.z displays uncompressed forms of the three files t1.Z, t2.Z, and t3.Z.

10.3.7 The **pack** and **unpack** Commands

The pack and unpack commands also can be used to compress and uncompress files. The output file generated by pack has a .z (lowercase) extension. The commands use **Huffman coding** to encode and decode text files and do not work well for small files with a uniform distribution of characters. If pack cannot compress a file, it informs you of this and quits, which usually happens for small files. The command also cannot consistently compress files larger than 8MB. For these reasons, you should use compress (and uncompress).

The pack and unpack commands do not work as well or as efficiently as compress and uncompress, so we do not describe them any further. If you are interested in knowing more about these commands, we encourage you to read the manual pages.

In the following In-Chapter Exercises, you will use the compress, uncompress, gzip, gunzip, gzmore, and zcat commands to appreciate their syntax and semantics.

IN-CHAPTER EXERCISES ━━━━━━━━━━━

10.3   Create the t2 file used in this section. Use the compress command to compress the file. What command line did you use?   *(continued)*

10.4 Create the bash.man file used in this section. Use the `gzip` command to compress the file. What command line did you use?

10.5 Display the compressed version of the t2 file on the display screen. What command line did you use?

10.6 Give the command line for uncompressing the compressed files generated in Exercise 10.1 and 10.2. Where does the uncompressed (original) file go? Also, repeat shell sessions shown in Sections 10.3.1 through 10.3.6.

10.4   Sorting Files

Sorting means ordering a set of items according to some criteria. In computer jargon, it means ordering a set of items (e.g., integers, a character, or strings) in *ascending* (the next item is greater than or equal to the current item) or *descending* (the next item is less than or equal to the current item) order. So, for example, a set of integers {10, 103, 75, 22, 97, 52, 1} would become {1, 10, 22, 52, 75, 97, 103} if sorted in ascending order, and {103, 97, 75, 52, 22, 10, 1} if sorted in descending order. Similarly, words in a dictionary are listed in ascending sorted order. Thus, the word *apple* appears before the word *apply*.

Sorting is a commonly used operation and is also performed in a variety of software systems. Systems in which sorting is used include:

- ❖ Words in a dictionary
- ❖ Names of people in a telephone directory
- ❖ Airline reservation systems that display arrival and departure times for flights sorted according to flight numbers at airport terminals
- ❖ Names of people displayed in a pharmacy with ready prescriptions
- ❖ Names of students listed in class lists coming from the registrar's office

The sorting process is based on using a field, or portion of each item, known as the **sort key**. The items in a list are compared (usually two at a time) by using their key fields to determine the position of each item in the sorted list. Which field is used as the key depends on the items to be sorted. If the items are personal records (e.g., student employee records), last name, student ID, and social security number are some of the commonly used keys. If the items are arrival and departure times for the flights at an airport, flight number and city name are commonly used keys.

The UNIX `sort` utility can be used to sort items in text (ASCII) files. The following is a brief description of this utility.

SYNTAX

sort [options] [file-list]

Purpose:	Sort lines in the ASCII files in 'file-list'
Output:	Sorted file to standard output

(continued)

Commonly used options/features: *(continued)*

Commonly used options/features:

-b	Ignore leading blanks
-d	Sort according to usual alphabetical order: ignore all characters except letters, digits, and then blanks
-f	Consider lowercase and uppercase letters to be equivalent
+n1[-n2]	Specify a field as the sort key, starting with +n1 and ending at -n2 (or end of line if -n2 is not specified); field numbers start with 0
-r	Sort in reverse order

If no file is specified in 'file-list', sort takes input from standard input. The output of the sort command goes to standard output. By default, sort takes each line starting with the first column to be the key. In other words, it rearranges the lines of the file, that is, strings separated by the newline character, according to the contents of all the fields, going from left to right. The following session illustrates the use of the sort utility with and without some options. The students file contains the items (student records, one per line) to be sorted. Each line contains four fields: first name, last name, e-mail address, and phone number. Each field is separated from the next by one or more space characters.

```
$ cat students
John Johnsen        john.johnsen@tp.com      503.555.1111
Hassaan Sarwar      hsarwar@k12.st.or        503.444.2132
David Kendall       d_kendall@msnbc.org      229.111.2013
John Johnsen        jjohnsen@psu.net         301.999.8888
Kelly Kimberly      kellyk@umich.gov         555.123.9999
Maham Sarwar        msarwar@k12.st.or        713.888.0000
Jamie Davidson      j.davidson@uet.edu       515.001.2932
Nabeel Sarwar       nsarwar@xyz.net          434.555.1212
$ sort students
David Kendall       d_kendall@msnbc.org      229.111.2013
Hassaan Sarwar      hsarwar@k12.st.or        503.444.2132
Jamie Davidson      j.davidson@uet.edu       515.001.2932
John Johnsen        jjohnsen@psu.net         301.999.8888
John Johnsen        john.johnsen@tp.com      503.555.1111
Kelly Kimberly      kellyk@umich.gov         555.123.9999
Maham Sarwar        msarwar@k12.st.or        713.888.0000
```

```
Nabeel Sarwar        nsarwar@xyz.net        434.555.1212
$
```

Note that the lines in the students file are sorted in ascending order by all characters, going from left to right (the whole line is used as the sort key). The following command sorts the file by using the whole line, starting with the last name–the second field (field number 1)–as the sort key.

```
$ sort +1 students
Jamie Davidson       j.davidson@uet.edu     515.001.2932
John  Johnsen        jjohnsen@psu.net       301.999.8888
John  Johnsen        john.johnsen@tp.com    503.555.1111
David Kendall        d_kendall@msnbc.org    229.111.2013
Kelly Kimberly       kellyk@umich.gov       555.123.9999
Hassaan Sarwar       hsarwar@k12.st.or      503.444.2132
Maham Sarwar         msarwar@k12.st.or      713.888.0000
Nabeel Sarwar        nsarwar@xyz.net        434.555.1212
$
```

The following command sorts the file in reverse order by using the phone number as the sort key and ignoring leading blanks (spaces and tabs). The +3 option specifies the phone number to be the sort key (as phone number is the last field), the −r option informs sort to display the sorted output in reverse order, and the −b option asks the sort utility to ignore the leading white spaces between fields.

```
$ sort +3 -r -b students
Maham Sarwar         msarwar@k12.st.or      713.888.0000
Kelly Kimberly       kellyk@umich.gov       555.123.9999
Jamie Davidson       j.davidson@uet.edu     515.001.2932
John  Johnsen        john.johnsen@tp.com    503.555.1111
Hassaan Sarwar       hsarwar@k12.st.or      503.444.2132
Nabeel Sarwar        nsarwar@xyz.net        434.555.1212
John  Johnsen        jjohnsen@psu.net       301.999.8888
David Kendall        d_kendall@msnbc.org    229.111.2013
$
```

The −b option is important if fields are separated by more than one space and the number of spaces differ from line to line, as is the case for the students file. The reason is that the space character is "smaller" (in terms of its ASCII value) than all letters and digits, and not skipping blanks will generate unexpected output. The sort keys can be combined, with one being the primary key and others being secondary keys, by specifying them in the order of preferences (the primary key occurring first). The following command sorts the students file with the last name as the primary key and the phone number as the secondary key.

```
$ sort +1 -2 +3 -b students
Jamie Davidson        j.davidson@uet.edu        515.001.2932
John Johnsen          jjohnsen@psu.net          301.999.8888
John Johnsen          john.johnsen@tp.com       503.555.1111
David Kendall         d_kendall@msnbc.org       229.111.2013
Kelly Kimberly        kellyk@umich.gov          555.123.9999
Hassaan Sarwar        hsarwar@k12.st.or         503.444.2132
Maham Sarwar          msarwar@k12.st.or         713.888.0000
Nabeel Sarwar         nsarwar@xyz.net           434.555.1212
$
```

The primary key is specified as +1 -2, meaning that the key starts with the last name (+1) and ends before the e-mail address field (-2) starts. The secondary key starts at the phone number field (+3) and ends at the end of line. As no field follows the phone number, it alone comprises the secondary key. For our file, however, the end result will be the same as for the command sort +1 students because the first John Johnsen's e-mail address is "smaller" than the second's.

10.5 Searching for Commands and Files

At times, you will need to find whether a particular command or file exists in your file structure. Or, if you have multiple versions of a command, you might want to find out which one executes when you run the command. We discuss three commands that can be used for this purpose: find, whereis, and which.

You can use the find command to search a list of directories that meet the criteria described by the expression (*see* command description) passed to it as an argument. The command searches the list of directories recursively; that is, all subdirectories at all levels under the list of directories are searched. The following is a brief description of the command.

---

find directory-list expression

Purpose:	Search the directories in 'directory-list' to locate files that meet the "criteria" described by the 'expression' (the second argument); the expression comprises one or more "criteria" (*see* the examples)
Output:	None unless it is explicitly requested in *expression*
Commonly used "criteria" in expression:	
-exec CMD	The file being searched meets the criteria if the command 'CMD' returns 0 as its exit status (true value for commands that execute successfully); 'CMD' must terminate with a quoted semicolon, that is, \;
-inum N	Search for files with inode number 'N' *(continued)*

SYNTAX

find directory-list expression (continued)	
–links N	Search for files with 'N' links
–name pattern	Search for files that are specified by the 'pattern'
–newer file	Search for files that were modified after 'file' (i.e., are newer than file)
–ok CMD	Like -exec except that the user is prompted first
–perm octal	Search for files if permission of the file is 'octal'
–print	Display the pathnames of the files found by using the rest of the criteria
–size ±N[c]	Search for files of size 'N' blocks; 'N' followed by 'c' can be used to measure size in characters; +N means size > N blocks, and –N means size < N blocks
–user name	Search for files owned by the user name or ID 'name'
\(expr \)	True if 'expr' is true; used for grouping criteria combined with OR or AND
! expr	True if 'expr' is false

More criteria are presented in Appendix A. You can use [-a] or a space to logically AND, and –o to logically OR two criteria. Note that at least one space is needed before and after a bracket, [or], and before and after –o. A complex expression can be enclosed in parentheses, \(and \). The following are some illustrative examples.

```
$ find . \( -name core -o -name '*.ps' -o -name '*.o' \) -print -exec rm {} \;
[ output of the command ]
$
```

The most common use of the find command is to search one or more directories for a file, as shown in the first example. Here, the command searches for the Pakistan.gif file in your home directory and displays the pathname of the directory that contains it. If the file being searched occurs in multiple directories, the pathnames of all the directories are displayed.

```
$ find ~ -name Pakistan.gif -print
/users/faculty/sarwar/myweb/Pakistan.html
$
```

The next command searches the /usr/include directory recursively for a file named socket.h and prints the absolute pathname of the file.

```
$ find /usr/include -name socket.h -print
/usr/include/sys/socket.h
$
```

You might want to know the pathnames for all the hard links (discussed in Chapter 11) to a file. The following command recursively searches the /usr and . (present working directory) directories for all the files that have an inode number 258072 and prints the absolute path-names of all such files.

```
$ find /usr . -inum 258072 -print
/users/faculty/sarwar/myweb/UnixTcpIP
$
```

The following command searches the present working directory for files that have the name core or have extensions .ps or .o, displays their absolute pathnames, and removes them from the file structure. Parentheses are used to enclose a complex criterion. Be sure that you use spaces before and after \(and -o. The command does not prompt you for permission to remove; in order to be prompted, replace -exec with -ok.

```
$ find . \( -name core -o -name '*.ps' -o -name '*.o' \) -print -exec rm {} \;
...
$
```

You can use the whereis command to find out whether your system has a particular command, and if it does, where it is in the file structure. You typically need to get such information when you are trying to execute a command that you know is a valid command but that your shell cannot locate because the directory containing the executable for the command is not in your search path (*see* Chapters 4 and 7). Under these circumstances, you can use the whereis command to find the location of the command and update your search path. Although whereis is a BSD command, most UNIX systems today have it because they have a BSD compatibility package. Depending on the system you are using, the command not only gives you the absolute pathname for the command that you are searching for, but it also gives you the absolute pathnames for its manual page and source files if they are available on your system. The following is a brief description of the command.

---

whereis [options] [file-list]

Purpose: Locate binaries (executables), source codes, and manual pages for the commands in 'file-list'—a space-separated list of command names

Output: Absolute pathnames for the files containing binaries, source codes, and manual pages for the commands in 'file-list'

Commonly used options/features:

    -b   Search for binaries (executables) only

    -s   Search for source code only

The following examples illustrate use of whereis command. The first command is used to locate the whereis command. The second command is used to locate the executable file for the cat command. The last command locates the information for the find, compress, and tar commands.

```
$ whereis ftp
ftp: /usr/bin/ftp /usr/ucb/ftp /usr/man/man1/ftp.1
$ whereis -b cat
cat: /usr/bin/cat
$ whereis find compress tar
find: /usr/bin/find /usr/man/man1/find.1
compress: /usr/bin/compress /usr/local/bin/compress /usr/man/man1/compress.1
tar: /etc/tar /usr/bin/tar /usr/sbin/tar /usr/include/tar.h /usr/man/man1/tar.1
$
```

In the outputs of these commands, the directories /usr/bin, /usr/local/bin, /usr/ucb/, and /usr/sbin contain the executables for commands, the directory /usr/man contains several subdirectories that contain various sections of the UNIX online manual, the file /etc/tar is a symbolic link to /usr/sbin/tar, and the /usr/include directory contains **header files**.

In a system that has multiple versions of a command, the which utility can be used to determine the location (absolute pathname) of the version that is executed by the shell you are using when you type the command. When a command does not work according to its specification, the which utility can be used to determine the absolute pathname of the command version that executes. A local version of the command may execute because of the way the search *path* is set up in the *PATH* variable (*see* Chapters 4 and 7). And, the local version has been broken due to a recent update in the code; perhaps it does not work properly with the new libraries that were installed on the system. The which command takes a command-list (actually a file-list for the commands) as argument and returns absolute pathnames for them to standard output.

In the following In-Chapter Exercises, you will get practice using the find, sort, and whereis commands as well as appreciate the difference between the find and whereis commands.

IN-CHAPTER EXERCISES

10.7 Give a command for sorting the students file by using the whole line starting with the e-mail address.

10.8 Give a command for finding out where the executable code for the traceroute command is on your system.

10.9 You have a file called Phones somewhere in your directory structure, but you don't remember where it is. Give the command to locate it.

10.6   Searching Files

UNIX has powerful utilities for file searching that allow you to find lines in text files that contain a particular expression, string, or pattern. For example, if you have a large file that contains the records for a company's employees, one per line, you might want to search the file for line(s) containing information on John Johnsen. The utilities that allow file searching are grep, egrep, and fgrep. The following is a brief description of these utilities.

grep [options] pattern [file-list]
egrep [options] [string] [file-list]
fgrep [options] [expression] [file-list]

Purpose:	Search the files in 'file-list' for the given pattern, string, or expression; if no 'file-list', take input from standard input
Output:	Lines containing the given pattern, string, or expression on standard output

Commonly used options/features:

-c	Print the number of matching lines only
-i	Ignore the case of letters during the matching process
-l	Print only the names of files with matching lines
-n	Print line numbers along with matched lines
-s	Useful for shell scripts, this option suppresses error messages (the 'return status' is set to 0 for success and nonzero for no success—*see* Chapter 13)
-v	Print nonmatching lines
-w	Search for the given pattern as a string

Of the three, the `fgrep` command is the fastest but most limited; `egrep` is the slowest but most flexible, allowing full use of regular expressions; and `grep` has reasonable speed and is fairly flexible in terms of its support of regular expressions. In the following sessions, we illustrate the use of these commands with some of the options shown in the description. We use the same students file in these sessions that we used in describing the `sort` utility in Section 10.4. We display the file by using the `cat` command.

```
$ cat students
John Johnsen        john.johnsen@tp.com      503.555.1111
Hassaan Sarwar      hsarwar@k12.st.or        503.444.2132
David Kendall       d_kendall@msnbc.org      229.111.2013
John Johnsen        johnsen@psu.net          301.999.8888
Kelly Kimberly      kellyk@umich.gov         555.123.9999
Maham Sarwar        msarwar@k12.st.or        713.888.0000
Jamie Davidson      j.davidson@uet.edu       515.001.2932
Nabeel Sarwar       nsarwar@xyz.net          434.555.1212
$
```

The most common and simple use of the `grep` utility is to display the lines in a file containing a particular string, word, or pattern. In the following session, we display those lines in the students file that contain the string sarwar. The lines are displayed in the order they occur in the file.

```
$ grep sarwar students
Hassaan Sarwar      hsarwar@k12.st.or      503.444.2132
Maham Sarwar        msarwar@k12.st.or      713.888.0000
Nabeel Sarwar       nsarwar@xyz.net        434.555.1212
$
```

The grep command can be used with the -n option to display the output lines with line numbers. In the following session, the lines in the students file containing the string sarwar are displayed with line numbers.

```
$ grep -n sarwar students
2:Hassaan Sarwar     hsarwar@k12.st.or      503.444.2132
7:Maham Sarwar       msarwar@k12.st.or      713.888.0000
8:Nabeel Sarwar      nsarwar@xyz.net        434.555.1212
$
```

You can use the grep command to search a string in multiple files with regular expressions and shell metacharacters. In the following session, grep searches for the string "include" in all the files in the present working directory that end with .c (C source files). Note that the access permissions for server.c were set so that grep couldn't read it—the user running the command did not have read permission for the server.c file.

```
$ grep -n include *.c
client.c: 21:      #include           <stdio.h>
client.c: 22:      #include           <ctype.h>
client.c: 23:      #include           <string.h>
lab1.c: 13:        #include           <stdio.h>
grep: can't open server.c
$
```

You can also use the grep command with the -l option to display the names of files in which the pattern occurs. However, it does not display the lines that contain the pattern. In the following session, the ~/States directory is assumed to contain one file for every state in the United States, and this file is assumed to contain the names of all the cities in the state (e.g., Portland). The grep command, therefore, displays the names of files that contain the word *Portland*, that is, the names of states that have a city called Portland.

```
$ grep -l Portland ~/States
Maine
Oregon
$
```

The following command displays the lines in the students file that start with letters
A through H. In the command, ^ specifies the beginning of a line.

```
$ grep '^[A-H]' students
Hassaan Sarwar      hsarwar@k12.st.or      503.444.2132
David Kendall       d_kendall@msnbc.org    229.111.2013
$
```

The following command displays the lines from the students file that contain at least eight
consecutive lowercase letters.

```
$ grep '[a-z]\{8\}' students
John Johnsen        jjohnsen@psu.net       301.999.8888
Jamie Davidson      j.davidson@uet.edu     515.001.2932
$
```

The following command displays the lines that contain a word starting with the word
(string) Ke. Note that \< is used to indicate start of a word. Single quotes are used in '\<Ke'
to ensure that the shell does not interpret any letter in the pattern as a shell metacharacter.

```
$ grep '\<Ke' students
David Kendall       d_kendall@msnbc.org    229.111.2013
Kelly Kimberly      kellyk@umich.gov       555.123.9999
$
```

The string \> is the end of the word anchor. Thus, the following command displays the
lines that contain words that end with net. If we replace the string net with the string war,
what would be the output of the command?

```
$ grep 'net\>' students
John Johnsen        jjohnsen@psu.net       301.999.8888
Nabeel Sarwar       nsarwar@xyz.net        434.555.1212
$
```

In the following command, the regular expression "Kimberly|Nabeel" is used to have
egrep display the lines, and their numbers, that contain either Kimberly or Nabeel. Note
that the regular expression uses the pipe symbol (|) to logically OR the two strings.

```
$ egrep -n "Kimberly|Nabeel" students
6:Kelly Kimberly    kellyk@umich.gov       555.123.9999
8:Nabeel Sarwar     nsarwar@xyz.net        434.555.1212
$
```

You can use the **-v** option to display the lines that do not contain the string specified in the command. The following command produces all the lines not containing the words Kimberly and Nabeel.

```
$ grep -v "Kimberly|Nabeel" students
John Johnsen        john.johnsen@tp.com      503.555.1111
Hassaan Sarwar      hsarwar@k12.st.or        503.444.2132
David Kendall       d_kendall@msnbc.org      229.111.2013
John Johnsen        jjohnsen@psu.net         301.999.8888
Maham Sarwar        msarwar@k12.st.or        713.888.0000
Jamie Davidson      j.davidson@uet.edu       515.001.2932
$
```

The following command displays the lines in the students file that start with letter J. Note the use of ^ to indicate the beginning of a line.

```
$ egrep "^J" students
Jamie Davidson      j.davidson@uet.edu       515.001.2932
John Johnsen        jjohnsen@psu.net         301.999.8888
John Johnsen        john.johnsen@tp.com      503.555.1111
$
```

The following command displays the lines in the students file that start with letters J or K. Note that ^J and ^K represent lines starting with the letters J and K.

```
$ egrep "^J|^K" students
Jamie Davidson      j.davidson@uet.edu       515.001.2932
John Johnsen        jjohnsen@psu.net         301.999.8888
John Johnsen        john.johnsen@tp.com      503.555.1111
Kelly Kimberly      kellyk@umich.gov         555.123.9999
$
```

In the following In-Chapter Exercises, you will use the commands of the grep family to understand their various characteristics.

IN-CHAPTER EXERCISES

10.10 Give a command for displaying the lines in the ~/Personal/Phones file that contain the words starting with the string "David."

10.11 Give a command for displaying the lines in the ~/Personal/Phones file that contain phone numbers with area code 212. Phone numbers are stored as xxx-xxx-xxxx, where x is a digit from 0 through 9.   *(continued)*

IN-CHAPTER EXERCISES *(continued)*

10.12 Display the names of all the files in your home directory that contain the word "main" (without quotes).

10.7 Cutting and Pasting

You can process files that store data in the form of tables in UNIX by using the cut and paste commands. A table consists of lines, each line comprises a record, and each record has a fixed number of fields. Fields are usually separated by tabs or spaces, although any field separator can be used. The cut command allows you to cut one or more fields of a table in one or more files and send them to standard output. In other words, you can use the cut command to slice a table vertically in a file across field boundaries. The following is a brief description of the command.

---

cut -blist [-n] [file-list]
cut -clist [file-list]
cut -flist [-dchar] [-s] [file-list]

| **Purpose:** | Cut out fields of a table in a file |
| **Output:** | Fields cut by the command |

Commonly used options/features:

–b list	Treat each byte as a column and cut bytes specified in the 'list'
–c list	Treat each character as a column and cut characters specified in the 'list'
–d char	Use the character 'char' instead of the <Tab> character as field separator
–f list	Cut fields specified in the 'list'
–n	Do not split characters (used with –b option)
–s	Do not output lines that do not have the delimiter character

SYNTAX

Here, 'list' is a comma-separated list with – used to specify a range of bytes, characters, or fields. The following sessions illustrate some of the commonly used options and features of the cut command. In this section, we use the file student_addresses, whose contents are displayed by the cat command.

```
$ cat student_addresses
John     Doe      jdoe@xyz.com      312.111.9999      312.999.1111
Pam      Meyer    meyer@uop.uk      666.222.1212      666.555.1212
Jim      Davis    jamesd@aol.com    713.999.5555      713.413.0000
Jason    Kim      j_kim@up.org      434.000.8888      434.555.2211
```

```
Amy       Nash      nash@state.gov      888.111.4444      888.827.3333
$
```

The file has five fields numbered 1 through 5, from left to right: first name, last name, e-mail address, home phone number, and work phone number. Although we could have used any character as the field separator, we chose the <Tab> character to give a "columnar" look to the table and the output of the following cut and paste commands. You can display a table of first and last names by using the -f option. Note that -f1,2 specifies the first and the second fields of the student_addresses file.

```
$ cut -f1,2 student_addresses
John      Doe
Pam       Meyer
Jim       Davis
Jason     Kim
Amy       Nash
$
```

We generated a table of names (first and last) and work phone numbers by slicing the first, second, and fifth fields of the table in the student_addresses file.

```
$ cut -f1,2,5 student_addresses
John      Doe       312.999.1111
Pam       Meyer     666.555.1212
Jim       Davis     713.413.0000
Jason     Kim       434.555.2211
Amy       Nash      888.827.3333
$
```

To generate a table of names and e-mail addresses, we used the following command. Here, -f1-3 specifies fields 1 through 3 of the student_addresses file.

```
$ cut -f1-3 student_addresses
John      Doe       jdoe@xyz.com
Pam       Meyer     meyer@uop.uk
Jim       Davis     jamesd@aol.com
Jason     Kim       j_kim@up.org
Amy       Nash      nash@state.gov
$
```

We recommend that you run this command on your machine to determine whether the desired output is produced. If the desired output is not produced, you have not used the

<Tab> character as the field separator for some or all of the records. In such a case, correct the table and try the command again.

In the preceding sessions, we have used the default field separator, the <Tab> character. Depending on the format of your file, you can use any character as a field separator. For example, as we discussed in Chapters 3 and 7, the /etc/passwd file uses the colon character (:) as the field separator. You can therefore use the cut command to extract information such as the login name, real name, group ID, and home directory for a user. Because the real name, login name, and home directory are the fifth, first, and sixth fields, respectively, the following command can be used to generate a table of names of all users, along with their login IDs and home directories.

```
$ cut -d: -f5,1,6 /etc/passwd
root:0000-Admin(0000):/
daemon:0000-Admin(0000):/
bin:0000-Admin(0000):/usr/bin
sys:0000-Admin(0000):/
adm:0000-Admin(0000):/var/adm
lp:0000-lp(0000):/usr/spool/lp
...
sarwar:Mansoor Sarwar:/users/faculty/sarwar:
...
$
```

Note that −d option is used to specify : as the field separator, and it is also displayed as the field separator in the output of the command. For blank delimited files, use a blank (space) after −d\, as shown in the following example. The cat sample command is used to display the blank delimited file, called sample, and the cut −d\ -f1,6 sample command is used to display fields 1 and 6 of this file.

```
$ cat sample
1 John CS Senior john@net2net.com 3.45
2 Jane CS Junior jane@net2net.com 3.76
3 Sara CS Senior sara@net3net.com 3.33
$ cut -d\  -f1,6 sample
1 3.45
2 3.76
3 3.33
$
```

The paste command complements the cut command; it concatenates files horizontally (the cat command concatenates files vertically). Hence, this command can be used to paste tables in columns. The following is a brief description of the command.

S Y N T A X

paste [options] file-list

Purpose: Horizontally concatenate files in 'file-list'; use standard input if—is used as a file

Output: Files in 'file-list' pasted (horizontally concatenated)

Commonly used options/features:

–d list   Use 'list' characters as line separators; <Tab> is the default character

Consider the file student_records that contains student names (first and last), major, and current GPA.

```
$ cat student_records
John      Doe      ECE      3.54
Pam       Meyer    CS       3.61
Jim       Davis    CS       2.71
Jason     Kim      ECE      3.97
Amy       Nash     ECE      2.38
$
```

We can combine the two tables horizontally and generate another by using the following command. In order to keep the resultant table small, we have used a shortened version of the original student_addresses file that contains the first name, last name, and work phone number only. Note that the output of the paste command is displayed on the display screen and is not stored in a file. The resultant table has seven fields.

```
$ paste student_records student_addresses
John      Doe      ECE      3.54    John     Doe      312.999.1111
Pam       Meyer    CS       3.61    Pam      Meyer    666.555.1212
Jim       Davis    CS       2.71    Jim      Davis    713.413.0000
Jason     Kim      ECE      3.97    Jason    Kim      434.555.2211
Amy       Nash     ECE      2.38    Amy      Nash     888.827.3333
$
```

Suppose that you want to use student_addresses and student_records tables to generate and display a table that has student names, majors, and home phone numbers. You may do so in one of two ways. When you use the first method, you cut appropriate fields of the two tables, put them in separate files with fields in the order you want to display them, paste the two tables in the correct order, and remove the tables. The following session illustrates this procedure and its result. Note that the new table is not saved as a file when the following commands are executed. If you want to save the new table in a file, use the paste table1 table2 > students_table command. The students_table contains the columns of table1 and table2 (in that order) pasted together.

```
$ cut -f1-3 student_records > table1
$ cut -f4 student_addresses > table2
$ paste table1 table2
John      Doe      ECE      312.111.9999
Pam       Meyer    CS       666.222.1212
Jim       Davis    CS       713.999.5555
Jason     Kim      ECE      434.000.8888
Amy       Nash     ECE      888.111.4444
$ rm table1 table2
$
```

The procedure just outlined is expensive in terms of space and time because you have to execute four commands, generate two temporary files (table1 and table2), and remove these files after the desired table has been displayed. You can use a different method to accomplish the same thing with the following command.

```
$ paste student_records student_addresses | cut -f1-3,7
John      Doe      ECE      312.111.9999
Pam       Meyer    CS       666.222.1212
Jim       Davis    CS       713.999.5555
Jason     Kim      ECE      434.000.8888
Amy       Nash     ECE      888.111.4444
$
```

Here, you first combine the tables in the two files into one table with nine columns by using the `paste student_records student_addresses` command and then displaying the desired table by using the `cut -f1-3,7` command. Clearly, this second method is the preferred way to accomplish the task because no temporary files are created and only one command is needed. If you want to save the resultant table in the students_table file, use the command `paste student_records student_addresses | cut -f1-3,7 > students_table`.

10.8 Encoding and Decoding

In Chapter 6, we discussed electronic mail and various UNIX utilities that can be used to send and receive e-mail. E-mail messages are transported in clear (plain) text, and some e-mail systems are fussy about certain characters contained in the body of the message, such as the tilde character (`~`) in the first column for the `mail` and `mailx` utilities. This is a serious problem for mail systems, such as `mail`, that do not have convenient support for attachments and you need to attach items such as pictures or executable programs (binaries). The sender can use the uuencode (UNIX-to-UNIX encode) utility to convert a file to be mailed to a format that contains readable ASCII characters only, with a letter in the first column. The receiver can use the uudecode utility to convert the uuencoded file to the original format. In this section, we discuss these two utilities, beginning with a brief description of them expressed as commands.

S Y N T A X

uuencode [source-file] decode_label

Purpose: Encode 'source-file' from binary to ASCII

Output: The encoded version of 'source-file' to standard output

Commonly used options/features:

None

uudecode [option] [encoded-file]

Purpose: Decode 'encoded-file' from ASCII to binary

Output: The binary version of 'encoded-file' into a file called 'decode-label', the second parameter of the uuencode command

Commonly used options/features:

-p   Send the binary version of the uuencoded file to standard output

The uuencode command sends the encoded (ASCII) version of the file to standard output. The command takes input from standard input if no 'source-file' is specified in the command. The output has 'decode_label' in the header (first line) of the ASCII version.

The uudecode utility recreates the original binary file from the uuencoded (ASCII) file and puts it in a file called decode_label. With the –p option, the command sends the binary version to standard output. This option uses the uudecode command in a pipeline (*see* Chapter 12). Both the uuencode and uudecode commands retain the original files that they translate. The diagram shown in Figure 10.1 illustrates the process of uuencoding and uudecoding.

You can redirect the output to a file by using the > symbol, as shown in the uuencode a.out alarm.out > sarwar.out command in the following session. When you do so, the encoded output goes to the file sarwar.out with a decode_label of alarm.out.

```
$ more a.out
  À  _ _  @ D*  @
Ô"àÂ@
@@#   āȼh®â"^L@K  \@K ¢ OÂ  ^  a
                        Kè `Â dâ h€®âH   à@4 Ò d  à
$ uuencode a.out alarm.out > sarwar.out
$ head sarwar.out
begin 700 alarm.out
M@0,!"P ( " , " @ \$" T .@0)(#H$25
M*B "E *@!)0"0 H7 0U"++@N , C" &((@) 0* 0! 0 "@$
M ! "- 0 $ )&<(Z @0 ( $ ! @! 0 )WCOV@O (KA7b
M*!$ bo$b(,0 2Y(0( "l$ (d@.@7$ $n4$" @@*(@(!* $\!
MPa.@7h"@80l2@ !+ 0 .@#h&#" z!dx@.@:*0% &2!( 1+p "*x5xdb0
M$" E! @!1<@ "6$N "F! %D #2:$" IA ") " !32 z!de! @!Q<@
M "6$N 2F! %D "N:$ 4+p "*x5xg01 (d!(b&t ".2$" JA
```

```
M",(#H&B  D  !  H  "R\   BN%>)(D  3  $I(0  !&4$"  '%R   )82X!*8$  5
M0   %YH0(  #"  Z!PH  3  >8CH'SJ(Z"  [".@A  ,   C"  &((PB.@B  ,  !#"
$ uudecode sarwar.out
$ more alarm.out
   À  _  _   @  D*  @
Ô"àÂ@
@@#   āȼh®â"^L@K   \@K  ¢  OÂ  ^  a
                              Kè  `Â  dâ  h€®âH     à

$
```

Note the label alarm.out on the first line of the uuencoded file sarwar.out. The uudecode command translates the file sarwar.out and puts the original in the file alarm.out. As expected, a.out and alarm.out contain the same data. If you want to re-create the original file in a.out, use a.out as the label in the uuencode command, as in uuencode a.out a.out > sarwar.out. The uudecode sarwar.out command produces the original binary file in the a.out file.

The output generated by uuencode is about 35 percent *larger* than the original file. Thus, for efficient use of the network bandwidth, you should compress binary files before uuencoding them and uncompress them after uudecoding them. Doing so is particularly important for large picture files or files containing multimedia data such as movies.

10.9   File Encryption and Decryption

We briefly described encryption and decryption of files in Chapter 8. Here, we describe these processes in more detail with the help of the UNIX command crypt.

Recall that encryption is a process by which a file is converted to a form completely different from its original version and that the transformed file is called encrypted file; and that the reverse process of transforming the encrypted file to its original form is known as decryption. Figure 10.2 illustrates these processes.

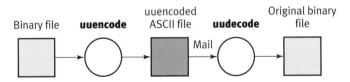

Figure 10.1 The process of uuencoding and uudecoding

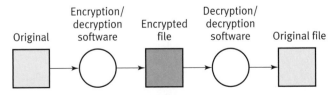

Figure 10.2 The process of encryption and decryption

You encrypt files to prevent others from reading them. You can also encrypt your e-mail messages to prevent hackers from understanding your message even if they are able to tap a network as your message travels through it. On a UNIX system, you can use the crypt command to encrypt and decrypt your files. The following is a brief description of the command.

SYNTAX

crypt [option]

Purpose:	Encrypt (decrypt) standard input and send it to standard output
Output:	Encrypted (decrypted) version of the input text

Commonly used options/features:

key	Password to be used to perform encryption (and decryption)
−k	Use the value of the environment variable CRYPTKEY

By default, the crypt command takes input from standard input and sends its output to standard output. The optional argument key is a password used in the encryption and decryption processes. The command is used mostly with actual files, not keyboard input, so the commonly used syntax for the crypt command is

```
crypt key < original_file > encrypted_file
```

To decrypt an encrypted file, the process is reversed according to the syntax

```
crypt key < encrypted_file > original_file
```

Remember that the 'key' must be the same for both commands. The file name after the greater-than symbol (>) is chosen by the user. Multiple files can be specified as source files, but the command encrypts only the first file and ignores the remaining files. The semantics of these commands are shown in Figure 10.3. Note that the original file (the file to be crypted) remains intact and must be explicitly removed from the system after the encrypted version has been generated.

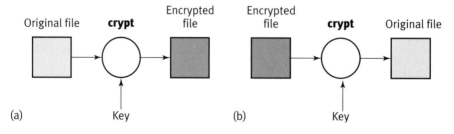

Figure 10.3 Encryption and decryption of a file by using the 'crypt' command

The following session illustrates the use of crypt for encrypting and decrypting a file called memo1. The crypt !hskr45#$ < memo1 > secret_memo1 command encrypts memo1 (in the present working directory) by using !hskr45#$ as the key and puts the encrypted version in the file secret_memo1, also in the present working directory. The cat commands before and after the crypt command show the contents of the original and encrypted files. Note that the contents of the encrypted file, secret_memo1, are not readable, which is the objective.

$ cat memo1

Dear Jim:

This is to inform you that second quarter earnings do not look very good and that this will be made public on Monday next week when The Wall Street Journal reports the company earnings. Of course, the company stock will take a hit, but we need to keep the morale of our employees high. I am calling a meeting of the vice presidents tomorrow morning at 8:00 to talk about this issue in the main conference room. See you then. Make sure this information does not get out before time.

Nadeem

$ crypt hskr45#$ < memo1 > secret_memo1

$ cat secret_memo1

```
.  _¬&Ôü _k!í
¶ë÷C_Ä_K6āÕ‰Ó
œw6ê!Y__À í)]QJ©,/M‰U„-_t¯;§C_nm  Ō   LŌ_ìô_VF}å_€@ªFì
‡°   5ù@kss‡._-ì_Bv{Ÿy¨íd__æ
'&Ê  d2?ŌKS]Qœê ìV„T1!bâp-Ā-/ªê_   ø  ùW_  )€ïW‹ç%|_Nì_fbÛÃHI!Üe  W€_-©¨£
HâWfàß7Ÿ«  ·Ûy‡:~€œTÊy…_v|-)¿¿-à HÒ+ÛTXO [ŌZÓÀPm°_!tÑ
„y©P"XAw›u _ha"  œ]Ë[ø-Ï«Ù_)º
   ÛË__%_)A&ÚÊÇZYcØ          …-CE'ªÙ>$  :$à_āPx _‹6„·_?N
Ì:NMÕ\Ú4€&Y_-ÄU Q)}Ú_ÌHu
I¸aU gf€ €Ë É_`   Ñ}_ò|ª:[EÊL ó N§^\Ãd_GùI8m óôÚœófâ«Ôù-Ï·ò?Û98˘œ©`  m __
ì_'(ø  €
ø û0_Ã@·+
-S
#óøÄ´ÄÄ´Å29.
_Ä.´Ä.
  ´:ù/´Å
      ÄÄ¿/
_  ÄÄÚ
Ä 58
```

$

The command for decrypting the file secret_memo1 and putting the original version in the file original_memo1 is as follows. The cat command confirms that the original file has been restored.

```
$ crypt hskr45#$ < secret_memo1 > original_memo1
$ cat original_memo1
```

Dear Jim:

This is to inform you that second quarter earnings do not look very good
and that this will be made public on Monday next week when The Wall Street
Journal reports the company earnings. Of course, the company stock will take
a hit, but we need to keep the morale of our employees high. I am calling
a meeting of the vice presidents tomorrow morning at 8:00 to talk about this
issue in the main conference room. See you then. Make sure this information
does not get out before time.

Nadeem

```
$
```

Again, the crypt command does not remove the file that it encrypts (or decrypts), and it is your responsibility to remove the original file after encrypting it. Note also that the encryption algorithm used by the crypt command is not the same as that used for encrypting user passwords, as found in the /etc/passwd or /etc/shadow files. Also, even a superuser cannot decrypt an encrypted file without having the correct key. The crypt command uses an encryption technique that was used in the German *Enigma machine* during World War II, although some of the parameters used in crypt make the output generated by the command more difficult to decipher than that of the Enigma machine. However, the methods of attack are well known for such machines. The level of security provided by crypt is therefore minimal, and the command must not be used on documents that require an extremely high level of security. However, an average user is not familiar with these attack methods, and the use of crypt is a fairly decent method of protecting your files.

The following In-Chapter Exercises will give you practice using the crypt, cut, paste, uudecode, and uuencode commands and help you to understand their semantics with a hands-on session.

IN-CHAPTER EXERCISES

10.13 Create the student_addresses and student_records files used in Section 10.7. Then run the cut and paste commands described in this section to see how these commands work.

10.14 Copy the executable code for a command from the /usr/bin directory and uuencode it. Run the ls -l command and report the size of the encoded file. Then uudecode the encoded file to convert it back to the original file.

10.15 Try the sessions for the crypt command given in this section on your system.

Summary

Several advanced file processing operations have to be performed from time to time. These operations include compressing and uncompressing, sorting, searching for files and commands in the file structure, searching files for certain strings or patterns, performing database like operations of cutting fields from a table or pasting tables together, transforming non-ASCII files to ASCII, and encrypting and decrypting files. Several tools are available in the UNIX operating system that can be used to perform these tasks.

Some of these tools have the ability to specify a set of items by using a single character string. This is done by using a set of nondigit and nonletter characters and a set of rules called regular expressions. The utilities that allow the use of regular expressions are awk, ed, egrep, grep, sed, and vi. In this chapter, we described regular expressions and their use in vi, egrep, and grep.

The compress and gzip commands can be used to compress and uncompress files, with gzip being the more flexible of the two. The uncompress, gunzip, and gzip –d commands can be used to uncompress files, compressed with the compress and gzip commands, respectively. The gzexe command can be used to compress executable files, and the gzexe –d command can be used to uncompress them. Files compressed with gzexe can be executed without explicitly uncompressing them. Files compressed with gzexe can be executed without explicitly uncompressing them. The zcat and zmore commands can be used to display compressed files without explicitly uncompressing them.

The sort command can be used to sort text files. Each line comprises a record with several fields, and the number of fields in all the lines is the same. Text files can be processed like tables by using the cut and paste commands that allow cutting of columns in a table and pasting of tables, respectively. The sort, cut, and paste commands can be combined via a pipeline (*see* Chapter 12) to generate tables based on different sets of criteria.

The find and whereis commands can be used to search the UNIX file structure to determine locations (absolute pathnames) of files and commands. The find command, in particular, is very powerful and lets you search for files based on several criteria, such as file size. The which command can be used to determine which version of a command executes, in case there are several versions available on a system.

UNIX provides a family of powerful utilities for searching text files for strings, expressions, and patterns. These utilities are grep, egrep, and fgrep. Of the three, fgrep is the fastest but most limited; egrep is the most flexible but slowest of the three; and grep is the middle-of-the-road utility—reasonably fast and fairly flexible.

The uuencode and uudecode utilities are useful in situations when users want to e-mail non-ASCII files such as multimedia files, but the mailing system does not allow attachments. The uuencode utility can be used to transform a non-ASCII file into an ASCII file, and uudecode can transform the ASCII file back into the original non-ASCII version. The uuencode utility is therefore used by the sender before sending a non-ASCII file, and uudecode is used by the receiver of a uuencoded file to convert it back to the original form.

In the UNIX system, the `crypt` command can be used to encrypt and decrypt files that the user wants to keep secret. Techniques for converting a crypted file back to original are well known. However, the average user is not familiar with these techniques, so the use of `crypt` results in a fairly good scheme for protecting files.

Problems

1. List five file processing operations that you consider advanced.

2. What are regular expressions?

3. Give the `vi` command for replacing all occurrences of the string "DOS" with the string "UNIX" in the whole document that is currently being edited. What are the commands for replacing all occurrences of the strings "DOS" and "Windows" with the string "UNIX" from the lines that start or end with these strings in the document being edited?

4. Give the `vi` command for deleting all four-letter words starting with B, F, b, and f in the file being edited.

5. Give the `vi` command for renaming all C source files in a document to C++ source code files. Note: C source files end with .c and C++ source files end with .C.

6. What is file compression? What do the terms *compressed files* and *decompressed files* mean? What commands are available for performing compression and decompression in UNIX? Which are the preferred commands? Why?

7. Take three large files in your directory structure—a text file, a PostScript file, and a picture file—and compress them by using the `compress` command. Which file was compressed the most? What was the percentage reduction in file size? Compress the same file by using the `gzip` command. Which resulted in better compression, `compress` or `gzip`? Uncompress the files by using `uncompress` and `gunzip` commands. Show your work.

8. What is sorting? Give an example to illustrate your answer. Name four applications of sorting. Name the UNIX utility that can be used to perform sorting.

9. Go to the http://cnn.com/weather Web site and record the high and low temperatures for the following majors cities in Asia: Kuala Lumpur, Karachi, Tokyo, Lahore, Manila, New Delhi, and Jakarta. In a file called asiapac.temps, construct an ASCII table comprising one line per city in the order: city name, high temperature, and low temperature. The following is a sample line.

    Tokyo 78 72

    Give commands to perform the following operations.

    a. Sort the table by city name.

    b. Sort the table by high temperature.

    c. Sort the table by using the city name as the primary and low temperature as the secondary key.

10. For the students file in Section 10.4, give a command to sort the lines in the file by using last name only as the sort key.

11. What commands are available for file searching? State the purpose of each.

12. Give the command that searches your home directory and displays pathnames of all the files created after the file /etc/passwd.

13. Give a command that searches your home directory and removes all PostScript and .gif files. The command must take your permission (prompt you) before removing a file.

14. On your UNIX system, how long does it take to find all the files that are larger than 1,000 bytes in size? What command(s) did you use?

15. What does the command `grep -n '^' student_addresses` do? Assume that student_addresses is the same file we used in Section 10.7.

16. Give the command that displays lines in student_addresses that start with the letter K or have letter J in them. The output of the command should also display line numbers.

17. What do the following commands do?

    a. `grep [A-H] students`

    b. `grep [A,H] students`

18. Give a command that displays names of all the files in your ~/courses/ece446 directory that contain the word UNIX.

19. Give a command that generates a table of user names for all users on your system, along with their personal information. Extract this information from the /etc/passwd file.

20. Use the tables student_addresses and student_records to generate a table in which each row contains last name, work phone number, and GPA.

21. Imagine that you have a picture file campus.bmp that you would like to e-mail to a friend. Give the sequence of commands that are needed to convert the file to ASCII form, reduce its size, and encrypt it before e-mailing it.

22. What is the purpose of file encryption? Name the UNIX command that you can use to encrypt and decrypt files. Give the command for encrypting a file called ~/personal/memo7 and store it in a ~/personal/memo_007 file. Be sure that, when the encrypted file is decrypted, it is put back in the ~/personal/memo7 file. Give the command to decrypt the encrypted file.

23. What is the difference between the following:

    a. encryption and encoding?

    b. encoding and compression?

    c. `compress` and `zip`?

File Sharing

Objectives

- To explain different ways of sharing files
- To discuss the UNIX schemes and commands for implementing file sharing
- To describe UNIX hard and soft (symbolic) links in detail and discuss their advantages and disadvantages
- To cover the commands and primitives
  `*, ~, ln, ln -f, ln -s, ls -i, ls -l`

11.1   Introduction

When a group of people work together on the same project, they need to share information. If the information to be shared is on a computer system, group members have to share files and directories. For example, authors collaborating on a book or software engineers working on a software project need to share files and directories related to their project. In this chapter, we discuss several ways of implementing file sharing in a computer system. The discussion of file sharing in this chapter focuses on how a file can be accessed from various directories by various users in a UNIX system. Under the topic of "version control" in Chapter 20, we address how members of a team can work on one or more files simultaneously without losing their work.

Several methods can be used to allow a group of users to share files and directories. In this chapter, we describe duplicate shared files, common login for members of a team, setting appropriate access permissions on shared files, common group for members in a team, and sharing via links. All these methods can be used to allow a team of users to share files and directories in a UNIX system. Although we describe each of these techniques, the chapter is dedicated primarily to a discussion of sharing via links in a UNIX-based computer system.

11.2   Duplicate Shared Files

The simplest way of sharing files is to make copies of these files and give them to all team members. The members can put these copies anywhere in their own accounts (directory structures) and manipulate them in any way they desire. This scheme works well if members of the team are to work on the shared file(s) sequentially, but it has obvious problems if team members are to work on these files simultaneously. In the former case, team members work on one copy of the shared files one by one and complete the task at hand. In the latter case, because the members work on their own copies, the copies become inconsistent and no single copy of the shared files reflects the work done by all the team members. This outcome defeats the purpose of sharing.

11.3   Common Login for Members of a Team

In this scheme, the system administrator creates a new user group comprising the members of a team and gives them a new account to which they all have access; that is, they all know the login name and password for the account. All the files and directories created by any team member under this account are owned by the team, and everyone has access to them.

It is a simple scheme that works quite well, particularly in situations in which the number of teams is small and teams are stable; that is, they stay together for long periods of time. Such is the case for teams of authors writing a book or programming teams working on large software projects that take several months to finish. However, this scheme also has a couple of drawbacks. First, team members have to use a separate account for their current project and cannot use their regular accounts to access shared files and directories. Second, the system administrator has to create a new account for every new team formed in the organization. Having to do so could create a considerable amount of extra work for the administrator if the duration of projects is short and new teams are formed for every new project. The scheme could be a real headache for the system administrator in a college-like environment where student teams are formed to work on class projects, resulting in a large number of teams every semester or quarter.

11.4 Setting Appropriate Access Permissions on Shared Files

In this scheme, team members decide to put all shared files under one member's account, and the access permissions on these files are set so that all team members can access them. This scheme works well if *only* this team's members form the user group (recall the discussion of owner, group, and others in Chapter 8) because, if the group has other users in it, they will also have access to the shared files. For example, suppose that two professors, Art Pohm and Jim Davis, at a university belong to the user group 'faculty'. They decide to put their shared files in Davis's account but set the group access permissions to read, write, and execute for all shared files. All the professors in the user group 'faculty' then will have the same access permissions to these files, which will pose security problems. In particular, if the information to be shared is a small portion of the total amount of information residing in a member's account (say, two ordinary files out of tens of files and directories that the member owns), the risk of opening the door to all users in a group is too high, and a better technique must be used.

11.5 Common Group for Members of a Team

This scheme works just like the preceding one, except that the system administrator creates a new user group consisting of the members of the team only. All team members get individual logins and set access permissions for their files so that they are accessible to other team/group members. This file-sharing scheme is effective and is used often, particularly in conjunction with some version control mechanism.

11.6 File Sharing Via Links

As described in Chapter 7, the attributes of a UNIX file are stored in its inode on disk. When a file is opened, its inode is copied into the main memory, allowing speedy access to its contents. In this section, we describe how the use of an inode results in a mechanism that allows you to access a file from various directories by specifying the file name only. System administrators commonly use this scheme to allow access to some files and directories through various directories. Thus, for example, all the files for executable commands can be accessed via the /bin or /usr/bin directories.

A **link** is a way to establish a connection between the file to be shared and the directory entries of the users who want to have access to this file. Thus, when we say that a file has N links, we mean that the file has N directory entries. The links therefore aid file sharing by providing different access paths to files to be shared. The level of sharing, however, is controlled by setting appropriate access permissions for these files. You can create links to files to which you do not have any access, but that gets you nowhere. Hence, file sharing via links is accomplished first by creating access paths to shared paths by establishing links to them and then by setting appropriate access permissions on these files.

UNIX supports two types of links: **hard links** and **soft/symbolic** links. Both types are created by using the ln command. The remainder of this chapter discusses methods of creating both types of links and their internal implementation in the UNIX system.

11.6.1 Hard Links

A hard link is a pointer to the inode of a file. When a file is created in UNIX, the system allocates a unique inode to the file and creates a directory entry in the directory in which the file is created. As we discussed before, the directory entry comprises an ordered pair (inode #, filename). The inode number for a file is used to access its attributes, including contents of the file on disk for reading or writing (changing) them (*see* Chapter 7). Suppose that you create a file Chapter3 in your present working directory and the system allocates inode number 53472 to this file. Therefore, the directory entry for this file is (52473, Chapter3).

If we assume that the present working directory previously contained files Chapter1 and Chapter2, its logical structure is shown in Figure 11.1(a). The new file has been highlighted with a gray shade. Figure 11.1(b) shows contents of the disk block that contains the present working directory. The connection between this directory entry and the file's contents is shown in Figure 11.1(c). The inode number in file Chapter3's directory entry is used to index an inode table in the main memory in order to access that file's inode. The inode contains attributes of Chapter3, including its location on disk.

In UNIX, you can create a link to a file by using the ln command. This command allows you to give another name to Chapter3 in the same directory that contains the file—or in some other directory. The Syntax box below is a brief description of the ln command.

SYNTAX

ln [options] existing-file new-file
ln [options] existing-file-list directory

Purpose: First syntax: Create a hard link to 'existing-file' and name it 'new-file'

Second syntax: Create hard links to the ordinary files in 'existing-file-list' in 'directory'; links have the same names as the original file

Commonly used options/features:

   -f   Force creation of link; don't prompt if 'new-file' already exists

   -n   Don't create the link if 'new-file' already exists

   -s   Create a symbolic link to 'existing-file' and name it 'new-file'

The ln command without any option creates a hard link to a file provided the user has execute permission for all the directories in the path leading to the file (the last component of the pathname). The following session illustrates how the ln command can be used to create a hard link in the same directory that contains 'existing-file'. The only purpose of this example is to illustrate how the ln command is used; it isn't representative of how you would establish and use hard links in practice.

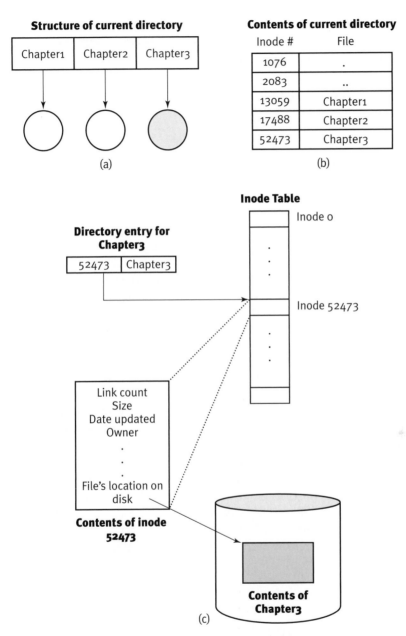

Figure 11.1 (a) Logical structure of current directory; (b) contents of current directory; and (c) relationship among a directory entry, inode, and file contents

```
$ ls -il
13059 -rwx------  1   sarwar faculty   398   Mar 11 14:20    Chapter1
17488 -rwx------  1   sarwar faculty   5983  Jan 17 11:57    Chapter2
52473 -rwx------  1   sarwar faculty   9352  May 28 23:09    Chapter3
$ ln Chapter3 Chapter3.hard
$ ls -il
13059 -rwx------  1   sarwar faculty   398   Mar 11 14:20    Chapter1
17488 -rwx------  1   sarwar faculty   5983  Jan 17 11:57    Chapter2
52473 -rwx------  2   sarwar faculty   9352  May 28 23:09    Chapter3
52473 -rwx------  2   sarwar faculty   9352  May 28 23:09    Chapter3.hard
$
```

The ls -il command shows the attributes of all the files in the present working directory, including their inode numbers. The command ln Chapter3Chapter3.hard creates a hard link to the file Chapter3; the name of the hard link is Chapter3.hard. The system creates a new directory entry (52473, Chapter3.hard) for Chapter3 in the present working directory. Thus, you can refer to Chapter3 by accessing Chapter3.hard as well, because both names point to the same file on disk. The second ls -il command is used to confirm that Chapter3.hard and Chapter3 are two names for the same file, as both have the same inode number, 52473, and hence the same attributes. Therefore, when a hard link is created to Chapter3, a new pointer to its inode is established in the directory where the link (Chapter3.hard, in this case) resides, as illustrated in Figure 11.2.

Note that the output of the ls -il command also shows that both files Chapter3 and Chapter3.hard have link counts of 2 each. Thus, when a hard link is created to a file, the link count for the file increments by 1. That is, the same file exists in the file structure with two names. When you remove a file that has multiple hard links, the UNIX system decrements the link count (in file's inode) by 1. If the resultant link count is 0, the system removes the directory entry for the file, releases the file's inode for recycling, and de-allocates disk blocks allocated to the file so that they can be used to store other files and/or directories created in the future. If the new link count is not 0, only the directory entry for the removed file is deleted; the file contents and other directory entries for the file (hard links) remain intact. The following session illustrates this point.

```
$ rm Chapter3
$ ls -il
13059 -rwx------  1   sarwar faculty   398   Mar 11 14:20    Chapter1
17488 -rwx------  1   sarwar faculty   5983  Jan 17 11:57    Chapter2
52473 -rwx------  1   sarwar faculty   9352  May 28 23:09    Chapter3.hard
$
```

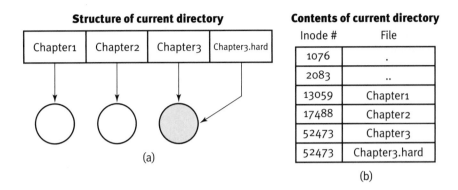

Structure of current directory

Chapter1	Chapter2	Chapter3	Chapter3.hard

(a)

Contents of current directory

Inode #	File
1076	.
2083	..
13059	Chapter1
17488	Chapter2
52473	Chapter3
52473	Chapter3.hard

(b)

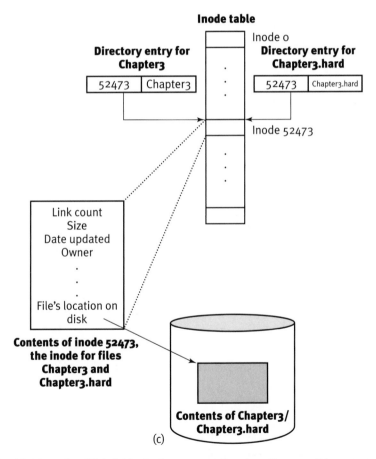

Inode table

Inode 0

Directory entry for Chapter3

52473	Chapter3

Directory entry for Chapter3.hard

52473	Chapter3.hard

Inode 52473

Link count
Size
Date updated
Owner
.
.
.
File's location on disk

Contents of inode 52473, the inode for files Chapter3 and Chapter3.hard

Contents of Chapter3/ Chapter3.hard

(c)

Figure 11.2 Establishing a hard link: (a) logical structure of current directory; (b) contents of current directory; and (c) hard link implementation by establishing a pointer to include of the file

This session clearly shows that removing Chapter3 results in the removal of the directory entry for this file but that the file still exists on disk and is accessible via Chapter3.hard. This link has the inode number and file attributes that Chapter3 had, except that the link count, as expected, has been decremented from 2 to 1.

The following `ln` command can be used to create a hard link called memo6.hard in the present working directory to a file ~/memos/memo6. The `ls -il` command is used to view attributes of the file ~/memos/memo6 before the hard link to it is created.

```
$ ls -il ~/memos/memo6
83476 -rwx------ 1 sarwar faculty 1673 May 29 11:22 /users/faculty/sarwar/memos/memo6
$ ln ~/memos/memo6 memo6.hard
$
```

After executing the `ln` command, you can run the `ls -il` command to confirm that both files (~/memos/memo6 and memo6.hard) have the same inode number and attributes.

```
$ ls -il ~/memos/memo6
83476 -rwx------ 1 sarwar faculty 1673 May 29 11:22 /users/faculty/sarwar/memos/memo6
$ ls -il memo6.hard
83476 -rwx------- 2 sarwar faculty 1673 May 29 11:22 memo6.hard
$
```

The output shows two important things: first, the link count is up by 1; and second, both files are represented by the same inode, 83476. Figure 11.3 shows the hard link pictorially.

In the following session, the `ln` command creates hard links to all nondirectory files in the directory ~/unixbook/examples/dir1. The hard links reside in the directory ~/unixbook/examples/dir2 and have the names of the original files in the dir1 directory. The second argument, dir2, must be an existing directory, and you must have execute and write permissions to it. Note that the link counts for all the files in dir1 and dir2 are 2. The `-f` option is used to force creation of hard link in case any of the files f1, f2, or f3 already exists in the ~/unixbook/examples/dir2 directory.

```
$ cd unixbook/examples
$ more dir1/f1
Hello, World!
This is a test file.
$ ls -l dir1
-rw------- 1 sarwar faculty 35 Jun 22 22:21 f1
-rw------- 1 sarwar faculty 35 Jun 22 22:21 f2
-rw------- 1 sarwar faculty 35 Jun 22 22:22 f3
$ ln -f ~/unixbook/examples/dir1/* ~/unixbook/examples/dir2
$ ls -l dir1
-rw------- 2 sarwar faculty 35 Jun 22 22:21 f1
```

```
-rw------- 2 sarwar faculty 35 Jun 22 22:21 f2
-rw------- 2 sarwar faculty 35 Jun 22 22:22 f3
$ ls -l dir2
-rw------- 2 sarwar faculty 35 Jun 22 22:21 f1
-rw------- 2 sarwar faculty 35 Jun 22 22:21 f2
-rw------- 2 sarwar faculty 35 Jun 22 22:22 f3
$ more dir2/f1
Hello, World!
This is a test file.
$
```

You can run the following `ln` command to create a hard link in your home directory to the file /users/sarwar/unixbook/examples/demo1. The hard link appears as a file demo1 in your home directory. If demo1 already exists in your home directory, you can overwrite it with the `-f` option. If demo1 exists in the home directory and you don't use the `-f` option, an error message is displayed on the screen informing you that the demo1 file exists. You must have execute permission for the directories in the pathname /users/sarwar/unixbook/examples/demo1, and demo1 must be a file.

```
$ ln -f /users/sarwar/unixbook/examples/demo1 ~
$
```

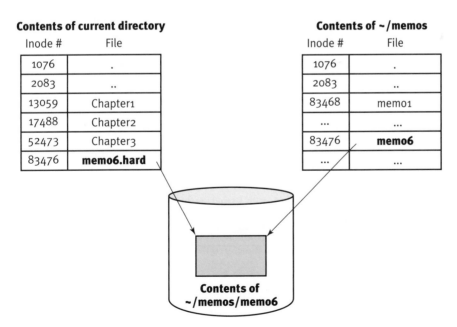

Figure 11.3 Pictorial representation of hard link between ~/memos/memo6 and memo6.hard in the current directory

The user sarwar can run the following command to create a hard link demo1 in a directory dir1 in bob's home directory that points to the file /users/sarwar/ unixbook/examples/demo1. The name of the link in bob's directory is demo1, the same as the original file. Figure 11.4 shows the establishment of the link.

```
$ ln -f /users/sarwar/unixbook/examples/demo1 /users/bob/dir1
$
```

The user sarwar must have execute permission for bob's home directory and execute and write permission to dir1 (the directory in which the link is created). The user bob must have proper access permissions to demo1 in sarwar's directory structure to access this file. Thus, if sarwar and bob are in the same user group and bob needs to edit demo1, sarwar must set the group access privileges for the file to read and write. Then, bob is able to edit demo1 by using, for example, the vi demo1 command from his home directory.

The following command accomplishes the same task. Remember that sarwar runs this command.

```
$ ln -f ~/unixbook/examples/demo1 /users/bob/dir1
$
```

You can run the following ln command to create hard links to all nondirectory files in your ~/unixbook/examples directory. The hard links reside in the directory unixbook/examples in user john's home directory and have the names of the original files. The user john must first create the unixbook directory in his home directory and the examples directory in his unixbook directory. You must have execute permission for john's unixbook directory and execute and write permission for his examples directory.

```
$ ln -f ~/unixbook/examples/* /users/john/unixbook/examples
$
```

11.6.2 Drawbacks of Hard Links

Hard links are the traditional way of *gluing* the file system structure of a UNIX system, which comprises several file systems. Hard links, however, have some problems and limitations that make them less attractive to the average user.

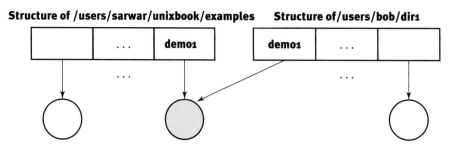

Structure of /users/sarwar/unixbook/examples   **Structure of /users/bob/dir1**

Figure 11.4 A hard link between /users/sarwar/unixbook/examples/demo1 and /users/bob/dir1

The first problem is that hard links cannot be established between files that are on different file systems. This inability is not an issue if you are establishing links between files in your own directory structure, with your home directory as the top-level directory, or with files in another user's directory structure that is on the same file system as yours. However, if you want to create a hard link between a file (command) in the /usr/bin directory and a file in your file structure, it most likely will not work because on almost all systems the /usr/bin directory and your directory structure reside on different file systems. The following command illustrates this point. In this example, we try to give the name del to the UNIX command rm that resides in the directory /usr/bin. Because the rm command is in one file system and our directory structure is in another, UNIX doesn't allow us to create a hard link, del, between a file in the current directory and /usr/bin/rm.

```
$ ln /usr/bin/rm del
ln: del: Cross-device link
$
```

This problem also shows up when a file with multiple links is moved to another file system. The following session illustrates this point. The ls -il command shows that Chapter3 and Chapter3.hard are hard links to the same file (note the same inode number). The mv command is used to move the file Chapter3 to the /tmp directory, which is a different file system than the one that currently contains Chapter3 (and Chapter2). Note that, after the mv command is executed, the link count for Chapter2 and /tmp/Chapter3 is 1 each and that the files have different inodes (/tmp/Chapter3 has inode 6 and Chapter3.hard has the same old inode 52473). The ln command cannot link /tmp/Chapter3 to temp.hard because the two files are in different file systems.

```
$ ls -il
13059 -rwx------  1  sarwar  faculty  398   Mar 11 14:20  Chapter1
17488 -rwx------  1  sarwar  faculty  5983  Jan 17 11:57  Chapter2
52473 -rwx------  2  sarwar  faculty  9352  May 28 23:09  Chapter3
52473 -rwx------  1  sarwar  faculty  9352  May 28 23:09  Chapter3.hard
$ mv Chapter3 /tmp
$ ls -il /tmp
6 -rwx ------  1  sarwar  faculty  9352  May 29 11:57  Chapter3
$ ls -il Chapter3.hard
52473 -rwx------  1  sarwar  faculty  9352  May 28 23:09  Chapter3.hard
$ ln /tmp/Chapter3 temp.hard
ln: temp.hard: Cross-device link
$
```

The second problem is that only a superuser can create a hard link to a directory. The ln command gives an error message when a nonsuperuser tries to create a hard link to a directory myweb, as in

```
$ ln ~/myweb myweb.hard
/users/sarwar/myweb is a directory
$
```

The third problem is that some editors remove the existing version of the file you are editing and put the new versions in new files. When that happens, any hard links to the removed file do not have access to the new file, thereby defeating the purpose of linking (file sharing). Fortunately, none of the commonly used editors do so. Thus, all the text editors discussed in Chapter 5 (pico, vi, and emacs) are safe to use.

In the following In-Chapter Exercises, you will use the ln and ls -il commands to create and identify hard links, and to verify a serious limitation of hard links.

IN-CHAPTER EXERCISES

11.1 Create a file Ch11Ex1 in your home directory that contains this problem. Establish a hard link to this file, also in your home directory, and call the link Ch11Ex1.hard. Verify that the link has been established by using the ls -il command. What field in the output of this command did you use for verification?

11.2 Execute the ln /tmp ~/tmp command on your UNIX system. What is the purpose of the command? What happens when you execute the command? Does the result make sense? Why or why not?

11.6.3 Soft/Symbolic Links

Soft/symbolic links take care of all the problems inherent in hard links and are therefore used more often than hard links. They are different from hard links both conceptually and in terms of how they are implemented. They do have a cost associated with them, which we discuss in Section 11.6.4, but they are extremely flexible and can be used to link files across machines and networks.

You can create soft links by using the ln command with the -s option. The following session illustrates the creation of a soft link.

```
$ ls -il
13059 -rwx------ 1  sarwar  faculty  398   Mar 11 14:20  Chapter1
17488 -rwx------ 1  sarwar  faculty  5983  Jan 17 11:57  Chapter2
52473 -rwx------ 2  sarwar  faculty  9352  May 28 23:09  Chapter3
52473 -rwx------ 1  sarwar  faculty  9352  May 29 23:09  Chapter3.hard
$ ln -s Chapter3 Chapter3.soft
$ ls -il
13059 -rwx------ 1  sarwar  faculty  398   Mar 11 14:20  Chapter1
17488 -rwx------ 1  sarwar  faculty  5983  Jan 17 11:57  Chapter2
```

```
52473 -rwx------- 1   sarwar    faculty  9352   May 29 12:09    Chapter3
52479 lrwxrwxrwx  1   sarwar faculty 8 May 29 12:09 Chapter3.soft -> Chapter3
$
```

The `ln -s Chapter3 Chapter3.soft` command is used to create a symbolic link to the file Chapter3 in the present working directory, and the symbolic link is given the name Chapter3.soft. The output of the `ls -il` command shows a number of important items that reveal how symbolic links are implemented and how they are identified in the output. First, the original file (Chapter3) and the link file (Chapter3.soft) have different inode numbers: 52473 for Chapter3 and 52479 for Chapter3.soft, which means that they are different files. Second, the original file is of ordinary file type – (ordinary file) and the link file is of link type l (link file). Third, the link count field is 1 for both files, which further indicates that the two files are different. Fourth, the file sizes are different: 9352 bytes for the original file and 8 bytes file the link file. Last, the name of the link file is followed by →Chapter3, the pathname for the file that Chapter3.soft is a symbolic link to; this is specified as the first argument in the `ln -s` command. The pathname of the existing file is content of the link file, which also explains the size of the link file (8 characters in the word Chapter3). Figure 11.5 shows the logical file structure of the current directory, directory entries in the current directory, and a diagram that shows that Chapter3 and Chapter3.soft are truly separate files and that the link file contains the pathname of the file to which it is a link.

In summary, when you create a symbolic link, a new file of type link is created. This file contains the pathname of the existing file as specified in the `ln -s` command. When you make a reference to the link file, the UNIX system sees that the type of the file is link and reads the link file to find the pathname for the actual file to which you are referring. For example, for the `cat Chapter3.soft` command, the system reads the contents of Chapter3.soft to get the name of the file to display (Chapter3 in this case) and send its contents to standard output. Hence, you see the contents of Chapter3 displayed.

You can create soft links across file systems, as illustrated by the following session. Here, the file Chapter3 is copied from one file system (that contains this file) to another that contains the /tmp directory. Then, the command `ln -s /tmp/Chapter3 temp.soft` is used to create a symbolic link to the copied file. The command works without any problem, establishing a symbolic link to /tmp/Chapter3 in temp.soft. Note that inode numbers for the two files are different, indicating that the two files are separate; temp.soft contains the pathname to the file for which it is a symbolic link, /tmp/Chapter3. Recall that in Section 11.6.1 a similar call to establish a hard link between /tmp/Chapter3 and temp.hard failed.

```
$ cp Chapter3 /tmp
$ ln -s /tmp/Chapter3 temp.soft
$ ls -il /tmp/Chapter3 temp.soft
6 -rwx------ 1 sarwar faculty 7119 May 29 12:36 /tmp/Chapter3
52497 lrwxrwxrwx 1 sarwar faculty 13 May 29 12:37 temp.soft -> /tmp/Chapter3
$
```

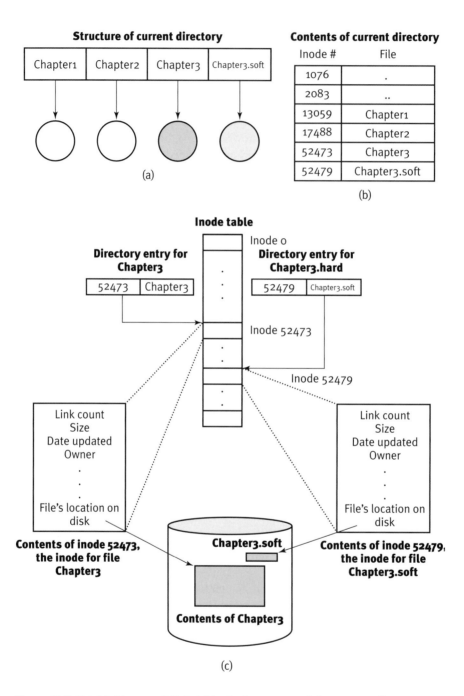

Figure 11.5 Establishing a soft link: (a) logical structure of the current directory; (b) contents of the current directory; and (c) soft link implementation by establishing a "pointer" to (pathname of) the existing file in the link file

The following session shows how symbolic links can be created to all the files, including directory files, in a directory. The `ln -sf ~/unixbook/examples/dir1/* ~/unix-book/examples/dir2` command creates soft links to all the files in a directory called ~/unixbook/examples/dir1 and puts them in the directory ~/unixbook/examples/dir2. You must have execute and write permissions for the dir2 directory, and execute permission to all the directories in the pathname. The `-f` option is used to force creation of the soft link in case any of the files f1, f2, or f3 already exist in ~/unixbook/examples/dir2. On some systems, the `-f` and `-s` options may not work together, in which case you will use only the `-s` option.

```
$ cd ~/unixbook/examples
$ more dir1/f1
Hello, World!
This is a test file.
$ ls -l dir1
-rw------- 1 sarwar faculty 35 Jun 22 22:21 f1
-rw------- 1 sarwar faculty 35 Jun 22 22:21 f2
-rw------- 1 sarwar faculty 35 Jun 22 22:22 f3
$ ln -sf ~/unixbook/examples/dir1/* ~/unixbook/examples/dir2
$ ls -l dir2
lrwxrwxrwx 1 sarwar faculty 38 Jun 22 22:54 f1 -> /users/sarwar/unixbook/examples/dir1/f1
lrwxrwxrwx 1 sarwar faculty 38 Jun 22 22:54 f2 -> /users/sarwar/unixbook/examples/dir1/f2
lrwxrwxrwx 1 sarwar faculty 38 Jun 22 22:54 f3 -> /users/sarwar/unixbook/examples/dir1/f3
$ more dir2/f1
Hello, World!
This is a test file.
$
```

You can run the following command to create a symbolic link in your home directory to the file /users/sarwar/unixbook/examples/demo1. The soft link appears as a file called demo1 in your home directory. If demo1 already exists in your home directory, you can overwrite it with the `-f` option. If demo1 exists in the home directory and you don't use the `-f` option, an error message is displayed on the screen informing you that the demo1 file exists. You must have execute permission for the directories in the pathname /users/sarwar/unixbook/examples/demo1, and demo1 must be a file.

```
$ ln -sf /users/sarwar/unixbook/examples/demo1 ~
$
```

The user sarwar can run the following command to create a soft link called demo1 in a directory dir1 in bob's home directory that points to the /users/sarwar/unixbook/examples/demo1 file. Figure 11.6 shows how the soft link is established.

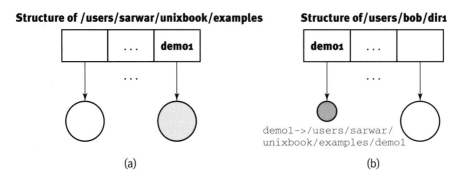

Figure 11.6 A soft link between (a) /users/sarwar/unixbook/examples/demo1 and(b) /users/bob/dir1

The user sarwar must have execute permission for bob's home directory, and execute and write permission for dir1 (the directory in which the soft link is created). The user bob must have proper access permissions for demo1 in sarwar's directory structure to access this file. Thus, if sarwar and bob are in the same user group and bob needs to be able to edit memo1, sarwar must set the group access privileges on the file to read and write. The user bob can then edit demo1 by using, for example, the `vi demo1` command from his home directory.

```
$ ln -sf /users/sarwar/unixbook/examples/demo1 /users/bob/dir1
$
```

The following command accomplishes the same task. Remember that sarwar runs this command.

```
$ ln -sf ~/unixbook/examples/demo1 /users/bob/dir1
$
```

You can run the following `ln` command to create soft links to all the files, including directory files, in your ~/unixbook/examples directory. These soft links reside in the directory called unixbook/examples in john's home directory and have the names of the original files. The user john must create the unixbook directory in his home directory and the examples directory in his unixbook directory. You must have execute permission for john's unixbook directory and execute and write permission for his examples directory.

```
$ ln -sf ~/unixbook/examples/* /users/john/unixbook/examples
$
```

11.6.4 Pros and Cons of Symbolic Links

As previously mentioned, symbolic links do not have the problems and limitations of hard links. Thus, symbolic links can be established between files across file systems and to directories. Also, files that symbolic links point to can be edited by any kind of editor without any ill effects, provided that the file's pathname doesn't get changed—that is, the original file is not moved.

Symbolic links do have a problem of their own that is not associated with hard links: If the file that the symbolic link points to is moved from one directory to another, it can no longer be accessed via the link. The reason is that the link file contains the pathname for the original location of the file in the file structure. The following session illustrates this point. Suppose that temp.soft is a symbolic link to the file /tmp/Chapter3. The mv command is used to move /tmp/Chapter3 to the present working directory. The cat command fails because the soft link still points to the file with pathname /tmp/Chapter3. This result is quite logical but is still a drawback; in hard links, the cat command would not fail so long as the moved file stays within the same file system.

```
$ mv /tmp/Chapter3 .
$ cat temp.soft
temp.soft: No such file or directory
$
```

Some other drawbacks of the symbolic links are that UNIX has to support an additional file type (the link type) and a new file has to be created for every link. Creation of the link file results in space overhead for an extra inode and disk space needed to store the pathname of the file to which it is a link. Symbolic links also result in slow file operations because, for every reference to the file, the link file has to be opened and read in order for you to reach the actual file. The actual file is then processed for reading or writing, requiring an extra disk read to be performed if a file is referenced via a symbolic link to the file.

In the following In-Chapter Exercises, you will use the ln -s and ls -il commands to create and identify soft links, and to verify that you can create soft links across file systems.

IN-CHAPTER EXERCISES

11.3 Establish a soft link to the file Ch11Ex1 that you created in Exercise 11.1. Call the soft link Ch11Ex1.soft. Verify that the link has been established. What commands did you use to establish the link and verify its creation?

11.4 Execute the ln-s /tmp ~/tmp command on your UNIX system. What is the purpose of the command? What happens when you execute the command? Does the result make sense? Why or why not?

_ Summary

Any of several techniques can be used to allow a team of users to share UNIX files and directories. Some of the most commonly used methods of file sharing are duplicating the files to be shared and distributing them among team members, establishing a common account for team members, setting appropriate permissions on the files to be shared, setting up a UNIX user group for the team members, and establishing links to the files to be shared files in the directories of all team members. File sharing via hard and soft links is the main topic of this chapter. However, the issue of simultaneous access of shared files by team members is not discussed here (*see* Chapter 20).

Hard links allow you to refer to an existing file by another name. Although hard links are the primary mechanism used by UNIX to glue the file structure, they have several shortcomings. First, an existing file and its links must be in the same file system. Second, only a superuser can create hard links to directories. Third, moving a file to another file system breaks all links to it.

Soft links can be used to overcome the problems associated with hard links. When a soft link to a file is created, a new file is created that contains the pathname of the file to which it is a link. The type of this file is link. Soft links are expensive in terms of the time needed to access the file and the space overhead of the link file. The time overhead during file access occurs because the link file has to be opened in order for the pathname of the actual file to be read, and only then does the actual read take place. The space overhead is caused by the link file that contains the pathname of the original file.

Hard and soft links are established with the `ln` command. For creating soft links, the `-s` option is used with the command. The `ls -il` command is used to identify (or confirm establishment of) links. The first field of the output of this command identifies the inode numbers for the files in a directory, and all hard links to a file have the same inode number as the original file. The first letter of the second field represents file type ('l' for soft link), and the remaining specify file permissions. The third field identifies the number of hard links to a file. Every simple file has one hard link at the time it is created. The last field identifies file names; a soft link's name is followed by `->` filename, where filename is the name of the original file. The `-f` option can be used to force the creation of a link, that is, to overwrite an existing file with the newly created link.

Problems

1.   What are the five methods that can be used to allow a team of users to share files in UNIX?

2.   What is a link in UNIX? Name the types of link that UNIX supports. How do they differ from each other?

3.   What are the problems with hard links?

4.   Remove the file Ch11Ex1 that you created in In-Chapter Exercise 11.1. Display the contents of Ch11Ex1.hard and Ch11Ex1.soft. What happens? What command did you use for displaying the files? Does the result make sense? Why or why not?

5.   Search the /usr/bin directory on your system and identify three links in it. Write down the names of these links. Are these hard or soft links? How do you know?

6. While in your home directory, can you establish a hard and soft link to /etc/passwd on your system? Why? What commands did you use? Are you satisfied with the results of the command execution?

7. Every UNIX directory has at least two hard links. Why?

8. Can you find the number of hard and soft links to a file? If so, what command(s) do you need to use?

9. Suppose that a file called shared in your present directory has five hard links to it. Give a sequence of commands to display absolute pathnames of all of these links. (*Hint:* Use the `find` command.)

10. Create a directory, dir1, in your home directory and three files, f1, f2, and f3, in it. Ask a friend to create a directory, dir2, in his or her home directory, with dir1.hard and dir1.soft as its subdirectories. Create hard and soft links to all the files in your dir1 in your friend's ~/dir2/dir1.hard and ~/dir2/dir1.soft directories. Give the sequence of commands that you executed to do so.

11. For Problem 10, what are the inode numbers of the hard links and soft links? What command did you use to determine them? What are the contents of the link (both hard and soft) files? How did you get your answers?

12. What are the pros and cons of symbolic links?

13. Clearly describe how file sharing can be accomplished by using links (hard and soft) in UNIX. In particular, do you need to do anything other than establish links to the files to be shared?

14. Suppose you have a collection of data file, say file1.data, ..., file9.data, that need to be shared (read-only) among 100 programs in your group. Discuss the overhead involved for each of the following:

    a. Setting permissions

    b. Creating hard links

    c. Creating soft links

    d. Making individual private copies of each file

Redirection and Piping

Objectives

- To describe the notion of standard files—standard input, standard output, and standard error files—and file descriptors

- To describe input and output redirection for standard files

- To discuss the concept of error redirection and appending to a file

- To explain the concept of pipes in UNIX

- To describe how powerful operations can be performed by combining pipes, file descriptors, and redirection operators

- To discuss error redirection in the C shell

- To explain the concept of FIFOs (also known as named pipes) and their command line use

- To cover the commands and primitives `&, |, <, >, >>, cat, diff, grep, lp, mkfifo, more, pr, sort, stderr, stdin, stdout, tee, tr, uniq, wc`

12.1　Introduction

All computer software (commands) performs one or more of the following operations: input, processing, and output; a typical command performs all three. The question for the operating system is: where does a shell command (internal or external) take its input from, where does it send its output to, and where are the error messages sent to? If the input is not part of the command code (i.e., data within the code in the form of constants or variables), it must come from an outside source. This outside source is usually a file, although it could be an I/O device such as a keyboard or a network interface card. Command output and error messages can go to a file as well. In order for a command to read from or write to a file, it must first open the file.

There are default files where a command reads its input and sends its output and error messages: called standard input, standard output, and standard error. In UNIX, these files are known as *standard files* for the command. The input, output, and errors of a command can be redirected to other files by using *file redirection facilities* in UNIX. This allows you to connect several commands together to perform a complex task that cannot be performed by a single existing command. We discuss the notion of standard files and redirection of input, output, and error in UNIX in this chapter.

12.2　Standard Files

In UNIX, three files are automatically opened by the kernel for every command for the command to read input from and send its output and error messages to. These files are known as standard input (stdin), standard output (stdout), and standard error (stderr). By default, these files are associated with the terminal on which the command executes. More specifically, the keyboard is standard input, and the display screen (or the console at which you are logged in) is standard output and standard error. Therefore, every command, by default, takes its input from the keyboard and sends its output and error messages to the display screen (or the console window), as shown in Figure 12.1. Recall our explanation of the per process file

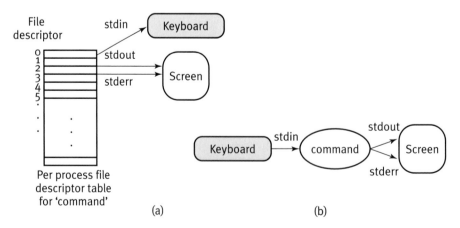

Figure 12.1 Standard files and file descriptors: (a) file descriptors; (b) semantics of a command execution

descriptor table in Chapter 7. In the remainder of this chapter, we use the terms *monitor screen*, *display screen*, *console window*, and *display window* interchangeably.

12.3   Input Redirection

Input redirection is accomplished by using the less-than symbol (<). This syntax is used to detach the keyboard from the standard input of 'command' and attach 'input-file' to it. Thus, if 'command' reads its input from standard input, this input will come from 'input-file', not the keyboard attached to the terminal on which the command is run. The semantics of the command syntax are shown in Figure 12.2.

Note that the 'command' input comes from the 'input-file'.

---

command < input file

Purpose: Input to 'command' comes from 'input-file' instead of from the keyboard

SYNTAX

For example, the command `cat < tempfile` takes its input from tempfile (as opposed to the keyboard because standard input for `cat` has been attached to tempfile) and sends its output to the display screen. So, effectively, the contents of tempfile are displayed on the monitor screen. This command is different from `cat tempfile`, in which tempfile is passed as a command line argument to the `cat` command; the standard input of `cat` does not change.

Similarly, in `grep "John" < Phones`, the `grep` command takes its input from the Phones file in the current directory, not from the keyboard. The output and error messages of the command go to the display screen. Again, this command is different from `grep "John" Phones`, in which Phones is passed as an argument to `grep`; the standard input of `grep` does not change and is still the keyboard attached to the terminal on which the command executes.

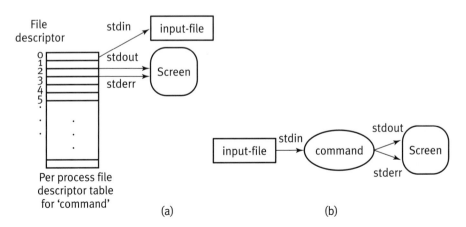

Figure 12.2 Input redirection: (a) file descriptors and standard files for 'command'; (b) semantics of input redirection

The `cat` and `grep` commands take input from the standard input if they are not passed as file arguments from the command line. The `tr` command takes input from the standard input only and sends its output to standard output. The command does not work with a file as a command line argument. Thus, input redirection is often used with the `tr` command, as in `tr -s ' ' ' ' < Bigfile`. When this command is executed, it substitutes multiple spaces in Bigfile with single spaces.

12.4   Output Redirection

Output redirection is accomplished by using the greater-than symbol (`>`).

This syntax is used to detach the display screen from the standard output of 'command' and attach 'output-file' to it. Thus, if 'command' writes/sends its output to standard output, the output goes to 'output-file', not the monitor screen attached to the terminal on which the command runs. The error messages still go to the display screen, as before. The semantics of the command syntax are shown in Figure 12.3.

S Y N T A X

command > output-file

Purpose: Send output of 'command' to the file 'output-file' instead of to the monitor screen

Consider the `cat > newfile` command. Recall that the `cat` command sends its output to standard output, which is the display screen by default. This command syntax detaches the display screen from standard output of the `cat` command and attaches newfile to it. The standard input of `cat` remains attached to the keyboard. When this command is executed, it creates a file called newfile whose contents are whatever you type on the keyboard until you hit `<Ctrl-D>` in the first column of a new line. If newfile exists, by default it is overwritten.

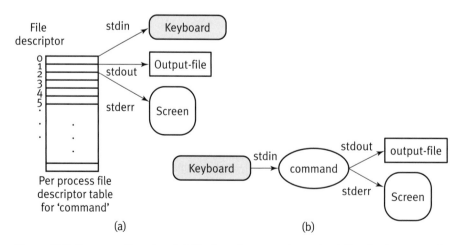

Figure 12.3 Output redirection: (a) file descriptors and standard files for 'command'; (b) semantics of output redirection

Similarly, the command `grep "John" Phones > Phone_John` sends its output (lines in the Phones file that contain the word "John") to a file called Phone_John, as opposed to displaying it on the monitor screen. The input for the command comes from the Phones file. The command terminates when `grep` encounters the end-of-file (eof) character in Phones.

In a network environment, the following command can be used to sort datafile, residing on the computer the 'client', that you are currently logged on to on the computer called 'server'. If your environment does not allow execution of the `rsh` (remote shell) command, you can try using the `ssh` (secure shell) command. Figure 12.4 illustrates the semantics of this command.

```
$ rsh server sort < datafile
$
```

This command is a good example of how multiple computers can be used to perform various tasks concurrently in a network environment. It is a useful command if your computer (call it 'client') has a large file, datafile, to be sorted and you do not want to make multiple copies of the file on various computers on the network to prevent inconsistency in them. This command allows you to perform the task. Such commands also are useful if server has specialized UNIX tools that you are allowed to use but not allowed to make copies of on your machine. (*See* Chapter 14 for network-related UNIX commands and utilities.) We have used this example to illustrate the power of the UNIX I/O redirection feature, not to digress on computing in a network environment.

12.5   Combining Input and Output Redirection

Input and output redirections can be used together, according to the syntax given in the following command description.

---

command < input-file > output-file
command < output-file > input-file

Purpose: Input to 'command' comes from 'input-file' instead of the keyboard, and the output of 'command' goes to 'output-file' instead of the display screen

SYNTAX

When this syntax is used, 'command' takes its input from 'input-file' (not from the keyboard attached to the terminal) and sends its output to 'output-file' (not to the display screen), as shown in Figure 12.5.

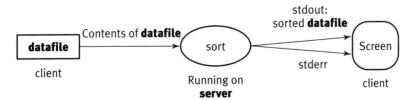

Figure 12.4 Semantics of the `rsh server sort < datafile` command run on 'mymachine'

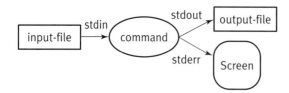

Figure 12.5 Combined use of input and output redirection

In the command line `cat < lab1 > lab2`, the `cat` command takes its input from the lab1 file and sends its output to the lab2 file. The net effect of this command is that a copy of lab1 is created in lab2. Therefore, this command line is equivalent to `cp lab1 lab2`, if lab2 does not exist. If lab2 is an existing file, the two commands have different semantics. The `cat < lab1 > lab2` command truncates lab2 (sets its size to zero and read/write pointer to the first byte position) and overwrites it by the contents of lab1. Because lab2 is not re-created, its attributes (e.g., access permissions and link count) are not changed. In case of the `cp lab1 lab2` command, not only is the data in lab1 copied into lab2, but also its attributes from its inode are copied into the inode for lab2. Thus, the `cp` command results in a true copy (data and attributes) of lab1 into lab2.

In the following In-Chapter Exercises, you will practice the use of input and output direction features of UNIX.

IN-CHAPTER EXERCISES

12.1   Write a shell command that counts the number of characters, words, and lines in a file called 'memo' in your present working directory and shows these values on the display screen. Use input redirection.

12.2   Repeat Exercise 12.1, but redirect output to a file called 'counts.memo'. Use I/O redirection.

12.6   I/O Redirection with File Descriptors

As described in Section 7.7, the UNIX kernel associates a small integer number with every open file, called the file descriptor for the file. The file descriptors for standard input, standard output, and standard error are 0, 1, and 2, respectively. The Bourne, Korn, Bash, and POSIX shells allow you to open files and associate file descriptors with them; the C shell does not allow the use of file descriptors. The other descriptors usually range from 3 through 19 and are called user-defined file descriptors. We discuss details of shell-based file I/O in Section 12.13. In the following sections, we describe I/O and error redirection under the Bourne, Korn, Bash, and POSIX shells. We discuss the C shell syntaxes and give examples toward the end of this chapter under separate sections.

By making use of file descriptors, standard input and standard output can be redirected in the Bourne, Korn, Bash, and POSIX shells by using the `0<` and `1>` operators, respectively. Therefore, `cat 1> outfile`, which is equivalent to `cat > outfile`, takes input from standard input and sends it to outfile; error messages go to the display screen. Similarly, ls -l foo 1> outfile is equivalent to ls -l foo > outfile. The output of this command (the long listing for foo) goes into a file called outfile, and error messages generated by it go to the display screen.

The file descriptor 0 can be used as a prefix with the < operator to explicitly specify input redirection from a file. In the command shown, the input to the grep command is the contents of tempfile in the present working directory.

```
$ grep "John" 0< tempfile
... command output ...
$
```

12.7 Redirecting Standard Error

The standard error of a command can be redirected by using the 2> operator (associating the file descriptor for the standard error with the > operator) as follows.

---

command 2> error-file

Purpose: Error messages generated by 'command' and sent to stderr are redirected to 'error-file'

SYNTAX

With this syntax, 'command' takes its input from the keyboard, sends its output to the monitor screen, and any error messages produced by 'command' are sent to 'error-file'. The semantics of the command syntax are shown in Figure 12.6. Command input may come from a file passed as a command line argument.

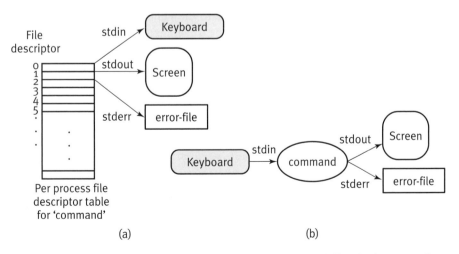

(a)   (b)

Figure 12.6 Error redirection: (a) file descriptors and standard files for 'command'; (b) semantics of error redirection

The command `grep "John" Phones 2> error.log` takes input from the Phones file, sends output to the display screen, and any error message produced by `grep` goes to a file error.log. If error.log exists, it is overwritten; otherwise, it is created. The following example shows how standard error of `ls -l` can be redirected to a file.

```
$ ls -l foo 2> error.log
... long listing for foo if no errors ...
$
```

The output of `ls -l foo` goes to the display screen, and error messages go to error.log. Thus, if foo does not exist, the error message `ls: foo: No such file or directory` goes into the error.log file, as shown. The actual wording of the message varies from system to system, but it basically informs you that foo does not exist. On an IBM AIX machine running under the Korn shell, the message was `ls: 0653-341 The file foo does not exist`.

```
$ ls -l foo 2> error.log
$ cat error.log
ls: foo: No such file or directory
$
```

Keeping standard error attached to the display screen and not redirected to a file is useful in many situations. For example, when the `cat lab1 lab2 lab3 > all` command is executed to concatenate files lab1, lab2, and lab3 into a file called all, you would want to know whether any of the three input files are nonexistent or if you do not have permission to read any of them. In this case, redirecting the error message to a file does not make much sense because you want to see the immediate results of the command execution.

12.8 Redirecting stdout and stderr in One Command

Standard output and standard error can be redirected to the same file. One obvious way to do so is to redirect stdout and stderr to the same file by using file descriptors with the > symbol, as in the following command. In this case, the input of the `cat` command comes from the lab1, lab2, and lab3 files, its output goes to the cat.output file, and any error message to the cat.errors file, as shown in Figure 12.7. Note that, although not shown in Figure 12.7(b), files lab1, lab2, and lab3 have file descriptors assigned to them when they are opened for reading by the `cat` command. The command produces an error message if any one of the three lab files does not exist or if you do not have read permission for any file.

```
$ cat lab1 lab2 lab3 1> cat.output 2> cat.errors
$
```

The following command redirects stdout and stderr of the `cat` command to the cat.output.errors file. Thus, the same file (cat.output.errors) contains the output of the `cat` command, along with any error messages that may be produced by the command.

```
$ cat lab1 lab2 lab3 1> cat.output.errors 2>&1
$
```

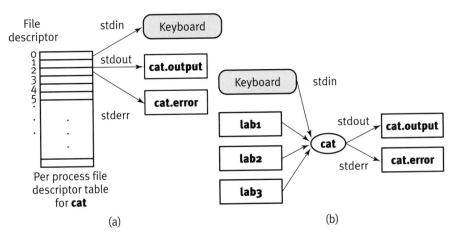

Figure 12.7 Error redirection: (a) file descriptors and standard files for cat lab1 lab2 lab3 1> cat.output 2> cat.errors (b) semantics of the cat command

In this command, the string 2>&1 tells the command shell to make descriptor 2 a duplicate of descriptor 1, resulting in error messages going to the same place that the command output goes to. Similarly, the string 1>&2 can be used to tell the command shell to make descriptor 1 a duplicate of descriptor 2. Thus, the following command accomplishes the same task. Figure 12.8 shows the semantics of the two commands.

```
$ cat lab1 lab2 lab3 2> cat.output.errors 1>&2
$
```

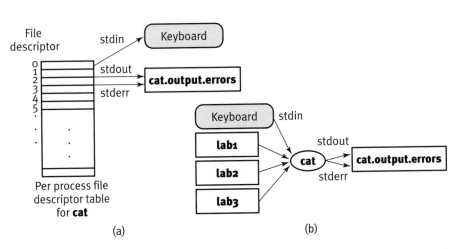

Figure 12.8 Error redirection: (a) file descriptors and standard files (b) semantics of the cat lab1 lab2 lab3 1> cat.output.errors 2>&1 and cat lab1 lab2 lab3 2> cat.output.errors 1>&2 commands

The evaluation of the command line content for file redirection is left to right. Therefore, redirections must be specified in left-to-right order if one notation is dependent on another. In the preceding command, first stderr is changed to the filecat.output.errors, and then stdout becomes a duplicate of stderr. Thus, the output and errors for the command both go to the same file, cat.output.errors.

The following command therefore does *not* have the effect of the two commands just discussed. The reason is that, in this command, stderr is made a duplicate of stdout *before* output redirection. Therefore, stderr becomes a duplicate of stdout (the display screen at this time) first, and then stdout is changed to the file cat.output.errors. Thus, the output of the command goes to cat.output.errors and errors go to the display screen. The sequence shown in Figure 12.9 illustrates the semantics of this command.

```
$ cat lab1 lab2 lab3 2>&1 1> cat.output.errors
$
```

Note that Figures 12.9(a) and 12.9(b) are identical because the execution of cat lab1 lab2 lab3 2>&1 does not make any changes in stdout and stderr—they stay attached to the display screen before and after the command is executed.

12.9   Redirecting stdin, stdout, and stderr in One Command

Standard input, standard output, and standard error can be redirected in a single command according to the following syntax.

SYNTAX

command o< input-file 1> output-file 2> error-file

Purpose: Input to 'command' comes from 'input-file' instead of the keyboard, output of 'command' goes to 'output-file' instead of the display screen, and error messages generated by 'command' are sent to 'error-file' Standard input, standard output, and standard error can be redirected in a single command according to the following syntax.

The file descriptors 0 and 1 are not required because they are the default values. The semantics of this command syntax are shown in Figure 12.10. Evaluation of the command line content for file redirection *is* left to right, so the order of redirection is important. Consider the following command syntaxes. For the first command, if 'input-file' is not found, the error message is sent to the display screen because stderr has not been redirected yet. For the second command, if 'input-file' is not found, the error message goes to 'error-file' because stderr has been redirected to this file.

```
command 1> output-file o< input-file  2> error-file
command 2> error-file  1> output-file o< input-file
```

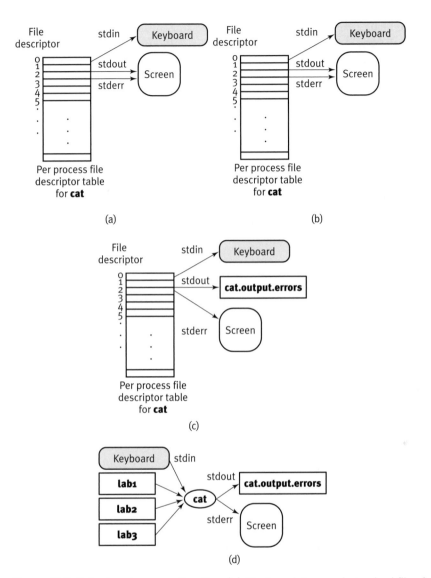

Figure 12.9 Output and error redirection: (a) file descriptors and standard files for the `cat` command; (b) standard files after `cat lab1 lab2 lab3 2>&1` with no change in stdout and stderr; (c) standard files after `cat lab1 lab2 lab3 2>&1 cat.output.errors`; and (d) command semantics

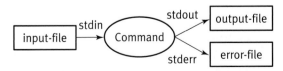

Figure 12.10 Redirecting stdin, stdout, and stderr in a single command

The following `sort` command sorts lines in a file called students and stores the sorted file in students.sorted. If the `sort` command fails to start because the students file does not exist, the error message goes to the display screen, not to the file sort.error. The reason is that, at the time the shell determines that the students file does not exist, the stderr is still attached to the console.

```
$ sort 0< students 1> students.sorted 2> sort.error
$
```

For the following command, the error message goes to the sort.error file if the `sort` command fails because the students file does not exist. The reason is that the error redirection is processed by the shell before it determines that the students file is nonexistent.

```
$ sort 2> sort.error 0< students 1> students.sorted
$
```

12.10   Redirecting without Overwriting File Contents (Appending)

By default, output and error redirections overwrite contents of the destination file. To *append* output or errors generated by a command at the end of a file, replace the > operator with the >> operator. The default file descriptor with >> is 1, but file descriptor 2 can be used to append errors to a file. In the following command, the output of `ls -l` is appended to the output.dat file, and the error messages are appended to the error.log file.

```
$ ls -l 1>> output.dat 2>> error.log
$
```

The following command appends contents of the files memo and letter at the end of the file stuff. If the command produces any error message, it goes to the error.log file. If error.log is an existing file, its contents are overwritten with the error message.

```
$ cat memo letter >> stuff 2> error.log
$
```

If you want to keep the existing contents of error.log and append new error messages to it, use the following command. For this command the previous contents of error.log are appended with any error message produced by the `cat` command.

```
$ cat memo letter >> stuff 2>> error.log
$
```

The Bourne shell, by default, overwrites a file when stdout or stderr of a command is redirected to it, but the Korn, C, and Bash shells have a `noclobber` option that prevents you from overwriting important files accidentally. We discuss this option for the C shell in Section 12.13 but discuss this option for the Korn and Bash shells here.

You can set the `noclobber` option in the Korn and Bash shells by using the `set` command with the `-o` option as shown. Of course, if you want to set this option permanently, put the command in your ~/.profile file.

```
$ set -o noclobber
$
```

In the Bash shell, you can also set the option by using the `set -C` command. When you set the `noclobber` option, you can force overwriting of a file by using the `>|` operator.

In the following In-Chapter Exercises, you will practice the use of input, output, and error redirection features of UNIX shells (excluding C shell) in a command line.

IN-CHAPTER EXERCISES

12.3   Write a command that counts the number of characters, words, and lines in a file called 'memo' in your present working directory and writes these values into a file 'memo.size'. If the command fails, the error message should go to a file 'error.log'. Use I/O and error redirections.

12.4   Write a shell command to send the contents of a 'greetings' file to 'doe@ domain.com' by using the `mail` command. If the `mail` command fails, the error message should go to a file 'mail.errors'. Use input and error redirection.

12.5   Repeat Exercise 12.2, but append error messages at the end of 'mail.errors'.

12.11   UNIX Pipes

The UNIX system allows stdout of a command to be connected to stdin of another command. You can make it do so by using the *pipe character* (|) according to the following syntax.

> **commands1 | commands2 | command3 | ... | commandN**
>
> **Purpose:**   Standard output of 'command1' is connected to stdin of 'command2', stdout of 'command2' is connected to stdin of 'command3', ..., and stdout of 'commandN-1' is connected to stdin of 'commandN'
>
> SYNTAX

Figure 12.11 illustrates the semantics of this command.

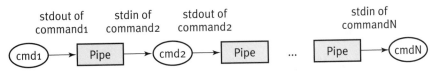

Figure 12.11 The semantics of a pipeline with *N* commands

Thus, a pipe allows you to send output of a command as input to another command. The commands that are connected via a pipe are called filters. A **filter** belongs to a class of UNIX commands that take input from stdin, process it in some specific fashion, and send it to stdout. Pipes and filters are frequently used in UNIX to perform complicated tasks that cannot be performed with a single command. Some commonly used filters are `cat`, `compress`, `crypt`, `grep`, `lp`, `pr`, `sort`, `tr`, `uniq`, and `wc`.

For example, in `ls -l | more`, the `more` command takes output of `ls -l` as its input. The net effect of this command is that the output of `ls -l` is displayed one screen at a time. The pipe really acts like a water pipe, taking output of `ls -l` and giving it to `more` as its input, as shown in Figure 12.12.

This command does not use a disk to connect standard output of `ls -l` to standard input of `more` because pipe is implemented in the main memory. In terms of the I/O redirection operators, the command is equivalent to the following sequence of commands.

```
$ ls -l > temp
$ more < temp (or more temp)
[contents of temp]
$ rm temp
$
```

Not only do you need three commands to accomplish the same task, but the command sequence is also extremely slow because file read and write operations are involved. Recall that files are stored on a secondary storage device, usually a disk. On a typical contemporary computer system, disk operations are about one million times slower than main memory (RAM) operations. The actual performance gain in favor of pipes, however, is much smaller, owing to efficient caching of file blocks by the UNIX kernel.

You can use the `sort` utility discussed in Chapter 10 to sort lines in a file. Suppose that you have a file called student_records that you want to sort and that the file may have some repeated lines that you want to appear only once in the sorted file. The `sort -u` student_records command can accomplish this task. As we discussed in Chapter 9, the `uniq` command can also do the task if it is given the sorted version of student_records with repeated lines in it. One way to do the task is to use the following commands. The `more` command is used to show the contents of student_records.

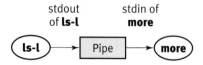

Figure 12.12 The semantics of the `ls -l | more` command

```
$ more student_records
John Doe        ECE     3.54
Pam Meyer       CS      3.61
Jim Davis       CS      2.71
John Doe        ECE     3.54
Jason Kim       ECE     3.97
Amy Nash        ECE     2.38
$ sort student_records > student_records_sorted
$ uniq student_records_sorted
Amy Nash        ECE     2.38
Jason Kim       ECE     3.97
Jim Davis       CS      2.71
John Doe        ECE     3.54
Pam Meyer       CS      3.61
$
```

The same task can be accomplished in one command line by using a pipe, as in,

```
$ sort student_records | uniq
Amy Nash        ECE     2.38
Jason Kim       ECE     3.97
Jim Davis       CS      2.71
John Doe        ECE     3.54
Pam Meyer       CS      3.61
$
```

At times, you may need to connect several commands. The following command line demonstrates the use of multiple pipes, forming a *pipeline* of commands. In this command line, we have used the grep and sort filters.

```
$ who | sort | grep "John" | mail -S "John's Terminal" doe@coldmail.com
$
```

This command sorts the output of who and sends the lines containing the string "John" (if any exists) as an e-mail message to doe@coldmail.com, with the subject line "John's Terminal". In terms of input and output redirection, this command line is equivalent to the following command sequence.

```
$ who > temp1
$ sort < temp1 > temp2
$ grep "John" temp2 > temp3
```

```
$ mail -S "John's Terminal" doe@coldmail.com < temp3
$ rm temp1 temp2 temp3
$
```

The command with pipes does not use any disk files, but the preceding command sequence needs three temporary disk files and six disk I/O (read and write) operations. The number of I/O operations may be a lot more, depending on the sizes of these files, the system load in terms of number of users currently using the system, and the run-time behavior of other processes running on the system.

A pipe, therefore, is a UNIX feature that allows two UNIX commands (processes) to communicate with each other. Hence, a pipe is also known as an interprocess communication (IPC) mechanism. More specifically, it allows two related processes on the same system to talk to each other. Typically, processes have parent-child relationships, and communication between processes is one-way only. For example, in ls | more, the output of ls is read by more as input. Thus, the one-way communication is from ls to more. For a two-way communication between processes, at least two pipes must be used. This cannot be accomplished at the command shell level, but it can be done in C/C++ by using the pipe( ) system call. Further discussion of this topic is beyond the scope of this book, but if you are interested, you can refer to any book on UNIX interprocess communication.

I/O redirection and pipes can be used in a single command, as follows.

```
$ grep "John" < Students | lpr —Pspr
$
```

Here, the grep command searches the Students file for lines that contain the string John and sends those lines to the lpr command to be printed on a printer named spr. Figure 12.13 illustrates the semantics of this command.

In the following command, egrep takes its input from ee446.grades and sends its output (lines ending with the character A) to the sort utility, which sorts these lines and stores them in the file ee446.As.sorted. The end result is that the names, scores, and grades of all the students who have A grades in ECE446 are stored in the ee446.As.sorted file. Figure 12.14 illustrates the semantics of this command.

```
$ egrep 'A$' < ee446.grades | sort > ee446.As.sorted
$
```

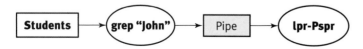

Figure 12.13 The semantics of the grep "John" < Students | lpr —Pspr command

Figure 12.14 The semantics of egrep 'A$' < ee446.grades | sort > ee446.As.sorted

Suppose that, before running the `rsh server sort < datafile` command in Section 12.3, you want to be sure that datafile on your local system is consistent with the updated copy on the server, called datafile.server. You can copy datafile.server and compare it with your local copy, datafile. But then you will have three copies, and if you are not careful you might remove the wrong copy. In this case, you can run the following command to see the differences between your local copy and the copy on the server without copying datafile.server on your (local) computer.

```
$ rsh server cat ~/research/pvm/datafile.server | diff datafile -
$
```

In this case, the `cat` command runs on the server, and its output is fed as input to the `diff` command executed on the local machine. The output of the `diff` command also goes to the display screen on the local machine. Figure 12.15 illustrates the semantics of this command.

12.12   Redirection and Piping Combined

You cannot use the redirection operators and pipes alone to redirect stdout of a command to a file and connect it to stdin of another command in a single command. However, you can use the `tee` utility to do so. You can use this utility to tell the command shell to send stdout of a command to one or more files, as well as to another command. The following is a brief description of the `tee` utility.

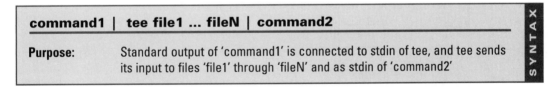

> **command1 | tee file1 ... fileN | command2**
>
> **Purpose:**   Standard output of 'command1' is connected to stdin of tee, and tee sends its input to files 'file1' through 'fileN' and as stdin of 'command2'
>
> SYNTAX

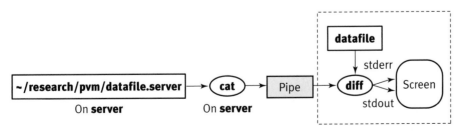

Figure 12.15 The semantics of rsh server cat ~/research/pvm/datafile.server | diff datafile - command

The semantics of this command syntax are that 'command1' is executed and that its output is stored in files 'file1' through 'fileN' and sent to 'command2' as its input. One use of the `tee` utility is given in the following command.

```
$ cat names students | grep "John Doe" | tee file1 file2 | wc -l
$
```

This command extracts the lines from the names and students files that contain the string "John Doe", pipes these lines to the `tee` utility, which puts copies of these lines in file1 and file2, and sends them to wc -1, which sends its output to the display screen. Thus, the lines in the names and students files that contain the string "John Doe" are saved in file1 and file2, and the line count of such lines is displayed on the monitor screen. Figure 12.16 illustrates the semantics of this command line. Such commands are useful in a shell script where different operations have to be performed on file1 and file2 later in the script.

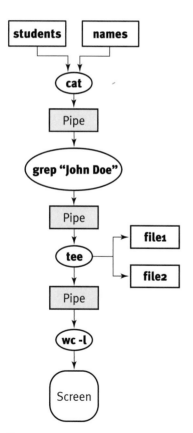

Figure 12.16 The semantics of the cat names students | grep "John Doe" | tee file1 file2 | wc -l command

12.13 Error Redirection in the C Shell

The input, output, and append operators (<, >, >>) work in the C shell as they do in other shells, as previously discussed. However, file descriptors cannot be used with these operators in the C shell. Also, error redirection works differently in the C shell than it does in other shells. In the C shell, the operator for error redirection is >&.

---

command >& file

Purpose: Redirect stdout and stderr of 'command' to 'file'

SYNTAX

For example, the following command redirects output and errors of the ls -l foo command to the error.log file. The standard input of the command is still attached to the keyboard. (We have used the % sign as the shell prompt, which is the default for the C shell.)

```
% ls -l foo >& error.log
%
```

The C shell does not have an operator for redirecting stderr alone. However, stdout and stderr of a command can be attached to different files if the command is executed in a subshell (by enclosing the command in parentheses). The following commands illustrate this point.

```
% find ~ -name foo -print >& output.error.log
% (find ~ -name foo -print > foo.paths) >& error.log
%
```

All external shell commands are executed by the children of your current shell, also known as subshells (*see* Chapter 13). When the first command executes, the output and errors of the find command go to the output.error.log file. As the subshell is not created until the whole command line has been processed (interpreted), the stdout and stderr of the parent shell are redirected to the error.log file because of the >& operator. Therefore, the subshell also has its stdout and stderr redirected to the error.log file.

In the second command line, the find command is executed under a subshell and inherits the standard files of the parent shell. When the find command in parentheses executes, it redirects stdout of the command to the foo.paths file; the stderr of the command remains attached to error.log. Thus, the output of the find command goes to the foo.paths file, and the errors generated by the command go to the error.log file. Figure 12.17 illustrates the semantics of the second find command.

You can use the >>& operator to redirect and append stdout and stderr to a file. For example, ls -l foo >>& output.error.log redirects stdout and stderr of the ls command and appends them to the error.log file.

The C shell also allows stdout and stderr of a command to be attached to the stdin of another command with the |& operator. The following is a brief description of this operator.

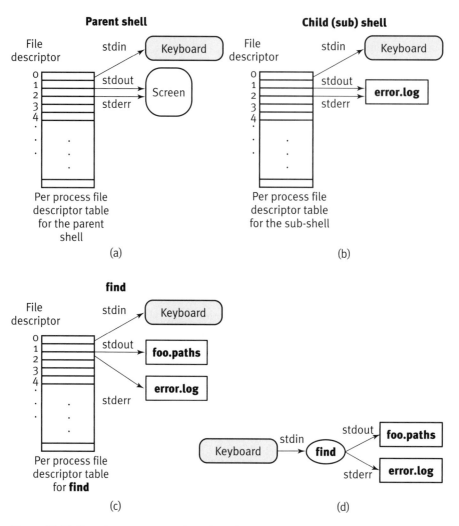

Figure 12.17 Step-by-step semantics of the (`find ~ -name foo -print > foo.paths`) `>&` `error.log` command

In the following command, the stdout and stderr of the `cat` command are attached to the stdin of the `grep` command. Thus, the output of the `cat` command, or any error produced by it (e.g., owing to no read permission for file1 or file2), is fed as input to the `grep` command.

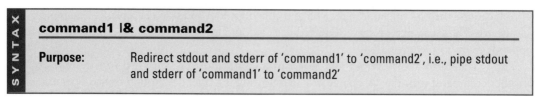

SYNTAX

command1 |& command2

Purpose: Redirect stdout and stderr of 'command1' to 'command2', i.e., pipe stdout and stderr of 'command1' to 'command2'

```
% cat file1 file2 |& grep "John Doe"
%
```

The I/O redirection and piping operators (| and |&) can be used in a single command. This command is an extension of the previous command in which the stdout of the `grep` command is attached to the stdin of the sort command. Furthermore, the stdout and stderr of the `sort` command are attached to the stdin of the `wc -1` command.

```
% cat file1 file2 |& grep "John Doe" | sort |& wc -1
%
```

In the following In-Chapter Exercises, you will practice the use of UNIX pipes, the `tee` command, and the error redirection feature of C shell.

IN-CHAPTER EXERCISES

12.6 Write a shell command that sorts a file 'students.records' and stores the lines containing 'Davis' in a file called 'Davis.record'. Use piping and I/O redirection.

12.7 Write a command to copy a file 'Scores' to 'Scores.bak' and send a sorted version of 'Scores' to 'professor@university.edu' via the `mail` command.

12.8 Write a C shell command for copying a file 'Phones' in your home directory to a file called 'Phones.bak' (also in your home directory) by using the `cat` command and the `>&` operator.

The C shell has a special built-in variable that allows you to protect your files from being overwritten with output redirection. This variable is called `noclobber` and, when set, prevents overwriting of existing files with output redirection. You can set the variable by using the `set` command and unset it by using the `unset` command. Or, you can place the `set noclobber` command in your ~/.cshrc file (or some other startup file).

```
% set noclobber
[your interactive session]
...
% unset noclobber
%
```

If the `noclobber` variable is set, the command `cat file1 > file2` generates an error message if file2 already exists. If file2 does not exist, it is created and file1 data are copied into it. The command `cat file1 >> file2` works fine if file2 exists and `noclobber` is set, but an error message is generated if file2 does not exist. You can use the `>!`, `>>!`, and `>>&!` operators to override the effect of the `noclobber` variable if it is set. Therefore, even if the `noclobber` variable is set and file2 exists, the command `cat file1 >! file2` copies data from file1 to file2. For the `cat file1 >>! file2` command, if the `noclobber` variable is set and file2 does not exist, file2 is created and file1 data are copied into it. The `>>&!` operator works in a manner similar to the `>>!` operator.

12.14 Recap Of I/O and Error Redirection

Table 12.1 summarizes the input, output, and error redirection operators in the Bourne, Korn, and C shells. We did not discuss some of these operators in this chapter; we discuss them in detail in Chapters 15–19 under shell programming. We included these operators in this table because it seems to be the most appropriate place to show all of them together.

TABLE 12.1 Redirection Operators and Their Meaning in Bourne, Korn, and C Shells

Operator	Bourne Shell	Korn Shell	C Shell
< file	Input redirection	Input redirection	Input redirection
> file	Output redirection	Output redirection	Output redirection
>> file	Append standard output	Append standard output	Append standard output
0< file	Input redirection	Input redirection	
1> file	Output redirection	Output redirection	
2> file	Error redirection	Error redirection	
1>> file	Append standard output to 'file'	Append standard output to 'file'	
2>> file	Append standard error to 'file'	Append standard error to 'file'	
<&m	Attach standard input to file descriptor m	Attach standard input to file descriptor m	
>&m	Attach standard output to file with descriptor m	Attach standard output to file with descriptor m	
m>&n	Attach file descriptor m to file descriptor n	Attach file descriptor m to file descriptor n	
<&-	Close standard input	Close standard input	
>&-	Close standard output	Close standard output	
m<&- or m>&-	Close file descriptor m	Close file descriptor m	

(continued)

TABLE 12.1 (continued)

>& file			Output and error redirection
>l file		Ignore noclobber and assign standard output to 'file'	
>>l file		Ignore noclobber and append standard output to 'file'	
>! file			Ignore noclobber and assign standard output to 'file'
>>! file			Ignore noclobber and append standard output to 'file'; if 'file' does not exist, create it
>>&! file			Ignore noclobber and append standard output and standard error to 'file'
cmd1 | cmd2	Connect standard output of command 'cmd1' to standard input of command 'cmd2'	Connect standard output of command 'cmd1' to standard input of command 'cmd2'	Connect standard output of command 'cmd1' to standard input of command 'cmd2'
cmd1 | &cmd2			Connect standard output and standard error of command 'cmd1' to standard input of command 'cmd2'
(cmd>/dev/tty)>&file			Redirect standard error of the 'cmd' command to 'file.
|&			Allow stdout and stderr of a command to be attached to stdin of another command

12.15   FIFOS

FIFOs, also known as named pipes, can also be used for communication between two processes executing on a system. Whereas processes communicating with pipes must be related to each other through a common ancestor process that you execute, processes communicating with FIFOs do not have to have this kind of relationship–they can be independently executed programs on a system. For command line use of pipes and FIFOs, this means that pipes can be used only for communication between commands connected via a pipeline and FIFOs can be used for communication between separately run commands. Another difference between pipes and FIFOs is that whereas a pipe is a main memory buffer and has no name, a FIFO is created on disk and has a name like a filename. This means that, like files, FIFOs have to be created and opened before they can be used for communication between processes.

You can use the mknod() system call or mkfifo() library call to create a FIFO in a process and the mkfifo command to create a file in a shell session. We discuss the command line use of FIFOs in this section. Here is a brief description of the mkfifo command.

---

mkfifo [option] file-list

Purpose	Create FIFOs with pathnames given in 'file-list'
Output:	FIFOs for pathnames given in 'file-list'

Commonly used options/features:

−m mode	Set access permissions for newly created FIFOs to 'mode'; the access permissions are specified in 'mode' as they are with the chmod command, such as 666, meaning read and write permissions for everyone and execute permission for nobody

---

In the following session, we use the first command to create a FIFO, called myfifo1, with default permissions based on the current value of umask (*see* discussion in Chapter 8). We use the second command to create a FIFO, called myfifo2, with read and write permissions for owner and no permissions for all other users. We use the ls −al command to display access permissions of the two FIFOs.

```
$ mkfifo myfifo1
$ mkfifo -m 600 myfifo2
$ ls -al
total 0
total 0
drwxr-xr-x    2   msarwar   faculty    512   Dec  7   15:05   .
drwx------   14   msarwar   faculty   1024   Dec  7   15:04   ..
prw-r--r--    1   msarwar   faculty      0   Dec  7   15:04   myfifo1
prw-------    1   msarwar   faculty      0   Dec  7   15:05   myfifo2
$
```

The general method by which two commands, cmd1 and cmd2, can communicate with a FIFO, called myfifo1, is shown in the following command sequence. Note that we run the first command in background (*see* Chapter 13 for background processes) so that we could run cmd2. When we execute cmd1, it blocks because myfifo1 is empty. Note that this cmd1 won't block if myfifo1 is a file; instead, cmd1 will return immediately. When output of cmd2 is sent to myfifo1 and the cmd3 command via the tee utility, cmd1 unblocks and starts processing data in myfifo1. Outputs of commands cmd1 and cmd3 are sent to standard output (i.e., the display screen). Figure 12.18 shows these semantics with the help of a diagram.

```
cmd1 < myfifo1 &
cmd2 infile | tee myfifo1 | cmd3
```

In the following session, the command sequence displays status of all the processes running on the system, the number of daemon processes, and the total number of processes running on the system. The two cat commands block until something is written into myfifo1 and myfifo2. The ps −e command sends status of all the processes running on the system to the tee command, which redirects this data to the two FIFOs as well as sends it to the wc −1 command. Thus, the first cat command displays the status of all the processes running on the system. The output of the second command is the number of processes running on the system and that of the third command is the number of daemons running on the system. As shown by the last two lines of the output, at the time of running this command sequence, the system was running 119 processes and 30 daemons.

```
$ cat myfifo1 &
    [1]    9208
$ cat myfifo2 | wc -1 &
    [2]    9211
$ ps -e | tee myfifo1 myfifo2 | grep 'd$' | wc -1
PID TTY     TIME      CMD
   0 ?      0:01      sched
   1 ?      0:10      init
   2 ?      0:00      pageout
   3 ?      282:23    fsflush
...
 639 ?      0:44      httpd
 643 ?      0:43      httpd
 642 ?      0:45      httpd
 640 ?      0:44      httpd
...
 9208   pts/6    0:00    cat
 8609   pts/33   0:00    bash
 9211   pts/6    0:00    wc
 9213   pts/6    0:00    tee
 9214   pts/6    0:00    sh
 9113   pts/33   0:01    emacs
28690   pts/25   0:00    bash
   30
  119
$
```

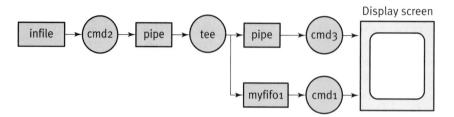

Figure 12.18 Semantics of execution of the command sequence cmd1 < myfifo1 & followed by cmd2 infile | tee myfifo1 | cmd3

The sequence of output in this session is dependent on the scheduling of the three commands; the output shown above is what was produced by our system and is the most likely output. An interesting exercise will be to come up with a sequence of commands to insure that the output is always produced in the same order as seen here.

When you no longer need to use a FIFO, you can remove it just like you remove an ordinary file. This means that you can use the unlink() system call (from within a process) or the rm command for removing a FIFO from your file system hierarchy. In the following session, we use the rm command for removing the myfifo1 and myfifo2 FIFOs. The output of the ls command before and after the rm command show that the two FIFOs have in fact been removed.

```
$ ls
myfifo1 myfifo2
$ rm myfifo1 myfifo2
$ ls
$
```

The following In-Chapter Exercises are designed to give you practice using the mkfifo command and help you to understand its semantics with a hands-on session.

IN-CHAPTER EXERCISES

12.9 Create three FIFOs, called fifo1, fifo2, and fifo3, with a single command. Write down the command that you used to perform the given task.

12.10 Create a FIFO, called fifo4, with its access privileges set to read and write for owner and group, and no privileges for others. Show the command that you used to accomplish the given task.

12.11 Try the shell session given in this section on your system. Does your system produce output in the same order as shown in our session? If not, show the output produced on your system.

Summary

UNIX automatically opens three files for every command for it to read input from and send its output and error messages to. These files are called standard input (stdin), standard output (stdout), and standard error (stderr). By default, these files are attached to the terminal on which the command is executed. Thus, the shell makes the command input come from the keyboard and its output and error messages to go to the monitor screen. These default files can be changed to other files by using redirection operators: < for input redirection and > for output and error redirection.

The stdin, stdout, and stderr can be referred to by using the integers 0, 1, and 2, called file descriptors for the three standard files, respectively. All open files in UNIX are referred to by similar integers that are used by the kernel to perform operations on these files. In the Bourne, Korn, Bash, and POSIX shells, the greater-than symbol (>) is used in conjunction with descriptors 1 and 2 to redirect standard output and standard error, respectively.

The standard output of a command can be connected to the standard input of another command via a UNIX pipe. Pipes are created in the main memory and are used to take output of a command and give it to another command without creating a disk file, effectively making two commands talk to each other. For this reason, a pipe is called an interprocess communication (IPC) mechanism, which allows related commands on the same machine to communicate with each other at the shell and application levels.

The I/O and error redirection features and pipes can be used together to implement powerful command lines. However, redirection operators and pipes alone cannot be used to redirect standard output of a command to a file, as well as connect it to standard input of another command. The tee utility can be used to accomplish this task, sending standard output of a command to one or more files and to another command.

The C shell does not support I/O and error redirection with file descriptors. Also, redirecting standard output and standard error of a command to different files is specified differently in the C shell than it is in the other shells.

FIFOs, also known as named pipes, allow related or unrelated processes on a system to communicate. Unlike a pipe, which is an in-memory buffer, a FIFO is a file created on the disk. For command line use, you can create a FIFO with the mkfifo command. When you no longer need a FIFO, you can remove it with the unlink() system call from within a program or the rm command at the command line.

Problems

1. What are standard files? Name them and state their purpose.

2. Briefly describe input, output, and error redirection. Write two commands of each to show simple and combined use of the redirection operators.

3. What are file descriptors in UNIX? What are the file descriptors of standard files? How can the I/O and error redirection operators be combined with the file descriptors of standard files to perform redirection in the Bourne, Korn, Bash, and POSIX shells?

4. Sort a file 'data1' and put the sorted file in a file called 'data1.sorted'. Give the command that uses both input and output redirection.

5. Give the command to accomplish the task in Problem 4 by using a pipe and output redirection.

6. Give a set of commands equivalent to the command ls -l | grep "sarwar" > output.p3 that use I/O redirection operators only. How does the performance of the given command compare with your command sequence? Explain.

7. What is the purpose of the tee command? Give a command equivalent to the command in Problem 6 that uses the tee command.

8. Write UNIX shell commands to carry out the following tasks.

   a. Count the number of characters, words, and lines in the file called 'data1' and display the output on the display screen.

   b. Count the number of characters, words, and lines in the output of the ls -l command and display the output on the display screen.

   c. Same as in part (b), but redirect the output to a file called 'data1.stats'.

9. Give the command for searching a file 'datafile' for the string "Internet", sending the output of the command to a file called 'Internet.freq' and any error message to a file 'error.log'. Draw a diagram for the command, similar to the ones shown in the chapter, to illustrate its semantics.

10. Give a command for accomplishing the task in Problem 9, except that both the output of the command and any error message go to a file called 'datafile'.

11. Give a command to search for lines in /etc/passwd that contain the string "sarwar". Store the output of the command in a file called 'passwd.sarwar' in your current directory. If the command fails, the error message must also go to the same file.

12. What is the UNIX pipe? How is pipe different from output redirection? Give an example to illustrate your answer.

13. What do the following commands do under the Bourne shell?

   a. cat 1> letter 2> save 0< memo

   b. cat 2> save 0< memo 1> letter

   c. cat 1> letter 0< memo 2>&1

   d. cat 0< memo | sort 1> letter 2> /dev/null

   e. cat 2> save 0< memo | sort 1> letter 2> /dev/null

14. Consider the following commands under the Bourne shell.

   i. cat memo letter 2> communication 1>&2

   ii. cat memo letter 1>&2 2> communication

   Where do output and error messages of the cat command go in each case if

   a. both files (memo and letter) exist in the present working directory, and

   b. one of the two files does not exist in the present working directory?

15. Send an e-mail message to 'doe@domain.com', using the `mail` command. Assume that the message is in a file called 'greetings'. Give one command that uses input redirection and one that uses a pipe. Any error message should be appended to a file 'mail.error'.

16. What happens when the following commands are executed on your UNIX system? Why do these commands produce the results that they do?

    a. `cat letter >> letter`

    b. `cat letter > letter`

17. By using output redirection, send a greeting message "Hello, World!" to a friend's terminal.

18. Give a command for displaying the number of users currently logged on to a system.

19. Give a command for displaying the login name of the user who was the first to log on to a system.

20. What is the difference between the following commands?

    a. `grep "John Doe" Students > /dev/null 2>&1`

    b. `grep "John Doe" Students 2>&1 > dev/null`

21. Give a command for displaying the contents of (the files names in) the current directory, three files per line.

22. Give a command that reads its input from a file called 'Phones', removes unnecessary spaces from the file, sorts the file, and removes duplicate lines from it.

23. Repeat Problem 22 for a version of the file that has unnecessary spaces removed from the file but still has duplicate lines in it.

24. What do the following commands do?

    a. `uptime | cat - who.log >> system.log`

    b. `zcat secret_memo.Z | head -5`

25. Give a command that performs the task of the following command but the `diff` command runs on the machine called 'server'. `rsh server cat ~/research/pvm/datafile.server | diff datafile -`

26. Give a command for displaying the lines in a file called 'employees' that are not repeated. What is the command for displaying repeated lines only?

27. Give a command that displays a long list for the most recently created directory.

28. Create a FIFO, called myfifo1. What are the default access privileges set for it? Create a FIFO, myfifo2, with read and write access privileges for everyone. Show your commands and their output for performing these tasks.

29. Give a set of commands for producing the output of the session given in Section 12.15. Your command sequence should insure that the order of output is always the following: the status of all the processes running on the system, the number of daemons running on the system, and the total number of processes running on the system.

Processes

Objectives

- To describe the concept of a process, and execution of multiple processes on a computer system with a single CPU
- To explain how a shell executes commands
- To discuss process attributes
- To explain the concept of foreground and background processes, including a description of a daemon and its uses
- To describe sequential and parallel execution of commands
- To discuss process and job control in UNIX: foreground and background processes, sequential and parallel processes, suspending processes, moving foreground processes into background and vice versa, and terminating processes
- To describe the UNIX process hierarchy
- To cover the commands and primitives
  `<^C>, <^D>, <^Z>, <^\>, ;, &, ( ),` bg, fg, jobs, kill, nice, nohup, ps, sleep, ptree, top

13.1 Introduction

As we have mentioned before, a process is a program in execution. The UNIX system creates a process every time you run an external command, and the process is removed from the system when the command finishes its execution. Process creation and termination are the only mechanisms used by the UNIX system to execute external commands. In a typical time-sharing system such as UNIX, which allows multiple users to use a computer system and run multiple processes simultaneously, hundreds and thousands of processes are created and terminated every day. Remember that the CPU in the computer executes processes and that a typical system has only one CPU. The question is: How does a system with a single CPU execute multiple processes simultaneously? A detailed discussion of this topic is beyond the scope of this textbook, but we briefly address it in Section 13.2. Later in the chapter, we discuss foreground and background processes, daemons, jobs, process and job attributes, and process and job control.

13.2 Running Multiple Processes Simultaneously

On a typical computer system that contains a single CPU and runs a time-sharing operating system, multiple processes are simultaneously executed by quickly switching the CPU from one process to the next. That is, one process is executed for a short period of time, and then the CPU is taken away from it and given to another process. The new process executes for a short period of time and then the CPU is given to the next process. This procedure continues until the first process in the sequence gets to use the CPU again. The time a process is "in" the CPU burst before it is switched "out" of the CPU is called a **quantum** or **time slice**. The quantum is usually very short: 1 sec for a typical UNIX system. When the CPU is free (not used by any process), the kernel uses an algorithm to decide which process gets to use the CPU next. The technique used to choose the process that gets to use the CPU is called **CPU scheduling**.

In a time-sharing system, a priority value is assigned to every process, and the process that has the highest priority gets to use the CPU next. Several methods can be used to assign a priority value to a process. One simple method is based on the time that it enters the system. In this scheme, typically the process that enters the system first is assigned the highest priority; the result is called a **firstcome, first-serve (FCFS) scheduling algorithm**. Another scheme is to assign a priority value based on the amount of time a process has used the CPU. Thus, a newly arriving process, or a process that spends most of its time performing input and/or output (I/O) operations, gets the highest priority. Processes that spend most of their time performing I/O are known as **I/O-bound processes**. An example of an I/O-bound process is a text editor such as `vi`. Another method, in which a process gets to use the CPU for one quantum and then the CPU is given to another process, the next process in the queue of processes waiting to use the CPU, is known as the **round robin (RR) scheduling algorithm**. This algorithm is a natural choice for time-sharing systems, wherein all users like to see progress by their processes. If you are interested in the other CPU scheduling algorithms, we encourage you to read a book on operating system principles and concepts. The operating system code that implements the CPU scheduling algorithm is known as the **processor scheduler**. The scheduler for most operating systems, including UNIX, is in the kernel. The operating system code that takes the CPU away from the current process and hands it over to the newly scheduled process is known as the **dispatcher**.

The UNIX scheduling algorithm is a blend of all of the algorithms mentioned. It uses a simple formula to assign a priority value to every process in the system that is ready to run. The priority value for every process in the system is recalculated every second. When it is time for scheduling, the CPU is given to the process with the *smallest* priority number. If multiple processes have the same priority number, the decision is made on the FCFS basis. The formula used to compute the priority value is,

Priority value = Threshold priority + Nice value + (Recent CPU usage/2),

where **threshold priority** is an integer usually having a value of 40 or 60, **nice value** is a positive integer with a default value of 20, and **CPU usage** is the number of **clock ticks** (1/60 or 1/50 sec for System V, where 60 or 50 is the frequency of the power line in Hz) for which the process has used the CPU. The CPU usage for every process is updated every clock tick, which increases the tick count for the process currently using the CPU. The tick count for every process is divided by 2 before process priorities are recalculated by using the formula shown. The CPU usage value therefore increases for the process using the CPU and decreases for all other processes. You can assign a higher nice value to your processes by using the `nice` command, but the nice value can never be a negative number. A higher nice value means a higher priority value and hence, a lower priority. So, when you increase the nice value of your process, you are being nice to other user processes. The formula clearly indicates that the higher the recent CPU usage of a process, the higher is its priority value and the lower is its priority. Thus, UNIX favors processes that have used less CPU time in the recent past. A text editor such as `vi` gets higher priority than a process that computes the value of pi (π) because `vi` spends most of the time doing I/O (reading keyboard input and displaying it on the screen), and the process that computes π spends most of its time doing calculations (using the CPU). Recalculating priority values of all the processes every second causes process priorities to change dynamically (up and down). In Section 13.5, we further explain the UNIX scheduling concept.

13.3   UNIX Process States

A UNIX process can be in one of many **states**, as it moves from one state to another, eventually finishing its execution (normally or abnormally) and getting out of the system. A process terminates normally when it finishes its work and exits the system gracefully. A process terminates abnormally when it exits the system because of an exception (error) condition or intervention by its owner or the superuser. The owner of the process can intervene by using a command or a particular keystroke to terminate the process. We discuss these commands and keystrokes later in the chapter. The primary states that a process can be in are shown in the state diagram in Figure 13.1.

The waiting state encompasses several states; we use the term here to keep the diagram simple. Some of the states belonging to the waiting state are listed under the oval representing the state. Table 13.1 gives a brief description of these UNIX process states. In the interest of brevity, and due to the scope of this book, the other states that a UNIX process can be in are not included in this discussion.

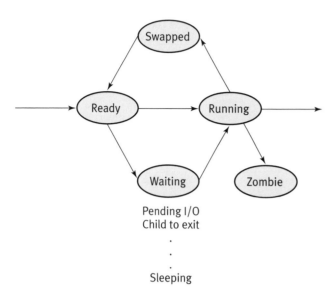

Figure 13.1 UNIX process state diagram

TABLE 13.1 A Brief Description of the UNIX Process States

State	Description
Ready	The process is ready to run but does not have the CPU. Based on the scheduling algorithm, the scheduler decided to give the CPU to another process. Several processes can be in this state, but on a machine with a single CPU, only one can be executing (using the CPU).
Running	The process is actually running (using the CPU).
Waiting	The process is waiting for an event. Possible events are an I/O (e.g., disk/terminal read or write) is completed, a child process exits (parent waits for one or more of its children to exit), or the sleep period expires for the process.
Swapped	The process is ready to run, but it has been temporarily put on the disk (on the swap space); perhaps it needs more memory and there is not enough available at this time.
Zombie	A dying process is said to be in a zombie state. Usually, when the parent of a process terminates before it executes the exit call, it becomes a zombie process. The process finishes and finds that the parent is not waiting. The zombie processes are finished for all practical purposes and do not reside in the memory, but they still have some kernel resources allocated to them and cannot be taken out of the system. All zombies (and their live children) are eventually adopted by the granddaddy, the init process, which removes them from the system.

13.4   Execution of **shell** Commands

A shell command can be internal or external. An **internal (built-in) command** is one whose code is part of the shell process. Some of the commonly used internal commands are . (dot command), bg, cd, continue, echo, exec, exit, export, fg, jobs, pwd, read, readonly, return, set, shift, test, times, trap, umask, unset, and wait. An **external command** is one whose code is in a file; contents of the file can be binary code or a shell script. Some of the commonly used **external commands** are grep, more, cat, mkdir, rmdir, ls, sort, ftp, telnet, lp, and ps. A shell creates a new process to execute a command. While the command process executes, the shell waits for it to finish. In this section, we describe how a shell (or any process) creates another process and how external commands are executed by the shell.

A UNIX process can create another process by using the fork system call, which creates an exact main memory copy of the original process. Both processes continue execution, starting with the statement that follows 'fork'. The forking process is known as the **parent process**, and the created (forked) process is called the **child process**, as shown in Figure 13.2. Here, we show a Bourne shell that has created a child process (another Bourne shell).

For executing an external binary command, a mechanism is needed that allows the child process to become the command to be executed. The UNIX system call exec can be used to do exactly that, allowing a process to overwrite itself with the executable code for another command. A shell uses the fork and exec calls in tandem to execute an external binary command. The sequence of events for the execution of an external command sort (whose code is in a binary file) are given in Figure 13.3.

The execution of a shell script (a series of shell commands in a file; *see* Chapters 15–18) is slightly different from the execution of a binary file. In the case of a shell script, the current shell creates a child shell and lets the child shell execute commands in the shell script, one by one. Each command in the script file is executed in the same way that commands from the keyboard are—that is, the child shell creates a child for every command that it executes. While the child shell is executing commands in the script file, the parent shell waits for the child to terminate. When the child shell hits the eof marker in the script file, it terminates. The only purpose of the child shell (like any other shell) is to execute commands, and eof means no more commands. When the child shell terminates, the parent shell comes out of the waiting state and resumes execution. This sequence of events is shown in Figure 13.4, which also shows the execution of a find command in the script file.

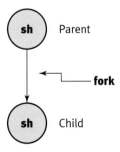

Figure 13.2 Process creation via the fork system call

Step 1: Shell uses **fork** to create a child

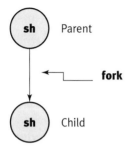

Step 2: Child uses **exec** to overwrite itself with the executable file corresponding to the **sort** command.

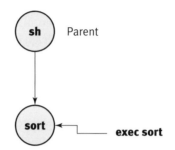

Step 3: **sort** starts execution while 'sh' waits for the command to finish. When **sort** finishes, the child process terminates and 'sh' starts execution again, waiting for the user to give it another command to execute.

Figure 13.3 Steps for execution of a binary program sort by a UNIX shell

Unless otherwise specified in the file containing the shell script, the child shell has the type of the parent shell. That is, if the parent is a Bourne shell, the child is also a Bourne shell. Thus, by default the shell script is executed by a "copy" of the parent shell. However, shell script written for any shell (C, Bourne, Korn, etc.) can be executed regardless of the type of the current shell. To do so, simply specify the type of the child shell (under which the script should be executed) in the first line of the file containing the shell script as #!full-path-name-of-the-shell. For example, the following line dictates that the child shell is C shell, so the script following this line is executed under the C shell.

#!/bin/csh

Also, you can execute commands in another shell by running that shell as a child of the current shell, executing commands under it, and terminating the shell. A child shell is also called a **subshell**. Recall that the commands to run various shells are sh for the Bourne shell, csh for the C shell, ksh for the Korn shell, and bash for the Bourne again shell. To start a new shell process, simply run the command corresponding to the shell you want to run. In the following session, the current shell is the C shell and the Bourne shell runs as its child. The echo command is executed under the Bourne shell. Then a Korn shell is started, and the echo command is executed under it. The ps command shows the three shells running. Finally, both the Korn and Bourne shells are terminated when <Ctrl-D> is pressed in succession, and control goes back to the original shell, the C shell. The first <Ctrl-D> terminates the Korn shell, giving control back to the Bourne shell. Figure 13.5 illustrates all the steps involved, showing the parent-child relationship between processes.

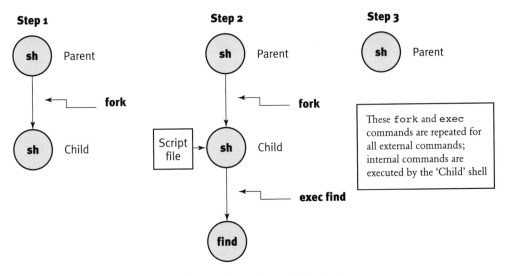

Figure 13.4 Steps for execution of a shell script by a UNIX shell

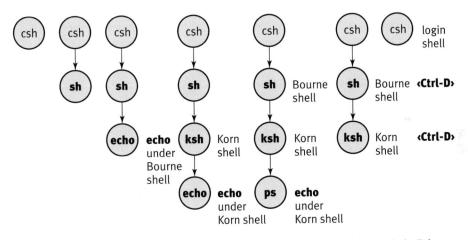

Figure 13.5 Execution of commands under the child shells (also called subshells)

```
% ps
   PID      TTY       TIME      CMD
   15672    pts/0     :03       -csh
% sh
$ echo This is Bourne shell.
This is Bourne shell.
$ ksh
$ echo This is Korn shell.
```

```
This is Korn shell.
$ ps
    PID      TTY       TIME       CMD
    15672    pts/0     0:03       -csh
    15772    pts/0     0:00       sh
    15773    pts/0     0:00       ksh
$ ^D
$ ^D
%
```

13.5   Process Attributes

Every UNIX process has several attributes, including owner's ID, process name, process ID (PID), process state, PID of the parent process, and length of time the process has been running. From the user's point of view, one of the most useful of these attributes is the PID, which is used as a parameter in several process control commands (discussed later in this chapter). The ps command can be used to view the attributes of processes running on a system. System V and BSD UNIX systems have their own versions of this command, and the outputs of the two commands are slightly different. The following is a brief description of the System V version of the ps command.

ps [options]

Purpose: Report process status

Output: Attributes of process running on the system

Commonly used options/features:

-a	Display information about the processes executing on your terminal except the session leader (your login shell)
-e	Display information about all the processes running on the system
-l	Display long list (14 columns) of the status report
-u uidlist	Display information about processes belonging to the users with the UIDs in 'uidlist' (UIDs separated by commas)

The following sessions demonstrate use of the ps command with and without options. We ran all of them on an IBM AIX (System V–based) machine running the Korn shell and a Sun Sparc with Solaris2 running the C shell. The command runs shown are for the AIX machine. The output of the ps command shows four fields. The output shows that three processes are attached to the terminal pts/1: -ksh (a Korn shell), ps, and vi (editor) belonging to the user who ran the command. The – in front of ksh indicates that it is the login shell. The PIDs of ksh, ps, and vi are 19440, 18786, and 20668, respectively. Furthermore, -ksh, ps, and vi have run for 2, 0, and 10 sec, respectively.

```
$ ps
   PID        TTY      TIME    CMD
 19440      pts/1     0:02    -ksh
 18786      pts/1     0:00    ps
 20668      pts/1     0:10    vi
$
```

You can use the –a option to display all processes except **session leaders** and nonterminal associated processes. In the following session, the session leader, the login shell (–ksh), is the only process not displayed.

```
$ ps –a
   PID        TTY      TIME    CMD
 20668      pts/     10:10    vi
 21534      pts/1     0:00    ps
$
```

You can use the –u option to display the status of all the processes belonging to the users with user IDs in 'uidlist' specified after the option. In this case, all the processes belonging to the user with UID 147 are displayed.

```
$ ps -u 147
  UID        PID       TTY     TIME    CMD
  147      18802      pts/1    0:00    ps
  147      19440      pts/1    0:02    ksh
  147      20668      pts/1    0:10    vi
$
```

The `ps -1` command shows the long list of processes on the system. Although relatively new users of UNIX do not need to use this option, we describe the details of its output for the sake of completeness, as well as to explain briefly some important concepts related to UNIX process scheduling. Table 13.2 briefly describes the meaning of various fields in the output of the command. Depending on the particular implementation of UNIX that you are using, the output (and its order) may be slightly different, but the output will contain almost the same fields.

```
$ ps –l
       F S UID    PID    PPID   C  PRI  NI  ADDR   SZ  WCHAN    TTY  TIME  CMD
  200001 A 147  18630   19440  13   66  20  fedf  288           pts/1 0:00  ps
  240001 A 147  19440   19496   1   60  20  9e93  476           pts/1 0:02  ksh
20200011 T 147  20668   19440   0   64  24  ceb9  356           pts/1 0:10  vi
$
```

We have talked about some of the fields already, and descriptions of the others in the table are fairly self-explanatory. Three fields in the output of the `ps -l` command are important in terms of how the UNIX scheduler works (*see* Section 13.2). These fields are C (CPU usage), NI (nice value), and PRI (priority value of the process). Recall that the priority number of a process is given by,

Priority value = Threshold priority + Nice value + (Recent CPU usage/2).

In terms of the fields listed in Table 13.2, the priority value (PRI) of a process is given by,

PRI = Threshold priority + (C/2) + NI.

■ **TABLE 13.2** Brief Description of Various Fields of the Output of the ps −l Command

Field	Meaning
F	Flags: Flags associated with the process indicate things like whether the process is a user or kernel process and why the process stopped or went to sleep

S	State: State of the process
	    O Currently running (using the CPU)
	    R Ready to run but not presently running
	    S Sleeping for an event
	    T Stopped (background process, suspended, or being traced)
	    Z Zombie process (finished but is still using some kernel resources; created, for example, when parent dies before the process finishes)

UID	User ID: Process owner's user ID
PID	Process ID: ID of the process
PPID	Parent PID: PID of the parent process
C	CPU Usage: Recent CPU utilization, a parameter used in computing a process's priority for scheduling purposes
PRI	Priority: Priority value of a process that dictates when the process is scheduled; the smaller the priority value of a process, the higher its priority
NI	Nice value: The nice value of a process; another parameter used in the computation of a process's priority value
ADDR	Address: The memory or disk address of a process, that is, its location in the main memory or disk (for a swapped-out process)
SZ	Size: The size of the memory image of a process in blocks
WCHAN	Wait channel: Null for running processes; processes that are ready to run and are waiting for the CPU to be given to them; for a waiting or sleeping process, shows the event the process is waiting for
TTY	Terminal: Shows the terminal name a process is attached to

(continued)

TABLE 13.2 *(continued)*

TIME	Time: The length of time (in minutes and seconds) a process has been running, or ran for before sleeping or stopping
CMD	Command: Lists the command used to start this process; the -f option is needed to see the full command in System V UNIX; otherwise, only the last component of the pathname is displayed

In the preceding session, the output of the ps -l command clearly shows that the higher the value of C for a process, the higher its priority value and the lower its scheduling priority. In other words, the more CPU time a process has used in the recent past, the lower its priority becomes. In that session, the vi process is currently stopped with a CPU usage of 0 and has a nice value of 24. The shell process (-ksh) is not using the CPU presently, its CPU usage is 1, and it has a nice value of 20. The priority values for vi and -ksh are 64 and 60, respectively. Thus, the next time the UNIX scheduler runs, it will assign the CPU to the shell process. By rearranging terms and substituting these values of C, PRI, and NI into the formula, we can compute the threshold priority used by our UNIX system:

Threshold priority $= 66 - 20 - 6 = 40.$

We can now use this threshold priority value to compute the priority value of a process that has a nice value of 20 and a CPU usage of 30:

PRI $= 40 + (30/2) + 20 = 75.$

Thus, the priority value of the process is 75.

In the following In-Chapter Exercises, you will use the ps command with and without options to appreciate the command output.

IN-CHAPTER EXERCISES

13.1 Use the ps command to display the status of processes that are running in your current session. Can you identify your login shell? What is it?

13.2 Run the command to display the status of all the processes running on your system. What command did you run? What are their PIDs? What are the PIDs of the parents of all the processes?

13.3 Try the above sessions for the top command on your system. How many processes are running on your system? What are the priority and nice values for the highest priority process?

If you want to monitor the CPU activity in real time, you can use the top command. It displays the status of the first 15 of the most CPU-intensive tasks on the system as well as the CPU activity and allows you to manipulate processes interactively. It refreshes its output every five seconds and allows you to sort tasks by CPU usage, memory usage, and run time.

Most features can either be selected by an interactive command or by specifying the feature in the personal or systemwide configuration file. Sometimes this command is available only to the superuser. Here is a sample run of the top command on our Solaris 2 system.

```
$ top
load averages: 0.09, 0.08, 0.07 06:51:18
81 processes:  79 sleeping, 1 stopped, 1 on cpu
CPU states:    93.0% idle, 4.6% user, 2.4% kernel, 0.0% iowait, 0.0% swap
Memory:        2048M real, 1559M free, 148M swap in use, 5394M swap free
  PID USERNAME THR PRI NICE  SIZE    RES   STATE   TIME   CPU     COMMAND
 3054 zartash   1   0   0     10M   7088K  sleep   0:00   1.25%   emac
 3053 msarwar   1  58   0    2624K  1584K  cpu/0   0:00   0.10%   top
 2375 zartash   1  48   0    2528K  1864K  sleep   0:00   0.03%   bash
  578 root      1  59   0    1728K  1040K  sleep   0:59   0.02%   ntpstat
 2992 msarwar   1  48   0    2528K  1864K  sleep   0:00   0.02%   sh
  570 root      1  58   0    8680K  8000K  sleep   9:20   0.00%   sunsniff
 1276 root      1  59   0    8680K  8032K  sleep   7:28   0.00%   sunsniff
  640 virtual   1  58   0    9096K  6568K  sleep   1:19   0.00%   httpd
 1607 virtual   1  58   0    8936K  6488K  sleep   1:16   0.00%   httpd
 1667 virtual   1  58   0    8896K  6408K  sleep   1:16   0.00%   httpd
  642 virtual   1  58   0    8816K  6064K  sleep   1:16   0.00%   httpd
  639 virtual   1  58   0    7248K  4544K  sleep   1:15   0.00%   httpd
 1666 virtual   1  58   0    8832K  6216K  sleep   1:14   0.00%   httpd
 1608 virtual   1  58   0    7296K  4624K  sleep   1:14   0.00%   httpd
  643 virtual   1  58   0    7312K  4584K  sleep   1:14   0.00%   httpd
...
<Ctrl-C>
$
```

The output shows that there are a total of 81 processes on the system; that 79 are sleeping, one is stopped, and; one is currently executing; that CPU usage is 93%; and various other statistics that show used and available main memory and swap space. The output also shows that the emacs process belonging to the user zartash is the highest priority process with priority and nice values as 0. At the top right is the current time, which is updated when the top command refreshes its output.

You can interact with top as it runs by using various commands. When you use an interactive command, top prompts you with one or more questions related to the chore that you want it to perform. For example, when you press <n>, top prompts you for the number of processes to display. You enter the number and hit the <Enter> key for top to start displaying the number of processes that you entered. Similarly, if you want to terminate a process, press <k> and top prompts you for the PID of the process to be terminated. You enter the PID of the process to be terminated and hit <Enter> for top to terminate the process. You can press <h> to display the various commands that allow you to interact with top. Here is the output of pressing <h> on our system.

```
Top version 3.5beta12, Copyright © 1984 through 1996, William LeFebvre
A top users display for UNIX
These single-character commands are available:
         ^L       —redraw screen
         q        —quit
    h or ?        —help; show this text
         d        —change number of displays to show
         e        —list errors generated by last "kill" or "renice" command
         i        —toggle the displaying of idle processes
         I        —same as 'i'
         k        —kill processes; send a signal to a list of processes
    n or #        —change number of processes to display
         o        —specify sort order (size, res, cpu, time)
         r        —renice a process
         s        —change number of seconds to delay between updates
         u        —display processes for only one user (+ selects all users)
```

So if you want to display real-time status of the processes owned by the user bob, you press <u> and enter the login name of the user. The following output shows monitoring of bob's processes.

```
Username to show: bob
load averages: 0.04, 0.05, 0.05 07:52:36
74 processes: 73 sleeping, 1 on cpu
CPU states: 98.4% idle, 0.0% user, 1.6% kernel, 0.0% iowait, 0.0% swap
Memory: 2048M real, 1484M free, 139M swap in use, 5403M swap free
 PID    USERNAME  THR  PRI  NICE  SIZE   RES    STATE   TIME  CPU     COMMAND
 8123   bob        1    58   0    2608K  1584K  cpu/1   0:00  0.12%   top
 7997   bob        1    48   0    2528K  1864K  sleep   0:00  0.01%   sh
```

13.6   Process and Job Control

UNIX is responsible for several activities related to process and job management, including process creation, process termination, running processes in the foreground and background, suspending processes, and switching processes from foreground to background and vice versa. As a UNIX user, you can request the above process and job control tasks by using the shell commands discussed in this section.

13.6.1 Foreground and Background Process and Related Commands

When you type a command and hit <Enter>, the shell executes the command and returns by displaying the shell prompt. While your command executes, you do not have access to your shell and therefore cannot execute any commands until the current command finishes and the shell returns. When commands execute in this manner, we say that they execute in the foreground. More technically, when a command executes in the **foreground**, it keeps control of the keyboard and the display screen.

At times, you will need to run a UNIX command (or any program) that takes a long time to finish and—while the command executes—you will want to do other work. You cannot do so if the command runs in the foreground because the shell does not return until the command completes. UNIX allows you to run a command so that—while the command executes—you get the shell prompt back and can do other work. This capability is called running the command in the **background**. You can run a command in the background by ending the command with an ampersand (&).

Background processes run with a larger nice value and hence, a lower priority. Thus, they get to use the CPU only when no higher priority process needs it. When a background process generates output that is sent to the display screen, the screen looks garbled, but if you are simultaneously using another application, your work is not altered in any way. You can get out of the application and then get back into it to obtain a cleaner screen. Some applications such as vi allow you to redraw the screen without quitting it. In vi (*see* Chapter 5), pressing <Ctrl-L> in the command mode allows you to do so.

The syntaxes for executing a command in the foreground and background are as follows. Note that no space is needed between the command and & but that you can use space for clarity.

SYNTAX

command (for foreground execution)
command & (for background execution)

Now consider the following command. It searches the whole file structure for a file called foo and stores the pathnames of the directories that contain this file in the file foo.paths; error messages are sent to the file /dev/null, which is the UNIX black hole: Whatever goes in never comes out. (Note that, for the C shell, 2> should be replaced with >&.) This command may take several minutes, perhaps hours, depending on the size of the file structure, system load in terms of the number of users logged on, and the number of processes running on the system. So if you want to do some other work on the system while the command executes, you cannot do so because the command executes in the foreground.

```
$ find / -name foo -print > foo.paths 2> /dev/null
...
$
```

The find command is a perfect candidate for background execution because, while it runs, you have access to the shell and can do other work. Thus, the preceding command should be executed as follows.

```
$ find / -name foo -print > foo.paths 2> /dev/null &
[1] 23467
$
```

The number shown in brackets is returned by the shell and is the **job number** for the process; the other number is the PID of the process. Here, the job number for this `find` command is 1, and the PID is 23467. A **job** is a process that is not running in the foreground and is accessible only at the terminal with which it is associated. Such processes are typically executed as background or suspended processes.

The commands that perform tasks that do not involve user intervention and take a long time to finish are good candidates for background execution. Some examples are sorting large files (`sort` command), compiling (`cc` or `make` command), and searching a large file structure for one or more files (`find` command). Commands that do terminal I/O, such as the `vi` editor, are not good candidates for background execution. The reason is that, when such a command executes in the background, it stops as it reads input from the keyboard. The command needs to be brought back to the foreground before it can start running again. The `fg` command allows you to bring a background process to the foreground. Following is a brief description of the syntax for this command.

---

fg[%jobid]

Purpose: Resume execution of the process with job number 'jobid' in the foreground or move background processes to the foreground

Commonly used values for '%jobid':

% or %+	Current job
%-	Previous job
%N	Job number N
%Name	Job beginning with 'Name'
%?Name	Command containing 'Name'

SYNTAX

When the `fg` command is executed without a 'jobid', it brings the current job into the foreground. The job using the CPU at any particular time is called the **current job**. In the following session, three `find` commands are executed in the background. When the `fg` command is executed, it brings the `find / -inum 23456-print > pathnames 2> /deve/null &` command into the foreground. The `fg` command can be executed with a job number as its argument to bring a particular job into the foreground. In the following session, the `fg %3` command brings job number 3 into the foreground. A string that uniquely identifies a job can also be used in place of a job number. The string is enclosed in double quotes if it has spaces in it. The third `fg` command illustrates this convention. Using `find` alone will not work because more than one command starts with this string.

```
$ find / -inum 23456 -print > pathnames 2> /dev/null &
[1] 13590
$ find / -name foo -print > foo.paths 2> /dev/null &
[2] 13591
$ find / -name foobar -print > foobar.paths 2> /dev/null &
[3] 13596
$ ps
   PID    TTY     TIME    CMD
 13495   pts/0    0:03    -ksh
 13583   pts/0    0:11    find / -inum 23456 -print > pathnames 2> /dev/null
 13586   pts/0    0:05    find / -name foo -print > foo.paths 2> /dev/null
 13587   pts/0    0:03    find / -name foobar -print > foobar.paths 2> /dev/null
$ fg
find / -inum 23456 -print > pathnames 2> /dev/null
<Ctrl-C>
$ fg %3
find / -name foobar -print > foobar.paths 2> /dev/null
<Ctrl-Z>
$ fg %"find / -name foob"
$ jobs
[1] + Stopped (SIGTSTP)     find / -inum 23456 -print
[2] - Running               find / -name foo > foo.paths 2> /dev/null&
[3] Running                 find / -name foobar > foobar.paths 2> /dev/null&
[4] Stopped (SIGTSTP) vi chapter13
$ jobs -l
[1] + 13583 Stopped (SIGTSTP) find / -inum 23456 -print
[2] - 13586 Running          find / -name foo > foo.paths 2> /dev/null&
[3] 13587 Running            find / -name foobar > foobar.paths 2>
/dev/null&
[4] 13589 Stopped (SIGTSTP) vi chapter13
$ bg
[1]      find / -inum 23456 -print&
$ jobs
[1]      + Running           find / -inum 23456 -print
[2]      - Running           find / -name foo > foo.paths 2> /dev/null&
[3]        Running           find / -name foobar > foobar.paths 2> /dev/null&
[4]        Stopped (SIGTSTP) vi chapter13
$ bg %4
[4]      vi chapter13&
```

```
$ jobs
[1]       + Running            find / -inum 23456 -print
[2]       - Running            find / -name foo > foo.paths 2> /dev/null&
[3]       Running              find / -name foobar > foobar.paths 2> /dev/null&
[4]       Stopped (SIGTSTP) vi chapter13
find / -name foobar -print > foobar.paths 2> /dev/null
```

While running a command in the foreground, you might need to *suspend* it in order to go back to the shell, do something under the shell, and then return to the suspended process. For example, say that you are in the middle of editing a C program file with vi and need to compile the program to determine whether some errors have been corrected. You can save changes to the file, suspend vi, compile the program to view the results of the compilation, and return to vi. You can suspend a foreground process by pressing <Ctrl-Z>. You can put a suspended process in the foreground by using the fg command and in the background by using the bg command (described later in this section). So you can suspend vi by pressing <Ctrl-Z>, compile the program to identify any other errors, and resume the suspended vi session by using the fg command. This sequence of events is shown in the following session.

```
$ ps
    PID    TTY     TIME    CMD
  19984   pts/3    0:00    ps
  20996   pts/3    0:02    -ksh
$
$ vi
#include <stdio.h>
#define SIZE 100
main (int argc, char *argv[])
{
...
~
~
~
<Ctrl-Z>
[1]+ Stopped (SIGTSTP) vi
$ ps
    PID    TTY     TIME    CMD
  19906   pts/3    0:00    ps
  19988   pts/3    0:10    vi
  20996   pts/3    0:02    -ksh
$ cc -o lab8 lab8.c
$ fg %1
```

```
#include <stdio.h>
#define SIZE 100
main (int argc, char *argv[])
{
...
~
~
~
:q!
$
```

In the preceding session, the cc -o lab8 lab8.c command is used to compile the C program in the lab8.c file and put the executable in a file called lab8. Understanding what compilation means is not the point here, and a fuller discussion of the semantics of the cc command is presented in Chapter 20. Here, we are merely emphasizing that processes that take a long time to start or those that have executed for a considerable amount of time are usually suspended; the example of suspending the vi command is presented only as an illustration.

You can move the foreground and suspended processes to the background by using the bg command. The syntax of this command is exactly like that of the fg command.

S Y N T A X

bg[%jobid-list]

Purpose: Resume execution of suspended processes/jobs with job numbers in 'jobid-list' in the background

Commonly used values for '%jobid':

% or %+	Current job
%-	Previous job
%N	Job number N
%Name	Job beginning with 'Name'
%?Name	Command containing 'Name'

If there are multiple suspended processes, the fg command without an argument brings the current process into the foreground, and the bg command without an argument resumes execution of the current process in the background. You can use the jobs command to display the job numbers of all suspended (stopped) and background processes and which one is the current process. The current process is identified by a + and the previous process by a − in the output of the jobs command. The following is a brief description of the command.

jobs [option][%jobid-list]

Purpose: Display the status of the suspended and background processes specified in 'jobid-list'; with no list, display the status of current job

Commonly used options/features:

−1   Also display PID of jobs

S Y N T A X

The optional argument 'jobid-list' can be a list of job numbers starting with % and separated by spaces. The following session shows the command usage with and without the only option and arguments. The jobs command reports the status of all jobs without their PIDs. The command with the −1 option also displays PIDs of the jobs. The following session shows the outputs of the jobs, jobs −1, bg, and bg %4 commands. Again, in the output of the jobs command, the current job is marked with the + sign and the previous job is marked with the − sign. Furthermore, processes executing in the background are in the running state and the suspended processes are in the stopped state. The string SIGTSTP in parentheses indicates that job numbers 1 and 4 received the stop signal (discussed in Section 13.6.3), which means that the user pressed <Ctrl-Z> when each job was running in the foreground. The bg command puts the current job in the background, as indicated by the output of the command (note the & at the end of the command). The immediately following jobs command indicates that the job moved into the background is in the running state. The bg %4 command moves job number 4 (the vi process) into the background. Moreover, the immediately following jobs command shows that vi became the current job and that the string SIGTSTP changed to SIGTTOU, meaning that this process can do terminal output but cannot do terminal input. That is, as long as vi is in the background, it cannot read keyboard input. So, the vi process is still in the stopped state.

As indicated in the command description, the bg command can be passed a list of job numbers for moving multiple suspended jobs into the background. Thus, the bg %1 %3 command can be used to move jobs 1 and 3 into the background.

In the following In-Chapter Exercise, you will practice creation and management of foreground and background processes by using the bg, fg, and jobs commands.

IN-CHAPTER EXERCISE

13.4 Run the sessions presented in this section on your system to practice foreground and background process creation and switching processes from the foreground to the background (the bg command) and vice versa (the fg command). Use the jobs command to display job IDs of the active and suspended processes.

13.6.2 UNIX Daemons

Although any process running in the background can be called a daemon, in UNIX jargon a **daemon** is a system process running in the background. Daemons are frequently used in UNIX to offer various types of services to users and handle system administration tasks. For example, the print, e-mail, and finger services are provided via daemons. The printing services are provided by the printer daemon, lpd. The finger services (*see* Chapter 14) are handled by the finger daemon, fingerd. The inetd, commonly known as the UNIX superserver, handles various Internet related services by spawning several daemons at system boot time. Access the /etc/inetd.conf file to view the services offered by this daemon on your system. This file has one line for every service that inetd offers.

13.6.3 Sequential and Parallel Execution of Commands

You can type multiple commands on one command line for sequential and/or parallel execution. The following is a brief description of the syntax for **sequential execution** of commands specified in one command line.

SYNTAX

cmd1; cmd2; ...; cmdN

Purpose: Execute the 'cmd1', 'cmd2', ..., 'cmdN' commands sequentially

---

Note that the semicolon is used as a command separator (delimiter) and does not follow the last command. No spaces are needed before and after a semicolon, but you can use spaces for clarity. These commands execute one after the other, as though each were typed on a separate line. In the following session, the date and echo commands execute sequentially as separate processes.

```
$ date; echo Hello, World!
Fri Jun 18 23:43:39 PDT 2004
Hello, World!
$
```

You can specify **parallel execution** of commands in a command line by ending each command with an ampersand (&). The commands that terminate with & also execute in the background. No spaces are required before or after an &, but you can use spaces for clarity. The following is a brief description of the syntax for parallel execution of shell commands specified in one command line.

SYNTAX

cmd1& cmd2& ... cmdN&

Purpose: Execute commands 'cmd1', 'cmd2', ..., 'cmdN' in parallel as separate processes

---

In the following session, the date and echo commands execute in parallel, followed by the sequential execution of the uname and who commands. The job and process IDs of the date command are 1 and 15575 and that of the echo command are 2 and 15576, respectively. One interesting and important point to note is that the output of the echo command is displayed before the date command, even though the date command appears first in the command line and starts as a separate process before the echo command. This order is due to the scheduling of processes and the amount of time each takes to execute. Also, the date and echo commands execute in the background, and the uname and who commands execute in the foreground.

```
$ date& echo Hello, World!& uname; who
[1] 15575
[2] 15576
Hello, World!
[2] Done echo Hello, World!
Sat Jun 19 10:13:14 PDT 2004
[1] Done date
SunOS
kuhn console Jun 12 14:17
sarwar pts/0 Jun 19 10:10
$
```

When the same command was executed on an AIX machine running the Korn shell, the following output was produced. Note that this output is different from the preceding output, further making the point that processes are executed in a random order as determined by the scheduler. Furthermore, as the commands used here do not take much time to execute, their order of execution will most likely be the same on your machine whenever you run this command line.

```
$ date& echo Hello, World!& uname; who
[1] 5078
[2] 17516
$ AIX
johnsen pst/3 Jun 19 11:17
sarwar pts/0 Jun 19 10:20
Hello, World!
Sat Jun 19 10:21:49 PDT 2004
[2] + Done date& echo Hello, World!& uname; who
[1] + Done date& echo Hello, World!& uname; who
$
```

In a command line, the last & puts all the commands after the previous & in one process. In the following command line, therefore, the date command executes as one process and all the commands in who; whoami; uname; echo Hello, World!& as another process. The process IDs are 15586 and 15587, and the job IDs for the processes are 1 and 2, respectively. Note again that the output of the date command appears after the output of the who command, owing to the scheduling of the two processes.

```
$ date& who; whoami; uname; echo Hello, World!&
[1] 15586
[2] 15587
$ kuhn console Jun 12 14:17
sarwar pts/0 Jun 19 10:10 (upibm7.egr.up.edu)
Sat Jun 19 10:10:23 PDT 2004
[1] Done date
$ sarwar
SunOS
Hello, World!
[2] Done ( who; whoami; uname; echo Hello, World! )
$
```

UNIX allows you to group commands and execute them as one process by separating commands using semicolons and enclosing them in parentheses. This is called **command grouping**. Because all the commands in a command group execute as a single process, they are executed by the same subshell. However, all the commands execute sequentially. The following is a brief description of the syntax for command grouping.

SYNTAX

(cmd1; cmd2; ...; cmdN)

Purpose: Execute commands 'cmd1', 'cmd2', ..., 'cmdN' sequentially, but as one process

---

In the following session, therefore, the date and echo commands execute sequentially, but as one process.

```
$ (date; echo Hello, World!)
Sat Jun 19 09:27:38 PDT 2004
Hello, World!
$
```

You can combine command grouping with sequential execution by separating command groups with other commands or command groups. In the following session, the date and echo commands execute as one process, followed by execution of the who command as a separate process.

```
$ (date; echo Hello, World!); who
Sat Jun 19 09:30:01 PDT 2004
Hello, World!
```

```
deborahs  ttyA0    Jun 19    08:05
kittyt    ttyA1    Jun 19    07:19
nelson    ttyC0    Jun 19    10:16
sarwar    ttyC1    Jun 19    09:27
$
```

Command groups can be nested. Hence, ((date; echo Hello, World!); who) and ((date; echo Hello, World!); (who; uname)) are valid commands and produce the expected results. Command grouping makes more sense when groups are executed as separate processes, as shown in the following session. In the second group of commands, (date; echo Hello, World) and (who; uname) execute in the background and the whoami command executes in the foreground; all three commands execute in parallel. Again, note the order of outputs: The output of whoami is displayed first, and the outputs of the other two processes are interleaved. On some systems, you need to press <Enter> after the first Hello, world! output is produced.

```
$ (date ; echo Hello, World!)&
[1] 2891
$ Fri Jun 18 23:43:10 PDT 2004
Hello, World!
[1] Done ( date; echo Hello, World! )
$
$ (date; echo Hello, World)& (who; uname)& whoami
[1] 15643
[2] 15645
sarwar
kuhn console Jun 12 14:17
Sat Jun 19 11:58:54 PDT 2004
Hello, World
[1] Done ( date; echo Hello, World )
$ sarwar pts/0 Jun 19 10:10
SunOS
[2] Done ( who; uname )
$
```

In the following In-Chapter Exercises, you will practice sequential and parallel execution of UNIX commands.

IN-CHAPTER EXERCISES ▬▬▬▬▬▬▬▬▬▬▬▬▬▬▬▬▬▬▬▬▬▬▬▬▬

13.5 Run the sessions presented in this section on your system to practice sequential and parallel execution of shell commands. *(continued)*

13.6 Which of the following commands run sequentially and which run in parallel? How many of the processes run in parallel? (who; date) & (cat temp; uname & whoami)

13.6.4 Abnormal Termination of Commands and Processes

When you run a command, it terminates normally after successfully completing its task. A command (process) can terminate prematurely because of a bad argument that you passed to it, such as a directory argument to the cp command. At times, you might also need to terminate a process abnormally. The need for abnormal termination occurs when you run a process with a wrong argument (e.g., a wrong file name to a find command) or when a command is taking too long to finish. Here, we address abnormal termination in relation to both foreground and background processes.

You can terminate a foreground process by pressing <Ctrl-C>. You can terminate a background process in one of two ways: (1) by using the kill command, or (2) by first bringing the process into the foreground by using the fg command and then pressing <Ctrl-C>. The primary purpose of the kill command is to send a signal (also known as a **software interrupt**) to a process. The UNIX operating system uses a signal to get the attention of a process. Any one of more than 40 signal types can be sent to a UNIX process. A process can take one of three actions upon receiving a signal:

1. Accept the default action as determined by the UNIX kernel
2. Ignore the signal
3. Intercept the signal and take a user-defined action

For most signals, the default action, in addition to some other events, always results in termination of the process. Ignoring a signal does not have any impact on the process. A user-defined action is specified in the process as a program statement, and it can take control of the process at a specific piece of code in the process. In a shell script, these actions can be specified by using the trap command in the Bourne shell. The C shell provides a limited handling of signals via the onintr instruction. In a C program, these actions are specified by using the signal system call. We discuss the trap and onintr commands in detail in Chapters 16 and 18, respectively. The description of the signal system call is beyond the scope of this textbook, but you can consult a book on UNIX systems programming to learn how this call is used. Or, for a quick look, view its manual page by using the man -s2 signal command.

Signals can be generated for various reasons. Some of these reasons are caused by the process itself, whereas others are external to the process. A signal caused by an event internal to a process is known as an **internal signal**, or a **trap** (not to be confused with the trap command). A signal caused by an event external to a process is called an **external signal**. For example, an internal signal is generated for a process when the process tries to execute a nonexisting instruction or to access memory that it is not allowed to access (e.g., memory belonging to some other process or memory belonging to the UNIX kernel). An external signal can be generated by pressing <Ctrl-C>, by logging out, or by using the kill command. The kill command can be used to send any type of signal to a process. The following is a brief description of the kill command.

kill [-signal_number] proc-list
Kill -l

Purpose: Send the signal for 'signal_number' to processes whose PIDs or jobIDs are specified in 'proc-list'; jobIDs must start with %. The command kill -l returns a list of all signals and their names (on some systems, numbers are not displayed)

Commonly used signal_numbers:

1	Hangup
2	Interrupt (<Ctrl-C>)
3	Quit (<Ctrl-\>)
9	Sure kill
15	Software signal (default signal number)

The 'hangup' signal is generated when you log out, the 'interrupt' signal is generated when you press <Ctrl-C>, and the 'quit' signal is generated when you press <Ctrl-\>. The kill command sends signal number 15 to the process whose PID is specified as an argument. The default action for this signal is termination of the process that receives it. This signal can be intercepted and ignored by a process, as can most of the other signals. In order to terminate a process that ignores signal 15 or other signals, signal number 9, known as **sure kill**, has to be sent to it. The kill command terminates all the processes whose PIDs are given in the 'PID-list', provided that these processes belong to the user who is using kill. The following session presents some instances of how the kill command can be used. But don't kill the shell process (PID 13495 in the following session) because it will log you out.

```
$ ps
PID      TTY     TIME    CMD
13495    pts/0   0:03    -ksh
13583    pts/0   9:11    find / -inum 23456 -print
13586    pts/0   5:03    find / -name foo -print
13587    pts/0   23:11   find / -name foobar -print
20577    pts/0   31:07   a.out
20581    pts/0   12:53   sort bigfile > bigfile.sorted
$ kill 13583
[1] + Killed      find / -inum 23456 -print &
$ kill -2 13587
```

```
[3] + Killed find / -name foobar -print &
$ kill -9 20577
[4] - Killed a.out &
$
```

In the first case, signal number 15 is sent to a process with PID 13583. In the second case, signal number 2 (`<Ctrl-C>`) is sent to a process with PID 13587. In both cases, if the specified signal numbers are not intercepted, the processes are terminated. In the third case, the a.out process ignores signal numbers 2 (`<Ctrl-C>`) and 15 (software signal), and therefore cannot be terminated unless signal number 9 (sure kill) is sent to it. The `kill` command can be used to terminate a number of processes with one command line. For example, the command `kill -9 13586 20581` terminates processes with PIDs 13586 and 20581. Process ID 0 can be used to refer to all the processes created during the current login. Thus, the `kill -9 0` command terminates all processes resulting from the current login.

The `kill` command also works with job numbers. Hence, the following command can be used to terminate a process with job number 1. Multiple processes can be terminated by specifying their job numbers in the command line. For example, `kill -9 %1 %3` can be used to terminate processes with job numbers 1 and 3.

```
$ kill -9 %1
[1] +    Killed find / -name foo -print > foo.paths &
$
```

When you log out, all the processes running in your session get a hangup signal (signal number 1) and are terminated per the default action. If you want processes to continue to run even after you have logged out, you need to execute them so that they ignore the hangup signal when they receive it. You can use the UNIX command nohup to accomplish this task. The following is a brief description of the syntax for this command.

SYNTAX

nohup command [args]

Purpose: Run 'command' and ignore the hangup signal

You need to use the nohup command for processes that take a long time to finish, such as a program sorting a large file containing hundreds of thousands of customer records. Obviously, you would run this type of program in the background so that it runs at a lower priority. The following is a simple illustration of the use of the nohup command. Here, the `find` command runs in the background and is not terminated when you log out or send it signal number 1 (hangup) via the `kill` command. If output of the command is not redirected, it is appended to the nohup.out file by default.

```
$ nohup find / -name foo -print 1> foo.paths 2> /dev/null &
[1] 15928
$
```

You can run multiple commands with nohup if they are separated by semicolons. In the following session, GenData generates some data and puts it in a file called employees, and the sort command sorts the file and stores the sorted version in the employees.sorted file.

```
$ nohup GenData > employees ; sort employees > employees.sorted &
[2] 15931
$
```

In the following In-Chapter Exercises, you will use the kill command to practice abnormal termination of processes, and the nohup and ps -a commands to appreciate how you can run processes that do not terminate when you log out.

IN-CHAPTER EXERCISES

13.7 Give a command for terminating processes with PID 10974 and jobID 3.

13.8 Run the first of the nohup commands presented, use ps to verify that the command is executing, log out, log in again, and use the ps -a command to determine whether the find command is running.

13.7 Process Hierarchy in UNIX

When you turn on your UNIX system, the kernel–after doing some checks and other household tasks–creates the first process from scratch. This process, which has no parent, is called the **init process** and is the granddaddy of all the processes that are created, so long as the system is up and running. The init process has a PID of 1 and runs with superuser privileges. (The **swapper process** has the PID 0.) The executable binary for the process is in the file /etc/init. This process, after doing several setups, as given in the /etc/rc file, reads the /etc/ttys file to determine which I/O (terminal) lines are to be active. For each active line, init starts a getty process from /etc/getty file. The **getty process**, also running in superuser mode, sets terminal attributes, such as baud rate, as specified in the file /etc/termcap. It then displays the login: prompt, inviting you to log on to the terminal.

At the login: prompt, when you type your login name and press <Return>, the getty process forks a child. The child execs to become a login process with your login name as its parameter. The **login process** prompts you for your password and checks the validity of your login name and password. If it finds both to be correct, the login process execs to become your login shell. If the login process does not find your login name in the /etc/passwd file or finds that the password that you entered does not match the one in the /etc/passwd file, it displays an error message and terminates. Control goes back to the getty process, which redisplays the login: prompt. Once in your login shell, you can do your work and terminate the shell by pressing <Ctrl-D>. When you do so, the shell process terminates and control goes back to the getty process, which displays the login: prompt, and life goes on.

Figure 13.6 shows schematically the process hierarchy of a UNIX system. This process diagram shows a system with one user running two processes, sort and find, with the Bourne shell as the user's login shell.

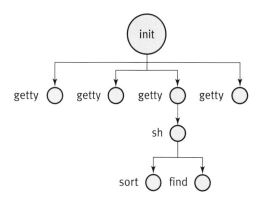

Figure 13.6 UNIX process hierarchy

Thus, when you log on to a UNIX system, the system creates the first process for you, called your login shell. In Chapters 2 and 7, we explained how you determine the type of your login shell (Bourne, C, Korn, etc.). The login shell interprets/executes your commands by creating processes for all the commands that you execute (*see* Section 13.3 for details of command execution).

Two UNIX processes exist throughout the lifetime of a system: the swapper and init processes. The getty process, which monitors a terminal line, lives for as long as the terminal is attached to the system. Your login shell process lives for as long as you are logged on. All other processes are usually short-lived and stay for as long as a command or utility executes.

You can use the `ptree` command to display the process tree of the currently running processes on the system in a graphical form, showing the parent-child relationship. You can print process trees for a process or for a user. In the following session, we use the `ptree –a davis` command to show the process hierarchy for the user davis. The output shows that the granddaddy of all of the processes run by davis is, as expected, the 'init' process. The output further shows that davis is using the system through a telnet session and is currently using the Bourne shell, which is running under Bash. Without the –a option, the line for the 'init' process, the parent of process 360 (i.e., the inetd daemon) is not displayed.

```
$ ptree -a davis
   1 /etc/init -
      360 /usr/sbin/inetd -s
         2288 in.telnetd
            2290 -bash
               2344 sh
                  2356 ptree -a davis
$
```

▬ Summary ▬▬▬▬▬▬▬▬▬▬▬▬▬▬▬▬▬▬▬▬▬▬▬▬▬▬▬▬▬

A process is a program in execution. Being a time-sharing system, UNIX allows execution of multiple processes simultaneously. On a computer system with one CPU, processes are executed concurrently by scheduling the CPU time and giving it to each process for a short time called a quantum. Each process is assigned a priority by the UNIX system, and when the CPU is available, it is given to the process with the highest priority.

The shell executes commands by creating child processes by using the fork and exec system calls. When a process uses the fork system call, the UNIX kernel creates an exact main memory image of the process. An internal command is executed by the shell itself. An external binary command is executed by the child shell overwriting itself by the code of the command via an exec call. For an external command comprising a shell script, the child shell executes the commands in the script file one by one.

Every UNIX process has several attributes, including process ID (PID), process ID of the parent (PPID), process name, process state (running, suspended, swapped, zombie, etc.), the terminal the process was executed on, the length of time the process has run, and process priority. The ps command can be used to display these attributes.

UNIX processes can be run in the background or the foreground. A foreground process controls the terminal until it finishes, so the shell cannot be used for anything else while a foreground process runs. When a process runs in the background, it returns the shell prompt so that the user can do other work as the process executes. Because a background process runs at a lower priority, a command that takes a long time is a good candidate for background execution. The background system processes that provide various services are called daemons. A set of commands can be run in a group as separate processes or as one process. Multiple commands can be run from one command line as separate processes by using a semicolon (;) as the command separator; enclosed in parentheses, these commands can be executed as one process. Commands can be executed concurrently by using ampersand (&) as the command separator.

Suspending processes, moving them from the foreground to the background and vice versa, having the ability to display their status, interrupting them via signals, and terminating them are all known as job control, and UNIX has a set of commands that allow these actions. Foreground processes can be moved to the background by suspending them by pressing <Ctrl-Z>, followed by executing the bg command. Background processes can be moved to the foreground by using the fg command. Commands that are suspended or run in the background are also known as jobs. The jobs command can be used to view the status of all your jobs. A foreground process can be terminated by pressing <Ctrl-C>.

The kill command can terminate a process with its PID or job ID. The command can be used to send various types of signals, or software interrupts, to processes. Upon receipt of any signal except one, a process can take the default (kernel-defined) action, take a user-defined action, or ignore it. No process can ignore the sure kill, which was put in place by the UNIX designers to make sure that every process running on a system could be terminated. Commands executed with the nohup command keep running even after a user logs out.

You can use the `ptree` command under a Bourne shell to display tree structures for your or some other user's processes. With the –a option, the output displayed contains a line for the granddaddy 'init' process.

Problems

1. What is a process? How is it known inside the UNIX system?

2. What is CPU scheduling? How does a time-sharing system run multiple processes on a computer system with a single CPU? Be brief but precise.

3. Name three famous CPU scheduling algorithms. Which are parts of the UNIX scheduling algorithm?

4. What are the main states that a process can be in? What does each state indicate about the status of the process?

5. What is the difference between built-in (internal) and external shell commands? How does a UNIX shell execute built-in and external commands? Explain your answer with an example.

6. Name three process attributes.

7. What is the purpose of the `nice` command in UNIX?

8. What are foreground and background processes in UNIX? How do you run shell commands as foreground and background processes? Give an example for each.

9. In UNIX jargon, what is a daemon? Give examples of five daemons.

10. What are signals in UNIX? Give three examples of signals. What are the possible actions that a process can take upon receiving a signal? Write commands for sending these signals to a process with PID 10289.

11. Give the command that displays the status of all running processes on your system.

12. Give the command that returns the total number of processes running on your system.

13. Compute the priority number of a UNIX process with a recent CPU usage of 31, a threshold priority of 60, and a nice value of 20. Show your work.

14. Give the sequence of steps (with commands) for terminating a background process.

15. Create a zombie process on your UNIX system. Use the `ps` command to show the process and its state.

16. Give two commands to run the `date` command after 10 sec. Make use of the `sleep` command; read the manual page for this command to find out how to use it.

17. Run a command that would remind you to leave for lunch after one hour by displaying the message "Time for Lunch!"

18. Give a command line for running the `find` and `sort` commands in parallel.

19. Give an example of a UNIX process that does not terminate with <Ctrl-C>.

20. Run the following commands on one command line so that they do not terminate when you log out. What command line did you use?

    ```
    find / -inum 23476 -print > all.links.hard 2> /dev/null

    find / -name foo -print > foo.paths 2> /dev/null
    ```

21. Run the following sequence of commands under your shell. What are the outputs of the three pwd commands? Why are the outputs of the last two pwd commands different?

    ```
    $ pwd
    $ sh
    $ cd /usr
    $ pwd
    ...
    $ <Ctrl-D>
    $ pwd
    ...
    $
    ```

22. Run the top command on your system. What are the priority and nice values of the highest priority process? Run commands to have top display information about top-10 processes and refresh its output every seven seconds. What commands did you use?

23. As you monitor the top session, display processes for the user john. What command did you use? Show your work.

24. Use the ptree command to display the tree structure for the processes running in your current session. What command did you use? Which process is the grandparent of all your processes and what is its process ID? What command will you use to display the tree hierarchy for the processes that the user kent has run on your system?

25. What are the names of processes with process IDs 0, 1, 2, and 3 on your UNIX system? How did you get the answer to the question? Show your work.

26. Suppose you are running various programs in a session—pine, vi, etc.—and the terminal locks up or the remote login program crashes, causing you to be disconnected from the host. Or, perhaps your keyboard or mouse suddenly stops working. Explain how you could log in from another terminal and use a sequence of UNIX commands to recover. Give the sequence of UNIX commands you would use to recover from the situation.

Networking and Internetworking

Objectives

- To describe networks and internetworks and explain why they are used

- To discuss briefly the TCP/IP protocol suite, IP addresses, protocol ports, and Internet services and applications

- To explain what the client-server software model is and how it works

- To discuss various network software tools for electronic communication, remote login, file transfer, remote command execution, and status reporting

- To describe briefly the secure shell

- To cover the commands and primitives `dig, finger, ftp, ifconfig, host, netstat, nslookup, ping, rcp, rlogin, rsh, ruptime, rwho, scp, sftp, slogin, ssh, talk, telnet, traceroute`

14.1   Introduction

The history of computer networking and the Internet goes back to the late 1960s when the Advanced Research Projects Agency (ARPA) started funding networking research. This research resulted in a wide area network, called ARPANET, by the late 1970s, with five nodes–UCLA, Stanford, UC Santa Barbara, University of Utah, and BBN. In 1982, a prototype Internet that used Transmission Control Protocol/Internet Protocol (TCP/IP) became operational and was utilized by a few academic institutions, industrial research organizations, and the U.S. military. By early 1983, all U.S. military sites connected to ARPANET were on the Internet, and computers on the Internet numbered 562. By 1986, this number had more than quadrupled to 2,308. From then on, the size of the Internet doubled every year for the next 10 years, until it served about 9.5 million computers by 1996. The first Web browser, called Mosaic, was developed at the National Center for Supercomputer Applications (NCSA) and launched in 1991. As a result, World Wide Web (shortened to the www, or just the Web) browsing surpassed File Transfer Protocol (FTP) as the major use of the Internet by 1995. Today, the Internet serves over 200 million hosts, over 900 million users, over 35 million domain names, over 46 million Web sites, and over 225 of 246 countries in the world. It is projected that by 2010, over 75% of the planet will be connected by the Internet. UNIX has a special place in the world of networking in general and internetworking in particular because most of the networking protocols were initially implemented on UNIX platforms. Also, most of the Internet services are provided by server processes running on UNIX-based computers.

14.2   Computer Networks and Internetworks

When two or more computer hardware resources (computers, printers, scanners, plotters, etc.) are connected, they form a computer network. A hardware resource on a network or an internetwork is usually referred to as a host. Figure 14.1(a) shows a schematic diagram of a network with six hosts, H1 through H6.

Computer networks are categorized as local area networks (LANs), metropolitan area networks (MANs), and wide area networks (WANs), based on the maximum distance between two hosts on the network. Networks that connect hosts in a room, building, or buildings of a campus are called LANs. The distance between hosts on a LAN can be anywhere from a few meters to about one kilometer. Networks that are used to connect hosts within a city, or between small cities, are known as MANs. The distance between hosts on a MAN is about one to 20 kilometers. Networks that are used to connect hosts within a state or country are known as WANs. WANs are also known as long-haul networks. The distance between the hosts on a WAN is in the range of tens of kilometers to a few thousand kilometers.

An internetwork is a network of networks. Internetworks can be used to connect networks within a campus or networks that are thousands of kilometers apart. The networks in an internetwork are connected to each other via specialized computers called routers or gateways. The Internet is the ubiquitous internetwork of tens of thousands of networks throughout the world. Figure 14.1(b) shows an internetwork of four networks. The four networks, Net1 through Net4, are connected via five routers, R1 through R5. Not all the networks are directly connected, and two networks can be connected to each other via multiple routers. In Figure 14.1(b), for example, Net2 and Net4 are not directly connected and Net3 and Net4 are

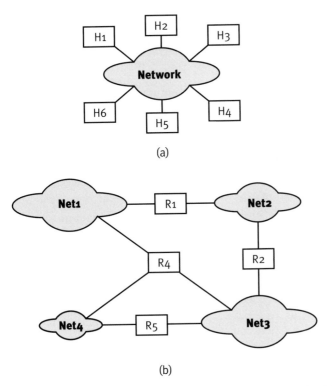

Figure 14.1 (a) A network of six hosts; (b) An internetwork of four networks

connected to each other directly via two routers, R4 and R5. Note that the router R4 also connects directly Net3 and Net1. Routers such as R4 that can connect more than two networks are known as multi-port routers.

14.3   The Reasons for Computer Networks and Internetworks

There are numerous reasons for using networks of computers as opposed to stand-alone, powerful minicomputers, mainframe computers, or supercomputers. The main reasons include the following.

- ❖ Sharing of computing resources: Users of a computer network can share computers, printers, plotters, scanners, files, and application software.
- ❖ Network as a communication medium: A network is an inexpensive, fast, and reliable communication medium between people who live far from each other.
- ❖ Cost efficiency: For the same price, you get more computing power with a network of workstations than with a minicomputer or mainframe computer.
- ❖ Less performance degradation: With a single powerful minicomputer, mainframe computer, or supercomputer, the work comes to a screeching halt if anything goes wrong with the computer, such as a bit in the main memory going bad. With a network of computers, if one computer crashes, the remaining computers on the network are still up and running, allowing continuation of work.

14.4   Network Models

Various questions arose in the design and implementation of networks. These questions dictated the design of the two best-known network models.

1. The type of physical communication medium, or communication channel, used to connect hardware resources. It can be a simple RS-232 cable, telephone line, coaxial cable, glass fiber, microwave link, or satellite link.

2. The topology of the network, that is, the physical arrangement of hosts on a network. Some commonly used topologies are bus, ring, mesh, and general graph.

3. The set of rules, called protocols, used to allow a host on a network to access the physical medium before initiating data transmission.

4. The protocols used for routing application data (e.g., a Web page) from one host to another in a LAN or from a host in one network to a host in another network in an internetwork.

5. The protocols used for transportation of data from a process on a host to a process on another host in a LAN or from a process on a host in one network to a process on a host in another network in an internetwork.

6. The protocols used by network-based software to provide specific applications such as telnet.

The two best-known network models are the International Standards Organization's Open System Interconnect Reference Model (commonly known as ISO's OSI 7-Layer Reference Model) and the TCP/IP 5-Layer Model. The OSI model was proposed in 1981 and the TCP/IP model in the late 1970s. By 1982, the TCP/IP model was being used by the U.S. military. The TCP/IP model, which has its roots in the Department of Defense Advanced Research Projects Agency (ARPA), is the basis of the Internet and is, therefore, also known as the Internet Protocol Model. This model consists of five layers, each having a specific purpose and a set of protocols associated with it. The diagram in Figure 14.2 shows the two models, along with an approximate mapping between the two.

ISO		Issue		TCP/IP	Task Handled
7	Application				
6	Presentation	6	5	Application	User process: Application details
5	Session				
4	Transport	5	4	Transport	
3	Network	4	3	Network	Kernel and Hardware: Communications details
2	Data Link	3	2	Link	
1	Physical	1 and 2	1	Device/Physical	
	ISO			TCP/IP	

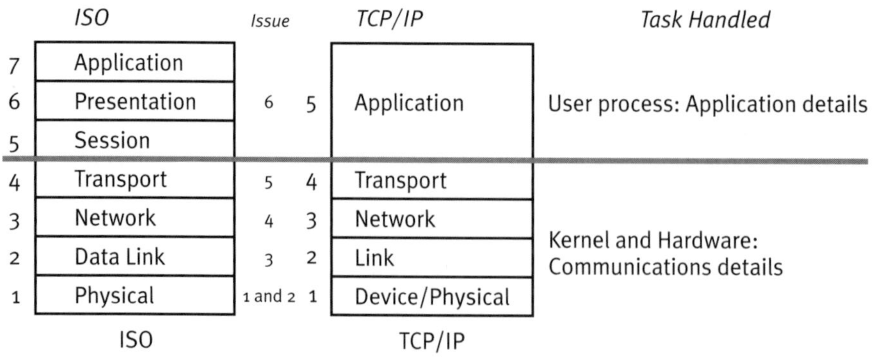

Figure 14.2 ISO and TCP/IP layered models, mapping between the two, and the general purpose of a group of layers

Because the TCP/IP model is used in the Internet, this will be our focus. In terms of the six issues previously listed, the first layer in the TCP/IP model deals with the first two issues, the second layer deals with the third issue, the third layer deals with the fourth issue, the fourth layer deals with the fifth issue, and the fifth layer deals with the sixth issue. In terms of their implementation, the first four layers deal with the details of communication between hosts, and the fifth layer deals with the details of the Internet services provided by various applications. Most of the first layer is handled by hardware (type of communication medium used, attachments of hosts to the medium, etc.). The rest of the first layer and all of the second layer are handled by the network interface card (NIC) in a host. Layers 3 and 4 are fully implemented in the operating system kernel on most existing systems. The first two layers are network hardware specific, whereas the remaining layers work independently of the physical network. On newer systems, the network layer is implemented in hardware.

IN-CHAPTER EXERCISES

14.1 Ask your system administrator: How many hosts are connected on your LAN? What type of computers are they (PCs or workstations)?

14.2 What is the physical medium for your network (coaxial cable, twisted pair, or glass fiber)? Ask your instructor or system administrator about the topology of your network (bus, ring, etc.).

14.3 The **Ethernet** is the most commonly used link-level protocol for LANs. Does your LAN use Ethernet? If not, what does it use?

14.5 The TCP/IP Protocol Suite

Several protocols are associated with various layers in the TCP/IP model. These protocols result in what is commonly known as the TCP/IP suite, which is illustrated in Figure 14.3.

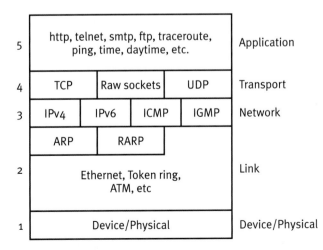

Figure 14.3 The TCP/IP

The description of most of the protocols in the suite is beyond the scope of this textbook, but we briefly describe the purpose of those that are most relevant to our discussion. As a user, you see the application layer in the form of applications and utilities that can be executed to invoke various Internet services. Some of the commonly used applications are for electronic mail, Web browsing, file transfer, and remote login. We discuss some of the most useful applications in Section 14.8.

14.5.1 The TCP and UDP

The purpose of the transport layer is to transport application data from your machine to a remote machine and vice versa. This delivery service can be a simple, best effort service that does not guarantee reliable delivery of the application data or one that guarantees reliable and in-sequence delivery of the application data. The best effort delivery service is offered by the User Datagram Protocol (UDP), and the completely reliable, in-sequence delivery is offered by the Transmission Control Protocol (TCP). The UDP is a connectionless protocol; that is, it simply sends the application data to the destination without establishing a virtual connection with the destination before transmitting the data. Hence, the UDP software on the sender host does not "talk" to the UPD software on the receiver host before sending data. The TCP is a connection-oriented protocol that establishes a virtual connection between the sender and receiver hosts before transmitting application data, leading to reliable, error-free, and in-sequence delivery of data. Of course, the overhead for establishing the connection makes TCP more costly than UDP. Thus, the UDP is like the U.S. Postal Service handling of first-class mail and the TCP is like the UPS (or FedEx) package delivery service. Most Internet applications such as telnet use TCP. In the Internet jargon, a data packet transported by TCP is called a segment and a data packet transported by UDP is called a datagram.

Because multiple client and server processes might be using the TCP and/or UDP at any one time, these protocols identify every process running on a host by 16-bit positive integers from 0 though 65,535, called port numbers. Port numbers from 0 through 1023 are called well-known ports and are controlled by the Internet Assigned Numbers Authority (IANA). Well-known services such as ftp are assigned ports that fall in the well-known range (excluding 0). Some of these services allow the use of either TCP or UDP, and IANA tries to assign the same port number to a given service for both TCP and UDP. For example, the ftp service is assigned port number 21, and the http (Web) server is assigned port number 80 for both the TCP and UDP. Most clients can run on any port and are assigned a port by the operating system at the time the client process starts execution. Some clients such as rlogin and rsh require the use of a reserved port as part of the client-server authentication protocol. These clients are assigned ports in the range 513 through 1023.

14.5.2 Routing of Application Data–The Internet Protocol (IP)

As we mentioned before, the network layer is responsible for routing application data to the destination host. The protocol responsible for this is the Internet Protocol (IP), which transports TCP segments or UDP datagrams containing application data in its own packets called IP datagrams. The routing algorithm is connectionless, which means that IP routing is best effort routing and it does not guarantee delivery of TCP packets (segments) or UDP packets (datagrams). Applications that need guaranteed delivery use TCP as their transport level protocol or have it built into the application itself. The current version of IP is IPv4, and the new version (not available in most operating systems yet) is IPv6 (commonly known as IPng: Internet Protocol–the Next Generation). In this textbook, we primarily discuss IPv4. The discussion on the actual routing algorithms used by IP is beyond our scope here. However, we describe a key component of routing on the Internet–the IP addressing (naming) scheme to identify uniquely a host on the Internet.

The key to routing is the IP assignment of a unique identification to every host on the Internet. IP does so by uniquely identifying the network it is on and then uniquely identifying the host on that network. The ID, a 32-bit positive integer in IPv4 and a 128-bit positive integer in IPv6, is known as the host's IP address. Every IP datagram has a sender's and a receiver's IP address in it. The sender's IP address allows the receiver host to identify and respond to the sender. Hosts and routers perform routing by examining the destination IP address on an IP datagram.

In IPv4, the IP address is divided into three fields: address class, network ID, and host ID. The address class field identifies the class of the address and dictates the number of bits used in the network ID and host ID fields. This scheme results in five address classes: A, B, C, D, and E, with classes A, B, and C being the most common. Figure 14.4 shows the structures of the five address types. The IP addresses belonging to classes D and E have special use, and their discussion is beyond the scope of this textbook. All IP addresses are assigned by a central authority, the Network Information Center (NIC–www.internic.net).

The maximum number of class A, B, and C networks that can be connected to the Internet is given by the expression: 2^{71} 2^{14} 2^{112}. Here, 7, 14, and 21 are the number of bits used to specify network IDs in class A, B, and C addresses, respectively. Thus, there are 2^7 class A networks, 214 class B networks, and 2^{21} class C networks. The sum of these numbers gives a total of 2,113,664 networks. Similarly, the number of bits used to identify host IDs in the three classes of addresses can be used to get the maximum number of hosts that can be connected to the Internet. Thus, there are roughly 2^{24} hosts per class A network, 2^{16} hosts per

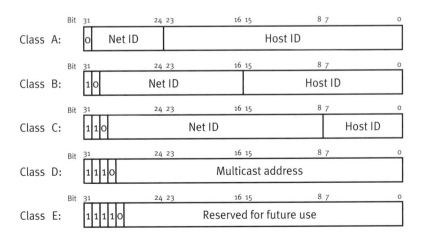

Figure 14.4 IPv4 address classes

class B network, and 2^8 hosts per class C network. The sum of all the hosts on the three types of networks is a total of 3,758,096,400 hosts. The actual numbers of class A, B, and C networks and hosts are somewhat smaller than the numbers shown, due to some special addresses (e.g., broadcast and localhost addresses). The broadcast addresses are used to address all hosts on a network. The localhost address is used by a host to send a datagram to itself. Hence, an IP datagram with localhost as its destination address is never put on the network.

The number of class A addresses is very small, so these addresses are assigned only to very large commercial organizations, educational institutions, and government agencies, such as U.S. national laboratories, Massachussetts Institute of Technology (MIT), University of California at Berkeley, Bell Labs, and NASA. The number of class B addresses is relatively large, and these addresses are assigned to large commercial organizations and educational institutions. Hence, corporations such as IBM and Oracle and institutions such as the Oregon Graduate Institute (OGI) and numerous other national and international universities have been assigned class B addresses. The total number of class C addresses is quite large, so these addresses are assigned to individuals and small- to medium-sized organizations, such as local Internet service providers, small consulting and software companies, community colleges, and universities.

Although the IPv4 addressing scheme can be used to identify a large number of networks and hosts, it will not be able to cope with the rapid growth of the Internet. Among the many advantages of IPv6 is that an extremely large number of hosts can be connected. With the 128-bit address, the maximum number of hosts on the Internet will increase to roughly 2^{128}, which is greater than 3.4×10^{38}. This number is roughly 6×2^{28} times the present world population. One disadvantage of IPing is that, as the address size is very large, remembering IPv6 addresses becomes very difficult. However, because most users prefer to use symbolic names, remembering IPv6 addresses should not present a problem. Also, some compact notations, such as the **colon hexadecimal notation**, similar to DDN have been proposed for IPv6 addresses as well. Some of the newer commands, such as dig (*see* Section 14.5.5), allow the use of this notation for IPv6 addresses and DDN for IPv4 addresses.

14.5.3 IPv4 Addresses in Dotted Decimal Notation

Although hosts and routers process IPv4 addresses as 32-bit binary numbers, they are difficult for people to remember. For this reason, the IPv4 addresses are given in **dotted decimal notation (DDN)**. In this notation, all four bytes of an IPv4 address are written in their decimal equivalents and are separated by dots. Thus, the 32-bit IP address,

```
11000000  01100110  00001010  00010101
```

is written as,

```
192.102.10.21
```

in dotted decimal notation. The ranges of valid IP addresses belonging to the five address classes in dotted decimal notation are shown in Table 14.1. Some of the addresses given in the table are special addresses.

TABLE 14.1 IPv4 Address Classes and Valid IP Addresses

Address Class	Range of Valid IP Addresses	
	Lowest	Highest
A	0.0.0.0	127.255.255.255
B	128.0.0.0	191.255.255.255
C	192.0.0.0	223.255.255.255
D	224.0.0.0	239.255.255.255
E	240.0.0.0	247.255.255.255

The internetwork shown in Figure 14.5 connects four networks via four routers, R1 through R4. Net1 is a class A network, Net3 is a class B network, and Net2 and Net4 are class C networks. The way to identify the class of a network is to look at the left-most decimal number in the IP address of a host on the network, in this case, the IP addresses of the routers. Note that the routers are assigned as many IP addresses as the number of networks they connect. Here, for example, router R1, which connects Net1 and Net2, has IP addresses 121.1.1.1 and 192.102.10.1. Similarly, R4 is assigned three IP addresses, as it interconnects three networks Net1, Net2, and Net3.

Of the special addresses, 127.0.0.0 (or 127.x.x.x, where x can be any number between 0 and 255), also known as localhost, is used by a host to send a data packet to itself. It also is commonly used for testing new applications before they are used on the Internet. Another special address, in which the host ID field is all 1s, is the directed broadcast address. This address is used to send a data packet to all hosts on a network, that is, for broadcasting on a local network whose host is using the address as a destination address.

14.5.4 Symbolic Names

People prefer to use symbolic names rather than numeric addresses because names are easier to remember, especially with the transition to the 128-bit long numeric addresses in IPv6. Also, symbolic names can remain the same even if numeric addresses change. Like its IP address,

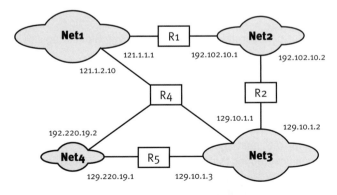

Figure 14.5 An internetwork of four networks with one class A, one class B, and two class C networks

the symbolic name of a host on the Internet must be unique. The Internet allows the use of symbolic names by using a hierarchical naming scheme. The symbolic names have the format

```
hostname.domain_name
```

where domain_name is the symbolic name referring to the site and is assigned by various registrars whose list is maintained by Internet's Network Information Center. The hostname is assigned and controlled by the site that is allocated the domain_name. The domain_name consists of two (or more) strings separated by a period (.). The right-most string in a domain name is called the top-level domain. The string to the left of the right-most period identifies an organization and can be chosen by the organization and assigned to it by the Network Information Center. If the string has already been assigned to another organization under the same top-level domain, another string is assigned in order to keep the domain names unique. There are three types of top-level domains: special, generic, and country codes. Details of these domains are given in Table 14.2.

■ TABLE 14.2 Top-Level Internet Domains

Domain Type	Top-Level Domain	Assigned to/for	Administered/ Sponsored/Operated by
Special	ARPA	Used exclusively for Internet-infrastructure purposes; currently includes the following second-level domains: e164.arpa, in-addr.arpa, ip6.arpa, uri.arpa, urn.arpa	IANA under the guidance of IAB www.iana.org
Generic	AERO	Reserved for members of air-transport industry	Société Internationale de Télécommunications Aéronautiques (SITA) www.nic.aero
	BIZ	Reserved for business	NeuLevel, Inc. www.neulevel.biz www.nic.biz
	COM	Reserved for commercial organizations	VeriSign Global Registry Services www.verisign.com
	COOP	Reserved for cooperative associations	Dot Cooperation LLC www.cooperative.org
	EDU	Reserved for U.S. post-secondary educational institutions that are accredited by an agency on the U.S. Department of Education's list of Nationally Recognized Accrediting Agencies	Educause www.educause.edu

(continued)

TABLE 14.2 *(continued)*

	GOV	Reserved for the U.S. government	U.S. General Services Administration `www.nic.gov`
	INFO	First unrestricted top-level domain since .com, so it can be used by anyone—businesses, marketers, etc.	Afilias Limited `www.afilias.info`
	INT	Reserved for organizations established by treaties between governments	IANA .int Domain Registry `www.iana.org`
	MIL	Reserved for the U.S. military	U.S. DoD Network Information Center `www.nic.mil`
	MUSEUM	Reserved for museums	Museum Domain Management Association (MuseDoma) `musedoma.museum`
	NAME	Reserved for individuals	Global Name Registry `www.gnr.name`
	NET	Intended for Internet Service Providers (ISPs) and telephone service providers	VeriSign Global Registry Services `www.verisign.com`
	ORG	Intended for noncommercial community but all are eligible to register	Public Interest Registry `www.pir.org`
	PRO	Restricted to credentialed professionals (this domain is being established)	RegistryPro `www.nic.pro`
Country Code	AU DE FI JP PK ... UK US	Australia Germany (Deutschland) Finland Japan Pakistan United Kingdom United States of America	Administration of these domains is the prerogative of individual countries

For the domain names that consist of more than two strings, the remaining strings are assigned by the organization that owns the domain. Some example domain names are: up.edu, intel.com, whitehouse.gov, uu.net, omsi.org, egr.up.edu, amazon.com.jp, ptv.com.pk, www.beavton.k12.or.us, www.lumensoft.biz, www.abc.tv, www.nato.int, www.darpa.mil, example.info, and bbc.co.uk. The strings to the left of a country domain are assigned by authorities in that country. Figure 14.6 illustrates the domain name hierarchy.

Attaching the name of a host to a domain name with a period between them yields the **fully qualified domain name (FQDN)** for the host—for example, egr.up.edu, where egr is the name of a host in the School of Engineering at the University of Portland. However, fully qualified domain names for the hosts on the Internet do not always have three parts. Most organizations allow various groups within the organization to choose the primary names for the hosts that they control and are responsible for. For example, the School of Engineering at the University of Portland, which uses the primary name egr.up.edu, uses www.egr.up.edu as the FQDN for its http server. The School of Business Administration, which uses the primary name bus.up.edu, can use the host name www.bus.up.edu for its Web server.

14.5.5 Translating Names to IP Addresses—The Domain Name System

Because Internet software deals with IP addresses and people prefer to use symbolic names, application software translates symbolic names to equivalent IP addresses. This translation involves use of a service provided by the Internet known as the **Domain Name System (DNS)**. The DNS implements a distributed database of name-to-address mappings. A set of dedicated hosts run server processes called **name servers** that take requests from application software (also called the client software; *see* Section 14.7) and work together to map domain names to the corresponding IP addresses. Every organization runs at least one name server, usually the Berkeley Internet Name Domain (BIND) program. The applications use resolver functions such as `gethostbyname` to invoke the DNS service. The `gethostbyname` resolver function maps a hostname (simple or fully qualified) to its IP address, and `gethostbyaddr` maps an IP address to its hostname.

An alternative, and old, scheme for using the DNS service is to use a static hosts file, usually /etc/hosts. This file contains the domain names and their IP addresses, one per line. The following command displays a sample /etc/hosts file.

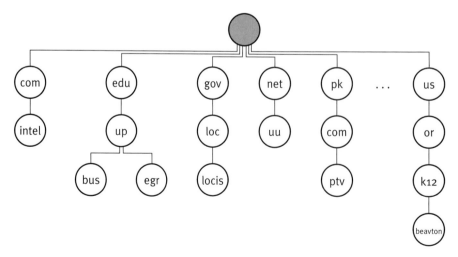

Figure 14.6 A portion of the Internet domain name hierarchy

```
$ cat /etc/hosts
#
# Internet host table
#
127.0.0.1               localhost
203.128.0.6             yamsrv1.ece.gatech.edu   loghost
203.128.0.1             shahalami
192.168.1.1             suraj-ge0
$
```

There are two problems with this scheme. First, its implementation depends on how the system administrator configures the system. Second, owing to the sheer size of the Internet and its current rate of growth, the static file can be extremely large.

You can use the ifconfig command to view the IP address and other information about your host's interface to the network. The following is an example run of the command. The command output shows that the host that you are logged on to has two IP addresses: 127.0.0.1 and 192.102.10.89. The address 127.0.0.1 is the destination address for itself (the localhost), whereas 192.102.10.89 is your host's actual IP address, by which it is known to the outside world.

```
$ ifconfig -a
lo0: flags=849<UP,LOOPBACK,RUNNING,MULTICAST> mtu 8232
            inet 127.0.0.1 netmask ff000000
le0: flags=863<UP,BROADCAST,NOTRAILERS,RUNNING,MULTICAST> mtu 1500
            inet 192.102.10.89 netmask ffffff00 broadcast 192.102.10.255
$
```

The ifconfig command is normally located in the /sbin directory. If you get an error message such as ifconfig: Command not found, include the /sbin directory in your search path (*see* Chapters 4 and 7) and reexecute the command. You can run the cat /etc/hosts command to display the domain names and IP addresses of the hosts on your network.

You can use the nslookup, host, or dig command to do the DNS lookup for a host whose domain name is passed as a command line argument to it. However, because the nslookup command might not be available in newer versions of operating systems, we do not discuss it here.

The host command allows you to display IP address(es) for a domain name or vice versa. In the following session, we use the host ibm.com command to display the IP addresses of the hosts that handle the domain name ibm.com. The output of the command shows that the ibm.com domain is handled by four hosts with IP addresses 129.42.16.99, 129.42.17.99, 129.42.18.99, and 129.42.19.99. The output of the second command shows that the domain name for the host with IP address 192.102.10.10 is guardian.egr.up.edu. The output of the third command shows that the host with IP address 216.109.118.69 runs the Yahoo Web server. The output of the fourth command shows that the IP address 73.10.40.1 has not been assigned to any domain (i.e., it is a nonexistent domain). Finally, the output of the last command shows that the name server failed to map the IP address 198.175.96.33 to any domain name, which does not mean that the domain does not exist.

```
$ host ibm.com
ibm.com has address 129.42.19.99
ibm.com has address 129.42.16.99
ibm.com has address 129.42.17.99
ibm.com has address 129.42.18.99
$ host 192.102.10.10
10.10.102.192.in-addr.arpa domain name pointer guardian.egr.up.edu.
$ host 216.109.118.69
69.118.109.216.in-addr.arpa domain name pointer p6.www.dcn.yahoo.com.
$ host 73.10.40.1
Host 1.40.10.73.in-addr.arpa not found: 3(NXDOMAIN)
$ host 198.175.96.33
Host 33.96.175.198.in-addr.arpa not found: 2(SERVFAIL)
$
```

The dig (domain information groper) command is a more flexible tool that allows you to interact with DNS servers and display their responses to queries. It is often used by system administrators to troubleshoot DNS problems. Unless it is told to contact a particular name server, dig queries each name server specified in the /etc/resolv.conf file to perform a DNS search. Here is a brief description of the command.

dig [options]	
Purpose:	Interact with name servers specified in /etc/resolv.conf and display their responses
Output:	Responses of name servers for queries sent to them
Commonly used options/features:	
-f file	For batch operation, take domain names (or IP addresses) from 'file'
-p port	Interact with a name server at 'port' instead of the default port 53

The dig command can be used in interactive or batch mode. In order to invoke the batch mode, you use the -f option and specify command arguments (e.g., domain names or IP addresses), the one per line. In the interactive mode, it takes arguments at the command line. Without an argument, dig interacts with the root server, as shown below. Note that 13 servers are used as the root of the DNS service: A.ROOT-SERVERS.NET through M.ROOT-SERVERS.NET.

```
$ dig
; <<>> DiG 9.2.1 <<>>
;; global options:  printcmd
;; Got answer:
;; ->>HEADER<<- opcode: QUERY, status: NOERROR, id: 37373
;; flags: qr rd ra; QUERY: 1, ANSWER: 13, AUTHORITY: 0, ADDITIONAL: 1
;; QUESTION SECTION:
;.                                  IN      NS

;; ANSWER SECTION:
.                       514045      IN      NS      B.ROOT-SERVERS.NET.
.                       514045      IN      NS      C.ROOT-SERVERS.NET.
.                       514045      IN      NS      D.ROOT-SERVERS.NET.
.                       514045      IN      NS      E.ROOT-SERVERS.NET.
.                       514045      IN      NS      F.ROOT-SERVERS.NET.
.                       514045      IN      NS      G.ROOT-SERVERS.NET.
.                       514045      IN      NS      H.ROOT-SERVERS.NET.
.                       514045      IN      NS      I.ROOT-SERVERS.NET.
.                       514045      IN      NS      J.ROOT-SERVERS.NET.
.                       514045      IN      NS      K.ROOT-SERVERS.NET.
.                       514045      IN      NS      L.ROOT-SERVERS.NET.
.                       514045      IN      NS      M.ROOT-SERVERS.NET.
.                       514045      IN      NS      A.ROOT-SERVERS.NET.

;; ADDITIONAL SECTION:
J.ROOT-SERVERS.NET.     600445      IN      A       192.58.128.30

;; Query time: 4 msec
;; SERVER: 203.128.0.2#53(203.128.0.2)
;; WHEN: Sat Dec 27 16:35:35 2003
;; MSG SIZE  rcvd: 244

$
```

The output of the following command shows that mit.edu is handled by three class A machines (18.7.21.70, 18.7.22.69, and 18.7.21.69). It further shows that the MIT site runs three name servers, BITSY.mit.edu, W20NS.mit.edu, and STRAWB.mit.edu, and that the IP addresses of BITSY.mit.edu and W20NS.mit.edu are 18.72.0.3 and 18.70.0.160, respectively.

```
$ dig mit.edu

; <<>> DiG 9.2.1 <<>> mit.edu
;; global options:  printcmd
;; Got answer:
;; ->>HEADER<<- opcode: QUERY, status: NOERROR, id: 31576
;; flags: qr rd ra; QUERY: 1, ANSWER: 3, AUTHORITY: 3, ADDITIONAL: 2

;; QUESTION SECTION:
;mit.edu.                       IN     A

;; ANSWER SECTION:
mit.edu.              60        IN     A      18.7.21.70
mit.edu.              60        IN     A      18.7.22.69
mit.edu.              60        IN     A      18.7.21.69

;; AUTHORITY SECTION:
mit.edu.              21600     N      NS     BITSY.mit.edu.
mit.edu.              21600     IN     NS     W20NS.mit.edu.
mit.edu.              21600     IN     NS     STRAWB.mit.edu.

;; ADDITIONAL SECTION:
BITSY.mit.edu.        21466     IN     A      18.72.0.3
W20NS.mit.edu.        21494     IN     A      18.70.0.160

;; Query time: 266 msec
;; SERVER: 203.128.0.2#53(203.128.0.2)
;; WHEN: Thu Dec 25 18:36:01 2003
;; MSG SIZE  rcvd: 166

$
```

14.5.6 Request For Comments (RFCs)

The TCP/IP standards are described in a series of documents, known as **Request for Comments (RFCs)**. RFCs are first published as **Internet Drafts** and are made available to all Internet users for review and feedback by placing them in known RFC repositories. After the review process is complete, a draft can become a standard. But not all RFCs are Internet Standards documents; some are for information only and others are experimental.

An RFC citation has the following format:

```
####     Title. Authors (up to three). Issue date. (Format: TXT=size-in-bytes,
         PS=size-in-bytes, PDF=size-in-bytes) (Obsoletes xxx) (Obsoleted by
         RFC####) (Updates RFC####) (Updated by RFC####) (Also FYI ####)
         (Status: sssss)
```

where, #### is a 4-digit decimal number; Format can be TXT (ASCII), PS (PostScript), and PDF (Portable Document Format); and Status can be UNKNOWN, PROPOSED STANDARD, DRAFT STANDARD, STANDARD, INFORMATIONAL, EXPERIMENTAL, or HISTORIC. Here is an example citation:

```
1180     TCP/IP tutorial. T.J. Socolofsky, C.J. Kale. Jan-01-1991.
         (Format: TXT=65494 bytes) (Status: INFORMATIONAL)
```

You can view and download an RFC by accessing any of the repositories maintained on FTP or Web sites. The most common method of accessing an RFC is to browse the Web page at http://www.ietf.org/rfc.html. As of the writing of this chapter, there are 3,765 RFCs available in the RFC index maintained on this Web page. If you want to be notified of the announcement of a new RFC, you can subscribe to the following distribution list:

http://mailman.rfc-editor.org/mailman/listinfo/rfc-dist

The following In-Chapter Exercises are designed to enhance your depth of understanding of your own network environment by way of learning the domain names and IP addresses of hosts on your network. You will also use the host and dig commands to translate domain names to IP addresses, and vice versa.

IN-CHAPTER EXERCISES ━━━━━━━━━━━━━━━

14.4   Give the domain names of some hosts on your LAN. Ask your instructor for help if you need any.

14.5   List the IP addresses of the hosts identified in Exercise 14.4 in dotted decimal notation. What is the class of your network (A, B, or C)? How did you find out?

14.6   Run the host and dig utilities to confirm the IP addresses of the hosts identified in Exercise 14.4.

14.7   Repeat the shell sessions given in this section on host and dig commands on your system. Do you get the same results? If not, how do outputs of your commands differ from those shown in this section?

14.8   Browse the Web page at http://www.ietf.org/rfc.html, find the citation for RFC1118, and write it down.

14.6 Internet Services and Protocols

Most users do not understand the intricacies of the Internet protocols and its architecture—nor do they need to. They access the Internet by using programs that implement the application-level protocols for various Internet services. Some of the most commonly used services and the corresponding protocols are listed in Table 14.3. The services are listed in alphabetic order and not according to their frequency of use. You can see the /etc/services file on your host to view the Internet services and their well-known port numbers.

■ **TABLE 14.3** Popular Internet Services and Corresponding Protocols

Service	Protocol
Electronic mail	SMTP (Simple Mail Transfer Protocol)
File transfer	FTP (File Transfer Protocol)
Remote login	Telnet
Time	Time
Web browsing	HTTP (Hyper Text Transfer Protocol)

The UNIX operating system has some network-related services that are not necessarily available in other operating systems. They include services for displaying all the users logged on to the hosts in a LAN, remote execution of a command, real-time chat in a network, and remote copy. We discuss utilities for most of these services in Section 14.8.

14.7 The Client-Server Software Model

Internet services are implemented by using a paradigm in which the software for a service is partitioned into two parts. The part that runs on the host on which the user running the application is logged on to is called the client software. The part that usually starts running when a host boots is called the server software. On the one hand, the server runs forever, waiting for a client request to come. Upon receipt of a request, it services the client request and waits for another request. On the other hand, a client starts running only when a user runs the program for a service that the client offers. It usually prompts the user for input (command and/ or data), transfers the user input to the server, receives the server's response, and forwards the response to the user. Most clients terminate with some sort of 'quit' or 'exit' command.

Most of the applications are connection-oriented client-server models, in which the client sends a connection request to the server and the server either accepts or rejects the request. If the server accepts the request, client and server are said to be connected through a **virtual connection**. From this point on, the client sends user commands to the server as requests. The server process serves client requests and sends responses to the client, which sends them to the user in a particular format. Communication between client and a server– and the client's interaction with the user–are dictated by the protocol for the service offered by an application. Figure 14.7 shows an overview of the client-server software model.

Thus, when you run a program that allows you to surf the Web, such as Netscape Navigator, an http client process starts running on your host. By default, most clients display the **home page** of the organization that owns the host on which the client runs, although it can be set to any page. When you want to view the Web page of a site, you give the site's **Universal Resource Locator (URL)** to the client process. For displaying a home page, the URL has the format,

```
http://host/page
```

where 'host' can be the fully qualified domain name or IP address (in dotted decimal notation) of the computer that has the home page you want to display, 'page' is the pathname for the file containing the page to be displayed—for example, http://cnn.com, http://192.201.18.91, http://lhotse.up.edu/~koretsky/index.html, and http://www.egr.up.edu/index.html. The client tries to establish a connection with the http server process on the site corresponding to the URL. If the site has the http server running and no security protections such as a password are in place, a connection is established between client and server. The server then sends the Web page to the client, which displays it on the screen, with any audio or video components sent to appropriate devices. Note that 'http' can be replaced with 'ftp' if you want to access an ftp site through your browser, or with 'telnet' if you want to remote log on via the telnet protocol.

You can invoke the client programs for most Internet services by specifying a domain name or IP address, as well as the particular port number, of the host on which a server runs. A client software that has such flexibility built in is known as a **fully parameterized client**. Such clients are important in terms of the flexibility they offer. They also allow testing of updated server software because server software can be run on a port that is not well-known and contacted by the client. A telnet client, discussed in Section 14.8, is a good example of a fully parameterized client.

14.8   Application Software

Numerous programs that implement the application-level protocols just discussed are available on networks of UNIX hosts and the Internet. Of the most commonly used applications described here, some are available on UNIX-based systems only, whereas others are available to all the hosts on the Internet.

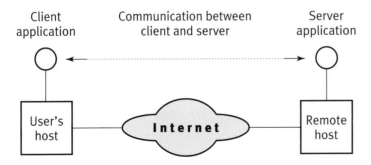

Figure 14.7 Depiction of the client-server software model

14.8.1 Displaying the Host Name

Network-based applications use the user@host address format to identify a user on a network on the Internet. You can use the hostname and uname commands (*see* Chapter 3) to display the name of the host you are logged on to. On some systems, the host name is shown in the short, simple name format, and on others it is displayed in the long, fully qualified domain name format. If you have to identify the host on the network that you are logged on to, you can use the hostname -s command to display the short format, which is simply the name of the host (the left-most string in the FQDN format). Some systems do not allow you to use the -s option unless you are the superuser. You can use the uname -n command to display the host name of the computer that you are logged on to in the FQDN format. The uname -a command displays complete information about a host, including the operating system it is running and the name of the CPU. The following are some examples of the hostname and uname commands.

```
$ hostname
yamsrv1.ece.gatech.edu
$ uname -n
yamsrv1.ece.gatech.edu
$ uname -a
SunOS yamsrv1.ece.gatech.edu 5.8 Generic_108528-22 sun4u sparc SUNW,Ultra-250
$
```

14.8.2 Displaying List of Users Using Hosts on a Network

You can use the rwho (remote who) command to display information about the users currently using machines on your network. The output of this command is like that of the who command. An output line contains the login name of a user, the computer and terminal the user is logged on to, and the date and time of login. The last field is blank if the user is currently typing at the terminal; otherwise, it shows the number of hours and minutes since the user last typed on the keyboard. You can use the rwho command with the -a option to include the users who are currently idle. The following session shows how the command is used, without and with the -a option.

```
$ rwho | more
bobk        upibm7:ttyC4      Jul 26 12:03
dfrakes     upibm47:ttyp2     Jul 26 11:49
lulay       upsun17:pts/0     Jul 26 10:17
oster       upsun17:pts/2     Jul 26 12:28
sarwar      upibm7:ttyp2      Jul 26 11:15
$ rwho -a | more
bobk        upibm7:ttyC4      Jul 26 12:03
```

```
dfrakes      upibm47:ttyp2      Jul 26 11:49
kent         upibm48:ttyp0      Jul 26 03:41 8:49
kittyt       upibm9:ttyp0       Jul 26 07:36 1:28
kuhn         upsun29:console     Jul 16 13:11 99:59
lulay        upsun17:pts/0       Jul 26 10:17
oster        upsun17:pts/2       Jul 26 12:28
pioster      upsun20:pts/0       Jul 26 09:53 2:41
sarwar       upibm7:ttyp2       Jul 26 11:15
sarwar       upsun29:pts/0       Jul 26 11:24 1:00
$
```

You can use the `rusers` (remote users) command to display the names of the users logged on to the machines on your local network. The login names of the users currently using a machine are displayed in one line per machine format. The following is a brief description of the command.

---

rusers [options] [host_list]

Purpose: Display the login names of the users logged on to all the machines on your local network

Output: Information about the users logged on to the hosts on your local network in one line per machine format

Commonly used options/features:

    -a   Display a host name even if no user is using it

    -l   Display the user information in a long format similar to that displayed by the `who` command

---

The `rusers` command broadcasts a query to all the hosts on the network, asking them to reply with user information. It collects all the replies and displays the information in the order received. The following is a simple run of the command. Note that host names are displayed in a 16-character field, which is why the edu part of the names is not completely displayed. As shown in the output of the command, the user kent is logged in twice on the upibm8.egr.up.edu host, sarwar is logged on to upsun29.egr.up.edu, and users kittyt and deborahs are logged on to upibm6.egr.up.edu, with kittyt logged on twice.

```
$ rusers | more
upibm48.egr.up.e kent kent
upsun29.egr.up.e sarwar
upibm6.egr.up.ed kittyt kittyt deborahs
$
```

You can display the names of the users logged on to a particular host by specifying the host as an argument to the rusers command. The following command displays the login names of the users logged on to the upibm7 host.

```
$ rusers upibm7
upibm7.egr.up.edu upppp44 upppp upppp26 kathek khnguyen upppp14 lesliesarwar sarwar
$
```

As shown in the following session, you can use the rusers command with the -a option to display host names even if no user is logged on to them. Doing so allows you to find out the names of all the hosts on your network.

```
$ rusers -a | more
upsun12.egr.up.e
...
upsun27.egr.up.e
upibm48.egr.up.e kent kent
upsun29.egr.up.e sarwar
upsqnt.egr.up.ed
...
upibm3.egr.up.ed
upibm6.egr.up.ed kittyt kittyt deborahs
$
```

14.8.3 Displaying the Status of Hosts on a Network

You can use the ruptime (remote uptime) command to display the status of all the computers connected to your LAN. Each line of the output has the following format: computer (host) name, system status (up/down), the amount of time the computer has been up (or down; the number before the 1 sign indicates the number of days), the number of users logged on to each host, and the load factor for each host. The following is a brief description of the command.

ruptime [options]	
Purpose:	Show status of machines on the local area network
Output:	Status of machines, including machine name, up/down status, time a machine has been up (or down) for—called machine uptime, and the number of users logged on the machine
Commonly used options/features:	
-1	Display output after sorting it with load average
-t	Display output after sorting it by machine uptime
-u	Display output after sorting it by the number of users

The following sessions demonstrate use of the `ruptime` command without and with the -u option.

```
$ ruptime | more
upibm0       up      1+09:16,      0 users,     load 0.00, 0.00, 0.00
...
upsun29      up      69+23:51,     2 user,      load 1.48, 1.35, 1.32
$ ruptime    -u | more -u
upibm7       up      1+09:25,     10 users,     load 0.00, 0.00, 0.00
upibm47      up      12+01:01,     4 users,     load 0.10, 0.04, 0.04
upsun17      up      8:25,         2 users,     load 0.00, 0.00, 0.03
upsun29      up      69+23:57,     1 user,      load 1.30, 1.31, 1.31
...
$
```

Note that upsun29 has been up for almost 70 days.

In the following In-Chapter Exercises, you will use the `ruptime`, `rwho`, and `rusers` commands to appreciate their syntax and output. You will also get a feel for what the Internet is primarily used for.

IN-CHAPTER EXERCISES ━━━━━━━━━━━━━━━━━━━━━━━━━━━━━

14.9   Use the `ruptime` command on your system to find out how many hosts are connected to your LAN.

14.10 Use the `rwho` and `rusers` commands to display information about the users who are currently logged on to the hosts on your network.

14.11 Ask your friends and fellow students about the two network services they use most often. Which services are they? Which is more popular of the two? How many people did you ask?

14.8.4 Testing a Network Connection

You can test the status of a network or a particular host on it by using the `ping` command. If the `ping` command does not work on your system, use the `whereis ping` command to find its location, update your search path, and try the command again. It is normally in the /usr/sbin directory. The following is a brief description of the command.

SYNTAX

ping [options] hostname

Purpose: Send an IP datagram to 'hostname' to test whether it is on the network (or Internet); if the host is alive, it simply echoes the received datagram

Output: Message(s) indicating whether the machine is alive

Commonly used options/features:

-c count Send and receive 'count' packets

-f Send 100 packets per second or as many as can be handled by the network; only the superuser can use this option

-s packetsize Send 'packetsize' packets; the default is 56 bytes (plus an 8-byte header)

The following session illustrates the use of the ping command with and without options. The output of the command is different for some systems, with the command displaying the echoed messages until you press <^c>. We used the -c option in the following session to send and receive three messages. The -c and -s options are used in the last command to send and receive three messages 2,040 bytes in size (plus an 8-byte ICMP header).

```
$ ping cse.ogi.edu
cse.ogi.edu is alive
$ ping -c 3 cse.ogi.edu
PING cse.ogi.edu: (129.95.20.2): 56 data bytes
64 bytes from 129.95.20.2: icmp_seq=0 ttl=245 time=13 ms
64 bytes from 129.95.20.2: icmp_seq=1 ttl=245 time=12 ms
64 bytes from 129.95.20.2: icmp_seq=2 ttl=245 time=15 ms
—cse.ogi.edu PING Statistics—
4 packets transmitted, 4 packets received, 0% packet loss
round-trip min/avg/max 5 12/13/15 ms
$ ping -c 3 -s 2040 cse.ogi.edu
PING cse.ogi.edu: (129.95.20.2): 2040 data bytes
2048 bytes from 129.95.20.2: icmp_seq=0 ttl=245 time=55 ms
2048 bytes from 129.95.20.2: icmp_seq=1 ttl=245 time=56 ms
2048 bytes from 129.95.20.2: icmp_seq=2 ttl=245 time=58 ms
—cse.ogi.edu PING Statistics—
3 packets transmitted, 3 packets received, 0% packet loss
round-trip min/avg/max 5 55/56/58 ms
$
```

You can use the IP address of a host in place of its hostname. For example, you can use ping 129.95.20.2 instead of ping cse.ogi.edu.

14.8.5 Displaying Information About Users

You can use the `finger` command to display information about users on a local or remote host. The information displayed is extracted from a user's ~/.plan and ~/.project files. The following is a brief description of the command.

---

finger [options] [user_list]

Purpose: Display information about the users in 'user_list'; without a 'user_list', the command displays a short status report about all the users currently logged on to the specified hosts

Output: User information extracted from the ~/.project and ~/.plan files

Commonly used options/features:

 −m   Match 'user_list' to login names only

 −s   Display output in a short format

The following session shows the simplest use of the command in which information about a single user, Birch Tree, on the host is displayed.

```
$ finger Birch
Login name: btree              In real life: Birch Tree
Directory: /users/faculty/tree    Shell: /bin/ksh
On since Dec 29 05:55:32 on pts/0 from upibm7.egr.up.edu
No unread mail
Project: Hacking UNIX for its sake ...
Plan: To turn from a Windows lizard to a UNIX wizard ...
$
```

You can use the `finger` command with the `-s` option to display the command's output in a short format and the `-m` option to match 'user-list' to login names only. The finger −m Tree command displays the same information as the `finger Birch` command if the login name of the user is tree (uppercase and lowercase letters are considered the same by networking commands). However, as the login name of the user is btree and the login name birch does not exist in the system, the `finger` command displays the message informing you accordingly. The following sessions show the use of these options.

```
$ finger -s Birch
Login          Name          TTY          Idle    When
birch          Birch Tree    pts/0                Fri 16:16
$ finger -m Birch
Login name:    Birch         In real life: ???
$
```

You can use the `finger` command to display information about a user on a host on the Internet, provided that the host offers the finger service and has the finger server (finger daemon: fingerd) running. Remote finger is disabled on many systems. The following command can be used to display information about a user christopher at the mit.edu domain (site).

```
$ finger christopher@mit.edu
[mit.edu]
Student data loaded as of Jan 11, Staff data loaded as of Jan 11.
Notify Personnel or use WebSIS as appropriate to change your information.
Our on-line help system describes
     How to change data, how the directory works, where to get more info.
     For a listing of help topics, enter finger help@mit.edu. Try finger
     help_about@mit.edu to read about how the directory works.
     Directory bluepages may be found at http://mit.edu/communications/bp.
There was 1 match to your request.
name: Christopher, Jason W
          email:  jasc@MIT.EDU
          phone:  (617) 123-4567
        address:  Simmons Hall # 779
     department:  Electrical Eng & Computer Sci
         school:  School Of Engineering
           year:  3
          alias:  J-christopher
$
```

The format of the output is generally the same, but it can vary from one site to another. Try the command for some name at mit.edu to see differences in output.

When run without any argument, the `finger` command returns the status of all the users who are currently logged on to your machine. The amount of information displayed varies somewhat, depending on the UNIX system that your host runs. However, every system displays at least the following information. With *@hostname as its argument, the command displays the status of all the users who are currently logged on to 'hostname'. Some sites put restrictions on use of the wild card *. For example, the sites mit.edu and osu.edu require the use of at least two characters in all queries. The following sessions display the status of all the users on the host that you are logged on to and on a remote host, iastate.edu, that allows use of the wild card *. Note that without an argument, `finger` assumes that input is an empty line.

```
$ finger
[upibm7.egr.up.edu]
Login          Name            TTY      Idle      Login Time
kathek         Kathe Koretsky  C4       59        Jul 30 13:55
oster          Peter Osterberg C3       29        Jul 30 16:12
```

```
sarwar          Mansoor Sarwar     p0        25          Jul 30 15:21
upppp           PPP kent           C6        11:02       Jul 30 05:40
upppp44         PPP sarwar         C2        1:22        Jul 30 15:21
$ finger *@iastate.edu
[iastate.edu]
Iowa State University site-wide finger server.
Use `finger "/h"@iastate.edu` for help information.
Net-Id:         Real Name:         Office:
- - - - - - - - - - - - - - - - - - - - - - - - - - - - - - -
diano           Dian Octaviani     221 Sheldon Ave #7      451-0983
jerry           *unknown*          nowhere                 00000000
rbcarter        **you-know-me**    **Apt num 3 Czech Republ (515)292-5979
snave           ***Snav3***        428 Stonehaven          #21
$
```

If a host does not run the finger server, the `finger` command displays the 'Connection refused' message for you, as in,

```
$ finger sarwar@egr.up.edu
[egr.up.edu] connect: Connection refused
$
```

If DNS cannot find a mapping for a domain name, the `finger` command returns an appropriate error message, as in,

```
$ finger jadavis@iastate.com
unknown host: iastate.com
$
```

When this happens, you can run the `host` command to find the IP address for the destination host and re-run the `finger` command by using the IP address instead of the domain name. If the host runs the finger server and has the user that you are looking for, the `finger` command display displays the relevant output, as shown below. Because the DNS table has been updated with the new mapping, the `finger williams@iastate.edu` command would also work.

```
$ host iastate.edu
iastate.edu has address 129.186.1.99
$ finger jadavis@129.186.1.99
[129.186.1.99]
Iowa State University site-wide finger server.
Use `finger "/h"@iastate.edu` for help information.
ISU Net-Id:        jadavis        Real name: Jeremy A Davis
```

```
Address:            219 N East St

Office Phone:       134-2664        Home Phone:

Net-Id              TTY             Login at   Idle Machine From host

User not logged in.
$
```

In the following In-Chapter Exercises, you will use the ping and finger commands to understand their syntax and various characteristics.

IN-CHAPTER EXERCISES

14.12 Run the ping command to determine whether a remote host that you know about is up.

14.13 Give the command for displaying information about yourself on your UNIX host.

14.14 Give the command for displaying information about a user on your host, with John as his first or last name.

14.15 Give a command for displaying information about all the users who are currently logged on to the site cmu.edu.

14.8.6 Remote Login

Most UNIX systems support two commands that allow you to log on to a remote host. One is based on the Internet service for remote login, telnet, and the other is a BSD command (supported by most UNIX systems) known as rlogin. We discuss both commands, but start with the more generic telnet command.

TELNET

The telnet protocol is designed to allow you to connect to a remote computer over a network. This protocol allows you to log on not only to UNIX-based computer systems but also to any computer system that supports the telnet protocol and has a telnet server process running on it. For example, you can connect a UNIX-based computer system such as a Sun workstation to a Windows-based PC. Although you usually need to have a valid account on the remote system, some remote machines allow you to log on without having an account. After the connection has been established, your host or terminal (or display window in a GUI environment) acts as a terminal connected to the remote host. From this point on, every keystroke on your terminal is sent to the remote host. As we mentioned before, telnet is implemented as client-server software. In other words, the host to which you want to connect must have a telnet server process running on a well-known port designated for it, and your command execution starts a telnet client process on your host. The well-known port for the telnet server is port number 23. Because the telnet protocol is based on TCP, the telnet client and server processes establish a virtual connection before prompting you for input. Multiple telnet client processes running on the same host or different hosts can communicate with the same telnet server process, that is, multiple users can use a remote host via telnet.

The UNIX command for starting a telnet client process is telnet. The following is a brief description of the command.

---

telnet [options] [host [port]]

Purpose: To connect to a remote system 'host' via a network; the 'host' can be specified by its name or IP address in dotted decimal notation

Commonly used options/features:

　-a　　　Attempt automatic login

　-l　　　Specify a user for login

The telnet client operates in two modes: input mode and command mode. When executed without an argument, the client enters the command mode and displays the 'telnet>' prompt. When run with a host argument, the client displays the 'login:' prompt to take your login name and password. Once a connection has been established between your client and the server, you interact directly with the telnet client. After establishing a connection with the server, the client enters the input mode. In this mode, the client takes character-at-a-time or line-at-a-time input mode, depending on what the server on the remote host supports; the default mode is character-at-a-time. All input mode data, except ^], known as the telnet escape character, are commands for the remote operating system, transferred to it via the telnet server process. The telnet escape character puts telnet in the command mode. Once it is in the command mode, you can use the ? or help command to display a brief summary of the telnet commands. Table 14.4 shows some useful telnet commands and their purpose.

■■ **TABLE 14.4** Commonly Used telnet Commands

Command	Meaning
? or help	Display a list of telnet commands and their purpose
close or quit	Close the telnet connection
mode	Try to enter line or character mode
open host	Make a telnet connection to 'host'
z	Suspend the telnet session and return to the local host; resume the telnet session with the fg command

The most common use of the telnet command is without an option. The following session shows the use of telnet to log on to another host, upsun29, on your network. As shown, after the connection with upsun29 has been established, you are prompted for login name and password (shown as a sequence of * characters). You must have a valid user account on upsun29 to be able to use it via telnet.

```
$ telnet upsun29
```

```
Trying 192.102.10.89...

Connected to upsun29.egr.up.edu.

Escape character is '^]'.

UNIX(r) System V Release 4.0 (upsun29.egr.up.edu)

login: sarwar

Password: **********

Last login: Sat Dec 27 05:05:37 from up

You have mail.

DISPLAY = (')

TERM = (vt100)

$
```

The following session shows how you can use the `telnet` command for logging on to a host on a remote site (network). Note that you have to use the FQDN of the host to which you want to telnet. The IP address of the host is 191.220.19.2, so you can execute the `tel-net 191.220.19.2` command to achieve the same result. The session also shows that you can put telnet into the command mode by pressing ^] and run various `telnet` commands before quitting. Some commands, such as `status`, return you to the input mode after completing their task. In the following session, we show that you can use the `z` command to suspend the telnet client and transfer control to the shell on the local host. The `ps` command shows the status of processes on the local machine. The `fg` command reverts to the telnet client. The ^] command puts telnet into the command mode, and the `quit` command terminates the telnet session.

```
$ telnet pccaix.sycrci.pcc.edu

Trying 192.220.19.2...

Connected to pccaix.sycrci.pcc.edu.

Escape character is '^]'.

telnet (pccaix)

AIX Version 4

(C) Copyrights by IBM and by others 1982, 1996.

login: msarwar

msarwar's Password:

Last login: Mon Jul 28 16:57:29 PDT 2003 on /dev/pts/1 from
192.220.11.131

[YOU HAVE NEW MAIL]

$

...

^]

telnet> z
```

```
Suspended
$ ps
        PID     TTY     STAT    TIME    COMMAND
        837     p0      S       0:00    -ksh
        920     p1      S       0:00    telnet upsun29
        1027    p2      T       0:00    telnet pccaix.sycrci.pcc.edu
        1028    p2      R       0:00    ps
$ fg
telnet pccaix.sycrci.pcc.edu
^]
telnet> quit
$
```

The following session shows use of the –a option to connect automatically to the Library of Congress Information System (LOCIS) at the locis.loc.gov site. Once connected to the LOCIS, you log in as 'guest' and browse through various resources available on the system.

```
$ telnet -a locis.loc.gov
Trying 140.147.254.3...
Connected to locis.loc.gov.
Escape character is '^]'.
L O C I S:  LIBRARY OF CONGRESS INFORMATION SYSTEM


To make a choice: type a number, then press ENTER


        1   Copyright Information      - files available and up-to-date
        2   Braille and Audio          - files frozen mid-August 1999
        3   Federal Legislation        - files frozen December 1998
        *   *   *   *   *   *   *   *   *   *   *   *   *   *   *
The LC Catalog Files are available at:
                                http://lcweb.loc.gov/catalog/
        *   *   *   *   *   *   *   *   *   *   *   *   *   *
        8   Searching Hours and Basic Search Commands
        9   Library of Congress General Information
       10   Library of Congress Fast Facts
       12   Comments and Logoff
            Choice:

...

^]
```

```
telnet> quit
$
```

As shown in the following session, you can use the `telnet` command to connect to a telnet server that is not running on a well-known port. In this case, the server is running on port number 5000. But be sure not to register for anything.

```
$ telnet chess.net 5000
Trying 216.22.45.192...
Connected to chess.net.
Escape character is '^]'.
Welcome to . . .
                                       /\
           /\_/\_/\                    \/
          (<> <>(<>)   /\ /\ /\   <>*<>*<>
          /<>\___\<>/  \/ \/ \/       /\
          /<*>/    (<>) (*) <> (*) (^) \/ (^)    (^><^><^)    (^><^><^)
          /<*>/       \/  | \/<>\/ | \*/^__^\*/  /<>/  \(<>) /<>/  \(<>)
         (<*>(             <<><><><>> <<>(__      <<>(___  \/ <<>(___  \/
         (<*>(             \*(<>)*/  /<><><>\    \__<*>\    \__<*>\
          \<*>\      /\   /*/<>\*\  \<><><>/        )<>)        )<>)
          \<*>\___(<>) <<>(   )<>> <<>(       /\   /<>/   /\   /<>/
          \<>/***/<>\ |<>|   |<>| |<>(__/^\ (<>)_)<>/   (<>)_)<>/      __
         (<>_<>(<>) (<>)   (<>) (_<>__<>) \_<>_/    \_<>_/      (<>)
          \/ \/ \/    \/     \/     \/ \/     \/        \/          \/


                       _/\_          /\
                      (<><>)        (<>)
                     / \<>/ \      /**/ (^><^><^) (^><^><^><^)
                     /<*>/\(*)\   /<>/  /*/ \(<>)       /**/
                     /(*)/  \(*)> /<>/  /*(      \/      /<>/
                     /(*)/   \(*)/<>/  ><><><>        /<>/
                     /(*)/    \ /<>/  /*(  /\        /<>/
                    / \/       \/\/  /<>\_(<>)      /<>/
                    (<>)       (<>) (_<>_<>_/      (<>)
                     \/         \/    \/ \/         \/
```

Login Screen By Aussie and Isis.
Welcome to Chess.net! Come in and join the fun!
At the login prompt, please enter your handle. If you do not yet have an

account please type 'guest' and speak to an administrator(*) about
\   registering.

You can do this by typing '/register'. Thank you, and we hope you enjoy your
stay.

login: **guest**

You are "guest609". You may use this name to play unrated games.

After logging in, do '/help register' for more info on how to register.

Press return to enter chess.net as "guest609":

^]

telnet> **quit**

$

You can run the `telnet` command with a well-known port number as an optional parameter to invoke various Internet services such as smtp. In the following session, the `telnet`
command invokes the daytime service at cs.berkeley.edu. The daytime service is offered at the
well-known port 13. Execution of the command causes the daytime server at cs.berkeley.edu
to send the current time (including day and date) to your client and close the connection.
Your client displays the time and returns to the shell process.

$ **telnet cs.berkeley.edu 13**

Trying 169.229.60.163...

Connected to cs.berkeley.edu.

Escape character is '^]'.

Sat Dec 27 04:06:38 2003

Connection closed by foreign host.

$

In Section 14.8.5, we used the `finger` command without an argument to display information about the users currently logged on to a computer. When run without a command
line argument, `finger` assumes an empty line to be its input (hitting <Enter> makes it
assume that). The `finger` command does not respond with some output automatically;
instead, it waits for your input before sending its response. We can connect to a finger server
with the `telnet` command, too. When we do so, the finger server waits for our input (i.e.,
as a user name whose information we would like displayed on the screen). In the following
session, we use the `telnet` command to connect with the finger server at iastate.edu and display information about the user Triska.

$ **telnet iastate.edu 79**

Trying 129.186.1.99...

Connected to iastate.edu.

Escape character is '^]'.

Triska

```
Iowa State University site-wide finger server.
Use `finger "/h"@iastate.edu` for help information.


  Net-Id:      Real Name:            Office:
  ------       ---------             -------
  triska       James C Triska        EE CPE  (515)294-4676
Connection closed by foreign host.
$
```

If there are multiple users on a site with the name that you enter, information about all of them is displayed. For example, in the following session, information is displayed about all those users at mit.edu who have Michael as part of their names.

```
$ telnet mit.edu 79
Trying 18.7.22.69...
Connected to mit.edu.
Escape character is '^]'.
Michael
Student data loaded as of Jan 8, Staff data loaded as of Jan 8.
Notify Personnel or use WebSIS as appropriate to change your information.
Our on-line help system describes
  How to change data, how the directory works, where to get more info.
  For a listing of help topics, enter finger help@mit.edu. Try finger
  help_about@mit.edu to read about how the directory works.
  Directory bluepages may be found at http://mit.edu/communications/bp.
There were 5 matches to your request.
Complete information will be shown only when one individual matches
your query. Resubmit your query with more information.
For example, use both firstname and lastname or use the alias field.
             name:   Michael, David
            title:   MIT Affiliate
            alias:   D-michael
             name:   Michael, Holly A
       department:   Civil And Environmental Eng
             year:   G
            alias:   H-michael
             name:   Michael, Lance F
       department:   Lincoln Lab
            title:   Staff
```

```
         alias:   L-michael
          name:   Michael, Philip C
     department:   Plasma Science and Fusion Center
          title:   Research Scientist, Experimental
          alias:   P-michael
          name:   Michael, Steven
     department:   Lincoln Lab
          title:   Staff
          alias:   S-michael
Connection closed by foreign host.
$
```

The `rlogin` Command

The `rlogin` command allows you to log on to a host on your local network. All the hidden files that are executed for a regular login are also executed for remote login. After logging on, therefore, you are put in your home directory and your login shell is executed. As we mentioned before, the `rlogin` command was originally designed for BSD UNIX, but it works on all the systems that have BSD support built into them (e.g., AIX, which is based on System V). The following is a brief description of the `rlogin` command.

---

rlogin [options] host

Purpose: To connect to a remote UNIX 'host' via a network; the 'host' can be specified by its name or IP address in the dotted decimal notation

Commonly used options/features:

  `-ec`   Set the escape character to 'c' (the default is ~)

  `-l user`   Use 'user' as the login name on the remote host

S Y N T A X

You can use the `rlogin` command to log on to a UNIX host on your network, provided you have a valid login name and password on the remote host. The following session shows how you can use the command to connect to a UNIX host upsun29 on your network. Note that, unlike the setup on our system, the `rlogin` command might not prompt you for a login name and password if they are the same on the local and remote hosts. Because the `rlogin` command can be used with an IP address in place of the hostname, the `rlogin 192.102.10.29` command accomplishes the same task. After using the remote system, you can use the `logout` command to log out from the remote system and return to the local system. In the following session, we also show that you can use the `hostname` and `whoami` commands to confirm that you are logged in as the same user (sarwar) and that the machine you log on to is upsun29.

```
$ rlogin upsun29
Password:
```

"This system is for the use of authorized users only. Individuals using this computer system without authority or in the excess of their author- ity are subject to having all their activities on this system monitored and recorded by system personnel. In the course of monitoring individuals improperly using this system or in the course of system maintenance, the activities of authorized users may also be monitored. Anyone using this system expressly consents to such monitoring and is advised that if such monitoring reveals possible evidence of illegal activity or violation of University regulations, system personnel may provide the evidence of such monitoring to University authorities and/or law enforcement officials."

NOTICE:

1.) This machine is rebooted at 4:15 AM daily.

2.) Please keep accounts below 100 MB. (du)

3.) All files not accessed during the last 360 days will be removed.

4.) Please help out and keep your email inbox empty. Move files to other folders. This will also make pine run faster for you!

5.) Limit TOTAL modem connect times to ONE hour from the hours of 5:pm to midnight.

```
You have mail.
DISPLAY = (')
TERM = (vt100)
$ hostname
upsun29.egr.up.edu
$ whoami
sarwar
$ logout
Terminal session terminated by sarwar
rlogin: connection closed.
$ hostname
upsun25.egr.up.edu
$
```

You can use the -l option to log on remotely with a login name different from the one you used to log on to the local host. You can use the following command to log on to the remote host upsun with the user name perform. (Note that upsun is on the same local area network as your host.) The rlogin command prompts you for your password, and you must have the password for the user perform for a successful login. If you do not have the right password, rlogin lets you try other login names (or the same login name) a few times.

```
$ rlogin upsun -l perform
Password:
Last login: Mon Dec 18 12:08:12 from upsun21.up.edu
SunOS Release 4.1.3 (UPSUN_SERVER) #5: Mon Nov 14 17:31:44 PST 1994
DISPLAY 5 (upx46:0.0)
TERM 5 (vt100)
$ whoami
perform
$ hostname
upsun.egr.up.edu
$
```

The following session shows remote login to a UNIX host that is not on your local network. Here, cs00.syi.pcc.edu is the FQDN of a host on the Internet, and the user is msarwar. Of course, you must enter the valid password for msarwar to be able to log in. You could have used the `rlogin -l msarwar@cs00.syi.pcc.edu` command to establish this session.

```
$ rlogin cs00.syi.pcc.edu -l msarwar
msarwar's Password:
Last login: Sat Dec 27 06:41:41 2003 on /dev/pts/2 from upibm7.egr.up.edu
[YOU HAVE NEW MAIL]
$ whoami
msarwar
$ hostname
cs00
$
```

In the following In-Chapter Exercises, you will use the `rlogin` and `telnet` commands to understand how they can be used to log on to a remote host on your network or on the Internet.

IN-CHAPTER EXERCISES

14.16 Use the `telnet` and `rlogin` commands to establish remote login sessions on a host on your LAN. Note that you will not be able to establish these sessions if the remote system does not run the corresponding server processes (e.g., 'telnetd' or 'in.telnetd'—use the `ps -el` command to determine this).

14.17 Try to establish a telnet session with the host locis.loc.gov and browse through the library at your pace.

14.18 Repeat all of the sessions shown in this section on telnet on your system. Do your results match ours?

14.8.7 Remote Command Execution

You can use the `rsh` (remote shell) command to execute a command on a remote host on your local network. Remote login is a relatively time-consuming process, but the `rsh` command gives you a faster way to execute commands on remote machines if the purpose of your remote login is to execute only a few commands. We used this command in Chapter 12 to illustrate the power of I/O redirection in UNIX. Now we discuss it formally. The following is a brief description of the command.

S Y N T A X

rsh [options] host [command]

Purpose: To execute a command on a remote machine, 'host', on the same network; the `rlogin` command is executed if no 'command' is specified

Commonly used options/features:

   -l user   Use 'user' as the login name on the remote host

When you execute a command on a remote machine, your current directory on the remote machine is set to your home directory and your login shell on the remote machine is used to execute the command. Only the shell environment hidden files (.cshrc for the C shell, .kshrc for the Korn shell, etc.) are executed before the `rsh` command is executed. The general environment files (.login and .profile) are not executed. The standard files (stdin, stdout, and stderr) for the `remote` command are attached to the standard files used for your local commands (your terminal by default). Thus, when I/O redirection is used, the redirected files are taken from your local machine unless the command to be executed is enclosed in single quotes. We discuss this concept later in this section, and in all cases we assume that upsun10 is the local machine and that upsun29 is the remote machine.

The following command line executes the `ps` command on upsun29, a "trusted host," and its output is sent to the display screen of upsun10 (the local machine). The semantics of the command line are depicted in Figure 14.8.

```
$ rsh upsun29 ps
    PID   TTY      TIME    CMD
   6525   pts/0    0:02    -ksh
   6565   pts/0    0:00    -ksh
   6566   pts/0    0:00    sort data | uniq > sorted_data
$
```

The following command line executes the `sort students` command on upsun29, taking input from the students file on upsun29, and sends the results back to the sorted_students file on the local machine, upsun10. If the students file does not exist, the error message is also sent back to upsun10. The semantics of the command are illustrated in Figure 14.9.

```
$ rsh upsun29 sort students > sorted_students
$
```

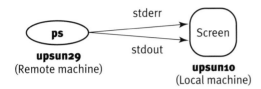

Figure 14.8 The semantics of the `rsh upsun29 ps` command

In the following command line, however, the `sort` command takes input from the students file on the local machine, upsun10. As with the previous command, the output is sent to the sorted_students file on the local machine.

```
$ rsh upsun29 sort < students > sorted_students
$
```

If you want the `sort` command to take input from a local file students and store the sorted results in a sorted_students file on the remote machine, you must quote the `remote` command with output redirection, as in,

```
$ cat students | rsh upsun29 'sort > sorted_students'
$
```

You can combine the I/O redirection operators with the pipe operator to create powerful command lines that take input from local and remote files, execute commands on local and remote machines, and send the final results to a file on the local or remote machine. We discussed a few such command lines in Chapter 12, which you should revisit at this time.

When used without an argument (which is optional), the `rsh` command reverts to the `rlogin` command. All the rules for the `rlogin` command apply in this case, and all the

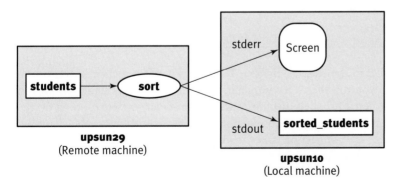

Figure 14.9 The semantics of the `rsh upsun29 sort students > sorted_students` command

hidden files that are executed during a normal login are executed. The following session shows the use of the rsh command without an argument. In the first example, the command is used to log on to upsun29 on the same network. In the second example, the rsh command is used to log on to a host on a different network on the Internet.

```
$ rsh upsun29
Last login: Mon Jan 12 18:31:17 from upibm7.egr.up.ed
Sun Microsystems Inc.    SunOS 5.5.1     Generic May 1996
) SPLAY 5 (
TERM 5 (vt100)
$
$ rsh cs00.syi.pcc.edu -l msarwar
msarwar's Password:
Last login: Mon Jan 12 18:56:07 PDT 2004 on /dev/pts/2 from upibm7.egr.up.edu
[YOU HAVE NEW MAIL]
$
```

14.8.8 File Transfer

You can use the ftp (file transfer protocol) command to transfer files to and from a remote machine on the same network or another network. This command is commonly used to transfer files to and from a remote host on the Internet. The following is a brief description of the command.

SYNTAX

ftp [options] [host]

Purpose: To transfer files from or to a remote 'host'

Commonly used options/features:

   -d   Enable debugging

   -i   Disable prompting during transfers of multiple files

   -v   Show all remote responses

As we mentioned earlier in the chapter, the File Transfer Protocol is a client-server protocol based on TCP. When you run the ftp command, an ftp client process starts running on your host and attempts to establish a connection with the ftp server process running on the remote host. If the ftp server process is not running on the remote host before the client initiates a connection request, the connection is not made and an Unknown host error message is displayed by the ftp command. Once an ftp connection has been established with the remote ftp site (a site running an ftp server process is called an ftp site), you can run several ftp commands for effective use of this utility. However, you must have appropriate access permission to be able to transfer files to the remote site. Most ftp sites allow you to transfer files into your system but not vice versa. Table 14.5 presents some useful ftp commands.

■ **TABLE 14.5** A Summary of Useful ftp Commands

Command	Meaning
! [cmd]	Runs 'cmd' on the local machine; without the 'cmd' argument, invokes an interactive shell
Help [cmd]	Displays a summary of 'cmd'; without the 'cmd' argument, displays a summary of all ftp commands
ascii	Puts the ftp channel into ASCII mode; used for transferring ASCII-type files such as text files
binary	Puts the ftp channel into binary mode; used for transferring non-ASCII files such as files containing executable codes or pictures
cd	Changes directory; similar to the UNIX cd command
close	Closes the ftp connection with the remote host, but stays inside ftp
dir remotedir localfile	Saves the listing of 'remotedir' into 'localfile' on the local host; useful for long directory listings, as pipes cannot be used with the ftp commands
get remotefile [localfile]	Transfer 'remotefile' to 'localfile' in the present working directory on the local machine; if 'localfile' is not specified, 'remotefile' is used as the name of the local file
ls [dname]	Shows contents of the designated directory; 'dname', current directory if none specified
mget remotefiles	Transfers multiple files from the remote host to the local host
mput localfiles	Transfers multiple files from the local host to the remote host
open [hostname]	Attempts to open a connection with the remote host; prompts if hostname not specified as parameter
put localfile [remotefile]	Transfers 'localfile' to 'remotefile' on the remote host; if 'remote-file' is not specified, use 'localfile' as name of remote file
quit	Terminates the ftp session
user [login_name]	If unable to log on, log on as a user on the remote host by specifying the 'user_name' as the command argument; prompt appears if 'user_name' is not specified

Most ftp sites require that you have a valid login name and password on that site to be able to transfer files to or from that site. A number of sites allow you to establish ftp sessions with them by using 'anonymous' as the login name and 'guest' or your full e-mail address as the password. Such sites are said to allow anonymous ftp.

The following session illustrates the use of the `ftp` utility to do an anonymous ftp with the site ftp.uu.net and transfer some files. In the process, we demonstrate the use of `ftp` commands `cd`, `ls`, `get`, and `mget`. We also demonstrate execution of the `ls` command on the local host. Finally, we terminate the ftp session with the `quit` command. This site requires use of the user's e-mail address as the password for anonymous ftp. If you are interested in their contents, uncompress the files that you transfer in the following session and "untar" them (*see* Chapter 19) to see what they contain.

```
$ ftp ftp.uu.net
Connected to ftp.uu.net.
220 FTP server ready.
Name (ftp.uu.net:msarwar): anonymous
331 Guest login ok, send your complete e-mail address as password.
Password:
230-
230-                   Welcome to the UUNET archive.
230- A service of UUNET Technologies Inc, Falls Church, Virginia
230- For information about UUNET, call +1 703 206 5600, or see the files
230- in /uunet-info
230-
230- Please see http://www.us.uu.net/support/usepolicy/ for Acceptable
230- Use Policy
230-
230- Access is allowed all day. Current time is Sun Jan 11 07:05:45 2004 GMT.
230-
230- All transfers are logged with your host name and email address.
230- If you don't like this policy, disconnect now!
230-
230- If your FTP client crashes or hangs shortly after login, try using a
230- dash (-) as the first character of your password. This will turn off
230- the informational messages which may be confusing your ftp client.
230-
230-
230- Please read the file /info/README.ftp
230- it was last modified on Fri Jun 29 00:54:02 2001 - 926 days ago
230- Please read the file /info/README
230- it was last modified on Fri Jun 29 00:54:02 2001 - 926 days ago
230- Guest login ok, access restrictions apply.
ftp> cd pub/shells/tcsh
250- Files within this subtree are automatically mirrored from
```

```
250- tesla.ee.cornell.edu:/pub/tcsh
250-
250- CWD command successful.
ftp> ls
200- PORT command successful.
150- Opening ASCII mode data connection for file list.
FAQ.Z
Ported.Z
tcsh-6.06.tar.gz
tcsh.man.Z
226 Transfer complete.
47 bytes received in 0.022 seconds (2.13 Kbytes/s)
ftp> get tcsh-6.06.tar.gz
200 PORT command successful.
150 Opening ASCII mode data connection for tcsh-6.06.tar.gz (524469 bytes).
226 Transfer complete.
local: tcsh-6.06.tar.gz remote: tcsh-6.06.tar.gz
526399 bytes received in 32 seconds (15.96 Kbytes/s)
ftp> !ls -l tcsh-6.06.tar.gz
total 1462
total 1462
-rw-r--r--    1 msarwar   faculty    524469 Jan 11 12:13 tcsh-6.06.tar.gz
ftp> mget tcsh*
mget tcsh-6.06.tar.gz? n
mget tcsh.man.Z? y
200 PORT command successful.
150 Opening ASCII mode data connection for tcsh.man.Z (75767 bytes).
226 Transfer complete.
local: tcsh.man.Z remote: tcsh.man.Z
76186 bytes received in 13 seconds (5.85 Kbytes/s)
ftp> quit
221-You have transferred 602585 bytes in 2 files.
221-Total traffic for this session was 604616 bytes in 4 transfers.
221-Thank you for using the FTP service on neo-ftp.uu.net.
221 Goodbye.
$
```

Once you have established an ftp connection, most sites put you in binary mode so that you can transfer non-ASCII files such as files containing audio and video clips. You can explicitly put the ftp session into binary mode by using the binary command, which ensures proper file transfer. You can revert to the ASCII mode by using the `ascii` command.

In the following In-Chapter Exercise, you will use the `ftp` command to transfer a file from a remote host on the Internet.

IN-CHAPTER EXERCISE

14.19   Establish an anonymous ftp session with the host ftp.uu.net and transfer the tcsh-6.06.tar.gz file into your system.

14.8.9 Remote Copy

You can use the `ftp` command to transfer files to and from a remote host on another network, but doing so requires that you log on to the remote host. You can use the `rcp` (remote copy) command to copy files to and from a remote machine on the same LAN, without logging on to the remote host. This command is not needed in a local area environment if you are using a network-based file system such as the **Network File System (NFS)**. In this case, the storage of your files is completely transparent to you, and you can access them from any host on your network, without specifying the name of the host that contains them. The following is a brief description of the command.

SYNTAX

rcp [options] [host:]sfile [host:]dfile
rcp [options] [host:]sfile [host:]dir

Purpose: To copy 'sfile' to 'dfile'

Commonly used options/features:

    -p   Attempt to preserve file modify and access times; without this option, the command uses the current value of umask to create file permissions

    -r   Recursively copy files at 'sfile' to 'dir'

As is obvious from the syntax, you can transfer files from your host to a remote host or from one remote host to another. The `rcp` command fails if the remote host does not "trust" your local host. The name of your local host must be in the /etc/hosts.equiv file on the remote machine for it to be a **trusted host** and for you to be able to use the `rcp`, `rsh`, and `rlogin` commands. You must also have a valid username and password to transfer files to and from the remote host. The format of a line in the file is,

```
hostname [username]
```

A '2' character can precede both a hostname and a username to deny access. A '1' character can be used in place of hostname or username to match any host or user. The following are a few such entries.

```
uphpux sarwarAllows access to the user sarwar on the host uphpux
+ sarwarAllows the user sarwar access from any host
upaix-sarwarDenies access to the user sarwar on the host upaix
-pc1Denies access to all users on the host pc1
pccvmAllows access to all users on the host pccvm
```

If the host you are using is not a trusted host (i.e., it is not listed in the /etc/hosts.equiv file), you need to create an entry in a file called .rhosts in your home directory on the remote host that contains the name of your host (from which you would use the rcp command) and your login name on this host. Thus, if the remote host is upsun29 and you want to use the rcp command on a host called upsun10, the entry in the ~/.rhosts file on upsun29 will be the following (assuming that your login name on upsun10 is sarwar).

```
upsun10    sarwar
```

This entry informs the networking software, which is in the UNIX kernel, that sarwar is a trusted user on the host upsun10.

The following rcp command copies all the files with html extension from your ~/myweb directory to the ~/webmirror directory on upsun29.

```
$ rcp ~/myweb/*.html upsun29:webmirror
$
```

The following rcp command copies the files Chapter[1–9].doc from the ~/unixbook directory on your system to the ~/unixbook.backup directory on upsun29.

```
$ rcp ~/unixbook/Chapter[1-9].doc upsun29:unixbook.backup
$
```

The following rcp command copies all C and C++ source files from your ~/ece446/projects directory on upsun29 to your ~/swprojects.backup directory on your machine.

```
$ rcp upsun29:ece446/projects/*.[c,C] ~/swprojects.backup
$
```

As we mentioned before, you can also use the rcp command to copy files from one remote host to another remote host. The following rcp command is used to copy the whole home directory from the www1 host to the www2 host. Note use of the -r option to copy subdirectories recursively and use of the -p option to preserve existing modification times and access permissions.

```
$ rcp -rp www1:* www2:
$
```

The following In-Chapter Exercise gives you practice using the rcp command in your environment.

IN-CHAPTER EXERCISE

14.20   Use an rcp command to copy a file from your machine to another machine on your network. What command line did you use? What did it do?

14.8.10 Secure Shell and Related Commands

There is a secure version of rsh, called ssh (secure shell). Whereas rsh (and other UNIX 'r' commands such as rlogin and rcp) communicate with the remote host in cleartxt, ssh uses **strong cryptography** for transmitting data, including commands, password, and files. For these reasons, ssh has become a de facto standard for secure terminal connections within a network or the Internet. The encrypted sessions used by ssh and scp prevent anyone from making sense of the ongoing communication while **sniffing** it. Also, authentication methods used in ssh prevent any kind of **spoofing** such as IP spoofing.

The *ssh* COMMAND

The ssh command allows you to perform the tasks that you can perform with the rlogin and rsh commands, but in a more secure manner. You are allowed to log in to the remote host or execute a command on it if the ssh server finds your machine name in the /etc/host.equiv or /etc/shosts.equiv file and your login name is the same on your machine and the remote machine. You are also allowed to log in to the remote host if your login names are different on the local and remote hosts, and your local machine's name and your login name on it are contained in the ~/.rhosts or ~/.shosts file. ssh uses additional security features, including **public-key cryptography**, to authenticate a user and its host before allowing the user to log in to the remote machine. We describe only some of the rather basic features of the ssh command that are needed for remote login and remote execution of commands.

You can log in to a remote host or execute a command on a remote host with the ssh command just like you do with the rsh command. For example, in the following session, the first command allows you to start an ssh session on the upsun29.egr.up.edu host, the second command lets you log in to the upsun host on the same local area network as the user called perform, and the last command lets you log in to a remote host cs00.syi.pcc.edu as msarwar.

```
$ ssh upsun29.egr.up.edu
...
$ rlogin upsun -l perform
...
$ ssh -l msarwar cs00.syi.pcc.edu
...
$
```

We now discuss remote execution of commands with ssh. All of the rsh commands discussed in Section 14.8.7 will work if you replace rsh with ssh. Here are some additional commands. The following command executes the ps -el | grep 'd$' command on cs00.syi.pcc.edu and displays the status of all the daemon processes on it on the local machine. You might be prompted for a password if your machine is not a trusted host.

```
$ ssh cs00.syi.pcc.edu "ps -el | grep d$"

19   T    0      0      0     0    0 SY   ?    0     ?            0:03   sched
...
 8   S  1517   1666    587    0   41 20   ? 1353    ?   ?         6:50   httpd
 8   S  1517   1665    587    0   41 20   ? 1369    ?   ?         6:53   httpd
 8   O    0   11667  11652   48   99 20   ? 1218    ? 190         5:50   mysqld
$
```

In the following session, the ps -el | grep d$ command runs on the remote machine and its output is piped to the grep '\<httpd'$ command that runs on the local machine. The output of the command line is status of the http daemons running on the remote host.

```
$ ssh cs00.syi.pcc.edu "ps -el | grep d$" | grep '\<httpd'$
 8   S  1517   1607    587    0   41 20   ? 1344    ?   ?         6:39   httpd
 8   S    0     522      1    0   40 20   ?  605    ?   ?         0:01   httpd
 8   S    0     587      1    0   40 20   ?  853    ?   ?         0:02   httpd
 8   S  1517   1608    587    0   41 20   ? 1345    ?   ?         6:36   httpd
 8   S  1517    641    587    0   41 20   ? 1368    ?   ?         7:05   httpd
 8   S  1517    639    587    0   41 20   ? 1315    ?   ?         7:03   httpd
 8   S  1517    643    587    0   40 20   ? 1341    ?   ?         6:51   httpd
 8   S  1517    642    587    0   41 20   ? 1359    ?   ?         6:37   httpd
 8   S  1517    640    587    0   41 20   ? 1329    ?   ?         6:47   httpd
 8   S  1517   1667    587    0   41 20   ? 1331    ?   ?         6:59   httpd
 8   S  1517   1666    587    0   41 20   ? 1353    ?   ?         6:50   httpd
 8   S  1517   1665    587    0   41 20   ? 1369    ?   ?         6:53   httpd
$
```

The scp COMMAND

The scp command is the secure version of the rcp command. It means that copying takes place under encrypted sessions after proper authentication of the local host and user. All of the commands discussed in Section 14.8.9 will work if rcp is replaced with scp. The following command copies the prog4.c file in your current directory into your ~/courses/cs213/programs/ directory on upsun29.

```
$ scp prog4.c upsun29:~/courses/cs213/programs/
$
```

The following command recursively copies the courses directory in your home directory on the upsun21.egr.up.edu host to your current directory.

```
$ scp -r upsun21.egr.up.edu:courses .
$
```

The following command recursively copies your home directory on the www1 host to your home directory on the www2 host, preserving existing modification times and access permissions for all files and directories. You might be prompted for a password on a remote machine.

```
$ scp -rp www1:* www2:
$
```

The sftp COMMAND

The sftp command is the secure version of the ftp command. It works just like the ftp command, except that stronger authentication takes place before file transfer takes place, and transfer takes place in encrypted sessions.

The following In-Chapter Exercise gives you practice using the ssh and scp commands in your environment.

IN-CHAPTER EXERCISE

14.21 Use the ssh and scp commands to access a remote host on your local area network, execute a command remotely, and copy a file from your machine to another machine on your network. What did you use? What are their semantics?

14.8.11 Interactive Chat

You can use the talk command for an interactive chat with a user on your host or on a remote host over a network. The following is a brief description of the command.

SYNTAX

talk user [tty]

Purpose: To initiate interactive communication with 'user' who is logged in on a 'tty' terminal

---

The 'user' parameter is the login name of the person if he or she is on your host. If the person you want to talk to is on another host, use login_name@host for 'user'. The 'tty' parameter is needed if the person is logged on to the same host more than once.

When you use the talk command to initiate a communication request, the other user is interrupted with a message on his or her screen informing that person of the request. The other user needs to execute the `talk` command to respond to you. That establishes a communication channel, and both users' display screens are divided in half. The upper half contains the text that you type, and the lower half contains the other user's responses. Both you and the other user can type simultaneously. The `talk` command simply copies the characters that you type at your keyboard on the screen of the other user. The chat session can be terminated when either of you presses `<Ctrl-C>`. If you are using the `vi` editor and your screen is corrupted during the communication, you can use `<Ctrl-L>` to redraw the screen.

Suppose that user sarwar wants to talk to another user, bob, and that both are logged on to the same host. The following command from sarwar initiates a talk request to bob.

```
$ talk bob
```

As soon as sarwar hits `<Enter>`, the following message is displayed at the top of bob's screen.

```
[Waiting for your party to respond]
Message from Talk_Daemon@upibm7.egr.up.edu at 13:36 ...
talk: connection requested by sarwar@upibm7.egr.up.edu.
talk: respond with: talk sarwar@upibm7.egr.up.edu
```

When bob runs the `talk sarwar` command, both bob's and sarwar's screens are divided in half, with the upper halves containing the message '[Connection established]' and the cursor moved to the top of both screens. Both bob and sarwar are now ready to talk. If bob wants to ignore sarwar's request while using a shell, he can simply press `<Enter>`.

If bob is logged in on another host—say, upsun29—sarwar needs to run the following command to initiate the talk request.

```
$ talk bob@upsun29
```

If sarwar is logged in once on upibm7 and bob wants to communicate with sarwar, his response to the preceding request should be talk sarwar@upibm7.

If bob is logged in on upsun29 multiple times, the following command from sarwar initiates a talk request on terminal ttyp2 (one of the terminals bob is logged on to).

```
$ talk bob@upsun29 ttyp2
```

If you want to block all talk requests because users keep bothering you with too many requests, execute:

```
$ mesg n
$
```

This command works only for your current session. If you want to block all talk and write requests whenever you log on, put this command in your ~/.profile file (on System V) or ~/.login file (on BSD). Doing so simply takes away the write permission on your terminal file in the /dev directory for group and others. Without any argument, the `mesg` command displays the current status.

In the following In-Chapter Exercise, you will use the `talk` command to establish a chat session with a friend on your network and appreciate the various characteristics of the command.

IN-CHAPTER EXERCISE

14.22 Establish a chat session using the `talk` command with a friend who is currently logged on.

14.8.12 Tracing the Route from One Site to Another Site

You can use the `traceroute` command to display the route (the names of the routers in the path) that your e-mail messages, `telnet` commands, and downloaded files from an ftp site can take from your host to the remote host, and vice versa. It also gives you a feel for the speed of the route. Because this command poses some security threats, most system administrators disable its execution. The security threat stems from the fact that, by displaying a route to a host on the Internet, someone can figure out the internal structure of the network to which the host is connected and the IP addresses of some machines on the network. The following is a simple execution of the command to show its output and demonstrate the inner workings of the Internet a bit more. The following command shows the route from our host to cs.berkeley.edu.

```
$ traceroute cs.berkeley.edu
traceroute: Warning: cs.berkeley.edu has multiple addresses; using 169.229.60.163
traceroute to cs.berkeley.edu (169.229.60.163), 30 hops max, 40 byte packets
 1  up (192.102.10.9)  0.491 ms  0.287 ms  0.263 ms
 2  64-251-255-65.up.edu (64.251.255.65)    0.357 ms  0.328 ms  0.320 ms
 3  loki_bc_ext.up.edu (64.251.255.1)  2.257 ms  1.896 ms  2.115 ms
 4  s3-0-1.gw01.ptld.eli.net (216.190.151.213)  3.097 ms  2.588 ms  2.561 ms
 5  srp2-0.cr02.ptld.eli.net (208.186.20.132)  2.642 ms  2.615 ms  2.519 ms
 6  p9-0.cr01.rcrd.eli.net (207.173.115.42)  16.830 ms  16.777 ms  16.853 ms
 7  srp3-0.cr02.rcrd.eli.net (208.186.20.242)  17.039 ms  17.005 ms  16.871 ms
 8  p9-0.cr01.sntd.eli.net (207.173.114.57)  20.239 ms  19.874 ms  20.027 ms
 9  so-0-0-0--0.er01.plal.eli.net (207.173.114.138)  20.877 ms  20.460 ms  20.463 ms
10  pa-paix.cenic.net (198.32.176.15)  20.837 ms  20.735 ms  20.566 ms
11  dc-svl-dc1--paix-px1-ge.cenic.net (137.164.22.146)  21.195 ms  21.299 ms  20.841 ms
12  dc-oak-dc1--svl-dc1-10ge.cenic.net (137.164.22.31)  22.245 ms  22.159 ms  22.053 ms
13  dc-oak-dc2--oak-dc1-ge.cenic.net (137.164.22.37)  22.461 ms  22.145 ms  22.045 ms
14  ucb--oak-dc2-ge.cenic.net (137.164.23.30)  22.443 ms  22.426 ms  22.061 ms
15  doecev-soda-br-6-4.EECS.Berkeley.EDU (128.32.255.170)  22.584 ms  27.032 ms  22.576 ms
16  sbd2a.EECS.Berkeley.EDU (169.229.59.226)  23.836 ms  26.594 ms  27.258 ms
```

```
17 relay2.EECS.Berkeley.EDU (169.229.60.28)  23.842 ms  39.446 ms  22.827 ms
$
```

A line in the trace contains the times taken by the three packets sent by `traceroute` as they go from one router to the next. In this instance, one-way travel time for data is about 1 sec from our host in Portland, Oregon, all the way to cs.berkeley.edu in Berkeley, California. The output also contains the IP addresses of the various routers (i.e., hops) on the way from our host to the destination host. A total of 17 hops are traversed by anything that goes from our host to cs.berkeley.edu. The Berkeley machine is on a class A network with network ID 169.229.60.

14.9   Important Internet Organizations

Table 14.6 lists the names of some of the important organizations that manage the Internet and formulate plans and policies for its growth.

■ **TABLE 14.6** Important Organizations That Manage the Internet and Formulate Plans and Policies for Its Growth

Organization	Purpose
Internet Society (ISOC) `www.isoc.org`	An international, nonprofit organization that was established to encourage and promote the use of the Internet. ISOC is the host for Internet Architecture Board (IAB).
Internet Architecture Board (IAB) `www.iab.org`	A group of people responsible for setting policies and standards for the Internet and the TCP/IP protocol suite.
Internet Engineering Task Force (IETF) `www.ietf.org`	An open group of individuals (network designers, vendors, operators, and researchers) who are responsible for the evolution of the Internet architecture and the Internet's smooth operation. IETF has the responsibility to design and test new technologies for the Internet and the TCP/IP protocol suite. IETF is the technical arm of IAB.
Internet Research Task Force (IRTF) `www.irtf.org`	A group of individuals who are responsible for promoting research that is important for the evolution of the Internet in all relevant areas: protocols, applications, architecture, and technology. IETF is the research arm of IAB.
Internet Assigned Numbers Authority (IANA) `www.iana.org`	Assignment of domain names and protocol port numbers for well-known Internet services, such as ftp.

(continued)

TABLE 14.6 *(continued)*

Internet's Network Information Center (InterNIC) `www.internic.net`	Maintains a list of the currently operating registrars of top-level domains, information about new top-level domains, problem reports about registrars, and information about registered domains.
Internet Corporation for Assigned Names and Numbers (ICANN) `www.icann.org`	ICANN is a technical coordination body whose primary objective to insure the stability of the Internet's system of assigned names and numbers. Every business that wants to become a registrar with a direct access to ICANN-designated top-level domains must be accredited by ICANN for this purpose.

14.10 Web Resources

Table 14.7 lists useful Web sites for network- and Internet-related concepts, organizations, and UNIX commands.

■■ **TABLE 14.7** Web Resources for Network- and Internet-related Policies, Documents, and UNIX commands

URL	Description
`www.openssh.com`	The home page for openssh, a free version of ssh (secure shell).
`www.iana.org/domain-names.htm`	This page gives detailed information about domain names and domain name services.
`www.chiark.greenend.org.uk/~sgtatham/putty/`	A home page for PuTTY (a free implementation of telnet and ssh for UNIX and Win32 platform).
`www.linuxgazette.com/issue64/dellomodarme.html`	An introductory article on the `ssh` command suite: sftp, scp, etc.
`www.ietf.org/rfc.html`	The home page for Request For Comments (RFCs).

(continued)

TABLE 14.7 (continued)

`www.isi.edu`	The home page for the Information Sciences Institute (ISI) at the University of Southern California (USC). ISI is a useful resource for Internet-related information, such as the history of the Internet, country codes, and protocol port numbers for the well-known Internet services.
`www.isoc.org/internet/history/`	This page contains many documents on the history of the Internet, including its infrastructure, standards, growth, and future. A good article to read is "Internet History and Growth" by William Slater III.
`http://www.zakon.org/robert/internet/timeline/`	This page has a detailed time line for the history of the Internet, including statistical data for the number of users, hosts, and domains served by the Internet.

Summary

Computer networking began more than 35 years ago with the development of ARPANET in the late 1960s. Today, computing without networking is unthinkable because of the ubiquitous Internet. Web browsing, file transfer, interactive chat, electronic mail, and remote login are some of the well-known services commonly used by today's computer users. The e-commerce phenomenon has started to change the way people do everyday chores and conduct business. UNIX has a special place in the world of networking in general and internetworking in particular because most of the networking protocols were initially implemented on UNIX platforms. Today, most of the Internet services are provided by server processes running on UNIX-based computers.

The core of internetworking software is based on the TCP/IP protocol suite. This suite includes, among several other protocols, the well-known TCP and IP protocols for transportation and routing of application data. The key to routing in the Internet is 32-bit IP addresses (in IPv4). The most heavily used Internet services are for Web browsing (and all the services that it offers, such as e-commerce), electronic mail, file transfer, and remote login. Not only do UNIX systems support all the Internet services, but they also have additional utilities to support local network activities.

The topics discussed in this chapter include the general structure of a network and an internetwork, networking models, the TCP/IP protocol suite, IP addresses, the domain name system (DNS), Internet protocols and services, and UNIX utilities for performing networking- and internetworking-related tasks. These utilities are implemented by using the client-server software model. The utilities discussed in this chapter are `finger` (for finding information about users on a host), `ftp` and `sftp` (for file transfer), `dig`, `ifconfig`, `host`, and `nslookup` (for translation of domain names to IP addresses), `ping` (to find the status of a host), `rcp` and `scp` (to remote copy on a UNIX host), `rlogin` (to remote login on a UNIX host), `rsh` and `ssh` (for logging on to a remote host on a network), `ruptime` (to display information about UNIX hosts on a LAN), `rwho` (to display users who are currently logged on to UNIX hosts in a LAN), `talk` (for interactive chat), `telnet` (for remote login), and `traceroute` (for tracing the route of data from your host to a destination host).

Problems

1. What are computer networks and why are they important?

2. What is an internetwork? What is the Internet?

3. What are the key protocols that form the backbone of the Internet? Where were they developed?

4. What is an IPv4 address? What is its size in bits and bytes? What is dotted decimal notation? What is the size of an IPv6 address in bits and bytes?

5. What are the classes of IPv4 addresses? Given an IPv4 address in binary, how can you tell which class the address belongs to? How can you tell the class of the address when it is expressed in the dotted decimal notation?

6. What is DNS? Name the UNIX command that can be used to translate a host name to its IP address.

7. List two domain names each for sites that are in the following top-level domains: edu, com, gov, int, mil, net, org, au, de, ir, kw, pk, and uk. How did you find them? Do not use examples given in this textbook.

8. Read the ftp://ftp.isi.edu/in-notes/iana/assignments/port-numbers file to identify port numbers for the following well-known services: ftp, http, time, daytime, echo, ping, and quote-of-the-day.

9. What is the timeout period for the finger protocol? How did you get your answer?

10. How many users have Johnston as part of their name at the osu.edu domain? How did you find out? Write down your command.

11. Give a command that accomplishes the same task that the following command does.

    `rsh upsun29 sort < students > sorted_students`

12. Show the semantics of the following command by drawing a diagram similar to the ones shown in Figures 14.8 and 14.9. Assume that the name of the local machine is upsun10.

    `cat students | ssh upsun29 sort | ssh upsun21 uniq > sorted_uniq_students`

13. Display the /etc/services file on your system and list port numbers for well-known ports for the following services: daytime, time, quote-of-the-day (qotd), echo, smtp, and finger. Did you find all of them? Do the port numbers match those found in Problem 8?

14. Use the `telnet` command to get current time via the daytime service at mit.edu. Write down your command line.

15. Fetch the files history.netcount and history.hosts from the directory nsfnet/statistics using anonymous ftp from the host nic.merit.edu. These files contain the number of domestic and foreign networks and hosts on the NSFNET infrastructure. What is the size of Internet in terms of the number of networks and hosts according to the statistics in these files? Although the statistics are somewhat dated, what is your prediction of its size a year from now? Why? Show your work.

16. You create the following entries in your ~/.rhosts file on a host on your network.

    `host1      john.doe`

    `host2      mike.brich`

    What are the consequences if john.doe and mike.birch are users on hosts host1 and host2 in your network? Both users belong to your user group.

17. Give a command for displaying simple names of all the hosts on your network.

18. Use the `telnet` command to display information about all the users at mit.edu who have Smith as part of their name. Show the command that you used to obtain your answer.

19. Give the command for displaying page-by-page information about the users who have Chen as part of their name at mit.edu. How many such users exist?

20. Describe the semantics of the following command. Clearly state which commands are executed locally and which are executed on the remote host. What is the output of the command?

    `ssh cs00.syi.pcc.edu "ps -el | grep d$" | grep '\<httpd'$ | wc -l`

21. Use the `traceroute` command to determine the route from your host to locis.loc.gov. What is the approximate travel time for data from your host to locis.loc.gov?

22. Find a host that offers the quote-of-the-day (qotd) service. What is the quote of the day today?

Introductory Bourne Shell Programming

Objectives

- To introduce the concept of shell programming
- To discuss how shell programs are executed
- To describe the concept and use of shell variables
- To discuss how command line arguments are passed to shell programs
- To explain the concept of command substitution
- To describe some basic coding principles
- To write and discuss some shell scripts
- To cover the commands and primitives
  `*`, `=`, `"`, `'`, `` ` ``, `&`, `<`, `>`, `;`, `|`, `\`, `/`, `[ ]`, `:`, `break`, `case`, `continue`, `exit`, `export`, `env`, `for`, `if`, `ls`, `read`, `readonly`, `set`, `sh`, `shift`, `test`, `while`, `until`, and `unset`

15.1 Introduction

The Bourne shell is more than a command interpreter. It has a programming language of its own that can be used to write shell programs for performing various tasks that cannot be performed by any existing command. A shell program, commonly known as a **shell script**, consists of shell commands to be executed by a shell and is stored in an ordinary UNIX file. The shell allows use of a read/write storage place, known as a **shell variable**, for users and programmers to use as a scratch pad for completing a task. The shell also contains **program control flow commands** (also called **statements**) that allow nonsequential execution of the commands in a shell script and repeated execution of a block of commands–similar to programming languages like C.

15.2 Running a Bourne Shell Script

There are three ways to run a Bourne shell script. The first method is to make the script file executable by adding the execute permission to the existing access permissions for the file. You can do so by running the following command, where script_file is the name of the file containing the shell script. Clearly, in this case you make the script executable for yourself only. However, you can set appropriate access permissions for the file if you also want other users to be able to execute.

```
$ chmod u+x script_file
$
```

Now, you can type `script_file` as a command to execute the shell script. As described in Chapter 13, the script is executed by a child of the current shell. Note that, with this method, the script executes properly if you are using the Bourne shell but not if you are using any other shell. In this case, execute the `/bin/sh` command to run the Bourne shell.

The second method of executing a shell script is to run the `/bin/sh` command with the script file as its parameter. Thus, the following command executes the script in script_file. If your search path (the *PATH* variable) includes the /bin directory, you can simply use the `sh` command.

```
$ /bin/sh script_file
$
```

The third method, which is also the most commonly used, is to force the current shell to execute a script in the Bourne shell, regardless of your current shell. You can do so by beginning a shell script with,

```
#!/bin/sh
```

All you need to do is set execute permission for the script file and run the file as a command. When your current shell encounters the string `#!`, it takes the rest of the line as the absolute pathname for the shell to be executed under which the script in the file is executed. If your current shell is the C shell, you can replace this line with a colon (:), which is known as the **null command** in the Bourne shell. When the C shell reads **:** as the first character, it runs a Bourne shell process that executes the commands in the script. The **:** command returns true. We discuss the return values of commands later in the chapter.

15.3   Shell Variables and Related Commands

A **variable** is a main memory location that is given a name. That allows you to reference the memory location by using its name instead of its address (*see* Chapter 3). The name of a shell variable can comprise digits, letters, and underscore, with the first character being a letter or underscore. Because the main memory is read/write storage, you can read a variable's value or assign it a new value. For the Bourne shell, the value of a variable is always a string of characters, even if you store a number in it. There is no theoretical limit on the length of a variable's value.

Shell variables can be one of two types: **shell environment variables** and **user-defined variables**. Environment variables are used to customize the environment in which your shell runs and for proper execution of shell commands. A copy of these variables is passed to every command that executes in the shell as its child. Most of these variables are initialized when the /etc/profile file executes as you log on. This file is written by your system administrator to set up a common environment for all users of the system. You can customize your environment by assigning different values to some or all of these variables in your ~/.profile startup file, which also executes when you log on. Table 15.1 lists most of the environment variables whose values you can change. We described some of these variables in the previous chapters.

■ **TABLE 15.1** Some Important Writable Bourne Shell Environment Variables

Environment Variable	Purpose of the Variable
CDPATH	Contains directory names that are searched, one by one, by the cd command to find the directory passed to it as a parameter; the cd command searches the current directory if this variable is not set
EDITOR	Default editor used in programs such as the e-mail program
ENV	Path along which UNIX looks to find configuration files
HOME	Name of home directory, when user first logs on
MAIL	Name of user's system mailbox file
MAILCHECK	How often (in seconds) the shell should check user's mailbox for new mail and inform user accordingly
PATH	Variable that contains user's search path—the directories that a shell searches to find an external command or program
PPID	Process ID of the parent process
PS1	Primary shell prompt that appears on the command line, usually set to $

(continued)

TABLE 15.1 *(continued)*

PS2	Secondary shell prompt displayed on second line of a command if shell thinks that the command is not finished, typically when the command terminates with a backslash (\ ), the escape character
PWD	Name of the current working directory
TERM	Type of user's console terminal

These shell environment variables are writable, and you can assign any values to them. Other shell environment variables are *read-only*, which means that you can use (read) the values of these variables but cannot change them. These variables are most useful for processing **command line arguments** (also known as **positional arguments**), or parameters passed to a shell script at the command line. Examples of command line arguments are the source and destination files in the cp command. Some other read-only shell variables are used to keep track of the process ID of the current process, the process ID of the most recent background process, and the exit status of the last command. Some important read-only shell environment variables are listed in Table 15.2.

User-defined variables are used within shell scripts as temporary storage places whose values can be changed when the program executes. These variables can be made read-only as well as passed to the commands that execute in the shell script in which they are defined. Unlike most other programming languages, in the Bourne shell programming language you do not have to declare and initialize shell variables. An uninitialized shell variable is initialized to a **null string** by default.

■ TABLE 15.2 Some Important Read-Only Bourne Shell Environment Variables

Environment Variable	Purpose of the Variable
$0	Name of program
$1–$9	Values of command line arguments 1 through 9
$*	Values of all command line arguments
$@	Values of all command line arguments; each argument individually quoted if $@ is enclosed in quotes, as in "$@"
$#	Total number of command line arguments
$$	Process ID (PID) of current process
$?	Exit status of most recent command
$!	PID of most recent background process

You can display the names of all shell variables (including user-defined variables) and their current values by using the set command without any parameters. As described later in this chapter, the set command can also be used to change the values of some of the read-only shell environment variables. The following is a sample run of the set command on an AIX-based computer. To keep you focused, we provide only a brief partial list.

```
$ set
AUTHSTATE=compat
CGI_DIRECTORY=/usr/lpp/internet/server_root/cgi-bin
DEFAULT_BROWSER=netscape
DOCUMENT_DIRECTORY=/usr/lpp/internet/server_root/pub
DOCUMENT_SERVER_MACHINE_NAME=pccaix
DOCUMENT_SERVER_PORT=80
ERRNO=10
FCEDIT=/usr/bin/ed
HOME=/home/inst/msarwar
IFS='
'
IMQCONFIGCL=/etc/IMNSearch/dbcshelp
IMQCONFIGSRV=/etc/IMNSearch
LANG=en_US
LINENO=1
LOCPATH=/usr/lib/nls/loc
LOGIN=msarwar
LOGNAME=msarwar
MAIL=/usr/spool/mail/msarwar
MAILCHECK=600
MAILMSG='[YOU HAVE NEW MAIL]'
NLSPATH=/usr/lib/nls/msg/%L/%N:/usr/lib/nls/msg/%L/%N.cat
ODMDIR=/etc/objrepos
OPTIND=1
PATH=/usr/lpp/workbench/bin:/usr/lpp/Java/bin:/usr/bin:/
etc:/usr/sbin:/usr/ucb:/usr/local/bin:/usr/local/share/
bin:/home/inst/msarwar/bin:/usr/bin/X11:/sbin:.
PPID=18632
PS1='$ '
PS2='> '
PS3='#? '
PS4='+ '
PWD=/home/inst/msarwar
RANDOM=22177
SECONDS=8204
SHELL=/usr/bin/ksh
TERM=vt100
```

```
TERM_DEFAULT=lft
TMOUT=0
TZ=PST8PDT
USER=msarwar
$
```

You can also use the env (System V) and printenv (BSD) commands to display environment variables and their values, but the list is not as complete as the one displayed by the set command. In particular, the output does not include any user-defined variables. The following is a sample output of the env command on the same AIX-based computer that we ran the set command on.

```
$ env
LANG=en_US
LOGIN=msarwar
NLSPATH=/usr/lib/nls/msg/%L/%N:/usr/lib/nls/msg/%L/%N.cat
IMQCONFIGCL=/etc/IMNSearch/dbcshelp
PATH=/usr/lpp/workbench/bin:/usr/lpp/Java/bin:/usr/bin:/
etc:/usr/sbin:/usr/ucb:/usr/local/bin:/usr/local/share/
bin:/home/inst/msarwar/bin:/usr/bin/X11:/sbin:.
IMQCONFIGSRV=/etc/IMNSearch
CGI_DIRECTORY=/usr/lpp/internet/server_root/cgi-bin
LOGNAME=msarwar
MAIL=/usr/spool/mail/msarwar
LOCPATH=/usr/lib/nls/loc
USER=msarwar
DOCUMENT_SERVER_MACHINE_NAME=pccaix
AUTHSTATE=compat
SHELL=/usr/bin/ksh
ODMDIR=/etc/objrepos
DOCUMENT_SERVER_PORT=80
HOME=/home/inst/msarwar
TERM=vt100
MAILMSG=[YOU HAVE NEW MAIL]
PWD=/home/inst/msarwar
DOCUMENT_DIRECTORY=/usr/lpp/internet/server_root/pub
TZ=PST8PDT
$
```

In the following In-Chapter Exercises, you will create a simple shell script and make it executable. Also, you will use the `set` and `env` commands to display the names and values of shell variables in your environment.

IN-CHAPTER EXERCISES

15.1   Display the names and values of all the shell variables on your UNIX machine. What command(s) did you use?

15.2   Create a file that contains a shell script comprising the `date` and `pwd` commands, one on each line. Make the file executable and run the shell script. List all the steps for completing this task.

15.3.1 Reading and Writing Shell Variables

You can use the following syntax to assign a value to (write) one or more shell variables (environment or user-defined). The command syntax `variable=value` comprises what is commonly known as the assignment statement, and its purpose is to assign `value` to `variable`. The following is the general syntax of the **assignment statement** in the Bourne shell.

---

variable1=value1 [variable2=value2 ... variableN=valueN]

Purpose: Assign values 'value1, ..., valueN' to variables 'variable1, ..., variableN', respectively—no space allowed before and after the equals sign

S Y N T A X

Note that there is no space before and after the equals sign (`=`) in the syntax. If a value contains spaces, you must enclose the value in quotes. Single and double quotes work differently, as discussed later in this section. You can refer to (read) the current value of a variable by inserting a dollar sign (`$`) before the name of a variable. You can use the `echo` command to display the values of shell variables.

The following session shows how shell variables can be read (interpreted) and written (created).

```
$ name=John
$ echo $name
John
$ name=John Doe
Doe: not found
$ name="John Doe"
$ echo $name
John Doe
$ name=John*
$ echo $name
```

```
John.Bates.letter John.Johnsen.memo John.email
$ echo "$name"
John*
$ echo "The name $name sounds familiar!"
The name John* sounds familiar!
$ echo \$name
$ name
$ echo '$name'
$ name
$
```

If values that include spaces are not enclosed in quotes, the shell tries to execute the second word in the value as a command and displays an error message if the word does not correspond to a valid command. Also, after the name=John* statement has been executed and *$name* is not quoted in the echo command, the shell lists the file names in your present working directory that match John*, with * considered as the shell metacharacter. The variable *$name* must be enclosed in quotes to refer to John*, as in echo "$name".

Thus, the use of double quotes allows variable substitution by special processing of the dollar sign ($), but most other shell metacharacters, including the character *, are processed literally. As a result, running the echo * command would display the names of all the files in your current directory in one line. The preceding session also shows that you can use single quotes to process the whole string literally. The backslash character can be used to escape the special meaning of any single character, including $, and treat it literally.

A command consisting of $variable only results in the value of *variable* executed as a shell command. If the value of *variable* comprises a valid command, the expected results are produced. If *variable* does not contain a valid command, the shell, as expected, displays an appropriate error message. The following session makes this point with some examples. The variable used in the session is *command*.

```
$ command=pwd
$ $command
/users/faculty/sarwar/unixbook/examples
$ command=hello
$ $command
sh: hello: command not found
$
```

15.3.2 Command Substitution

When a command is enclosed in backquotes (also known as *grave accents*), the shell executes the command and substitutes the command (including backquotes) with the output of the command. This process is referred to as **command substitution**. The following is a brief description of command substitution.

'command'

Purpose: Substitute its output for `command`

The following session illustrates the concept. In the first assignment statement, the `variable` command is assigned a value pwd. In the second assignment statement, the output of the pwd command is assigned to the `command` variable.

```
$ command=pwd
$ echo "The value of command is: $command."
The value of command is: pwd.
$ command=`pwd`
$ echo "The value of command is: $command."
The value of command is: /users/faculty/sarwar/unixbook/examples.
$
```

Command substitution can be specified in any command. For example, in the following session, the output of the date command is substituted for `date` before the echo command is executed.

```
$ echo "The date and time is `date`."
The date and time is Fri May 7 13:26:42 PDT 2004.
$
```

We demonstrate the real-world use of command substitution in various ways throughout this chapter and Chapter 16.

The following In-Chapter Exercises are designed to reinforce the creation and use of shell variables and the concept of command substitution.

IN-CHAPTER EXERCISES

15.3 Assign your full name to a shell variable called *myname* and echo its value. How did you accomplish the task? Show your work.

15.4 Assign the output of echo "Hello, world!" command to the *myname* variable and then display the value of *myname*. List the commands that you executed to complete your work.

15.3.3 Exporting Environment

When a variable is created, it is not automatically known to subsequent shells. The export command passes the *value* of a variable to subsequent shells. Thus, when a shell script is called and executed in another shell script, it does not get automatic access to the variables defined in the original (caller) script unless they are explicitly made available to it. The export command can be used to pass the value of one or more variables to any subsequent script. All read/write shell environment variables are available to every command, script, and subshell, so they are exported at the time they are initialized. The following is a brief description of the export command.

SYNTAX

export [name-list]

Purpose: Export the names and copies of the current values in 'name-list' to every command executed from this point on

---

The following session presents a simple use of the command. The *name* variable is initialized to John Doe and is exported to subsequent commands executed under the current shell and any subshells that run under the current shell.

```
$ name="John Doe"
$ export name
$
```

We now illustrate the concept of exporting shell variables via some simple shell scripts. Consider the following session.

```
$ cat display_name
echo $name
exit 0
$
$ name="John Doe"
$ display_name

$
```

Note that the shell script in the display_name file displays a null string even though we initialized the *name* variable just before executing this script. The reason is that the *name* variable is not exported before running the script, and the *name* variable used in the script is *local* to the script. Because this local variable *name* is uninitialized, the echo command displays the null string–the default value of every uninitialized variable.

You can use the exit command to transfer control to the calling process–the current shell process in the preceding session. The only argument of the exit command is an optional integer number, which is returned to the calling process as the **exit status** of the terminating process. All UNIX commands return an exit status of 0 upon *success* (if they successfully perform their tasks) and nonzero upon *failure*. The return status value of a command is stored in the read-only environment variable $? and can be checked by the calling process. In shell scripts, the status of a command is commonly checked and subsequent action taken. We show the use of $? in some shell scripts later in the chapter. When the `exit` command is executed without an argument, the UNIX kernel sets the return status value for the script.

In the following session, the *name* variable is exported after it is initialized, thus making it available to the display_name script. The session also shows that the return status of the display_name script is 0.

```
$ name="John Doe"
$ export name
$ display_name
John Doe
$ echo $?
0
$
```

We now show that a copy of an exported variable's value is passed to any subsequent command. In other words, a command has access to the value of the exported variable only; it cannot assign a new value to the variable. Consider the script in the export_demo file.

```
$ cat export_demo
#!/bin/sh
name="John Doe"
export name
display_change_name
display_name
exit 0
$ cat display_change_name
#!/bin/sh
echo $name
name="Plain Jane"
echo $name
exit 0
$ export_demo
John Doe
Plain Jane
John Doe
$
```

When the export_demo script is invoked, the *name* variable is set to John Doe and the variable is exported so that it becomes part of the environment of all the commands that execute under `export_demo` as its children. The first `echo` command in the display_change_name script displays the value of the exported variable, *name*. It then initializes a local variable, *name*, to Plain Jane. The second echo command therefore echoes the current value of the local variable *name* and displays Plain Jane. When the display_change_name script has finished, the display_name script executes and displays the value of the exported (nonlocal) *name*, thus displaying John Doe.

15.3.4 Resetting Variables

A variable retains its value as long as the script in which it is initialized. You can reset the value of a variable to null (the default initial value of all variables) by either explicitly initializing it to null or by using the unset command. The following is a brief description of this command.

SYNTAX

unset [name-list]

Purpose: Reset or remove the variable or function corresponding to the names in 'name-list', where 'name-list' is a list of names separated by spaces

---

We discuss functions in the Bourne shell in Chapter 16, so we limit the discussion of the unset command here to variables only. The following session shows a simple use of the command. The variables *name* and *place* are set to John and Corvallis, respectively, and the echo command displays the values of these variables. The unset command resets *name* to null. Thus, the echo "$name" command displays a null string (a blank line).

```
$ name=John place=Corvallis
$ echo "$name $place"
John Corvallis
$ unset name
$ echo "$name"

$ echo "$place"
Corvallis
$
```

The following command removes the variables *name* and *place*.

```
$ unset name place
$
```

Another way to reset a variable is to assign it explicitly a null value by assigning it no value and simply hitting <Enter> after the = sign, as in

```
$ country=
$ echo "$country"

$
```

15.3.5   Creating Read-Only Defined Variables

When programming, you sometimes need to use constants. You can use **literal constants**, but using **symbolic constants** is good programming practice, primarily because it makes your code more readable. Another reason for using symbolic names is that a constant used at various places in code might need to be changed. With a symbolic constant, the change is made at one place only, but a literal constant must be changed every place it was used. A symbolic constant can be created in the Bourne shell by initializing a variable with the desired value and making it read-only by using the `readonly` command. This command is rarely used in shell scripts, but we discuss it briefly for the sake of complete coverage of shell variables. The following is a brief description of the command.

---

readonly [name-list]

Purpose: Prevent assignment of new values to the variables in 'name-list'

SYNTAX

In the following session, the *name* and *place* variables are made read-only after initializing them with John and Ames, respectively. Once they have become read-only, assignment to either variable fails.

```
$ name=Jim
$ place=Ames
$ readonly name place
$ echo "$name $place"
John Ames
$ name=Art place="Ann Arbor"
place: is read only
$ name=Art
name: is read only
$
```

When the `readonly` command is executed without arguments, it displays all read-only variables and their values. In the following session, note that *LOGNAME* is a shell environment variable whose value is the login name of the owner of the account, and it makes sense to keep it a read-only variable. The variables *name* and *place* are user-defined read-only variables created in the preceding session.

```
$ readonly
LOGNAME=msarwar
name=Jim
place=Ames
$
```

15.3.6 Reading from Standard Input

So far, we have shown how you can assign values to shell variables statically at the command line level or by using the assignment statement in your programs. If you want to write an interactive shell script that prompts the user for keyboard input, you need to use the `read` command to store the user input in a shell variable. This command allows you to read one line of standard input. The following is a brief description of the command.

SYNTAX

read variable-list

Purpose: Read one line from standard input and assign words in the line to variables in 'name-list'

A line is read in the form of words separated by white spaces (`<space>` or `<Tab>` characters, depending on the value of the shell environment variable *IFS*). The words are assigned to the variables in the order of their occurrence, from left to right. If the number of words in the line is greater than the number of variables in 'variable-list', the last variable is assigned the extra words. If the number of words in a line is less than the number of variables, the remaining variables are reset to null.

We illustrate the semantics of the `read` command by way of the following script in the read_demo file.

```
$ cat read_demo
#!/bin/sh
echo "Enter input: \c"
read line
echo "You entered: $line"
echo "Enter another line: \c"
read word1 word2 word3
echo "The first word is: $word1"
echo "The second word is: $word2"
echo "The rest of the line is: $word3"
exit 0
$
```

We now show how the input that you enter from the keyboard is read by the `read` command in that script. In the following run, you enter the same input: `UNIX rules the network computing world!` (you can never overemphasize the power of UNIX). The first `read` command takes the whole input and puts it in the shell variable *line* without the newline character. In the second `read` command, the first word of your input is assigned to the variable *word1*, the second word is assigned to the variable *word2*, and the rest of the line (without the newline character) is assigned to the variable *word3*. The outputs of the echo commands for displaying the values of these variables confirm this point.

```
$ read_demo
Enter input: UNIX rules the network computing world!
You entered: UNIX rules the network computing world!
Enter another line: UNIX rules the network computing world!
The first word is: UNIX
The second word is: rules
The rest of the line is: the network computing world!
$
```

The \c character at the end of the two echo commands that prompt your input is a **special character**, which is used to force the cursor to stay at the same line after you hit <Enter>. If you do not use this character, the cursor moves to the next line, which is what you like to see happen while displaying information and error messages. However, when you prompt the user for keyboard input, you should keep the cursor in front of the prompt for a more user-friendly interface. Several other special characters can be used in the echo command. These characters along with their meanings are listed in Table 15.3. Note that on some UNIX systems, you may have to use double backslash (\\ ) instead of single backslash for the special characters to work. For example, use \\c instead of \c to keep the cursor on the same line.

The BSD version of the echo command supports only the –n option for suppressing the newline character, thus displaying a line without moving the cursor to the next line. Standard ASCII control sequences can be used to display other special characters, such as <^H> for backspace and <^G> for bell. The System V version of the echo command also supports these control sequences.

In the following In-Chapter Exercises, you will use the read and export commands to practice reading from stdin in shell scripts and exporting variables to child processes.

IN-CHAPTER EXERCISES

15.5 Give commands for reading a value into the *myname* variable from the keyboard and exporting it so that commands executed in any child shell have access to the variable.

15.6 Copy the value *myname* variable to another variable, *anyname*. Make the *anyname* variable readonly and unset both the *myname* and *anyname* variables. What happened? Show all your work.

15.4 Passing Arguments to Shell Scripts

In this section, we describe how command line arguments can be passed to shell scripts and manipulated by them. As we discussed in Section 15.3, you can pass command line arguments, or positional parameters, to a shell script. The values of up to the first nine of these arguments are stored in variables $1 through $9, respectively. You can use the names of these variables to refer to the values of these arguments. If the positional argument that you refer to is not passed an argument, it has a value of null. The environment variable $# contains the total number of arguments passed in an execution of a script. The variables $* and $@ both contain the values of all of the arguments, but $@ has each individual argument in quotes if it is used as "$@". The variable name $0 contains the name of the script file (the command name). The shell script in the cmdargs_demo file shows how you can use these variables.

■■ **TABLE 15.3** Special Characters for the echo Command*

Character	Meaning
\b	Backspace
\c	Prints line without moving cursor to next line
\f	Form feed
\n	Newline (move cursor to next line)
\r	Carriage return
\t	Horizontal tab
\v	Vertical tab
\\	Backslash (escape special meaning of backslash)
\0N	Character whose ASCII number is octal N

* You might have to use \\ instead of \ on some UNIX systems.

```
$ cat cmdargs_demo
#!/bin/sh
echo "The command name is: $0."
echo "The number of command line arguments passed as parameters are $#."
echo "The value of the command line arguments are: $1 $2 $3 $4 $5 $6 $7 $8 $9."
echo "Another way to display values of all of the arguments: $@."
echo "Yet another way is: $*."
exit 0
$ cmdargs_demo a b c d e f g h i
The command name is: cmdargs_demo.
The number of command line arguments passed as parameters are 9.
The value of the command line arguments are: a b c d e f g h i.
Another way to display values of all of the arguments: a b c d e f g h i.
Yet another way is: a b c d e f g h i.
$ cmdargs_demo One Two 3 Four 5 6
The command name is: cmdargs_demo.
The number of command line arguments passed as parameters are 6.
The value of the command line arguments are: One Two 3 Four 5 6 .
Another way to display values of all of the arguments: One Two 3 Four 5 6.
```

```
Yet another way is: One Two 3 Four 5 6.
$
```

Although the shell maintains as many as nine command line arguments at a time, you can write scripts that take more than nine arguments. To do so, use the `shift` command. By default, the command shifts the command line arguments to the left by one position, making *$2* become *$1*, *$3* become *$2*, and so on. The first argument, *$1*, is shifted out. Once shifted, the arguments cannot be restored to their original values. The number of positions to be shifted can be more than one and specified as an argument to the command. The following is a brief description of the command.

---

shift [N]

Purpose: Shift the command line arguments *N* positions to the left

SYNTAX

The script in the shift_demo file shows the semantics of the `shift` command. The first `shift` command shifts the first argument out and the remaining arguments to the left by one position. The second `shift` command shifts the current arguments to the left by three positions. The three `echo` commands are used to display the current value of the program name (*$0*), the values of all positional parameters (*$@*), and the values of the first three positional parameters, respectively. The results of execution of the script are obvious.

```
$ cat shift_demo
#!/bin/sh
echo "The program name is $0."
echo "The arguments are: $@"
echo "The first three arguments are: $1 $2 $3"
shift
echo "The program name is $0."
echo "The arguments are: $@"
echo "The first three arguments are: $1 $2 $3"
shift 3
echo "The program name is $0."
echo "The arguments are: $@"
echo "The first three arguments are: $1 $2 $3"
exit 0
$ shift_demo 1 2 3 4 5 6 7 8 9 10 11 12
The program name is shift_demo.
The arguments are: 1 2 3 4 5 6 7 8 9 10 11 12
The first three arguments are: 1 2 3
The program name is shift_demo.
```

```
The arguments are: 2 3 4 5 6 7 8 9 10 11 12
The first three arguments are: 2 3 4
The program name is shift_demo.
The arguments are: 5 6 7 8 9 10 11 12
The first three arguments are: 5 6 7
$
```

The values of positional arguments can be altered by using the set command. The most effective use of this command is in conjunction with command substitution. The following is a brief description of the command.

SYNTAX

set [options][argument-list]

Purpose: Set values of the positional arguments to the arguments in 'argument-list'; when executed without an argument, the set command displays names of all shell variables and their current values (as shown in Section 15.3)

The following session involves a simple interactive use of the set command. The date command is executed to show that the output has six fields. The set `date` command sets the positional parameters to the output of the date command. In particular, $1 is set to Fri, $2 to May, $3 to 7, $4 to 13:26:42, $5 to PDT, and $6 to 2004. The echo "$@" command displays the values of all positional arguments. The third echo command displays the date in a commonly used form.

```
$ date
Fri May 7 13:26:42 PDT 2004
$ set `date`
$ echo "$@"
Fri May 7 13:26:42 PDT 2004
$ echo "$2 $3, $6"
May 7, 2004
$
```

An option commonly used with the set command is − −. It is used to inform the set command that, if the first argument starts with a−, it should not be considered an option for the set command. The script in set_demo shows another use of the command. When the script is run with a file argument, it generates a line that contains the file name, the file's inode number, and the file size (in bytes). Note that on some systems, the size variable needs to be set to $5. The set command is used to assign the output of the ls -il command as the new values of the positional arguments $1 through $9. If you do not remember the format of the output of the ls -il command, we suggest you run this command on a file before studying the code. The special character \t in the first and third echo commands is used to display a <Tab> character.

```
$ cat set_demo
#!/bin/sh
filename="$1"
set `ls -il $filename`
inode="$1"
size="$6"
echo "Name\tInode\tSize"
echo
echo "$filename\t$inode\t$size"
exit 0
$ set_demo lab3
Name    Inode      Size

lab3    856110     591
$
```

> **Warning:** strange results show up if `lab3` is not there. Also, if your system produces output like the following for the `ls` command, you need to insert the `shift 4` command before the `inode="$1"` command.
>
> ```
> $ ls -il set_demo
> total 4
> total 4
>     1014337 -rwxr-xr-x   1 msarwar   faculty     138 May 20 22:46 set_demo
> $
> ```

In the following In-Chapter Exercises, you will use the `set` and `shift` commands to reinforce the use of command line arguments and their processing.

IN-CHAPTER EXERCISES ━━━━━━━━━━━━━━━━━━━━━━━━━━━━

15.7   Write a shell script that displays all command line arguments, shifts them to the left by two positions, and redisplays them. Show the script along with a few sample runs.

15.8   Update the shell script in Exercise 15.7 so that, after accomplishing the original task, it sets the positional arguments to the output of the `who | head -1` command and displays the positional arguments again.

15.5   Comments and Program Headers

You should develop the habit of putting **comments** in your programs to describe the purpose of a particular series of commands. At times, you should even briefly describe the purpose of a variable or assignment statement. Also, you should use a **program header** for every shell script that you write. These are simply good software engineering practices. Program headers and comments help a programmer who has been assigned the task of modifying or enhancing your code to understand it quickly. They also help you understand your own code, in particular if you reread it after some period of time. Programs written long ago, when putting comments in the program code or creating separate documentation for programs was not a common practice, are very difficult to understand and enhance. These programs are commonly known as **legacy code**.

A good program header must contain at least the following items. In addition, you can insert any other items that you believe to be important or are commonly used in your organization or group as part of its **coding rules**.

1. Name of the file containing the script
2. Name of the author
3. Date written
4. Date last modified
5. Purpose of the script (in one or two lines)
6   A brief description of the algorithm used to implement the solution to the problem at hand

A comment line (including every line in the program header) must start with the number sign (#), as in,

```
# This is a comment line.
```

However, a comment does not have to start at a new line; it can follow a command, as in,

```
set -- `ls -l lab1`    # Assign new values to positional parameters and
                       # if the first argument starts with a -, do not
                       # consider it an option for the set command.
                       # This is to handle the output of the ls -l
                       # command if lab1 is an ordinary file.
```

The following is a sample header for the set_demo script.

```
# File Name:            ~/Bourne/examples/set_demo
# Author:               Syed Mansoor Sarwar
# Date Written:         August 10, 1999
# Date Last Modified:   May 21, 2004
# Purpose:              To illustrate how the set command works
# Brief Description:    The script runs with a filename as the only command
#                       line argument, saves the filename, runs the set
#                       command to assign output of ls -il command to
#                       positional arguments ($1 through $9), and displays
#                       file name, its inode number, and its size in bytes.
```

We do not show the program headers for all the sample scripts in this textbook for the sake of brevity.

15.6   Program Control Flow Commands

The program control flow commands/statements are used to determine the sequence in which statements in a shell script execute. There are three basic types of statements for controlling the flow of a script: two-way branching, multiway branching, and repetitive execution of one or more commands. The Bourne shell statement for two-way branching is the `if` statement, the statements for multiway branching are the `if` and `case` statements, and the statements for repetitive execution of some code are the `for`, `while`, and `until` statements.

15.6.1 The `if-then-elif-else-fi` Statement

The most basic form of the `if` statement is used for two-way branching, but the statement can also be used for multiway branching. The following is a brief description of the statement. The words in monospace type are called keywords and must be used as shown in the syntax. Everything in brackets is optional. All the command lists are designed to enable you to accomplish the task at hand.

```
if expression
    then
        [elif expression
        then
            then-command-list]
        ...
        [else
            else-command-list]
fi
```

Purpose: To implement two-way or multiway branching

Here, an 'expression' is a list of commands. The execution of commands in 'expression' returns a status of true (success) or false (failure). We discuss three versions of the `if` statement that together comprise the statement's complete syntax and semantics. The first version of the `if` statement is without any optional features, which results in the syntax for the statement that is commonly used for two-way branching.

```
if expression
    then
            then-commands
fi
```

Purpose: To implement two-way branching

If 'expression' is true, the 'then-commands' are executed; otherwise, the command after `fi` is executed. The semantics of the statement are illustrated in Figure 15.1.

The 'expression' can be evaluated with the `test` command. It evaluates an expression and returns true or false. The command has two syntaxes: One uses the keyword `test` and the other uses brackets. The following is a brief description of the command.

SYNTAX

test [expression]
Or
[[expression]]

Purpose: To evaluate 'expression' and return true or false status

---

An important point about this second syntax is that normal brackets indicate an optional expression and that bold brackets are required because they comprise the test statement. Also, at least one space is required before and after an operator, a parenthesis, a bracket, or an operand. If you need to continue a test expression to the next line, you must use a backslash (\ ) before hitting <Enter> so that the shell does not treat the next line as a separate command. (Recall that \ is a shell metacharacter.) We demonstrate use of the `test` command in the first session but then use the simpler syntax of [ ].

The `test` command supports many operators for testing files and integers, testing and comparing strings, and logically connecting two or more expressions to form complex expressions. Table 15.4 describes the meanings of the operators supported by the `test` command on most UNIX systems.

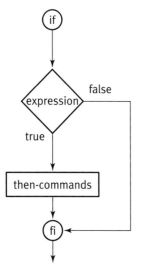

Figure 15.1 Semantics of the `if-then-fi` statement

TABLE 15.4 Operators for the `test` Command

File Testing		Integer Testing		String Testing	
Expression	**Return Value**	**Expression**	**Return Value**	**Expression**	**Return Value**
`-d file`	True if 'file' is a directory	`int1 -eq int2`	True if 'int1' and 'int2' are equal	`str`	True if 'str' is not an empty string
`-f file`	True if 'file' is an ordinary file	`int1 -ge int2`	True if 'int1' is greater than or equal to 'int2'	`str1 = str2`	True if 'str1' and 'str2' are the same
`-r file`	True if 'file' is readable	`int1 -gt int2`	True if 'int1' is greater than 'int2'	`str1 != str2`	True if 'str1' and 'str2' are not the same
`-s file`	True if length of 'file' is nonzero	`int1 -le int2`	True if 'int1' is less than or equal to 'int2'	`-n str`	True if the length of 'str' is greater than zero
`-t [filedes]`	True if file descriptor 'filedes' associated with the terminal	`int1 -lt int2`	True if 'int1' is less than 'int2'	`-z str`	True if the length of 'str' is zero
`-w file`	True if 'file' is writable	`int1 -ne int2`	True if 'int1' is not equal to 'int2'		
`-x file`	True if 'file' is executable				

Operators for Forming Complex Expressions			
`!`	Logical NOT operator: true if the following expression is false	`('expression')`	Parentheses for grouping expressions; at least one space before and one after each parenthesis
`-a`	Logical AND operator: true if the previous (left) and next (right) expressions are true	`-o`	Logical OR operator: true if the previous (left) or next (right) expression is true

We use the `if` statement to modify the script in the set_demo file so that it takes one command line argument only and checks on whether the argument is a file or a directory. The script returns an error message if the script is run with no or more than one command line argument or if the command line argument is not an ordinary file. The name of the script file is if_demo1.

```
$ cat if_demo1
#!/bin/sh
if test $# -eq 0
    then
            echo "Usage: $0 ordinary_file"
            exit 1
fi
if test $# -gt 1
    then
            echo "Usage: $0 ordinary_file"
            exit 1
fi
if test -f "$1"
    then
            filename="$1"
            set `ls -il $filename`
```
Figure X.X
```
            inode="$1"
            size="$6"
            echo "Name\tInode\tSize"
            echo
            echo "$filename\t$inode\t$size"
            exit 0
fi
echo "$0: argument must be an ordinary file"
exit 1
$ if_demo1
Usage: if_demo1 ordinary_file
$ if_demo1 lab3 lab4
Usage: if_demo1 ordinary_file
$ if_demo1 dir1
if_demo1: argument must be an ordinary file
$ if_demo1 lab3
Name      Inode     Size

lab3      856110     591
$
```

In the preceding script, the first `if` statement displays an error message and exits the program if you run the script without any command line argument. The second `if` statement displays an error message and exits the program if you run the script with more than one argument. The third `if` statement is executed if conditions for the first two are false—that is, if you run the script with one argument only. This `if` statement produces the desired results if the command line argument is an ordinary file. If the passed argument is not an ordinary file, the condition for the third `if` statement is false and the error message `if_demo1: argument must be an ordinary file` is displayed. Note that the exit status of the script is 1 when it exits because of an erroneous condition and 0 when the script executes successfully and produces the desired results.

An important practice in script writing is to correctly indent the commands/statements in it. Proper indentation of programs enhances their readability and makes them easier to understand and upgrade. Note the indentation style used in our sample scripts and follow it when you write your own scripts.

We now discuss the second version of the `if` statement, which also allows two-way branching. The following is a brief description of the statement.

---

if expression
    then
        then-command
    else
        else-command
fi

Purpose: To implement two-way branching

SYNTAX

If 'expression' is true, the commands in 'then-commands' are executed; otherwise, the commands in 'else-commands' are executed, followed by the execution of the command after `fi`. The semantics of the statement are depicted in Figure 15.2.

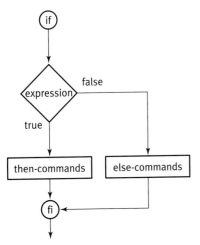

Figure 15.2 Semantics of the `if-then-else-fi` statement

Next, we rewrite the if_demo1 program, using the `if-then-else-fi` statement, and use the alternative syntax for the `test` command. The resulting script is in the if_demo2 file, as shown in the following session. Note that the program looks cleaner and more readable.

```
$ cat if_demo2
#!/bin/sh
if [ $# -eq 0 ]
   then
       echo "Usage: $0 ordinary_file"
       exit 1
fi
if [ $# -gt 1 ]
   then
       echo "Usage: $0 ordinary_file"
       exit 1
fi
if [ -f "$1" ]
   then
       filename="$1"
       set `ls -il $filename`
       inode="$1"
       size="$6"
       echo "Name\tInode\tSize"
       echo
       echo "$filename\t$inode\t$size"
       exit 0
   else
       echo "$0: argument must be an ordinary file"
       exit 1
fi
$
```

Finally, we discuss the third version of the `if` statement, which is used to implement multiway branching. The following is a brief description of the statement.

if expression1
   then
      then-commands
   elif expression2
      elif1-commands

(continued)

---

if expression1 (continued)

elif expression3
    elif2-commands

  ...

  else
    else-command
fi

Purpose: To implement multiway branching

If 'expression1' is true, the commands in 'then-commands' are executed. If 'expression1' is false, 'expression2' is evaluated, and if it is true, the commands in 'elif1-commands' are executed. If 'expression2' is false, 'expression3' is evaluated. If 'expression3' is true, 'elif2-commands' are executed. If 'expression3' is also false, the commands in 'else-commands' are executed. The execution of any command list is followed by the execution of the command after `fi`. You can use any number of `elif`s in an `if` statement to implement multiway branching. The semantics of the statement are depicted in Figure 15.3.

We modify the script in the if_demo file so that, if the command line argument is a directory, the program displays the number of files and subdirectories in the directory, excluding hidden files. In addition, the program ensures that the command line argument is an existing file or directory in the current directory before processing it. We also use the `if-then-elif-else-fi` statement in the implementation. The resulting script is in the if_demo3 file, as shown in the following session.

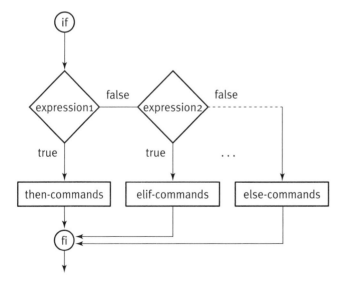

Figure 15.3 Semantics of the `if-then-elif-else-fi` statement

```
$ cat if_demo3
#!/bin/sh
if [ $# -eq 0 ]
    then
        echo "Usage: $0 file"
        exit 1
    elif [ $# -gt 1 ]
    then
        echo "Usage: $0 file"
        exit 1
    elif [ -d "$1" ]
        then
            nfiles=`ls "$1" | wc -w`
            echo "The number of files in the directory is $nfiles"
            exit 0
    else
        ls "$1" 2> /dev/null | grep "$1" 2> /dev/null 1>&2
        if [ $? -ne 0 ]
        then
            echo "$1: not found"
            exit 1
        fi
        if [ -f "$1" ]
            then
                filename="$1"
                set `ls -il $filename`
                # Please see the warning at the end of section 15.4
                shift 4
                inode="$1"
                size="$6"
                echo "Name\tInode\tSize"
                echo
                echo "$filename\t$inode\t$size"
                exit 0
            else
                echo "$0: argument must be an ordinary file or directory"
                exit 1
        fi
fi
```

```
$ if_demo3 /bin/ls
Name      Inode     Size


/bin/ls   50638     18844
$ if_demo3 file1
file1: not found
$ if_demo3 dir1
The number of files in the directory is 4
$ if_demo3 lab3
Name      Inode        Size


lab3      856110       591
$
```

If the argument is a directory, the number of files in it (including directories and hidden files) is saved in the *nfiles* variable. The command ls "$1" 2> /dev/null | grep "$1" 2> /dev/null 1>&2 is executed to check whether the file passed as the command line argument exists. The standard error is redirected to /dev/null (the UNIX black hole), and standard output is redirected to standard error by using 1>&2. Thus, the command does not produce any output or error messages; its only purpose is to set the command's return status value in $?. If the command line argument exists, the ls command is successful and $? contains 0; otherwise, it contains a nonzero value. If the command line argument is a file, the required file-related data is displayed. Note the use of command substitution.

In the following In-Chapter Exercises, you will practice the use of the if statement, command substitution, and manipulation of positional parameters.

IN-CHAPTER EXERCISES ━━━━━━━━━━━━━━━━━━━━━━━━━━━━━━━━━━━━

15.9 Create the if_demo2 script file and run it with no argument, more than one argument, and one argument only. While running the script with one argument, use a directory as the argument. What happens? Does the output make sense?

15.10 Write a shell script whose single command line argument is a file. If you run the program with an ordinary file, the program displays the owner's name and last update time for the file. If the program is run with more than one argument, it generates meaningful error messages.

15.6.2 The **for** Statement

The for statement is the first of three statements that are available in Bourne shell for repetitive execution of a block of commands in a shell script. These statements are commonly known as **loops**. The following is a brief description of the statement.

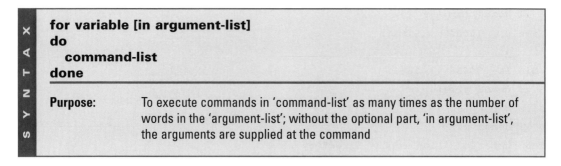

for variable [in argument-list]
do
   command-list
done

Purpose: To execute commands in 'command-list' as many times as the number of words in the 'argument-list'; without the optional part, 'in argument-list', the arguments are supplied at the command

The words in 'argument-list' are assigned to 'variable' one by one, and the commands in 'command-list', also known as the body of the loop, are executed for every assignment. This process allows the execution of commands in 'commandlist' as many times as the number of words in 'argument-list'. Figure 15.4 illustrates the semantics of the for command.

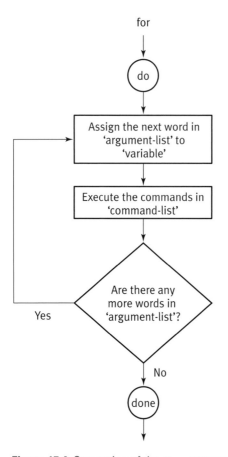

Figure 15.4 Semantics of the for statement

The following script in the for_demo1 file shows use of the `for` command with optional arguments. The variable *people* is assigned the words in 'argumentlist' one by one, and each time the value of the variable is echoed until no word remains in the list. At that time, control comes out of the `for` statement, and the command following done is executed. Then the code following the `for` statement (the exit statement only in this case) is executed.

```
$ cat for_demo1
#!/bin/sh
for people in Debbie Jamie John Kitty Kuhn Shah
do
    echo "$people"
done
exit 0
$ for_demo1
Debbie
Jamie
John
Kitty
Kuhn
Shah
$
```

The following script in the user_info file takes a list of existing (valid) login names as command line arguments and displays each login name and the full name of the user who owns the login name, one per login. In the sample run, the first value of the user variable is dheckman. The echo command displays dheckman: followed by a <Tab>, and the cursor stays at the current line. The grep command searches the /etc/passwd file for the login name dheckman and pipes it to the cut command, which displays the fifth field in the /etc/passwd line for dheckman (his full name). The process is repeated for the remaining two login names (ghacker and msarwar). No user is left in the list passed at the command line, so control comes out of the `for` statement and the `exit 0` command is executed to transfer control back to shell. The command substitution "^"`echo $user":"` in the grep command can be replaced by "^"$user":".

```
$ cat user_info
#!/bin/sh
for user
do
# Don't display anything if a login name is not found in /etc/passwd
grep "^"`echo $user":"` /etc/passwd 1> /dev/null 2>&1
if [ $? -eq 0 ]
    echo "$user:\t\c"
```

```
          grep "^"`echo $user":"` /etc/passwd | cut -f5 -d':'
    fi
    done
    exit 0
    $ user_info dheckman ghacker msarwar
    dheckman:  Dennis R. Heckman
    ghacker:   George Hacker
    msarwar:   Mansoor Sarwar
    $
```

15.6.3 The `while` Statement

The `while` statement, also known as the `while` loop, allows repeated execution of a block of code based on the condition of an expression. The following is a brief description of the statement.

SYNTAX
while expression **do**   **command-list** **done**
Purpose: To execute commands in 'command-list' as long as 'expression' evaluates to true

The 'expression' is evaluated and, if the result of this evaluation is true, the commands in 'command-list' are executed and 'expression' is evaluated again. This sequence of expression evaluation and execution of 'command-list', known as one **iteration**, is repeated until the 'expression' evaluates to false. At that time, control comes out of the `while` statement and the statement following `done` is executed. Figure 15.5 depicts the semantics of the `while` statement.

The variables and/or conditions in the expression that result in a true value must be correctly manipulated in the commands in 'command-list' for well-behaved loops—that is, loops that eventually terminate and allow execution of the rest of the code in a script. Loops in which the expression always evaluates to true are known as **nonterminating**, or **infinite**, **loops**. Infinite loops, usually a result of poor design and/or programming, are bad because they continuously use CPU time without accomplishing any useful task. However, some applications do require infinite loops. For example, all the servers for Internet services such as ftp are programs that run indefinitely, waiting for client requests. Once a server has received a client request, it processes it, sends a response to the client, and waits for another client request. The only way to terminate a process with an infinite loop is to kill it by using the `kill` command. Or, if the process is running in the foreground, pressing <Ctrl-C> would also do the trick, unless the process is designed to ignore <Ctrl-C>. In that case, you need to put the process in the background by pressing <Ctrl-Z> and use the `kill -9` command to terminate it.

The script in the while_demo file shows a simple use of the `while` loop. When you run this script, the *secretcode* variable is initialized to agent007 and you are prompted to make a

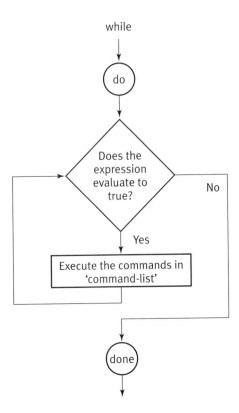

Figure 15.5 Semantics of the `while` statement

guess. Your guess is stored in a local variable *yourguess*. If your guess is not agent007, the condition for the `while` loop is true and the commands between `do` and `done` are executed. This program displays a message tactfully informing you of your failure and prompts you for another guess. Your guess is again stored in the *yourguess* variable, and the condition for the loop is tested. This process continues until you enter agent007 as your guess. This time, the condition for the loop becomes false and the control comes out of the `while` statement. The echo command following `done` executes, congratulating you for being part of a great gene pool!

```
$ cat while_demo
#!/bin/sh
secretcode=agent007
echo "Guess the code!"
echo "Enter your guess: \c"
read yourguess
while [ "$secretcode" != "$yourguess" ]
do
    echo "Good guess but wrong. Try again!"
```

```
    echo "Enter your guess: \c"
    read yourguess
done
echo "Wow! You are a genius!!"
exit 0
$ while_demo
Guess the code!
Enter your guess: star wars
Good guess but wrong. Try again!
Enter your guess: columbo
Good guess but wrong. Try again!
Enter your guess: agent007
Wow! You are a genius!!
$
```

15.6.4 The until Statement

The syntax of the until statement is similar to that of the while statement, but its semantics are different. Whereas in the while statement the loop body executes as long as the expression evaluates to true, in the until statement the loop body executes as long as the expression evaluates to false. The following is a brief description of the statement.

S Y N T A X	**until expression** **do** **command-list** **done**
	Purpose: To execute commands in 'command-list' as long as 'expression' evaluates to false

Figure 15.6 illustrates the semantics of the until statement. The code in the until_demo file performs the same task that the script in the while_demo file does (*see* Section 15.6.3), but it uses the until statement instead of the while statement. Thus, the code between do and done (the loop body) is executed for as long as your guess is not agent007.

```
$ cat until_demo
#!/bin/sh
secretcode=agent007
echo "Guess the code!"
echo "Enter your guess: \c"
read yourguess
until [ "$secretcode" = "$yourguess" ]
```

```
do
      echo "Good guess but wrong. Try again!"
      echo "Enter your guess: \c"
      read yourguess
done
echo "Wow! You are a genius!!"
exit 0
$ until_demo
Guess the code!
Enter your guess: Inspector Gadget
Good guess but wrong. Try again!
Enter your guess: Peter Sellers
Good guess but wrong. Try again!
Enter your guess: agent007
Wow! You are a genius!!
$
```

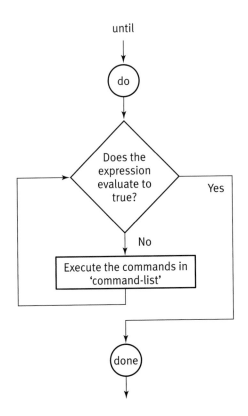

Figure 15.6 Semantics of the until statement

15.6.5 The **break** and **continue** Commands

The break and continue commands can be used to interrupt the sequential execution of the loop body. The break command transfers control to the command following done, thus terminating the loop prematurely. The continue command transfers control to done, which results in the evaluation of the condition again and hence, continuation of the loop. In both cases, the commands in the loop body following these statements are not executed. Thus, they are typically part of a conditional statement such as an if statement. Figure 15.7 illustrates the semantics of these commands.

In the following In-Chapter Exercises, write shell scripts with loops by using the for, while, and until statements.

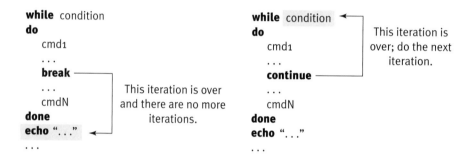

Figure 15.7 Semantics of the break and continue commands

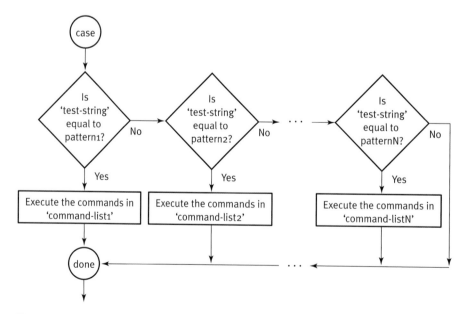

Figure 15.8 Semantics of the case statement

IN-CHAPTER EXERCISES

15.11   Write a shell script that takes a list of host names on your network as command line arguments and displays whether the hosts are up or down. Use the `ping` command to display the status of a host and the `for` statement to process all host names.

15.12   Rewrite the script in Exercise 15.11, using the `while` statement. Rewrite it again, using the `until` statement.

15.6.6 The `case` Statement

The `case` statement provides a mechanism for multiway branching similar to a nested `if` statement. However, the structure provided by the `case` statement is more readable. You should use the `case` statement whenever nesting of an `if` statement becomes deeper than three levels (i.e., you are using three `elif`s). The following is a brief description of the statement.

```
case test-string in
    pattern1)   command-list1
                ;
    pattern2)   command-list2
                ;;

    ...
    patternN)   command-listN
                ;;
esac
```

| **Purpose:** | To implement multiway branching like a nested `if` |

The `case` statement compares the value in 'test-string' with the values of all the patterns one by one until either a match is found or no more patterns with which to match 'test-string' remain. If a match is found, the commands in the corresponding 'command-list' are executed and control goes out of the `case` statement. If no match is found, control goes out of `case`. However, in a typical use of the `case` statement, a wild card pattern matches any value of 'test-string'. Also known as the *default case*, it allows execution of a set of commands to handle an exception (error) condition for situations in which the value in 'test-string' does not match any pattern. Back-to-back semicolons (`;;`) are used to delimit a 'commandlist'. Without `;;` the first command in the command list for the next pattern is executed, resulting in unexpected behavior by the program. Figure 15.8 depicts the semantics of the `case` statement.

The following script in the case_demo file shows a simple but representative use of the `case` statement. It is a menu-driven program that displays a menu of options and prompts you to enter an option. Your option is read into a variable called *option*. The `case` statement then matches your option with one of the four available patterns (single characters in this case) one by one, and when a match is found, the corresponding 'command-list' (a single command in this case) is executed. Thus, at the prompt, if you type d and hit `<Enter>`, the date command is executed and control goes out of `case`. Then, the program exits after the `exit 0` command executes. A few sample runs of the script follow the code in this session.

```
$ cat case_demo
#!/bin/sh
echo "Use one of the following options:"
echo "    d:   To display today's date and present time"
echo "    l:   To see the listing of files in your present working directory"
echo "    w:   To see who's logged in"
echo "    q:   To quit this program"
echo "Enter your option and hit <Enter>: \c"
read option
case "$option" in
        d)   date
             ;;
        l)   ls
             ;;
        w)   who
             ;;
        q)   exit 0
             ;;
esac
exit 0
$ case_demo
Use one of the following options:
        d:   To display today's date and present time
        l:   To see the listing of files in your present working directory
        w:   To see who is logged in
        q:   To quit this program
Enter your option and hit <Enter>: d
        Thu June 10 17:05:55 PDT 2004
$ case_demo
Use one of the following options:
        d:   To display today's date and present time
        l:   To see the listing of files in your present working directory
        w:   To see who is logged in
        q:   To quit this program
Enter your option and hit <Enter>: w
kuhn      console  Aug 10 10:18
sarwar    pts/0    Aug 10 16:57
$ case_demo
```

```
Use one of the following options:
         d:    To display today's date and present time
         l:    To see the listing of files in your present working directory
         w:    To see who is logged in
         q:    To quit this program
Enter your option and hit <Enter>: a
$
```

Note that, when you enter a valid option, the expected output is displayed. However, when you enter input that is not a valid option (a in the preceding session), the program does not give you any feedback. The reason is that the case statement matches your input with all the patterns, one by one, and exits when there is no match. We need to modify the script slightly so that when you enter an invalid option, the script tells you so and then terminates. To do so we add the following code.

```
    *)    echo "Invalid option; try running the program again."
          exit 1

          ;;
```

We also enhance the script so that uppercase and lowercase inputs are considered to be the same. We use the pipe symbol (|) in the patterns to specify a logical OR operation. The enhanced code and some sample runs are shown in the following session.

```
$ cat case_demo
#!/bin/sh
echo " Use one of the following options:"
echo " d or D:   To display today's date and present time"
echo " l or L:   To see the listing of files in your present working directory"
echo " w or W:   To see who's logged in"
echo " q or Q:   To quit this program"
echo "Enter your option and hit <Enter>: \c"
read option
case "$option" in
      d|D)      date
                ;;
      l|L)      ls
                ;;
      w|W)      who
                ;;
      q|Q)      exit 0
                ;;
      *)        echo "Invalid option; try running the program again."
                exit 1
```

```
                    ;;
esac
exit 0
$ case_demo
Use one of the following options:
        d or D:   To display today's date and present time
        l or L:   To see the listing of files in your present working directory
        w or W:   To see who is logged in
        q or Q:   To quit this program
Enter your option and hit <Enter>: D
Sat June 12 18:14:22 PDT 2004
$ case_demo
Use one of the following options:
        d or D:   To display today's date and present time
        l or L:   To see the listing of files in your present working directory
        w or W:   To see who is logged in
        q or Q:   To quit this program
Enter your option and hit <Enter>: a
Invalid option; try running the program again.
$
```

— Summary

Every UNIX shell has a programming language that allows you to write programs for performing tasks that cannot be performed by existing commands. These programs are commonly known as shell scripts. In its simplest form, a shell script consists of a list of shell commands that are executed by a shell one by one, sequentially. More advanced scripts contain program control flow statements for implementing multiway branching and repetitive execution of a block of commands in a script. The shell programs that consist of Bourne shell commands, statements, and features are called Bourne shell scripts.

The shell variables are main memory locations that are given names and can be read from and written to. There are two types of shell variables: environment variables and user-defined variables. The environment variables are initialized by the shell at the time of user login and are maintained by the shell to provide a nice work environment. The user-defined variables are used as scratch pads in a script to accomplish the task at hand. Some environment variables such as positional parameters are read-only in the sense that you cannot change their values without using the set command. User-defined variables can also be made read-only by using the readonly command.

The Bourne shell commands for processing shell variables are = (for assigning a value to a variable), set (for setting values of positional parameters and displaying values of all environment variables), env (for displaying values of all shell variables), export (for allowing subsequent commands to access shell variables), `read` (for assigning values to variables from the keyboard), `readonly` (for making user-defined variables read-only), `shift` (for shifting command line arguments to the left by one or more positions), `unset` (to reset the value of a read/write variable to null), and `test` (to evaluate an expression and return true or false).

The program control flow statements `if` and `case` allow the user to implement multiway branching; the `for`, `until`, and `while` statements allow the user to implement loops; and the `break` and `continue` statements allow the user to interrupt sequential execution of a loop in a script. I/O redirection can be used with control flow statements as with other shell commands (*see* Chapter 16).

Problems ————————————————

1. What is a shell script? Describe three ways of executing a shell script.

2. What is a shell variable? What is a read-only variable? How can you make a user-defined variable read-only? Give an example to illustrate your answer.

3. Which shell environment variable is used to store your search path? Change your search path interactively to include the directories ~/bin and (.). What would this change allow you to do? Why? If you want to make it a permanent change, what would you do? (See Chapter 4 if you have forgotten how to change your search path.)

4. What will be the output if the shell script read_demo in Section 15.3.6 is executed and you give * as input each time you are prompted?

5. Write a shell script that takes an ordinary file as an argument and removes the file if its size is zero. Otherwise, the script displays file's name, size, number of hard links, owner, and modify date (in this order) on one line. Your script must do appropriate error checking.

6. Write a shell script that takes a directory as a required argument and displays the name of all zero length files in it. Do appropriate error checking.

7. Write a shell script that removes all zero length ordinary files from the current directory. Do appropriate error checking.

8. Modify the script in Problem 6 so that it removes all zero length ordinary files in the directory passed as an optional argument. If you don't specify the directory argument, the script uses the present working directory as the default argument. Do appropriate error checking.

9. Run the script in if_demo2 in Section 15.6.1 with if_demo2 as its argument. Does the output make sense to you? Why or why not?

10. Write a shell script that takes a list of login names on your computer system as command line arguments and displays these login names and full names of the users who own these logins (as contained in the /etc/passwd file), one per line. If a login name is invalid (not found in the /etc/passwd file), display the login name but nothing for full name. The format of the output line is login name: user name.

11. What happens when you run a stand-alone command enclosed in backquotes (grave accents), such as `` `date` ``? Why?

12. What happens when you type the following sequence of `shell` commands?

   a. `name=date`

   b. `$name`

   c. `` `$name` ``

13. Look at your ~/.profile and /etc/profile files and list the environment variables that are exported along with their values. What is the purpose of each variable?

14. Write a Bourne shell script that takes a list of login names as its arguments and displays the number of terminals that each user is logged on to in a LAN environment.

15. Write a Bourne shell script domain2ip that takes a list of domain names as command line arguments and displays their IP addresses. Use the `nslookup` command. The following is a sample run of this program.

```
$ domain2ip up.edu redhat.com
Name: up.edu
Address: 192.220.208.9
Name: redhat.com
Address: 207.175.42.154
$
```

16. Modify the script in the case_demo file in Section 15.6.6 so that it allows you to try any number of options and quits only when you use the `q` option.

17. Write a Bourne Shell script that displays the following menu and prompts you for one-character input to invoke a menu option, as follows.

   a. List all files in the present working directory

   b. Display today's date and time

   c. Invoke shellscript for Problem 13

   d. Display whether a file is a "simple" file or a "directory"

   e. Create a backup for a file

   f. Start a telnet session

   g. Start an ftp session

   h. Exit

   Option (c) requires that you ask for a list of login names; and for options (d) and (e), insert a prompt for file names before invoking a shell command/program. For options (f) and (g), insert a prompt for a domain name (or IP address) before initiating a telnet or ftp session. The program should allow you to try any option any number of times and should quit only when you give s option **x** as input. A good programming practice for you to adopt is to build code incrementally—that is, write code for one option, test it, and then go to the next option.

Advanced Bourne Shell Programming

Objectives

- To discuss numeric data processing
- To describe how standard input of a command in a shell script can be redirected from data within the script
- To explain the signal/interrupt processing capability of the Bourne shell
- To describe how file I/O can be performed by using file descriptors and how standard files can be redirected from within a shell script
- To explain functions in the Bourne shell
- To discuss debugging of Bourne shell scripts
- To cover the commands and primitives
  `|`, `<`, `>`, `>>`, `clear`, `exec`, `expr`, `grep`, `kill`, `more`, `read`, `sort`, `stty`, `trap`

16.1 Introduction

We discuss several important, advanced features of the Bourne shell in this chapter. They include processing of numeric data, the here document, signals and signal processing, and redirection of standard files from within a shell script. We also discuss the Bourne shell's support of functions that allow the programmer to write general purpose and modular code. Finally, we describe how Bourne shell scripts can be debugged.

16.2 Numeric Data Processing

The values of all Bourne shell variables are stored as character strings. Although this feature makes symbolic data processing fun and easy, it does make numeric data processing a bit challenging. The reason is that integer data is actually stored in the form of character strings. In order to perform arithmetic and logic operations on them, you need to convert them to integers, and be sure the result is converted back to a character string for its proper storage in a shell variable. Fortunately, the Bourne shell command `expr` does the trick. The following is a brief description of the command.

expr args	
Purpose:	Evaluate the expression arguments, 'args', and send the result to standard output
Commonly used operators/features:	
`|`	Return the first expression if it is not null or 0; else return the second expression
`\&`	Return the first expression if neither is null or 0; else return 0
`=, \>, \>=,` `=` `\<, \<=, !`	Integer comparison operators: equal, greater than, greater than or equal to, less than, less than or equal to, not equal
`+, -, \*, /, %`	Integer arithmetic operators: add, subtract, multiply, integer divide (return quotient), remainder

The shell metacharacters such as * must be escaped in an expression so that they are treated literally and not as shell metacharacters. In the following session, the first `expr` command increments the value of the shell variable *var1* by 1. The second `expr` command computes the square of *var1*. The last two `echo` commands show the use of the `expr` command to perform integer division and integer remainder operations on *var1*.

```
$ var1=10
$ var1=`expr $var1 + 1`
$ echo $var1
11
$ var1=`expr $var1 \* $var1`
$ echo $var1
```

```
121
$ echo `expr $var1 / 10`
12
$ echo `expr $var1 % 10`
1
$
```

The following countup script takes an integer as a command line argument and displays the range of numbers from 1 to the given number. In the script, we use a simple while loop to display the current number (starting with 1) and then compute the next numbers, until the current number becomes greater than the target number, (which is passed as the command line argument). Note that if \c does not work on your system, use \\c instead.

```
$ cat countup
#!/bin/sh
if [ $# != 1 ]
    then
        echo "Usage: $0 integer-argument"
        exit 1
fi
target="$1"    # Set target to the number passed at the command line
current=1      # The first number to be displayed

# Loop here until the current number becomes greater than the target
while [ $current -le $target ]
do
        echo "$current \c"
        current=`expr $current + 1`
done
echo
exit 0
$ countup 5
1 2 3 4 5
$
```

The following script, addall, takes a list of integers as command line arguments and displays their sum. The while loop adds the next number in the argument list to the running sum, (which is initialized to 0), updates the count of numbers that have been added, and shifts the command line arguments left by one position. The loop then repeats until all command line arguments have been added. The sample run following the code takes the list of the first seven perfect squares and returns their sum.

```
$ cat addall
#!/usr/bin/sh
# File Name:     ~/unixbook/examples/Bshell/addall
# Author:        Syed Mansoor Sarwar
# Written:       August 18, 2004
# Modified:      August 18, 2004
# Purpose:       To demonstrate use of the expr command in processing
#                numeric data
# Brief Description:   Maintain running sum of numbers in a numeric
#                variable called sum, starting with 0. Read
#                the next integer and add it to sum. When all
#                elements have been read, stop and display the
#                answer.
# If run with no arguments, inform the user of command syntax
if [ $# = 0 ]
   then
       echo "Usage: $0 number-list"
       exit 1
fi


sum=0 Running sum initialized to 0


count=0   # Count the count of numbers passed as arguments
while [ $# != 0 ]
do
   sum=`expr $sum + $1`       # Add the next number to the running sum
   count=`expr $count + 1`    # Update count of numbers added so far
   shift                      # Shift the counted number out
done
# Display final sum
echo "The sum of the given $count numbers is $sum."
exit 0
$ addall
Usage: addall number-list
$ addall 1 4 9 16 25 36 49
The sum of the given 7 numbers is 140.
$
```

Although this example neatly explains numeric data processing, it is nothing more than an integer adding machine. We now present a more useful example that uses the UNIX file system. The fs (for files' size) file contains a script that takes a directory as an optional argument and returns the size (in bytes) of all nondirectory files in it. On some UNIX systems, running the fs command invokes xfs. If this happens on your system, change the name of this script to 'files'.

When you run the program without a command line argument, the script treats your current directory as the argument. If you specify more than one argument, the script displays an error message and terminates. When you execute it with one nondirectory argument only, again the program displays an error message and exits.

The gist of this script is the following code.

```
ls $directory | more |
while read file
do
    ...
done
```

This code generates a list of files in *directory* (with the ls command), converts the list into one file name per line list (with the more command), and reads each file name in the list (with the read command) until no file remains in the list. The read command returns true if it reads a line and returns false when it reads the eof marker. The body of the loop (the code between do and done) adds the file size to the running total if the file is an ordinary file. When no name is left in the directory list, the program displays the total space (in bytes) occupied by all nondirectory files in the directory and terminates.

If the value of the file variable is not an existing file, the [-d "$file"] expression returns false and the error message Usage: fs [directory name], as shown in a sample run below where foo is a nonexisting directory. The file="$directory"/"$file" statement is used to construct the relative path name of a file with respect to the directory specified as the command line argument. Without this, the set -- `ls -l "$file"` command will be successful only if the directory contains the name of the current directory.

```
$ cat fs
#!/bin/sh
# File Name:      ~/unixbook/examples/Bshell/fs
# Author:        Syed Mansoor Sarwar
# Written:       August 18, 2004
# Modified:      August 20, 2004; May 8, 2004
# Purpose:       To add the sizes of all the files in a directory passed as
#                command line argument
# Brief Description: Maintain running sum of file sizes in a numeric variable
#                called sum, starting with 0. Read all the file names
#                by using the pipeline of ls, more, and while commands.
```

```
#                      Get the size of the next file and add it to the running
#                      sum. Stop when all file names have been processed and
#                      display the answer.
if [ $# = 0 ]
  then
     directory="."
  elif [ $# != 1 ]
  then
     echo "Usage: $0 [directory name]"
     exit 1
  elif [ ! -d "$1" ]
  then
     echo "Usage: $0 [directory name]"
     exit 1
  else
     directory="$1"
fi
# Get file count in the given directory; for empty directory, display a
# message and quit.
file_count=`ls $directory | wc -w`    # Get count of files in directory
if [ $file_count -eq 0 ]
  then
     echo "$directory: Empty directory."
     exit 0
fi
# for each file in the directory specified, add the file size to the running
# total. The more command is used to output file names one per line so can
# read command can be used to read file names.

sum=0# Running sum initialized to 0.
ls "$directory" | more |
while read file
do
    file="$directory"/"$file"     # Store the relative path name for each file
    if [ -f "$file" ]             # If it is an ordinary file
       then                       # then
          set -- `ls -l "$file"`  # set command line arguments
          sum=`expr $sum + $4`    # Add file size to the running total.
                                  # Wrks for Solaris; change 4 to 5 on AIX
```

```
fi
# Code to decrement the file_count variable and display the final sum
# if the last file has been processed.
if [ "$file_count" -gt 1 ]  # Are more files left?
  then
     file_count=`expr $file_count - 1`
  else
     # Spell out the current directory
     if [ "$directory" = "." ]
       then
          directory="your current directory"
     fi
     echo "The size of all ordinary files in $directory is $sum bytes."
  fi
done
```

$ **fs dir1 dir2**
Usage: fs [directory name]
$ **fs foo**
Usage: fs [directory name]
$ **fs**
The size of all ordinary files in your current directory is 7587 bytes.
$ **fs .**
The size of all ordinary files in your current directory is 7587 bytes.
$ **fs ..**
The size of all ordinary files in .. is 6360521 bytes.
$ **fs ../Bshell**
The size of all ordinary files in ../Bshell is 7587 bytes.
$ **fs ~/unixbook**
The size of all ordinary files in /home/sarwar/unixbook is 6851778 bytes.
$

In the following In-Chapter Exercise, you will create a Bourne shell script that processes numeric data by using the expr command.

IN-CHAPTER EXERCISE

16.1   Create the addall script in your directory and run it with the first 10 numbers in the Fibonacci series. What is the result? Does the program produce the correct result? If you are not familiar with the Fibonacci series, see Section 18.3.

16.3 The Here Document

The **here document** feature of the Bourne shell allows you to redirect standard input of a command in a script and attach it to data in the script. Obviously, this feature works with commands that take input from standard input. The feature is used mainly to display menus, although there are some other important uses of this feature. The following is a brief description of the here document.

SYNTAX

command « [-] input_marker
... input data ...
input_marker

Purpose: To execute 'command' with its input coming from the here document—data between the input start and end markers 'input_marker'

The 'input_marker' is a word that you choose to wrap the input data in for 'command'. The closing marker must be on a line by itself and cannot be surrounded by any spaces. The command and variable substitutions are performed before the here document data is directed to the stdin of the command. Quotes can be used to prevent these substitutions or to enclose any quotes in the here document. The 'input_marker' can be enclosed in quotes to prevent any substitutions in the entire document, as in,

```
command <<'Marker'
...
'Marker'
```

A hyphen (-) after << can be used to remove leading tabs (not spaces) from the lines in the here document and the input ending marker. This feature allows the here document and the delimiting marker to conform to the indentation of the script. The following session illustrates this point.

```
while [ ... ]
do
    grep ...  <<- DIRECTORY
            John Doe ...
            ...
            Art Pohm ...
        DIRECTORY
    ...
done
```

One last, but very important point: Output and error redirections of the command that uses the here document must be specified in the command line, not following the here document ending marker. The same is true of connecting the standard output of the command with other

commands via a pipeline, as shown in the following session. Note that the grep ... <<-
DIRECTORY 2> errorfile | sort command line can be replaced by (grep ... 2> error-
file | sort) <<- DIRECTORY.

```
while [ ... ]
do
    grep ... <<- DIRECTORY 2> errorfile | sort
       John Doe ...

       ...

       Art Pohm ...
    DIRECTORY
  ...
done
```

We can illustrate the use of the here document feature with a simple instance of redirecting stdin of the cat command from the here document. The script in the heredoc_demo file
is used to display a message for the user and then send a message to the person whose e-mail
address is passed as a command line argument. In the following session, we use two here documents: one begins with << DataTag and ends with DataTag; and the other begins with
<< WRAPPER and ends with WRAPPER.

```
$ cat heredoc_demo
#!/bin/sh

cat << DataTag
This is a simple use of the here document. These data are the
input to the cat command.
DataTag

# Second example
mail -s "Weekly Meeting Reminder" $1 << WRAPPER
Hello,

This is a reminder for the weekly meeting tomorrow.

Mansoor

WRAPPER
echo "Sending mail to $1 ... done."
exit 0
$ heredoc_demo eecsfaculty
This is a simple use of the here document. These data are the
input to the cat command.
Sending mail to eecsfaculty ... done.
$
```

The following script is more useful and makes a better utilization of the here document feature. The dext (for directory expert) script maintains a directory of names, phone numbers, and e-mail addresses. The script is run with a name as a command line argument and uses the grep command to display the directory entry corresponding to the name. The -i option is used with the grep command in order to ignore the case of letters.

```
$ more dext
#!/bin/sh
if [ $# = 0 ]
    then
            echo "Usage: $0 name"
            exit 1
fi
user_input="$1"
grep -i "$user_input" << DIRECTORY
        John Doe      555.232.0000      johnd@somedomain.com
        Jenny Great   444.6565.1111     jg@new.somecollege.edu
        David Nice    999.111.3333      david_nice@xyz.org
        Don Carr      555.111.3333      dcarr@old.hoggie.edu
        Masood Shah   666.010.9820      shah@Garments.com.pk
        Jim Davis     777.000.9999      davis@great.adviser.edu
        Art Pohm      333.000.8888      art.pohm@great.professor.edu
        David Carr    777.999.2222      dcarr@net.net.gov
DIRECTORY

exit 0
$ dext
Usage: ./dext name
$ dext Pohm
        Art Pohm      333.000.8888      art.pohm@great.professor.edu
$
```

The advantage of maintaining the directory within the script is that it eliminates extra file operations such as open and read that would be required if the directory data was maintained in a separate file. The result is a much faster program.

If there are multiple entries for a name, the grep command displays all the entries. You can display the entries in sorted order by piping the output of the grep command to the sort command and enclosing them in parentheses, as in (grep -i "$user_input" | sort). We enhance the dext script in Section 16.6 to include this feature, as well as take multiple names from the command line.

The following In-Chapter Exercise is designed to reinforce your understanding of the here document feature of a Bourne shell.

16.2   Create the `dext` script on your system and run it. Try it with as many different inputs as you can think of. Does the script work correctly?

16.4   Interrupt (Signal) Processing

We discussed the basic concept of signals in Chapter 13 where we defined them as software interrupts that can be sent to a process. We also stated that there are three possible actions that the process receiving a signal can take:

1. Accept the default action as determined by the UNIX kernel,

2. Ignore the signal, or

3. Take a programmer-defined action

In UNIX, several types of signals can be sent to a running program. Some of these signals can be sent via hardware devices such as the keyboard, but all can be sent via the `kill` command, as discussed in Chapter 13. The most common event that causes a hardware interrupt (and a signal) is generated when you press <Ctrl-C> and is known as the **keyboard interrupt**. This event causes the foreground process to terminate (the default action). Other events that cause a process to receive a signal include termination of a child process, a process accessing a main memory location that is not part of its **address space** (the main memory area that the process owns and is allowed to access), and a software termination signal caused by execution of the `kill` command without any signal number. Table 16.1 presents a list of some important signals, their numbers (which can be used to generate those signals with the `kill` command), and their purpose.

■■ **TABLE 16.1** Some Important Signals, Their Numbers, and Their Purpose

Signal Name	Signal #	Purpose
SIGHUP (hang up)	1	Informs the process when the user who ran the process logs out, and the process terminates
SIGINT (keyboard interrupt)	2	Informs the process when the user presses <Ctrl-C> and the process terminates
SIGQUIT (quit signal)	3	Informs the process when the user presses <Ctrl-|> or <Ctrl-\\> and the process terminates
SIGKILL (sure kill)	9	Definitely terminates the process when the user sends this signal to it with the `kill -9` command

(continued)

TABLE 16.1 (continued)

SIGSEGV (segmentation violation)	11	Terminates the process upon memory fault when a process tries to access memory space that does not belong to it
SIGTERM (software termination)	15	Terminates the process when the `kill` command is used without any signal number
SIGTSTP (suspend/stop signal)	18	Suspends the process, usually `<Ctrl-Z>`
SIGCHLD (child finishes execution)	20	Informs the process of termination of one of its children

The interrupt processing feature of the Bourne shell allows you to write programs that can ignore signals or execute a particular sequence of commands when particular types of signals are sent to them. This feature is much more powerful than that of the C shell, which allows programs to ignore a keyboard interrupt (`<Ctrl-C>`) only (see Chapter 18). The `trap` command can be used to intercept signals. The following is a brief description of the command.

trap ['command-list'] [signal-list]

Purpose: To intercept signals specified in 'signal-list' and take default kernel-defined action, ignore the signals, or execute the commands in 'command-list'; note that quotes around 'command-list' are required

When you use the `trap` command in a script without any argument (no 'command-list' and no 'signal-list'), the default actions are taken when signals are received by the script. Thus, using the `trap` command without any argument is redundant. When the `trap` command is used without any commands in single quotes, the signals in 'signal-list' are ignored by the process. When both a 'command-list' and a 'signal-list' are specified, the commands in 'command-list' execute when a signal in 'signal-list' is received by the script.

Next, we enhance the script in the while_demo file in Chapter 15 so that you cannot terminate execution of this program with `<Ctrl-C>` (signal number 2), the `kill` command without any argument (signal number 15), or the `kill –1` command (to generate the SIGHUP signal). The enhanced version is in the trap_demo file, as shown in the following session. Note that the `trap` command is used to ignore signals 1, 2, 3, 15, and 18. A sample run illustrates this point.

```
$ more trap_demo
#!/bin/sh

# Intercept signals and ignore them
trap '' 1 2 3 15 18
```

```
# Set the secret code
secretcode=agent007
# Get user input
echo "Guess the code!"
echo "Enter your guess: \c"
read yourguess

# As long as the user input is the secret code (agent007 in this case),
# loop here: display a message and take user input again. When the user
# input matches the secret code, terminate the loop and execute the
# following echo command.
while [ "$secretcode" != "$yourguess" ]
do
    echo "Good guess but wrong. Try again!"
    echo "Enter your guess: \c"
    read yourguess
done
echo "Wow! You are a genius!"
exit 0
$ trap_demo
Guess the code!
Enter your guess: codecracker
Good guess but wrong. Try again!
Enter your guess: <Ctrl-C>
Good guess but wrong. Try again!
Enter your guess: agent007
Wow! You are a genius!
$
```

To terminate programs that ignore terminal interrupts, you have to use the `kill` command. You can do so by suspending the process by pressing <Ctrl-Z>, using the `ps` command to get the PID of the process, and terminating it with the `kill` command.

You can modify the script in the trap_demo file so that it ignores signals 1, 2, 3, 15, and 18, clears the display screen, and turns off the echo. Whatever input you enter from the keyboard, then, is not displayed. Next, it prompts you for the code word twice. If you do not enter the same code word both times, it reminds you of your bad short-term memory and quits. If you enter the same code word, it clears the display screen and prompts you to guess the code word again. If you do not enter the original code word, the display screen is cleared and you are prompted to guess again. The program does not terminate until you have entered the original code word. When you do enter it, the display screen is cleared, a message is displayed at the top left of the screen, and echo is turned on. Because the terminal interrupt is ignored, you cannot terminate the program by pressing <Ctrl-C>. The stty -echo command turns off the echo. Thus when you type the original code word (or any guesses), it is not displayed on the screen. The clear command clears the display screen and positions the cursor at the top-left corner. The stty echo command turns on the echo. The resulting script is in the canleave file, as shown in the following session.

```
$ more canleave
#!/bin/sh

# Ignore signals 1, 2, 3, 15, and 18
trap '' 1 2 3 15 18

# Clear the screen, locate the cursor at the top-left corner,
# and turn off echo
clear
stty -echo

# Set the secret code
echo -n "Enter your code word:"
read secretcode
echo " "

# To make sure that the user remembers the code word
echo -n "Enter your code word again:"
read same
echo " "
if [ $secretcode != $same ]
   then
       echo "Work on your short-term memory before using this code!"
       exit 1
fi
# Get user guess
clear
echo -n "Enter the code word:"
read yourguess
echo " "

# As long as the user input is not the original code word, loop here: display
# a message and take user input again. When the user input matches the secret
# code word, terminate the loop and execute the following echo command.
while [ "$secretcode" != "$yourguess" ]
```

```
do
  clear
  echo -n "Enter the code word:
  read yourguess
done
# Set terminal to echo mode
clear
echo "Back again!"
stty echo
exit 0
$
```

You can use this script to lock your terminal before you leave it to pick up a printout (or get a can of soda); hence, the name canleave (can leave). Using it saves you the time otherwise required for the logout and login procedures.

The following In-Chapter Exercise is designed to reinforce your understanding of the signal handling feature of a Bourne shell.

IN-CHAPTER EXERCISE

16.3   Test the scripts in the trap_demo and canleave files on your UNIX system. Do they work as expected? Be sure that you understand them.

16.5   The **exec** Command and File I/O

The **exec** command is the command-level version of the UNIX loader. Although it is normally used to execute a command instead of the current shell without creating a new process, (it overwrites the current shell with the code of the command to be executed), the **exec** command is used for two distinct purposes:

1. To execute a command/program instead of the current process (under which **exec** is executed, usually a shell), and
2. To open and close file descriptors

When the **exec** command is used in conjunction with the redirection operators, it allows commands and shell scripts to read/write any type of files, including devices. In this section, we describe both uses of this command but focus primarily on the second use.

16.5.1 Execution of a Command Without Creating a New Process

The **exec** command can be used to run a command instead of the process (usually a shell) that executes this command. It works with all shells. The following is a brief description of the command.

S Y N T A X	**exec command**

Purpose: Overwrite the code for 'command' on top of the process that executes the exec command (the calling process), which makes 'command' run in place of the calling process without creating a new process

You cannot return to the calling process; once the command has finished, control goes back to the parent of the calling process. If the calling process is your login shell, control goes back to the getty process when the exec command finishes execution, as in,

```
$ exec date
Tue Jun 29 15:09:15 PDT 2004
login:
```

When exec date finishes, control does not go back to the shell process but to the getty process (the parent of the login shell). The semantics of this command execution are shown in Figure 16.1.

If the command is run under a subshell of the login shell, control goes back to the login shell, as clarified in the following session. Here, a C shell is run as a child of the login shell (a Korn shell) and exec date is run under the C shell. When the exec date command finishes, control goes back to the login Korn shell. The sequence shown in Figure 16.2 depicts the semantics of these steps.

```
$ ps
    PID    TTY    TIME    COMD
    1271   p0     0:00    -ksh
    1373   p0     0:00    ps
$ csh
% ps
    PID    TTY    TIME    COMD
    1271   p0     0:00    -ksh
    1375   p0     0:00    csh
    1398   p0     0:00    ps
% exec date
Tue Jun 29 15:17:20 PDT 2004
$ ps
    PID    TTY    TIME    COMD
    1271   p0     0:00    -ksh
    1373   p0     0:00    ps
$
```

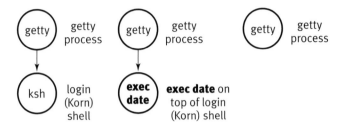

Figure 16.1 Execution of the exec date command under the login shell

16.5.2 File I/O via the exec Command

The Korn shell allows you to work with as many as 10 file descriptors at a time. Three of these descriptors are set aside for standard input (0), standard output (1), and standard error (2). All 10 descriptors can be used for I/O by using the redirection operators with the exec command. Table 16.2 describes the syntax of the exec command for file I/O.

When executed from the command line, the exec < sample command causes each line in the sample file to be treated as a command and executed by the current shell. That happens because the exec command is executed by the shell process whose only purpose is to read commands from stdin and execute them; as the file sample is attached to the stdin, the shell reads its commands from this file. The shell terminates after executing the last line in sample. When executed from within a shell script, this command causes the stdin of the remainder of the script to be attached to sample. The following session illustrates the working of this command when it is executed from the command line. As shown, the sample file contains two commands: date and echo. A Korn shell process is run under the login shell, (which is also Korn and is shown as -ksh in the output of the ps command), via the ksh command. When the exec < sample command is executed, the commands in the sample file are executed, the child Korn shell terminates after finishing execution of the last command in sample (the output of the third ps command shows that only the login shell runs after the exec < sample command is done), and control returns to the login shell.

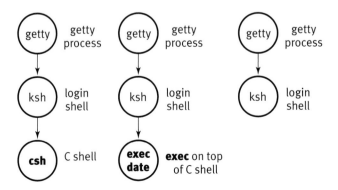

Figure 16.2 Execution of the exec date command under a subshell of the login shell

■■■ TABLE 16.2 Syntax of the `exec` Command for File I/O

Syntax	Meaning
`exec < file`	Opens 'file' for reading and attaches standard input of the process to 'file'
`exec > file`	Opens 'file' for writing and attaches standard output of the process to 'file'
`exec >> file`	Opens 'file' for writing, attaches standard output of the process to 'file', and appends standard output to 'file'
`exec n< file`	Opens 'file' for reading and assigns it the file descriptor 'n'
`exec n> file`	Opens 'file' for writing and assigns it the file descriptor 'n'

`exec n<< tag`
`...`
`tag`
	Opens a here document (data between << 'tag' and 'tag') for reading; the opened file is assigned a descriptor 'n'

`exec n>> file`	Opens 'file' for writing, assigns it file descriptor 'n', and appends data to the end of 'file'
`exec n>&m`	Duplicates 'm' into 'n'; whatever goes into 'file' with file descriptor 'n' will also go into 'file' with file descriptor 'm'
`exec <&-`	Closes standard input
`exec >&-`	Closes standard output
`exec n<&-`	Closes 'file' with descriptor 'n' attached to stdin
`exec n >&-`	Closes 'file' with descriptor 'n' attached to stdout

So, effectively, when the `exec < sample` command is executed from the command line, it attaches stdin of the current shell to the sample file. When this command is executed from a shell script, it attaches stdin of the shell script to the sample file. In either case, the `exec < /dev/tty` command must be executed to reattach stdin to the terminal. Here, /dev/tty is the pseudo terminal that represents the terminal on which the shell is executed. The following session illustrates use of this command from the command line. The semantics of these steps are shown in Figure 16.3.

```
$ cat sample
date
echo Hello, World!
$ ps
    PID    TTY    TIME    CMD
  24022   pts/1   0:00    ps
  28486   pts/1   0:00    -ksh
$ ksh
$ ps
```

```
    PID    TTY    TIME    CMD
  18752   pts/1   0:00    ps
  24020   pts/1   0:00    ksh
  28486   pts/1   0:00    -ksh
$ exec < sample
$ Tue Jun 29 23:38:53 PDT 2004
$ Hello, World!
$
$ ps
     PID    TTY    TIME    CMD
   24022   pts/1   0:00    ps
   28486   pts/1   0:00    -ksh
$
```

Similarly, when the `exec > data` command is executed from the command line, it causes outputs of all subsequent commands executed under the shell (that normally go to the monitor screen) to go to the data file. Thus, you do not see the output of any command on the screen. In order to see the output on the screen again, you need to execute the `exec >` `/dev/tty` command. After doing so, you can view the contents of the data file to see the outputs of all the commands executed prior to this command. When the `exec > data` command is executed from a shell script, it causes the outputs of all subsequent commands (that normally go to the monitor screen) to go to the data file until the `exec > /dev/tty` command is executed from within the shell script.

Thus, effectively, when the `exec > data` command is executed from the command line, it attaches stdout of the current shell to the data file. When this command is executed from a shell script, it attaches stdout of the shell script to the data file. In either case, the `exec >`

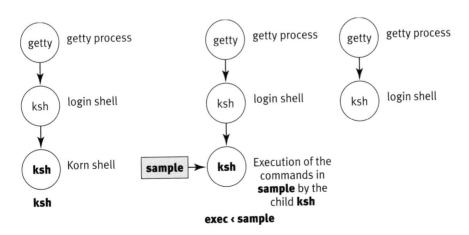

Figure 16.3 Execution of the `ksh` and `exec < sample` commands under the login shell

/dev/tty command needs to be executed to reattach stdout to the terminal. The following session illustrates use of this command from the command line. Note that, after the exec > data command has executed, the outputs of all subsequent commands (date, echo, and more) go to the data file. In order to redirect the output of commands to the screen, the exec > /dev/tty command must be executed, as shown in the following session.

```
$ exec > data
$ date
$ echo Hello, World!
$ uname -a
$ exec > /dev/tty
$ date
Tue Jun 29 23:57:30 PDT 2004
$ cat data
Tue Jun 29 23:56:03 PDT 2004
Hello, World!
AIX pccaix 3 4 000001336700
$
```

Similarly, you can redirect standard output and standard error for a segment of a shell script by using the following command.

```
exec > outfile 2> errorfile
```

In this case, output and error messages from the shell script following this line are directed to outfile and errorfile, respectively. (Obviously, file descriptor 1 can be used with > to redirect output.) If output needs to be reattached to the terminal, you can do so by using,

```
exec > /dev/tty
```

Once this command has executed, all subsequent output goes to the monitor screen. Similarly, you can use the exec 2> /dev/tty command to send errors back to the display screen.

Consider the following shell session. When exec.demo1 is executed, 'file1' gets the line containing Hello, world!, 'file3' gets the contents of 'file2', and 'file4' gets the line >. This is great!. The shell script between the commands exec < file2 and exec < /dev/tty takes its input from 'file2'. Therefore, the command cat > file3 is really cat < file2 > file3. The cat > file4 command takes input from the keyboard as it is executed after the exec < /dev/tty command has been executed (which reattaches the stdin of the script to the keyboard). Figure16.4 illustrates the semantics of the three cat commands in the shell script.

```
$ cat exec.demo1
cat > file1
exec < file2
```

```
cat > file3
exec < /dev/tty
cat > file4
$ chmod 755 exec.demo1
$ exec.demo1
```

Hello, world!

<Ctrl-D>

This is great!

<Ctrl-D>

$

Now, we develop a shell script, diff2, that uses file I/O features of the Bourne shell. It takes two files as command line arguments and compares them line by line. If the files are the same, it displays a message that says so, and the program terminates. If one file is smaller than the other, it displays a message informing you of that and exits. As soon as the program finds the lines at which the two files differ, it displays an error message informing you of the lines from both files that are different and terminates. The following is the script and a few sample runs.

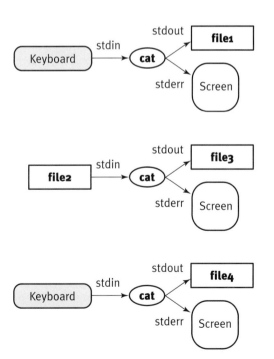

Figure 16.4 Detachment and reattachment of stdin and stdout inside a shell script

```
$ cat diff2
#!/bin/sh

# File Name: ~/unixbook/examples/Bshell/diff2
# Author:   Syed Mansoor Sarwar
# Written:  August 28, 2004
# Modified: August 28, 2004
# Purpose:  To see if the two files passed as command line arguments
#           are same or different
#           Brief Description: Read a line from each file and compare them. If
#                              the lines are the same, continue. If they are
#                              different, display the two lines and exit. If one
#                              of the files finishes before the other, display a
#                              message and exit. Otherwise, the files are the
#                              same; display an appropriate message and exit
if [ $# != 2 ]
   then
      echo "Usage: $0 file1 file2"
      exit 1
   elif [ ! -f "$1" ]
   then
      echo "$1 is not an ordinary file"
      exit 1
   elif [ ! -f "$2" ]
   then
      echo "$2 is not an ordinary file"
      exit 1
   else
      :
fi
file1="$1"
file2="$2"

# Open files for reading and assign them file descriptors 3 and 4

exec 3< "$file1"
exec 4< "$file2"

# Read a line each from both files and compare. If both reach EOF, then files
# are the same. Otherwise, they are different. 0<&3 is used to attach standard
# input of the read line1 command to file descriptor 3, 0<&4 is used to attach
```

```
# standard input of the read line2 command to file descriptor 4.

while read line1 0<&3
do
    if read line2 0<&4
        then
            # if lines are different, the two files are not the same
            if [ "$line1" != "$line2" ]
                then
                    echo "$1 and $2 are different."
                    echo " $1: $line1"
                    echo " $2: $line2"
                    exit 1
            fi
        else
            # if EOF for file2 reached, file1 is bigger than file2
            echo "$1 and $2 are different and $1 is bigger than $2."
            exit 1
    fi
done
# if EOF for file1 reached, file2 is bigger than file1. Otherwise, the two
# files are the same. 0<&4 is used to attach standard input of read to file
# descriptor 4
if read line2 0<&4
    then
        echo "$1 and $2 are different and $2 is bigger than $1."
        exit 1
    else
        echo "$1 and $2 are the same!"
        exit 0
fi

# Close files corresponding to descriptors 3 and 4
exec 3<&-
exec 4<&-
$ diff2
Usage: diff2 file1 file2
$ diff2 test1
Usage: diff2 file1 file2
```

```
$ diff2 test1 test2 test3
Usage: diff2 file1 file2
$ diff2 test1 test2
test1 and test2 are different and test1 is bigger than test2.
$ diff2 test1 test1
test1 and test1 are the same!
$ diff2 test1 test3
test1 and test3 are different.
     test1: Not the same!
     test3: Not the same.
$ cat test1
Hello, world!
Not the same!
Another line.
$ cat test2
Hello, world!
$ cat test3
Hello, world!
Not the same.
$
```

The exec command is used to open and close files. The exec 3< "$file1" and exec 4< "$file2" commands open the files passed as command line arguments for reading and assigns them file descriptors 3 and 4. From this point on, you can read the two files by using these descriptors. The commands read line1 0<&3 and read line2 0<&4 read the next lines from the files with files descriptors 3 (for 'file1') and 4 (for 'file2'), respectively. The commands exec 3<&- and exec 4<&- close the two files. The : in the else part of the first if statement is a null statement that simply returns true.

In the following In-Chapter Exercises, you will use the exec command to redirect I/O of your shell to ordinary files. The concept of I/O redirection from within a shell script and file I/O by using file descriptors is also reinforced.

IN-CHAPTER EXERCISES

16.4   Write command lines for changing stdin of your shell to a file called data and stdout to a file called out, both in your present working directory. If the data file contains the following lines, what happens after the commands are executed?

```
echo "The time now is: \c"
date
echo "The users presently logged on are: \c"
who
```

(continued)

16.5   After finishing the steps in Exercise 16.4, what happens when you type commands at the shell prompt? Does the result make sense to you? Write the command needed to bring your environment back to normal.

16.6   Create a file that contains the diff2 script and try it with different inputs.

16.6   Functions in the Bourne Shell

The Bourne shell allows you to write functions. **Functions** consist of a series of commands, called the **function body**, that are given a name. You can invoke the commands in the function body by using the function name.

16.6.1 The Reasons for Functions

Functions are normally used if a piece of code is repeated at various places in a script. By making a function of this code, you save typing time. Thus if a block of code is used at, say, 10 different places in a script, you can create a function of it and invoke it where it is to be inserted by using the name of the function. The trade-off is that the mechanism of transferring control to the function code and returning it to the calling code (from where the function is invoked/called) takes time, which slightly increases the running time of the script.

Another way of saving typing time is to create another script file for the block of code and invoke this code by calling the script as a command. The disadvantage of using this technique is that, as the script file is on the disk, invocation of the script requires loading the script from the disk into the main memory—an expensive operation. Whether they are located in ~/.profile, defined interactively in a shell, or defined in the script, the function definitions are always in the main memory. Thus, invocation of functions is several times faster than invoking shell scripts (which are on the disk).

16.6.2 Function Definition

Before you can use a function, you have to define it. For often-used functions, you should put their definitions in your ~/.profile file. This way, the shell records them in its environment when you log on and allows you to invoke them while you use the system. You must execute the ~/.profile file with the **.** (dot) command after defining a function in it and before using it without logging off and logging on. You can also define functions while interactively using the shell. These definitions are valid for as long as you remain in the session that you were in when you defined the functions.

The definitions for functions that are specific to a script are usually put in the file that contains the script. However some definitions of general-purpose functions are still placed in the ~/.profile file. Functions can be exported (by using the `export` command) to make them available to all the child processes of the process that contains these functions. If the process containing the function definitions is a shell process, the functions can be invoked by any process that executes under the shell.

The format of function definition is,

```
function_name ( )
{
   command-list
}
```

The 'function_name' is the name of the function that you choose, and the commands in 'command-list' comprise the function body. The opening brace (() and the function name can be on the same line. To define a function interactively, type the function name and parentheses at the shell prompt, followed by a { on a line, one command per line (function grouping can be used), and a } on the last line.

16.6.3 Function Invocation/Call

The commands in a function body are not executed until the function is invoked (called). You can invoke a function by using its name as a command. When you call a function, its body is executed and control comes back to the command following the function call. If you invoke a function at the command line, control returns to the shell after the function finishes its execution.

16.6.4 Examples of Functions

The following is a simple example of a function, called `machines`, defined interactively in a shell and invoked. This function returns the names of all the computers on your local network.

```
$ machines ()
> {
> date
> echo "These are the machines on the network:"
> ruptime | cut -f1 -d' ' | more
> }
$ machines
Thu Feb 19 17:05:00 PDT 2004
These are the machines on the network:
upibm0
...
upsun1
...
upsun29
$
```

You can use the `set` command to view all the function definitions in your current environment. The following is a sample run of the command. For the sake of brevity, we show only one function definition as part of the output.

```
$ set
...
machines(){
date
echo "These are the machines on the network:"
ruptime | cut -f1 - d' ' | more
}
$
```

We now enhance the **dext** script described in Section 16.3 so that it can take multiple names at the command line. The enhanced version also uses a function OutputData to display one or more output records (lines in the directory) for every name passed as the command line argument. In the case of multiple lines for a name, this function displays them in sorted order. A few sample runs are shown following the script.

```
$ cat dext
#!/bin/sh

if [ $# = 0 ]
   then
      echo "Usage: $0 name"
      exit 1

fi

OutputData()
{
   echo "Info about $user_input"
   (grep -i "$user_input" | sort) << DIRECTORY
   John Doe       555.232.0000      johnd@somedomain.com
   Jenny Great    444.6565.1111     jg@new.somecollege.edu
   David Nice     999.111.3333      david_nice@xyz.org
   Don Carr       555.111.3333      dcarr@old.hoggie.edu
   Masood Shah    666.010.9820      shah@Garments.com.pk
   Jim Davis      777.000.9999      davis@great.adviser.edu
   Art Pohm       333.000.8888      art.pohm@great.professor.edu
   David Carr     777.999.2222      dcarr@net.net.gov
DIRECTORY
   echo    # A blank line between two records
}

# As long as there is at least one command line argument (name), take the
# first name, call the OutputData function to search the DIRECTORY and
```

```
# display the line(s) containing the name, shift this name left by one
# position, and repeat the process.

while [ $# != 0 ]
do
    user_input="$1"     # Get the next command line argument (name)
    OutputData          # Display info about the next name
    shift               # Get the following name
done
exit 0
$ dext
Usage: ./dext name
$ dext john
Info about john
    John Doe        555.232.0000  johnd@somedomain.com

$ dext john masood carr
Info about john
    John Doe        555.232.0000  johnd@somedomain.com

Info about masood
    Masood Shah    666.010.9820  shah@Garments.com.pk

Info about carr
    David Carr     777.999.2222  dcarr@net.net.gov
    Don Carr       555.111.3333  dcarr@old.hoggie.edu
$
```

In the following In-Chapter Exercise, you will write a simple function and a Bourne shell script that uses it.

IN-CHAPTER EXERCISE

16.7 Write a function called menu that displays the following menu. Then write a shell script that uses this function.

```
Select an item from the following menu:
    d. to display today's date and current time,
    f. to start an ftp session,
    t. to start a telnet session, and
    q. to quit.
```

16.7   Debugging Shell Programs

You can debug your Bourne shell scripts by using the **-x** (echo) option of the **sh** command. This option displays each line of the script after variable substitution but before its execution. You can combine the **-x** option with the **-v** (verbose) option to display each line of the script (as it appears in the script file) before execution. You can also invoke the **sh** command from the command line to run the script, or you can make it part of the script, as in **#!/bin/sh -xv**. In the latter case, remove the **-xv** options after debugging is complete.

In the following session, we show how a shell script can be debugged. The script in the debug_demo file prompts you for a digit. If you enter a value between 1 and 9, it displays Good input! and quits. If you enter any other value, it simply exits. When the script is executed and you enter 4, it displays the message debug_demo: [4: not found.

```
$ cat debug_demo
#!/bin/sh

echo "Enter a digit: \c"
read var1
if ["$var1" -ge 1 -a "$var1" -le 9 ]
   then
      echo "Good input!"
fi
exit 0
$ debug_demo
Enter a digit: 4
debug_demo: [4: not found
$
```

We debug the program by using the **sh -xv debug_demo** command. The shaded portion of the run-time trace shows the problem area. In this case, the error is generated because of a problem in the condition for the **if** statement. A closer examination of the shaded area reveals that missing space between [and 4 is the problem. After we take care of this problem, the script works properly.

```
$ sh -xv debug_demo
#!/bin/sh

echo -n "Enter a digit: "
+ echo -n Enter a digit:
Enter a digit: read var1
+ read var1
```

4

```
if ["$var1" -ge 1 -a "$var1" -le 9 ]
   then
      echo "Good input!"
fi
+ [4 -ge 1 -a 4 -le 9 ]
debug_demo: [4:not found
exit 0
+ exit 0
$
```

The following In-Chapter Exercise is designed to enhance your understanding of interrupt processing and debugging features of the Bourne shell.

IN-CHAPTER EXERCISE

16.8 Test the scripts in the onintr_demo and canleave files on your UNIX system. Do they work as expected? Make sure you understand them. If your versions do not work properly, use the sh –xv command to debug them.

Summary

The Bourne shell does not have the built-in capability for numeric integer data processing in terms of arithmetic, logic, and shift operations. In order to perform arithmetic and logic operations on integer data, the expr command must be used.

The here document feature of the Bourne shell allows standard input of a command in a script to be attached to data within the script. The use of this feature results in more efficient programs because no extra file-related operations, such as file open and read, are needed, because the data is within the script file and has probably been loaded into the main memory when the script was loaded.

The Bourne shell also allows the user to write programs that ignore signals such as keyboard interrupt (<Ctrl-C>). This useful feature can be used, among other things, to disable program termination when it is in the middle of updating a file. The trap command can be used to invoke this feature.

The Bourne shell has powerful I/O features that allow explicit processing of files. The exec command can be used to open a file for reading or writing and to associate a small integer, called a file descriptor, with it. The command line exec n< file opens a file for reading and assigns it a file descriptor n. The command line exec n> file opens a file for writing and assigns it a file descriptor n. This feature allows writing scripts for processing files. The command line exec n<&- can be used to close a file with descriptor n. The exec command provides various other file-related features, including opening a here document and assigning it a file descriptor, which allows the use of a here document anywhere in the script.

The Bourne shell programs can be debugged by using the -x and -v options of the sh command. This technique allows viewing the commands in the user's script after variable substitution but before execution.

Problems

1. Why is the expr command needed?

2. What is the here document? Why is it useful?

3. Write a Bourne shell script cv that takes the side of a cube as a command line argument and displays the volume of the cube.

4. Modify the countup script in Section 16.2 so that it takes two integer command line arguments. The script displays the numbers between the two integers (including the two numbers) in ascending order if the first number is smaller than the second, and in descending order if the first number is greater than the second. Name the script count_up_down.

5. Write a Bourne shell script that prompts you for a userID and displays your login name, your name, and your home directory.

6. Write a Bourne shell script that takes a list of integers as the command line argument and displays a list of their squares and the sum of the numbers in the list of squares.

7. Write a Bourne shell script that takes a machine name as an argument and displays a message informing you whether the host is on the local network.

8. What are signals in UNIX? What types of signals can be intercepted in the Bourne shell scripts?

9. Write a Bourne shell script that takes a file name and a directory name as command line arguments and removes the file if it is found under the given directory and is a simple file. If the file (the first argument) is a directory, it is removed (including all the files and subdirectories under it).

10. Write a Bourne shell script that takes a directory as an argument and removes all the ordinary files under it that have .o, .ps, and .jpg extensions. If no argument is specified, the current directory is used.

11. Enhance the diff2 script in Section 16.5 so that it displays the line numbers where the two files differ.

12. Enhance the diff2 script of Problem 11 so that, if only one file is passed to it as a parameter, it uses standard input as the second file.

13. Write a Bourne shell script for Problem 16 in Chapter 15, but use functions to implement the service code for various options.

Introductory C Shell Programming

Objectives

- To introduce the concept of shell programming
- To describe how shell programs can be executed
- To explain the concept and use of shell variables
- To discuss how command line arguments are passed to shell programs
- To discuss the concept of command substitution
- To describe some basic coding principles
- To write and discuss some shell scripts
- To cover the commands and primitives
  *, =, ", ', `, &, <, >, ;, |, \, /, [], (),
  continue, csh, exit, env, foreach, goto,
  head, if, ls, set, setenv, shift, switch,
  while, unset, unsetenv

17.1   Introduction

The C shell is more than a command interpreter: it has a programming language of its own that can be used to write shell programs for performing various tasks that cannot be performed by any existing command. Shell programs, commonly known as shell scripts, in the C shell consist of shell commands to be executed by a shell and are stored in ordinary UNIX files. The shell allows use of read/write storage places called shell variables to provide a comfortable work environment for users of the system and for programmers to use as scratch pads for completing a task. The C shell also has program control flow commands/statements that allow the user to implement multiway branching and repeated execution of a block of commands.

17.2   Running a C Shell Script

You can run a C shell script in one of three ways. The first method is to make the script file executable by adding the execute permission to the existing access permissions for the file. To do so, run the following command, where script_file is the name of the file containing the shell script. In this case, you make the script executable for yourself (the owner) only. However, you can set appropriate access permissions for the file if you also want to allow other users to execute it.

```
% chmod u+x script_file
%
```

Now, you can type `script_file` as a command to execute the shell script. As described in Chapter 13, the script is executed by a child of the current shell; the script executes properly if you are using the C shell. It does not work properly if you are using any other shell, such as the Bourne shell, because you would be trying to run a C shell script under a non–C shell process. In this case, execute the `/bin/csh` command to run the C shell.

The second method of executing a shell script is to run the `/bin/csh` command with the script file as its parameter. Thus, the following command executes the script in script_file. If your search path (the *path* variable) includes the /bin directory, you can simply use the `csh` command.

```
% /bin/csh script_file
%
```

The third method, which is also the most commonly used, is to force execution of a script in the C shell, regardless of your current shell. You can do so by beginning a shell script with,

```
#!/bin/csh
```

All you need to do is set execute permission for the script file and run the file as a command. When your current shell reads the string #!, it takes the rest of the line as the absolute pathname of the shell to be executed, under which the script in the file is executed.

17.3   Shell Variables and Related Commands

A **variable** is a main memory location that is given a name. This allows you to reference the memory location by using its name instead of its address (*see* Chapter 3). The name of a shell variable is comprised of digits, letters, and underscore, with the first character being a letter or underscore. Because the main memory is read/write storage, you can read a variable's value or assign it a new value. Under the C shell, the value of a variable can be a string of characters or a numeric value. There is no theoretical limit to the length of a variable's value stored as a string.

Shell variables can be one of two types: **shell environment variables** and **user-defined variables**. You can use environment variables to customize the environment in which your shell runs and for proper execution of shell commands. A copy of these variables is passed to every command that executes in the shell as its child. Most of these variables are initialized when you log on, according to the environment set by your system administrator. You can customize your environment by assigning appropriate values to some or all of these variables in your ~/.login and ~/.cshrc start-up files, which also execute when you log on. (*See* Chapter 4 for a discussion of start-up files.) Table 17.1 lists most of the environment variables whose values you can change.

■ **TABLE 17.1** Some Important Writable C Shell Environment Variables

Environment Variable	Purpose of the Variable
cdpath	Directory names that are searched, one by one, by the cd command to find the directory passed to it as a parameter; the cd command searches the current directory if this variable is not set
home	Name of your home directory, when you first log on
mail	Name of your system mailbox file
path	Variable that contains your search path—the directories that a shell searches to find an external command or program
prompt	Primary shell prompt that appears on the command line, usually set to %
prompt2	Secondary shell prompt displayed on the second line of a command if the shell thinks that the command is not finished, typically when the command line terminates with a backslash (\ ), the escape character
cwd	Name of the current working directory
term	Type of user's console terminal

The shell environment variables listed in Table 17.1 are writable, and you can assign them any values to make your shell environment meet your needs. Other shell environment variables are read-only. That is, you can use (read) the values of these variables, but you cannot change them directly. These variables are most useful for processing command line arguments (also known as positional arguments), the parameters passed to a shell script at the command line. Examples of command line arguments are the source and destination files in the cp command. Some other read-only shell variables are used to keep track of the process ID of the current process, the process ID of the most recent background process, and the exit status of the last command. Some important read-only shell environment variables are listed in Table 17.2.

■■ **TABLE 17.2** Some Important Read-Only C Shell Environment Variables

Environment Variable	Purpose of the Variable
$argv[0] or *$0*	Name of the program
$argv[1] - $argv[9] or *$1–$9*	Values of command line arguments 1 through 9
$argv[*] or *$**	Values of all of the command line arguments
$#argv or *$#*	Total number of command line arguments
$$	Process ID (PID) of the current process; typically used as a file name extension to create (most probably) unique file names
$!	PID of the most recent background process

User-defined variables are used within shell scripts as temporary storage places whose values can be changed when the program executes. These variables can be made global and passed to the commands that execute in the shell script in which they are defined. As with most programming languages, you have to declare C shell variables before using them. A reference to an uninitialized C shell variable results in an error.

You can display the values of all shell variables (environment and user-defined) and their current values by using the set command without any argument. The following is a sample run of the set command on a Sun Sparc workstation running Solaris 2. It is just a partial list here to keep you focused.

```
% set
argv      ()
cdpath    (/ /usr)
cwd       /usr1.d/sarwar
dirstack      /usr1.d/sarwar
echo_style        bsd
gid       152
group     faculty
history   100
home      /usr1.d/sarwar
manpath   /opt/man:/usr/X11/man:/usr/local/lang/man:/usr/
local/lotus/man:/usr/open win/share/man:/usr/local/stp50/
man:/usr/local/man:/usr/man
notify
path      (/opt/bin /usr/ccs/bin /usr1.d/sarwar/pvm3/bin/
ARCH /usr/local/pvm3/lib/SUN4 /usr/local/linda/bin
/usr/local/lang/pascal /usr/local/lang/CC/sun4 /usr/local/
```

```
lang . /usr1.d/sarwar/bin /usr/ucb /bin /usr/bin /usr/
include /usr/X11/lib /usr/lib /etc /usr/etc /usr/local/
bin /usr/local/lib /usr/local/games /usr/X11/bin /usr/
openwin/bin /usr/openwin/lib)
prompt    upsun29.egr.up.edu:~ ! %
prompt2   %R?
savehist      50
shell     /bin/tcsh
term      vt100
thishost      upsun29.egr.up.edu
tty       pts/0
uid       121
user      sarwar
%
```

You can use the env (System V) and printenv (BSD) commands to display both the environment variables and their values. The following is a sample output of the env command on the same Sun Sparc workstation that we ran the set command on.

```
% env
HOME=/usr1.d/sarwar
PATH=/opt/bin:/usr/ccs/bin:/usr1.d/sarwar/pvm3/bin/ARCH:/
usr/local/pvm3/lib/SUN4:/usr/local/linda/bin:/usr/local/
lang/pascal:/usr/local/lang/CC/sun4:/usr/local/lang:.:/
usr1.d/sarwar/bin:/usr/ucb:/bin:/usr/bin:/usr/include:/
usr/X11/lib:/usr/lib:/etc:/usr/etc:/usr/local/bin:/usr/
local/lib:/usr/local/games:/usr/X11/bin:/usr/openwin/bin:/
usr/openwin/lib
LOGNAME=sarwar
HZ=100
TERM=vt100
TZ=US/Pacific
SHELL=/bin/csh
MAIL=/var/mail/sarwar
HOSTTYPE=sun4
VENDOR=sun
OSTYPE=solaris
MACHTYPE=sparc
SHLVL=2
PWD=/usr1.d/sarwar
```

```
USER=sarwar
GROUP=faculty
HOST=upsun29.egr.up.edu
REMOTEHOST=upibm7.egr.up.edu
OPENWINHOME=/usr/openwin
PVM_ROOT=/usr/local/pvm3
PVM_ARCH=SUN4
SUNVISION=/usr/local/sunvision
XGLHOME=/usr/local/sunvision
LD_LIBRARY_PATH=/opt/lib:/usr/X11/lib:/usr/openwin/lib:/usr/dt/lib
SUN_SOURCE_BROWSER_EX_FILE=/usr/local/lang
EDITOR=vi
EXINIT=set redraw
MAILER=comp -e vi
MANPATH=/opt/man:/usr/X11/man:/usr/local/lang/man:/usr/
local/lotus/man:/usr/open win/share/man:/usr/local/stp50/
man:/usr/local/man:/usr/man
NNTPSERVER=news.egr.up.edu
VISUAL=pico
inbox=/usr1.d/sarwar/Mail/inbox
SIGNATURE=sarwar@egr.up.edu
WWW_HOME=http://www.egr.up.edu/
XKEYSYMDB=/usr/lib/X11/XKeysymDB
LANG=C
DISPLAY=upsun22.egr.up.edu:0.0
TERMCAP=d0|vt100|vt100-am|vt100am:do=^J:co#80:li#24:cl=50\
E[;H\E[2J:sf=5\ED:le=^H:bs:am:cm=5\E[%i%d;%dH:nd=2\
E[C:up=2\E[A:ce=3\E[K:cd=50\E[J:so=2\E[7m:se=2\E[m: us=2\
E[4m:ue=2\E[m:md=2\E[1m:mr=2\E[7m:mb=2\E[5m:me=2\E[m:is=\
E[1;24r\E[24;1H:rf=/usr/share/lib/tabset/vt100:rs=\E>\
E[?3l\E[?4l\E[?5l\E[?7h\E[?8h:ks=\E[?1h\E=:ke=\E[?1l\
E>:ku=\EOA:kd=\EOB:kr=\EOC:kl=\EOD:kb=^H:ho=\E[H:k1=\
EOP:k2=\EOQ:k3=\EOR:k4=\EOS:pt:sr=5\EM:vt#3:xn:sc=\E7:rc=\
E8:cs=\E[%i%d;%dr:
%
```

In the following In-Chapter Exercises, you will create a simple shell script and make it executable. Also, you will use the set and env commands to display the names and values of shell variables in your environment.

IN-CHAPTER EXERCISES

17.1 Display the names and values of all shell variables on your UNIX machine. What command(s) did you use?

17.2 Create a file that contains a shell script comprising the `date` and `who` commands, one on each line. Make the file executable and run the shell script. List all the steps for completing this task.

17.3.1 Reading and Writing Shell Variables

You can use any of three commands to assign a value to (write) one or more shell variables (environment or user-defined): `@`, `set`, and `setenv`. The `set` and `setenv` commands are used to assign a string to a variable. The difference is that the `setenv` command declares and initializes a **global variable** (equivalent to an assignment statement followed by execution of the `export` command in the Bourne shell), whereas the `set` command declares and initializes a **local variable**. You can use the `@` command to assign a numeric value to a local variable. The following are brief descriptions of the `@` and `set` commands. We describe the `setenv` command in Section 17.3.3.

SYNTAX

set [variable1[=strval1] [variable2 [=strval2] ... variableN [=strvalN]
@ [variable1=numval1] [variable2 [=numval2] ... variableN [=numvalN]

Purpose: Assign values 'strval1', ..., 'strvalN' or 'numval1', ..., 'numvalN' to variables 'variable1, ..., variableN', respectively, where a value can be 'strval' for a string value and 'numval' for a numeric value

No space is required before or after the = sign for the `@` and `set` commands, but spaces can be used for clarity. If a value contains spaces, you must enclose the value in parentheses. The `set` command with only the name of a variable declares the variable and assigns it a null value. Unlike the Bourne shell, where every variable is automatically initialized, in the C shell you must declare a variable in order to initialize and use it. Without any arguments, the `set` and `@` commands display all shell variables and their values. Multiword values are displayed in parentheses. (We discuss the `@` command in detail in Chapter 18.) You can refer to (read) the current value of a variable by inserting a dollar sign (`$`) before the name of a variable. You can use the `echo` command to display values of shell variables.

In the following session, we show how shell variables can be read and written.

```
% echo $name
name: Undefined variable.
% set name
```

```
% echo $name
% set name = John
% echo $name
John
% set name = John Doe II
% echo $name
John
% echo $Doe $II
% set name = (John Doe)
% echo $name
John Doe
% set name = John*
% echo $name
John.Bates.letter    John.Johnsen.memo    John.email
% echo "$name"
John*
% echo "The name $name sounds familiar\!"
The name John* sounds familiar!
% echo \$name
$name
% echo '$name'
$name
%
```

The preceding session shows that, if values that include spaces are not enclosed in quotes, the shell assigns the first word to the variable and the remaining as null-initialized variables. In other words, the command set name = John Doe II initializes the *name* variable to John, and declares *Doe* and *II* as string variables. Also, after the set name=John* command has been executed and $name is not enclosed in quotes in the echo command, the shell lists the file names in your present working directory that match John*, with * considered as the shell metacharacter. Thus, running the echo * command would display the names of all the files in your current directory in one line. The preceding session also shows that single quotes can be used to process the value of the *name* variable literally. In fact, you can use single quotes to process the whole string literally. The backslash character can be used to escape the special meaning of any single character, including $, and treat it literally. In the C shell, you must use a backslash before the ! symbol if it is followed by any character other than a space. An alternative is to escape its special meaning by using \! instead.

A command line consisting of $variable alone results in the value of *variable* being executed as a shell command. If the value of *variable* comprises a valid command, the expected results are produced. If *variable* does not contain a valid command, the shell, as expected, displays an appropriate error message. The following session illustrates this point with some samples. The variable used in this session is *command*.

```
% set command = pwd
% $command
/users/faculty/sarwar/unixbook/examples
% set command = hello
% $command
hello: command not found
%
```

17.3.2 Command Substitution

When a command is enclosed in backquotes (also known as *grave accents*), the shell executes the command and substitutes the output of the command for the command (including back-quotes). This process is referred to as command substitution. The following is a brief description of command substitution.

`command`

Purpose: Substitute its output for `command`

SYNTAX

The next session illustrates the concept. In the first assignment statement, the variable called *command* is assigned the value pwd. In the second assignment statement, the output of the pwd command is assigned to the *command* variable.

```
% set command = pwd
% echo "The value of command is: $command."
The value of command is: pwd
% set command = `pwd`
% echo "The value of command is: $command."
The value of command is: /users/faculty/sarwar/unixbook/examples
%
```

Command substitution can be specified in any command. For example, in the following command line, the output of the date command is substituted for 'date' before the echo command is executed.

```
% echo "The date and time is `date`."
The date and time is Sat Aug 7 13:26:42 PDT 2004.
%
```

The following In-Chapter Exercises are designed to reinforce the creation and use of shell variables and the concept of command substitution.

IN-CHAPTER EXERCISES

17.3 Assign your full name to a shell variable *myname* and echo its value. How did you accomplish the task? Show your work.

17.4 Assign the output of echo "Hello, world!" command to the *myname* variable and then display the value of *myname*. List the commands that you executed to complete this task.

17.3.3 Exporting Environment

When a variable is created, it is not automatically known to subsequent shells. The setenv command passes the *value* of a variable to subsequent shells. Thus when a shell script is called and executed in another shell script, it does not get automatic access to the variables defined in the original (caller) script unless they are explicitly made available to it. You can use the setenv command to assign a value to a string variable and pass the value of the variable to subsequent commands that execute as children of the script. Because all read/write shell environment variables are available to every command, script, and subshell, they are initialized by the setenv command. The following is a brief description of the setenv command.

SYNTAX

setenv [variable [strval]]

Purpose: Assigns to 'variable' a string value 'strval' and exports 'variable' and a copy of its value so that it is available to every command executed from this point on

---

The following command line shows a simple use of the command. The *name* variable is initialized to John Doe and is exported to subsequent commands executed under the current shell and any subshell that runs under the current shell. Note that unlike the set command, the setenv command requires that you enclose multiword values in double quotes, not in parentheses.

```
% setenv name "John Doe"
%
```

The next session illustrates the concept of exporting shell variables via some simple shell scripts.

```
% cat display_name
#!/bin/csh
echo $name
exit 0
```

```
%
% set name=(John Doe)
% display_name
name: Undefined variable.
%
```

Note that the script in the display_name script file displays an undefined variable error message, even though we initialized the *name* variable just before executing this script. The reason is that the *name* variable declared interactively is not exported before running the script, and the *name* variable used in the script is local to the script. As this local variable *name* is uninitialized, the echo command displays the error message. As stated before, unlike the Bourne shell, the C shell requires declaration of a variable before its use.

You can use the exit command to transfer control out of the executing program and pass it to the calling process, the current shell process in the preceding session. The only argument of the exit command is an optional integer number that is returned to the calling process as the exit status of the terminating process. All UNIX commands return an exit status of 0 upon *success* (if they successfully perform their task) and nonzero upon *failure*. The return status value of a command is stored in the read-only environment variable *$?* and can be checked by the calling process. In shell scripts, the status of a command is checked and then subsequent action is taken. Later in the chapter we show the use of the read-only environment variable *$?* in some shell scripts. When the exit command is executed without an argument, the UNIX kernel sets the return status value for the script.

In the following session, the *name* variable is exported after it has been initialized, thus making it available to the display_name script. The session also shows that the return status of the display_name script is 0.

```
% setenv name "John Doe"
% display_name
John Doe
% echo $?
0
%
```

We now show that a copy of an exported variable's value is passed to any subsequent command. That is, a command has access only to the value of an exported variable; it cannot assign a new value to the variable. Consider the following script in the export_demo file.

```
% cat export_demo
#!/bin/csh
setenv name "John Doe"
display_change_name
echo "$name"
exit 0
```

```
% cat display_change_name
#!/bin/csh
echo "$name"
set name = (Plain Jane)
echo "$name"
exit 0
% export_demo
John Doe
Plain Jane
John Doe
%
```

When the export_demo script is invoked, the *name* variable is set to John Doe and exported so that it becomes part of the environment of the commands that execute under export_demo as its children. The first echo command in the display_change_name script displays the value of the exported variable *name*. It then initializes a local variable called *name* to Plain Jane. The second echo command therefore echoes the current value of the local variable *name* and displays Plain Jane. When the display_change_name script finishes, the display_name script executes the echo command and displays the value of the exported *name* variable, thus displaying John Doe.

17.3.4 Resetting Variables

A variable retains its value for as long as the script in which it is initialized executes. You can remove a variable from the environment by using the unset and unsetenv commands. The following are brief descriptions of the commands.

SYNTAX

unset variable-list
unsetenv variable

Purpose: Remove the specified variables from the environment. The variables in 'variable-list' are separated by spaces. The unset command is used for the variables declared by using the set or @ commands. The unsetenv command is used for variables declared by using the setenv command.

Next we show a simple use of the unset command. The variables *name* and *place* are set to John and Corvallis, respectively, and the echo command displays the values of these variables. The unset command resets *name* to null. Thus, the echo "$name" command displays a null string (a blank line).

```
% set name=John place=Corvallis
% echo "$name $place"
John Corvallis
```

```
% unset name
% echo "$name"
name: Undefined variable.
% echo "$place"
Corvallis
%
```

The following command removes the variables *name* and *place* from the environment.

```
% unset name place
%
```

To reset a variable, explicitly assign it a null value by using the set command with the variable name only. Or you can assign the variable no value and simply hit <Enter> after the = sign, as in,

```
% set country=
% echo "$country"
% set place
% echo $place
%
```

Here, the set command is used to reset the *country* and *place* variables to null.

17.3.5 Reading from Standard Input

So far, we have shown how you can assign values to shell variables statically at the command line or by using the assignment statement. If you want to write an interactive shell script that prompts the user for keyboard input, you need to use the set command in order to store the user input in a shell variable, according to the following syntax.

---

set variable = $<
set variable = `head -1`

Purpose: Read one line from stdin into 'variable'; `head -1` is between backquotes

SYNTAX

These commands allow you to read one line of keyboard input into 'variable'. Some C shell implementations (e.g., under Sun Solaris 2) do not support the first set command, but the second set command works in all implementations. You can use the syntax for the second command to assign the first line of keyboard input to 'variable'. Unlike that of the Bourne shell, the keyboard input feature of the C shell does not allow assignment of words in a line to multiple variables. However, the words in a line are stored in the form of an array, and you can access them by using the name of the variable (we discuss arrays in Chapter 18).

We illustrate the semantics of the second set command with a script in the keyin_demo file, as follows.

```
% cat keyin_demo
#!/bin/csh
echo -n "Enter input: "
set line = `head -1`
echo "You entered: $line"
exit 0
%
```

In the following run, enter UNIX rules the network computing world! (you can never overemphasize the power of UNIX). The set command takes the whole input and puts it in the shell variable *line* without the newline character. The output of the echo command displays the contents of the shell variable *line*.

```
% keyin_demo
Enter input: UNIX rules the network computing world!
You entered: UNIX rules the network computing world!
%
```

The –n option is used with the echo command (*see* Table 15.3) to keep the cursor on the same line. If you do not use this option, the cursor moves to the next line, which is what you want to see happen while displaying information and error messages. However, when you prompt the user for keyboard input, you should keep the cursor in front of the prompt for a more user-friendly interface. The C shell on most UNIX systems that are based on BSD UNIX runs the BSD version of the echo command, which does not support the \c and other options supported by the System V version of the echo command. The BSD version does support Standard ASCII control sequences that can be used to display other special characters, such as <Ctrl-H> for backspace and <Ctrl-G> for bell.

In the following In-Chapter Exercise, you will use the set command to practice reading from stdin in shell scripts.

IN-CHAPTER EXERCISE

17.5   Write commands for reading a value into the *myname* variable from the keyboard and exporting it so that the commands executed in any child shell have access to the variable.

17.4   Passing Arguments to Shell Scripts

In this section, we describe how command line arguments can be passed to shell scripts and manipulated by them. As we discussed in Section 17.3, you can pass command line arguments, also called positional parameters, to a shell script. The values of up to the first nine of these arguments can be referenced by using the names $argv[1] through $argv[9] (the names $1 through $9 can also be used) for the first through nine arguments, respectively. If a positional argument referenced in your script is not passed as an argument, it has a value of null. You can use the names $#argv or $# to refer to the total number of arguments passed in an execution of the script. The names $argv[*], argv, or $* refer to the values of all of the arguments. The variable name $argv[0] or $0 contains the name of the script file (the command name). In the following session, we use the shell script in the cmdargs_demo file to show how you can use these variables.

```
% cat cmdargs_demo
#!/bin/csh
echo "The command name is: $0."
echo "The number of command line arguments is $#argv."
echo -n "The values of the command line arguments are: "
echo "$argv[1] $argv[2] $argv[3] $argv[4] $argv[5] $argv[6] $argv[7] $argv[8] $argv[9]."
echo "Another way to display values of all of the arguments: $argv[*]."
exit 0
% cmdargs_demo a b c d e f g h i
The command name is: cmdargs_demo.
The number of command line arguments are 9.
The value of the command line arguments are: a b c d e f g h i.
Another way to display values of all of the arguments: a b c d e f g h i.
% cmdargs_demo One Two 3 Four 5 6
The command name is: cmdargs_demo.
The number of command line arguments are 6.
The value of the command line arguments are: One Two 3 Four 5 6    .
Another way to display values of all of the arguments: One Two 3 Four 5 6.
%
```

Although the shell maintains as many as nine command line arguments at a time, you can write scripts that take more than nine arguments. To do so, use the shift command. By default, this command shifts the command line arguments to the left by one position, making $argv[2] become $argv[1], $argv[3] become $argv[2], and so on. The first argument, $argv[1], is shifted out. Once shifted, the arguments cannot be restored to their original values. More than one position can be shifted if specified as an argument to the command. The following is a brief description of the command.

shift [variable]

Purpose: Shift the words in 'variable' one position to the left; if no variable name is specified, the command line arguments are assumed

SYNTAX

The script in the shift_demo file shows the semantics of the `shift` command with the implicit 'variable', the command line arguments. The `shift` command shifts the first argument out and the remaining arguments to the left by one position. The three `echo` commands are used to display the current values of program names, all positional arguments ($#argv[*]), and the values of the first three positional parameters, respectively. The results of execution of the script are obvious.

```
% cat shift_demo
#!/bin/csh
echo "The name of the program is $0."
echo "The arguments are: $argv[*]."
echo "The first three arguments are: $argv[1] $argv[2] $argv[3]."
shift
echo "The name of the program is $0."
echo "The arguments are: $argv[*]."
echo "The first three arguments are: $argv[1] $argv[2] $argv[3]."
exit 0
% shift_demo 1 2 3 4 5 6 7 8 9 10 11 12
The program name is shift_demo.
The arguments are: 1 2 3 4 5 6 7 8 9 10 11 12.
The first three arguments are: 1 2 3.
The program name is shift_demo.
The arguments are: 2 3 4 5 6 7 8 9 10 11 12.
The first three arguments are: 2 3 4.
%
```

The values of positional arguments can be altered by using the `set` command by using *argv* as its variable argument. The most effective use of this command is in conjunction with command substitution. The following is a brief description of the command.

SYNTAX	**set argv = [argument-list]**
	Purpose: Set values of the positional arguments to the arguments in 'argument-list'

The following is a simple interactive use of the command. The `date` command is executed to show that the output has six fields. The `set argv = `date`` command sets the positional parameters to the output of the `date` command. In particular, $argv[1] is set to Sat, $argv[2] to Aug, $argv[3] to 7, $argv[4] to 13:26:42, $argv[5] to PDT, and $argv[6] to 2004. The `echo $argv[*]` command displays the values of all positional arguments. The third `echo` command displays the date in a commonly used form.

```
% date
Sat Aug 14 11:33:38 PDT 2004
% set argv = `date`
% echo $argv[*]
Sat Aug 14 11:33:38 PDT 2004
% echo "$argv[2] $argv[3], $argv[6]"
Aug 14 2004
%
```

The script in set_demo shows another use of the command. When the script is run with a file argument, it generates a line that contains the file name, the file's inode number, and the file size (in bytes). The set command is used to assign the output of ls -il command as the new values of the positional arguments $argv[1] through $argv[9]. We show the output of the ls -il command in case you do not remember the format of the output of this command.

```
% cat set_demo
#!/bin/csh
set filename = $argv[1]
set argv = `ls -il $filename`
echo "The command line arguments are: $argv[*]"
set inode = $argv[1]
set size = $argv[5]
echo "Name     Inode  Size"
echo
echo "$filename $inode $size"
exit 0
% set_demo lab3
The command line arguments are: 856162 -rwx------ 1 sarwar 668 Aug 13 20:24 lab3
Name   Inode    Size
lab3   856162   668
%
```

In the following In-Chapter Exercises, you will use the set and shift commands in order to reinforce the use and processing of command line arguments.

IN-CHAPTER EXERCISES

17.6 Write a shell script that displays all command line arguments, shifts them to the left by two positions, and redisplays them. Show the script along with a few sample runs.

(continued)

IN-CHAPTER EXERCISES *(continued)*

17.7 Update the shell script in Exercise 17.1 so that, after accomplishing this task, it sets the positional arguments to the output of the who | head –1 command and displays the positional arguments again.

17.5 Comments and Program Headers

You should develop the habit of putting comments in your programs describing the purpose of a particular series of commands. At times, you might even want to describe briefly the purpose of a variable or assignment statement. Also, you should use a program header for every shell script that you write. Program headers and comments help a programmer who has been assigned the task of modifying or enhancing your code to understand it quickly. They also help you understand your own code, in particular if you reread it after a lengthy period of time. Programs written many years ago, when putting comments in the program code or creating separate documentation for programs was not a common practice, are difficult to understand and enhance. These programs are commonly known as legacy code.

A good program header must contain at least the following items. In addition, you can insert any other items that you feel are important or are commonly used in your organization/group as part of its coding rules.

1. Name of the file containing the script
2. Name of the author
3. Date written
4. Date last modified
5. Purpose of the script (in one or two lines)
6. A brief description of the algorithm used to implement the solution to the problem at hand

A comment line (including every line in the program header) must start with the number sign (#), as in,

```
# This is a comment line.
```

However, a comment does not have to start at a new line; it can follow a command, as in,

```
set Var1=a Var2 Var3=b # Assign "a" to Var1, "b" to Var3, and declare
                       # a variable Var2 with an initial value of null.
```

The following is a sample header for the set_demo script.

```
# File Name:            ~/Cshell/examples/set_demo
# Author:               Syed Mansoor Sarwar
# Date Written:         August 10, 1999
# Date Last Modified:   May 21, 2004
```

# Purpose:	To illustrate how the set command works
# Brief Description:	The script runs with a filename as the only
#	command line argument, saves the filename, runs
#	the set command to assign output of ls -il
#	command to positional arguments ($1 through
#	$9), and displays file name, its inode number,
#	and its size in bytes.

We do not show the program headers for all of the sample scripts in this textbook in order to save space.

17.6   Program Control Flow Commands

The program control flow commands/statements are used to determine the sequence in which statements in a shell script execute. The three basic types of statements for controlling the flow of a script are two-way branching, multiway branching, and repetitive execution of one or more commands. The C shell statement for two-way branching is the if statement, the statements for multiway branching are the if and switch statements, and the statements for repetitive execution of some code are the foreach and while statements. In addition, the C shell has a goto statement that allows you to jump to any command in a program.

17.6.1 The if-then-else-endif Statement

The most basic form of the if statement is used for two-way branching, but the statement can also be used for multiway branching. The following is a brief description of the statement. The words in monospace type are keywords and must be used as shown in the syntax. Everything in brackets is optional. All the command lists are designed to help you accomplish the task at hand.

```
if (expression) then
    then-command-list
    [else if (expression) then
            then-command-list
    ...
    else
        else-command-list]
endif
```

Purpose: To implement two-way or multiway branching

Here, an 'expression' is a list of commands. The execution of commands in 'expression' returns a status of true (success) or false (failure). The word then must appear on the same line as the word if; otherwise you get the error message if: Empty if. We discuss the complete syntax and semantics of the if statement by presenting three versions of it. The most basic use of the if statement is without any optional features and results in the following syntax for the statement, which is commonly used for two-way branching.

if (expression) then
    then-commands
endif

Purpose: To implement two-way branching

If 'expression' is true, the 'then-commands' are executed; otherwise, the command after, `endif` is executed. The semantics of the statement are shown in Figure 17.1.

You can form an expression by using many operators for testing files, testing and comparing integers and strings, and logically connecting two or more expressions to form complex expressions. Table 17.3 describes the operators that can be used to form expressions, along with their meanings. Operators not related to files are listed in the order of their precedence (from high to low): parentheses, unary, arithmetic, shift, relational, bitwise, and logical.

■ **TABLE 17.3** C Shell Operators for Forming Expressions

Operator	Function	Operator	Function
Parentheses		**Relational operators**	
( )	To change the order of evaluation	>	Greater than
		<	Less than
		>=	Greater than or equal to
		<=	Less than or equal to
		!=	Not equal to (for string comparison)
		==	Equal to (for string comparison)
Unary operators		**Bitwise operators**	
–	Unary minus	&	AND
~	One's complement	^	XOR (exclusive OR)
!	Logical negation (NOT)	|	OR
Arithmetic operators		**Logical operators**	
%	Remainder	&&	AND
/	Divide	||	OR
*	Multiply		
–	Subtract		
+	Add		

(continued)

TABLE 17.3 *(continued)*

Shift operators

>>	Shift right
<<	Shift left

File- and String-Related Operators					
Operator	**Function**	**Operator**	**Function**	**Operator**	**Function**
−d file	True if 'file' is a directory	**−e** file	True if 'file' exists	**−f** file	True if 'file' is ordinary file
−o file	True if user owns 'file'	**−r** file	True if 'file' is readable	**−w** file	True if 'file' is writable
−x file	True if 'file' is executable	**−z** file	True if length of 'file' is zero bytes		

We use the preceding syntax of the `if` command to modify the script in the set_demo file so that it takes one command line argument only and checks on whether the argument is a file or a directory. The script returns an error message if the script is run with none or more than one command line argument or if the command line argument is not an ordinary file. The name of the script file is if_demo1.

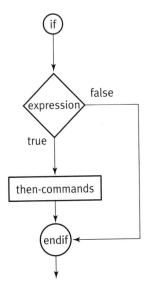

Figure 17.1 Semantics of the `if−then−if` statement

```
% cat if_demo1
#!/bin/csh
if ( ($#argv == 0) || ($#argv > 1) ) then
    echo "Usage: $0 ordinary_file"
    exit 1
endif
if ( -f $argv[1] ) then
    set filename = $argv[1]
    set fileinfo = `ls -il $filename`
    set inode = $fileinfo[1]
    set size = $fileinfo[5]
    echo "Name    Inode   Size"
    echo
    echo "$filename    $inode $size"
    exit 0
endif
echo "$0: argument must be an ordinary file"
exit 1
% if_demo1
Usage: if_demo1 ordinary_file
% if_demo1 lab3 lab4
Usage: if_demo1 ordinary_file
% if_demo1 dir1
if_demo1: argument must be an ordinary file
% if_demo1 lab3
Name      Inode    Size
lab3      856110   591
%
```

In the preceding script, the first version of the if statement contains a compound expression that displays an error message and exits the program if you run the script without a command line argument or with more than one argument. The second if statement is executed if the condition for the first if is false, that is, if you run the script with one command line argument only. This if statement produces the desired results if the command line argument is an ordinary file. If the passed argument is not an ordinary file, the condition for the second if statement is false and the error message if_demo1: argument must be an ordinary file is displayed. Note that the exit status of the script is 1 when it exits because of an erroneous condition, and 0 when the script executes successfully and produces the desired results.

An important practice in script writing is to correctly indent the commands/statements in it. Proper indentation of programs enhances their readability, making them easier to understand and upgrade. Note the indentation style used in the sample scripts presented in this textbook and follow it when you write scripts.

The second version of the `if` statement syntax also allows two-way branching. The following is a brief description of the statement.

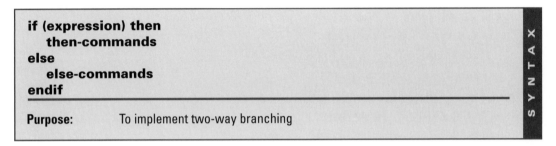

```
if (expression) then
    then-commands
else
    else-commands
endif
```

Purpose: To implement two-way branching

If 'expression' is true, the commands in 'then-commands' are executed; otherwise, the commands in 'else-commands' are executed, followed by the execution of the command after `endif`. The semantics of the statement are shown in Figure 17.2.

We rewrite the if_demo1 program by using the `if-then-else-endif` statement. The resulting script is in the if_demo2 file, as shown in the following session. Note that the program looks cleaner and more readable.

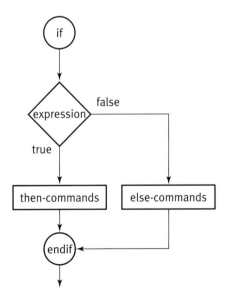

Figure 17.2 Semantics of the `if-then-else-endif` statement

```
% cat if_demo2
#!/bin/csh
if ( ($#argv == 0) || ($#argv > 1) ) then
    echo "Usage: $0 ordinary_file"
    exit 1
endif
if ( -f $argv[1] ) then
    set filename = $argv[1]
    set fileinfo = `ls -il $filename`
    set inode = $fileinfo[1]
    set size = $fileinfo[5]
    echo "Name     Inode Size"
    echo
    echo "$filename     $inode $size"
    exit 0
    else
    echo "$0 : argument must be an ordinary file"
    exit 1
endif
%
```

The third version of the if statement is used to implement multiway branching. The following is a brief description of the statement.

SYNTAX

> **if (expression1) then**
>   **then-commands**
> **else if (expression2) then**
>   **else-if1-commands**
> **else if (expression3) then**
>   **else-if2-commands**
> **...**
> **else**
>   **else-commands**
> **endif**
>
> **Purpose:**   To implement multiway branching

If 'expression1' is true, the commands in 'then-commands' are executed. If 'expression1' is false, 'expression2' is evaluated, and if it is true, the commands in 'else-if1-commands' are executed. If 'expression2' is false, 'expression3' is evaluated. If 'expression3' is true, 'else-if2-commands' are executed. If 'expression3' is also false, the commands in 'else-commands' are executed. The execution of any command list is followed by the execution of the command after endif. You can use any number of else-ifs in an if statement to implement multi-way branching. The semantics of the statement are illustrated in Figure 17.3.

We enhance the script in the if_demo2 script so that if the command line argument is a directory, the program displays the number of files and subdirectories in the directory, excluding hidden files. Implementation also involves use of the if-then-else-endif statement. The resulting script is in the if_demo3 file, as shown in the following session.

```
% cat if_demo3
#!/bin/csh
    if ( ( $#argv == 0 ) || ( $#argv > 1 ) ) then
        echo "Usage: $0 file"
        exit 1
    else
        if ( -f $argv[1] ) then
            set filename = $argv[1]
            set fileinfo = `ls -il $filename`
            set inode = $fileinfo[1]
            set size = $fileinfo[5]
            echo "Name    Inode Size"
            echo
            echo "$filename $inode $size"
        else if ( -d $argv[1] ) then
            set nfiles = `ls $argv[1] | wc -w`
```

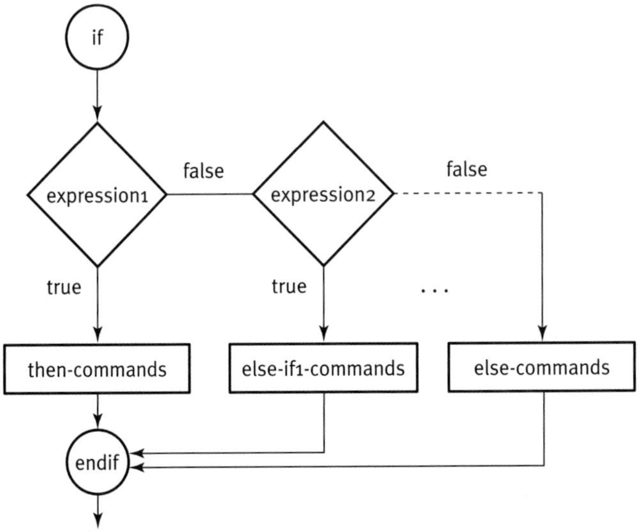

Figure 17.3 Semantics of the if-then-else-if-else-endif statement

```
                echo "The number of files in the directory is: $nfiles."
         else
                echo "$0 : argument must be an existing file or directory"
                exit 1
         endif
    endif
endif
exit 0
% if_demo3
Usage: if_demo3 file
% if_demo3    foo
if_demo3 : argument must be an existing file or directory
% if_demo3    foo foobar
Usage: if_demo3 file
% if_demo3    if_demo3
Name         Inode     Size
if_demo3     1005892   658
% if_demo3 ../main.h
Name         Inode     Size
../main.h    825745    121
% if_demo3 .
The number of files in the directory is: 3.
% if_demo3 ~/unixbook
The number of files in the directory is: 81.
%
```

If the command line argument is an existing file, the required file-related data is displayed. If the argument is a directory, the number of files in it (including directories and hidden files) is saved in the nfiles variables and displayed. If the argument is a nonexisting file or directory, the error message if_demo3: argument must be an existing file or directory is displayed. The sample runs of the script given above show these cases. The same runs also show the expected outputs when the script is run without an argument and more than one argument.

In the following In-Chapter Exercises, you will practice the use of if statement, command substitution, and manipulation of positional parameters.

IN-CHAPTER EXERCISES

17.8   Create the if_demo2 script file and run it with no argument, more than one argument, and one argument only. While running the script with one argument, use a directory as the argument. What happens? Does the output of the script make sense?

(continued)

17.9   Write a shell script whose single command line argument is a file. If you run the program with an ordinary file, the program displays the owner's name and last update time for the file. If the program is run with more than one argument, it generates meaningful error messages.

17.6.2 The **foreach** Statement

The foreach statement is the first of two statements available in the C shell for repetitive execution of a block of commands in a shell script. These statements are commonly known as loops. The following is a brief description of the statement.

---

foreach variable (argument-list)
    command-list
end

Purpose: To execute commands in 'command-list' as many times as the number of words in 'command-list'; if 'argument-list' is $argv, the arguments are taken from the command line arguments

S Y N T A X

The words in 'argument-list' are assigned to 'variable' one by one, and the commands in 'command-list', also known as the body of the loop, are executed for every assignment. This process allows execution of the commands in 'command-list' as many times as the number of words in 'argument-list'. Figure 17.4 depicts the semantics of the foreach command.

The following script in the foreach_demo1 file shows use of the foreach command with optional arguments. The variable *people* is assigned the words in 'argument-list' one by one each time the value of the variable is echoed, until no words remain in the list. At this time, control comes out of the foreach statement, and the command following end is executed. Then, the code following the foreach statement (the exit statement only in this case) is executed.

```
% cat foreach_demo1
#!/bin/csh
foreach people ( Debbie Jamie John Kitty Kuhn Shah )
    echo "$people"
end
exit 0
% foreach_demo1
Debbie
Jamie
John
Kitty
Kuhn
Shah
%
```

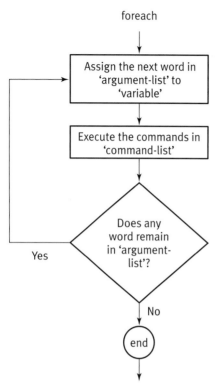

foreach

Assign the next word in
'argument-list' to
'variable'

Execute the commands in
'command-list'

Does any
word remain
in 'argument-
list'?

Yes

No

end

Figure 17.4 Semantics of the `foreach` statement

The following script in the user_info file takes a list of existing (valid) login names as command line arguments and displays each login name and the full name of the *user* who owns the login name, one per login. In the sample run, the first value of the user variable is dheckman. The echo command displays dheckman: followed by a `<Tab>`, and the cursor stays at the current line. The `grep` command searches the /etc/passwd file for dheckman and pipes it to the cut command, which displays the fifth field in the /etc/passwd line for dheckman (his full name). The process is repeated for the remaining two login names (ghacker and msarwar). As no user is left in the list passed at the command line, control comes out of the `foreach` statement and the `exit 0` command is executed to transfer control back to shell.

```
% cat user_info
#!/bin/csh
foreach user ( $argv )
     echo -n "$user :   "
grep "^"$user":" /etc/passwd | cut -f5 -d':'
end
exit 0
```

```
% user_info dheckman ghacker msarwar
dheckman:      Dennis R. Heckman
ghacker:       George Hacker
msarwar:       Mansoor Sarwar
%
```

17.6.3 The `while` Statement

The `while` statement, also known as the *while loop*, allows repeated execution of a block of code based on the condition of an expression. The following is a brief description of the statement. Figure 17.5 illustrates the semantics of the `while` statement.

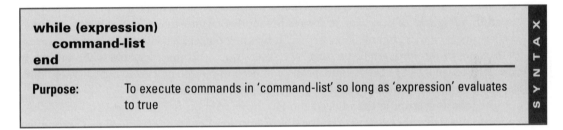

while (expression)
    command-list
end

Purpose: To execute commands in 'command-list' so long as 'expression' evaluates to true

SYNTAX

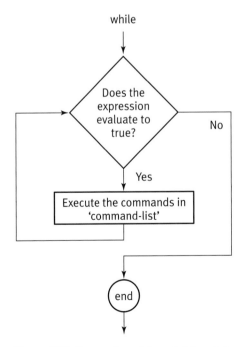

Figure 17.5 Semantics of the `while` statement

The 'expression' is evaluated and, if the result of this evaluation is true, the commands in 'command-list' are executed and 'expression' is evaluated again. This sequence of expression evaluation and execution of 'command-list', known as one iteration, is repeated until the 'expression' evaluates to false. At that time, control comes out of the while statement and the statement following end is executed.

The variables and/or conditions in the expression that result in a true value must be properly manipulated in the commands in 'command-list' for well-behaved loops, that is, loops that eventually terminate and allow execution of the rest of the code in a script. Loops in which the expression always evaluates to true are known as nonterminating, or infinite, loops. Infinite loops, usually a result of poor design and/or programming, are bad because they continuously use CPU time without accomplishing any useful task. However, some applications require infinite loops. For example, all the servers for Internet services, such as ftp, are programs that run indefinitely, waiting for client requests. Once a server has received a client request, it processes it, sends a response to the client, and waits for another client request. The only way to terminate a process with an infinite loop is to kill it by using the kill command. Or, if the process is running in the foreground, pressing <Ctrl-C> would do the trick, unless the process is designed to ignore <Ctrl-C>. In that case, you need to put the process in the background by pressing <Ctrl-Z> and using the kill -9 command to terminate it.

The following script in the while_demo file shows a simple use of the while loop. When you run this script, the *secretcode* variable is initialized to agent007, and you are prompted to make a guess. Your guess is stored in the local variable *yourguess*. If your guess is not agent007, the condition for the while loop is true and the commands between while and end are executed. This program displays a tactful message informing you of your failure and prompts you for another guess. Your guess is again stored in the *yourguess* variable and the condition for the loop is tested. This process continues until you enter agent007 as your guess. This time, the condition for the loop becomes false, and control comes out of the while statement. The echo command following done executes, congratulating you for being part of a great gene pool!

```
% cat while_demo
#!/bin/csh
set secretcode = agent007
echo "Guess the code\!"
echo -n "Enter your guess: "
set yourguess = `head -1`
while ("$secretcode" != "$yourguess")
    echo "Good guess but wrong. Try again\!"
    echo -n "Enter your guess: "
    set yourguess = `head -1`
end
echo "Wow! You are a genius\!"
exit 0
```

```
% while_demo
Guess the code!
Enter your guess: star wars
Good guess but wrong. Try again!
Enter your guess: columbo
Good guess but wrong. Try again!
Enter your guess: agent007
Wow! You are a genius!
%
```

17.6.4 The `break`, `continue`, and `goto` Commands

The `break` and `continue` commands can be used to interrupt the sequential execution of the loop body. The `break` command transfers control to the command following `end`, thus terminating the loop prematurely. A good programming use of the `break` command is to transfer control out of a nested loop. The `continue` command transfers control to `end`, which results in the evaluation of the loop condition again, hence continuation of the loop. In both cases, the commands in the loop body following these statements are not executed. Thus they are typically part of a conditional statement such as an `if` statement. The `goto` command can be used to transfer control to any command in the script. The following is a brief description of the command.

		SYNTAX
goto label		
Purpose:	To execute the command at the 'label'	

The `goto` command transfers control to the command at label:, a tag for the command. The use of `goto` is considered a bad programming practice because it makes debugging of programs a daunting task. For this reason, we do not recommend its use, with the exception perhaps of transferring control out of a nested loop (all loops and not just the one that has the `goto` command in it). Figure 17.6 illustrates the semantics of these commands.

In the following In-Chapter Exercises, you will write the C shell scripts with loops by using the `foreach` and `while` statements.

IN-CHAPTER EXERCISES

17.10 Write a shell script that takes a list of host names on your network as command line arguments and displays whether the hosts are up or down. Use the `ping` command to display the status of a host and the `foreach` statement to process all host names.

17.11 Rewrite the script in Exercise 17.10 by using the `while` statement.

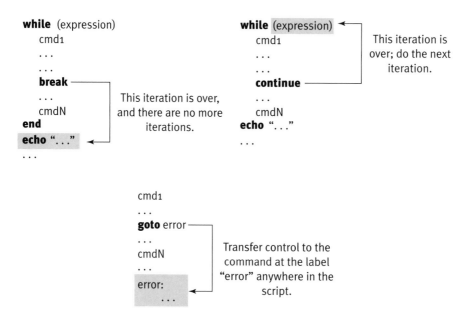

Figure 17.6 Semantics of the `break`, `continue`, and `goto` commands

17.6.5 The `switch` Statement

The `switch` statement provides a mechanism for multiway branching similar to a nested `if` statement. However, the structure provided by the `switch` statement is more readable. You should use the `switch` statement whenever the nesting level of an `if` statement becomes deeper than three levels (i.e., you are using three `else-if`s). The following is a brief description of the statement.

```
switch (test-string)
    case pattern1:
        command-list1
    breaksw
    case pattern2:
        command-list2
    breaksw
    ...
    ...
    default:
        command-listN
    breaksw
endsw
```

Purpose: To implement multiway branching as with a nested `if`

The switch statement compares the value in 'test-string' with the values of all the patterns one by one until either a match is found or there are no more patterns to match 'test-string' with. If a match is found, the commands in the corresponding 'command-list' are executed and control goes out of the switch statement. If no match is found, control goes to commands in 'command-listN'. Figure 17.7 illustrates the semantics of the switch statement.

The following script in the switch_demo file shows a simple but representative use of the switch statement. It is a menu-driven program that displays a menu of options and prompts you to enter an option. Your input is read into a variable called *option*. The switch statement then matches your option with one of the four available patterns (single characters in this case) one by one, and when a match is found, the corresponding 'command-list' (a single command in this case) is executed. Thus if you type <d> and hit <Enter> at the prompt, the date command is executed and control goes out of switch. The exit 0 command is then executed for normal program termination. Note that items enclosed in brackets are logically OR'ed. Thus, here, uppercase and lowercase letters are treated the same. A few sample runs of the script follow the code.

```
% cat switch_demo
#!/bin/csh
echo "Use one of the following options:"
echo " d or D: To display today's date and present time"
echo " l or L: To see the listing of files in your present working directory"
echo " w or W: To see who is logged in"
```

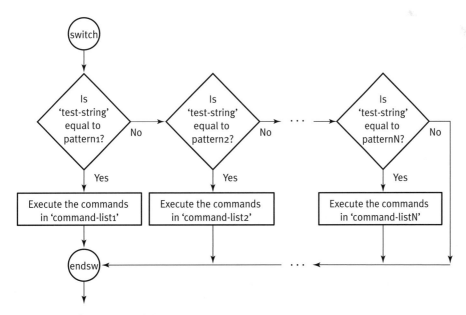

Figure 17.7 Semantics of the switch statement

```
echo " q or Q: To quit this program"
echo -n "Enter your option and hit <Enter>: "
set option = `head -1`
switch ("$option")
    case [dD]:
        date
    breaksw
    case [lL]:
        ls
    breaksw
    case [wW]:
        who
    breaksw
    case [qQ]:
        exit 0
    breaksw
    default:
        echo "Invalid option; try running the program again."
        exit 1
    breaksw
endsw
exit 0
```

% switch_demo

```
Use one of the following options:
    d or D: To display today's date and present time
    l or L: To see the listing of files in your present working directory
    w or W: To see who is logged in
    q or Q: To quit this program
Enter your option and hit <Enter>: d
Sun Aug 15 00:59:07 PDT 2004
```

% switch_demo

```
Use one of the following options:
d or D:  To display today's date and present time
            l or L: To see the listing of files in your present working directory
            w or W: To see who is logged in
            q or Q: To quit this program
Enter your option and hit <Enter>: W
dfrakes    console  Aug 14 22:18
```

```
sarwar     pts/0      Aug 14 23:41
% switch_demo
Use one of the following options:
d or D:  To display today's date and present time
         l or L: To see the listing of files in your present working directory
         w or W: To see who is logged in
         q or Q: To quit this program
Enter your option and hit <Enter>: a
Invalid option; try running the program again.
%
```

▬ Summary ▬▬▬▬▬▬▬▬▬▬▬▬▬▬▬▬▬▬▬▬▬▬▬

Every UNIX shell has a programming language that allows you to write programs for performing tasks that cannot be performed by using the existing commands. These programs are commonly known as shell scripts. In its simplest form, a shell script consists of a list of shell commands that are executed by a shell sequentially, one by one. More advanced scripts use program control flow statements for implementing multiway branching and repetitive execution of a block of commands in the script. The shell programs that consist of C shell commands, statements, and features are called C shell scripts.

The shell variables are the main memory locations that are given names and can be read from and written to. There are two types of shell variables: environment variables and user-defined variables. Environment variables, initialized by the shell at the time the user logs on, are maintained by the shell to provide a user-friendly work environment. User-defined variables are used as scratch pads in a script to accomplish the task at hand. Some environment variables, such as the positional parameters, are read-only in the sense that the user cannot change their values without using the set command.

The C shell commands for processing shell variables are set and setenv (for setting values of positional parameters and displaying values of all environment variables), env (for displaying values of all shell variables), unset and unsetenv (for removing shell variables from the environment), set with $< or set with "head –1" (for assigning keyboard input as values of variables), and shift (for shifting command line arguments to the left by one or more positions).

The program control flow statements if and switch allow the user to implement multiway branching, and the foreach and while statements can be used to implement loops. The continue, break, and goto commands can be used to interrupt the sequential execution of a shell program and transfer control to a statement that (usually) is not the next statement in the program layout.

Problems ━━━━━━━━━━━━━━

1. What is a shell script? Describe three ways of executing a shell script.

2. What is a shell variable? What is a read-only variable? How can you make a user-defined variable read-only? Give an example to illustrate your answer.

3. Which shell environment variable is used to store your search path? Change your search path interactively to include the directories ~/bin and (.). What would this change allow you to do? Why? If you want to make it a permanent change, what would you do? (*See* Chapter 4 if you have forgotten how to change your search path.)

4. What will be the output if the shell script keyin_demo in Section 17.3.5 is executed and you give * as input each time you are prompted?

5. Write a shell script that takes an ordinary file as an argument and removes the file if its size is zero. Otherwise, the script displays file's name, size, number of hard links, owner, and modify date (in this order) on one line. Your script must do appropriate error checking.

6. Write a shell script that takes a directory as a required argument and displays the name of all zero length files in it. Do appropriate error checking.

7. Write a shell script that removes all zero length ordinary files in the current directory. Do appropriate error checking.

8. Modify the script in Problem 6 so that it removes all zero length ordinary files in the directory passed as an optional argument. If you do not specify the directory argument, the script uses the present working directory as the default argument. Do appropriate error checking.

9. Run the script in if_demo2 in Section 17.6 with if_demo2 as its argument. Does the output make sense to you? Why?

10. Write a shell script that takes a list of login names on your computer system as command line arguments and displays these login names and full names of the users who own these logins (as contained in the /etc/passwd file), one per line. If a login name is invalid (not found in the /etc/passwd file), display the login name but nothing for full name. The format of the output line is the following.

     login name: user name

11. What happens when you run a stand-alone command enclosed in backquotes (grave accents), such as `'date'`? Why?

12. What happens when you execute the following sequence of shell commands?

     a. `set name=date`

     b. `$name`

     c. `` `$name` ``

13. Take a look at your ~/.login and ~/.cshrc files and list the environment variables that are exported, along with their values. What is the purpose of each variable?

14. Write a shell script that takes a list of login names as its arguments and displays the number of terminals that each user is logged on to in a LAN environment.

15. Write a C shell script domain2ip that takes a list of domain names as command line arguments and displays their IP addresses. Use the `nslookup` command. The following is a sample run of this program.

    ```
    % domain2ip up.edu redhat.com
    Name: up.edu
    Address: 192.220.208.9

    Name: redhat.com
    Address: 207.175.42.154

    $
    ```

16. Modify the script in the switch_demo file in Section 17.6.5 so that it allows you to try any number of options and quits only when you use the `q` option.

17. Write a C shell script that displays the following menu and prompts for one-character input to invoke a menu option, as shown.

    a. List all files in the present working directory

    b. Display today's date and time

    c. Invoke the shell script for Problem 13

    d. Display whether a file is a "simple" file of a "directory"

    e. Create a backup for a file

    f. Start a telnet session

    g. Start an ftp session

    h. Exit

    Option (c) requires that you ask the user for a list of login names. For options (d) and (e), prompt the user for file names before invoking a `shell` command/program. For options (f) and (g), prompt the user for a domain name (or PI address) before initiating a telnet or ftp session. The program should allow the user to try any option any number of times and should quit only when the user gives option (h) as input.

    A good programming practice is to build code incrementally—that is, write code for one option, test it, and then go to the next option.

Advanced C Shell Programming

Objectives

- To discuss numeric data processing
- To describe array processing
- To discuss how standard input of a command in a shell script can be redirected to data within the script
- To explain signal/interrupt processing capability of the C shell
- To cover the commands and primitives
  `=, +=, -=, *=, /=, %=, <, >, |, &, (), <<, @,`
  `<^Z>, clear, onintr, set, stty`

18.1   Introduction

We did not discuss four features of C shell programming in Chapter 17: processing of numeric data, array processing, the here document feature, and interrupt processing. In this chapter, we discuss these features and give some example scripts that use them. We also describe how C shell scripts can be debugged.

18.2   Numeric Data Processing

The C shell has a built-in capability for processing numeric data. It allows you to perform arithmetic and logic operations on numeric integer data without explicitly converting string data to numeric data and vice versa. You can use the @ command to declare numeric variables, the variables that contain integer data. This command allows declaration of local variables only. The following is a brief description of the command.

SYNTAX

@ variable [operator expression] [variable [operator expression]] ...

Purpose: To declare 'variable' to be a numeric variable, evaluate the arithmetic 'expression', apply the operator specified in 'operator' on the current value of 'variable' and the value of 'expression', and assign the result to 'variable'

Expressions are formed by using the arithmetic and logic operators summarized previously in Table 17.4. Although octal numbers can be used in expressions by starting them with 0, the final value of an arithmetic expression is always expressed in decimal numbers. The elements of an expression must be separated by one or more spaces unless the elements are (,), &, |, <, and >. Table 18.1 describes the assignment operators that can be used as 'operator'.

■ **TABLE 18.1**   Assignment Operators for the @ Command

Operator	Meaning
=	Assigns the value of the expression on the right-hand side of = to the variable preceding it
+=	Adds the value of the expression on the right-hand side of = to the current value of the variable preceding it and assigns the result to the variable
-=	Subtracts the value of the expression on the right-hand side of = from the current value of the variable preceding it and assigns the result to the variable
*=	Multiplies the value of the expression on the right-hand side of = with the current value of the variable preceding it and assigns the result to the variable
/=	Divides the value of the variable preceding = by the value of the expression on the right-hand side of = and assigns the result (quotient) to the variable *(continued)*

TABLE 18.1 *(continued)*

Divides the value of the variable preceding = by the value of the expression on the right-hand side of = and assigns the remainder to the variable

In the following interactive session, the numeric variables *value1* and *value2* are initialized to 10 and 15, respectively. The echo command is used to show that the assignments work properly.

```
% @ value1 = 10
% @ value2 = 15
% echo "$value1 $value2"
10  15
%
```

In the following session, the @ command declares two variables, *difference* and *sum*, and initializes them to the values of the expressions. These actions result in the variables *difference* and *sum* taking the values −5 and 25, respectively.

```
% @ difference = ($value1 - $value2) sum = ($value1 + $value2)
% echo $difference $sum
-5  25
%
```

You can use the ++ and -- operators to increment or decrement a variable's value by 1. For example, the following three commands are equivalent, all incrementing the value of the *results* variable by 1.

```
% @ results++
% @ results += 1
% @ results = ( $results + 1 )
```

You can also use the variables declared by using the set command to store numeric data. Thus, in the following session, the variables *side*, *area*, and *volume* are declared by using the set command and are assigned numeric values by using the @ command.

```
% set side = 10 area volume
% @ area = $side * $side
% @ volume = $side * $side * $side
% echo $side $area $volume
10  100  1000
%
```

In the following In-Chapter Exercise, you will perform numeric data processing by using the set and @ commands.

IN-CHAPTER EXERCISE

18.1 Declare two numeric variables *var1* and *var2* initialized to 10 and 30, respectively. Give two versions of a command that will produce and display their sum and product.

18.3   Array Processing

An **array** is a named collection of items of the same type stored in contiguous memory locations. Array items are numbered, with the first item being 1. You can access an array item by using the name of the array followed by the item number in brackets. Thus, you can use *people [k]* to refer to the *k*th element in the array called *people*. This process is known as **array indexing**. You can declare arrays for strings and integers by using the set command in the following manner.

SYNTAX

set array_name = (array elements)

Purpose: To declare 'array_name' to be an array variable containing 'array elements' in parentheses

---

You can access the contents of the whole array by using the array name preceded by the dollar sign ($), such as $name. You can access the total number of elements in an array by using the array name preceded by $#, as in $#name. The $?name is 1 if the named array has been initialized and 0 if it has not been initialized.

In the following session, we define a string array of six items, called students, initialized to the words enclosed in parentheses. The contents of the whole array can be accessed by using $students, as shown in the first echo command. Thus, the echo $#students command displays 6 (the size of the students array), and the echo $?students command displays 1, informing you that the array has been initialized.

```
% set students = (David James Jeremy Brian Art Charlie)
% echo $students
David James Jeremy Brian Art Charlie
% echo $#students
6
% echo $?students
1
%
```

In the following session, we show how elements of the *students* array can be accessed and changed. You can access the *i*th element in the *students* array by indexing it as *$students [i]*. Thus, the first echo command displays the second item in the students array. The set command changes the value of the second element from James to Mansoor Sarwar. Figure 18.1 depicts the original and modified *students* arrays.

```
% echo $students[2]
James
% set students[2] = "Mansoor Sarwar"
% echo $students
David Mansoor Sarwar Jeremy Brian Art Charlie
% echo $students[2]
Mansoor Sarwar
%
```

Like other variables, an array variable can be removed from the environment by using the unset command. In the following session, the unset command is used to deallocate the *students* array. The echo command is used to confirm that the array has actually been deallocated.

```
% unset students
% echo $students
students: Undefined variable.
%
```

Therefore, any shell variable assigned multiple values with the set command becomes an array variable. Thus, when a variable is assigned a multiword output of a command as a value, it becomes an array variable and contains each field of the output in a separate array slot. In the following session, *files* is an array variable whose elements are the names of all the files in the present working directory. The *numfiles* variable contains the number of files in the current directory. The echo $files[3] command displays the third array element.

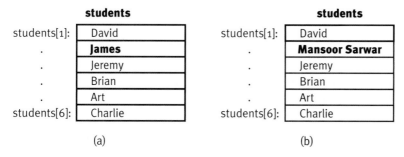

Figure 18.1 The *students* array (a) before and (b) after changing the contents of the second slot

```
% set files = `ls` numfiles = `ls | wc -w`
% echo $files
cmdargs_demo foreach_demo1 if_demo1 if_demo2 keyin_demo
% echo $numfiles
5
% echo $files[3]
if_demo1
%
```

You can also use an array declared with the `set` command to contain numeric data. In the following session, the num_array_demo file contains a script that uses an array of integers, called *Fibonacci*, computes the sum of integers in the array, and displays the sum on the screen. The *Fibonacci* array contains the first 10 numbers of the **Fibonacci series**. If you are not familiar with the Fibonacci series, the first two numbers in the series are 0 and 1 and the next Fibonacci number is calculated by adding the preceding two numbers. Therefore, the first 10 numbers in the Fibonacci series are 0, 1, 1, 2, 3, 5, 8, 13, 21, and 34. Thus, the Fibonacci series may be expressed mathematically as

$$F_1 = 0, \; F_2 = 1, \; \ldots \; , \; F_n = F_{n-1} + F_{n-2} \quad (\text{for } n \geq 3).$$

The following script in the num_array_demo file is well documented and fairly easy to understand. It displays the sum of the first 10 Fibonacci numbers. A sample run of the script follows the code.

```
% cat num_array_demo
# File Name:    ~/unixbook/examples/Cshell/num_array_demo
# Author:        Syed Mansoor Sarwar
# Written:       August 16, 2004
# Last Modified: August 16, 2004
# Purpose:       To demonstrate working with numeric arrays
# Brief Description: Maintain running sum of numbers in a numeric variable called
# sum, starting with 0. Read the next array value and add it to
# sum. When all elements have been read, stop and display the
# answer.
#!/bin/csh


# Initialize Fibonacci array to any number of Fibonacci numbers - first ten in this case
set Fibonacci = ( 0 1 1 2 3 5 8 13 21 34 )
@ size = $#Fibonacci    # Size of the Fibonacci array
@ index = 1             # Array index initialized to point to the first element
@ sum = 0               # Running sum initialized to 0
```

```
while ( $index <= $size )
    @ sum = $sum + $Fibonacci[$index]    # Update the running sum
    @ index++                            # Increment array index by 1
end
echo "The sum of the given $#Fibonacci numbers is $sum."
exit 0
% num_array_demo
The sum of the given 10 numbers is 88.
%
```

Although this example clearly explains numeric array processing, is of no practical use. We now present a more useful example, wherein the fs file contains a script that takes a directory as an optional argument and returns the size (in bytes) of all ordinary files in it. If no directory name is given at the command line, the script uses the current directory.

When you run the program without a command line argument, it treats your current directory as the argument. If you specify more than one argument, the script displays an error message and terminates.

When executed with one nondirectory argument only, the program again displays an error message and exits. When executed with one argument only and the argument is a directory, the program initializes the string array variable *files* to the names of all the files in the specified directory (or current directory if none is specified) by using command substitution, or `ls $directory`. A numeric variable *nfiles* is initialized to the number of files in the current directory by using the @ nfiles = $#files command. Then, the size of every ordinary file in the *files* array is added to the numeric variable *sum* (which is initialized to *0*). When no more names are left in the *files* array, the program displays the total space (in bytes) used by all ordinary files in the directory, then terminates.

```
% cat fs
# File Name:   ~/unixbook/examples/Cshell/fs
# Author:      Syed Mansoor Sarwar
# Written:     August 16, 1999
# Modified:    August 16, 1999; May 11, 2000
# Purpose:     To add the sizes of all the files in a directory passed as
#              command line argument
# Brief Description:   Maintain running sum of file sizes in a numeric variable
#                      called sum, initialized to 0. Read all the file names
#                      in a string array called files. Get the size of a file
#                      and add it to the running total in sum. Stop when all file
#                      names have been processed and display the answer.
#!/bin/csh

if ( $#argv == 0 ) then
```

```
        set directory = "."
else if ( $#argv > 1 ) then
        echo "Usage: $0 [directory name]"
        exit 0
else if ( ! -d $argv[1] ) then
        echo "Usage: $0 [directory name]"
exit 0
else
        set directory = $argv[1]
endif

# Initialize files array to file names in the specified directory
set files = `ls $directory`
@ nfiles = $#files # Number of files in the specified directory into nfiles
@ index = 1        # Array index initialized to point to the first file name
@ sum = 0          # Running sum initialized to 0

while ( $index <= $nfiles )              # For as long as a file name is left in files
            set thisfile = "$directory"/"$files[$index]"
      if ( -f $thisfile ) then           # If the next file is an ordinary file
            set argv = `ls -l $thisfile` # Set command line arguments
            @ sum = $sum + $argv[4]      # On AIX change 4 to 5; Solaris does not
                                         # display group name
            @ index++                    # Add file size to the current total
      else
            @ index++
            endif
end

# Spell out the current directory
if ( "$directory" == "." ) then
        set directory = "your current directory"
endif
echo "The size of all non-directory files in $directory is $sum bytes."
exit 0
% fs fs
Usage: fs [directory name]
% fs dir1 dir2
Usage: fs [directory name]
% fs dir1
```

```
Usage: fs [directory name]
% fs
The size of all non-directory files in your current directory is 3090 bytes.
% fs ..
The size of all non-directory files in .. is 6875330 bytes.
% fs $home
The size of all non-directory files in /home/sarwar is 14665746 bytes.
%
```

In the following In-Chapter Exercise, you will write a C shell script that uses the numeric data processing commands for manipulating numeric arrays.

IN-CHAPTER EXERCISE

18.2 Write a C shell script that contains two numeric arrays, *array1* and *array2*, initialized to values in the sets {1,2,3,4,5} and {1,4,9,16,25}, respectively. The script produces and displays an array whose elements are the sum of the corresponding elements i the two arrays. Thus the first element of the resultandt arry is $1 + 1 = 2$, the second element is $2 + 4 = 6$, and so on.

18.4 The Here Document

The here document feature of the C shell allows you to redirect standard input of a command in a script and attach it to data within the script. Obviously, then, this feature works with commands that take input from standard input. The feature is used mainly to display menus, although it also is useful in other ways. The following is a brief description of the here document.

---

command << input_marker
... input data ...
input_marker

Purpose: To execute 'command' with its input coming from the here document— data between the input start and end markers 'input_marker'

SYNTAX

The 'input_marker' is a word that you choose to wrap the input data in for 'command'. The closing marker must be on a line by itself and cannot be surrounded by any spaces. We explain the use of the here document with a simple redirection of standard input of the cat command from the document. The following script in the heredoc_demo file displays a message for the user and then sends a mail message to the person whose e-mail address is passed as a command line argument.

```
% cat heredoc_demo
#!/bin/csh

# First example
cat << DataTag
This is a simple use of the here document. These data are the
input to the cat command.
DataTag

# Second example
mail $argv[1] << WRAPPER
Hello,

This is a reminder for the weekly meeting tomorrow.

Mansoor
WRAPPER

echo "Sending mail to $argv[1] ... done"
exit 0
% heredoc_demo eecsfaculty
This is a simple use of the here document. These data are the
input to the cat command.
Sending mail to eecsfaculty ... done
%
```

The following script is more useful and a better use of the here document feature. This script, dext (for directory expert), maintains a directory of names, phone numbers, and e-mail addresses. The script is run with a name as a command line argument and uses the grep command to display the directory entry corresponding to the name. The -i option is used with the grep command in order to ignore the case of letters. The backslashes are used to continue the grep command and visually segregate the directory data from it.

```
% more dext
#!/bin/csh

if ( $#argv == 0 ) then
    echo "Usage: $0 name"
    exit 1
else
    set user_input = "$argv[1]"
    grep -i "$user_input" \
\
<< Directory_Data
```

```
John Doe        555.232.0000    johnd@somedomain.edu

Jenny Great     444.656.1111    jg@new.somecollege.edu

David Nice      999.111.3333    david_nice@xyz.org

Jim Davis       777.000.9999    davis@great.adviser.edu

Art Pohm        333.000.8888    art.pohm@great.professor.edu

Directory_Data


endif

exit 0

%
```

The advantage of maintaining the directory within the script is that it eliminates some extra file operations such as open and read that would be required if the directory data were maintained in a separate file. The result is a much faster program.

Completing the following In-Chapter Exercise will enhance your understanding of the here document feature of C shell.

IN-CHAPTER EXERCISE

18.3   Create the dext script on your system and run it. Try it with as many different inputs as you can think of. Does the script work correctly?

18.5   Interrupt (Signal) Processing

We discussed the basic concept of signals in Chapter 13, where we defined them as software interrupts that can be sent to a process. We also stated that the process receiving a signal can take any one of three possible actions:

1. accept the default action as determined by the UNIX kernel,
2. ignore the signal, or
3. take a programmer-defined action.

In UNIX, several types of signals can be sent to a process. Some of these signals can be sent via the hardware devices such as the keyboard, but all can be sent via the kill command, as discussed in Chapter 13. The most common event that causes a hardware interrupt (and a signal) is generated when you press <Ctrl-C> and is known as the keyboard interrupt. This event causes the foreground process to terminate (the default action). Other events that cause a process to receive a signal include termination of a child process, a process accessing a main memory location that is not part of its address space (the main memory area that the program owns and is allowed to access), and a software termination signal caused by execution of the kill command without any signal number. Table 18.2 presents a list of some important signals, their numbers (which can be used to generate those signals with the kill command), and their purpose.

■ **TABLE 18.2** Some Important Signals, Their Numbers, and Their Purpose

Signal Name	Signal #	Purpose
SIGHUP (hang up)	1	Informs the process when the user who ran the process logs out and terminates the process
SIGINT (keyboard interrupt)	2	Informs the process when the user presses `<Ctrl-C>` and terminates the process
SIGQUIT (quit signal)	3	Informs the process when the user presses `<Ctrl-|>` or `<Ctrl-\>` and terminates the process
SIGKILL (sure kill)	9	Definitely terminates the process when the user sends this signal to it with the `kill -9` command
SIGSEGV (segmentation violation)	11	Terminates the process upon memory fault when a process tries to access memory space that doesn't belong to it
SIGTERM (software termination)	15	Terminates the process when the kill command is used without any signal number
SIGTSTP (suspend/stop signal)	18	Suspends the process, usually `<Ctrl-Z>`
SIGCHLD (child finished execution)	20	Informs the process of termination of one of its children

The signal processing feature of the C shell allows you to write programs that cannot be terminated by a terminal interrupt (`<Ctrl-C>`). In contrast to the Bourne shell support for signal processing, this feature is very limited. The command used to intercept and ignore `<Ctrl-C>` is onintr. The following is a brief description of the command.

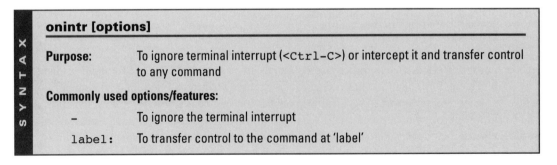

onintr [options]

Purpose: To ignore terminal interrupt (`<Ctrl-C>`) or intercept it and transfer control to any command

Commonly used options/features:

    –   To ignore the terminal interrupt

    `label:`   To transfer control to the command at 'label'

When you use the onintr command without any option, the default action of process termination takes place when you press `<Ctrl-C>` while the process is running. Thus, using the `onintr` command without any option is redundant. Here, we enhance the script in the while_demo file in Chapter 17 so that you cannot terminate execution of this program with <Ctrl-C>. The enhanced version is in the onintr_demo file, as shown in the following session. Note that the `onintr` command is used to transfer control to the command at the `interrupt_label:` label when you press <Ctrl-C> while executing this program. The code at this label is a `goto` command that transfers control to the `onintr interrupt` command to reset the interrupt handling capability of the code, effectively ignoring <Ctrl-C>. A sample run illustrates this point.

```
% cat onintr_demo
#!/bin/csh
# Intercept <Ctrl-C> and transfer control to the command at
backagain:
     onintr interrupt

# Set the secret code
set secretcode = agent007

# Get user input
echo "Guess the code\!"
echo -n "Enter your guess: "
set yourguess = `head -1`
# As long as the user input is not the secret code (agent007 in this case),
# loop here: display a message and take user input gain. When the user
# input matches the secret code, terminate the loop and execute the
# following echo command.
while ( "$secretcode" != "$yourguess" )
     echo "Good guess but wrong. Try again\!"
     echo -n "Enter your guess: "
     set yourguess = `head -1`
end
echo "Wow! You are a genius\!"
exit 0
# Code executed when you press <Ctrl-C>
interrupt:
     echo "Nice try -- you cannot terminate me by <Ctrl-C>\!"
     goto backagain

% onintr_demo
Guess the code!
Enter your guess: codecracker
```

```
Good guess but wrong. Try again!
Enter your guess: <Ctrl-C>
Nice try -- you cannot terminate me by <Ctrl-C>!
Guess the code!
Enter your guess: agent007
Wow! You are a genius!
%
```

The net effect of using the `onintr` command in the preceding script is to ignore keyboard interrupt. You can achieve the same effect by using the command with the – option. Thus, the whole interrupt handling code in the onintr_demo program can be replaced by the `onintr` – command; no code is needed at any label, but then the code does not display any message for you when you press `<Ctrl-C>`.

To terminate programs that ignore terminal interrupts, you have to use the `kill` command. You can do so by suspending the process by pressing `<Ctrl-Z>`, using the `ps` command to get the PID of the process, and terminating it with the `kill` command.

You can modify the script in the onintr_demo file so that it ignores the keyboard interrupt, clears the display screen, and turns off the echo. Whatever you enter at the keyboard, then, is not displayed. Next, it prompts you for the code word twice. If you do not enter the same code word both times, it reminds you of your bad short-term memory and quits. If you enter the same code word, it clears the display screen and prompts you to guess the code word again. If you do not enter the original code word, the screen is cleared and you are prompted to guess again. The program does not terminate until you have entered the original code word. When you do enter it, the display screen is cleared, a message is displayed at the top left of the screen, and echo is turned on. Because the terminal interrupt is ignored, you cannot terminate the program by pressing `<Ctrl-C>`. The `stty -echo` command turns off the echo. Thus, when you type the original code word (or any guesses), it is not displayed on the screen. The `clear` command clears the display screen and locates the cursor at the top left corner. The `stty echo` command turns on the echo. The resulting script is in the `canleave` file shown in the following session.

```
% more canleave
#!/bin/csh

# Ignore terminal interrupt
onintr -

# Clear the screen, locate the cursor at the top-left corner,
# and turn off echo
clear
stty -echo

# Set the secret code
echo -n "Enter your code word: "
```

```
set secretcode = `head -1`
echo " "

# To make sure that the user remembers the code word
echo -n "Enter your code word again: "
set same = `head -1`
echo " "
if ( $secretcode != $same ) then
    echo "Work on your short-term memory before using this code\!"
    exit 1
endif

# Get user guess
clear
echo -n "Enter the code word: "
set yourguess = `head -1`
echo " "

# As long as the user input is not the original code word, loop here: display
# a message and take user input gain. When the user input matches the secret
# code word, terminate the loop and execute the following echo command.
while ( "$secretcode" != "$yourguess" )
    clear
    echo -n "Enter the code word: "
    set yourguess = `head -1`
end

# Set terminal to echo mode
clear
echo "Back again\!"
stty echo
exit 0
%
```

You can use this script to lock your terminal before you leave it to pick up a printout or get a can of soda; hence, the name canleave (can leave). Using it saves you the time otherwise required for the logout and login procedures.

18.6 Debugging Shell Programs

You can debug your C shell scripts by using the **-x** (echo) option of the **csh** command. This option displays each line of the script after variable substitution but before execution. You can combine the **-x** option with the **-v** (verbose) option to display each line of the script (as it appears in the script file) before execution. You can also invoke the **csh** command from the command line to run the script, or you can make it part of the script, as in **#!/bin/csh -xv**.

In the following session, we show how a shell script can be debugged. The script in the debug_demo file prompts you for a digit. If you enter a value between 1 and 9, it displays **Good input!** and quits. If you enter any other value, it simply exits. When the script is executed, enter 4, and it displays the message **debug_demo: [4: not found.**

```
% cat debug_demo
#!/bin/csh

echo -n "Enter a digit: "
set var1 = `head -1`
if ( ( "$var1" >= 1 ) && ( "$var1" <= 9 ) ) then
    echo "Good input!"
endif
exit 0
% debug_demo
Enter a digit: 4
": Event not found
%
```

We debug the program by using the **csh -xv debug_demo** command. The last two lines of output of the run-time trace shows the problem area. In this case, the error is generated because of the bang sign (**!**) in the echo **"Good input!"** statement. The problem is taken care of by escaping **!**, as in **\!**. Another solution is to put a space after the **!** symbol. After we take care of this problem, the script works properly.

```
$ csh -xv debug_demo

echo -n "Enter a digit: "
echo -n Enter a digit:
Enter a digit: set var1 = `head -1`
set var1 = `head -1`
head -1
4
if ( ( "$var1" > = 1 ) && ( "$var1" < = 9 ) ) then
if ( ( 4 > = 1 ) && ( 4 < = 9 ) ) then
echo "Good input!"
": Event not found
$
```

The following In-Chapter Exercise has been designed to enhance your understanding of the interrupt processing and debugging features of C shell.

IN-CHAPTER EXERCISE

18.4   Test the scripts in the onintr_demo and canleave files on your UNIX system. Do they work as expected? Be sure that you understand them. If your versions do not work properly, use the `csh -xv` command to debug them.

Summary

The C shell has the built-in capability for numeric integer data processing in terms of arithmetic, logic, and shift operations. Combined with the array processing feature of the language, this allows the programmer to write useful programs for processing large data sets with relative ease. The numeric variables can be declared and processed by using the @ and `set` commands.

The here document feature of the C shell allows standard input of a command in a script to be attached to data within the script. The use of this feature results in more efficient programs. The reason is that no extra file-related operations, such as file open and read, are needed, as the data is within the script file and has probably been loaded into the main memory when the script was loaded.

The C shell also allows the user to write programs that ignore signals such as terminal interrupt (`<Ctrl-C>`). This useful feature can be used, among other things, to disable program termination when it is in the middle of updating a file. The `onintr` command can be used to invoke this feature.

The C shell programs can be debugged by using the `-x` and `-v` options of the `csh` command. This technique allows viewing the commands in the user's script after variable substitution but before execution.

Problems

1.   Is the `expr` command needed in the C shell?

2.   What is the here document? Why is it useful?

3.   Modify the num_array_demo script in Section 18.3 so that it takes the numbers to be added as the command line arguments. Use the `while` control structure and integer arrays.

4.   The `dext` script in Section 18.4 takes a single name as a command line argument. Modify this script so that it takes a list of names as command line arguments. Use the `foreach` control structure to implement your solution.

5. The script in the canleave file discussed in Section 18.5 is designed to ignore keyboard interrupt. How can this program be terminated? Be precise.

6. Write a C shell script that takes integer numbers as command line arguments and displays their sum on the screen.

7. Write a C shell script that takes an integer number from the keyboard and displays the Fibonacci numbers equal to the number entered from the keyboard. Thus, if the user enters 7, your script displays the first seven Fibonacci numbers.

8. What are signals in UNIX? What types of signals can be intercepted in C shell scripts?

9. Enhance the code of Problem 7 so that it cannot be terminated by pressing `<Ctrl-C>`. When the user presses `<Ctrl-C>`, your script gives a message to the user and continues.

10. Modify the script in Problem 6 so that it reads integers to be added as a here document.

File System Backup

Objectives

- To describe how files and directories can be archived and restored in UNIX
- To explain recovery of a subset of archived files
- To cover the commands and primitives
  `|`, `>`, `cd`, `compress`, `file`, `ls`, `pwd`, `tar`, `uncompress`

19.1   Introduction

The UNIX operating system has several utilities that allow you to archive your files and directories in a single file. System administrators normally use a tape as the storage medium for archiving complete file system structures as backups so that, when a system crashes for some reason, files can be recovered. UNIX-based computer systems normally crash for reasons beyond the operating system's control, such as a disk head crash because of a power surge. UNIX rarely causes a system to crash because it is a well-designed, coded, and tested operating system. In a typical installation, backup is done every day during off hours (late night or early morning) when the system is not normally in use.

As a normal UNIX user, you can also archive your work if you want to. You normally need to do this to archive files related to a project so that you can transfer them to someone via e-mail, ftp, or secondary storage medium (tape, floppy, DVD, or CD-ROM). The primary reason for making an archive is the convenience of dealing with (sending or receiving) a single file instead of a complete directory hierarchy. Without an archive, the sender might have to send several files and directories (a file structure) that the receiver would have to restore in the correct order. Without an archiving facility, depending on the size of the file structure, the task of sending, receiving, and reconstructing the file structure can be very time-consuming. UNIX has several utilities that can be used for archiving files, including `cpio`, `dump`, and `tar`. We discuss `tar` only, as it is the most commonly used of these utilities.

19.2   Archiving and Restoring Files via `tar`

In Chapter 10, we discussed file compression by using the `compress` and `pack` commands and pointed out that compression saves disk space and transmission time. However, compressing small files normally does not result in much compression. Moreover, compressing files of one **cluster** in size (the minimum unit of disk storage; one or more sectors) or less does not help save disk space even if compression does result in smaller files, because the system ends up using one cluster to save the compressed file anyway. But if compression does result in a smaller file, you do save time in transmitting the compressed version. If the disk block size is 512 bytes and a cluster consists of more than two blocks, you can use the `tar` command to *pack* files together in one file, with a 512-byte tar header at the beginning of each file, as shown in Figure 19.1.

The `tar` (tape archive) utility was originally designed to save file systems on tape as a backup so that files could be recovered in the event of a system crash. It is still used for that purpose, but it is also commonly used now to pack a directory hierarchy as an ordinary disk file. Doing so saves disk space and transmission time while a directory hierarchy is being transmitted electronically. The saving in disk space results primarily from the fact that empty space within a cluster is not wasted. A brief description of the `tar` utility follows.

19.2.1 Archiving Files

You can use the `tar` command for archiving (also known as packing) a list of files and/or directories by using the `c` or `r` option. The `c` option creates a new archive, whereas the `r` option appends files at the end of the current archive. The most common use of the `tar` command is with the `c` option.

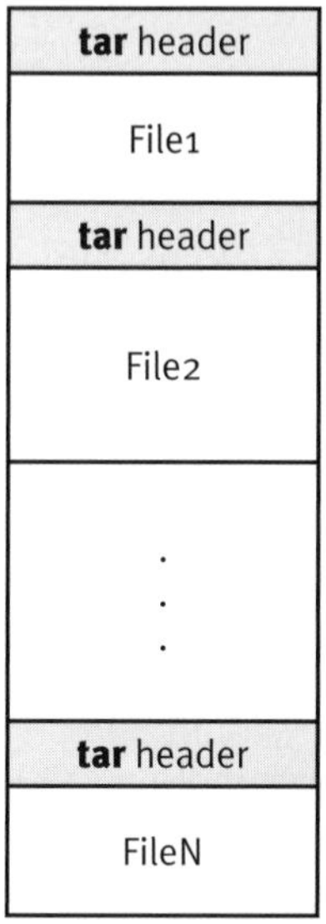

Figure 19.1 Format of a `tar` file

---

tar [options] [files]
The use of – in front of an option is not mandatory

Purpose:	Archive (copy in a particular format) 'files' to or restore files from tape, (which can be an ordinary file); directories are archived and restored recursively

Commonly used options/features:

Option Format:	Function_letter [Modifier]
Function_letter:	
c	Create a new tape and record archive 'files' on it
r	Record 'files' at the end of tape (append operation)
t	List tape's contents (names of files archived on it) in a format such as `ls -l`
u	Update tape by adding 'files' on it if not on or if modified since last written to tape
x	Extract (restore) 'files' from tape; entire tape if none specified
Modifier:	
b N	Use 'N' as the blocking factor (1 default; 20 maximum) *(continued)*

S Y N T A X

tar [options] [files] *(continued)*		
f Arch	Use 'Arch' as the archive for archiving or restoring files; default is /dev/mto. If 'Arch' is –, standard input is read (for extracting files), or standard output is written (for creating an archive)—a feature used when `tar` is used in a pipeline	
h	Follow symbolic links	
l	Display error message if links are not found	
o	Change ownership (user ID and group ID) to the user running `tar`	
v	Use verbose mode: Display function letter x for extraction or for an archive	

In the examples presented in this chapter, we use the directory structure shown in Figure 19.2.

The following session shows that there are two directories under the unixbook directory: called current and final. In addition, each of these directories contains six files (*see* Figure 19.2), displayed by the `ls –l` commands.

```
$ cd unixbook
$ pwd
/users/sarwar/unixbook
% ls -l
drwx------   2   sarwar    512   Jul 22 13:21   current
drwx------   2   sarwar    512   Jul 22 13:21   final
$ cd current
$ ls -l
-rw-------   1   sarwar   204288   Jul 19 13:06   ch07.doc
-rw-------   1   sarwar    87552   Jul 19 13:06   ch08.doc
-rw-------   1   sarwar    86016   Jul 19 13:06   ch09.doc
-rw-------   1   sarwar   121344   Jul 19 13:06   ch10.doc
-rw-------   1   sarwar   152576   Jul 19 13:06   ch11.doc
-rw-------   1   sarwar   347648   Jul 19 13:06   ch12.doc
$ cd ..
$ cd final
$ ls -l
-rw-------   1   sarwar    41984   Jul 19 13:06   ch1.doc
-rw-------   1   sarwar    54272   Jul 19 13:06   ch2.doc
-rw-------   1   sarwar   142848   Jul 19 13:06   ch3.doc
-rw-------   1   sarwar    86528   Jul 19 13:06   ch4.doc
-rw-------   1   sarwar   396288   Jul 19 13:06   ch5.doc
-rw-------   1   sarwar   334848   Jul 19 13:06   ch6.doc
$
```

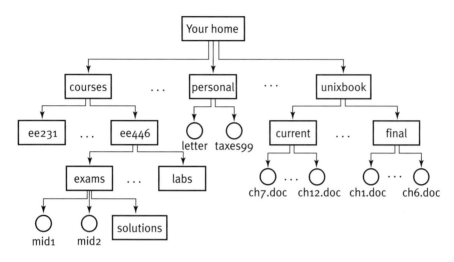

Figure 19.2 A sample file structure

If you want to create an archive of the unixbook directory on a tape drive /dev/rmt/t0 (the name might be different on your system), you can use the following command after changing directory to unixbook. The v (verbose) option is used to view the files and directories that are being archived. Unless you are the system administrator, in all likelihood you do not have access permission to use (read or write) the tape drive. Thus, the shell will give you the following error message. However, if you do have proper access permissions for the tape drive, an archive of the unixbook directory is created on the tape. Not only do you need access privileges to /dev/rmt/t0, but you also need to *mount* it first.

```
$ tar cvf /dev/rmt/t0 .
tar: /dev/rmt/t0: Permission denied
$
```

However, you can create an archive on a disk file—in a directory that you have the write permission for—by using the following command. Here we made ~/unixbook our current directory and created a `tar` archive of this directory in a file called unixbook.tar. Note that .tar is not an extension required by the `tar` utility. We have used this extension because it allows us to identify `tar` archives by looking at the file name. With no such extension, we have to use the `file` command to identify our `tar` archive files, as shown in the last command line in the session (in case you forgot what the `file` command does).

```
$ cd ~/unixbook
$ tar cvf unixbook.tar .
a ./ 0K
```

```
tar: ./unixbook.tar same as archive file
a ./final/ 0K
a ./final/ch1.doc 41K
a ./final/ch2.doc 53K
a ./final/ch3.doc 140K
a ./final/ch4.doc 85K
a ./final/ch5.doc 387K
a ./final/ch6.doc 327K
a ./current/ 0K
a ./current/ch07.doc 200K
a ./current/ch08.doc 86K
a ./current/ch09.doc 84K
a ./current/ch10.doc 119K
a ./current/ch11.doc 149K
a ./current/ch12.doc 340K
$ ls -l

drwx------     2    sarwar      512    Jul 22 13:21    current
drwx------     2    sarwar      512    Jul 22 13:21    final
-rw-------     1    sarwar  2064896    Jul 22 13:47    unixbook.tar
$ file unixbook.tar
unixbook.tar:       USTAR tar archive
$
```

You can also create the `tar` archive of the current directory by using the following command line. The – argument informs `tar` that the archive is to be sent to standard output, which is redirected to the unixbook.tar file. As we discussed in Chapter 15, the back quotes (grave accents) are used for command substitution, that is, to execute the `find` command and substitute its output for the command, including the grave accents. The output of the `find . -print` command (the names of all the files and directories in the current directory) are passed to the `tar` command as its parameters. These file and directory names are taken as the list of files to be archived by the `tar` command. Thus, the net effect of the command line is that a `tar` archive of the current directory is created in unixbook.tar.

```
$ tar cvf - `find . -print` > unixbook.tar
$
```

In the following In-Chapter Exercise, you will use the `tar` command with the c option to create an archive of a directory.

IN-CHAPTER EXERCISE

19.1   Create a `tar` archive of the labs directory hierarchy in your home directory. What command line(s) did you use? What is the name of your archive file?

19.2.2 Restoring Archived Files

You can restore (unpack) an archive by using the function option x of the `tar` command. To restore the archive created in Section 19.2.1 and place it in a directory called ~/backups, you can run the following command sequence. The `cp` command copies the archive file, assumed to be in your home directory, to the directory (~/backups) where the archived files are to be restored. The `cd` command is used to make the destination directory the current directory. Finally, the `tar` command is used to do the restoration. Note that the destination directory is the current directory.

```
$ cp unixbook.tar ~/backups
$ cd ~/backups
$ tar xvf unixbook.tar
x ., 0 bytes, 0 tape blocks
x ./final, 0 bytes, 0 tape blocks
x ./final/ch1.doc, 41984 bytes, 82 tape blocks
x ./final/ch2.doc, 54272 bytes, 106 tape blocks
x ./final/ch3.doc, 142848 bytes, 279 tape blocks
x ./final/ch4.doc, 86528 bytes, 169 tape blocks
x ./final/ch5.doc, 396288 bytes, 774 tape blocks
x ./final/ch6.doc, 334848 bytes, 654 tape blocks
x ./current, 0 bytes, 0 tape blocks
x ./current/ch07.doc, 204288 bytes, 399 tape blocks
x ./current/ch08.doc, 87552 bytes, 171 tape blocks
x ./current/ch09.doc, 86016 bytes, 168 tape blocks
x ./current/ch10.doc, 121344 bytes, 237 tape blocks
x ./current/ch11.doc, 152576 bytes, 298 tape blocks
x ./current/ch12.doc, 347648 bytes, 679 tape blocks
$ ls -l
drwx------   2   sarwar      512   Jul 22 13:21   current
drwx------   2   sarwar      512   Jul 22 13:21   final
-rw-------   1   sarwar   2064896   Jul 22 13:47   unixbook.tar
$
```

Note that the unixbook.tar file remains intact after it has been unpacked. This result makes sense considering that the primary purpose of the `tar` archive is to back up files, and it should remain intact after restoration in case the system crashes after the file is restored but before it is archived again. After restoration of the unixbook.tar file, your directory structure looks like that shown in Figure 19.3.

At times, you might need to restore a subset of files in a `tar` archive. System administrators often do this after a system crashes (usually caused by a disk head crash resulting from a power surge) and destroys some user files with it. In such cases, system administrators restore only those files from the tape archive that reside on the damaged portion of the disk. Selective restoration is possible with the function option `x` as long as the pathnames of the files to be restored are known. If you do not remember the pathnames of the files to be restored, you can use the function option `t` to display the pathnames of files and directories on the archive file. The output of the `tar` command with the `t` option is in a format similar to the output of the `ls -l` command, as shown in the following session. As marked in the sample, the first field specifies file type and access permissions, the second field specifies user_ID/group_ID of the owner of the file, the third field shows the file size in bytes, the next several fields show the time and date that the file was last modified, and the last field shows the pathname of the file as stored in the archive.

If an archive contains a large number of files, you can pipe the output of the `tar t` command to the `more` command for page-by-page view. If you know the name of the file but not its pathname, you can pipe output of the `tar` command with the `t` option to the `grep` command. Files can also be restored, or their pathnames viewed, selectively. The following session illustrates these points.

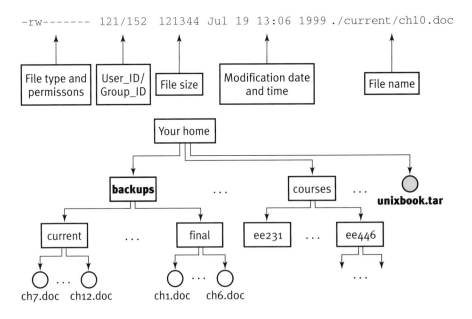

Figure 19.3 Restoring unixbook.tar in ~/backups

```
$ tar -tvf unixbook.tar
drwx------  121/152        0    Jul 22 13:47 1999  ./
drwx------  121/152        0    Jul 22 13:21 1999  ./final/
-rw-------  121/152    41984    Jul 19 13:06 1999  ./final/ch1.doc
-rw-------  121/152    54272    Jul 19 13:06 1999  ./final/ch2.doc
-rw-------  121/152   142848    Jul 19 13:06 1999  ./final/ch3.doc
-rw-------  121/152    86528    Jul 19 13:06 1999  ./final/ch4.doc
-rw-------  121/152   396288    Jul 19 13:06 1999  ./final/ch5.doc
-rw-------  121/152   334848    Jul 19 13:06 1999  ./final/ch6.doc
drwx------  121/152        0    Jul 22 13:21 1999  ./current/
-rw-------  121/152   204288    Jul 19 13:06 1999  ./current/ch07.doc
-rw-------  121/152    87552    Jul 19 13:06 1999  ./current/ch08.doc
-rw-------  121/152    86016    Jul 19 13:06 1999  ./current/ch09.doc
-rw-------  121/152   121344    Jul 19 13:06 1999  ./current/ch10.doc
-rw-------  121/152   152576    Jul 19 13:06 1999  ./current/ch11.doc
-rw-------  121/152   347648    Jul 19 13:06 1999  ./current/ch12.doc
$ tar -tvf unixbook.tar | grep ch10.doc
-rw-------  121/152   121344    Jul 19 13:06 1999  ./current/ch10.doc
$
```

If you want to restore the file ch10.doc in the ~/unixbook/current directory, you can use the following command sequence. Be sure that you give the pathname of the file to be restored, not just its name.

```
$ cd ~/unixbook
$ tar -xvf ~/backups/unixbook.tar current/ch10.doc
current/ch10.doc
$
```

The output of this `tar` command shows that the file ch10.doc has been restored in the ~/backups/current directory. You can confirm this result by using the `ls -l ~/backups/current` command.

In the following In-Chapter Exercises, you will use the `tar` command with t and x options to appreciate how attributes of the archived files can be viewed and how archived files can be restored.

IN-CHAPTER EXERCISES

19.2 List the attributes of the files in the archive that you created in Exercise 19.1 and identify the sizes of all the files in it. What command did you use? *(continued)*

19.3   Copy the archive file that you created in Exercise 19.1 to a file called mytar. Unarchive mytar in a directory called dir.backup in your home directory. Show the commands that you used for this task.

19.2.3 Copying Directory Hierarchies

You can use the `tar` command to copy one directory to another directory. You can also use the `cp -r` command to do so, but the disadvantage of using this command is that the file access permissions and file modification times are not preserved. The access permissions of the copied files and directories are determined by the value of *umask*, and the modification time is set to current time. Also, the `-r` option is not available on all UNIX systems.

More commonly, the `tar` command is used to archive the source directory, create the destination directory, and `untar` (unpack) the archived directory in this latter directory. The entire task can be performed with one command by using command grouping and piping. In the following session, the ~/unixbook/examples directory is copied to the ~/unixbook/examples.bak directory. The `tar` command to the left of pipe sends the archive to stdout, and the `tar` command to the right of pipe unpacks the archive it receives at its stdin.

```
$ (cd ~/unixbook/examples; tar -cvf - .) | (cd~/unixbook/examples.bak; tar -xvf -)
a ./ OK
a ./Bshell/Domain, 14 bytes, 1 tape blocks
a ./Bshell/IP, 18 bytes, 1 tape blocks
a ./Bshell/dns_demo1, 227 bytes, 1 tape blocks
...
a ./Bshell/fs.csh, 1531 bytes, 3 tape blocks
a ./Bshell/dir1, 0 bytes, 0 tape blocks
a ./Bshell/copy, 2222 bytes, 5 tape blocks
x ., 0 bytes, 0 tape blocks
x ./Bshell/Domain, 14 bytes, 1 tape blocks
x ./Bshell/IP, 18 bytes, 1 tape blocks
x ./Bshell/dns_demo1, 227 bytes, 1 tape blocks
...
x ./Bshell/fs.csh, 1531 bytes, 3 tape blocks
x ./Bshell/dir1, 0 bytes, 0 tape blocks
x ./Bshell/copy, 2222 bytes, 5 tape blocks
$
```

The advantages of using this command line are that both cd and tar commands are available on all UNIX systems and that the copied files have the access permissions and file modification times for the source files.

You can also use the tar command to copy directories to a remote machine on a network. In the following command line, the ~/unixbook/examples directory is copied to the ~/unixbook/examples.bak directory on a remote machine called upsun21. The rsh command (*see* Chapter 14) is used to execute the quoted command group on upsun21. Because the tar command is not run in verbose mode, it runs silently and you do not see any output on the display screen.

```
$ (cd ~/unixbook/examples; tar cf - .) | rsh upsun21 "cd ~/unixbook/example.bak; tar xf -"
$
```

19.3   Software Distribution in the tar Format

Companies often use the tar command to distribute their software because it results in a single file that the customer needs to copy, and it saves disk space compared to the unarchived directory hierarchies that might contain the software to be distributed. Also, most companies keep their distribution packs (in the tar format) on their Internet sites, where their customers can download them via the ftp command. Thus, the tar format also results in less "copying" time and reduced work by the customer, who uses only one get (or mget) command (an ftp command) versus several sequences of commands if directory hierarchies have to be downloaded.

Because the sizes of software packages are increasing due to their graphical interfaces and multimedia formats, archives are compressed before they are put on ftp sites. The users of the software need to uncompress the downloaded files before restoring them.

Now consider a file, tcsh-6.06.tar.Z, that we downloaded from an ftp site. In order to restore this file, we have to uncompress and untar it, as shown in the following command sequence.

```
$ uncompress tcsh-6.06.tar.Z
$ tar xvf tcsh-6.06.tar
... [command output]
$
```

If a software pack is distributed on a secondary storage medium (floppy, tape, DVD, or CD-ROM), you need to copy appropriate files to the appropriate directory and repeat these commands.

If you want to distribute some software that is stored in a directory hierarchy, you first need to make an archive for it by using the tar command and then compress it by using the compress command (or some other similar utility). These steps create a tar archive in a compressed file that can be placed in an ftp repository or on a Web page or sent as an e-mail attachment.

Disk file backups are also commonly used to pack large inactive or less frequently used files to save disk space.

The -z option of the GNU version of the `tar` utility can be used to generate the compressed version of the `tar` archive. This option can be used to restore the compressed version of the `tar` archive. The use of this option eliminates the use of the `gzip` (or `gunzip`) utility to compress or uncompress an archive and then the `tar` command; the two-step process can be performed by the `tar` command alone. In the following session, the first `tar` command generates a compressed `tar` archive of the current directory in the ~/unixbook/backups/ub.tar.gz file, and the second `tar` command restores the compressed `tar` archive from the same file into the current directory.

```
$ tar -zcf ~/unixbook/backups/ub.tar.gz .
$ tar -zxvf ~/unixbook/backups/ub.tar.gz
[ command output ]
$
```

Summary

UNIX has several utilities for creating archive (backup) copies of your files and directories, including `cpio`, `dump`, and `tar`. The `tar` command is the one most commonly used. The backups can be in the form of tape or disk files. For tape backups, not only does a user need access privileges to the tape device file, but the file also needs to be mounted first. Disk file backups are commonly used for software distribution but can also be used to pack large inactive files to save disk space. In a network of UNIX machines, users can create archives of their files and directories on remote machines by using command groups that use the `tar` and `rsh` commands. You can use the -z option of the GNU `tar` to generate the compressed version of the `tar` archive and to restore the compressed version of a `tar` archive. You can use the -z option of the GNU `tar` to generate the compressed version of the `tar` archive and to restore the compressed version of a `tar` archive.

Problems

1. What is the meaning of the term *archive*?

2. What is the `tar` command used for? Give all its uses.

3. What are the names of the device files for the tapes drives on your system? What are the access permissions for these files?

4. Give a command line for creating a `tar` archive of your current directory. Give commands for compressing and keeping the archive in the backups directory in your home directory.

5. Give commands for restoring the backup file in Problem 4 in the ~/backups directory.

6. Give a command line for copying your home directory to a directory called home.back so that access privileges and file modify time are preserved.

7. Why is the `tar` command preferred over the `cp -r` command for creating backup copies of directory hierarchies?

8. Suppose that you download a file, unixbook.tar.Z, from an ftp site. As the file name indicates, it is a `tar` archive file in compressed form. Give the sequence of commands for restoring this archive and installing it in your ~/unixbook directory.

9. Use the GNU `tar` command to create a compressed archive of your ~/courses directory in the ~/backups directory. Name the backup courses.tar.gz. Show the command line that you used to perform this task.

10. Use the GNU `tar` command to create a compressed archive of your ~/courses directory in the ~/backups directory. Name the backup courses.tar.gz. Show the command line that you used to perform this task.

11. Use the GNU `tar` command to restore the compressed `tar` archive in ~/backups/courses.tar.gz into the ~/mirrors directory. Show the command line that you used to perform this task, along with the output of the command.

UNIX Tools for Software Development

Objectives

- To summarize computer programming languages at different levels
- To discuss interpreted and compiled languages and the compilation process
- To briefly describe the software engineering life cycle
- To discuss LINUX program generation tools for C to perform the following tasks: editing, indenting, compiling (of C, C++, and Java programs), handling module-based software, creating libraries, source code management, and revision control
- To describe LINUX tools for static analysis of C programs: verifying code for portability and profiling
- To discuss LINUX tools for dynamic analysis of C programs: debugging, tracing, and monitoring performance
- To cover the commands and primitives
  `admin, ar, cc, ci, co, cvs, delta, emacs, g++, gcc, gdb, get, grep, help, ident, indent, javac, make, rcsmerge, nm, rcs, ranlib, rlog, strip, time`

20.1 Introduction

A typical UNIX system supports several high-level languages, both interpreted and compiled. These languages include C, C++, Pascal, Java, LISP, and FORTRAN. However, most of the application software for the UNIX platforms is developed in the C language, the language in which the UNIX operating system is written. Thus, a range of software engineering tools are available for use in developing software in this language. Many of these tools can also be used for developing software in other programming languages, C++ in particular.

The UNIX operating system has a wealth of software engineering tools for program generation and static and dynamic analysis of programs. They include tools for editing source code, indenting source code, compiling and linking, handling module-based software, creating libraries, profiling, verifying source code for portability, source code management, debugging, tracing, and performance monitoring. In this chapter, we describe some of the commonly used tools in the development of C-based software. The extent of discussion of these tools varies from brief to detailed, depending on their usefulness and how often they are used in practice. Before discussing these tools, however, we briefly describe various types of languages that can be used to write computer software. In doing so, we also discuss both interpreted and compiled languages.

20.2 Computer Programming Languages

Computer programs can be written in a wide variety of programming languages. The native language of a computer is known as its **machine language**, the language comprising the instruction set of the CPU inside the computer. Recall that the instruction set of a CPU consists of instructions that the CPU understands. These instructions enable the performance of various types of operations on data, such as arithmetic, logic, shift, and I/O operations. Today's CPUs are made of **bistate devices** (devices that operate in *on* or *off* states), so CPU instructions are in the form of 0s and 1s (0 for the off state and 1 for the on state). The total number of instructions for a CPU and the maximum length (in bytes) of an instruction is CPU dependent. Whereas reduced instruction set computer (RISC) based CPUs have several hundred simple instructions, complex instruction set computer (CISC) based CPUs have tens of complex instructions. Programs written in a CPU's machine language are known as **machine programs**, commonly known as **machine codes**. The machine language programs are the most efficient because they are written in a CPU's native language. However, they are the most difficult to write because the machine language is very different from any spoken language; the programmer has to write these programs in 1s and 0s, and a change in one bit can cause major problems. Debugging machine language programs is a very challenging and time-consuming task. For these reasons, programs today are rarely written in machine languages.

In assembly language programming, machine instructions are written in English-like words, called *mnemonics*. Because programs written in assembly language are closer to the English language, they are relatively easier to write and debug. However, these programs must be translated into the machine language of the CPU used in your computer before you can execute them. This process of translation is carried out by a program called an **assembler**. You have to execute a command to run an assembler, with the file containing an assembly language program as its argument. Although assembly languages are becoming less popular, they are still used to write time-critical programs for controlling real-time systems (e.g., the controllers in drilling machines for oil wells) that have limited amounts of main storage.

In an effort to bring programming languages closer to the English language—and make programming and debugging tasks easier—high-level languages (HLLs) were developed. Commonly used high-level languages are Ada, C, C++, Java, Javascript, BASIC, FORTRAN, LISP, Pascal, and Prolog. Some of these languages are interpreted (e.g., Javascript and LISP), whereas others are compiled (e.g., C, C++, and Java). On the one hand, programs written in an interpreted language are executed one instruction at a time by a program called an **interpreter**, without translating them into the machine code for the CPU used in the computer. On the other hand, programs written in compiled languages must be translated into the machine code for the underlying CPU before they are executed. This translation is carried out by a program called a **compiler**, which generates the assembly version of the high-level language program. The assembly version has to go through further translation before the executable code is generated. The compiled languages run many times faster than the interpreted languages because compiled languages are directly executed by the CPU, whereas the interpreted languages are executed by a piece of software (an interpreter).

However, the Java language is not compiled in the traditional sense. Java programs are translated into a form known as the Java Bytecode, which is then interpreted by an interpreter.

To simplify the task of writing computer programs even more, languages at a higher level even than the HLLs were developed. They include scripting and visual languages such as UNIX shell programming, Perl, visual BASIC, and visual C++. Some of these languages are interpreted; others are compiled. Figure 20.1 shows the proximity of various types of programming languages to the hardware, ease of their use, and relative speed at which programs are executed.

As the level of programming languages increases, the task of writing programs becomes easier and programs become more readable. The trade-off is that programs written in HLLs take longer to run. For interpreted programs, the increase in program running time is due to the fact that another program (the interpreter) runs the program. For compiled languages, the compilation process takes longer and the resulting machine code is usually much bigger than

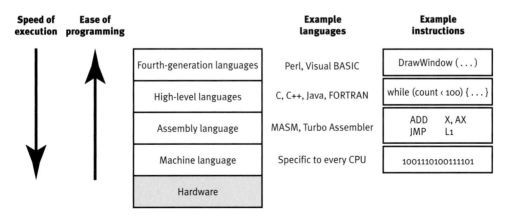

Figure 20.1 Levels of programming languages, with examples, ease of programming, and speed of execution

it would be if written in assembly language by hand. However, time is saved because of ease of programming in HLLs far outweighs the increase in code size. Figure 20.1 also shows some language statement examples to demonstrate the increased readability of programs as the level of programming languages increases.

20.3 The Compilation Process

Because our focus in this chapter is on UNIX tools–primarily for the C programming language (a compiled language)–we need to describe briefly the compilation process before moving on. As we stated in Section 20.2, computer programs written in compiled languages must be translated to the machine code of the CPU used in the computer system on which they are to execute. This translation is usually a three-step process consisting of *compilation*, *assembly*, and *linking*. The compilation process translates the source code (e.g., a C program) to the corresponding assembly code for the CPU used in the computer system. The assembly code is then translated to the corresponding machine code, known as object code. Finally, the object code is translated to the executable code. Figure 20.2 outlines the translation process.

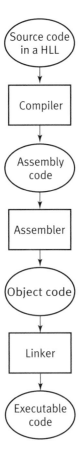

Figure 20.2 The process of translating a high-level language program to executable code

The object code consists of machine instructions, but it is not executable because the source program might have used some library functions that the assembler cannot resolve references to, because the code for these functions is not in the source file(s). The linker performs the task of linking (connecting) the object code for a program and the object code in a library, and generates the executable binary code.

The translation of C programs goes through a preprocessing stage before it is compiled. The **C preprocessor** translates program statements that start with the # sign. Figure 20.3 outlines the compilation process for C programs. The entire translation process is carried out by a single compiler command. We discuss various UNIX compilers later in this chapter.

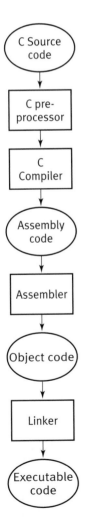

Figure 20.3 The process of translating C programs to executable code

20.4   The Software Engineering Life Cycle

A software product is developed in a sequence of phases, collectively known as the **software life cycle**. Several life-cycle models are available in the literature and used in practice. The life cycle used for a specific product depends on its size, the nature of the software to be developed (scientific, business, etc.), and the design methodology used (object-oriented or classical). Some of the commonly used life-cycle models are build-and-fix, water-fall, and spiral. The common phases in most life-cycle models are requirement analysis, specifications, planning, design, coding, testing, installation, and maintenance. A full discussion of life-cycle models and their phases is outside the scope of this textbook, but we discuss the coding phase in detail—in particular, the UNIX program development tools that can be used in this phase.

The program development process consists of three steps: *program generation, static analysis of the source code,* and *dynamic analysis of the executable code.* The purpose of the program generation phase is to create source code and generate the executable code for the source code. Hence, it involves tools for editing text files, indenting the source code properly, compiling the source code, handling module-based software, creating libraries, managing the source code, and controlling revisions. The *static analysis phase* consists of verifying the source code for portability and measuring metrics related to the source code (e.g., the number of calls to a function and the time taken by each function). The *dynamic analysis phase* comprises debugging, tracing, and monitoring the performance of the software, including testing it against product requirements. In the rest of this chapter, we describe UNIX tools for all three steps. The depth of discussion on each tool depends on its usefulness, the frequency of its use, and how widely it is available on various UNIX platforms.

20.5   Program Generation Tools

The program generation phase consists of creating source code and generating the executable code for it. Hence, it involves tools for editing text files, indenting the source code properly, compiling the source code, handling module-based software, creating libraries, managing the source code, and controlling revisions. Below, we discuss the UNIX tools for supporting the above tasks.

20.5.1 Generating C Source Files

Any text editor can be used to generate C program source files. We discussed the most frequently used UNIX editors (`pico`, `vi`, and `emacs`) in Chapter 5.

20.5.2 Indenting C Source Code

Proper indentation of source code is an important part of good coding practice, primarily because it enhances readability of the code, and readable code is easier to maintain (correct and enhance). The best known indentation style for C programs was proposed by Brian Kernighan and Dennis Ritchie in *The C Programming Language*, the first book on the C language. It is commonly known as the K&R (for Kernighan and Ritchie) indentation style. Most non-C programmers are not familiar with this style unless they have read the book. The UNIX utility `cb` (C program beautifier) can be used to indent a C program properly. The following is a brief description of the `cb` command.

cb [options] [file-list]

Purpose: This command reads syntactically correct programs specified in 'file-list', indents them according to some commonly accepted C program structures, and sends them to standard output

Commonly used options/features:

  -s   Indent code according to the K&R style

  -j   Put split lines back together

S Y N T A X

Without any file argument, the cb command takes input from standard input. By default, it preserves all user newline characters. Without the -s option, the cb utility produces Pascal-style indentation. When used with the -s option, the utility indents the C program according to the K&R style. In the following session, the C program file second.c needs to be indented. Note the difference in indentation with and without the -s option.

```
$ more second.c
#include <stdio.h>
main()
{
int i,j;

for (i=0,j=10; i < j; i++)
{
printf("UNIX Rules the Networking World!\n");
}
}
$ cb second.c
#include <stdio.h>
main()
{
    int i,j;
    for (i=0,j=10; i < j; i++)
    {
        printf("UNIX Rules the Networking World!\n");
    }
}
$ cb -s second.c
#include <stdio.h>
main()
{
    int  i, j;
```

```
    for (i = 0, j = 10; i < j; i++) {
        printf("UNIX Rules the Networking World!\n");
    }
}
$
```

The preceding session shows how cb can be used to change the format of a C program and display it on the screen. You need to use output redirection to save the output of cb into a file or use the tee utility to save the properly formatted program in a file as well as display it on the screen. The following session shows the two ways of performing this task. In both cases, the formatted version of second.c goes into the kr_second.c file.

```
$ cb -s second.c > kr_second.c
$ cb -s second.c | tee kr_second.c
#include <stdio.h>
main()
{
    int  i, j;

    for (i = 0, j = 10; i < j; i++) {
            printf("UNIX Rules the Networking World!\n");
    }
}
```

The indent utility can also be used for indenting and formatting a C program file. This utility has more features and options than the cb utility. The following is a brief description of the indent command.

SYNTAX

indent input-file [output-file] [options]

Purpose: This command reads a syntactically correct program specified in 'input-file', indents it according to some commonly accepted C program structure, and saves the formatted program in 'output-file' if it is specified in the command line. If the output file is not specified, the formatted version replaces the original version after saving the original version in a file that has the same name as 'input-file' and extension BAK.

Commonly used options/features:

`/*INDENT OFF*/` `/*INDENT ON*/`	The source code between these two comments is not formatted by indent
`-bl`	Format according to Pascal-like syntax
`-br`	Format according to the more commonly used K&R-like syntax, the default setup

Several other options allow you to format your code in various styles. You can specify these options before or after the file names. The indent command makes sure that the names of 'input-file' and 'output-file' are different; if they are the same, it gives an error message and quits. We show a simple use of the command in the following session. Note that the format is similar to that produced by the cb -s second.c command. The original contents of the second.c file are saved in second.c.BAK in the current directory. The second.c file is the same file used in the session for the cb utility.

```
$ indent second.c
$ cat second.c
#include <stdio.h>
main()
{

    int     i, j;

    for (i = 0, j = 10; i < j; i++) {
            printf("UNIX Rules the Networking World!\n");

    }

}
$
```

In the following In-Chapter Exercise, you will use the cb and indent commands to practice indentation of C programs.

IN-CHAPTER EXERCISE

20.1 Create the second.c file just described and indent it according to the K&R style by using the cb and indent commands. What command lines did you use?

20.5.3 Compiling C, C++, and JAVA Programs

Several C compilers are available on UNIX, including cc, xlc, and gcc. The most commonly used C compiler for UNIX is gcc (GNU C/C++ compiler). This compiler is written for ANSI C, the most recent standard for C language. The gcc command on LINUX systems is a symbolic link to gcc. All C++ compilers, such as g++ (GNU compiler for C++), can also be used to compile C programs. The g++ compiler invokes gcc with options necessary to make it recognize C++ source code. Although we primarily discuss the gcc compiler in this section, we do show a few small examples of the C++ and Java programs and their compilation with the g++ and javac compilers. We use the cc compiler for examples in the rest of the chapter; all of the examples work for the gcc compiler, too. The following is a brief description of the gcc command. Most of the options discussed in this section for the gcc compiler also work for the cc compiler.

The gcc command can be used with and without options. We describe some basic options here and some in later sections of this chapter. One of the commonly used options, even by the beginners, is –o. You can use this option to inform gcc that it should store the executable code in a particular file instead of the default a.out file. In the following session, we show compilation of the C program in the first.c file, with and without the –o option. The gcc first.c command produces the executable code in the a.out file and the gcc –o slogan first.c command produces the executable code in the slogan file. The ls command is used to show the names of the executable files generated by the two gcc commands.

---

gcc [options] file-list

Purpose: This command can be used to invoke the C compilation system. When executed, it preprocesses, compiles, assembles, and links to generate executable code. The executable code is placed in the a.out file by default. The command accepts several types of files and processes them according to the options specified in the command line. The files can be archive files (.a extension), C source files (.c extension), C++ source files (.C, .cc, or .cxx extension), assembler files (.s extension), preprocessed files (.i extension), or object files (.o extension). When a file extension is not recognizable, the command assumes the file to be an object or library/archive file. The files are specified in 'file-list'.

Commonly used options/features:

–ansi	Enforce full ANSI conformance
–c	Suppress the linking phase and keep object files (with .o extension)
–g	Create symbol table, profiling, and debugging information for use with the gdb (GNU DeBugger)
–llib	Link to the 'lib' library
–mconfig	Optimize code for 'config' CPU ('config' can specify a wide variety of CPUs, including Intel 80386, 80486, Motorola 68K series, RS6000, AMD 29K series, and MIPS processors)
–o file	Create executable in 'file', instead of the default file a.out
–O [level]	Optimize. You can specify 0–3 as 'level'; generally, the higher the number for 'level', the higher the level of optimization. No optimization is done if 'level' is 0.
–pg	Provide profile information to be used with the –profiling tool gprof
–S	Do not assemble or link the .c files, and leave assembly versions in corresponding files file .s extension
–v	Verbose mode: Display commands as they are invoked
–w	Suppress warnings
–W	Give extra and more verbose warnings

```
$ cat first.c
main ()
{
     printf("UNIX Rules the Networking World!\n");
}
$ ls
first.c    second.c
$ gcc first.c
$ ls
a.out     first.c second.c
$ a.out
UNIX Rules the Networking World!
$ gcc -o slogan first.c
$ ls
a.out      first.c second.c slogan
$ slogan
UNIX Rules the Networking World!
$
```

If your shell's search path does not include your current directory (.), you will get the message 'a.out: not found', as shown below. If this happens, then you have two options: you can either run the command as ./a.out (i.e., explicitly inform the shell that it should run the a.out file in your current directory) or include your current directory in your shell's search path and re-run the command as a.out. The following session illustrates both options. Note that the change in your search path is effective for your current session only; for a permanent change in the search path, you need to change the value of the *PATH* variable in your ~/.profile (or /etc/profile) file (*see* Chapter 4 for details).

```
$ a.out
a.out: not found
$ ./a.out
UNIX Rules the Networking World!
$ PATH=$PATH:.
$ export PATH
$ a.out
UNIX Rules the Networking World!
$
```

Dealing with Multiple Source Files

You can use the gcc command to compile and link multiple C source files and create an executable file, all in a single command line. For example, you can use the following command line to create the executable file called polish for the C source files driver.c, stack.c, and misc.c.

```
$ gcc driver.c stack.c misc.c -o polish
$
```

If one of the three source files is modified, you need to retype the entire command line, which creates two problems. First, all three files are compiled into their object modules, although only one needs recompilation, which results in longer compilation time, particularly if the files are large. Second, retyping the entire line may not be a big problem when you are dealing with three files (as here), but you certainly will not like having to do it with a much larger number of files. To avoid these problems, you should create object modules for all source files and then recompile only those modules that are updated. All the object modules are then linked together to create a single executable file.

You can use the gcc command with the -c option to create object modules for the C source files. When you compile a program with the -c option, the compiler leaves an object file in your current directory. The object file has the name of the source file and an .o extension. You can link multiple object files by using another gcc command. In the following session, we compile three source modules—driver.c, stack.c, and misc.c—separately to create their object files, and then use another gcc command to link them and create a single executable file, polish.

```
$ gcc -c driver.c
$ gcc -c stack.c
$ gcc -c misc.c
$ gcc misc.o stack.o driver.o -o polish
$ polish
[output of the program]
$
```

You can also compile multiple files with the -c option. In the first of the following command lines, we compile all three source files with a single command to generate the object files. The compiler shows the names of the files as it compiles them. The order in which files are listed in the command line is not important. The second command line links the three object files and generates one executable file, polish.

```
$ gcc -c driver.c stack.c misc.c
$ gcc misc.o stack.o driver.o -o polish
$
```

Now if you update one of the source files, you need to generate only the object file for that source file by using the gcc -c command. Then you link all the object files again (using the second of the gcc command lines) to generate the executable.

Linking Libraries

The C compilers on LINUX systems link appropriate libraries with your program when you compile it. Sometimes, however, you have to tell the compiler explicitly to link the needed libraries. You can do so by using the gcc command with the -1 option, immediately followed by the letters in the library name that follow the string lib and before the extension. Most libraries are in the /lib directory. You have to use a separate -1 option for each library that you need to link. In the following session, we link the math library (/lib/libm.a) to the object code for the program in the power.c file. We used the first gcc command line to show the error message generated by the compiler if the math library is not linked. The message says that the symbol pow is not found in the file power.o (the file in which it is used). The name of the math library is libm.a, so we use the letter m (that follows the string lib and precedes the extension) with the —1 option.

```
$ cat power.c
#include <math.h>

main()
{
    float  x,y;

    printf ("The program takes x and y from stdin and displays x^y.\n");
    printf ("Enter integer x: ");
    scanf  ("%f", &x);
    printf ("Enter integer y: ");
    scanf  ("%f", &y);
    printf ("x^y is: %6.3f\n", pow((double)x,(double)y));
}
$ gcc power.c -o power
/tmp/ccj67RX0.o: In function `main':
/tmp/ccj67RX0.o(.text+0x62): undefined reference to `pow'
collect2: ld returned 1 exit status
$ gcc power.c -lm -o power
$ power
The program takes x and y from stdin and displays x^y.
Enter integer x: 9.82
Enter integer y: 2.3
x^y is: 191.362
$
```

Compiling C++ Programs

We now show a simple C++ program, its compilation with the g++ compiler, and its execution. In the following session, we show a C++ program that reads from the keyboard temperature in Celsius and displays the corresponding temperature in Fahrenheit, its compilation with the g++ compiler, and a sample run of the resultant executable code. Note that whereas we use the .c extension for C program source file, we use the .cpp extension for C++ source files.

```
$ cat Convert.cpp
#include <iostream.h>
int main()
{
    float c, f;
    cout << "Degrees in Celsius? ";
    cin >> c;
    f = 9*c/5 + 32;
    cout << "Degrees in Fahrenheit: " << f << endl;
}
$ g++ Convert.cpp -o ConvertCPP
$ ./ConvertCPP
Degrees in Celsius? 15.78
Degrees in Fahrenheit: 60.404
$
```

We have not given any description of the g++ compiler options because they are the same as the options for the gcc compiler described earlier in this section. You can use the man g++ command to learn more about the g++ compiler.

Compiling JAVA Programs

Java source code is compiled (translated) into Java bytecode and is interpreted by the Java Virtual Machine (also known as the Java Interpreter). The Java compiler on our UNIX system is called javac, and the Java Virtual Machine is java. In the following session, we use the javac compiler to compile the Java program in the Convert.java file. It produces the Java bytecode and stores it in the Convert.class file, which is interpreted with the java command.

```
$ cat Convert.java
import java.io.*;
public class Convert
{
    public static void main(String args[]) throws IOException
    {
        BufferedReader buff = new BufferedReader(new InputStreamReader(System.in));
        System.out.println("Degrees in Celsius? ");
        String input = buff.readLine();
        double c = Double.parseDouble(input);
```

```
        double f = 9*c/5 + 32;

        System.out.println("Degrees in Fahrenheit? " + f);

    }
$ javac Convert.java
$ java Convert
Degrees in Celsius? 15.78
Degrees in Fahrenheit: 60.404
$
```

If you have a problem using the javac compiler, include /usr/java/j2sdk1.4.0/bin in your shell's search path.

In the following In-Chapter Exercise, you will use the gcc, g++, and javac compiler commands to compile simple C, C++, and Java programs on your UNIX system and run them.

IN-CHAPTER EXERCISE

20.2   Repeat the compilation sessions in this section on your UNIX system to appreciate the basic working of the three compilers and the Java Virtual Machine, java.

20.5.4 Handling Module-Based C Software

Most of the useful C software is usually divided in multiple source (.c and .h) files. This software structure has several advantages over a *monolithic* program stored in a single file. First, it leads to more modular software, which results in smaller program files that are less time-consuming to edit, compile, test, and debug. It also allows recompilation of only those source files that are modified, rather than the entire software system. Furthermore, the multimodule structure supports **information hiding**, the key feature of object-oriented (OO) design and programming.

However, the multimodule implementation also has its disadvantages. First, you must know the files that comprise the entire system, the interdependencies of these files, and the files that have been modified since you created the last executable system. Also, when you are dealing with multimodule C software, compiling multiple files to create an executable sometimes becomes a nuisance because two long command lines have to be typed: one to create object files for all C source files, and the other to link the object files to create one executable file. An easy way out of this inconvenience is to create a simple shell script that does this work. The disadvantage of this technique is that, even if a single source file (or a header file) is modified, all object files are re-created, most of them unnecessarily.

UNIX has a much more powerful tool, called make, that allows you to manage compilation of multiple modules into an executable. The make utility reads a specification file, called makefile, that describes how the modules of a software system depend on each other. The make utility uses this dependency specification in the makefile and the times when various components were modified, in order to minimize the amount of recompilation. This utility is very useful when your software system consists of tens of files and several executable programs. In such a system, remembering and keeping track of all header, source, object, and executable files can be a nightmare. The following is a brief description of the make utility.

---

make [-f makefile]

Purpose:	This utility updates a file based on the dependency relationship stored in a 'makefile''; the dependency relationship is specified in 'makefile' in a particular format

Commonly used options/features:

-f	This option allows you to instruct make to read interdependency specification from any file; without this option, the file name is treated as makefile or Makefile
-h	Display a brief description of all options
-n	Do not run any makefile commands; just display them
-s	Run in silent mode, without displaying any messages

The make utility is based on interdependencies of files, target files that need to be built (e.g., executable or object file(s)), and commands that are to be executed to build the target files. These interdependencies, targets, and commands are specified in the makefile as **make rules**. The following is the syntax of a make rule.

---

target-list: dependency-list
<Tab> command-list

Purpose:	The syntax of a make rule

Here, 'target-list' is a list of target files separated by one or more spaces, 'dependency-list' is a list of files separated by one or more spaces that the target files depend on, and 'command-list' is a list of commands–separated by the newline character–that have to be executed to create the target files. Each command in the 'command-list' starts with the <Tab> character. The comment lines start with the # character.

The makefile consists of a list of make rules that describe the dependency relationships between files that are used to create an executable file. The make utility uses the rules in the makefile to determine which of the files that comprise your program need to be recompiled and relinked to re-create the executable. Thus, for example, if you modify a header (.h) file, the make utility recompiles all those files that include this header file. The files that contain this header file must be specified in the corresponding makefile.

The following makefile can be used for the power program discussed in Section 20.5.3.

```
$ cat makefile
#  Sample makefile for the power program
#  Remember: each command line starts with a TAB
power: power.c
     cc power.c -o power -lm
$
```

If the executable file power exists and the source file power.c has not been modified since the executable file was created, running make will give the message that the executable file is up-to-date for power.c. Therefore, make has no need to recompile and relink power.c. At times, you will need to force remaking of an executable because (for example) one of the system header files included in your source has changed. In order to force re-creation of the executable, you will need to change the last update time. One commonly used method for doing so is to use the touch command, and rerun make. The following session illustrates these points.

```
$ make
make: 'power' is up to date.
$ touch power.c
$ make
cc power.c -o power -lm
$
```

When you use the touch command with one or more existing files as its arguments, it sets their last update time to the current time. When used with a nonexistent file as an argument, it creates a zero length file (empty file) with that name.

In the following In-Chapter Exercise, you will use the make command to create an executable for a single source file.

IN-CHAPTER EXERCISE

20.3   Create the executable code for the C program in the power.c file and place it in a file called XpowerY. Use the make utility to perform this task by using the makefile given above. Run XpowerY to confirm that the program works properly.

In order to show a next level use of the make utility, we partition the C program in the power.c file into two files: power.c and compute.c. The following session shows the contents of these files. The compute.c file contains the compute function, which is called from the main function in power.c. To generate the executable in the power file, we need to compile the two source files independently and then link them, as shown in the two cc command lines at the end of the session.

```
$ cat power.c
double compute(double x, double y);
main()
{
    float    x,y;
    printf   ("The program takes x and y from stdin and displays x^y.\n");
    printf   ("Enter integer x: ");
    scanf    ("%f", &x);
    printf   ("Enter integer y: ");
    scanf    ("%f", &y);
    printf   ("x^y is: %6.3f\n", compute(x,y));
}
$ cat compute.c
#include <math.h>
double compute (double x, double y)
{
    return   (pow ((double) x, (double) y));
}
$ cc -c compute.c power.c
compute.c:
power.c:
$ cc compute.o power.o -o power -lm
$
```

The dependency relationship of the two source files is quite simple in this case. To create the executable file power, we need two object modules: power.o and compute.o. If either of the two files power.c or compute.c is updated, the executable needs to be re-created. Figure 20.4 shows this first cut on the dependency relationship.

The make rule corresponding to this dependency relationship is, therefore, the following. Note that the math library has to be linked because the compute function in the compute.c file uses the pow function in this library.

```
power:   power.o compute.o
         cc power.o compute.o -o power -lm
```

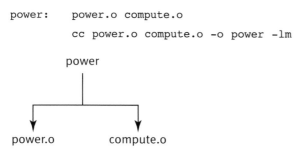

Figure 20.4 First cut on the make dependency tree

We also know that the object file power.o is built from the source file power.c and that the object file compute.o is built from the source file compute.c. Figure 20.5 shows the second cut on the dependency relationship.

Thus, the make rules for creating the two object files are the following.

```
power.o:       power.c
               cc -c power.c
compute.o:     compute.c
               cc -c compute.c
```

The final makefile is shown in the following session. Note that the rules are separated by one blank line (the minimum normally required), although the make utility on our Sun workstation (running SunOS 5.4) does not require the blank line between make rules.

```
$ cat makefile
power:         power.o compute.o
               cc power.o compute.o -o power -lm
power.o:       power.c
               cc -c power.c
compute.o:     compute.c
               cc -c compute.c
$
```

The following is an execution of the make utility with the preceding makefile. Note the order in which the commands for the three make rules execute. The command for generating the executable file, as expected, runs at the end.

```
$ make
cc -c power.c
cc -c compute.c
cc power.o compute.o -o power -lm
$
```

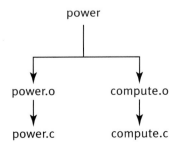

Figure 20.5 Second cut on the make dependency tree

In the following In-Chapter Exercise, you will use the make utility to create the executable code for a C source code that is partitioned into two files.

IN-CHAPTER EXERCISE ━━━━━━━━━━━━━━━━━━━━━━━━━━━━

20.4 Create the two source files power.c and compute.c and follow the steps just discussed to create the executable file power by using the make utility.

We now change the structure of this software and divide it into six files called main.c, compute.c, input.c, compute.h, input.h, and main.h. The contents of these files are shown in the following session. Note that the compute.h and input.h files contain declarations (prototypes) of the compute and input functions but not their definitions; the definitions are in the compute.c and input.c files. The main.h file contains two prompts to be displayed to the user.

```
$ cat compute.h
/* Declaration/Prototype of the "compute" function */
double compute(double, double);
$ cat input.h
/* Declaration/Prototype of the "input" function */
double input (char *);
$ cat main.h
/* Declaration of prompts to users */
#define PROMPT1 "Enter the value of x: "
#define PROMPT2 "Enter the value of y: "
$ cat compute.c
#include <math.h>
#include "compute.h"
double compute (double x, double y)
{
    return (pow ((double) x, (double) y));
}
$ cat input.c
#include "input.h"
double input(char *s)
{
    float x;

    printf ("%s", s);
    scanf ("%f", &x);
```

```
        return (x);
}
$ cat main.c
#include "main.h"
#include "compute.h"
#include "input.h"

main()
{
    double x, y;
    printf ("The program takes x and y from stdin and displays x^y.\n");
    x = input(PROMPT1);
    y = input(PROMPT2);
    printf ("x^y is: %6.3f\n", compute(x,y));
}
$
```

To generate the executable for the software, you need to generate the object files for the three source files and link them into a single executable. The following commands are needed to accomplish this task. Note that, as before, you need to link the math library while linking the compute.o file to generate the executable in the power file.

```
$ cc -c main.c input.c compute.c
$ cc main.o input.o compute.o -o power -lm
$
```

Figure 20.6 shows the dependency relationships among these files.

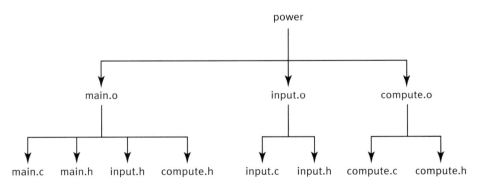

Figure 20.6 The make dependency tree for the sample C software

The makefile corresponding to this dependency relationship is,

```
$ cat makefile
power: main.o input.o compute.o
    cc main.o input.o compute.o -o power -lm

main.o: main.c main.h input.h compute.h
    cc -c main.c

input.o: input.c input.h
    cc -c input.c

compute.o: compute.c compute.h
    cc -c compute.c
$
```

Execution of the `make` command results in the execution of the rules associated with all targets in the makefile.

```
$ make
cc -c main.c
cc -c input.c
cc -c compute.c
cc main.o input.o compute.o -o power -lm
$
```

In the following In-Chapter Exercise, you will use the `make` utility to create an executable for a multi-module C source.

IN-CHAPTER EXERCISE ▬▬▬▬▬▬▬▬▬▬▬▬▬▬▬▬▬▬▬▬▬▬▬▬▬▬

20.5 Create the three source and header files just discussed, and then use the `make` command to create the executable in the file power. Use the preceding makefile to perform your task.

If the make rules are in a file other than makefile (or Makefile), you need to run the `make` command with the `-f` option, as in `make -f my.makefile`.

The make rules as shown in the preceding makefile contain some redundant commands that can be removed. The `make` utility has a predefined rule that invokes the `cc -c xxx.c -o xxx.o` command for every rule, as in,

```
xxx.o: xxx.c zzz.h
    cc -c xxx.c
```

Furthermore, the `make` utility recognizes that the name of an object file is usually the name of the source file. This capability is known as a standard dependency, and because of it you can leave xxx.c from the dependency list corresponding to the target xxx.o. The following makefile therefore, works as well as the one given previously.

```
$ cat makefile
power: main.o input.o compute.o
     cc main.o input.o compute.o -o power -lm
main.o: main.h input.h compute.h
input.o: input.h
compute.o: compute.c compute.h
     cc -c compute.c
$
```

Running the `make` command with this makefile produces the following result.

```
$ make
cc    -c main.c -o main.o
cc    -c input.c -o input.o
cc    -c compute.c -o compute.o
cc main.o input.o compute.o -o power -lm
$
```

The `make` utility supports simple macros that allow simple text substitution. You must define the macros before using them; they are usually placed at the top of the makefile. A macro definition has the following syntax.

Macro_name = text

With this rule in place, 'text' is substituted for every occurrence of $('macro_name') in the rest of the makefile. In addition, the `make` utility has some built-in macros, such as *CFLAGS*, that are set to default values and are used by the built-in rules, such as execution of the `cc` `$(CFLAGS)` -c xxx.c -o xxx.o command for a predefined rule, as previously described. The default value of the *CFLAGS* macro is usually -O (for optimization), but it can be changed to any other flag(s) for the `cc` compiler. On our system, *CFLAGS* is set to null; no options. The `make` utility uses several built-in macros for the built-in rules.

The following makefile shows the use of **user-defined macros** and some useful make rules that can be invoked at the command line. It also shows that the commands for make rules are not always compiler or linker commands; they can be any shell commands.

```
$ cat makefile
CC = cc
OPTIONS = -xO4 -o
OBJECTS = main.o input.o compute.o
SOURCES = main.c input.c compute.c
HEADERS = main.h input.h compute.h

power: main.c $(OBJECTS)
      $(CC) $(OPTIONS) power $(OBJECTS) -lm

main.o: main.c main.h input.h compute.h

input.o: input.c input.h

compute.o: compute.c compute.h

all.tar: $(SOURCES) $(HEADERS) makefile
     tar cvf - $(SOURCES) $(HEADERS) makefile > all.tar

clean:
     rm *.o
$
```

When the make command is executed, the commands for the last two targets (all.tar and clean) are not executed, as these targets do not depend on anything and nothing depends on them. You can invoke the commands associated with these targets by passing the targets as parameters to make. The advantage of putting these rules in the makefile is that you do not have to remember which files to archive (by using the tar command in this case) and which to remove once the final executable has been created. The make clean command invokes the rm *.o command to remove all object files that are created in the process of creating the executable for the software. The following session shows the output of make when executed with two targets as command line arguments. The tar archive is placed in the all.tar file.

```
$ make all.tar clean
tar cvf - main.c input.c compute.c main.h input.h compute.h makefile > all. tar
a main.c 1K
a input.c 1K
a compute.c 1K
a main.h 1K
a input.h 1K
a compute.h 1K
a makefile 1K
rm *.o
$
```

In the following In-Chapter Exercise, you will run the above sessions on your system to further enhance your understanding of the make utility.

IN-CHAPTER EXERCISE ━━━━━━━━━━━━━━━━━━━━━━━━━━━━━

20.6   Use the preceding makefile to create the executable in the file power.

20.5.5 Building Object Files into a Library

The UNIX operating system allows you to *archive* (bundle) object files into a single library file. In other words, this allows you to use the name of one file instead of a number of object files in a makefile and allows function-level software reuse of C programs. The ar tool, also called a **librarian**, allows you to perform this task. The following is a brief description of this utility.

ar key archive-name [file-list]	
Purpose:	This utility allows creation and manipulation of archives; for example, it can be used to create an archive of the object files in 'file-list' and store it in the file called 'archive-file'
Commonly used options/features:	
d	Delete a file from an archive
q	Append a file to an existing archive
r	Create a new archive or overwrite an existing archive
t	Display the table of contents of an archive
s	Force generation of the archive symbol table
x	Extract one or more files from an archive and store them in the current working directory
v	Generate a verbose output

(S Y N T A X)

The 'archive-name' must end with the .a extension. Once an archive file has been created for a set of object modules, these modules can be accessed by the C compiler and the UNIX loader (ld) by specifying the archive file as an argument. (The ld command can be used to explicitly link object files and libraries.) The compiler or the loader automatically links the object modules needed from the archive.

A key is like an option for a command. However, unlike with most UNIX commands, you do not have to insert a hyphen (-) before a key for the ar command, but you can use it if you want to. In the following examples of the ar command, we do not insert a hyphen before a key.

Creating an Archive

You can create an archive by using the ar command with the r key. The following command line creates an archive of the input.o and compute.o files in mathlib.a. Note that we have not used −r, although we could have.

```
$ ar r mathlib.a input.o compute.o
$
```

If mathlib.a exists, the command line overwrites it with the new archive. Once the archive has been created in your current directory, you can link it to the main.c file by using the compiler command.

```
$ cc main.c mathlib.a -o power
$
```

You can use the q key to append the object modules at the end of an existing archive. Thus, in the following example, the object modules input.o and compute.o are appended at the end of the existing archive mathlib.a. If the mathlib.a archive does not exist, it is created.

```
$ ar q mathlib.a input.o compute.o
$
```

Once you have created an archive of some object modules, you can remove the original modules, as in,

```
$ rm compute.o input.o
$
```

Displaying the Table of Contents

You can display the table of contents of an archive by using the ar command with the t key. The following command displays the table of contents of the mathlib.a archive.

```
$ ar t mathlib.a
compute.o
input.o
$
```

Deleting Object Modules from an Archive

You can delete one or more object modules from an archive by using the ar command with the d key. In the following session, the first ar command deletes the object module input.o from the mathlib.a archive, and the second displays the new table of contents (confirming the removal of input.o object module from the archive).

```
$ ar d mathlib.a input.o
$ ar t mathlib.a
compute.o
$
```

Extracting Object Modules from an Archive

You can extract one or more object modules from an archive by using the ar command with the x key. The following command line can be used to extract the object module cpstr.o from the stringlib.a archive and put it in your current directory.

```
$ ar x stringlib.a cpstr.o
$
```

Although we have shown the use of the ar command from the command line, you can also run the command as part of a makefile so that an archive of the object files of a software product is created after the executable file has been created. Doing so allows future use of any general-purpose object modules (one or more functions in these modules) created as part of the software. It is done at the end of a makefile with an explicit make rule, as in,

```
mathlib.a: input.o compute.o
        ar rv mathlib.a input.o compute.o
        rm input.o compute.o
```

You can create a library of object files by putting the name of each object module in parentheses, preceded by the name of the library. The following makefile is an enhancement of the makefile from the previous section that can be used to archive input.o and compute.o after creating them.

```
$ cat makefile
CC = cc
OPTIONS = -xO4 -o
OBJECTS = main.o input.o compute.o
SOURCES = main.c input.c compute.c
HEADERS = main.h input.h compute.h

power: main.o mathlib.a(input.o) mathlib.a(compute.o)
    $(CC) $(OPTIONS) power main.o mathlib.a -lm

main.o: main.h input.h compute.h

mathlib.a(input.o): input.h

mathlib.a(compute.o): compute.h
```

```
all.tar: $(SOURCES) $(HEADERS) makefile
    tar cvf - $(SOURCES) $(HEADERS) makefile > all.tar

clean:
    rm *.o
$
```

For each of these rules, the make utility executes the following sequence of built-in commands that generate the object module in parentheses by using the cc command and archives this object module by using the ar command. The following is a sample run of the preceding makefile.

```
$ make
cc    -c main.c -o main.o
cc    -c input.c -o input.o
ar rv mathlib.a input.o
r - input.o
ar: writing mathlib.a
cc    -c compute.c -o compute.o
ar rv mathlib.a compute.o
r - compute.o
ar: writing mathlib.a
cc -xO4 -o power main.o mathlib.a -lm
$
```

In the following In-Chapter Exercise, you will use the ar command with different options to appreciate its various characteristics in dealing with libraries of object files.

IN-CHAPTER EXERCISE

20.7   Use the commands just discussed to create an archive, delete an object file from the archive, display the table of contents for an archive, and extract an object file from the archive. Show your work.

20.5.6 Working with Libraries

A library is an archive of object modules. Working with libraries, therefore, involves creating libraries, ordering modules in a library, and displaying library information. We discussed library creation and manipulation in several ways in the previous section. In this section, we discuss the remaining two operations; ordering archives and displaying library information.

Ordering Archives

Object files are not maintained in any particular order in an archive file created by the `ar` command. On some UNIX systems, the caller function must occur before the called function regardless of whether they are in the same or different modules. This condition is a problem because the `cc` and `ld` commands cannot locate object modules unless they are properly ordered. When they cannot locate object modules, these commands display an `undefined symbol` error message when they encounter a call to a function in an object module in an archive. The easiest way to handle this problem is to use the `ranlib` utility, which adds a table of contents to one or more archives that are passed as its parameters. This utility performs the same task as the `ar` command with the `s` key. The following is a brief description of the `ranlib` utility.

---

ranlib [archive-list]

Purpose: This utility adds a table of contents to each archive in 'archive-list'

SYNTAX

The following `ranlib` command adds a table of contents to the mathlib.a archive. The `ar s mathlib.a` command can also be used to perform the same task.

```
$ ranlib mathlib.a
$
```

Displaying Library Information

The nm utility can be used to display the symbol table (names, types, sizes, entry points, etc.) of library and object files. The command displays one line for each object (function and global variable) in a library or object file. This output informs you about the functions available in a library and the functions that these library functions depend on. Each output line includes the size (in bytes) of an object, the type of the object (data object, function, file, etc.), scope of the object, and the name of the object. This information is quite useful for debugging libraries. The following is a brief description of the utility.

---

nm key archive-name [file-list]

Purpose: This utility allows display of the symbol table of the library and object files specified in 'file-list'

Commonly used options/features:

`-v`	Display the version number of the command
`-n`	Sort the external symbols by name before displaying them

(continued)

SYNTAX

---

nm key archive-name [file-list] *(continued)*

-p	Produce parsable output; each symbol is preceded by its value (see the manual page for various values and the corresponding symbols)
-s	Print section name instead of section index (e.g., .text instead of 2)
-v	Sort the external symbols by value before displaying them

The output of the nm command contains eight fields. Table 20.1 gives a brief description of the items in the output.

■ **TABLE 20.1** A Brief Description of the Items in the Output of the nm Command

Item Name	Description
Index	Index of the symbol
Value	Value of the symbol; it can be a symbol's offset in a relocatable file or a virtual address in an executable and dynamic library file
Size	Size of the associated object file in bytes
Type	Type of the object; the type can be NOTY (no type was specified), OBJT (a data item), FUNC (a function or any other executable code), SECT (a section symbol), or FILE (name of the source file)
Bind	Field shows the symbol's binding attribute; binding value can be LOCL (for symbols whose scope is limited to the object file containing their definitions), GLOB (for symbols whose scope is all the object files being combined), and WEAK (for symbols that are essentially global with a lower precedence than those with GLOB binding)
Other	Set to 0; reserved for future use
Shndx	One of the three special values (ABS, COMMON, UNDEF) or the section in which the symbol is defined (.text, .data, .rodata, etc.)
Name	Name of the symbol

In the following session, the nm –V command is used to display the version of the nm command, and the nm mathlib.a command is used to display the information about the mathlib.a library that we created in Section 20.4.

```
$ nm -V
nm: Software Generation Utilities (SGU) SunOS/ELF (LK-1.4 (S/I))
$ nm mathlib.a
Symbols from mathlib.a[input.o]:
[Index]  Value  Size   Type    Bind   Other   Shndx    Name
```

[1]		0		0	FILE		LOCL		0		ABS		input.c
[2]		0		0	SECT		LOCL		0		3		
[3]		0		0	NOTY		GLOB		0		UNDEF		scanf
[4]		0		0	NOTY		GLOB		0		UNDEF		printf
[5]		16		104	FUNC		GLOB		0		2		input

```
Symbols from mathlib.a[compute.o]:
```

[Index]	Value	Size	Type	Bind	Other	Shndx	Name
[1]	| 0|	0|FILE	|LOCL	|0	|ABS	|compute.c
[2]	| 0|	0|NOTY	|GLOB	|0	|UNDEF	|pow
[3]	| 16|	116|FUNC	|GLOB	|0	|2	|compute

```
$
```

The nm and grep commands are often run together in order to retrieve information about a specific object. In the following command, we retrieve information about the code function. The output shows that the function is in the object file compute.o and the source file compute.c. In addition, it informs us that the offset of the function is 16 and that the size of the executable is 116 bytes. The section field 2 means that it is a piece of code. On some systems, the output looks a little different. For example, the output may show the type of a symbol to be .text instead of 2. In the next session, we use the -s option to display the field name instead of its section index values.

```
$ nm mathlib.a | grep compute
Symbols from mathlib.a[compute.o]:
```

[1]		0		0	FILE		LOCL		0		ABS		compute.c
[3]		16		116	FUNC		GLOB		0		2		compute

```
$
```

The following commands demonstrate the use of the nm command on the math library (/usr/lib/libm.a), with and without options. The command lines are used to display information about the pow function that we used previously in this chapter. The -n and -s options are used to sort the symbols by name and display field names instead of section index values (such as .text instead of 2).

```
$ nm /usr/lib/libm.a | grep "pow"
Symbols from /usr/lib/libm.a[w_pow.o]:
```

[1]		0		0	FILE		LOCL		0		ABS		w_pow.c
[8]		0		0	NOTY		GLOB		0		UNDEF		__ieee754_pow
[11]		0		768	FUNC		WEAK		0		2		pow
[12]		0		768	FUNC		GLOB		0		2		__pow

```
Symbols from /usr/lib/libm.a[e_pow.o]:
```

[1]		0		0	FILE		LOCL		0		ABS		e_pow.c

```
[38]         |       0|    2764|FUNC  |GLOB      |0       |2         |__ieee754_pow
$ nm -s /usr/lib/libm.a | grep "pow"
Symbols from /usr/lib/libm.a[w_pow.o]:
[1]          |       0|       0|FILE  |LOCL      |0       |ABS       |w_pow.c
[8]          |       0|       0|NOTY  |GLOB      |0       |UNDEF     |__ieee754_pow
[11]         |       0|     768|FUNC  |WEAK      |0       |.text     |pow
[12]         |       0|     768|FUNC  |GLOB      |0       |.text     |__pow
Symbols from /usr/lib/libm.a[e_pow.o]:
[1]          |       0|       0|FILE  |LOCL      |0       |ABS       |e_pow.c
[38]         |       0|    2764|FUNC  |GLOB      |0       |.text     |__ieee754_pow
$ nm -ns /usr/lib/libm.a | grep "pow"
Symbols from /usr/lib/libm.a[w_pow.o]:
[8]          |       0|       0|NOTY  |GLOB      |0       |UNDEF     |__ieee754_pow
[12]         |       0|     768|FUNC  |GLOB      |0       |.text     |__pow
[11]         |       0|     768|FUNC  |WEAK      |0       |.text     |pow
[1]          |       0|       0|FILE  |LOCL      |0       |ABS       |w_pow.c
Symbols from /usr/lib/libm.a[e_pow.o]:
[38]         |       0|    2764|FUNC  |GLOB      |0       |.text     |__ieee754_pow
[1]          |       0|       0|FILE  |LOCL      |0       |ABS       |e_pow.c
$
```

20.5.7 Version Control

Studies have shown that about two-thirds of the cost of a software product is spent on maintenance. As we mentioned before, the maintenance of a software product comprises corrective maintenance and enhancement. In corrective maintenance, the errors and bugs found after installation are fixed. In enhancement, the product is enhanced to include more features, such as an improved user interface. Regardless of its type, maintenance means changing and/or revising the source code for the product and generating new executables. As you revise source code, you may need to undo changes made to it and go back to an earlier version of the software. Moreover, if a team of programmers is working on a piece of software, each team member should be able to check out and check in editable (modifiable) versions of the software. In the remainder of the chapter, we discuss the UNIX tools that support such features. We use the terms *revision*, *version*, *release*, and *delta* interchangeably.

Version control is the task of managing revisions to a software product. Typical software for version control allows you to

- ❖ Lock out other users from changing a file while one user is altering it (provide a check-out and check-in system of file access)
- ❖ Create different versions of a file
- ❖ Help identify revisions to a file
- ❖ Store and retrieve different versions of a file

❖ Merge multiple versions of the same file to create a new "final" file
❖ Maintain a history of all versions of every file related to a product
❖ Access earlier versions of all the files of a product
❖ Limit access to a file to a subset of users on the system

Several UNIX tools allow you to control versions of your files. The Source Code Control System (SCCS) and Revision Control System (RCS) are the most commonly available.

The Source Code Control System (SCCS)

To perform the previously mentioned tasks on a file using the **Source Code Control System (SCCS)**, you must convert it to a file in a special "sccs-format." This file is known as the SCCS history file, SCCS log file, or simply an SCCS file. You cannot edit this file by using normal UNIX text editors such as `vi`. But once this file has been created, you can access a version of your original file by using the SCCS-specific commands to create a new version, view the current editing activity on it, or view revisions made to it. We describe the SCCS commands for performing the most common tasks. All of the SCCS utilities are in the in/usr/ccs/bin directory. Include this directory in your search path (in the *PATH* or *path* variable) if it is not already there.

Creating an SCCS File   The `admin` utility is used to create an SCCS file and for several other purposes (e.g., limiting access to a file and locking versions) described later in the section. The following is a brief description of the utility.

---

admin [options] s.filename

Purpose: This utility allows creating and administering SCCS history files. Names of history files have an 's.' prefix. Using – as the file name allows entering file names from stdin, one file per line. If a directory name is used instead of an 's.filename', the `admin` command is applied to all s.files in the directory.

Commonly used options/features:

  -aname   Add the user specified in 'name' to the list of users who can obtain an editable version of the SCCS file; a group ID can be used instead of a user name to allow or deny check-out rights to all members of the group

  -dlist   Unlock the set of releases specified in 'list'

  -ename   Delete users specified in 'name' from the list of users who can obtain an editable version of the SCCS file

  -flist   Lock the set of releases specified in 'list'

  -iname   Create an SCCS history file called 's.name'

  -n   Create a new SCCS history file

Once the SCCS history file has been created, you should remove the original file from your directory. From now on, you will access the source file by using the SCCS-specific commands. In the following session, we create an SCCS history file called s.input.c.

```
$ ls
compute.c  compute.h  input.c  input.h  main.c   main.h
$ admin -iinput.c s.input.c
No id keywords (cm7)
$ ls -l s.input.c
-r--r--r--   1 sarwar          262 Oct  2 10:22 s.input.c
$
```

The admin command in the preceding session displays a message with a message number in parentheses, cm7. This kind of message can result from an erroneous use of an SCCS command, or it can be just a warning. You can use the help utility to find details about the error message. The following is a brief description of the help utility.

SYNTAX

help [message-key-list]

Purpose: This utility allows display of an explanation of any error or warning message(s) resulting from the use of an SCCS-related utility; the input is a list of message keys

---

In the following session, we first use the help command to get an explanation of the warning message resulting from the use of the admin utility in the preceding session. Following the help command, we use the admin command to try to create a history file that already exists, and admin gives an error message with the message key ad19. The second help command is used to display the explanation of this error message.

```
$ help cm7
cm7: "No id keywords"
No SCCS identification keywords were substituted for. You may not have
any keywords in the file, in which case you can ignore this warning.
If this message came from delta then you just made a delta without any
keywords. If this message came from get then the last time you made a
delta you changed the lines on which they appeared. It's a little late
to be telling you that you messed up the last time you made a delta,
but this is the best we can do for now, and it's better than nothing.
This isn't an error, only a warning.
$ admin -iinput.c s.input.c
ERROR [s.input.c]: file s. input.c exists (ad19)
$ help ad19
ad19: "file ... exists"
You are trying to create the named SCCS file, but it already exists.
$
```

In the following In-Chapter Exercise, you will use the admin command with the -i option to create an SCCS file.

IN-CHAPTER EXERCISE ────────────────────────────

20.8 Use the admin command to create an SCCS history file for input.c.

Checking Out a Copy of an SCCS File for Reading and Writing Once you have created an SCCS history file for a file, you have to use an SCCS utility to access the file for any type of operation. You cannot directly use an editor to edit an SCCS file. The get utility is used to check out a copy of a version of the file for reading or writing (editing). The following is a brief description of the get utility.

---

get [options] [s.file-list]

Purpose:	This utility allows retrieval of a version of an SCCS file specified in 's.file-list'; if no version number is supplied, the latest version is checked out

Commonly used options/features:

-e	Retrieve a version for editing, which locks the specified file so that nobody can make changes to the version that you have checked out
-p	Display the text in the retrieved version on stdout, without checking it out
-rSID	Retrieve the version corresponding to the given 'SID' (SCCS ID), commonly known as the version number
-s	Run in silent mode; do not report version number and statistics

(SYNTAX)

The SID (SCCS ID) for a given delta (the version number for the file being checked out) is a number, in dotted decimal format, comprising two or four fields: the release and level fields; and for branch deltas, the branch and sequence fields. For instance, an SID of 1.2 means release number 1 and level number 2. An SID of 1.2.3.4 means release 1, level 2, branch 3, and sequence 4. The level or sequence field of an SCCS file is automatically incremented by 1 every time you save changes to it. You must explicitly change the release number by using the get command with the -r option.

The following command shows the contents of the SCCS history file, s.input.c, created in the preceding section. Note that the file contents are sandwiched between an SCCS header and an SCCS trailer. The lines that start with <^A> contain SCCS-specific information. Thus, once an SCCS file has been created, you must check out the original file before processing it.

```
$ cat s.input.c
^Ah16227
^As 00011/00000/00000
^Ad D 1.1 04/10/02 10:22:24 sarwar 1 0
```

```
^Ac date and time created 04/10/02 10:22:24 by sarwar
^Ae
^Au
^AU
^Af e 0
^At
^AT
^AI 1
#include "input.h"

double input(char *s)
{
    float x;

    printf ("%s", s);
    scanf ("%f", &x);
    return (x);

}
^AE 1
$
```

Without any option, the `get` command retrieves a read-only copy of the latest version of a file. In the following session, we check out the s.input.c file so that we can access a read-only copy of the input.c file. The output of the command shows the SID and version number on the first line (1.1 here) and the number of lines in the file on the second line (11 lines here), in addition to the message (with message key cm7 here). We used the `ls -l` command to show that a read-only copy of the file is in fact checked out (*see* Chapter 8). Once you have checked out a file, you can display its contents by using a UNIX shell command such as `cat`. Also, multiple users can check out read-only copies of a release.

```
$ get s.input.c
1.1
11 lines
No id keywords (cm7)
$ ls -l input.c
-r--r--r--  1 sarwar          110 Oct  2 11:50 input.c
$
```

If you just want to display the contents of a file without checking out a read-only copy, you can use the `get` command with the `-p` option.

```
$ get -p s.input.c
1.1
#include "input.h"

double input(char *s)
{
    float x;

    printf ("%s", s);
    scanf ("%f", &x);
    return (x);
}
11 lines
No id keywords (cm7)
$
```

If you simply want to make changes to the input.c file, you must check out its editable (having read and write permissions) version by using the get command with the -e option. Thus, in the following session, the input.c file is checked out for editing. We used the ls -l command to show the read and write access privileges for the checked out file.

```
$ get -e s.input.c
1.1
new delta 1.2
11 lines
$ ls -l input.c
-rw--r--r--  1 sarwar         110 Oct  2 15:39 input.c
$
```

An attempt to check out the input.c file, which has already been checked out for editing, results in an error message because the editable check out results in the file getting locked for the duration of check out. For example, an attempt to check out input.c for read-only results in an error message because the file has been checked out for editing in the preceding session.

```
$ get s.input.c
ERROR [s.input.c]: writable 'input.c' exists (ge4)
$
```

In the following In-Chapter Exercises, you will use the admin command to check out a file and display a file without checking it out.

IN-CHAPTER EXERCISES

20.9 Check out a read-only copy of input.c and display its contents. What commands did you use?

20.10 Display input.c with the `admin -p` command. Write the entire command line.

Monitoring Editing Activity on SCCS Files You can monitor the current editing activity on one or more files by using the `sact` utility. You should run this utility to check the status of a file before trying to check it out. The following is a brief description of the utility.

<table>
<tr><td rowspan="6">S Y N T A X</td><td colspan="2">**sact [s.file-list]**</td></tr>
<tr><td>**Purpose:**</td><td>This utility allows display of the current editing activity on the SCCS files specified in 's.file-list'</td></tr>
<tr><td>**Output:**</td><td>The output contains the SID of the existing delta, the SID of the new delta, the user who has checked out the file with the `get -e` command, and the date and time the editable version of the file was checked out (i.e., the `get -e` command was executed)</td></tr>
</table>

The following command is used to show the current editing activity on the s.input.c file after it has been checked out with the `get -e s.input.c` command earlier in this section. The command output shows that the SID of the existing version is 1.1, the SID of the new version is 1.2, and the editable version of the file was checked out by the user sarwar on October 2, 2004, at 15:39:48.

```
$ sact s.input.c
1.1 1.2 sarwar 04/10/02 15:39:48
$
```

The `sact` utility takes the information that it displays from a file created when you check out an editable version of an SCCS file. The name of this file is the same as the SCCS file, with s. replaced by p., as in p.input.c. This file is called the `lock file` and is created for an SCCS file that has been checked out for editing. No such file is created when you check out a read-only copy of a file.

Checking In/Returning an SCCS File You can use the `unget` command to return a version of an SCCS file to the SCCS system right after executing the `get` command. It reverses the effect of `get` by restoring the SCCS file to the previous state, deleting the non-SCCS versions of the file, and unlocking the file so that other users can access it. The following is a brief description of the `unget` command.

---

unget [options] s.file-list

Purpose: This command allows returning an editable version of an SCCS file; if no version number is supplied, the latest version is returned

Commonly used options/features:

   −n   Return a copy of the file, leaving the checked-out version in place

   −rSID   Return the version corresponding to the given 'SID'

The following session illustrates the use of the `unget` command. The first `get` command is used to check out a read-only copy of the input.c file. The first `unget` command generates an error message because no p.input.c file is generated when a read-only copy of an SCCS file is checked out, informing you that you cannot return an SCCS file if it is checked out for read-only. (There is no need to check in a read-only copy of a file.) The second `get` command is used to check out an editable version of the s.input.c file. The `ls` command is used to show that the p.input.c file is generated, and the `cat` command is used to show the contents of this file. The `unget` command following the `cat` command is used to check in the s.input.c file. The `unget` command returns the s.input.c file to restore it to the previous state, delete its editable version, and unlock the file so that other users can access it. Finally, the `sact` command is used to show that no editing activity is taking place on the s.input.c file (as it has been returned); that is, there are no outstanding versions for the s.input.c file. You can use the `ls -l input.c` command to determine that the non-SCCS version of the file, input.c, no longer exists.

```
$ get s.input.c
1.1
11 lines
No id keywords (cm7)
$ unget s.input.c
ERROR [s.input.c]: 'p.input.c' nonexistent (ut4)
$ get -e s.input.c
1.1
new delta 1.2
11 lines
$ ls
compute.c   input.c     main.c     p.input.c
compute.h   input.h     main.h     s.input.c
$ cat p.input.c
1.1 1.2 sarwar 04/10/03 11:09:27
$ unget s.input.c
```

```
1.2
$ sact s.input.c
ERROR [s.input.c]: No outstanding deltas
$
```

Creating New Versions of SCCS Files After checking out an editable version of an SCCS file and modifying it, you must return it to the corresponding SCCS file by using the `delta` command. The new SID for the file is the old SID plus 1. The `delta` command also describes the changes made to the file and prompts you for any comments that you would like to put in the SCCS file related to the changes you made to it. After you have created the new version, the `delta` command removes the checked-out version.

---

delta [options] s.file-list

Purpose: This command allows creation of a new version of an SCCS file; if 's.file-list' is –, file names are read from stdin

Commonly used options/features:

–n	Leave the edited version in place
–rSID	Specify the 'SID' of the delta
–y[text]	Insert 'text' as comment

In the following session, we add a comment header to the input.c file and create a new version of the SCCS file by using the `delta` command.

```
$ cat input.c
/*
    This function prompts the user for an input number, reads
    user input, and returns this input to the caller function.
*/
#include "input.h"
double input(char *s)
{
...
}
$
$ delta s.input.c
comments? Added a comment at the top of the file.
No id keywords (cm7)
1.2
4 inserted
0 deleted
```

```
11 unchanged
$
```

As we stated before, the `delta` command removes the edited version during execution. If you want to keep the edited version, you need to use the `delta -n` command. You may want to do so in order to create a checkpoint and continue editing the file(s).

Displaying the History of SCCS Files   You can use the `prs` command to display the history of one or more SCCS files. The following is a brief description of the command.

---

prs [options] s.file-list

Purpose: Display the history of the SCCS files specified in 's.file-list'; if 's.file-list' is -, the file names are read from stdin

Commonly used options/features:

  −c[date]   Cutoff date and time in the format YY[MM[DD[HH[MM[SS]]]]]

  −e   Include deltas at SID or date and earlier (refer to options −c and −r)

  −rSID   Specify the 'SID' of the delta

SYNTAX

By default, the whole history of an SCCS file is displayed. If you want to display the history of a particular version, use the −r option. And if you want to display history to a particular delta or date, use the −e option. In the following example, we use the `prs` command to display the complete history of the s.input.c file. The five-digit numbers on the right-hand side, separated by slashes, give the number of lines inserted, deleted, and unchanged, respectively, in the last version. Thus, 4 lines were inserted in version 1.1 of s.input.c to create version 1.2, no lines were deleted, and 11 lines remained unchanged.

```
$ prs s.input.c
s.input.c:
D 1.2 04/10/03 13:57:07 sarwar 2 1      00004/00000/00011
MRs:
COMMENTS:
Added a comment at the top of the file.
D 1.1 04/10/02 10:22:24 sarwar 1 0      00011/00000/00000
MRs:
COMMENTS:
date and time created 04/10/02 10:22:24 by sarwar
$
```

The `prs -r1.2 s.input.c` command displays the history of version 1.2 of the s.input.c file. The `prs -e -r1.3 s.stack.c` command displays the history of all versions of the s.stack.c through version 1.3. The outputs of these commands are shown in the following session.

```
$ prs -r1.2 s.input.c
s.input.c:
D 1.2 04/10/03 13:57:07 sarwar 2 1          00004/00000/00011
MRs:
COMMENTS:
Added a comment at the top of the file.
$ prs -e -r1.3 s.stack.c
s.stack.c:
D 1.3 04/10/03 15:39:14 sarwar 3 2          00005/00000/00137
MRs:
COMMENTS:
Added a comment header at the top of the file.
D 1.2 04/10/01 18:37:14 sarwar 2 1          00035/00026/00102
MRs:
COMMENTS:
Changed stack data structure and implemented it by using a linked list.

D 1.1 04/09/26 10:22:24 sarwar 1 0 00128/00000/00000
MRs:
COMMENTS:
date and time created 04/09/26 10:22:24 by sarwar
$
```

You can use the `prs` command with the `-y` option to display the most recent delta table entry, one line per filename argument.

In the following In-Chapter Exercise, you will use the SCCS commands `get`, `delta`, and `prs` to practice check-in and check-out procedures, and to determine various versions of a file.

IN-CHAPTER EXERCISE

20.11 Check out an editable copy of input.c, add a comment line to it, and check it back in. Give the sequence of commands that you used to accomplish the task. How many versions of the input.c file do you have? What is the latest version? What is the oldest? How do you know? Give the command line that you used in your session.

Checking Out Copies of a Specific Version You can check out any version of an SCCS file by using the `get` command with the `-r` option. In the following session, we check out a read-only version of the compute.c file and an editable version of the input.c file. Note that the version of the read-only copy of the compute.c is 1.1 (as specified in the command line).

However, the version of the editable copy of input.c cannot be 1.2 (as specified in the command line), as this version already exists. The new version of input.c is a branch of 1.2, called version 1.2.1.1. We used the `ls -l p*` command to confirm that in fact an editable version of the input.c file is checked out.

```
$ get -r1.1 s.compute.c
1.1
8 lines
No id keywords (cm7)
$ get -e -r1.2 s.input.c
1.2
new delta 1.2.1.1
15 lines
$ ls -l p*
-rw--r--r--   1 sarwar        37 Oct   3 14:57 p.input.c
$
```

Figure 20.7 shows how revision numbers are related. As we mentioned before, the first (left-most) digit is the release number, the second digit is the level number, the third digit is the branch number, and the fourth (right-most) digit is the sequence number. For instance, if the revision number (SID) is 1.2, 1 is the release number and 2 is the level number. If the revision number is 1.2.3.4, 3 is the branch number and 4 is the sequence number. The level or sequence field of an SCCS file is automatically incremented by 1 every time you save a change to it. Thus, if you check out an editable copy of revision number 1.2.1.1 by using the `get -e` command, the new revision number allocated to the file will be 1.2.1.2; that is, the sequence number is automatically incremented by one. You have to explicitly change the release number by using the `get` command.

Editing Multiple Versions of a File You can edit multiple versions of a file simultaneously by checking them out, one by one, with the `get` command. Because multiple versions of a file are checked out in the same editable file (a file with the same name), you must move the existing copy to another file before checking out another copy. Otherwise, the `get` command gives an error message informing you that the writable file exists, as is the case in the second `get` command in the following session. We used the `mv` command to move the current input.c to input1.c before checking out the new version of input.c.

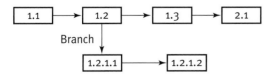

Figure 20.7 A tree of version numbers

```
$ get -e -r1.1 s.input.c
1.1
new delta 1.1.1.1
11 lines
$ get -e -r1.2 s.input.c
ERROR [s.input.c]: writable 'input.c' exists (ge4)
$ mv input.c input1.c
$ get -e -r1.2 s.input.c
1.2
new delta 1.2.1.1
15 lines
$
```

You can use the sact command to determine current activity on the s.input.c file. Thus, the following command reports that two versions, 1.1 and 1.2, of the input.c file have been checked out and that their version numbers at the check-in time will be 1.1.1.1 and 1.2.1.1, respectively.

```
$ sact s.input.c
1.1 1.1.1.1 sarwar 04/10/03 16:10:13
1.2 1.2.1.1 sarwar 04/10/03 16:10:56
$
```

After you finish editing the two versions and want to create their new deltas, you must specify their revision numbers in the delta command. Thus, the first delta command in the following session is used to create the new version for version 1.2, or 1.2.1.1. Not specifying the revision number results in an ambiguous return—two versions have been checked out—and the delta command so informs you. Be sure that you move all the checked-out files to the correct file, one by one, before checking them in. The following session also illustrates how to perform the return operations correctly. Note that you do not need to specify the revision number in the second delta command, as only one checked-out copy is left after the first delta command.

```
$ delta -r1.2 s.input.c
comments? Reformatted the file according to the K&R style.
No id keywords (cm7)
1.2.1.1
2 inserted
1 deleted
14 unchanged
$ mv input1.c input.c
$ delta s.input.c
```

comments? **None.**

No id keywords (cm7)

1.1.1.1

0 inserted

0 deleted

11 unchanged

$

In the following In-Chapter Exercise, you will use the get command with -e and -r options to check out and check in particular versions of a file.

IN-CHAPTER EXERCISE

20.12. Check out versions 1.1 and 1.2 of input.c by using your history file s.input.c. Modify them and check them in. Give the sequence of commands that you executed.

Creating a New Release of an SCCS File To create a new release of an SCCS file, you need to perform the following steps. First, use the get command with the -e and -r options to check out an editable version of the file with the new release number. Second, edit the file as needed. Third, save the new release by using the delta command. In the following session, we create release number 2.1 of the input.c file.

```
$ get -e -r2 s.input.c
1.3
new delta 2.1
15 lines
$ vi input.c
...
$ delta s.input.c
comments? Created a new release.
No id keywords (cm7)
2.1
10 inserted
0 deleted
15 unchanged
$
```

Removing Versions You can remove a version of an SCCS file by using the rmdel (remove delta) command. The release to be removed must be a leaf in the tree of version numbers (*see* Figure 20.7). Thus, for example, version 1.2 cannot be removed, but 1.2.1.2 can be. The following is the brief syntax of the command.

S Y N T A X

rmdel -rSID s.file-list

Purpose: Remove the specified version (with the given 'SID') of the SCCS files in
's.file-list'

In the following example, the rmdel command is used to remove version 1.2.1.2 of the
s.input.c file. As shown in Figure 20.7, release 1.2.1.2 is a leaf in the version tree for the file.

```
$ rmdel -r1.2.1.2 s.input.c
$
```

An error message is generated if you try to remove a nonleaf or a nonexistent version of a file.
In the following session, the first two rmdel commands generate error messages because version
1.1 is a nonleaf version and version 1.2.1.3 is nonexistent, as reported by the two error messages.
Version 1.3 of s.input.c can be removed because it is a leaf in the version tree of Figure 20.7.

```
$ rmdel -r1.1 s.input.c
ERROR [s.input.c]: not a 'leaf' delta (rc5)
$ rmdel -r1.2.1.3 s.input.c
ERROR [s.input.c]: nonexistent sid (rc3)
$ rmdel -r1.3 s.input.c
$
```

Combining SCCS Files You can combine or compress an SCCS file by using the comb utility. It removes all unnecessary versions of the given file and generates its latest version. For
each SCCS file, the utility produces a Bourne shell script at stdout, which must be run to generate the latest version of the source. After the comb utility has been executed on an SCCS
file, it contains only the most recent version of the source. This utility keeps the latest version and versions that have branches. The following is a brief description of the comb utility.

S Y N T A X

comb [options] s.file-list

Purpose: Generate shell scripts for the SCCS files specified in 's.file-list' that can
be used to combine all current versions of these files and generate their
latest versions; if 's.file-list' is –, file names are read from stdin

Commonly used options/features:

–clist	Preserve the versions given in 'list'
–o	Do not access the reconstructed file at the most recent ancestor but at the creation time, which may lead to smaller files
–pSID	Preserve the oldest delta specified in 'SID'

If no options are specified, comb preserves only the most recent (leaf) delta in a branch and the minimal number of ancestors needed to preserve the history. If a directory is specified instead of an SCCS file, the comb utility generates shell scripts for all the SCCS files in the directory and gives messages for all non-SCCS files in the directory.

In the following session, the s.input.c file is combed to generate its latest version. The first prs command is used to show the current state of the s.input.c file. Note that the file has four versions, with 1.2.1.1 being the latest version. The comb -o command is used to create a Bourne shell script in the comb.sh file for compressing the s.input.c file according to the version's creation time. This shell script is executed to generate the latest version of the SCCS file. The prs command displays the history of the new version. Note that a new sequence of version numbers is created. The latest updated version is 1.4 in this case.

```
$ prs s.input.c
s.input2.c:

D 1.2.1.1 04/10/05 10:09:52 sarwar 4 2    00003/00000/00017
MRs:
COMMENTS:
Added in-code comments

D 1.3 04/10/05 10:07:45 sarwar 3 2        00001/00000/00017
MRs:
COMMENTS:
Reformatted the header

D 1.2 04/10/05 10:06:35 sarwar 2 1        00006/00000/00011
MRs:
COMMENTS:
Added a comment header

D 1.1 04/10/05 10:04:42 sarwar 1 0        00011/00000/00000
MRs:
COMMENTS:
date and time created 04/10/05 10:04:42 by sarwar
$ comb -o s.input.c > comb.sh
$ chmod +x comb.sh
$ comb.sh
No id keywords (cm7)
$ prs s.input.c
s.input.c:

D 1.4 04/10/05 10:12:13 sarwar 3 2        00002/00000/00018
MRs:
```

```
COMMENTS:
Added in-code comments

D 1.3 04/10/05 10:12:11 sarwar 2 1        00001/00000/00017
MRs:
COMMENTS:
Reformatted the header

D 1.2 04/10/05 10:12:09 sarwar 1 0        00017/00000/00000
MRs:
COMMENTS:
This was COMBined
$
```

In the following In-Chapter Exercise, you will use the comb command to delete the unnecessary versions of a file in order to compress it.

IN-CHAPTER EXERCISE

20.13 Use the comb utility to compress s.input.c file. Show the history of s.input.c after it has been compressed.

Limiting Access Rights to SCCS Files Any user can check out an SCCS file, provided that the user has appropriate permissions for the file and has access to file's pathname. You can protect your SCCS files by restricting access to one or more users and/or groups by using the −a and −e options of the admin command. Restricting access of a user to an SCCS file allows that person to check out a read-only version of the file but not an editable version of the file. As mentioned in the brief description of the admin command, the −a option can be used to allow check-out rights to one or more users or everyone in a group. If a user name or group ID is preceded by an exclamation point (!), the specified user or group is denied check-out rights. The −e option can be used to remove a user from the list. Multiple −a and −e options can be used in a command line.

In the following session, we show the use of both options. The first admin command adds the user chris to the list of users who are allowed to check out the s.input.c file. The second admin command is used to add all the users in group number 102 to the list of users who can access the file. The third command removes hamid's check-out rights. The next two get commands show that hamid can still check out a read-only version of the input.c file but cannot check out an editable version of it. The fourth admin command allows sunil check-out rights for the s.input.c file. The last admin command denies davis access rights for editing input.c. Note that the −e option is equivalent to the −a\! option, as demonstrated by the third admin command in the session.

```
$ admin -achris s.input.c
$ admin -a102 s.input.c
$ admin -a\!hamid s.input.c
$ get s.input.c
```

```
1.4
20 lines
No id keywords (cm7)
$ get -e s.input.c
1.4
ERROR [s.input.c]: not authorized to make deltas (co14)
$ admin -asunil s.input.c
$ get -e s.input.c
1.4
new delta 1.5
20 lines
$ admin -edavis s.input.c
$
```

You can specify multiple -e or -o options in an admin command line to allow or deny access to different users. In the following command line, the users sarwar, davis, raj, and goldberg are allowed to access an editable version of the input.c file, and the editing rights are taken away from tanya, riz, and jacob.

```
$ admin -asarwar -adavis -araj -agoldberg -etanya -eriz -e jacob s.input.c
$
```

You can completely freeze one or more versions of an SCCS file so that no user can check them out for editing by locking the file. Locked files can be checked out only for reading or displaying on the screen. You can use the admin command to lock a single or all releases of an SCCS file. The -fl option locks releases, and the -dl option unlocks them. To lock (or unlock) a single release, insert a release number after the option. To lock (or unlock) all releases of an SCCS file, insert the letter a after the option. In the following session, the first admin command locks release 1 of the s.compute.c file. The second admin command locks all releases of the file s.input.c. The last admin command unlocks releases 1 and 3–7 of the s.input.c file. We used the get commands to show that the expected actions (of locking or unlocking of releases) actually do take place. The get -e command fails when applied to a locked release. You can check out a read-only copy of a locked release.

```
$ admin -fl1 s.compute.c
$ admin -fla s.input.c
$ get -e s.input.c
1.4
ERROR [s.input.c]: SCCS file locked against editing (co23)
$ get -e -r1.3 s.compute.c
1.3
ERROR [s.compute.c]: release '1' locked against editing (co23)
```

```
$ get -e -r1.4 s.compute.c
1.4
ERROR [s.compute.c]: release '1' locked against editing (co23)
$ admin -fl1,3-7 s.input.c
$ get -e -r3.1 s.input.c
3.1
ERROR [s.input.c]: release '3' locked against editing (co23)
$ get -e -r6.2 s.input.c
6.2
ERROR [s.input.c]: release '6' locked against editing (co23)
$ get -e -r1.4 s.input.c
1.4
new delta 1.5
20 lines
$
```

You can use the admin command with the -fceil and -ffloor options to specify a ceiling and a floor, respectively, on the release numbers that can be checked out. The default ceiling is 9999 and the default floor is 1.

In the following In-Chapter Exercise, you will use the admin command with the -f option to set different access rights on an SCCS file for different users.

IN-CHAPTER EXERCISE

20.14 Give a command line that allows users davis, doug, and arif editing rights to the s.input.c file and takes away the same rights from users jim, syed, mossman, and singh.

SCCS Special Character Sequences You can place any of several special character sequences in a comment header of a source file before checking it into an SCCS file. When you use the get command to check out a read-only copy of a file, these character sequences are processed specially. Table 20.2 shows some of these sequences and what replaces them.

■ **TABLE 20.2** SCCS Special Character Sequences and Their Values

Character Sequence	Replaced with
%D%	Current date
%H%	Current hour
%I%	SID number: release.level.branch.sequence
%M%	Name of the source file (not SCCS file)
%T%	Current time

   In the following session, we add some of these control characters in the module header for
the input.c file and display the read-only version of the file to see how the `get` command
interprets the control characters. The lines added to the input.c file are displayed by using the
head command. The effect of these lines is shown by displaying the read-only version of the
file with the `cat` command.

```
$ get -e s.input.c
1.4
new delta 1.5
20 lines
$ vi input.c
... editing session ...
$ head input.c
/*
     * Author:       Syed Mansoor Sarwar
     * Purpose:      Display the string passed as a parameter, prompt the
     *               the user for a float as input, and return it as a double.
     * Module:       %M%
     * SID:          %I%
     * Date & Time:     %D% %H%
*/
...
$ delta s.input.c
comments? Added SCCS control characters to the header.
No id keywords (cm7)
1.5
10 inserted
0 deleted
20 unchanged
$ get s.input.c
$ cat input.c
/*
     * Author:       Syed Mansoor Sarwar
     * Purpose:      Display the string passed as a parameter, prompt the
     *               user for a float as input, and return it as a double.
     * Module:       input.c
     * SID:          1.6
     * Date & Time:     04/10/05 15:10:14
*/
```

```
#include "input.h"

double input(char *s)
{
 …
}
$
```

The sccs *Front End*   You can also manage your files by using the sccs utility, which is the front end for the SCCS system. It allows you to run various SCCS utilities (admin, get, prs, unget, etc.) as subcommands under it. It supports some additional commands, such as delget and tell, which are not available as stand-alone SCCS commands. Each subcommand is applied to the indicated SCCS files, as is the case with the stand-alone SCCS commands. We show the use of the sccs utility by way of a few examples. The following is a brief description of the utility.

SYNTAX

sccs [options] subcommand [options] [s.file-list]

Purpose: Apply 'subcommand' to the SCCS files specified in 's.file-list'

The options for the sccs command must appear before the subcommand argument and, as expected, the options for a subcommand must appear after the subcommand. The sccs command normally expects the SCCS files to be in the SCCS directory in the current working directory. You can explicitly create this directory or it is automatically created when you create an SCCS version of a file by using the create subcommand under the sccs utility. If a filename is a directory, the subcommand is applied to all the s. files in the SCCS directory; error messages are generated for all non-SCCS files. Thus, the sccs get input.c command applies the get command to a history file named SCCS/s.input.c, whereas the sccs get SCCS command applies the get command to every s. file in the SCCS subdirectory.

To initialize the history file for a source file named input.c, make the SCCS directory a subdirectory and then use the sccs create input.c command. Both operations can also be performed by the sccs create input.c command alone. This command creates a file SCCS/s.input.c and a backup copy of the source file in ,input.c (the comma is part of the file name). Once the SCCS history file has been created, you can remove the backup file if you want to. In the following session, we create the SCCS directory and an SCCS history file called SCCS/s.input.c. Finally, we remove the backup file.

```
$ mkdir SCCS
$ sccs create input.c
input.c:
1.1
11 lines
$ rm ,input.c
$
```

You can run the following sequence of commands to check out an editable copy of input.c, edit it, and then check it back in. The `edit` subcommand is used to check out an editable copy of an SCCS file. The `delget` subcommand is used to check in an SCCS file.

```
$ sccs edit input.c
1.1
new delta 1.2
11 lines
$ vi input.c
... editing session ...
$ sccs delget input.c
comments? Added SCCS control strings
1.2
3 inserted
2 deleted
9 unchanged
1.2
12 lines
$
```

All the SCCS commands described in the previous sections–and more–can be used as subcommands with the `sccs` utility. Use the `man sccs` command on your system to see what additional commands are available under the SCCS front end.

The Revision Control System (RCS)

The **Revision Control System (RCS)** was designed to perform most of the tasks that can be performed by SCCS, but more simply. The two systems differ from each other in how they maintain versions of a file. In SCCS, the version numbers start with 1.1. When you request a particular version of a file, SCCS starts with version 1.1 and makes changes to it according to the different information stored in the s.file to construct the requested version. In contrast, RCS starts with the latest version and makes changes in it to re-create the requested version. The RCS way of creating a version is usually faster because most people work forward and create a newer version based on the current version, rather than on an older version. The version numbers in RCS are maintained in the same way that they are maintained in SCCS, that is, in the format release.level.branch.sequence.

Like SCCS, RCS maintains several versions of a file in a special "rcs-format." You cannot edit this file by using normal UNIX editors such as `vi`. But once this file has been created, you can access a version of your original file by using RCS-specific commands to create a new version (check-out and check-in procedures), view the current editing activity on an RCS file, or view revisions made to the file. We describe the commands for performing the most common tasks. All the RCS utilities are in the /usr/ccs/bin directory. Add this directory to your search path (in the shell variable PATH or path) if it isn't already there.

Working with RCS The first step to using RCS is to create a directory called RCS in the directory that contains the files you want to manage with RCS. This directory contains the revision control information on your files, including the latest version of each file, along with the information that can be used by RCS to create previous versions.

Creating an RCS History File The `ci` utility is used to create and manage RCS history files. The following is a brief description of the utility.

---

ci [options] filename

Purpose: This utility allows creating and administering RCS history files; names of history files have ',v' postfix

Commonly used options/features:

   -rver   Check in the modified file as version number 'ver'

   -u   Check out the created file in unreserved (read-only) mode

---

Once you have created an RCS history file, you can remove the original. From now on, you will access the source file by using the RCS-specific commands, and these files work with RCS history files only. In the following session, we use the `ci` utility to create (check in) an RCS history file called RCS/input.c,v.

```
$ ci input.c
RCS/input.c,v <- - input.c
enter description, terminated with single '.' or end of file:
NOTE: This is NOT the log message!
>>Initial version of the input.c file created by Syed Mansoor Sarwar
>> .
initial version: 1.1
done
$
```

After creating the RCS/input.c,v file, the `ci` command removes the original file, input.c. You can use the –u option to check in a file and keep a read-only copy of the original in the current directory.

In the following In-Chapter Exercise, you will use the `ci` command to create an RCS history file.

IN-CHAPTER EXERCISE

20.15 Create the RCS history file for input.c. What command(s) did you use? What is the pathname of the history file?

Checking Out an RCS File The co utility is used to check out a file. The following is a brief description of the utility.

---

co [options] filename

Purpose: This utility allows checking out of a file called 'filename' from the corresponding RCS history file

Commonly used options/features:

  -l   Check out a file for editing (in locked mode)

  -rver   Check out 'ver' version of the specified file

  -u   Check out an unreserved (read-only) version of the specified file

(margin: S Y N T A X)

Without any option, the co command checks out a read-only copy of the file. The -l option is used to check out a file for editing. The use of this option locks the file so that only one user can check it out for editing. You can use the following command to check out input.c for editing.

```
$ co -l input.c
RCS/input.c,v --> input.c
revision 1.1 (locked)
done
$
```

After you finish editing input.c, you can check in its new version by using the ci command. In the following session, we check in a new version of input.c and keep a read-only copy of it in the current directory.

```
$ ci -u input.c
RCS/input.c,v <-- input.c
new release: 1.2; previous revision: 1.1
enter log message, terminated with single '.' or end of file
>> Added a comment header to the file.
>> .
done
$
```

Note that the new version of input.c in RCS has the same release number (1) as the locked version but a new level number (2).

If a particular revision of a file has been checked out for editing, execution of a command for checking out the same version of the file results in an exception message that gives the user the opportunity to remove the checked-out version or exit. The following command line illustrates this point. We checked out version 1.1 of the input.c file before issuing the co command. The command prompts the user to remove the already checked-out version or abort check out. In this case, we just hit <Enter> at the prompt to abort check out.

```
$ co -l input.c
RCS/input.c,v  -->  input.c
revision 1.1 (locked)
writable input.c exists; remove it? [ny](n): <Enter>
co error: checkout aborted
$
```

In the following In-Chapter Exercise, you will use the co and ci commands to practice check-in and check-out procedures under RCS.

IN-CHAPTER EXERCISE

20.16 Check out an editable copy of input.c, make changes to it, and check in the new version. Write the sequence of commands that you used to perform this task.

Creating a New Version of a File If you want to retrieve a new version of a file, you must first create it. You can create a new version of a file by using the ci command with the -r option. In the following session, version 2.1 of the input.c file is created and stored in the RCS directory. Note that we use -r2 as a shortcut for -r2.1.

```
$ ci -r2 input.c
RCS/input.c,v <-- input.c
new revision: 2.1; previous revision 1.2
enter log message, terminated with single '.' or end of file
>> Just showing how a new version of a file can be created.
>> .
done
$
```

Checking Out Copies of Specific Versions In RCS, you can check out an existing version of a file by using the co command with the -r option. If the checked-out version has the highest revision number, the new version generated at check-in time has the same release number with the level number (or sequence number if the file is a branch of a particular release) automatically incremented by 1. If the checked-out version is not the latest, a branch of the file is generated.

In the following session, we check out version 1 of the input.c file for editing. By default, the co command always checks out the highest version of a release, or version 1.2 here. Note that we used the ci -r command in the previous section to create a new release (release 2) of this file. A higher release exists for the input.c file, so the ci command created a new branch at the checked-out level, resulting in version number 1.2.1.1.

```
$ co -l -r1 input.c
RCS/input.c,v --> input.c
revision 1.2 (locked)
done
$ vi input.c
... editing session ...
$ ci input.c
RCS/input.c,v <-- input.c
new revision: 1.2.1.1; previous revision 1.2
enter log message, terminated with single '.' or end of file
>> Just showing how a branch of a file can be created.
>> .
done
$
```

To create a branch of an RCS file explicitly, we specify a version number with the branch number of the version in the co command. In the following example, we create branch 1 of revision number 2.1 of input.c, resulting in the creation of version 2.1.1.1 of the file.

```
$ co -l -r2.1.1 input.c
RCS/input.c,v --> input.c
revision 2.1 (locked)
done
$ vi input.c
... editing session ...
$ ci input.c
RCS/input.c,v <-- input.c
new revision: 2.1.1.1; previous revision 2.1
enter log message, terminated with single '.' or end of file
>> Just showing how a branch of a file can be created explicitly.
>> .
done
$
```

Figure 20.8 illustrates how revision numbers of the input.c file are related. As we mentioned before, the first (left-most) digit is the release number, the second digit is the level number, the third digit is the branch number, and the fourth (right-most) digit is the sequence number.

In the following In-Chapter Exercise, you will use the co command with the -r option and the ci command to create specific versions of a file.

IN-CHAPTER EXERCISE

20.17 Create versions 1.2 and 2.1 of the input.c file. What command lines did you use?

Abandoning Changes If you made changes to a file that did not work out, you can undo the changes and uncheck out the file by using the rcs utility. The following is a brief description of the rcs utility.

rcs [options] filename	
Purpose:	This utility allows control of RCS files
Commonly used options/features:	
−a	Allow a list of users to check out an editable version of the specified file and check it back in
−e	Remove a user from the list of users who are allowed to check out an editable version of the specified file and check it back in
−l	Check out a file without overwriting it
−o	Remove a version of a file
−u	Abandon changes made to the file and uncheck out the file

You can use the rcs −u command to undo changes made to a file and uncheck out the file. The following command abandons the changes made to input.c; that is, the changes are undone and the file is unchecked out. After this command finishes execution, a copy of input.c is no longer available to you.

```
$ rcs -u input.c
$
```

Locking a File without Overwriting (Taking Care of a Mistake) When you execute the ci −u input.c command, a read-only copy of input.c is left in your current directory. A word of caution: If you change permissions for input.c to make it writable and make changes to it, these changes can be problematic because they cannot be installed in the RCS/filename,v file

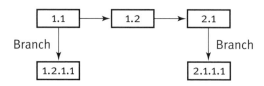

Figure 20.8 The version tree for input.c

in the RCS database. The reason is that you did not properly check out an editable version of the file by using the co -l input.c command.

You can overcome this problem by locking input.c with the rcs -l command without checking it out from the RCS directory and overwriting the existing file (that you updated by mistake). This command followed by the ci -u input.c command installs the changes in the RCS/input.c,v file and leaves a read-only copy in the current directory. This command creates a new version. The following session illustrates these points.

```
$ co -u input.c
RCS/input.c,v  -->  input.c
revision 1.2 (unlocked)
done
$ chmod 700 input.c
$ vi input.c
...
$ ci input.c
RCS/input.c,v  <--  input.c
ci error: no lock set by sarwar
$ rcs -l input.c
RCS file: RCS/input.c,v
1.2 locked
done
$ ci -u input.c
RCS/input.c,v  <--  input.c
new revision: 1.3; previous revision: 1.2
enter log message, terminated with single '.' or end of file
>> Demonstrated file locking.
>> .
done
$
```

Removing a Version   RCS allows you to remove any (including nonleaf) version of a file by using the rcs command with the -o option. If the removed version is an intermediate version, the remaining versions are not renumbered. In the following session, we remove version 1.1 of input.c.

```
$ rcs -o1.1 input.c
RCS file: RCS/input.c,v
deleting revision 1.1
done
$
```

The following In-Chapter Exercise is designed to enhance your understanding of the versions of a file in RCS. The exercise particularly asks you to use the `rcs -o` command to delete a version of a file.

IN-CHAPTER EXERCISE ▬▬▬▬▬▬▬▬▬▬▬▬▬▬▬▬▬▬

20.18 Can you remove version 1.2 of the input.c file just discussed in RCS? Give the command line for performing this task.

Working in Groups Working in groups is quite straightforward. All you need do is place the RCS subdirectory (or subdirectories) in a shared directory. You then run all RCS utilities by specifying the complete pathnames for the RCS files and editing files in your local directories. An alternative to creating a common shared directory is to maintain all RCS directories in one user's directory and create symbolic links (*see* Chapter 11) to this directory in the directories of the remaining members of the group.

In the following session, we check out an editable version of the input.c file, assuming that the only RCS directory is in the /users/shared directory.

```
$ co -l /users/shared/RCS/input.c,v
RCS/input.c,v --> input.c
revision 2.1.1.1 (locked)
done
$
```

After making changes to the input.c file, we can check it back in by using the following command. The –u option is used to keep a read-only copy in the current directory.

```
$ ci -u /users/shared/input.c
/users/shared/RCS/input.c,v <-- input.c
new revision: 2.1.1.2; previous revision 2.1.1.1
enter log message, terminated with single '.' or end of file
>> Illustrated working in groups.
>> .
done
$
```

The preceding command lines need long pathnames, so the users in the group might want to create one-line scripts to handle check-in and check-out procedures. The following are the Bourne shell scripts for the procedures checkin and checkout.

```
$ cat checkin
#!/bin/sh
```

```
# Check in command line; keep a read-only copy in the current directory
ci -u /users/shared/RCS/$1,v
$ cat checkout
#!/bin/sh
# Check out command line; check out an editable copy of the file
co -1 /users/shared/RCS/$1,v
$
```

After creating these scripts, you need to make them executable for yourself by using the chmod u+x command, as in,

```
$ chmod u+x checkin checkout
$
```

An alternative to creating script files checkin and checkout is for users in the group to create a symbolic link, called RCS, to the /users/shared/RCS directory and use short names (simple file names).

Displaying the History of RCS Files You can use the rlog utility to the display the history of an RCS file. The following is a brief description of the utility.

---

rlog [options] filename

Purpose: This utility allows the display of the history of an RCS file

Commonly used options/features:

  -L   Only look at files that have been checked out
  -R   Only display file names
  -luser   Specify files locked by 'user'

Without any option, the rlog command displays the history of all the revisions that have been made to the file. The following command displays the history of the input.c file.

```
$ rlog input.c
RCS file: RCS/input.c,v
Working file: input.c
head: 1.2
branch:
locks: strict
        sarwar: 1.2
access list:
symbolic names:
```

```
comment leader: " * "
keyword substitution: kv
total revisions: 2;  selected revisions: 2
description:
Just a test.
-------------------------
revision 1.2  locked by: sarwar;
date: 2004/10/10 11:59:53;  author: sarwar;  state: Exp;
lines: +1 -0
Testing repeated checkout.
-------------------------
revision 1.1
date: 2004/10/09 11:55:43;  author: sarwar;  state: Exp;
Initial revision
=============================================================
$
```

The following command line displays files that have been checked out by the user jonathan for editing. The files checked out for read-only are not included in this list.

```
$ rlog -L -R -ljonathan RCS/*
RCS/compute.c,v
RCS/input.c,v
$
```

In the following In-Chapter Exercise, you will display the check-in check-out history of an RCS file by using the `rlog` command.

IN-CHAPTER EXERCISE

20.19 Execute the `rlog input.c` command on your system. What did it display? Does the output make sense?

Breaking Locks If you must update a file (perhaps fix a bug in it) that has been checked out by another user in your group for editing, you can use the `rcs -u` command to uncheck out this file. Then check out an editable copy of the same file without overwriting the existing file, make appropriate changes to it, and check it back in. We show this sequence of events in the following session. The first `co` command checks out input.c. The second `co` command displays the message generated when the command is used to check out a file that has already been checked out. The `rcs -u input.c` command unchecks out the input.c file. The `rlog` command shows that input.c is no longer checked out. Once the file has been unlocked (unchecked out), the last three commands check out the input.c file, edit it, and check it back in (retaining a read-only version in the current directory).

```
$ co -l input.c
RCS/input.c,v   -->   input.c
revision 1.2 (locked)
done
$ co -l input.c
RCS/input.c,v   -->   input.c
revision 1.2 (locked)
writable input.c exists; remove it? [ny](n): n
co error: checkout aborted
$ rcs -u input.c
RCS file: RCS/input.c,v
1.3 unlocked
done
$ rlog -L -R -lsarwar input.c
$ co -l input.c
...
$ vi input.c
...
$ ci -u input.c
...
$
```

Displaying Differences between Versions   You can use the rcsdiff utility to display differences between versions of a file. Without any argument, it displays differences between the current and the last checked-in versions. The rcsdiff utility calls the diff command to produce the difference output. You can use this utility to find differences between two or more revisions of a file before merging them. The following is a brief description of the utility.

---

rcsdiff [options] filename

Purpose: This utility allows comparison of different versions of the same file and displays the differences between them

Commonly used options/features:

    -rver   Used to specify version number 'ver' for the file

SYNTAX

The following rcsdiff command line displays the differences between the current version and the last checked-in version of the input.c file.

```
$ rcsdiff input.c
================
RCS file: RCS/input.c,v
retrieving version 2.1
diff -r2.1 input.c
[output of the above diff command]
$
```

You can explicitly name the two versions to be compared by using the −r option. The following command line displays the difference output between versions 1.2 and 2.1 of input.c.

```
$ rcsdiff -r1.2 -r2.1 input.c
RCS file: RCS/input.c,v
retrieving revision 1.2
retrieving revision 2.1
diff -r1.2 -r2.1
1,2d0
< /* Just a test */
[remaining output of the above diff command]
$
```

Merging Versions   The `rcsmerge` utility can be used to merge the differences between two versions of a file. These versions are the current version and a version specified in the command line, or the two versions specified in the command line. The following is a brief description of the utility.

---

rcsmerge [options] filename

Purpose: This utility allows merging of two different versions of the same file

Commonly used options/features:

   −rver   Used to specify the version number 'ver' for the file

   −p   Output changes to a file other than the current version

---

If the currently checked-out version of input.c is 1.4 and you want to merge the changes made on version 1.1.1.2 into this file, you can run the following command. By default, the `rcsmerge` command overwrites the existing file with the merged file. You can use the −p option to redirect the merged version to stdout, which can then be redirected to another file. The use of −p option is highly recommended because the command sometimes does not work as you expect it to. If you do not use this option, the current version is changed and there is nothing to fall back on. In the following `rcsmerge` command, we combine the currently checked-out version (1.4) and version 1.1.1.2 of the input.c file and store it in merged_input.c. With the −p option, you can remove the merged_input.c file and go back to input.c.

```
$ rcsmerge -r1.1.1.2 -p input.c > merged_input.c
RCS file: RCS/input.c,v
retrieving revision 1.1.1.2
retrieving revision 1.4
Merging differences between 1.1.1.1 and 1.4 into input.c; result to stdout
$
```

You can merge any two versions of an RCS file by specifying them in the command line. For example, the following rcsmerge command merges versions 1.2 and 3.2 of input.c and stores the merged version in the merged_input.c file.

```
$ rcsmerge -r1.2 -r3.2 -p input.c > merged_input.c
RCS file: RCS/input.c,v
retrieving revision 1.2
retrieving revision 3.2
Merging differences between 1.2 and 3.2 into input.c; result to stdout
$
```

In the following In-Chapter Exercise, you will practice merging various versions of an RCS file.

IN-CHAPTER EXERCISE

20.20 Create a few versions of input.c file and execute the rcsmerge command to merge them all into the merged_input.c file.

Limiting Access Rights to RCS Files Any user can check out an RCS file, provided that the user has appropriate permissions for the file and has access to the file's pathname. You can protect your RCS files by restricting access to one or more users and/or groups by using the –a and –e options of the rcs command. As mentioned in the brief description of the rcs utility, you can use the –a option to allow check-out rights on a file to one or more users or everyone in a group. All other users are allowed to check out a read-only copy of the file. You can use the –e option to remove a user from the list. Multiple –a and –e options can be used in a command line.

In the following session, we demonstrate the use of both options. The first rcs command adds users matt, chang, and mona to the list of users allowed to check out an editable version of the input.c file and check it back in; no other user is allowed to perform these tasks. The second rcs command adds all the users in group number 102 to the list of users who can access the file. The last rcs command denies davis the access right for editing input.c.

```
$ rcs -amatt,chang,mona input.c
$ rcs -a102 input.c
$ rcs -edavis input.c
$
```

You can specify multiple -e or -o options with an rcs command line to allow or deny access to different users. In the following rcs command line, users sirini, chris, and kahn are allowed to access an editable version of the input.c file, but users liz and beena are not.

```
$ rcs -asirini,chris -akahn -eliz -ebeena input.c
$
```

In the following In-Chapter Exercise, you will use the rcs command with -a and -e options to set different access rights for different users on an RCS file.

IN-CHAPTER EXERCISE

20.21 Give a command line that allows users peter and aziz editing rights to the RCS/input.c,v file and takes away the same rights from user mary.

RCS Special Character Sequences You can place any of several special character sequences in a comment header of a source file. These character sequences are processed specially by RCS and are expanded to include information from the RCS log for the file. The general format for these special sequences is $string$. This sequence results in the expansion of 'string' by RCS. This expansion takes place when you check a file into the RCS directory and is in place the next time you check out the file. Table 20.3 shows some of these sequences and their expanded values.

◼◼ **TABLE 20.3** RCS Special Character Sequences and Their Expanded Values

Character Sequence	Replaced with
$Author$	Author's login name
$Date$	Current date and time
$RCSfile$	Name of the RCS file
$Revision$	The highest revision number
$Source$	Name of the source file

The comment header,

```
/*
 * Author:      $Author$
 * Date:        $Date$
 * Module:      $RCSfile$
 * Revision:    $Revision$
 * Status:      $Id$
 */
```

in the input.c file expands to,

```
/*
 * Author:      $Author: sarwar $
 * Date:        $Date: 2004/10/24 16:41:57 $
 * Module:      $RCSfile: input.c,v $
 * Revision:    $Revision: 1.6 $
 * Status:      $Id: input.c,v 1.6 2004/10/24 16:41:57 sarwar Exp $
 */
```

when the file is checked in.

The most commonly used sequence is Id, which is expanded by RCS to include the RCS file name, revision number, date, time, login name of the user making changes, and the RCS state of the file. If you want to put this information in an executable file, you need to include the following C/C++ code in the source file.

```
static char rcsid[] = "$Id$";
```

This code gets compiled into your C/C++ program.

You can use the `ident` utility to display the expanded RCS special character sequences in a file. It works on both source and binary files. The following `ident` command displays the expanded forms of the special strings in the input.c file.

```
$ ident input.c
input.c:
     $Author: sarwar $
     $Date: 1999/10/24 16:41:57 $
     $RCSfile: input.c,v $
     $Revision: 1.6 $
     $Id: input.c,v 1.6 1999/10/24 16:41:57 sarwar Exp $
$
```

Miscellaneous RCS Utilities   There are several other RCS utilities that an advanced user might need to learn. See the manual page for the `rcs` utility on your UNIX system to learn what commands are available and to learn more about them.

Using RCS from within `emacs`   You can check in and check out files and run other RCS utilities from within the `emacs` editor. To do so, you need to run the editor in the vc mode. The <^cvv> command does the next right thing in most cases. For example, if a file is read-only, <^cvv> will check it out for editing. If the file is an editable version, <^cvv> will check the file in. The <^cvu> command unchecks out the current file and reverts to the previous version. The <^cvl> command shows the RCS history (version log) of the file. The <^cvh> command inserts a special character sequence, the RCS Id header, at the current cursor position.

Beyond SCCS and RCS

Several freeware version control systems, mostly built on top of the RCS system, act as front ends to the RCS system. Many have been developed in-house by companies. One of the most popular of these systems is the freeware Concurrent Version System (CVS). It is optimized to allow you to apply RCS commands to multiple files in various directories and allows concurrent file check-outs without locking the file. The latter feature is implemented by using **lazy locking,** which allows multiple users to check out a file for editing that you have already checked out, without having to break your lock.

There are also graphical front ends to RCS and other version control systems. The main feature of these systems is that they are easier to use because of their GUI. Most of the newer, in-house systems have a Web interface.

20.6 Static Analysis Tools

Static analysis of a program involves analyzing the structure and properties of your program without executing it. These analyses are usually meant to determine the level of portability of your code for multiple platforms, the number of lines of code (LOC), the number of function calls/points (FPs) in your program, and the percentage of time taken by each function in the code. During the planning phase of a software project, parameters such as LOC and FPs are commonly used in **software cost models** that are used to estimate the number of person-months needed to complete a software project and, hence, the software cost.

Static analysis tools allow you to measure those parameters. In the following sections, we discuss some useful UNIX tools that allow you to perform these analyses. Our focus is the `lint` utility, but we also briefly describe the `prof` utility.

20.6.1 Verifying Code for Portability

Most C compilers do fairly well at checking for type mismatches, but few handle portability. You can use the `lint` utility to check your C software for portability. It is one of the most useful tools in UNIX for developing high-quality, clean, and portable C software, yet it is one of the least understood and used. It detects program features that are likely to be bugs, non-portable, or wasteful of system resources. Although `lint` can be used with many types of files, including C program, assembly, and preprocessor files, the discussion here is limited to its use with C program files.

In addition to performing tight type checking, `lint` also performs many other checks on a program to report structural problems such as unreachable statements, loops that are not entered at the top, local variables declared and not used, and logical expressions whose values are constant. The `lint` utility also reports messages if it finds functions that return values in some places and not in others, functions that are called with varying numbers or types of arguments, and functions that return values that are not used or whose return values are used but are not supposed to return any.

Most of the messages reported by `lint` are meaningful; they tell you what the problem is and where it is. However, some of its messages are difficult to understand and irrelevant. You simply have to learn to ignore such messages. The following is a brief description of the `lint` utility.

---

lint [options] file-list

Purpose: This utility allows checking of C programs, specified in 'file-list', for features that can be bugs, nonportable, or wasteful of system resources

Commonly used options/features:

`-c`	Check type casts (coercions) of questionable validity
`-s`	Produce one-line error messages (or warnings) only
`-u`	Suppress complaints about external variables and functions used and not defined, or vice versa; this option is useful for running `lint` on a subset of modules of a software
`-v`	Suppress complaints about unused arguments in functions

We demonstrate the use of `lint` with the simple program shown in the following session and stored in the cat.c file. The program reads input from stdin and sends it to stdout. It is in a sense, then, a simple version of the `cat` command. We have used the `nl` command with –ba option to number all the source lines (including blank lines) because the line numbers reported in `lint`'s error messages include blank lines.

```
$ nl -ba cat.c
     1   /*
     2    *    Copy stdin to stdout
     3    */
     4
     5   #include <stdio.h>
     6
     7   main (int argc,    char *argv[])
     8   {
     9        char         c;
    10        int          i,j;
    11
    12        while ((c = getchar()) != EOF)
    13             putchar(c);
    14   }
$
```

The program compiles without any error messages from the compiler. It also runs without a problem, echoing each line entered from the keyboard until you press <Ctrl-D> (the eof character in UNIX on a new line). The compilation and execution of the program is shown in the following session.

```
$ cc cat.c
$ a.out
Hello there!
Hello there!
Let's see how it goes.
Let's see how it goes.
That's all folks!
That's all folks!
<^D>
$
```

We now use the `lint` command to see if it detects any potentially problematic features in the cat.c program. Note that the output of `lint` informs you in the second and the second-to-last messages that the `main` function has no `return` statement. The first warning informs you of a common programming error, that is, the value returned by `getchar` is of type `int` and the variable `c` is of type `char`. This approach works on most machines, but it can cause catastrophic failure on some machines. The problem occurs when the program reads the eof character `<Ctrl-D>` if the input comes from the keyboard), as this character is usually a negative number, such as −1. Because a character variable is allocated 1 byte and −1 is not a character, the value stored in `c` is incorrect. The program, therefore, does not terminate. The third message is obvious: The parameters of the `main` function are not used. The fourth message reports that the `j` and `i` variables are declared but not used, resulting in memory space allocated for these two variables (four bytes each on most contemporary machines) but never used in the program. The last message says that `putc` returns a value that is ignored. This message can be ignored because `putc` is used to display a value on the display screen, and if it cannot do so then not much can be done about it—not even an error message can be displayed on the screen. The `lint` utility displays a similar message for `printf` (and related functions) that should also be ignored.

```
$ lint cat.c
(12) warning: nonportable character comparison : main
[14] warning: Function has no return statement : main

argument unused in function
     (7) argc in main
     (7) argv in main

variable unused in function
     (10) j in main
     (10) i in main

function falls off bottom without returning value
```

```
      (14) main
```

function returns value which is always ignored

```
      putchar
$
```

One last serious bug that lint reports is the use of a variable before it is initialized. You can take care of most of the problems reported by lint by making simple changes to your program. For example, in the above session, you can remove unused parameters from the header of the main function, change the type of c from char to int, remove the declaration for variables i and j, declare the return type for main to be void, and cast the return type of putchar to void to take care of the problems reported by lint. In the following session, we show the new version of the program, the output of the lint command when it is used with the new version, compilation of the new code, and a sample run. Note that lint did not report a single error. This is how production quality C code should be developed on UNIX platforms.

```
$ nl -ba cat.c
     1    /*
     2    *    Copy stdin to stdout
     3    */
     4
     5    #include <stdio.h>
     6
     7    void main ()
     8    {
     9              int      c;
    10
    11              while ((c = getchar()) != EOF)
    12                   (void) putchar(c);
    13    }
$ lint cat2.c
$ cc cat2.c
$ a.out
Long live lint!
Long live lint!
^D
$
```

The following In-Chapter Exercise is designed to give you an appreciation of the use of the lint utility and to help you understand some of the error messages that it produces.

IN-CHAPTER EXERCISE

> **20.22** Go through all the sessions presented in this section to appreciate how `lint` works. Does `lint` produce the same error messages on your system for the first version of cat.c?

You can put some special comments in your code that are treated specially by `lint`. When `lint` reaches these special comments, it takes an action specific to the comment. We discuss one special comment that informs `lint` of functions that never return.

System calls such as `exit()` and `exec()` that do not return are not understood by `lint`, nor is the return call. This condition causes a different type of wrong error reports (or warnings) from `lint`. The `/*NOTREACHED*/` comment can be placed after such calls, informing `lint` that this path through the program code can never be reached. When this comment is read by `lint`, it does not produce the bogus warning. Use of `/*NOTREACHED*/` is shown in the following session.

```
$ cat sample.c
...

    if (fd == -1)
        printf("File open failed.");
        exit(0);
        /*NOTREACHED*/

    }
...
$
```

The `lint` command can be run with several command line options. For example, the `-c` option checks type casts of questionable validity. Thus, `lint` reports a warning for the s = (char *) i; and s = (int *) i; statements in the following code.

```
$ cat test.c
...

    char *s;
    int i;
...

    s = (char *) i;
    s = (int *) i;
...
$ lint -c test.c
(8) warning: illegal combination of pointer and integer, op CAST
(9) warning: assignment type mismatch:
    pointer to char "=" pointer to int
$
```

We strongly recommend that you create a make rule for running the `lint` utility on your modules before compiling them. The following is a sample make rule and its execution.

```
$ cat makefile
SOURCES = compute.c input.c main.c
LINTFLAGS = -c
...
lint: $(SOURCES)
      lint $(LINTFLAGS) $(SOURCES)
...
$ make lint
lint -c compute.c input.c main.c
$
```

Although `lint` checks for most portability features, it does not check a few things. It does not check whether control strings in the printf calls match the types of corresponding variables. Nor does it ensure that variables are unique after the first seven characters. Other than these minor exceptions, `lint` is trouble-free and should be used regularly to remove sticky stuff from production software.

20.6.2 Source Code Metrics

You can use the UNIX tool `prof` to display a profile of your code in terms of the functions used and the percentage of time taken by each function. This information allows you to focus more closely on those functions that are causing bottlenecks in the software.

At times, you will want to know how long a program spends in each function when it is executed. You can use this information to improve the performance of certain portions of a program by optimizing them. UNIX has two main tools for analyzing the program performance: `prof` and `gprof`. Both tools enable your program to track down the number of times each function is called and the time spent in each function. The `gprof` tool provides more data than `prof`, but both are effective in identifying expensive portions of your program and execution paths in it. The use of both tools is very similar, and they generate similar output. We discuss `prof` only, but the steps shown work for `gprof` as well.

The first step in using `prof` is to compile your program with a particular option that asks the compiler to insert appropriate code in the object module for counting the number of times that each function is executed and the time spent in each function. For fully testing your program, use the `cc` compiler command with the `-p` option, as in,

```
$ cc -p matrix_mult.c -o mm
$
```

After your program has compiled successfully, run it. Execution produces the run-time data in a file called mon.out in a format that `prof` can read. You then use the `prof` utility with this file to display the program profile.

20.7 Dynamic Analysis Tools

Dynamic analysis of a program involves its analysis during run time. As we mentioned before, this phase comprises debugging, tracing, and performance monitoring of the software, including testing it against product requirements. In this section, we discuss the three useful UNIX tools for tracing the execution of a program (`ctrace`), debugging a program (`dbx`), and measuring the running time of a program in actual time units (`time`).

20.7.1 Tracing Program Execution

The simplest yet most effective method to debug a C program is to monitor its sequential execution by displaying the values of variables related to the problem. Most programmers perform this task by inserting printf statements at appropriate places in a program to display values of certain variables when the program control reaches these places. The `ctrace` utility allows you to display the values of all program variables and monitor program execution. The following is a brief description of this utility.

SYNTAX

ctrace [options] filename

Purpose: This utility allows monitoring execution of a program for debugging purposes

Commonly used options/features:

  `-ffcns`   Trace only the functions specified in 'fcns'

  `-pfcns`   Trace all but the functions specified in 'fcns'

The `ctrace` utility performs its task by reading the C program from the specified file (or from stdin), inserting statements in it to display program statements and values of the variables modified or referenced by them, and sending the modified program to standard output. You can save this program in a C source file and compile it to generate an executable. When you run the program, every statement, the name and value of any variables referenced or modified in the statement, and any output from the statement are displayed on the screen. The output of `trace` goes to the stdout, so you can save it in a file and view it by using an editor or a command such as `cat`, `more`, `head`, or `tail`.

In the output of a `ctraceb` program, the long and pointer variables are always printed as signed integers; *char*, *short*, and *int* variables are also printed as signed integers or as characters, if appropriate. Pointers to character arrays are printed as strings if appropriate. Double variables are printed as floating point numbers in scientific notation. You can request that variables be printed in additional formats, if appropriate, with various options. You can use the -o, -x, -u, and -e options to display values of variables in octal, hexadecimal, unsigned, or floating point format, respectively.

When loops are detected in the trace output, tracing stops until the loop exits or a different sequence of statements within the loop executes. A warning message is displayed after each 1,000 loop cycles to help you detect infinite loops.

In the following session, we present a simple C program in the `main.c` file that displays the sum of squares of the first 10 positive integers. When the program is compiled and run, nothing is displayed and the control does not return to shell. We used the `ctrace` utility to produce the traceable version of main.c in temp.c. We used the `ls -l` command to demonstrate the increase in the size of the source code after `ctrace` has inserted the trace code in it. The code in temp.c is compiled to generate the executable code in a.out. Execution of the `a.out` command generates the program trace. Note that the `for` loop in the program should execute 10 times, but it keeps on executing forever. This result shows that we have an infinite loop in our program. Because the trace code will keep displaying the `still repeating` ... message forever, we used the `a.out | more` command to paginate the output of the program. The trace shows that the value of i is always 10 before the assignment statement `j = i*i;` is executed. After carefully studying the statement that executes before the assignment statement (the `for` statement), we realize that, instead of using the assignment operator, `=`, we should have used the equality operator, `==`, in the `for` statement. When we correct this bug, the program works correctly.

```
$ nl -ba main.c
     1    main()
     2    {
     3    int       i,j;
     4
     5              for (i=0,j=0; i=10; i++)
     6              j = i*i;
     7              printf ("The sum of squares = %d\n", j);
     8    }
$ ctrace main.c > temp.c
$ ls -l
-rw--r--r--   1   sarwar     104  Oct     12     11:07   main.c
-rw--r--r--   1   sarwar     9789 Oct     12     11:08   temp.c
$ cc temp.c
$ a.out | more
     1 main()
     5    for (i=0,j=0; i=10; i++)
          /* i == 0 */
          /* j == 0 */
          /* i == 10 or '\n' */
     6        j = i*i;
              /* i == 10 or '\n' */
              /* j == 100 or 'd' */
     5    for (i=0,j=0; i=10; i++)
          /* i == 11 or '\v' */
          /* i == 10 or '\n' */
```

```
6           j = i*i;
            /* i == 10 or '\n' */
            /* j == 100 or 'd' */
/* repeating */
/* still repeating after 1000 times */
/* still repeating after 2000 times */
/* still repeating after 3000 times */
...
$
```

20.7.2 Source Code Debugging

The task of debugging software is time-consuming and difficult. It consists of monitoring the internal working of your code while it executes, examining values of program variables and values returned by functions, and executing functions with specific input parameters. As we stated before, most C programmers tend to use the printf calls at various places in their programs to find the origin of a bug and then remove it. This technique is simple and works quite well for small programs. However, for large size software, where an error may be hidden deep in a function call hierarchy, this technique ends up taking a lot of editing time for adding and removing printf calls in the source file. A more efficient debugging method under such circumstances is to use a **symbolic debugger**. Typical facilities available in a symbolic debugger include:

- Running programs
- Setting break points
- Single stepping
- Listing source code
- Editing source code
- Accessing and modifying variables
- Tracing program execution
- Searching for functions and variables

Several symbolic debuggers are available on UNIX platforms, the most common being dbx and gdb (freeware GNU debugger). They offer similar facilities. We describe dbx, as it is the standard debugger on most UNIX systems. Although dbx has several features for debugging C++ classes as well, we discuss its features for debugging C programs only. The following is a brief description of the utility.

SYNTAX

dbx [options] [execfile]

Purpose: This utility allows source-level debugging and execution of the program
                      in 'execfile', which was generated from a C, C++, FORTRAN, or Pascal
                      source file

(continued)

---

dbx [options] [execfile] (continued)

Commonly used options/features:

-r	Execute the 'execfile' immediately
-s startup	Read the initialization commands from the 'startup' file instated of .dbxrc
-sr startup	Read the initialization commands from the 'startup' file instated of .dbxrc and then remove startup

---

During startup under the Korn shell, dbx searches for .dbxrc. If it does not find .dbxrc, dbx prints a warning message and searches for .dbxinit. The search order is: ./.dbxrc and then ~/.dbxrc. The -s and -sr options allow you to use any file as a startup file.

Using dbx

Before debugging a program with dbx (or any other debugger), you must compile it with the -g compiler option to include the symbol table in the executable. We use the program in the bugged.c file to show various features of dbx. The program prompts you for keyboard input, displays the input, and exits. We use several functions to demonstrate the features of dbx for displaying the stack trace and setting break points at function boundaries. The following session shows program code, its compilation without the -g option, and its execution.

```
$ nl -ba bugged.c
     1    /*
     2    * Sample C program bugged with a simple, yet nasty error
     3    */
     4
     5    #include <stdio.h>
     6
     7    #define PROMPT     "Enter a string: "
     8    #define SIZE   255
     9
    10    void get_input(char *, char *);
    11    void null_function1 ();
    12    void null_function2 ();
    13
    14    void main ()
    15    {
    16        char *s_val, *temp;
    17
    18        temp = s_val;
    19        null_function1 ();
```

```
20          null_function2 ();
21          get_input(PROMPT, temp);
22          (void) printf("You entered: %s.\n", s_val);
23          (void) printf("The end of buggy code!\n");
24    }
25
26    void null_function1 ()
27    { }
28
29    void null_function2 ()
30    { }
31
32    void get_input(char *prompt, char *str)
33    {
34          (void) printf("%s", prompt);
35          for (*str = getchar(); *str != '\n'; *str = getchar())
36                str++;
37          *str = '\0'; /* string terminator */
38    }
```

```
$ cc bugged.c -o bugged
$ bugged
Enter a string: Need dbx!!
Segmentation Fault
$
```

Note that the program prompts you for input and faults without echoing what you enter from the keyboard. This happens frequently in C programming, particularly with programmers who are new to C or are not careful about initializing variables in their programs and rely on the compiler. It is time to use dbx!

Entering the dbx Environment As we mentioned before, in order to enter the dbx environment, you must compile your C program with the -g compiler option. This option creates an executable file that contains the symbol table and debugging, relocation, and profiling information for your program. After the code compiles successfully, you can then use the dbx command to debug your code, as in the following session. The output of the dbx command may vary from system to system. Note that (dbx) is the prompt for the dbx debugger.

```
$ cc -g bugged.c -o bugged
$ dbx bugged
The major new features of this release relative to 3.0.1 are
...
```

```
Reading symbolic information for bugged
Reading symbolic information for rtld /usr/lib/ld.so.1
Reading symbolic information for libc.so.1
Reading symbolic information for libdl.so.1
(dbx)
```

Once inside the dbx environment, you can run many commands to monitor the execution of your code. You can use the help command to get information about the dbx commands. Without any argument, the help command displays the names of all of the dbx commands. You can get information about any dbx command by passing the command name as an argument to the help command. In the following session, the help command shows the names of all dbx commands and the help trace command displays a brief description of the trace command. The following is a partial list of commands.

```
(dbx) help
Command Summary

Execution and Tracing
     cancel    catch     clear       cont      delete    fix

     ...

Displaying and Naming Data
     assign    call      demangle    display  down      dump      examine

     ...

Accessing Source Files
     bsear     ch        cd          edit      file      files     func
(dbx) help trace
Line tracing:
trace                     # Trace each source line
trace in <proc>           # Trace each source line while in proc
trace [ at ] <line#>      # Trace given source line

Call tracing:
trace <proc>              # Trace calls to the procedure
trace inmember <func>     # Trace calls to any member function named <func>
trace infunctin <func>    # Trace when any function named <func> is called
trace inclass <class>     # Trace calls to any member function of <class>

Value tracing:
trace <exp> at <line#>    # Print <exp> when <line> is reached
trace <var> [in <proc>]   # Trace changes to the variable

Any of the above forms may be followed by the form 'if <cond>' which acts
   like a filter; trace output is emitted only if <cond> evaluates to true.
```

The speed of trace is governed by setting the dbxenv variable trace_speed.
(dbx)

In addition to the **dbx**-specific commands, **dbx** also allows you to execute all shell commands.

Executing a Program   You can run your program inside the **dbx** environment by using the run command. The following command executes the bugged program. The program prompts you for input. When you enter the input (**Hello!** in this case) and hit <Enter>, the program fails when it tries to execute the command at line 35. The error message is quite cryptic for beginners and those who are not familiar with UNIX jargon. All the error message says is that a signal of type SEGV was received by the program when it was executing the statement at line 35. The message in the parentheses explains what SEGV means: that your program tried to access a memory location that did not belong to its process address space.

```
(dbx) run

Running: bugged

(process id 7400)

Enter a string: Hello!

signal SEGV (no mapping at the fault address) in get_input at line 35 in file "bugged.c"

    35    void null_function1 ()

(dbx)
```

Tracing Program Execution   To find out what went wrong, we use the **dbx** commands for tracing program execution. There are several ways of tracing a program, including line-by-line tracing of the whole program and tracing statements of a function, calls to a particular function, and changes to a variable. The command used for tracing program execution is **trace**. The following is a brief description of the command.

---

trace [options]

Purpose: This **dbx** command allows monitoring execution of a program for debugging purposes. Depending on its parameters, this command can be used for line tracing, function call tracing, and value tracing. Without any option, the command traces the whole program line by line.

Commonly used options/features:

func	Trace calls to the function `func`
infunc	Trace source lines in the function called 'func'
line#	Trace the statement at the program line number '#'
var[in func]	Trace changes to the 'var' variable
	Any of these options can be followed by the form 'if cond' to have the trace command send output only if 'cond' is true.

(margin label: SYNTAX)

After executing the `trace` command, you need to rerun the program to start tracing. The rerun command starts execution of the program from the beginning or as specified in the trace command. In the following session, we show line-by-line tracing of the whole program and tracing changes in the `s_val` variable in the `main` function.

```
(dbx) trace
(2) trace
(dbx) rerun
Running: bugged
(process id 7401)
entering function main
trace:    18        temp = s_val;
trace:    19        null_function1 ();
entering function null_function1
trace:    27        { }
leaving function null_function1
trace:    20        null_function2 ();
entering function null_function2
trace:    30        { }
leaving function null_function2
trace:    21        get_input(PROMPT, temp);
entering function get_input
trace:    34        (void) printf("%s", prompt);
trace:    35        for (*str = getchar(); *str != '\n'; *str = getchar ())
Enter a string: Need dbx!! signal SEGV (acess to address exceeded
 protections) in get_input at line
(dbx) trace s_val in main
(3) trace s_val in ma   in
(dbx) rerun
Running: bugged
(process id 7402)
initially (at line "bugged.c":18): s_val = (nil)
Enter a string: Hello!
signal SEGV (no mapping at the fault address) in get_input at line 35 in
file "bugged.c"
          35        for (*str = getcar(); *str != '\n'; *str = getchar())
(dbx)
```

The `trace` command returns an index number (2 and 3 here) that can be used with the `delete` command to turn off the corresponding trace, such as `delete 2` to turn off the line-by-line trace in the above session.

Setting Break Points You can also trace a program up to a particular statement or function by using the `stop` command. It allows you to run a program without interruption until the control reaches the statement or function that you want to study more closely. The process of stopping a program in this way is known as setting **break points**. A brief description of the `stop` command is given here.

SYNTAX

stop [options]

Purpose: This command allows setting break points at the line or function level

Commonly used options/features:

`at`line	Stop program execution at line number 'line'
`in`func	Stop program execution when 'func' is called

In the following session, we use the `stop at 21` command to set break points at line 21 and the `get_input` function. We then trace the program line by line. The first `stop` command is used to stop the program at the statement on line 21. The `rerun` command is used to run the program and stop its execution at line 21. The second `stop in get_input` command is used to stop execution of the program before execution of the `get_input` function begins. We now have set two break points, one at line 21 and the other before the function call `get_input` is executed. Again, the `rerun` command is used to run the program and stop its execution at the first statement of the `get_input` function. The `next` command is used to execute after the break point.

```
(dbx) stop at 21
(4) stop at "bugged.c":21
(dbx) rerun
Running: bugged
(process id 7404)
initially (at line "bugged.c":18): s_val = (nil)
stopped in main at line 21 in file "bugged.c"
    21    get_input(PROMPT, temp);
(dbx) stop in get_input
(5) stop in get_input
(dbx) rerun
Running: bugged
(process id 7405)
stopped in main at line 21 in file "bugged.c"
    21    get_input (PROMPT, temp);
(dbx) next
Enter a string: Hello!
```

```
signal SEGV (no mapping at the fault address) in get_input at line 35 in file "bugged.c"
   35    for (*str = getchar(); *str !='\n'; *str = getchar())
(dbx)
```

Like the `trace` command, the `stop` command returns an index number in parentheses, which can be used with the `delete` command to turn off the break point.

Single Stepping through Your Program Always set break points in your program to be able to view execution of all or part of your code statement by statement. The process of tracing program execution statement by statement is known as single stepping through your program. **Single stepping**, combined with tracing of variables, allows you to study program execution closely. Single stepping can be done with the `step` command, which executes the current statement and stops before the next instruction runs. If you are tracing a variable, it shows you the value of the variable when a statement within the scope of the variable executes. Run the `help scope` command to get more information about the scoping rules.

In the following session, we stop execution of the program at line 18, set tracing for the *s_val* variable in the `main` function, and single step through the program with the `step` command.

```
(dbx) stop at 18
(6) stop at "bugged.c":18
(dbx) trace s_val in main
(3) trace s_val in main
(dbx) run
Running: bugged
(process id 7406)
initially (at line "bugged.c":18): s_val = (nil)
stopped in main at line 18 in file "bugged.c"
   18        temp = s_val;
(dbx) step
stopped in main at line 19 in file "bugged.c"
   19        null_function1 ();
(dbx) step
stopped in null_function1 at line 27 in file "bugged.c"
   27        { }
(dbx) step
stopped in main at line 20 in file "bugged.c"
   20        null_function2 ();
(dbx)
```

Listing Program Code You can use the `list` command to display all or part of a source program. You can display lines of code in a particular function or on a range of lines. In the following example, the `list get_input` command is used to display the code for the get_input function, and the list 14,27 command is used to display the source program at lines 14–27. Use the help list command to get more information about the list command.

```
(dbx) list get_input
    29   void null_function2 ()
    30   { }
    31
    32   void get_input (char *prompt, char *str)
    33   {
    34        (void) printf("%s", prompt);
    35        for (*str = getchar(); *str != '\n'; *str = getchar())
    36             str++;
    37        *str = '\0'; /* string terminator */
    38   }
(dbx) list 14,27
    14   void main ()
    15   {
    16        char *s_val, *temp;
    17
    18        temp = s_val;
    19   null_function1 ();
    20   null_function2 ();
    21   get_input(PROMPT, temp);
    22   (void) printf("You entered: %s. \n", s_val);
    23   (void) printf("The end of bugged code!\n");
    24   }
    25
    26   void null_function1 ()
    27   { }
(dbx)
```

Searching for Identifiers You can use the search and bsearch commands to search for identifiers in your program and display lines that contain them. You can use the search command to perform a forward search, starting with the current position, and the bsearch command to do a backward search. In the following session, the first two search commands display source lines that contain the identifier str. The three bsearch commands perform a backward search for the same identifier.

```
(dbx) search str
    32        return (str);
```

```
(dbx) search str
dbx: End of file; did not find search string: str
(dbx) bsearch str
   31          str = str - i;
(dbx) bsearch str
   30          *str = '\0'; /* string terminator */
(dbx) bsearch str
   27          str++;
(dbx)
```

Accessing Identifiers (Variables and Functions)   You can access the location of an identifier (variable or function) in the program source and view its type, value, and places of use by using various dbx commands. Table 20.4 shows the syntaxes and brief descriptions of the commands used to perform these tasks.

■ **TABLE 20.4** The dbx Commands for Accessing Identifiers

Command Syntax	Purpose
print identifier	Display the current value of 'identifier'
whatis identifier	Display the type of 'identifier'
whereami	Display the location in the program code in terms of file name, function name, and line number
whereis identifier	Display the type of 'identifier' in terms of whether it is a variable or function and its context as described for the which command
which identifier	Display the context of 'identifier' in terms of the executable file, source file, and function it is in

In the following session, we illustrate the use of these commands with examples. Although the outputs of the commands are fairly self-explanatory, the outputs of the which and whereis commands need a bit of explanation. The output of the which str command shows that the str identifier is in the executable file called bugged, the corresponding source file is bugged.c, and the function in bugged.c that contains the identifier is get_input. The output of the whereis str command has the same format. The print str command displays the value of the str variable, and the whatis str command displays the type declaration of the str variable. The whereami command displays the next command to be executed.

```
(dbx) print str
str = (nil)
(dbx) whatis str
char *str;
(dbx) which str
```

```
`bugged`bugged.c`get_input`str
```
```
(dbx) whereis str
```
```
variable:       `bugged`bugged.c`get_input`str
```
```
(dbx) whereami
```
```
stopped in get_input at line 34 in file "bugged.c"
```
```
    34          (void) printf("%s", prompt);
```
```
(dbx)
```

In the following session, we use some of those commands with function arguments. Note that the format of the output of both commands is identical for variables and functions.

```
(dbx) whereis get_input
```
```
function:       `bugged`bugged.c`get_input
```
```
(dbx) whatis get_input
```
```
void get_input(char *prompt, char *str);
```
```
(dbx)
```

Fixing the Bug After finding out that the program faults at line 35, the first thing you should do is determine the variables involved in the statement that caused the fault. Then you should display the values of theses variables. You can use the dump command to display the values of all the variables in the current function—or any function, for that matter. The following is a brief description of the command.

SYNTAX

dump [function_name]

Purpose: Without a parameter, display the values of all the variables local to the current function; with a function argument, display values of all the variables local to the named function

---

In the following session, we run the program inside dbx and then display the values of all the variables in the get_input and main functions.

```
(dbx) run
```
```
Running: bugged
```
```
(process id 7412)
```
```
Enter a string: Hello!
```
```
signal SEGV (no mapping at the fault address) in get_input at line 35 in file
"bugged.c"
```
```
35    for (i=0, *str=getchar(); *str != '\n'; *str = getchar()) {
```
```
(dbx) dump
```
```
prompt = 0x20clc "Enter a string: "
```

```
str = (nil)
(dbx) dump main
s_val = (nil)
(dbx)
```

The session immediately reveals that the value of the actual parameter to the `get_input` function, `s_val`, is nil (0). This causes the formal parameter in the `get_input` function, *str*, to have a starting value of `nil`. When we dereference the *str* variable to store user input, we try to access memory location with address 0. This location belongs to the UNIX kernel space and is used to store the resident part of the operating system. Therefore, the program tries to write to a location that is outside its process address space (i.e., does not belong to it). This attempt is a clear violation that results in the SEGV (segmentation violation) signal sent to the running program, causing its termination (the default action on this signal). Hence, you see the error message `Segmentation Fault` when you run the program from the command line. Figure 20.9 illustrates segmentation violation.

To fix the bug in the program, all you need do is initialize the *s_val* pointer to a memory space that has been allocated to the program (statically or dynamically). We use a character array called *user_input* and set the *s_val* pointer to point to the first byte of the array. The revised `main` function is shown in the following session, along with its compilation and proper execution. The changes (additions in this case) in the code are additions of lines 2, 6, and 8 in the program (not counting the blank lines).

```
$ cat bugged.c
#define PROMPT   "Enter a string: "
#define SIZE 255
void get_input(char *, char *);
void main ()
{
    char user_input[SIZE];
    char *s_val, *temp;
    s_val = user_input;   /* initialize s_val */
    temp = s_val;
    null_function1();
    null_function2();
    get_input(PROMPT, temp);
    ...
}
...
$ cc -o bugged bugged.c
$ bugged
Enter a string: Hello!
```

```
You entered: Hello!.
The end of bugged code!
$
```

Leaving dbx *and Wrapping Up* You can use the quit command to leave dbx and return to your shell.

```
(dbx) quit
$
```

Once your code has been debugged, you can decrease the size of the binary file, releasing some disk space, by removing from it the information generated by the -g option of the C compiler to be used by debugging and profiling utilities. You can do so by using the strip command. The information stripped from the file contains the symbol table and relocation, debugging, and profiling information. In the following session, we show the long list for the bugged file before and after execution of the strip command. Note that the size of the file has decreased from 9,076 bytes to 4,552 bytes, resulting in about 50% saving in disk space. Alternatively, you can recompile the source to generate an optimized executable by using various options.

```
$ ls -l bugged
-rwxr-xr-x  1 sarwar        9076 Oct 18 17:14 bugged
$ strip bugged
$ ls -l bugged
-rwxr-xr-x  1 sarwar        4552 Oct 18 17:15 bugged
$
```

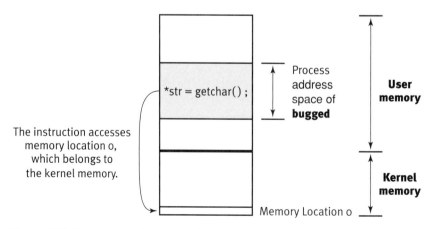

Figure 20.9 The memory (segmentation) access violation causing program failure

In the following In-Chapter Exercise, you will make extensive use of dbx to understand its various features.

IN-CHAPTER EXERCISE

20.23 Go through all dbx commands discussed in this section to appreciate how dbx works. If some of the commands used in this section do not work on your system, use the help command to list the dbx commands and use those that are available in your version of dbx.

20.7.3 Run-Time Performance

The **run-time performance** of a program or any shell command can be measured and displayed by using the time command. This command reports three times: real time, system time, and user time in the format hours:minutes:seconds. Real time is the actual time taken by the program to finish running, system time is the time taken by system activities while the program was executing, and user time is the time taken by execution of the program code. Because UNIX is a time-sharing system, real time is not always equal to the sum of system and user time, as many other users' processes may be running while your program executes. The following is a brief description of the command.

---

time [command]

Purpose: Report the run-time performance of 'command' in terms of its execution time; it reports three times: real time (actual time taken by command execution), system time (time spent on system activities while the command was executing), and user time (time taken by the command code itself)

SYNTAX

The time command sends its output to stderr. So, if you want to redirect the output of the time command to a disk file, you must redirect its stderr (not its stdout) to the file.

There are two versions of the time command: the built-in command for the C shell and the /usr/bin/time command. The output of the built-in time command is quite cryptic, whereas the output of the /usr/bin/time command is very readable. When the C shell version of the time command is executed without a command argument, it reports the length of time the current C shell has been running. The reported time includes the time taken by all its children, that is, all the commands that have run under the shell. The other version of the command does not have this feature.

The following time command, executed under the C shell, reports how long the current shell has been running: 2 hr, 33 min, and 17 sec. In the output, u represents user time and s represents system time.

```
% time
2.0u 4.0s 2:33:17 0% 0+0k 0+0io 0pf+0w
%
```

The following command reports the time taken by the `find` command. For the sake of brevity, we have not displayed the error messages generated by the `find` command because of improper access privileges for certain directories. Note how neat the output looks.

```
$ /usr/bin/time find /usr -name socket.h -print
real    57:26.6
user       24.8
sys      6:42.9
$
```

As mentioned before, the sum of user and system times does not always equal real time, especially if a program is idle and does not use the CPU for some time. That happens quite often because UNIX is a time-sharing system and many other processes may be running while your program is running. In the output of the first `time` command, the real time is 2 hr, 33 min, and 17 sec, which clearly does not equal the sum of user and system times (2 sec and 4 sec, respectively).

Because the `time` command can be used to measure the running time of any program, you can use it with an executable of your own—a binary image or a shell script. The following session shows the running time of the quick_sort program when it is executed to sort numbers in the in_data file. Note that the real time equals the system time plus the user time, as the command was run late at night when the system was not running any other user processes.

```
$ /usr/bin/time quick_sort in_data
real       51.2
user       48.6
sys         2.6
$
```

There are other ways of measuring the running time of a program that give you better precision. But, using the `time` command to perform this task is the easiest way, and we certainly recommend it for beginners.

20.8   Web Resources

Table 20.5 lists useful Web sites for various programming languages and UNIX commands and tools for program development.

Table 20.5 Web Resources for the Most Commonly Used Programming Languages, and UNIX Commands and Tools for Program Development

Reference	URL	Description
General Pages: Manpage Viewer and Program Development Tools		
1	www.npaci.edu/MT/tera-cgi/man.cg	Manpage viewer: a Web page for UNIX/LINUX manual pages *(continued)*

TABLE 20.5 *(continued)*

2	`http://tacpa.org/notes/linux/devTools.html`	A good page for UNIX/Linux development tools
Programming Languages		
1	`www.perl.com`	The Perl language homepage
2	`cm.bell-labs.com/cm/cs/who/dmr/chist.html`	History of the C language, by Dennis Ritchie
3	`www.research.att.com/~bs/C++.html`	C++ language page, maintained by Bjarne Stroustrup, the designer of the language
4	`java.sun.com`	The source of Java technology
5	`developer.java.sun.com/developer/onlineTraining/Programming/BasicJava1/`	Essentials of the Java programming language
6	`www.gnu.org/software/java/java.html`	GNU and the Java language
7	`www.haskell.org`	The Haskell home page
8	`home.planet.nl/~revorvo/cobol.htm`	Links to the most interesting COBOL sites
9	`www.sics.se/SICS-reports/SICS-T--93-01--SE/report_10.html`	A good Web page on the Prolog language
10	`www.eiffel.com`	The Eiffel language home page
11	`www.smalltalk.org`	The Smalltalk language home page
12	`www.visualbasic.org`	Association of Visual Basic Professionals
13	`gcc.gnu.org/onlinedocs/gcc-2.95.3/g77_12.html`	The GNU FORTRAN language
14	`www.acm.org/sigapl ACM'S`	ACM's Special Interest Group on APL and J
15	`www.users.cloud9.net/~bradmcc/APL.html`	A resourceful home page on APL
16	`allman.rhon.itam.mx/dcomp/awk.html`	A good introduction to the awk language
17	`www.gnu.org/software/gawk/gawk.html`	The Web page for GNU awk, gawk
18	`www.tcl.tk`	The tcl developers site
19	`www.w3.org/MarkUp/`	Home page for HTML activities

(continued)

TABLE 20.5 *(continued)*

UNIX Compilers		
20	`gcc.gnu.org/`	The home page for the gcc compiler
21	`www.delorie.com/gnu/docs/gcc/` `g++.1.html`	The manual page for GNU C++ compiler g++
22	`www.cs.wm.edu/cspages/computing/` `tutorial/gpp.html`	A good tutorial on g++
23	`developer.java.sun.com/developer/online` `Training/Programming/BasicJava1/`	Essentials of the Java programming language
24	`java.sun.com/products/jdk/1.1/docs/` `tooldocs/solaris/javac.html`	Manual page for the javac compiler
25	`jakarta.apache.org/ant/`	The Jakarta Project; this Web page describes Apache Ant, a Java-based build tool similar to the make utility
26	`fpt://ftp.ugcs.caltech.edu/pub/elef` `/autotools/toolsmanual.html`	A repository of tools for developing software with GNU
make and Similar Build Tools, ar, nm		
27	`http://heather.cs.ucdavis.edu/` `~matloff/UnixAndC/CLanguage/Make.html`	A good tutorial on make files and libraries
28	`jakarta.apache.org/ant/`	The Jakarta Project. This Web page describes Apache Ant, a Java-based build tool similar to the make utility
29	`fpt://ftp.ugcs.caltech.edu/pub/` `elef/autotools/toolsmanual.html`	A repository of tools for developing software with GNU
30	`www.opengroup.org/onlinepubs` `/007908799/xcu/ar.html`	The manual page for the ar utility
31	`www.opengroup.org/onlinepubs/` `007908799/xcu/nm.html`	The manual page for the nm utility
dbx, gdb, ddd, and GNU Tools for Software Testing		
32	`http://wings.buffalo.edu/computing/` `Documentation/unix/dbx.html`	A Web page for dbx documentation
33	`www.gnu.org/software/gdb/gdb.html`	The home page for the gdb: the GNU project debugger

(continued)

TABLE 20.5 *(continued)*

34	`www.gnu.org/manual/gdb-5.1.1/` `html_chapter/gdb_toc.html`	Debugging with `gdb` version 5.1.1
35	`www.gnu.org/software/ddd` `www.gnu.org/manual/ddd`	The home pages for GNU `ddd`, a graphical front end for `gdb` and other command-line debuggers
36	`fpt://ftp.ugcs.caltech.edu/pub/` `elef/autotools/toolsmanual.html`	A repository of tools for developing software with GNU
37	`www.bluemarsh.com/java/jswat`	A Web site for a stand-alone Java debugger `jswat`
38	`gcc.gnu.org/java`	Home page for the GNU compiler for Java, `gcj`
39	`www.redhat.com/devnet/articles` `/gcj.pdf`	A technical paper on using `gcj` to compile Java code into native machine code
40	`www.gnu.org/software/dejagnu/` `dejagnu.html`	GNU home page for DejaGnu, a framework for testing programs
Gprof		
41	`www.gnu.org/manual/gprof-2.9.1/` `gprof.html`	The home page for `gprof`: the GNU project profiler
42	`sam.zoy.org/doc/programming/` `gprof.html`	HOWTO: using `gprof` with multithreaded applications
43	`user-mode-linux.sourceforge.net/` `gprof.html`	Running `gprof` and `gcov`
RCS		
44	`www.gnu.org/software/rcs/rcs.html`	GNU page for RCS
45	`www.tldp.org/HOWTO/CVS-RCS-HOWTO-` `15.html`	Configuration management tools, including RCS and CVS

▬ Summary ▬▬▬▬▬▬▬▬▬▬▬▬▬▬▬▬▬▬▬▬▬▬▬▬▬▬▬▬▬▬▬▬▬▬▬▬▬▬

UNIX supports all contemporary high-level languages (both interpreted and compiled), including C, C++, Java, Javascript, FORTRAN, BASIC, and LISP. We described the translation process that a program in a compiled language such as C has to go through before it can be executed. We also described briefly a typical software engineering life cycle and discussed in detail the program development process and the tools available in UNIX for this phase of the life cycle. The discussion of tools focused on their use for developing production-quality C software.

The program development process comprises three phases: code generation, static analysis, and dynamic analysis. The UNIX code generation tools include text editors (emacs, pico, and vi) C language enhancers (cb and indent), compilers (cc, gcc, xlc, CC, cpp, and g++), tools for handling module-based software (make), tools for creating libraries (ar, nm, and ranlib), and tools for version control (SCCS, RCS, and their related commands).

The purpose of the static analysis phase is to identify features of the software that might be bugs or nonportable, and to measure metrics such as lines of code (LOC), function points (FPs), and repetition count for functions. The UNIX tools that can be used for this purpose include lint, prof, and dprof.

The purpose of the dynamic analysis phase is to analyze programs during their execution. The tools used during this phase are meant to trace program execution in order to debug them and measure their run-time performance in terms of their execution time. The commonly used UNIX tools for this phase of the software life cycle are debuggers (dbx, gdb, etc.), tracing tools (trace), and tools for measuring running times of programs (time).

UNIX has several tools for other phases of a software life cycle, but a discussion of them is outside the scope of this textbook.

Problems

1. What are the differences between compiled and interpreted languages? Give three examples of each.

2. Give one application area each for assembly and high-level languages.

3. Write the steps that a compiler performs on a source program in order to produce an executable file. State the purpose of each step. Be precise.

4. What are the -o, -l, and -xO options of the cc command used for? Give an example command line for each and describe what it does.

5. Give the compiler commands to create an executable called prog from C source files myprog.c and misc.c. Assume that misc.c uses some functions in the math library. What is the purpose of each command?

6. What are the three steps of the program development process? What are the main tasks performed at each step? Write the names of UNIX tools that can be used for these tasks.

7. Give a shell command that can be used to determine the number of lines of code (LOC) in the program stored in the scheduler.c file.

8. Write advantages and disadvantages of automating the recompilation and relinking process by using the make utility, as opposed to manually doing this task.

9. Consider the following makefile and answer the questions that follow.

```
CC = cc

OPTIONS = -xO4 -o
```

```
OBJECTS = main.o stack.o misc.o

SOURCES = main.c stack.c misc.c

HEADERS = main.h stack.h misc.h

polish: main.c $(OBJECTS)

    $(CC) $(OPTIONS) power $(OBJECTS) -lm

main.o: main.c main.h misc.h

stack.o: stack.c stack.h misc.h

misc.o: misc.c misc.h
```

List the following.

   a. Names of macros

   b. Names of targets

   c. Files that each target is dependent on

   d. Commands for constructing the targets named in part (b)

10. For the makefile in Problem 9, give the dependency tree for the software.

11. What commands are executed for the main.o, stack.o, and misc.o targets? How do you know?

12. For the makefile in Problem 9, what happens if you run the `make` command on your system? Show the output of the command.

13. Use the `nm` command to determine the size of the select call in the socket library (/usr/lib/libsocket.a). What is the size of the code for the call?

14. Give the command line for determining the library that contains the function `strcmp`. What is the size of this function?

15. Can you remove versions 1.1 and 1.3 from the version tree shown in Figure 20.7? Why or why not?

16. Can you remove versions 1.1 and 1.2 from the version tree shown in Figure 20.8? Why or why not?

17. Create version 2.1 of the s.input.c file after creating versions 1.1, 1.2, 1.3, and 1.2.1.1. What command did you use? Show the command with its output.

18. Suppose that the input.c file has versions 1.1–1.6 and that you need to delete version 1.3. How can you accomplish this task if the file is managed under

   a. SCCS (as s.input.c)?

   b. RCS (RCS/input.c,v)?

19. Under SCCS and RCS, you have checked out the latest version of the input.c file. What would happen if you tried to check out the same file again? Why?

20. Give the command line that restricts access of the SCCS log file s.input.c so that only users dale and kent can edit any version of this file. What is the command line for performing the same task for the RCCS/input.c,v file? What is the command line for taking editing rights away from users ahmed and tomn?

21. The following code is meant to prompt you for integer input from the keyboard, read your input, and display it on the screen. The program compiles with one warning, but it doesn't work properly. Use the dbx utility to find the bugs in the program. What are they? Fix the bugs, recompile the program, and execute it to be sure that the corrected version works. Show the working version of the program.

```
#include <stdio.h>

#define PROMPT   "Enter an integer: "

void get_input(char *, int *);

void main ()
{
    int     user_input;
    get_input(PROMPT, user_input);
    (void) printf("You entered: %d.\n", user_input);
}

void get_input(char *prompt, int *ival)
{
    (void) printf("%s", prompt);
    scanf ("%d", &ival);
}
```

22. What does the time sh command line do when executed under the C shell?

23. Give the command line to redirect the output of the /usr/bin/time polish command to a file called polish_output. Assume that you are using the Bourne shell.

UNIX
GUI Basics

Objectives

- To explain the relationship of the components of an X Window System/XFree86 Graphical User Interface to UNIX

- To describe the basic concepts and implementation of XFree86

- To give an overview of the KDE desktop management system

- To discuss the Mac OS X Aqua GUI and Darwin UNIX

- To provide Internet resources to supplement these objectives

21.1   Introduction

When you sit at a computer and work with an application program to accomplish specific tasks, you are primarily concerned with achieving the results that the computer provides. You are shielded from the details of exactly how the computer turns the motions of your hands and fingers into those results. You press a mouse button, for example, to signify a graphical "pick" in an application window shown on-screen. That choice, or event, is recognized by and acted upon by the **Graphical User Interface (GUI)** that controls the dialog between a single user and an application program. The intermediary between the user's requested event and the UNIX operating system, which accomplishes the event, is XFree86, the *Network Protocol*.

In this chapter, we first define XFree86 as a **Network Protocol** for graphical interaction between a user and one or more computer systems running UNIX. This means that it is a software system specifically designed to work over a network to pass user-generated events to the application program, and then channel graphical responses, or requests for graphical output, back to the user. The forms of interactivity, via event-driven input and multi-window display output, are detailed for XFree86, from the user perspective. Because one of the chief arbiters of the user-computer interactive dialog is the *window management system* or *desktop management system*, we then define and detail the functionality of these kinds of programs. Specifically, we describe the operations in the KDE desktop management systems, the most important implementations of desktop managers in all releases of UNIX. Then, we address the functions of window managers, particularly fvwm2 in a non-integrated installation, to expose you to the look and feel of a modern desktop manager and its capabilities. Finally, we give a list of Internet resources that enable you to find more information on all the topics presented in the chapter.

21.2   Basics of XFree86

One way of illustrating the process of a Graphical User Interface is shown in Figure 21.1 where you (depicted as the USER) harness the intermediary facilities of software and hardware components to work with the application program. The figure illustrates how a user's dialog with an application program is used efficiently to control the dialog between an application program, running on a stand-alone or networked computer, through the components of a GUI.

The fundamental assumption of this chapter is that a GUI can be used to most efficiently control the dialog between a single user and an application program running on a stand-alone or networked computer, using the intermediary of the UNIX operating systems. The components of a user's dialog with an application program can be simplified to the software component blocks shown in Figure 21.1. For example, a user presses a mouse button to signify a graphical "pick" in an application window shown on screen. That choice, or event, is recognized by and acted upon by the Window Manager controlling that window.

In the UNIX operating system, the components of the GUI recognize a user's request and process it using the protocols of XFree86. The event is passed along to the Desktop Manager, which then passes the request to the application software program for further disposition. Another example is the reverse of the previous one. An application software program generates a request for graphical service, passes this request to UNIX, which in

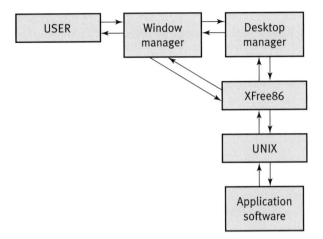

Figure 21.1 Components of a GUI

turn passes the request to XFree86. XFree86 uses the facilities of the Desktop Manager and Window Manager to display the graphical request on the screen of the user's computer.

It is important to note that you can either use the facilities of a *non-integrated GUI system* (i.e., one that only uses the functions of a window manager and XFree86 to work within the UNIX environment) or that of an *integrated GUI system*, which uses the Desktop Manager (and perhaps a Session Manager) as an intermediate software link in the chain shown in Figure 21.1. For example, if you install UNIX on your computer, you might want to install only XFree86 and a default window manager, such as fvwm2. This would constitute a non-integrated GUI installation. The event-generation chain of interactivity as seen in Figure 21.1 would start at User and proceed through Window Manager and then jump to XFree86. An integrated approach would involve installation of the Desktop Manager, such as KDE. The event-generation chain of interactivity would start at User and proceed through Window Manager, then Desktop Manager, and then to XFree86. Most users will use the integrated installation. Section 21.2 deals exclusively with a non-integrated installation. Section 21.3 deals with an integrated installation.

(Note that if you have done a non-integrated installation of UNIX, and you have *not* specified that the X Window System start automatically when your computer boots up, you must type `startx` at the UNIX command prompt in order for XFree86 and a default window manager to "take control" of your display.)

In this chapter, we first define XFree86 as a Network Protocol for graphical interaction between a user and one or more computer systems running UNIX. This means that it is a software system specifically designed to work over a network to pass user-generated events to the application program, and then channel graphical responses, or requests for graphical output, back to the user. The forms of interactivity, via event-driven input and multi-window display output, are detailed for XFree86, from the user perspective.

Since one of the chief arbiters of the user-computer interactive dialog is the *window management system* or *desktop management system*, we then define and detail the functionality of these kinds of programs. Specifically, we describe the operations in the KDE desktop management systems, the most important implementations of desktop managers in all releases of UNIX. We also give a functional overview of window managers, particularly fvwm2 in a non-integrated installation, to expose you to the look and feel of a modern desktop manager and its capabilities. Finally, we give a list of Internet resources that enable you to find more information on all the topics presented in the chapter.

21.2.1 What Is XFree86 Similar To, and What Advantage(s) Does It Have?

Contemporary user-computer interactivity falls into two basic categories, as mentioned in previous chapters. In one category, where a **character user interface**, or CUI, is implemented, the user types commands on a command line using a keyboard, and components of the operating system handle this input and take appropriate action. In the other category, the user gives input via a **graphical user interface**, or GUI, and components of the operating system take appropriate action. Of course there are also hybrid styles of interactivity that are a mixture of the above two categories. Up to this point in the book, you relied almost entirely on a CUI to activate the functionality of UNIX.

The two foremost questions for the beginner concerning XFree86 are: What is it similar to, and what advantage does it give me over the traditional UNIX character user interface (CUI)? The answer to the first question is twofold; XFree86 is a derivative of the X Window System, a network protocol developed to provide a GUI to the UNIX operating system. (For more information on the X Window System, *see* Internet Resource 1.) The major difference between XFree86 and the X Window System is that XFree86 contains device drivers for Intel-based PCs, specifically input/output devices and graphics devices. The current release of XFree86 (Release 4.2.1) is based on the most current release of the X Window System. (For more information on XFree86, *see* Internet Resource 2.) XFree86 on the surface appears similar to other popular operating system window managers, such as those found on the Macintosh and in Microsoft Windows. There is an important differentiation to make here, between window system, window manager, and desktop manager. Briefly stated, the **window system** provides the generic functionality of a GUI, a **window manager** simply has particular implementations of the functionality provided by the window system, and the **desktop manager** provides a graphical method of interacting with the operating system. For example, interactive resizing of a window by the user is a generic function of a window system, whereas using icons or slider buttons is how this is accomplished in a particular window manager. The desktop manager provides the user with the graphic means to work with operating system functions, such as file maintenance. A desktop manager might present a picture of folders connected in a tree-like structure, and allow the user to manipulate files in those folders by dragging and dropping icons. Certainly, a modern window manager can include some or all of the functional features of a desktop manager. The role that a window manager plays in XFree86, and examples of window manager functionality, are given in Section 21.2.3.

In the following In-Chapter Exercises, you will be asked to identify some common window managers.

IN-CHAPTER EXERCISES

21.1 What is the name of the window manager in Windows 95/98/2000/XP?

21.2 What is the name of the window manager on a Macintosh using OS X?

The first question can also be answered by giving an analogy: what XFree86 does for a user of networked computers is exactly like what an operating system does for the user of a stand-alone computer. On a stand-alone computer, the complex details of managing the resources of the hardware of the computer to accomplish tasks is left to the operating system. The user is shielded by the operating system from the complex details of actually accomplishing a task, such as copying a file from one place to another on a fixed disk. On a system of networked computers, XFree86 manages the resources of the hardware of possibly many computers across the network, to accomplish tasks for an individual user. Also, in a networked, distributed-system environment, where many machines are hooked up via a communications link, XFree86 serves as a manager of the components of your interaction with application programs and system resources *transparently*; in other words, you can run an application program on a machine that you are not sitting in front of, and the mechanics of interaction with the application work exactly as if the application were executing on a stand-alone machine right on the desk in front of you.

The most obvious answer to the second question is that you are able to quickly and easily accomplish pre-defined tasks by using a GUI under UNIX. For example, dragging icons to delete files is faster than typing commands to do the same thing, particularly if the file names are long and complex. Another not-so-obvious benefit to having a GUI for UNIX is that your style of interaction with the operating system will be very similar to your style of interaction with applications. For example, modern engineering applications are graphics-based, and have a common look and feel; pull-down menus almost always include functions such as cut, copy, paste, and so on. Having a GUI for UNIX makes for uniformity of interaction between operating system and application.

21.2.2 The Key Components of Interactivity—Events and Requests

When you work with a computer, you provide input in a variety of ways, and the computer, after doing some processing, gives you feedback in return. Limiting this feedback to text and graphics, the computer usually responds by displaying information on the screen.

On a modern computer workstation, you are able to use several devices, such as keyboard, mouse buttons, digitizing tablet, trackball, etc., to provide input to an application program in a style of interaction known as **interrupt-driven interaction**. The application is processing data or in a wait state until signaled by a particular input device. Interrupts are known as *input events* from one or more devices, which can be ordered in time by forming a list, or **queue**. With applications written for XFree86, the client application can then process this queue of input events, do the work necessary to form responses to the events, and then it can output the responses as *requests* for graphical output to the server. A schematic illustration of this is shown in Figure 21.2.

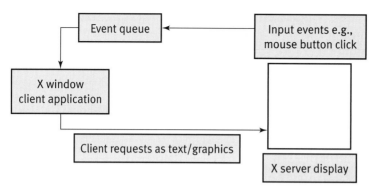

Figure 21.2 Event/request model

A key concept of XFree86 that sometimes causes confusion is the difference between *server* and *client*. One possible cause for confusion is that traditionally, on a computer network, a server is thought of as a machine that serves files to many other machines, which is certainly a different function than an XFree86 server. In XFree86, a server is the hardware and/or software that actually takes input from and displays output to the user. For example, the keyboard, mouse, and display screen in front of the user are part of the server; they graphically "serve" information to the user. The client is an application program that connects to the server, and receives input events from the server and makes output requests to the server. Be aware that sometimes in XFree86 jargon, the client is spoken of as a hardware device, like a workstation, or computer. For our purposes, we will use the term "client" to refer to an application, rather than a piece of hardware. In XFree86, a server and client can exist on the same workstation or computer, and use Interprocess Communications (IPC) mechanisms, such as UNIX pipes or sockets, to transfer information between them. A **local client** is an application that is running on the same machine that you are sitting in front of. A **remote client** is an application that is running on a machine connected to your server via a network connection. Whether a client application is local or remote, it still looks and feels exactly the same to the user of XFree86.

Looking at Figure 21.3 you will see three client applications, X, Y, and Z, displaying their output on an XFree86 server. Each of these applications is running on a different machine. Remote Client X is running on a machine linked to the XFree86 server via a Local Area Network hookup, an Ethernet. Remote Client Y is running on a machine linked to the XFree86 server via a Wide Area Network, the Internet. Local Client Z is running directly on the workstation that is the server, and uses UNIX sockets to display output requests on the server screen. Not illustrated in Figure 21.3 is that each of the clients, X, Y, and Z, gets input events via this server as well.

Another critical aspect of XFree86 is that the GUI for each client is independent of the GUI of the window manager itself. In other words, each client application can open a window on the server screen, use its own style of GUI buttons, icons, pull-down menus, etc., and the window manager, which is simply just another client application, handles the display of all other client windows. Figure 21.3 illustrates this point.

In the following In-Chapter Exercises, you will be asked about the client-server model.

IN-CHAPTER EXERCISES

21.3   If the client can queue events, do you think it would be advantageous for the server to queue requests? Why?

21.4   From what you know of network programming in UNIX, is the meaning of client-server the same in network programming as it is in XFree86? If it is not the same, what is the salient difference?

The important aspect of the window manager being just another client of the XFree86 server is that you can use any of the available XFree86 window managers, such as fvwm2, Sawfish, or twm, to suit your particular needs. You can even use your own window manager—if you actually have the time and resources it takes to write the program code for one. It is worth noting that only one window manager can be active on a given server at one time.

21.2.3 The Role of a Window Manager in the User Interface, and fvwm2

As implied in the previous section, the user interface of XFree86 has two basic parts: the **application user interface**, which is how each client application presents itself in one or more windows on the server screen display, and the window manager or **management interface**, which controls the display of and organizes all client windows. The application user interface is built into (i.e., written in a high-level programming language along with) a client application, and utilizes either subroutine calls to a library of basic X Window protocol operatives, or uses a standard X Window toolkit of pre-defined window elements, such as icons, buttons, sliders, etc. In this section we concentrate on the general functions that a window manager provides to control the appearance and operability of client application windows, and in particular we examine fvwm2, a standard window manager that comes ready to run with XFree86.

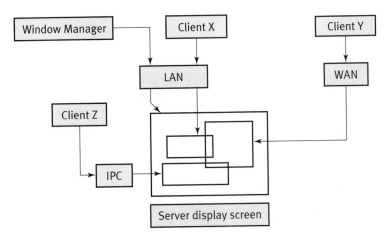

Figure 21.3 Client and server topologies

All window managers in XFree86 are highly customizable, both by the system administrator and by the user. Compare this to other operating system window managers that are built into the operating system and cannot be customized to any real extent. The appearance and functionality of fvwm2 can be modified by the user, as we will show in the final sub-sections of this section.

Note that the window manager that you install as part of your UNIX system can be one of either two major classes of fvwm window manager versions, that is, fvwm1 or fvwm2. There is a significant difference in the appearance and "customization" of these two versions. In the following text, we use an fvwm2 variant of the basic fvwm window manager, and describe the features and operability of that class of fvwm. Depending on your UNIX installation, you will have an .fvwmrc or .fvwm2rc configuration file in your home directory, and this is a simple way of finding out which version of fvwm you are using. As of this writing, fvwm1 is an obsolete window manager.

Functions and Appearance of the Window Manager Interface

If you have had some experience using Windows 98/2000/XP or a Macintosh, you will recognize many of the following general functions, shown in Table 21.1, that a window manager provides. Note that these functions are particular implementations of possibly more than one generic window system service, those provided by the XFree86 protocol.

It is worth examining and identifying the components of a typical XFree86 window display. Figure 21.4 illustrates some particular examples of implementations of the functions found in Table 21.1. This figure shows a full-screen display using the fvwm2 window manager.

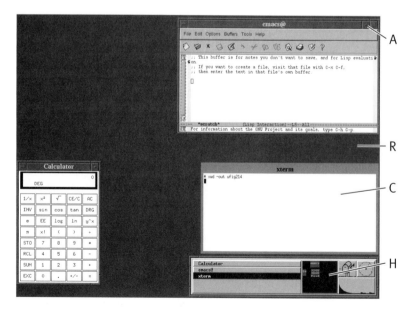

Figure 21.4 XFree86 fvwm2 screen display

■ TABLE 21.1 Window Manager General Functions

The Appearance and Operation of fvwm2

Item	Function	Description
A	(De)Iconify window	Reduce window to a small, representative picture, or enlarge to a full size window
B	Create new window	Launch or run a new client application
C	CUI to operating system	Allows user to open one or more windows and type commands into those windows
D	Desktop management	Graphical file maintenance, speed buttons, special clients such as time-of-day clock
E	Destroy window	Close connection between server and client
F	Event focus	Specifies which client is receiving events from devices such as mouse, keyboard, etc.
G	Modify window	Resize, move, stack, tile one or more windows
H	Virtual screens	More than one screen area mapped on to the physical screen of the server
I	Pop-up/pull-down menus	Utility menus activated by holding down mouse buttons to run client applications

There are a few general things to notice about the XFree86 screen display shown in Figure 21.4. The background of this screen display is known as the **root window**, and it is labeled R. All other windows that open on the screen are children of this parent window. In fact, a single parent window of one client can itself spawn many sub-windows, which are all children of that client's parent. An interesting and important aspect of this relationship is found when parent windows obscure or cover child windows, or when child windows cannot exist outside of the frame defined for the parent window. In the first instance, simply uncovering the child, if this is possible, allows you to operate in the child window. In the second instance, the parent window can become very cluttered due to the existence of too many uncovered children on top of it. Note that Figure 21.4 shows no covered windows, and visually is similar to what is known as a **tiled display**.

When you hold down the left-most, middle, or right-most mouse button when the graphics cursor is in the root window, you get the opportunity to utilize pop-up or cascading pull-down menus, Function I in Table 21.1. Typically, these menus fall into three general categories. Depending on how fvwm2 has been configured at installation, one button can present a cascading pull-down menu of pre-defined client applications that you can run by making a menu choice. To open a client-server connection and launch the application, you simply make the menu choice. An example of the cascading choices found on a typical pull-down menu of this type is shown in Figure 21.5. The cascading menus found in this figure are activated by pressing and holding down the left-most mouse button when the cursor is in the root window. A second button can display a list of all open windows, and allow you to bring any of them to the top of the stack of windows displayed on the screen, and make that

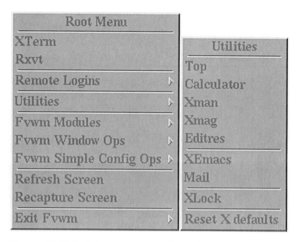

Figure 21.5 Pull-down menu to launch utilities

window the current window where you are doing operations. A third button can display a menu of window modification operations that you can perform by making a menu choice. Typically these modification operations are move, resize/re-proportion, raise in the stack to expose the window, lower the window in the stack, (de)iconify the window, (un)maximize the window, and destroy or close the window.

The (De)Iconify window function is accomplished by use of the button labeled A in Figure 21.4, and it is found in the title bar of the frame surrounding a client application window. Clicking the left-most mouse button on this screen button reduces the window to an icon, which is labeled A in the figure. Each client application window is surrounded by a frame containing several window manager components that allow the user to perform Function G, Modify window, from Table 21.1.

Another client application window, an xterminal, or *xterm* for short, is labeled C in the figure, and provides a CUI to the operating system of the computer this server is linked to by default. Some window modification components surrounding an xterm window are further described in Figure 21.6. The focus of the server is sometimes known as the *current position* of the graphics cursor in the screen display, and is represented by Function F in Table 21.1. When the focus of the server is in an xterm window, and the shell prompt appears at the upper-left corner of the window, you are able to type the UNIX commands–you learned in the previous 20 chapters of this book–to have the operating system of the client machine that is controlling this xterm take actions.

A typical virtual screen menu, which performs Function H from Table 21.1, is displayed at Label H. To use this menu of virtual screens, the user simply positions the graphics cursor with the mouse over one of the tiles in the virtual screen menu, clicks the left-most mouse button, and another portion of the root window is displayed, enabling the user to place other client application windows in that tile. The desktop is not limited by the size of the physical screen display, because a virtual screen display consists of the space that is defined by the area of all the tiles in the virtual screen menu.

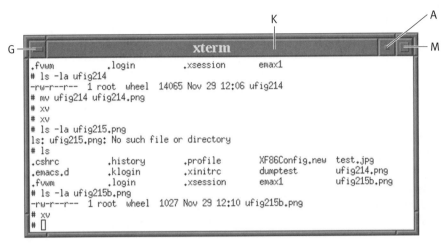

Figure 21.6 xterm window and modify components

The fvwm2 window modification components included in a frame that is placed around an xterm window are shown in Figure 21.6. These components provide Functions A, E, and G from Table 21.1.

The button labeled A in Figure 21.6 is used to iconify or deiconify the xterm window. When one screen tile becomes too cluttered with windows, it is possible to iconify some of the windows to unclutter the screen display.

The button labeled G in Figure 21.6 allows you to perform typical window modification operations. Be aware that, for many client applications, using the "destroy window" option available with this button does not gracefully terminate the client-server connection. Usually, within the application user interface provided by the client application, that is, inside the window, there is a pull-down menu choice or other action that allows for a graceful exit from the application, and a clean disconnect of client from server. There are several dangers inherent in not gracefully exiting an application, foremost of which is that you might lose important data that has not been saved. Also, on networks with software license managers, if you do not gracefully leave an application, it does not free up its token to other users of the network, which is bad network etiquette.

The button labeled M in Figure 21.6 allows you to modify the size of the window by *maximizing* the window in the current virtual screen tile. This simply means that you can quickly enlarge the window frame and its contents to take up the entire area of the current tile. To return the window to its original size, click the maximize button again.

The important functional elements not labeled in Figure 21.6 are the *resize handles*, which are activated by moving the graphics cursor to the extreme edges of the frame. They allow you to use the mouse and pointer button on it to interactively resize and re-proportion the window.

There is also another important component of this typical window frame that provides supplemental functions of the window manager. This is the title bar, labeled K in Figure 21.6. A function of the title bar is to allow you to re-position the entire window and its contents by using the pointing button on the mouse.

21.2.4 Customizing XFree86 and fvwm2

Now that you are familiar with the appearance and operations of the fvwm2 window manager and because XFree86, and fvwm2 in particular, are highly customizable to suit the interactive needs of a wide range of users, it is worthwhile to know how an individual user can effectively achieve that customization. We will examine three approaches to changing the appearance and functionality of the window system, and the window manager as well. The first approach involves changing the characteristics of applications that run under XFree86 by specifying command line options. The second approach involves modifying or creating an initialization file for the window system, and then invoking that initialization file, either by re-starting the window system, or by logging off and then logging back on. The third approach involves modifying or creating an initialization file for the window manager, in our case fvwm2, and then invoking that initialization file.

A word of caution is necessary at this point: If you do not know what a modification does to the operation of the window manager or system, do not make it. Certainly before making any modifications to the XFree86 environment, become familiar with the default operations that were set up at installation. Then make back-up copies of any initialization files you want to change, modify the files, and then if unexpected behavior results, you can always return to the defaults.

Command Line Changes to an XFree86 Application

Once you have seen and worked with the default operations of a particular application, it is possible to run that application with customized display characteristics by typing a command, along with appropriate options and arguments. In this section we will modify the display and operating characteristics of the xterm terminal emulator window, using the `xterm` command and its options. We will also run three other applications using command line options and arguments. A brief description of the `xterm` command is given as follows.

---

xterm [[+][-]toolkitoption ...] [[+][-]option ...]

Purpose:	Run a terminal emulation program in its own window to allow you to type UNIX commands; the + adds the option, the − subtracts the option
Output:	A window with display characteristics determined by toolkitoption and options
Commonly used options/features:	
−ah	This option indicates that xterm should always highlight the text cursor
−e program [arguments ...]	This option specifies the program (and its command line arguments) to be run in the xterm window
−sb	This option indicates that some number of lines that are scrolled off the top of the window should be saved and that a scroll bar should be displayed so that those lines can be viewed

(SYNTAX)

For example, in order to affect the kind of shell that is run in the xterminal window when it starts up, you would type the following at the command line:

```
$ xterm -ls &
```

This option indicates the shell that is started in the xterm window will be a login shell. In order to start an xterm window with an ordinary subshell running in it, you would type the following at the command line:

```
$ xterm +ls &
```

To have the window manager start the xterm window with a scroll bar, which would allow you to scroll backward or forward through the text displayed on-screen and retained in a buffer, type the following:

```
$ xterm -sb &
```

A more complete listing of toolkitoptions and options for the xterm command is given in the Command Reference Dictionary Appendix at the back of this book.

The following session shows how to run other applications using command line options. The three applications that we run below– xclock, xbiff, and xterm–are sized and positioned with the -geometry command line option and its arguments, which are the same for all three applications. Xclock displays an analog time-of-day clock on the screen as an icon. Xbiff displays a mailbox and flag on screen; the flag goes up when mail arrives for you in your system mailbox. Xterm opens a CUI to the UNIX operating system. In order to size and position the application windows on your display screen, you must be aware of the way in which the screen coordinates are derived. The coordinate system for screen locations in the XFree86 is shown in Figure 21.7.

Notice that the origin, 0 in X and 0 in Y, is in the upper-left corner of the screen, and the direction of increasing X is to the left and increasing Y is down. Of course the screen resolution of your display, in other words how many pixels in X and Y can be addressed, depends on what kind of monitor and graphics card you have available, and, how your XFree86 preferences are set. To run the applications in an xterm window, type the following:

```
$ xclock   -geometry   100 × 100 + 10 + 10      &
$ xbiff    -geometry   50 × 50 + 120 + 10       &
$ xterm    -geometry   80 × 24 + 200 + 10       &
$
```

The upper-left corner of Figure 21.8 shows the appearance and relative size and position of each of the applications windows after all three commands have been typed. The arguments for the -geometry option are as follows: X-pixel size of window, Y-pixel size of window, X-position of upper-left corner of window, Y-position of upper-left corner of window. So the line xclock -geometry 100 × 100 + 10 + 10 sizes the xclock to be 100 by 100 pixels, and positions its upper-left corner at the coordinates X = 10, Y = 10 relative to (0, 0.)

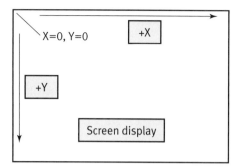

Figure 21.7 Screen coordinate system

To close down an XFree86 application gracefully, you can use the client application mechanisms, which might be a pull-down menu choice or a button press. To close xclock or xbiff, you can find the PID of each by using the ps command, and then issuing a kill signal for that PID. For example, if xclock had a PID of 904, as shown in the output from ps, then typing the command in an xterm window,

```
$ kill -9 904
```

would close the xclock application.

To find out more about the options for xclock and xbiff, refer to the UNIX manual pages on your system.

Figure 21.8 Three applications run with command line options

In the following In-Chapter Exercises, you will get more practice using the xterm command.

IN-CHAPTER EXERCISES

21.5 Run an xclock sized at 75 × 75 located at (200, 200).

21.6 If you run an xterm with no arguments, what is the default window size of the display on screen? How did you find this out?

21.7 After consulting the manual page for xterm, either on your system or in the Command Reference Dictionary Appendix at the back of this book, run an xterm with background color set to green.

21.8 Run an xterm with the scroll bars disabled or enabled.

Preference Changes in .Xdefaults and .xinitrc Initialization Files

Instead of typing command line options for applications you run on a regular basis, or to start specific applications whenever you begin an XFree86 session, you can group these types of common preference changes in two different initialization files. First, we will discuss some additions and modifications you can make to a file named .Xdefaults, which is your personal copy of the file that sets the systemwide defaults for XFree86. Your personal copy takes precedence over the systemwide default file. Then we will discuss other additions that you can make to an initialization file that starts up applications, named .xinitrc.

The following sample .Xdefaults file is a standard default file supplied by our system manager to control the appearance of windows and specify which resources will be used with either all or specific applications.

```
#  Standard .Xdefaults for U of P user accounts  (k.t. 5/7/20004 rev 6.0)

#

    .BorderWidth:           10

    .BitmapIcon:            on

    .MakeWindow.Background: white

    .MakeWindow.Border:     grey

    .MakeWindow.BodyFont:   cor

    .MakeWindow.Foreground: black

    .MakeWindow.Freeze:     on

    .MakeWindow.Mouse:      #e6f

    .MakeWindow.MouseMask:  black

    .MakeWindow.ClipToScreen:on

    .Menufreeze:            on

    .Menubackground:        white

    .Panefont:              8 × 13

    .SelectionFont:         8 × 13
```

```
            .SelectionBorder:          black
            .Paneborderwidth:          1
      TK*graphics_device: POSTGRAP
      TK*text_display: True
      Xv    -Graph.geometry:          800 × 650 + 0 + 50
      Xv    -Render.geometry:         700 × 500 + 50 + 100
      Xv    -Text.geometry:           800 × 650 + 20 + 70
      Xv    -ToolBar.geometry:        386 × 242 + 841 + 161
```

The first block of lines beginning with period (.) specifies display characteristics of all windows. Another way of doing this is to use the meta character asterisk (*) to specify all windows, for example,

```
      *Foreground        black
```

would change the foreground color of all unspecified windows to black. To modify only the display attributes of a particular application window, you could type,

```
      Application*Background: green
```

and that line would change the background of the main application window to the color green.

The remaining lines in the file set particular resources for specific applications. For example, the line `TK*graphics_device: POSTGRAP` sets the graphics output device, or printer, for the application TK Solver to be a PostScript device. The line `Xv-Render.geometry: 700 × 500 + 50 + 100` sets the size of the Xv Render viewport to be 700 by 500 pixels in size, and places that viewport at the coordinates 50 in X and 100 in Y away from the upper-left corner of the screen.

If you want to have certain key applications automatically start whenever you log in, you can create or modify an initialization file in your home directory named .xinitrc with your favorite text editor, and place the names of those key applications in that file. Obviously, these new defaults will not take effect until you log in for the next session after you make the changes. For example, the following .xinitrc file starts key applications and also sets a default color for the following root window.

```
      xsetroot -solid         green
      xterm      -geometry 120 × 80 + 20 + 40
      netscape -geometry 166 × 340 + 160 + 10
      fvwm2 &
```

The first line in this file sets the root window color to solid green. The second line opens a terminal emulator window, sized and positioned as indicated, as soon as you log in. The third line runs the Netscape browser at the size and position indicated. The fourth line starts the fvwm2 window manager.

Typical Changes in .fvwm2rc to Customize the fvwm2 Window Manager

To make specific changes in the look and feel of the fvwm2 window manager, you can create or modify the .fvwm2rc file in your home directory to accomplish the customization. If you do not already have a .fvwm2rc file in your home directory, obtain one from your system administrator or from within your own UNIX system. You can edit this file with your favorite text editor, such as `vi` or `emacs`, and use the facilities of that editor, such as search and replace, to accomplish efficient modifications. It will then be possible to customize fvwm2 to your preferences by making changes in the coded directives and commands in this file. The structure of coded directives and commands that should be in this file is shown in Table 21.2. In general, this shows you the extent to which customization can be done.

■ TABLE 21.2 The .fvwm2rc Directives

Function	What it does
Colors & Fonts	Changes colors and fonts used in window borders and menus
Activity Modes	Sets focus and icon placement
Desktop	Sets the style of the virtual desktop and pager
Modules	Sets the paths to modules and icons
Decorations	Sets the window styles and decorations, such as width of borders
Functions	Defines functions bound to mouse and mouse buttons
Menus	Defines user menus shown in the root window

Table 21.3 lists some samples of commands and directives listed in Table 21.2. Commented lines in the .fvwm2rc file begin with the pound sign (`#`); therefore, placing a `#` before a line in the file turns the directive found on that line into a comment, thus negating its effect.

■ TABLE 21.3 Examples of .fvwm2rc Directives

Example	What it does
`HiForeColor grey90`	Sets selected window's foreground color to grey
`Font -adobe-helvetica-medium -r-*-*-14 *-*-*-*-*-*-*`	Sets the font used for menus
`ClickToFocus`	Focus follows current position
`StickyIcons`	Shows all icons in all virtual windows
`DeskTopSize 8x2`	Sets the virtual desktop to be 8 × 2 times screen
`ModulePath /usr/lib/X11/fvwm2`	Sets the path to icon pixel maps
`Style "xclock" NoTitle, NoHandles, Sticky`	Sets decoration of clock on the desktop

For example, if you do not want all icons to follow you around the virtual desktop into every virtual screen, simply add a # in front of the line that reads StickyIcons. This is where the search and replace or find feature of your text editor comes in handy.

If you want to be able to move into any virtual screen simply by "rolling" the mouse, find the line in your .fvwm2rc file that reads,

```
EdgeScroll 100 100
```

and make sure that line is *not* commented out. The arguments of the EdgeScroll command let you flip through 100 percent of each virtual screen display as you roll the mouse and change the current position into any of the virtual screen tiles. Otherwise you would have to use the tiled display found in the lower-right hand corner of Figure 21.4, labeled H in that figure, and click in the appropriate tile in order to map that virtual tile into the physical screen coordinates.

To build complex functions into the .fvwm2rc file, you must remember to *forward reference* them in the file, which means that you should place them in the file before they are called in any way. Following is an example of a complex function which moves (changes screen placement) or raises (brings to the top of the window stack) a window using mouse movement and pointer-button clicks.

```
Function "Move-or-Raise"
    Move           "Motion"
    Raise          "Motion"
    Raise          "Click"
    RaiseLower     "DoubleClick"
EndFunction
```

The most useful aspect of window manager customization is being able to define your own menus activated by the mouse buttons when the current position is located in a specific place on screen. For example, when the current position is in the root window, the pop-up menus 'Utilities', 'Window Ops', and 'winlist', are activated by, or "bound" to, the mouse buttons. This is accomplished by the following three lines of code in the .fvwm2rc file:

```
Mouse  1        R        A     Popup        "Utilities"
Mouse  2        R        A     Popup        "Window Ops"
Mouse  3        R        A     Module       "winlist" Fvwm2Winlist transient
```

These menus are made up of a collection of menu choices that either run applications or generate other cascading submenu choices. For example, the module winlist calls on a resource to display a list of all open windows on screen. The R on each line means that this menu is activated in the root window. The A on each line means that you can use any keystroke modifier in addition to pressing the mouse button.

In order to define your own pop-up menu, the following example shows a customized pop-up menu definition that can be bound to the right-most (#3) mouse button.

```
# MORE EE
# A collection of three electrical engineering software tools plus another cascading pop-up # menu
Popup  "more ee"
      Title      "More EE Programs"
      Exec "spiceit - SPICE simulator"      exec /usr/local/bin/spiceit &
      Exec "xschedit - schematic editor"    exec /usr/local/bin/xschedit &
      Exec "xsymed - symbol editor"         exec /usr/local/bin/xsymed &
      Nop   ""
      Popup      "EMULATION"                 emulation
EndPopup
```

After the comments explaining the contents of the menu in brief, any menu must begin with a line that has the command Popup. A title that can be referenced by other menus follows the Popup command; in other words, if later in the .fvwm2rc file you want to call this menu as a submenu, you would refer to it with the name more ee. Next, a Title 'More EE Programs', which will appear as text at the top of the menu, is placed on its own line. The three programs, spiceit, xschedit, and xsymed, are placed after the Exec command, and the paths to those three programs are listed on each line following the entry that will appear in the pop-up menu for each. A blank line in the menu is achieved with the Nop command. Another cascading submenu, titled EMULATION, is placed on a line after a Popup command. The name of the menu that is activated when this choice is made is emulation, which was defined in lines of code *before* the more ee menu definition. Finally, the menu must end with the EndPopup command. Figure 21.9 shows how this menu will appear on-screen.

To actually bind this menu to the right-most mouse button, and have it activated when the current position is in the root window, the following lines must appear in .fvwm2rc. Notice that the previous binding of the winlist module to this mouse button was commented out of the file.

```
#Mouse   3   R   A    Module "winlist" Fvwm2Winlist transient
```

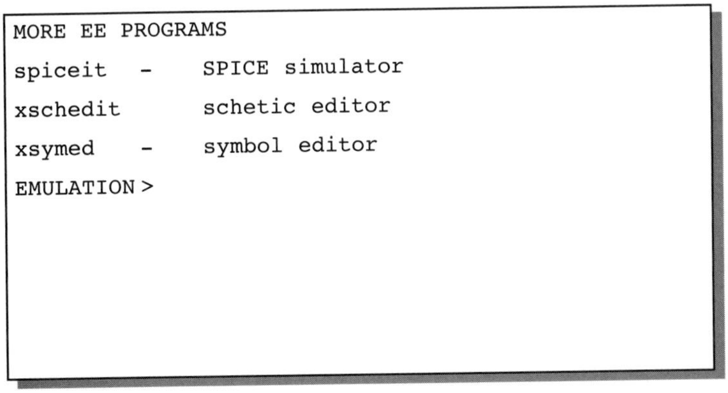

```
MORE EE PROGRAMS
spiceit    -    SPICE simulator
xschedit        schetic editor
xsymed     -    symbol editor
EMULATION >
```

Figure 21.9 A customized pop-up menu

```
Mouse    3    R    A    Popup "more ee"
```

For a more detailed description of the options available for customizing fvwm2, see the fvwm2 Manual Page link of reference 8 in Table 21.10. To gain more familiarity with the features and utilities of a non-integrated GUI installation, see Problems 1–12 at the end of this chapter.

21.3   The KDE Desktop Manager

KDE stands for the K Desktop Environment, and was developed by a volunteer organization of programmers. To find out more about the history and mission of the KDE organization, refer to Internet Resource 9 at the end of this chapter. The KDE desktop manager is an **integrated system**, in the sense that it provides a consistent and uniform implementation of functions such as an application programmers interface (API), object request broker (ORB), window management, desktop configuration tools, session management, and most important, application programs. The uniformity of these functions in an integrated system necessarily goes beyond the rudimentary provisions that XFree86 and the X Window System make for creating and maintaining a graphical interface to UNIX. The drawbacks of these systems are their size and complexity. In the sections that follow, we assume that when you installed your version of UNIX, you installed and specified the KDE desktop manager to start automatically. We show the appearance of KDE Version 3.0 running under FreeBSD UNIX 5.0 (Amnesiac), where we purposely skipped the KPersonalizer.

Note: If you have *not* specified that KDE starts automatically when your UNIX system boots up, but you have installed KDE as your default GUI, you can always begin a KDE session by typing `startx` at the UNIX shell prompt after you have logged in. We do not cover the installation of KDE as a package but leave this as Problems 16 and 17 at the end of the chapter.

21.3.1   Logging In and Logging Out

As your computer boots up, a login window appears on-screen allowing you to log on to your system with a GUI. Chapter 3, Section 3.4 showed you how to log on and off using a text-based interface. Depending on which integrated system you designated as the default when you or your system administrator installed UNIX, you will see a login dialog box for KDE. Similar to what you did in Chapter 3, you can now enter your username and password into the login dialog box. This dialog box also allows you to make other important system choices, such as changing the type of session you will have with the computer (generally a KDE GUI session), rebooting the operating system, or halting the operating system in preparation for powering down the hardware of the computer. Most ordinary users of UNIX on a network will only log in and out using this dialog box. If you have UNIX running on a stand-alone computer, you will sometimes have to restart or reboot the computer using the other dialog box choices. When halting the system, it is always a good idea to allow UNIX to completely unload itself before turning off the power to the computer.

After you have successfully logged in to a KDE session, your screen display should look similar to Figure 21.10.

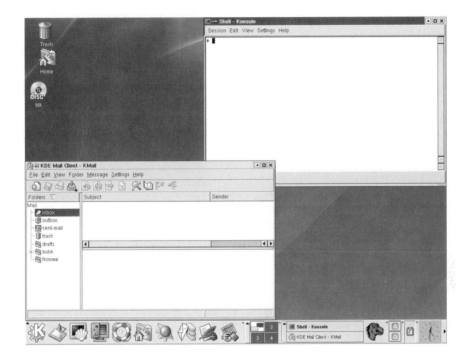

Figure 21.10 The KDE screen display

The KDE desktop has a very similar look and feel to many other desktop systems that you might be familiar with, such as those found on a Macintosh or a Windows 98/2000/XP computer system. One of the most notable differences between KDE and Windows or Mac operations is that when pointing and clicking to launch a program in KDE, you use a *single* click of the left-most mouse button to accomplish the launch. Looking at Figure 21.10, the first similarity you might notice is the grouping of pictures in the bar at the bottom of the screen display. This bar is known as the **Panel**, or **Kicker**, and it performs as an information center for many of the desktop's facilities, and as a launching pad for application programs. Next you see icons arranged along the left side of the screen display, for example, one that looks like a garbage can with the word 'Trash' beneath it. Objects dragged and dropped onto this icon are deleted from the computer. Most important, there are two open windows in the center of the screen display, one with the title bar heading 'Mail client', and the other with the title bar heading 'Shell-Konsole'. The first window is a KDE application window, known as Kmail, that allows you to work with e-mail, similar to what was shown in Chapter 6. The second window is an **Xterminal**, or xterm for short, that allows you to type UNIX commands and have the computer take actions based on the commands, similar to the console you would work in if you did not have a GUI to UNIX. If you click and hold down the right-most mouse button (assuming you have a three-button mouse) when the cursor is in the background area of the desktop, a menu appears which allows you to accomplish some common tasks, such as create a new folder on the desktop, or view and edit desktop icon properties. Figure 21.11 shows this menu.

At this point, if you want to log out of the current session, or take other system actions such as reboot or halt the UNIX operating system, you would make the Logout menu choice, as seen at the bottom of Figure 21.11. You could also use the **K Menu** icon found in the extreme lower-left corner of the screen display in Figure 21.10. If you left-click on this icon, a menu of choices appears as a pop-up menu, and the logout choice is at the bottom of this menu. In the following sections, we will be describing the above components and other important features of the KDE desktop.

21.3.2 The KDE Panel

By far the most important component on the KDE desktop is the KDE Panel, or Kicker. Referring to Figure 21.10, the default display of the Panel is across the bottom of the screen display. As listed in Figure 21.12 from left to right, the components of the Panel are named and briefly described in Table 21.4.

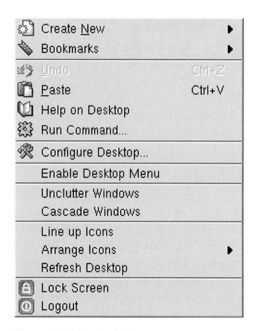

Figure 21.11 Right-click menu

Figure 21.12 KDE Panel Components

TABLE 21.4 KDE Panel Component Descriptions

Label	Component Name	Description
A	K Menu Icon	Allows you to launch applications and desktop utilities, similar to the Windows Start Menu
B	Terminal Icon	Opens a terminal window that contains a shell prompt
C	Application Start Icons	Allows you to launch applications
D	Pager Applet	Allows you to move between virtual tiles of the desktop
E	Taskbar	Displays all running applications as buttons
F	Lock/Logout	Two buttons to lock the screen or logout
G	System Tray	Swallows applications
H	Clock	Opens Clock/Date Applet
I	Hide button	Fades Panel off the screen to give you more room

The most important component of the Panel is the Main K Menu Icon, A in Figure 21.12. If you left-click on it, the Main Menu, as seen in Figure 21.13, appears, and contains fly-out menus enabling you to launch a preset list of applications and utilities. For example, as shown

Figure 21.13 Main K menu

in Figure 21.14, the Utilities fly-out menu of the Main Menu contains a large listing of useful utilities which can be launched from it. There are a number of other fly-out menus activated from the Main Menu that allow you to launch user applications, graphics applications, Internet tools, multimedia tools, and other system-wide applications and development applications. Finally, there are two buttons on the Main Menu that allow you to lock the screen with password protection so it cannot be tampered with when you are away from the display, and a Logout button.

Right-clicking on any of the objects in the panel activates a menu that allows you to manipulate that particular object. For example, if you right-click over any icon in the panel, you get menu choices that allow you to remove that button from the panel, move that button to a new location on the panel, or obtain and change properties of that application, as seen in Figure 21.15.

One of the most useful aspects of the KDE desktop is the ease with which you can reconfigure almost every component of it. This applies to the panel as well. For example, if you wanted to change the content and structure of the panel menus, this can be done by using

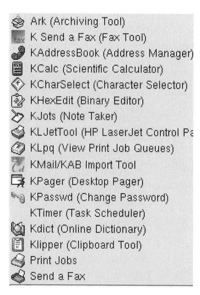

Figure 21.14 Utilities sub-menu of the KDE main menu

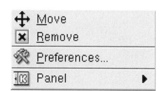

Figure 21.15 Right-click menu on a Panel object

the KDE menu editor. You launch this utility by making the fly-out menu choices Main Menu>System>Menu Editor. Figure 21.16 shows the general appearance of the menu editor. The following Practice Session will show you how to create a new application menu choice under the Main Menu>Editors, which assumes you are running KDE 3.0 on your UNIX system. It also assumes that as part of your UNIX system installation, the emacs package has been installed in /usr/local/bin/, but that there is no menu choice for it. If it has not been installed, skip ahead to Practice Session 21.2 and install emacs, similar to the installation of Xemacs, following the instruction steps in that Practice Session, then return to this Practice Session and follow the steps shown.

Practice Session 21.1

Step 0 You can verify the path to the emacs program by typing `konqueror` in an xterm Konsole window, and when the Konqueror file manager opens on screen, as seen in Figure 21.17, make sure that emacs is found along the path /usr/local/bin/emacs. If it is not found along that path, in a Konsole window, type `whereis emacs`. The path to the program should then be listed, and you can use this path specification in the Konqueror Location bar.

Step 1 From the Main Menu, make the fly-out menu choices System>Menu Editor. The Menu Editor window opens on your screen, similar to Figure 21.16.

Step 2 Two menus appear in that window, a menu tree shown on the left in Figure 21.16, and the default menu panel on the right.

Step 3 Left-click on the plus-sign to the left of the Editors icon in the menu tree. The available editors on your system will now appear as leaf nodes below the branch Editors.
If there is a menu choice for Emacs, use the Edit>Cut choice to cut that entry out of the leaf nodes.

Step 4 At the top of the Menu Editor window, left-click on the icon New Item. A New Item—Menu Editor dialog box appears on-screen, allowing you to enter a name for the new menu item. Type emacs, and then left-click on OK.

Step 5 On the right side of the Menu Editor window, type emacs into the Command text entry box, and type `/usr/local/bin/emacs` into the Work Path text entry box. Leave the Type set at Application, and do not enter a Comment.

Step 6 Left-click on the Apply button at the bottom of the Menu Editor window. Your display should look similar to Figure 21.18.

Step 7 Quit the Menu Editor by making the pull-down menu choice File>Quit.

Step 8 From the Main Menu on the Panel, make the fly-out menu choices Editors>emacs. You should now see a GNU emacs window appear on screen. Quit emacs by making the File>Exit Emacs choice.

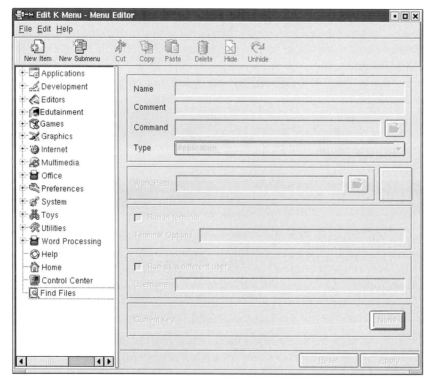

Figure 21.16 KDE Menu Editor window

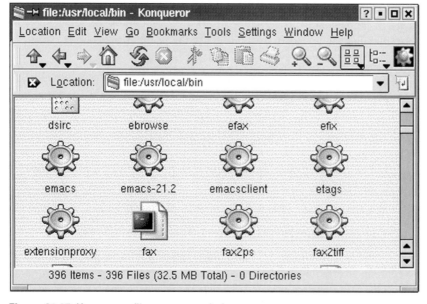

Figure 21.17 Konqueror file manager window

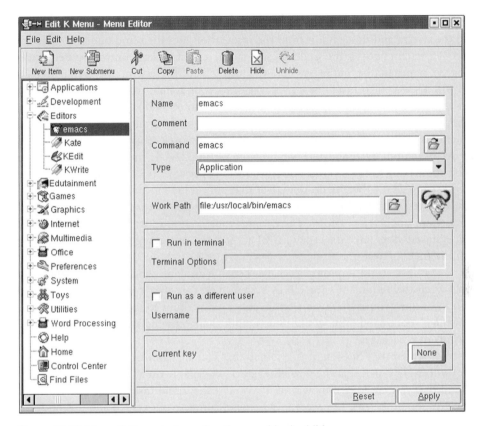

Figure 21.18 Menu Editor window after the graphical addition emacs

In the following In-Chapter Exercises, you will learn more about the Menu Editor.

IN-CHAPTER EXERCISES

21.9 Use the Menu Editor and add any application menu choices that you like to the Main Menu, using the methods described in Practice Session 21.1.

21.10 Using the Menu Editor, create application menu choices under Main Menu>Editors for vi, vim, and pico, and any other editors of your choice. On our system, Xemacs is already found as a menu choice under Editors. Be aware that the availability of these editors is influenced by what you installed with your UNIX system.

21.3.3 New Package Installation

At the time you install your UNIX system, or when the system administrator installs it, some useful applications, known as **packages**, may not have been installed. This is usually the case when a user wants an expeditious install, without having to individually specify each package to be installed. It is also the case when you do not know the capabilities of a package when you install the system and thus omit it from the installation, but then find out later what the capabilities of a certain package are, and now want to have that package on your system without having to re-install the entire system. On our FreeBSD system, the `sysinstall` command will allow you to install new packages onto your system from a CD. This utility command will also allow you to upgrade, or re-install on an individual basis or collectively, new and improved versions of packages which have been made available since your initial UNIX system installation. There are other methods of doing package upgrades, such as using a **Package Management System**, which we show in Section 21.4.4. You can also do package upgrades by connecting to the Internet and downloading packages from a distribution site, as we show in Section 21.4.4, but we do not cover that option here in this section.

What follows is a detailed description of how to install a new package, a graphics imaging and manipulation application known as xv, onto your computer using the `sysinstall` command. sysinstall does have the capability of adding and upgrading packages on your system via an Internet connection.

Also note that if new and improved packages become available, and you obtain them via the Internet from the vendor of your UNIX system, you can always move them to a hard drive location or onto your system via a removable disk medium to make them available to the `sysinstall` command. You would then simply change the default location for where sysinstall finds new packages.

In the following Practice Session, it is assumed that you are running FreeBSD version 5.0 (Amnesiac) with KDE 3.0.5, that the new package xv is available on a CD, xv is not initially installed, and that you are logged-in as root. If you did the initial installation yourself from CD-ROM, you should be able to proceed. Otherwise, contact your system administrator for help in installing new or upgraded packages.

Practice Session 21.2

Step 1   The first three steps will verify that you have the xv package available on a CD. Insert the CD with the new package into your CD-ROM drive. For FreeBSD, we inserted Disk 1. Your CD-ROM should be mounted, and a desktop icon for it should appear on-screen. Left-click on the CD-ROM icon and a Konqueror File Manager window should open on-screen, showing you the files and folders on the CD.

Step 2   Find the xv package by clicking on the folder **packages**, or whichever appropriate folder is available for your system. If it is not available on that particular CD, then insert the proper CD that contains this package. Then click on the folder **graphics**, and scroll down until you see the **xv-3.10a_3.tbz** file, similar to what is seen in Figure 21.19. Again, if it is not available on that CD, then insert the proper CD.

Step 3   Close the Konqueror File Manager window using the pull-down menu choice Location>Quit.

(continued)

Practice Session 21.2 *(continued)*

Step 4   From the KDE Panel, click on the Konsole icon to open a new terminal window.

Step 5   In the terminal window, type `sysinstall`. The sysinstall dialog session begins, and appears on screen, similar to Figure 21.20.

Step 6   Use the arrow keys on the keyboard to scroll down and highlight the Configure choice. Press the `<Enter>` key on the keyboard. The FreeBSD Configuration Menu appears on screen. Use the arrow keys on the keyboard to highlight the Packages choice, then press `<Enter>` on the keyboard. The Choose Installation Media menu appears on-screen. At this point you could install via ftp server. Press `<Enter>` on the keyboard to make the CD/DVD Install from a FreeBSD CD/DVD choice.

Step 7   If you have more than one CD-ROM or DVD drive listed in the Choose a CD/DVD type dialog box, use the arrow keys on the keyboard to highlight the CD-ROM drive which contained the medium from Steps 1–3 above. Press `<Enter>`.

Step 8   If you chose the correct CD-ROM drive, the Package Selection window appears on-screen. Use the arrow keys to scroll down to the graphics choice, and then press `<Enter>` on the keyboard.

Step 9   Use the arrow keys to scroll down to the choice **xv-3.10a**. Press `<Enter>` to signify that you want to install the xv package. An x appears in the square brackets, similar to [x]. Press the `<Tab>` key on the keyboard to make the OK choice.

Step 10 In the Package Selection window, use the right-arrow key to highlight the Install choice. Press `<Enter>`. The Package Targets window appears on-screen, similar to Figure 21.21. Press `<Enter>`. A dialog box appears informing you that the package is being added. The path to where the xv program is being added should be something like /usr/X11R6/bin.

Step 11 Exit the FreeBSD Configuration Menu by using the arrow keys to highlight the X Exit menu choice, and then use the `<Tab>` key to highlight the sysinstall Main Menu choice X Exit Install. Press `<Enter>` to exit. You will be returned to the command line. Use the `whereis` command to verify the location, or path, to the newly added xv program.

Step 12 Add a menu choice to your Main Menu Personal menu for the new application, by using the procedures from Practice Session 21.1. Similar to Step 5. of Practice Session 21.1, be sure to add the command xv into the Menu Editor Command line. Then launch xv using the new menu choice or button.

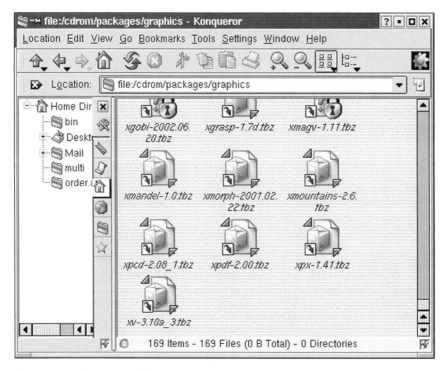

Figure 21.19 Contents of CD for loading new packages

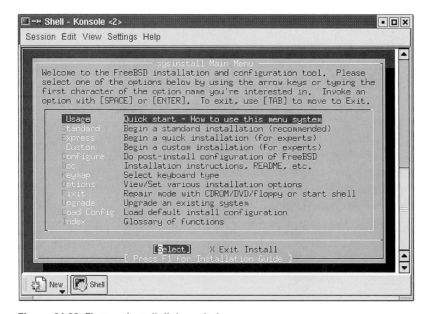

Figure 21.20 First sysinstall dialog window

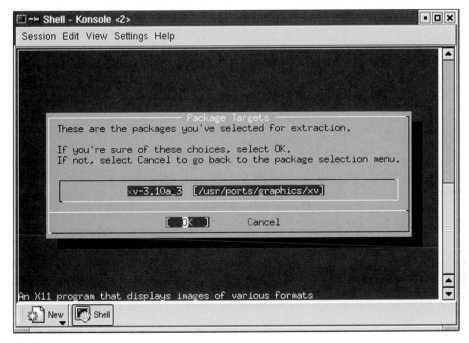

Figure 21.21 Package Targets display window

In the following In-Chapter Exercises, you will learn more about sysinstall.

IN-CHAPTER EXERCISES

21.11 Use sysinstall, or a similar graphical front-end package installation program, to install a useful new package on your UNIX system, and write down a verbal description of the steps required to do so.

21.12 Use sysinstall to upgrade existing packages on your system via an Internet connection, and write down a verbal description of the steps required to do so.

21.3.4 KWM Window Manager

The program that you most directly work with in the KDE desktop environment is the window manager. The appearance and interactivity of KDE windows, from simple terminal windows to application windows, is controlled by the window manager. The default window manager for KDE is called **KWM**. There are several other window managers available to you, the most popular being Sawfish, IceWM, WindowMaker, Enlightenment, AfterStep, and FVWM2. For more information on these window managers, see the Internet Resources at the end of this chapter, no. 5 through no. 8.

The KWM window manager gives a window dressing, or standard interactive techniques and their related features, to expedite your work within that window. For example, a scroll bar

(Item F in Figure 21.22) is provided in a Konsole window to allow you to graphically scroll backward or forward through the text that has been displayed on the screen. For more examples of these features, see Table 21.5 and the graphical references to Figure 21.22.

■ **TABLE 21.5** Konsole Window Components of a KWM Window

Item	Name	Description
A	Menu Button	Allows you to move, iconify, resize, make sticky
B	Title Bar	Shows current path and allows window movement
C	Control Buttons	Minimize, maximize, and kill window
D	Menus	Application-specific menu choices for xterminal
E	Body	Xterminal console display
F	Scroll Bar	Allows you to scroll contents of text in this window
G	Border	Allows re-sizing of window with "handles"
H	Sticky Button	Allows you to make window sticky, or always visible as you page through the virtual tiles of the desktop
J	Toolbar	Allows you to use application tools

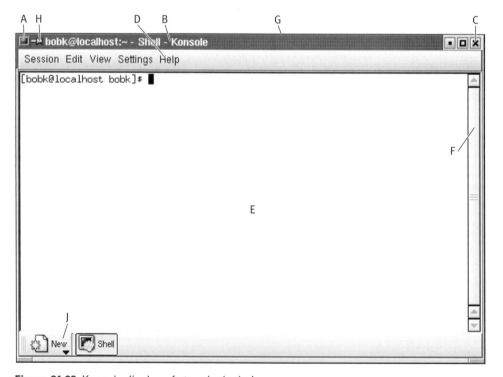

Figure 21.22 Konsole display of xterminal window

As previously mentioned, the window manager provides a frame within which the application can display its graphical output, and within which the user can interact with the application program through user-generated events. The look (appearance of buttons, style and color, its **theme**) and feel (how buttons work, how menus are activated) of the window manager is independent of the look and feel of the application running in Area E as seen in Figure 21.22. Because of this, it is possible to reconfigure the appearance, and also the interactivity, of the KWM window manager, and not affect the look or interactivity of any application running inside of the window manager's border. To understand the steps necessary to reconfigure the KWM window manager so that it has a different look and feel, do Practice Session 21.3. In this Practice Session, you will change a feature of the style of interaction with Sawfish known as focus policy. **Focus Policy** is the response of the graphical server to locations of the current position. For example, if you move the mouse, and the cursor on-screen rolls into a window, that window becomes the current window for input and output events. You will also change the appearance of KWM to the Wood theme. We assume that you are using the KWM window manager, and it has the Default Theme look as the default. We also assume that your virtual desktop tile is 1, as seen in the Panel pager.

Practice Session 21.3

Step 0 As preparation for this session, observe the response of KWM as you move the mouse and the screen cursor shifts between open windows. As you roll the mouse, does the current window become the one that the cursor is in? Also note the appearance of the borders and decorations around your open windows.

Step 1 From the Main Menu, make the menu choice Preferences>Look & Feel>Window Behavior. The Window Behavior – KDE Control Module window opens on screen, similar to Figure 21.23.

Step 2 In the Window Behavior – KDE Control Module window, under Focus Policy, change the text bar to read Focus follows mouse. If it already reads this, change it to Click to focus.

Step 3 Left-click on the Apply button in the Window Behavior – KDE Control Module window.

Step 4 Now move the mouse so that the cursor shifts between windows on-screen. The behavior of the Window Manager has changed, depending on what you set the focus policy to be.

Step 5 Left-click on the OK button at the bottom of the Window Behavior – KDE Control Module to close it.

(continued)

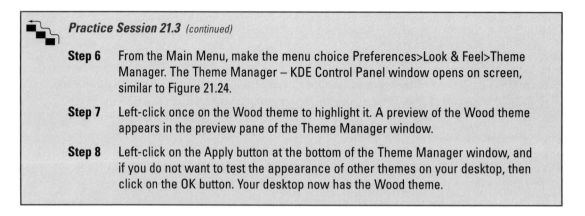

Practice Session 21.3 *(continued)*

Step 6   From the Main Menu, make the menu choice Preferences>Look & Feel>Theme Manager. The Theme Manager – KDE Control Panel window opens on screen, similar to Figure 21.24.

Step 7   Left-click once on the Wood theme to highlight it. A preview of the Wood theme appears in the preview pane of the Theme Manager window.

Step 8   Left-click on the Apply button at the bottom of the Theme Manager window, and if you do not want to test the appearance of other themes on your desktop, then click on the OK button. Your desktop now has the Wood theme.

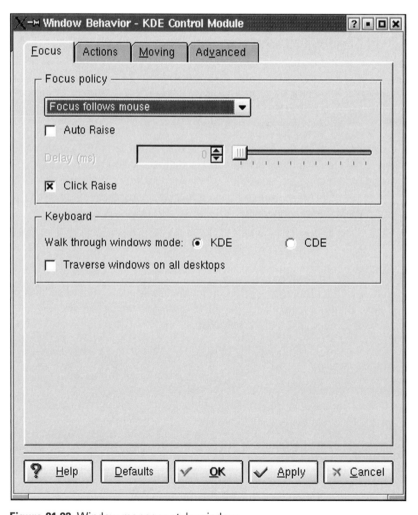

Figure 21.23 Window manager style window

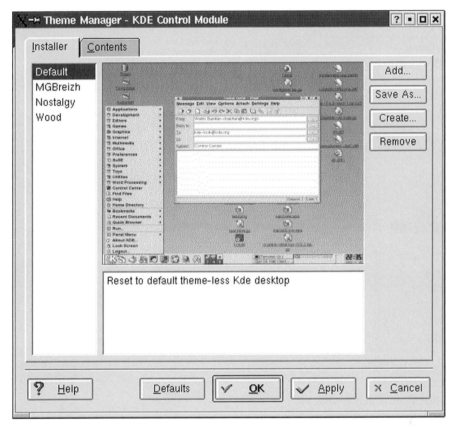

Figure 21.24 KDE Theme Manager window showing default theme

21.3.5 The KDE Control Center

The most important configuration tool available to you for the KDE desktop is the KDE Control Center. This utility allows configuration of single-user attributes, as well as systemwide attributes for all users. A single user with ordinary privileges is allowed to make a variety of changes in the performance of the KDE desktop. For example, as shown in Figure 21.25, you can use a series of on-screen menu choices to change the focus behavior within KDE windows, as you did in Practice Session 21.3 above. To launch the KDE Control Center, make the Main Menu choice Control Center. There are two important areas of the KDE Control Center window, as seen in Figure 21.25. The panel on the left is the menu tree of available options that you can modify using the Control Center on your system. By clicking on one of the main branches or sub-branches of this tree, you can see a configuration display in the right panel associated with that particular tree item. For example, if you left-click on the Look & Feel main branch after launching the Control Center, you have several sub-branch options available to you: one of these options, Window Behavior, allows you to change the focus policy. Once you click the Apply button at the bottom of the KDE Control Center window, that attribute or option change will immediately take effect.

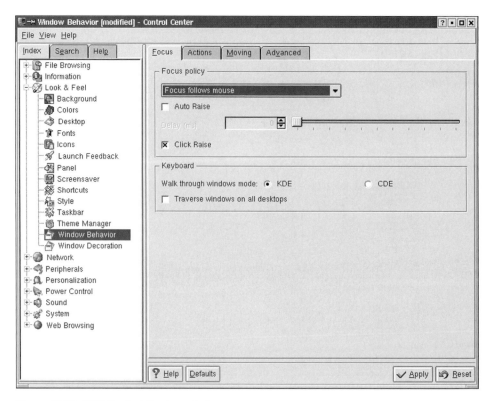

Figure 21.25 KDE Control Center window

In the following In-Chapter Exercises, you will learn more about the KDE Control Center.

IN-CHAPTER EXERCISES

21.13 Use the KDE Control Center to change the Look & Feel Screensaver to one that you like.

21.14 Use the KDE Control Center to undo or make similar modifications to what options and attributes are shown in Practice Session 21.7.

21.3.6 File Management with Konqueror

To obtain a graphical view of the files on your UNIX system, particularly the files you have in your home and working subdirectories, the Konqueror file manager allows you to quickly see and edit not only the ordinary files themselves, but also the directory structure that contains them. This capability is given to you by the UNIX file maintenance commands that appeared earlier in this textbook, but using a graphical approach usually saves time for the ordinary user, and it is also something that most users are more familiar with. In an xterm

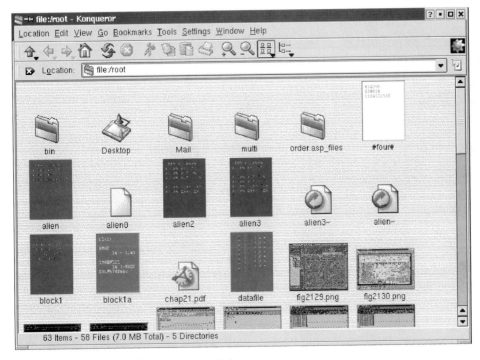

Figure 21.26 Konqueror file manager window

Konsole window, type **konqueror** and then press **<Enter>**. The Konqueror file manager window opens on screen, similar to Figure 21.26.

On our UNIX system by default Konqueror shows the contents of the current working directory, which is the Home directory, as seen in Figure 21.26. There are seven important functional areas of this window.

1. The title bar across the top of the window
2. The menu bar showing several drop-down menus
3. The toolbar icons at the top of the Konqueror window that allow you to take actions and change the appearance of file displays very quickly. For example, the Back icon button allows you to make the previously viewed directory the currently viewed directory.
4. The location bar which shows you the current path
5. The Bookmark Toolbar that allows you to add bookmarked paths or URLs
6. The main window which shows you icons of files in the current directory
7. The Status Bar along the bottom of the window which contains general information about whatever is at the current cursor position.

A listing of the important properties and actions you can affect and accomplish with the menu bar is given in Table 21.6.

■■ **TABLE 21.6** Properties and Actions of the Konqueror Pull-Down Menus

Pull-Down Menu Choices	Description
Location>New Window	Opens a new Konqueror window into the current directory
Location>Open Location	Opens a new Konqueror window into a specified directory
Location>Quit	Quits Konqueror
Edit>...	Copy, Paste, Delete file(s)
View>Tree View	Shows tree-structured picture of directories
View>Show Details	Shows various file attributes
Go>...	Navigates path structure
Tools>Find File	Allows file searching

One of the most useful choices of the pull-down menu is Tools>Find File, which allows you to designate a place in the file structure of the system at which to start the search, and allows you to designate a file name to search for. This utility is very similar to the text-based UNIX `find` command. For example, if you wanted to find all files starting at the root directory that ended in the file extension .png, you would make the Tools>Find File pull-down menu choice, and then supply the information in the proper text bars of the Find File window as shown in Figure 21.27. When you click on the Find button, you get a view in the main

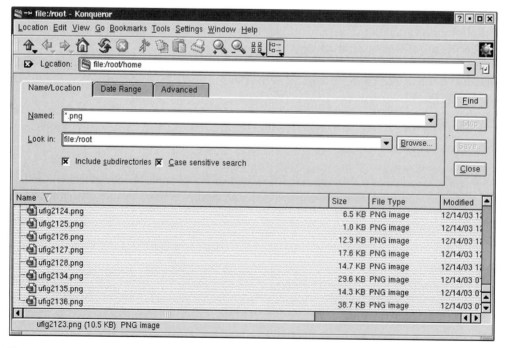

Figure 21.27 Find File window

window showing all files in the current working directory that match your search criteria or file specification. In this operation we chose Tree View for the display of the found files, rather than Icon View.

In the following In-Chapter Exercises, you will learn more about Konqueror.

IN-CHAPTER EXERCISES

21.15 Use the Konqueror's Find File utility to find all files starting at the root directory that end with the file extension .bmp. How many files were found? (*Hint:* We found 15 files in 15 subdirectories of root in 60 seconds.) Then use the button choice Change to this directory to change the Konqueror display to one of the sub-directories on your system that contains a .bmp file, and then, if the image does not appear in the main window, use the Konqueror pull-down menu choice Location>Open with Kview to open the found .bmp file. What do you see?

21.16 Use the Konqueror's `Find File` utility to find all files starting in your home directory that begin with the letter M (uppercase).

21.17 Create a menu choice on the Main KDE Menu for non-superuser Konqueror. Write down an outline of what steps you took to accomplish this. This is an important menu choice which should be added to customize your desktop.

To gain more familiarity with the features and utilities of the KDE Desktop, go on to Problems 12–19 at the end of this chapter.

21.4 The Mac OS X Aqua GUI

Another important and contemporary example of a UNIX GUI, one that does *not* rely on the X Window System or XFree86 to mitigate the dialog between user and application software, is the Aqua GUI used on Apple Macintosh computers running operating system OS X. Another way of looking at the dialog between a user and application software, which we showed earlier in Figure 21.1, and which is very similar to the ISO and TCP/IP layered models shown in Chapter 14, is illustrated in Figure 21.28. In this layered model, the application code, which you work with as a user, has access to the various other layers of software that directly drive or operate the hardware. The user can be thought of as occupying the space surrounding the application code and hardware, because these two layers are what the user works directly with. In a UNIX X Window System or XFree86 implementation of this model, the Graphics and Application Service is provided by various software components, such as a window manager, Xlib, and/or various toolkits. In the Mac UNIX OS X implementation of the same model, the Graphics and Application Service is provided by software such as Quartz Extreme, QuickTime and OpenGL, and proprietary software. In both implementations, the Operating System is UNIX; in the case of Mac OS X, Mac UNIX, known as Darwin, is derived from both BSD 4.4 UNIX and the UNIX Mach kernel.

One very distinct, and somewhat unfortunate but understandable difference between an X Window System or XFree86–based GUI and the Mac OS X GUI, is the fact that the former

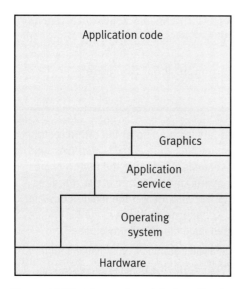

Figure 21.28 A layered model of application code—hardware

are totally open-source systems for which you can modify all of the actual source-code, and the latter is a proprietary and closed system. This means that for the Mac OS X Aqua GUI, the Graphics and Application Service layers shown in Figure 21.28 are essentially not available to you to make any substantive changes in. However, we do show you how to make some superficial changes and modifications to the appearance and functionality of the Aqua GUI in the sections below. An advantage of having a closed, proprietary system is that everything in it has been developed so that it works, which is not always the case in an open-source system.

Similar to what we did in Section 21.3, in the following sections, we will cover these aspects of the Mac OS X Aqua GUI: the appearance of the Mac desktop, the Dock, customizing the Dock, the Fink Package Manager, Aqua preference changes and Terminal appearance changes, other System Preference changes, and using the Finder. To illustrate our examples for this section, we used Mac OS X version 10.2.3 (Jaguar).

21.4.1 The Appearance of the Mac Desktop

On a Mac running OS X, you have two basic ways of interacting with the operating system: using a CUI in a terminal window, or using a GUI via what is known as the Desktop. By default, when you first log in, you are placed on the Desktop, which has the general appearance shown in Figure 21.29.

Desktop Components and the Terminal

There are several important graphical components found on the Desktop, and most of them perform similar functions to those found on the KDesktop in Section 21.3 above. These components, and a brief description of the functions they perform, are found in Table 21.7.

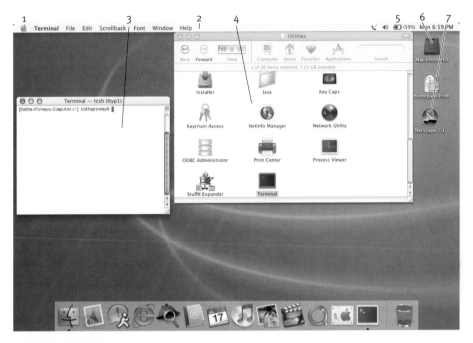

Figure 21.29 OS X Desktop

■ **TABLE 21.7** The Desktop Components

Item	Component	Description
1	Apple Menu	Gives you access to system functions
2	Application Menu	Gives you access to an application's functions
3	Terminal Window	Allows you to type in UNIX commands
4	Finder Window	Allows you to do graphical file maintenance
5	Menulet Bar	Allows you to launch system controls
6	Local Disk Icon	Allows you access to a local disk volume
7	Application Icon	Allows you to launch an application
8	Finder Icon	Allows you to launch a graphical file tool
9	The Dock	Contains icons for application running
10	Trash	Allows you to delete files and folders

Items 1, 2, and 5 are found on what is known as the **Menu Bar**. Item 1 is the **Apple Menu**, which allows you to execute several important system functions, such as setting system preferences, shutting-down, or logging-out. The pull-down menu choices found under the Apple Menu are show in Figure 21.30. Item 2, the Application Menu choices, shows several menu choices.

Figure 21.30 Apple menu choices

No matter what application is running, or currently active, the Menu Bar contains pull-down menus pertinent to that application. This is different from the KDesktop in Section 21.3, where each application program window contained, within the window manager's "dressing" or frame, its own pull-down menu choices that were used to execute functions in the application program. As shown in Figure 21.29, the currently active application is **The Terminal**, and the pull-down menus for that application are found across the top of the Desktop. You can run the Terminal application by clicking on its icon in the Macintosh HD/Applications/Utilities folder. The Terminal is a very important application that lets you type in and execute UNIX commands, and interact with the underlying UNIX system via a CUI. There are usually four standard pull-down menus available with every application menu: File, Edit, Window, and Help.

Note: The File>New Shell pull-down menu choice in the Terminal Application Menu allows you to open a new terminal window with the default attributes.

In the following In-Chapter Exercises, you will learn more about the Terminal application.

IN-CHAPTER EXERCISES

 21.18 Run the Terminal application on your Mac, and open several Terminal windows on-screen at the same time. What is the default shell running in each window? How do you know this, or how did you find this out?

 21.19 Are the OS X manual pages organized along the same lines as the other UNIX system manual pages we dealt with in earlier chapters?

 21.20 Is there a scroll bar available in the terminal window? How can you cut and paste between Terminal windows?

Having several Terminal windows open simultaneously is very advantageous, allowing you to execute several UNIX commands and retain the results on-screen at the same time, or start off several different processes and execute them in parallel. In the Terminal Application Menu, the Window pull-down menu, for example, allows you to switch the focus between and manipulate the currently open Terminal windows. These choices are shown in Figure 21.31. In the Window pull-down menu list, there are choices that allow you to switch between the two currently active windows, iconify them, or close them. You can achieve the same results by using the mouse and clicking on the buttons found on each Terminal window.

The Dock

The most prominent component of the OS X desktop is Item no. 9 in Figure 21.29, known as **The Dock**. It contains several icons that either execute applications when you click on them, or allow you access to devices, folders, or files. Item no. 8 in Figure 21.29 is an icon on the Dock that launches one of the most important applications in OS X: **The Finder**. This is the graphical file maintenance and search tool for the Mac, which allows you to examine not only local disk volumes and files and accessories such as an IPod, but that also gives you access to network files. Item no. 10 is the Trash, a handy icon that allows you to delete files when you drag-and-drop files or folders onto it or allows you to unmount externally-mounted Macintosh HDs, such as a ThumbDrive or JumpDrive. The features and icons of the Dock are illustrated in Figure 21.32 and summarized in Table 21.8.

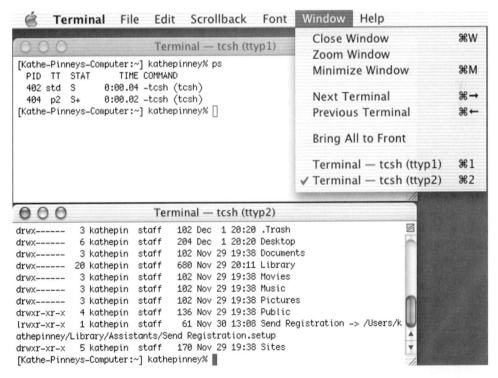

Figure 21.31 Terminal application window menu choices

Figure 21.32 The Dock

■■■ **TABLE 21.8** Dock Component Descriptions

Item	Component	Description
1	Finder icon	Launches the graphical file maintenance/search tool
2	Application icons	Launches utility applications, such as Internet Explorer
3	Active Application	Displays an icon for the active Terminal application
4	Divider	Segregates applications to the left, Trash to the right
5	Iconified folder	Displays an icon for an iconified Finder folder
6	Trash	Allows drag-and-drop to delete and unmount objects

Window Appearance

An open window on the OS X Desktop has many of the same features found in an open window on the KDesktop. A window can serve two basic purposes: It gives you a graphical interface into the application controlling the window content, or shows you a view of what is in a folder or file. A typical window, for example, one obtained when you double-click on Item no. 6 seen in Figure 21.29 (the Desktop icon representing the Macintosh HD on the computer) is seen in Figure 21.33.

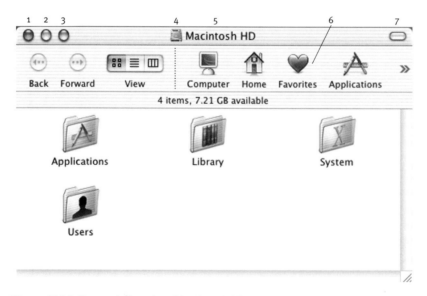

Figure 21.33 Open window into Macintosh HD

In the following In-Chapter Exercises, you will make some comparisons between KDE and the Mac Aqua GUI.

IN-CHAPTER EXERCISES

21.21 What are the significant differences, if any, between an Aqua window and a KDesktop window, in terms of functionality? Refer to Section 21.3.

21.22 What are the significant differences, if any, between the Dock in OS X and the Panel in the KDesktop? Refer back to Section 21.3.

The dressing, or functional features, found in this typical window are described in brief in Table 21.9. Items 1, 2, 3, 4, 5, and 7 are found on what is known as a **titlebar**. You can move the window by clicking and holding down the mouse button on the titlebar, and dragging your mouse so that the window is re-positioned.

TABLE 21.9 Features of a Typical Window

Item	Component	Description
1	**Close window button**	Allows you to close this window
2	**Iconify window button**	Minimizes this window into an icon on the Dock
3	**Zoom window button**	Expands or contracts the window size to default sizes
4	**Proxy icon**	Miniature version of the icon representing this device
5	**Pathname button**	Command-click on this to see the path to this file or device
6	**Toolbar icons**	Allows you to execute application commands graphically
7	**Toolbar button**	Shows or hides Item 6
8	**Resize handle**	Allows you to resize this window

21.4.2 The Dock

As described earlier, the Dock is an icon bar found at the bottom of the Aqua Desktop display, and is visible even though other applications and their windows are active. The icons currently on this bar allow you to run applications, move between active applications already running, and gain access to folders and files. To run an application whose icon is found on the Dock, click on the icon. Other ways of running an application are to double-click on its icon found on the desktop, or to double-click on its icon that you have located in the application folder. When an application first runs, its icon bounces up and down on the Dock, and then occupies a static position there, until you exit the application. When the application is running, a small black triangle appears under its icon on the Dock, as seen in Figure 21.32 under the Finder and System Preferences icons. When you have more than one application running at the same time, you can bring an application and its windows to the front by clicking on its icon in the Dock. When you quit an application by making its application menu Quit choice, its icon disappears from the Dock, unless it is permanently found there. See Section 21.4.3 to find out how to add or remove icons from the Dock.

Active applications have a Dock menu, which can be activated by either clicking on its icon in the Dock and holding down, or by holding down the `<Ctrl>` key on the keyboard and clicking on its icon. Typical actions you can take using these menus are quitting, showing a Finder window that contains the application icon, and retaining the application icon on the Dock.

Additional icons can be placed on the Dock that represent disk volumes (such as external hard drives), folders, or files. If you have placed a disk icon on the Dock, when you click on it, a Finder window will open showing you the contents of the disk. If you have placed a folder icon on the Dock, when you click on it, a Finder window will open showing you the contents of the folder. If you have placed a file icon on the Dock, when you click on it, the appropriate application launches to show you the contents of the file.

When you iconify a window, a small icon representing it appears on the Dock, just to the left of the Trash icon.

An icon representing the Finder is always found on the extreme left side of the Dock, and this icon cannot be removed from the Dock. See Section 21.4.7 for more information on how to use the Finder.

The "divider," which nominally separates application icons to the left, and folders, iconified windows and the Trash to the right, can be used to resize the Dock. To do this, move the cursor over the divider, and click-and-drag to make the Dock bigger or smaller.

The Trash serves as a means to mark objects on your computer's file system for deletion or ejection. An object, such as a folder, a file or group of files, or a disk icon (such as a CD-ROM disk or external ThumbDrive or JumpDrive), is first dragged onto the Trash icon in the Dock. In the case of folders and files, you must then confirm deletion by emptying the Trash via the Finder pull-down menu choice Finder>Empty Trash. In the case of disk volumes, the Trash serves to unmount these, or "eject" them, from the file system, and there is no need to confirm deletion.

21.4.3 Customizing the Dock

There are three modifications that you can make to the Dock to customize it.

1. Change the System Preferences that control its appearance
2. Resize or reposition it on the desktop
3. Add icons to it and remove icons from it.

The following sub-sections deal with the basic ways of accomplishing these three customizations.

Changing the Dock's System Preferences

To modify the look and feel of the Aqua interface, it is necessary to run an application known as System Preferences. When this application is executed, it presents a window containing several "panels," one of which allows you to modify the Dock. The panel for the Dock is found under Personal in the second row down. See Figure 21.36. In order to run the System Preferences application, you can either make the menu bar pull-down menu choice under the apple System Preferences…, and then click on the panel icon Dock, or click on the System Preferences icon on the Dock (The light switch next to the apple, seen as the fourth icon to the left of the Trash in Figure 21.32).

As shown in Figure 21.34, the Dock System Preferences panel opens, and contains several appearance-modifying choices. The toolbar icons at the top of the window allow you to quickly move to any of the other System preference windows to make other changes, such as to Displays, Sounds, Network, etc. From top to bottom, you can change the Dock size, individual icon magnification when the cursor is over the icon, position on screen, the effect used to iconify windows, whether or not the icons bounce when an application is first opened, and whether or not the entire Dock is hidden or visible when you are working on another portion of the desktop.

Resizing or Repositioning the Dock

In order to change the size of the Dock, or move it to a new location, you can use the System Preferences window shown in the previous sub-section. Another way to resize it is by clicking-and-holding on the divider in the dock, and dragging to resize it. A different way to reposition it is to hold down the <Ctrl> key on the keyboard, and click on the divider in the dock. This turns on a divider menu, which contains many of the choices found in the Dock System Preferences window seen in Figure 21.34.

Adding and Removing Icons

Probably the most useful changes you can make to the Dock are to add new application, folder, file, or disk icons to it permanently, or to remove default or old icons from it. The easiest way of accomplishing the addition of new icons onto the Dock is by dragging and dropping them from the Finder or the desktop onto the Dock. Figure 21.35 shows an example of an application

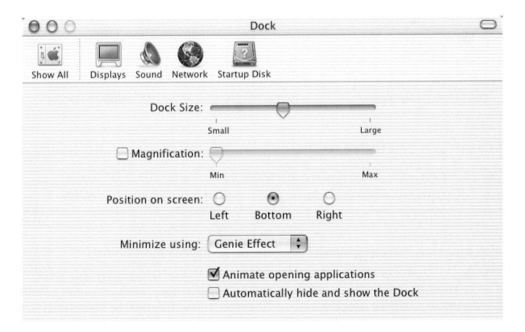

Figure 21.34 Dock System Preferences window

Figure 21.35 New dock icons

icon (Word X) added to the left of the divider, and a folder (the home folder), a file, and a disk drive added to the right of the divider. These icons were added by dragging and dropping icons from the Finder and desktop. Note that the original icons remain where they were, and dragging and dropping them onto the Dock simply creates aliases of them on the Dock.

The simplest way of deleting icons from the Dock is to drag them off the Dock. They disappear immediately. For example, to delete the application, folder, file and disk icons shown in Figure 21.35, you could just drag them off the Dock. This deletes their aliases.

Many of the operations that can be achieved graphically can also be done via the use of keyboard keystroke-combinations. Table 21.10 lists some common keystroke combinations that deal with the Dock.

■ **TABLE 21.10** Dock keystroke commands

Keystroke Combination	Action
`<Option>+<Cmd>+<D>`	Toggles Dock on or off
`<Cmd>+Click`	Shows the clicked-on icon in the Finder
`<Ctrl>+Click`	Shows the clicked-on icon's Dock menu
`<Option>+<Cmd>+Click`	Brings the clicked-on application to the front
`<Cmd>+<Tab>`	Brings the next active application to the front
`<Shift>+Cmd+<Tab>`	Brings the previous active application to the front.

IN-CHAPTER EXERCISE ━━━━━━━━━━━━━━━━━━━━━━

21.23 Which would you say is more customizable, the Dock or the KDE panel? Support your answer with some specific examples that contrast or compare the two facilities.

21.4.4 The Fink Package Manager for Installing UNIX Applications

On the Aqua GUI side of OS X, the normal way of installing a pre-compiled application that was *not* installed along with the rest of the system is to drag its application icon from a desktop folder or the medium it is archived on into the applications folder on the Macintosh HD. It then becomes fully functional.

On the Darwin UNIX side of OS X, some useful applications, known as **packages**, can be installed with the use of a **Package Management System**. A package is simply an application, its attendant documentation, and the files necessary to compile, link, and configure it so it can run on your computer. A package management system, such as the **Fink Package Manager**, allows you obtain UNIX packages from an on-line database containing thousands of applications, and easily and quickly install them on your system. The other alternative on the Darwin UNIX side, which we do not cover here, is to install applications from source code.

We will briefly cover how to obtain and install the Fink Package Manager (version 0.6.2), how to install a package, named **dosunix**–which converts DOS-formatted text into UNIX-formatted text–and how to use the package to convert UNIX text to DOS/Windows text.

(*Note:* You must have installed the OS X Developers Tools, or have a compiler available, for the Fink Package Manager to install packages you download from its on-line database.)

Obtaining and Installing Fink

To begin this process, you must use an Internet connection, preferably a high-bandwidth DSL line, although it is feasible to download the Fink Installer over a 56Kbaud modem line as well. The Fink Installer pre-compiled application is approximately 20 MB in size. You can download the fink-0.6.2-installer from:

http://fink.sourceforge.net/download/

In the following steps, we assume you have administrator privileges on this system, have access to Root's password, and can run the sudo command. We also assume that what you type on the keyboard is always followed by pressing the <Enter> key on the keyboard. The Fink application and files will be installed in the new directory sw on the disk and partition you specify in Step 4, thus not overwriting any other application or system files. Steps 1 through 6 are for obtaining and installing, and Step 7 is for configuration.

1. At the fink URL, click the link that will download the installer disk image for your version of OS X. Because we are using OS X version 10.2.3, we clicked on the link Fink 0.6.2 Binary Installer.

2. When the installer disk image is finished downloading, it should appear as an icon on your desktop, in our case fink-0.6.2-installer.dmg, and a disk icon should also appear, which in our case was named Fink 0.6.2 Installer.

3. Double-click the Fink Installer disk icon. A new window opens, showing a number of files, one of which is Fink_0.6.2_Installer.pkg (in our case the 0.6.2 was there for the version we used, yours may be different). Double-click on this icon to run the Fink installation program.

4. A number of dialog screens are presented (where you must enter your administrator's password, then agree to the terms of the license), and then you are asked which disk you want to install Fink on, and finally the Easy Install screen appears. Click on the Install button.

5. The installation proceeds and shows a monitor of its progress; during our install process, a Terminal window appeared in the middle of the install asking for confirmation of the creation of a .cshrc file in our home directory, which executes Fink configuration by running a shell script in /sw/bin/init.csh.

6. Click Close in the install window to finish the installation.

7. To configure Fink, run the Terminal, and on the command line type `sudo fink configure`. Following are the prompts from Fink and what you should type on the command line in response for a default configuration.

```
OK, I'll ask you some questions and update the configuration file in
'/sw/etc/fink.conf'.

In what additional directory should Fink look for downloaded tarballs? []
<Enter> Which directory should Fink use to build packages? (If you don't
know what this means, it is safe to leave it at its default.) [] <Enter>

    (1)  Quiet (don't show download stats)

    (2)  Low (don't show tarballs being expanded)

    (3)  Medium (shows almost everything)

    (4)  High (shows everything)

How verbose should Fink be? [2] <Enter>

Proxy/Firewall settings

Enter the URL of the HTTP proxy to use, or 'none' for no proxy. The URL
should start with http:// and may contain username, password or port
specifications. [none] <Enter>

Enter the URL of the proxy to use for FTP, or 'none' for no proxy. The
URL should start with http:// and may contain username, password or port
specifications. [none] <Enter>

Use passive mode FTP transfers (to get through a firewall)? [Y/n] Y

Mirror selection

All mirrors are set. Do you want to change them? [y/N] N

Writing updated configuration to '/sw/etc/fink.conf'...
```

Some useful documentation on Fink can be obtained by typing `fink–help` or `man fink`. Table 21.11 list the important `Fink` commands that may be typed on the command line, with a brief description of each.

■■ **TABLE 21.11** Fink Commands

Command	Description
fink install package	Downloads, configures, and builds package on your system
fink remove package	Removes package from your system *(continued)*

TABLE 21.8 (continued)

`fink update-all`	Updates all packages installed on your system
`fink list`	Lists all available packages at the time you installed Fink
`fink describe package`	Gives documentation on package
`fink configure`	Reruns the Fink configuration process

Installing a Package Using Fink

To begin this process, you must have a C compiler installed (gcc that came with the OS X Developers Tools, for example), and you must be connected to the Internet. You must also have successfully installed Fink, as shown in the previous sub-section. Our objective now is to download a package from the Fink database at the Sourceforge website. The package we will download is known as **dosunix**, and contains three utilities that will accomplish 1) the transformation of UNIX text into DOS/Windows text, 2) the translation of DOS/Windows text into UNIX text, and 3) the verification that a file is in either format. In the steps below, we assume you have administrator privileges on this system, have access to Root's password, and can run the `sudo` command.

1.   Type the following on the command line in a Terminal window

     ```
     sudo fink install dosunix
     ```

You are asked for your administrator password, the download from the website occurs, and then the progress of the many steps in compilation and installation of the package are echoed on screen.

2.   When Fink is done installing, it echoes "Setting up dosunix(1.0.13-1)..." and you are returned to the command line prompt. You may now go on to the next sub-section to apply this application to a UNIX text file.

Using the dosunix Application

There is a basic difference between a UNIX text file, one created by the text editor vi, and a DOS/Windows plain text file, one that you create or view in Notepad. The end-of-line character in the UNIX text file is a Line Feed (ASCII 10), whereas the end-of-line characters in DOS/Windows are the Carriage Return (ASCII 13) and the Line Feed. When you transfer a plain text file from a UNIX system to a DOS/Windows system, you must somehow substitute a Carriage Return and Line Feed for every Line Feed, or else the multi-line UNIX text file will look like a single line of text on the DOS/Windows screen display. There are several UNIX command line techniques available to do this, but the application we downloaded using the Fink Package Manager gives you the capabilities not only to transform UNIX text to DOS/Windows text, but also DOS/Windows text to UNIX text, and check whether or not your file is in either format. Following is a sample session conducted in both a Terminal window and in Windows XP Notepad, showing how to use the **unixdos** and **chktxt** applications and what the resulting files look like in a DOS/Windows application. It assumes that you have successfully installed the dosunix application previously mentioned in this chapter, and have created a file named unixtext with the vi text editor on your Mac OS X system, as seen below. You then do the **OS X Operations**, and transfer the two files to Windows XP for viewing with Notepad.

```
OS X Operations

[my_computer:~]me%      unixdosunixtext      dostext

UnixDos 1.0.13-Summary: A total of 7 end of line characters were modi-
fied.

[my_computer:~]me%      chktxt    unixtext

ChkTxt 1.0.13: unixtext is a Unix text file.

[my_computer:~]me%      chktxt    dostext

ChkTxt 1.0.13: dostext is a DOS text file.

[my_computer:~]me%
```

Windows XP Operations

How the file unixtext looks in Notepad

> This file is an example of multi-line UNIX text. It was created in the vi text editor....

> How the file dostext looks in Notepad-

> This file is an example of multi-line UNIX text.

> It was created in the vi text editor.

> Then it was transferred to a computer running Windows XP.

> The resulting display in Notepad shows a single line of text.

> Finally, it was run through the unixdos application.

> This output was then transferred to a computer running Windows XP.

> The resulting display in Notepad was the same as the UNIX text.

21.4.5 System Preference Changes and the Terminal Inspector

As well as being able to customize the dock by making System Preference changes, it is also desirable to customize the general appearance and functionality of the entire desktop itself, and specifically the appearance and functionality of the premier UNIX application that can run on the desktop: the Terminal.

General appearance changes can be achieved by using the System Preference panel icons that affect the look and feel of the Aqua interface. When you run the System Preferences application, by either making the pull-down menu choice System Preferences... from the Apple menu, or by clicking on the System Preferences icon in the Dock, a window opens on-screen, similar to Figure 21.36.

In order to change the look and feel of Terminal windows, it is necessary to run the Terminal application. As stated above, you can run the Terminal application by double-clicking

Figure 21.36 System Preferences Window

on its icon in the Macintosh HD/Applications/Utilities folder. When the Terminal application runs, in the application menu that appears at the top of the screen, make the pull-down menu choice File>Show Info. The Terminal Inspector window appears on-screen. If you select Window from the pop-up menu at the top of the Terminal Inspector window, you can change the display characteristics of the currently-open Terminal window, and also set these characteristics as the default for all Terminal windows. See Figure 21.37.

Not only can you set the size of the window, but you can also display important information in its title bar, such as the active process name, shell command name, tty name, and the shortcut keys that bring this terminal to the front. Table 21.12 lists the other pop-up menu choices, and some of the important characteristics you can change with them.

TABLE 21.12 Terminal Inspector Pop-Up Options

Pop-Up Menu	Options
Shell	Shows current shell and allows different exit operations
Processes	Shows currently running child processes of this window's shell
Emulation	Allows changes to VT-100-style interaction
Buffer	Allows you to set the number of lines of text previously displayed
Display	Allows cursor style, text font, character encoding changes
Color	Allows background, cursor, and text color changes
Window	Allows size and title bar content changes

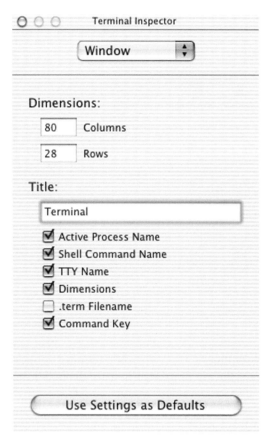

Figure 21.37 Terminal Inspector window settings

In the following In-Chapter Exercises, you will learn more about the Terminal Inspector.

IN-CHAPTER EXERCISES

21.24 You can change the default shell used in every Terminal window that opens by editing the NetInfo database. Run the NetInfo Manager, and go to the /users/ your_username directory, where your_username is your login name on the Mac. Find the shell property, and double-click on it to change it to some other shell, for example, the Bash.

21.25 Look back into Chapter 4 and review how to accomplish the same thing as what you did in Exercise 21.24 above, but from the UNIX command line. Which method do you prefer?

21.4.6 The Finder Preferences

As well as being able to change general System Preferences, another one of the most important applications you want to change the appearance and functionality of is the Finder, the

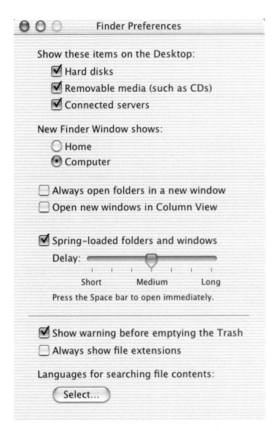

Figure 21.38 Finder Preferences window

application that allows you to work with your computer's file system. To change Finder preferences, from the Finder application menu, make the choice Finder>Preferences. The Finder Preferences window opens on-screen, as seen in Figure 21.38.

The choices available in this window, from top to bottom, are as follows:

1. *Show these items on the desktop.* You get the opportunity to display three different kinds of disk drive on your Desktop: hard disks, removable media (such as ThumbDrives or JumpDrives), and connected servers.

2. *New finder window shows.* Two choices for which is the default path folder which opens when you open a new finder window; either your Home folder or the Computer's folder.

3. *New windows.* You can specify whether or not you want a new window to open when you open a folder, and whether it opens in Column View or not.

4. *Spring-loaded folders and windows.* Determines how windows and folders behave when you drag an item over them; if no check mark is placed here, the item will be placed in the location it is dragged to.

5. *Show warning before emptying Trash.* Allows confirmation of deletion of folders and files.

6. *Always show file extensions.* If this is checked, filenames with extensions will appear in List Views of folders.

7. *Language searching.* Allows you to use multi-language search for content indexing and searching, and consequently shows those operations.

In the following In-Chapter Exercises, you will learn more about Finder Preferences.

IN-CHAPTER EXERCISES ━━━━━━━━━━━━━━━━━━━━━━━━━

21.26   In the Finder Preferences window, check the "Always show file extensions" button. Then go to a folder that contains files that have extensions. What are some of the file extensions you see listed?

21.27   What happens on your system when you insert a JumpDrive or ThumbDrive into a USB port on your Mac? What is the name of the drive that gets mounted? How can you name or rename this externally-mounted drive? How can you safely unmount the externally mounted drive?

21.4.7 Using the OS X Finder to Search the Entire File System

In your work with OS X, you are constantly called on to access directories (folders in Mac terminology), files, applications, and disk drives, particularly to do maintenance on these structures. The Finder is an application that allows you to see a graphic representation of different views of the folders, files, applications, and disk volumes on your computer's file system(s), and also allows you to quickly and easily search for folders and files.

In OS X, there are two levels of files which you can access: The upper-level, which most Mac users will work with and which is visible without modifying any Finder Preferences, and the lower-level, Darwin-specific UNIX files that are hidden from view in the Finder by default. The next section shows you how you can make these lower-level files visible in the Finder, so that you can search the entire file system structure using the graphic facilities of the Finder, rather than having to rely upon a CUI text-based search in the Terminal.

Finder Components

A typical Finder window and its components, one that can be seen when you click on the Finder icon in the dock, is shown in Figure 21.39. This particular view is known as a Column View, and shows the folders on the Macintosh HD disk drive, and the contents of the applications folder on that drive.

The three standard types of view you can have into folders and disk drives are seen in the toolbar at the top of Figure 21.39, where the column view is highlighted. These are:

1. The Icon View, which is similar to the column view, but shows a single column of folder, file, and application icons

2. The List View, which shows you a prioritized list of folders, files, and applications

3. The Column View, which is the current view type in Figure 21.39. The advantage of the column view is that you can quickly navigate upward and downward along the path structure of your computer's file system(s). The Back and Forward buttons found in the toolbar allow you to move backward (upward in the file structure), or forward (downward in the file structure), and as you do this in combination with clicking on a folder or drive of interest, you get more or fewer columns displayed in the main body of the window. Clicking on a folder makes that the current folder, similar to the UNIX current or present working directory. An example of doing this to descend down into your utilities folder, as seen in Figure 21.39, would be to click on the utilities folder icon (the one with the triangle to the right of it). If you did this, another column would open showing you the contents of the utilities folder, and the computer's main folder (the column showing Macintosh HD and Network) would close. The toolbar also contains handy icons that allow you to quickly go to your computer's main folder, your Home folder, your Favorites folder, or the Applications folder.

In the following In-Chapter Exercises, you will learn more about Finder components.

IN-CHAPTER EXERCISES

21.28 Using the Finder in Column View, show the icons in your Home folder. What are they? List the path structure from your computer folder to the Home folder, for example /Macintosh HD/Users/Your_Username. How many columns does it occupy?

21.29 Repeat Exercise 21.28 in a Terminal window, and list the path structure to your home directory, for example /Users/Your_Username. What command(s) did you use to accomplish this operation?

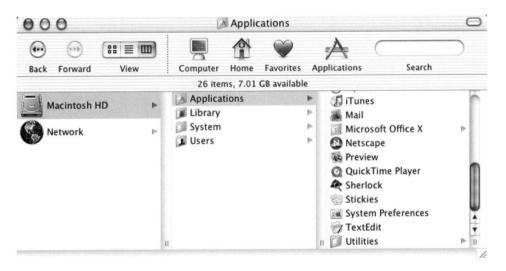

Figure 21.39 Typical Finder window and its components

Searching with the Finder

By far the most useful operation you can perform within the Finder is searching for folders, files, or applications. Of course, this can be done using several methods on the UNIX command line as well, if you are using a CUI. In the Mac Aqua GUI, searching is done graphically by either:

1. Typing a name, word, or expression into the Search field bar right above the Search button (the word "Search" at the far-right of the toolbar, as seen in Figure 21.39), and then pressing <Enter> on the keyboard
2. Using the Search button in the toolbar

   In the first method, depending on what the current folder is, a match is attempted between the name, word, or expression typed into the field and the contents of every folder downward, or below, the current folder. Whether or not the search finds any matches, the results are displayed in the Finder window into which you typed the search criterion. You can double-click on the resulting file or folder names, then change the view option to Column if it is not already that, and trace the path structure to the results by moving forward and backward through the file system using the Back and Forward buttons. In the second method, when you click on the Search button, a Find window opens, similar to Figure 21.40, that allows you to start the search at any location in the path structure of the file system of interest, and design search criteria.

   As seen in Figure 21.40, the word Utilities will be searched for *everywhere* on the file system. When you click the Search button in the Find window, every match will appear using a List View in a new Finder window.

Searching the Entire File System, and Seeing Darwin UNIX Files

As previously mentioned, the lower-level, Darwin UNIX-specific files by default are *not visible* in the Finder. If you wanted to locate the **bash** shell program, you could either use the whereis command in the Terminal application, or you could execute the following steps to

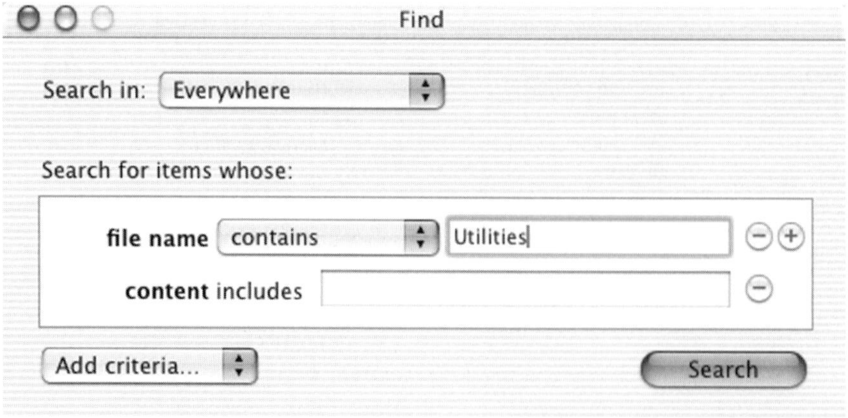

Figure 21.40 Find window

make files that are normally hidden in the Finder visible. This method involves making the following addition to the Finder Preferences file:

`/Users/Your_Username/Library/Preferences/com.apple.finder.plist.`

In the following steps, Your_Username is equivalent to your username on your Mac.

1. Run the Property List Editor at /Developer/Applications.
2. Open com.apple.finder.plist in /Users/Your_Username/Library/Preferences.
3. Click on the disclosure triangle next to Root to show Finder preferences.
4. Click on Root.
5. Click on New Child Button found in the upper-left of the Property List Editor window.
6. In the first column, type `AppleShowAllFiles`.
7. Click on the class column entry for this new item, and select Boolean from the pop-up list. Be sure you are changing the class for the new entry you made in Step 6.
8. Click in the Value column for this new entry, and verify that its value is Yes.
9. Save the plist file with File>Save from the Property List Editor window.
10. Quit the Property List Editor.
11. Force Quit the Finder and restart it, or restart your computer, for the changes to take effect.

Now you have the ability to see the Darwin UNIX-specific files with the Finder, along with what was previously visible to you. For example, to find the bash program, run the Finder by clicking its icon in the Dock. Then, using a column view, descend to the bin folder, and bash should appear in the right-most column, as seen near the top of the right-most column in Figure 21.41.

Compare the contents of the Finder window in Figure 21.39 with the contents in Figure 21.41. You can also use the second Search method shown in Section 21.4.7 to locate folders and files that are hidden. To do this, when you have the Find window open on-screen, choose the Add criteria… pop-up menu to add the criterion of visibility off or all.

Then your searches will find the hidden files as well as the traditional visible ones.

In the following In-Chapter Exercises, you will learn more about the Finder.

IN-CHAPTER EXERCISES

21.30 Use the Dock menu choice Show in Finder and the Finder in column view to list complete path structures for the icon of the System Preferences application on the Dock. (*Hint:* The name of the file is System Preferences.app).

21.31 Use the UNIX `find` command to accomplish the same thing you did in Exercise 21.30. List the exact syntax that you used for the `find` command to do this.

21.32 After making the com.apple.finder.plist changes shown above in this sub-section, use the Finder to find the file bashrc, and show its complete path structure in a Column View.

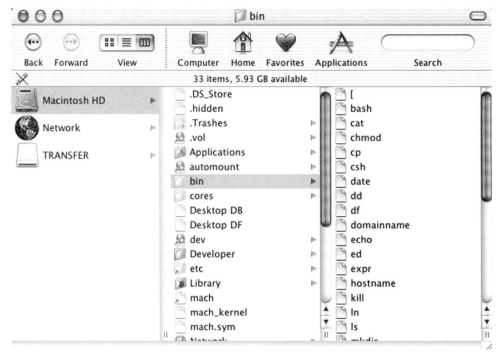

Figure 21.41 Finder showing bin directory

21.5 Web Resources

Table 21.13 is a listing of Web pages that you can explore to find out more about topics covered in this chapter. Many of these sites also include downloadable files that you can use to enhance and extend the GUI capabilities of your UNIX system.

■■ **TABLE 21.13** Internet Resources

Reference in text	URL	Description
1	`http://www.X.org`	X Window System management organization
2	`http://www.xfree86.org`	XFree86 management organization
3	`http://sawmill.sourceforge.net/`	Sawfish window manager
4	`http://icewm.sourceforge.net/`	IceWM window manager
5	`http://www.windowmaker.org`	WindowMaker window manager
6	`http://www.enlightenment.org`	Enlightenment window manager
7	`http://www.afterstep.org`	Afterstep window manager
8	`http://www.fvwm.org`	FVWM2 window manager *(continued)*

TABLE 21.13 *(continued)*

9	`http://www.kde.org`	KDE management organization
10	`http://fink.sourceforge.net`	Fink package management system

▄ Summary

The operability of UNIX is greatly improved from the user perspective by deployment of a Graphical User Interface(GUI). A common GUI system is built on a network protocol called the X Window System. This GUI system can be classified as either *integrated* or *non-integrated*. A non-integrated system generally utilizes only the functionality of a window manager. An integrated system generally couples the window manager with other higher-level programs that achieve *desktop management* and *session management*. An example of an integrated system is KDE.

XFree86 is a network protocol derived from the X Window System, but contains more device-specific drivers for Intel-based PC hardware. XFree86 is used for networked graphical interaction between a user and one or more computer systems running UNIX. The chief arbiter of the interactive dialog between user and computer system is the *window manager*. The fvwm2 window manager offers all of the amenities of other popular window systems, and additionally allows you to manage the graphic output from UNIX application programs. The user interface has two basic parts: the *application user interface*, which is how each client application presents itself in one or more windows on the server screen display, and the window manager or *management interface*, which controls the display of and organizes all client windows.

The basic model of interactivity in XFree86 is an event-request loop between application *client* and graphical *server*. With applications written for XFree86, the client application can process input events, do the work necessary to form a response to the events, and then it can output the responses as *requests* for graphical output to the server.

XFree86, and fvwm2 in particular, are highly customizable to suit the interactive needs of a wide range of users. In this chapter we covered three approaches to changing the appearance and functionality of a non-integrated window system, and the window manager as well. The first approach involved changing the characteristics of applications that run under XFree86 by specifying command line options. The second approach involved modifying or creating an initialization file for the window system, and then invoking that initialization file, either by re-starting the window system, or logging off and then logging back in. The third approach involved modifying or creating an initialization file for the window manager, fvwm2, and then invoking that initialization file.

We covered the functionality of the predominant open-source integrated desktop management system, KDE. We showed how this system can be used to expedite your work within the UNIX environment, particularly with regard to personal productivity and file management operations. We specifically showed the customization possible within this system to allow a user to work more efficiently.

We gave an introduction to a non-X Windows/XFree86-based GUI system, Apple's OS X. We detailed the appearance of the OS X Desktop, showed the basic elements of the Dock, explained how to customize the Dock, showed in detail how to use the Fink Package Manager to install Darwin UNIX-side packages on your system via an Internet database download, explained how to make Aqua preference changes, particularly Terminal appearance changes, and finally how to use the Finder for both Aqua and Darwin UNIX searches.

Problems

1. Give definitions, in your own words, for the following terms as they relate to the XFree86: window system, window manager, desktop manager, client, server, focus, iconify, maximize, minimize, xterm, application user interface, management interface.

2. Which XFree86 window manager is used on your computer system? How can you identify and recognize which window manager you are using by default?

3. Examine the window manager configuration file for the window manager you are using on your system (for example, /usr/lib/X11R6/lib/X11/.fvwm2rc). Then if one is available, examine your home directory, and compare your own personal copy of that same window manager configuration with the systemwide file. Make the following changes to your personal window manager configuration file if they are not already there, and note the changes in your style of interaction with the window manager:

   a. Comment out the ClickToFocus directive

   b. Comment out the StickyIcons directive

   c. Set DeskTopSize to 2 × 2

4. Which command allows another user to have her windows displayed on your screen under XFree86? What would be the advantages of doing this? What would be the disadvantages of doing this? Explain why this is even possible at all under XFree86.

5. Identify the xterm options that are set on your computer system. What is the default size of an xterm window? What is the default background color for an xterm window? What do you think are the most useful xterm options for you?

6. Which file must you make changes to in order to have the default window manager be mwm? Change your window manager in this file, and restart your system or log in using the new window manager. Note the differences in operation between your new window manager and your initial default window manager. Why would you *not* want to stop execution of the window manager in the middle of a session on your computer system?

7. When you hold down the left-most mouse button when the screen cursor is in the root window of your XFree86 display, what appears on your screen? What appears when you hold down the middle mouse button? What appears when you hold down the right-most mouse button? What controls the appearance and con-

tent of the menus that are presented to you when you take these actions? If you hold down the right-most mouse button when the screen cursor is over the title bar of a window on your display, what happens? What menu is presented to you?

8. Do all windows launched on your XFree86 display have the same components, (i.e., scroll bars, iconify button, title bar, resize handles)? What facility controls the look and feel of these components? How do these components compare in function and operation to what you might be familiar with from another GUI, for example on a Mac using OS X or under Windows98/2000/XP?

9. Use your favorite Web browser to explore the site http://www.xfree86.org. What are the objectives of this organization?

10. Use the xpaint application to design a bitmapped image for use as an icon in a pull-down menu. For example, if you were going to design a menu choice for reading from a file, your bitmapped image might look like a book that is open for reading. Save the image, and then use an image viewing application to view the image you designed.

11. After completing Problem 10, find an X-based application on your network that allows you to customize menu items. Then design icon images for use with the application using xpaint, and install them for use with the application.

12. If your system has a desktop manager, such as KDE, compare the file mainte-nance facilities of that XFree86 desktop manager with the UNIX commands that do file maintenance. What are the advantages of the desktop manager's file facilities? What are the advantages of the UNIX commands that do file mainte-nance? Can you see the advantage of using both at the same time?

13. What is a session manager, and how is it different from a desktop management system or a window manager?

14. What are the three major components of KDE? Give a brief description of each one of them.

15. How do you change the size and position of the KDE panel?

16. Outline the installation procedure for the KDE system if you obtain the software as packages over the Internet. When would it be necessary for you to do this installation?

17. How can you use sysinstall on a FreeBSD UNIX system to upgrade KDE com-ponents? What components of KDE would you add or upgrade? Are these components available on the distribution CD?

18. Why would someone want to do a non-integrated installation of UNIX, i.e., either without a GUI (with only a text-based interface to the system) or with only a bare-bones window manager, like fvwm2, running?

19. Why are server-class installations of UNIX done without a GUI?

20. Run the Terminal application under OS X, and using the Terminal Inspector, cre-ate a Terminal with different attributes from your system's defaults. Then save the new settings in a file. How can you open a Terminal window with the settings saved in that file?

21. What is "single user mode" on a Mac running OS X? When and how do you enter console mode? What would you use a login session in console mode for?

22. What keystroke combinations, when typed in a Terminal window, will close the Terminal window?

23. How can an Aqua window be resized?

24. Is it possible to completely remove the Dock from the OS X desktop? If not, what applications must stay there? Explain your answer.

25. Is there the equivalent of a KDE panel drawer on the OS X Dock? How do you implement a drawer in OS X?

26. Edit the NetInfo database and change your default shell in Terminal windows to zsh. What advantages does this shell give you over the default shell?

27. Does the Finder show dot files by default?

28. What changes would you make to restore the Finder to its default condition of *not* showing the UNIX Darwin files on your system?

Appendix: Command Dictionary

Prototype

This appendix provides information about each command in the following format

command name–A synopsis of what the command accomplishes when executed as a single command on the UNIX command line

Syntax:	(1) The command name, its option(s), the option argument(s) for each option, and the command argument(s), all separated by space characters. Anything in square brackets [ ] can be omitted and not change the way the command works.
	(2) Any other pertinent forms of the command's syntax.
Purpose:	A short description of the major purpose of the command.
Output:	The default output, either when no options are executed with the command, or the most important form of output when options are executed with the command.
Options and Option Arguments:	A complete list of each option, where each option is usually prefixed with a hyphen (–), and the option modifiers, enclosed in quotation marks that specify particular behaviors of the option.
Command Arguments:	A complete list of the targets, or objects on which the command works, for example, files, a username, etc.
Example(s):	Important or classic uses of the command, with options, option arguments, and command arguments presented if needed.

Commands That Create, Manipulate, and Delete Files and Directories

Command	Description
`ar`	Maintains a group of files that are in an archive
`awk`	Searches for and processes string or character patterns in a file
`cat`	Displays or joins files
`cd`	Changes the present working directory
`chgrp`	Changes group ownership of a file
`chmod`	Sets file access permissions
`chown`	Sets file ownership
`cmp`	Displays differences in files

(continued)

`comm`	Compares sorted files
`cp`	Duplicates or copies files
`cpio`	Copies files in to and out of an archive
`cut`	Manipulates fields and characters in a file or from the stdout
`dd`	Copies files between devices and converts formats
`diff`	Displays the differences between two files
`echo`	Displays strings, file references, or shell variables on the stdout
`emacs`	Runs a graphical editor for text file creation
`file`	Determines the type of a file
`find`	Finds files along a specified path
`fmt`	Line-oriented simple text editor
`grep`	Searches a file for a pattern of characters
`head`	Displays the first few lines of a file
`less`	Displays one screenful of a file at a time
`ln`	Creates hard or symbolic links to a file
`lpr`	Sends a job to the printer
`lprm`	BSD command to remove jobs from the print queue
`lpq`	BSD command to examine the contents of the print queue
`ls`	Lists names of files and directories on the stdout
`man`	Retrieves the manual, or help page, on a designated command
`mkdir`	Creates directories
`more`	Displays one screenful of a file at a time
`mv`	Moves a file to a new directory, or renames files or directories
`od`	Displays the octal representation of a file, including control characters
`paste`	Merges lines of text in files
`pr`	Paginates and prints files
`ranlib`	Converts archive files to random libraries
`rm`	Deletes files or directories
`rmdir`	Deletes directories
`sed`	Makes changes in files according to contents of a script file
`sort`	Sorts, merges, or sequence checks text files
`spell`	Reports spelling errors in files
`tail`	Displays last few lines of a file
`tar`	Creates a compressed archive of files or directories, or uncompresses them *(continued)*

`touch`	Changes file access and modification times
`tr`	Copies stdin to stdout with specified modifications
`umask`	Gets or sets the file access mode creation mask
`uniq`	Reports or filters out repeated lines in a file
`wc`	Displays a count of lines, words, or characters in a file
`whereis`	Locates the binary, source, and man pages for a command

Commands That Help You Develop C Programs	
Command	**Description**
`cb`	Prettifies a C language program
`cc`	Compiles a C language program
`ctrace`	A dynamic debugger for C programs
`indent`	Prettifies a C language program
`lint`	C program verifier
`make`	Maintains, updates, and regenerates related programs and files
`nm`	Prints the name list of an object file
`strip`	Strips symbol table and debugging line numbers from an object file
`test`	Shell program conditional execution construct
`trace`	A dynamic debugger tool for C programs

Commands That Help You Work on a Local Area Network or on the Internet	
Command	**Description**
`ftp`	Transfers files between hosts over a local network or the Internet
`mail`	Sends and reads e-mail to/from other local users, or on the Internet
`mesg`	Enables or disables write, talk, and other message utilities in a terminal
`pine`	Text-based full-screen e-mail system
`ping`	Establishes that a host is on a network and communicating
`rcp`	Copies files between hosts on a local network or the Internet
`rlogin`	Allows remote login on a host on a local network, or the Internet
`rsh`	Allows execution of a command on a remote host
`rwho`	Shows who is logged on to local or remote hosts
`scp`	Secures shell copy; allows copying within the secure shell between hosts
`sftp`	Secures shell ftp; allows file transfers within the Secure Shell

(continued)

`ssh`	Secures shell; establishes a secure shell connection between hosts
`talk`	Provides two-way, screen-oriented communications between users
`telnet`	Allows communication with another host computer on a network
`who`	Lists information about who is logged in to your UNIX system
`write`	Reads lines on the stdin and writes them to another user's terminal

Commands That Show the Status of the System, or Let You Change System Settings	
Command	**Description**
`at`	Executes commands at a later time
`crontab`	Arranges jobs to run at specified times
`df`	Reports the number of free disk blocks for a mounted device
`du`	Displays disk usage of files and directories
`expr`	Takes character strings and evaluates them as expressions
`finger`	Displays information about users on the system
`kill`	Terminates one or more process IDs by sending a kill signal
`nice`	Allows execution of UNIX commands at a lower priority than default
`nohup`	Executes commands after the user has logged off the system
`ps`	Displays process status of a user's currently running processes
`ruptime`	Displays the host status of the local host machine
`sleep`	Creates a process that waits a specified amount of time
`stty`	Sets stdin terminal's I/O options
`tee`	Duplicates stdout into a file
`tty`	Displays on the stdout the terminal tty of the stdin
`w`	Displays information about currently logged in users
`which`	Displays the pathname for a command
`xterm`	Opens an X terminal with specified characteristics and attributes

Commands for C Program Source Code Revision Control	
Command	**Description**
`admin`	Creates or modifies SCCS history files
`comb`	Generates a shell script that can reconstruct an SCCS file
`delta`	Checks in a record of line-by-line differences in a checked-out SCCS file
`get`	Retrieves a working copy from an SCS history file

(continued)

`help`	Retrieves information about SCCS warning or error messages
`prs`	Displays part or all of an SCCS file in a user-supplied format
`sccs`	Applies indicated SCCS commands to a history file
`unget`	Undoes a previous SCCS `get` command

Commands for General Document Revision Control	
Command	**Description**
`ci`	Stores new revisions of documents in an RCS file
`co`	Checks out a revision from an RCS file and saves it in the working file
`ident`	Identifies RCS keyword strings in a file.
`rcs`	Creates a new RCS file, or changes the attributes of an existing file
`rcsdiff`	Compares versions of an RCS file using the `diff` command
`rcsmerge`	Incorporates changes in two revisions of an RCS file into the working file
`rcslog`	Prints log messages and other information about RCS files

admin—Create an SCCS history file called `c.input.c`:

Syntax: **admin** [**-bhnz**] [**-a** 'username' |'groupid'] ... [**-d** 'flag']
... [**-e** 'username'|'groupid'] ... [**-f** 'flag' ['value']] ...
[**-i**['filename']] [**-m** 'mr-list'] [**-r** 'release']
[**-t**['description-file']] 's.filename' ...

Purpose: Create or modify the flags and other parameters of Source Code Control System (SCCS) history files

Output: New or modified SCSS-coded files

Options and Option Arguments:

-b   Force encoding of binary data

-h   Check the structure of an existing s.file and compare a newly computed check sum with one stored in the first line of that file

-n   Create a new SCCS history file

-z   Recompute the file check sum and store it in the first line of the s.file

-a'username'|'groupid'   Add a user name or a numerical group ID to the list of users who may check deltas in or out. If the list is empty, any user is allowed to do so.

-d'flag'   Delete the indicated 'flag' from the SCCS file

-e'username'|'groupid'   Erase a username or group ID from the list of users allowed to make deltas

-f'flag' ['value']   Set the indicated 'flag' to the (optional) 'value' specified. The following flags are recognized:

b	Enable branch deltas
c'ceil'	Set a ceiling on the releases that can be checked out; 'ceil' is a number less than or equal to 9,999. If c is not set, the ceiling is 9,999.
f'floor'	Set a floor on the releases that can be checked out
d'sid'	The default delta number, or SID, to be used by an SCCS `get` command
i	Treat the `'No id keywords'` message issued by an SCCS `get` or `delta` command as an error rather than a warning
j	Allow concurrent updates
l'release'[,'release'...]	Lock the indicated list of releases against deltas
n	Create empty releases when releases are skipped; these null (empty) deltas serve as anchor points for branch deltas
q'value'	Supply a 'value' to which the `%Q%` keyword is to expand when a read-only version is retrieved with the SCCS `get` command
m'module'	Supply a value for the module name to which the `%M%` keyword is to expand; if the m flag is not specified, the value assigned is the name of the SCCS file with the leading s. removed
t'type'	Supply a value for the module type to which the `%Y%` keyword is to expand
v['program']	Specify a validation 'program' for the MR numbers associated with a new delta; the optional 'program' specifies the name of an MR number validity checking 'program'
-i['filename']	Initialize the history file with text from the indicated file
-m['mr-list']	Insert the indicated modification request (MR) numbers in the commentary for the initial version
-r'release'	Specify release for the initial delta
-t['description-file']	Insert descriptive text from the file 'description-file'

Command Arguments:

's.filename' ....   Encoded SCSS history file(s)

Example(s):   Create an SCCS history file called c.input.c: `admin -iinput.c s.input.c`

---

ar–Maintain portable archive or library

Syntax:	`ar -d [-Vv] 'archive file'...`
	`ar -m [-abiVv] ['posname'] 'archive file'...`
	`ar -p [-sVv] 'archive' ['file'...]`
	`ar -q [-cVv] 'archive file'...`
	`ar -r [-abciuVv] ['posname'] 'archive file'...`
	`ar -t [-sVv] 'archive' ['file'...]`
	`ar -x [-CsTVv] 'archive' ['file'...]`
Purpose:	Maintain groups of files combined into a single archive file. Its main use is to create and update library files.
Output:	Archived files

Options and Option Arguments:

-a	Position new 'file's in 'archive' after the file named by the 'posname' operand
-b	Position new 'file's in 'archive' before the file named by the 'posname' operand
-c	Suppress the diagnostic message that is written to standard error by default when 'archive' is created
-C	Prevent extracted files from replacing like-named files in the file system
-d	Delete one or more 'file's from 'archive'
-i	Position new 'file's in 'archive' before the file named by the 'posname' operand
-m	Move 'file's to the end of the archive
-p	Print the contents of 'file's in 'archive' to standard output
-q	Quickly append 'file's to the end of 'archive'
-r	Replace or add 'file's in 'archive'
-s	Force the regeneration of the archive symbol table even if ar is not invoked with an option that will modify the archive contents
-t	Print a table of contents of 'archive'
-T	Allow file name truncation of extracted files whose archive names are longer than the file system can support
-u	Update older files
-V	Print its version number on standard error
-v	Give verbose output

Command Arguments:

'archive'	A pathname of the archive file
'file'	A pathname. Only the last component will be used when comparing it against the names of files in the archive. If two or more 'file' operands have the same last pathname component, the results are unspecified.
'posname'	The name of a file in the archive file used for relative positioning

Example(s): Replace library.a with object files from the current directory:
```
ar r library.a 'ls *.o'
```

---

at–Execute script at a specified time

Syntax:
```
at [-c|-k|-s] [-m] [-f 'file'] [-q 'queuename'] -t 'time'
at [-c|-k|-s] [-m] [-f 'file'] [-q 'queuename'] 'timespec'...
at -l [-q 'queuename'] ['at job id'...]
at -r 'at job id'...
```

Purpose: Read commands from standard input and group them together as an 'at-job', to be executed at a later time

Output: Results of running script

Options and Option Arguments:

-c	C shell; csh used to execute at-job

-k	Korn shell; `ksh` used to execute at-job
-s	Bourne shell; `sh` used to execute at-job
-f'file'	Specify path of a file to be used as the source of at-job
-l	Report all jobs scheduled for the invoking user if no 'at job id' operands are specified; if 'at job id's are specified, report only information for these jobs
-m	Send mail to invoking user after at-job has run, announcing its completion. Standard output and standard error produced by at-job will be mailed to the user as well, unless redirected elsewhere. Mail will be sent even if job produces no output.
	If –m is not used, the job's standard output and standard error will be provided to user by means of mail, unless they are redirected elsewhere; if there is no such output to provide, user is not notified of the job's completion
-q'queuename'	Specify in which queue to schedule a job for submission. When used with the –l option, limit search to that particular queue. Values for 'queuename' are limited to the lowercase letters a through z. By default, at-jobs will be scheduled in queue a. In contrast, queue b is reserved for batch jobs. Queue c is reserved for cron jobs, so it cannot be used with the –q option.
-r'at job id'	Remove the jobs with the specified 'at job id' operands previously scheduled by the at utility
-t'time'	Submit job to be run at the time specified by 'time'

Command Arguments:

'at job id'	Name reported by a previous invocation of the at command at the time the job was scheduled
'timespec'	Submit job to be run on date and at time specified
'time'	The 'time' can be specified as one, two, or four digits

Example(s):   Execute `stdin` commands at 12:45 on December 15: `at 12:45pm Dec 15`

---

awk–Process patterns in a file

Syntax:	**awk** [**-f** 'progfile'] [**-F**'c'] ["prog"] ['parameters'] ['filename'...]
	awk [**-F** 'ERE'] [**-v** 'assignment 'program" | **-f** 'progfile' ['argument' ...]
Purpose:	Search for patterns in file(s) and process them
Output:	Counter increment or lines of text to standard output

Options and Option Arguments:

-f'progfile'	Use the set of patterns it reads from 'progfile'
-F'c'	Use the character 'c' as the field separator character

Command Arguments: None

Example(s):   Print first and second fields from all lines that contain the string "seasoning" in the file named food: `awk '/seasoning/ {print $1 $2}' food`

cal–Display a calendar

Syntax:	**cal** [['month'] 'year']
Purpose:	Display a calendar on standard output
Output:	Display a calendar of month or year
Options:	None

Command Arguments: None

Example(s):   Display a calendar on stdout for December, 2004: `cal 12 2004`

---

cat–Concatenate and display files

Syntax:	**cat** [**-nbsuvet**] ['file'...]
Purpose:	Join one or more files sequentially or display them in the console window
Output:	Joined files or files output at the standard output
Options:	

-n	Precede each line output with its line number
-b	Number the lines, as with -n, but omit line numbers from blank lines
-u	Output not buffered (default is buffered output)
-s	cat silent about nonexistent files
-v	Print visibly nonprinting characters (with the exception of <Tabs>, newlines and formfeeds)
-e	Print $ character at the end of each line (prior to newline)
-t	Print <Tabs> as ^I's and formfeeds as ^L's; the -e and -t options are ignored if the -v option is not specified

Command Arguments:

'file'	Pathname of an input file; if no 'file' is specified, standard input is used
Example(s):	Display the entire contents of the file source.c at stdout: `cat source.c` Take lines typed at stdin and create a file named typedin.txt from them: `cat > typedin.txt`

---

cb–C program beautifier

Syntax:	**cb** [**-s**] [**-j**] [**-l** 'leng'] [**-v**] ['file'...]
Purpose:	Read syntactically correct program and indent them according to some commonly accepted C program structures
Output:	Properly indented code at standard output

Options and Option Arguments:

-s	Write code in the style of Kernighan and Ritchie, found in the C programming language
-j	Put split lines back together
-l'leng'	Split lines that are longer than length
-V	Print on standard error output the version of cb invoked

Command Arguments:

'file'...	Source file(s) to be properly indented

Example(s):   Splits any lines longer than 80 characters in the file korn.c:
```
cb -l 80 korn.c > korn_2.c
```

CC–Provide C compiler

Syntax: **cc** [options] 'sourcefile'... [**-l** 'library'...]

Purpose: Compile, assemble, and load 'sourcefile' into executable a.out

Output: Executable a.out

Options and Option Arguments:

-a	Insert code to count the number of times each basic block is executed; invokes a run-time recording mechanism that creates a .d file for every .c file (at normal termination). The .d file accumulates execution data for the corresponding source file.
-B'binding'	Specify whether bindings of libraries for linking are static or dynamic
-c	Suppress linking and produce a .o file for each source file; a single object file can be named explicitly by using the **-o** option
-C	Prevent the C preprocessor, cpp, from removing comments
-dryrun	Show but do not execute commands constructed by the compilation driver
-D'name'[='def']	Define a symbol 'name' to the C preprocessor
-E	Run the source file through the C preprocessor
-fast	Select the optimum combination of compilation options for speed
-help	Display helpful information about cc
-o'outputfile'	Name the output file 'outputfile'
-p	Prepare the object code to collect data for profiling
-S	Do not assemble the program but produce an assembly source file
-temp='directory'	Set directory for temporary files to be 'directory'
-time	Report execution times for the various compilation passes
-U'name'	Remove any initial definition of the symbol name
-v	Verbose; print version number of the compiler
-w	Do not print warnings

Command Arguments:

-l 'library'	Link with object library 'library'; must follow 'sourcefile'
'sourcefile'	The pathnames of the file(s) cc is to compile, assemble, and/or load

Example(s):   Compile program short.c, link it to library baked, and output executable image
as short: `cc —o short short.c —lbaked`

---

cd–Change working directory

Syntax: **cd** ['directory']
Purpose: Change the present working directory to 'directory' or return to home directory
Output: Present working directory set to 'directory'
Options: None

Command Arguments:

'directory'   Directory pathname to which you want to change

Example(s):   Descend to the subdirectory newfiles: `cd newfiles`
Ascend to the parent of the present working directory: `cd ..`
Make the present working directory /usr/local/bin: `cd /usr/local/bin`

---

chgrp–Change file group ownership

Syntax: **chgrp** [`-fhR`] 'group' 'file'
Purpose: Change the group associated with a file
Output: Modified group for specified file
Options:

-f   Force; do not report errors

-h   If file is a symbolic link, change group of the symbolic link; without this option,
the group of the file referenced by the symbolic link is changed

-R   Recursive; `chgrp` descends through the directory and any subdirectories, setting the
specified group ID as it proceeds; when a symbolic link is encountered, the group of
the target file is changed (unless the `-h` option is specified), but no recursion takes place

Command Arguments:

'group'   A group name from the group database or a numeric group ID. Either specifies a group
ID to be given to each file named by one of the 'file' operands. If a numeric 'group'
operand exists in the group database as a group name, the group ID number associated
with that group name is used as the group ID

'file'   Pathname of a file whose group ID is to be modified

Example(s):   Change the group of the file terms to user2: `chgrp user2 terms`

---

chmod–Change mode of a file

Syntax: **chmod** [options] 'mode' 'file'...
Purpose: Change file access modes of file(s)
Output: Modified access modes

Options:

-f   Force; do not report errors

-R   Recursive; with directories specified in file(s), chmod recursively descends the directory structure and changes specified files access modes

Command Arguments:

'mode'   Either a symbolic or absolute designation of class and access permission

'file...'   One or more files that the access is applied to

Example(s):   Add read permission to usergroup, and others for the file diagram.jpg:
```
chmod a+r diagram.jpg
```
Take away write permission for group for the file picture.pdf:
```
chmod g-w picture.pdf
```

---

chown–Change file ownership

Syntax: **chown** [**-fhR**] 'owner'[:'group'] 'file'...

Purpose: Change owner of a file or files

Output: Files with changed ownership

Options:

-f   Do not report errors

-h   If file is a symbolic link, change owner of the symbolic link; without this option, owner of the file referenced by the symbolic link is changed

-R   Recursive; chown descends through the directory, and any subdirectories, setting the ownership ID as it proceeds; when a symbolic link is encountered, the owner of the target file is changed (unless the -h option is specified), but no recursion takes place

Command Arguments:

'owner'[:'group']   A user ID and optional group ID to be assigned to 'file'. The 'owner' portion of this operand must be a username from the user database or a numeric user ID. Either specifies a user ID to be given to each file named by 'file'. If a numeric 'owner' exists in the user database as a username, the user ID number associated with that username will be used as the user ID. Similarly, if the 'group' portion of this operand is present, it must be a group name from the group database or a numeric group ID. Either specifies a group ID to be given to each file. If a numeric group operand exists in the group database as a group name, the group ID number associated with that group name will be used as the group ID.

'file'   A pathname of a file whose user ID is to be modified

Example(s):   Makes bobk the owner of all files in /usr1.b/bobk and its subdirectories:
```
chown —R bobk /usr1.b/bobk
```

ci–Check in RCS revisions

Syntax:	**ci** ['options'] 'file'...
Purpose:	Store new revisions of documents in RCS files
Output:	Each pathname matching an RCS suffix is taken to be an RCS file; all others are assumed to be working files containing new revisions

Options and Option Arguments:

-r'rev'	Check in revision 'rev'
-r	Bare option (without any revision)
-l['rev']	Similar to **-r**, except that it performs an additional co **-l** for the deposited revision
-u['rev']	Works like **-l**, except that the deposited revision is not locked
-f['rev']	Force a deposit; the new revision is deposited even it is not different from the preceding one
-k['rev']	Search the working file for keyword values to determine its revision number, creation date, state, and author and assign these values to the deposited revision, rather than computing them locally
-q['rev']	Quiet mode; diagnostic output not printed
-i['rev']	Initial check in; report an error if the RCS file already exists
-j['rev']	Just check in and do not initialize; report an error if the RCS file does not already exist
-I['rev']	Interactive mode; user is prompted and questioned even if standard input is not a terminal
-d['date']	Use 'date' for the check-in date and time
-M['rev']	Set modification time on any new working file to be date of retrieved revision
-m'msg'	Use the string 'msg' as the log message for all revisions checked in
-n'name'	Assign the symbolic name 'name' to the number of the checked-in revision
-N'name'	Same as **-n**, except that it overrides a previous assignment of 'name'
-s'state'	Set the state of the checked-in revision to the identifier 'state'
-t-'string'	Write descriptive text from the 'string' to the RCS file, deleting the existing text
-T	Set the RCS file's modification time to the new revision's time if the former precedes the latter and there is a new revision
-w'login'	Uses 'login' for the author field of the deposited revision
-V	Print RCS's version number
-V'n'	Emulate RCS version 'n'
-x'suffixes'	Specify suffixes for RCS files
-z'zone'	Specify date output format in keyword substitution and default time zone for 'date' in **-d**'date' option

Command Arguments:

'file'...   Working or output file name(s)

Example(s):   Retrieves the next revision for editing the RCS file named book:
```
ci —l —m"major edits" book
```

cmp–Compare two files

Syntax: **cmp** [**-l**] [**-s**] 'file1' 'file2' ['skip1'] ['skip2']

Purpose: Compare two files and locate where they first differ

Output: A zero flag if two files do not differ and a byte offset location of where the first difference is

Options:

-l   Write the byte number (decimal) and the differing bytes (octal) for each difference

-s   Write nothing for differing files; return exit statuses only

Command Arguments:

'file1'   Pathname of the first file to be compared; if 'file1' is -, standard input is used

'file2'   Pathname of the second file to be compared; if 'file2' is -, standard input is used

'skip1', 'skip2'   Initial byte offsets into 'file1' and 'file2'

Example(s):   Compares two files, first and second, and shows where they differ:
```
cmp first second
first second differ:   char 71, line 3
```

---

co–Check out RCS revisions

Syntax: **co** ['options'] 'file'...

Purpose: Retrieve a revision from each RCS file and store it in the corresponding working file

Output: Pathnames matching an RCS suffix are RCS files; all others are working files

Options and Option Arguments:

-r['rev']   Retrieve latest revision whose number is less than or equal to 'rev'

-l['rev']   Same as -r, except that it also locks the retrieved revision for the caller

-u['rev']   Same as -r, except that it unlocks the retrieved revision if it was locked by the caller

-f['rev']   Force overwriting of the working file

-kkv   Generate keyword strings, using the default form

-kkvl   Same as -kkv, except that a locker's name is always inserted if the given revision is currently locked

-kk   Generate only keyword names in keyword strings; omit their values

-ko   Generate the old keyword string, present in the working file just before it was checked in

-kb   Generate a binary image of the old keyword string

-kv   Generate only keyword values for keyword strings

-p['rev']   Print retrieved revision on standard output rather than storing it in the working file

-q['rev']	Quiet mode; diagnostics not printed
-I['rev']	Interactive mode; user prompted and questioned even if standard input is not a terminal
-d'date'	Retrieve latest revision on the selected branch whose check-in date/time is less than or equal to 'date'
-M['rev']	Set modification time on new working file to be date of the retrieved revision
-s'state'	Retrieve latest revision on the selected branch whose state is set to 'state'
-T	Preserve modification time on RCS file even if file changes because a lock is added or removed
-w['login']	Retrieve latest revision on the selected branch, which was checked in by user with login name 'login'
-j'joinlist'	Generate new revision that is the combination of the revisions on 'joinlist'
-V	Print RCS's version number
-V'n'	Emulate RCS version 'n', where 'n' can be 3, 4, or 5
-x'suffixes'	Use 'suffixes' to characterize RCS files

Command Arguments:

'file'...	Working or output file name(s)

Example(s): Retrieves an editable copy of RCS file named chap3, but locks it from other users:

```
co -l chap3
```

---

comb–Combine SCCS deltas

Syntax:	**comb** [**-os**] [**-c**'sid-list'] [**-p**'sid'] 's.filename'...
Purpose:	Generate a shell script that can be used to reconstruct the indicated s.files
Output:	The script is written to standard output

Options and Option Arguments:

-o	For each 'get -e' generated, access the reconstructed file upon release of the delta to be created
-s	Generate scripts to gather statistics, rather than combining deltas; when run, the shell scripts report file name, size (in blocks) after combining, original size (also in blocks), and percentage size change, computed by the formula 100 * ('original - combined') / 'original'
-c'sid-list'	Include the indicated list of deltas; all other deltas omitted. The 'sid-list' is a comma-separated list of SCCS delta IDs (SIDs). To specify a range of deltas, use a '-' separator instead of a comma between two SIDs in the list.
-p'sid'	The SID of the oldest delta to be preserved

Command Arguments:

's.filename'...	Reconstructed SCCS file

Example(s): Produces a shell script at stdout to calculate how much of an SCCS file named file1 will be reduced: comb -s file1

comm–Select or reject lines common to two files

Syntax:	**comm** [**-123**] 'file1' 'file2'
Purpose:	Show a line-by-line comparison of two sorted files
Output:	The comm command will read 'file1' and 'file2', which should be ordered in the current collating sequence, and produce three text columns as output: lines only in 'file1'; lines only in 'file2'; and lines in both files
Options:	
-1	Suppress output column of lines unique to 'file1'
-2	Suppress output column of lines unique to 'file2'
-3	Suppress output column of lines duplicated in 'file1' and 'file2'

Command Arguments:

'file1'	Pathname of first file to be compared; if 'file1' is -, standard input is used
'file2'	Pathname of second file to be compared; if 'file2' is -, standard input is used
Example(s):	Compares two lists from file1 and file2, and displays items in both lists: comm file1 file2

---

cp–Copy files

Syntax:	**cp** [**-fip**] 'source file' 'target file'
	cp [**-fip**] 'source file'... 'target'
	**cp -r	-R** [**-fip**] 'source dir'... 'target'
Purpose:	Copy one or more files in two basic ways: duplicate and to a directory
Output:	Duplicates of text or binary files in the same or another directory
Options:	
-f	Unlink; if a file descriptor for a destination file cannot be obtained, attempt to unlink the destination file and proceed
-i	Interactive; cp will prompt for confirmation whenever the copy would overwrite an existing 'target'. A y answer means that the copy should proceed. Any other answer prevents cp from overwriting 'target'.
-p	Preserve; cp duplicates not only the contents of 'source file', but it also preserves the owner and group id, permissions modes, and modification and access time
-r	Recursive; cp will copy the directory and all its files, including any subdirectories and their files to 'target'
-R	Same as -r, except that pipes are replicated, not read from

Command Arguments:

'source file'	Pathname of a regular file to be copied
'source dir'	Pathname of a directory to be copied
'target file'	Pathname of an existing or nonexisting file, used for the output when a single file is copied

'target'   Pathname of a directory to contain the copied files –; standard input is used

Example(s):   Copy all files that end in .pdf from the directory /usr/local/bin to the present
working directory: `cp *.pdf /usr/local/bin .`

Duplicate filea into fileb: `cp filea fileb`

---

cpio–Copy file archives in and out

Syntax: **cpio -i** [options] ['pattern'...]
cpio -o [options]
cpio -p [options] 'directory'

Purpose: Copy files into and out of an archive. The -i, -o, and -p options select the action
to be performed. The following modes describe each of the actions:

Copy In Mode
`cpio -i` (copy in) extracts files from standard input, which is assumed to be the
product of a previous `cpio -o`. Only files with names that match 'patterns' are
selected.

Copy Out Mode
`cpio -o` (copy out) reads the standard input to obtain a list of pathnames and copies
those files on to standard output, together with pathname and status information.

Pass Mode
`cpio -p` (pass) reads standard input to obtain a list of pathnames of files that are
conditionally created and copied into the destination 'directory' tree, based on the
options.

Output: Archived files, depending on the mode selected

Options and Option Arguments:

-i   (copy in) `cpio -i`; extract files from standard input

-o   (copy out) `cpio -o`; read standard input to obtain a list of pathnames and copy those
files to standard output

-p   (pass) `cpio -p`; read standard input to obtain a list of pathnames of files

The following options can be appended in any sequence to the -o, -i, or -p options:

-a   Reset access times of input files after they have been copied; access times are not reset
for linked files when `cpio -pla` is specified (mutually exclusive with -m)

-A   Append files to an archive; the -A option requires the -o option; valid only with
archives that are files or that are on floppy diskettes or hard disk partitions

-b   Reverse the order of the bytes within each word (use only with the -i option)

-B   Block input/output 5120 bytes to the record

-c   Read or write header information in ASCII character form for portability

-C'bufsize' Block input/output 'bufsize' bytes to the record, where 'bufsize' is replaced by a
positive integer

-d   Create directories as needed

-E'file'	Specify an input file ('file') that contains a list of filenames to be extracted from the archive (one filename per line)
-f	Copy in all files except those in 'patterns'
-H'header'	Read or write header information in 'header' format
-I'file'	Read contents of 'file' as an input archive
-k	Attempt to skip corrupted file headers and I/O errors that may be encountered
-l	Whenever possible, link files rather than copying them
-L	Follow symbolic links; the default is not to follow symbolic links
-m	Retain previous file modification time
-M'message'	Define a 'message' to use when switching media
-O'file'	Direct output of cpio to 'file'
-r	Interactively rename files
-R'id'	Reassign ownership and group information for each file to 'user ID'
-s	Swap bytes within each half word
-S	Swap half words within each word
-t	Print table of contents of the input; no files created
-u	Copy unconditionally (normally, an older file will not replace a newer file with the same name)
-v	Verbose; print a list of file names
-V	Special verbose; print a dot for each file read or written

Command Arguments:

'directory'	Pathname of an existing directory to be used as the target of cpio -p
'pattern'	Expressions making use of a pattern-matching notation similar to that used by the shell
Example(s):	Restore files with name "backup" from a diskdrive named hd0 into the present working directory, and recreates subdirectory structure on hd0: cpio —icdv "backup" < /dev/hd0

crontab–User crontab file

Syntax:	**crontab** ['filename'] **crontab** [**-elr**] 'username'
Purpose:	Arranges jobs to run at specified times
Output:	Unredirected stdout and stderr mailed to user
Options:	
-e	Edit a copy of the current user's crontab file or create an empty file to edit if crontab does not exist
-l	List the crontab file for the invoking user
-r	Remove a user's crontab file from the crontab directory

Command Arguments:

'filename'	Name of a file that contains the crontab commands; you may type commands at stdin and end with <Ctrl-D>

'username' Used by superuser to change the crontab file for a user

Example(s): List the contents of your current crontab file on stdout:
crontab −l

---

ctrace–C program debugger

Syntax: **ctrace** [options] ['file']

Purpose: Allow user to monitor sequentially the execution of a C program as each program statement executes

Output: The modified program to standard output

Options and Option Arguments:

-**f** functions Trace only these functions

-**v** functions Trace all but these functions

-**o** Octal

-**x** Hexadecimal

-**u** Unsigned

-**e** Floating point

-**l** n Check 'n' consecutively executed statements for looping trace output, instead of the default of 20

-**s** Suppress redundant trace output from simple assignment statement and string copy function calls

-**t** n Trace 'n' variables per statement instead of the default of 10

-**P** Preprocess input before tracing it

-**p** string Change the trace print function from the default of printf

-**r** f Use file f in place of the runtime.c trace function package

-**V** Print version information on stderr

-**Q**arg If arg is y, identification information about ctrace will be added to the output files

Command Arguments:

'file' C program for which you want to trace execution

Example(s): Trace the execution of the program named short, but suppress redundant output from assignment statements and string copy functions: ctrace −s short

---

cut–Cut out selected fields of each line of a file

Syntax: **cut −b** 'list' [−**n**] ['file'...]
cut −c 'list' ['file'...]
cut −f 'list' [−**d** 'delim'] [−**s**] ['file'...]

Purpose: Select characters or tab fields from an input file and send to stdout

Output: The output characters or fields specified at stdout

Options and Option Arguments:

'list'   A comma-separated or blank character–separated list of integer field numbers (in increasing order), with optional – to indicate ranges (e.g., 1,4,7; 1-3,8; -5,10 (short for 1-5,10); or 3- (short for third through last field)

−**b**'list'   The 'list' following −b specifies byte positions

−**c**'list'   The 'list' following −c specifies character positions

−**d**'delim'   The character following −d is the field delimiter (−f option only)

−**f**'list'   The 'list' following −f is a list of fields assumed to be separated in the file by a delimiter character (*see* −d)

−**n**   Do not split characters; when −b 'list' and −n are used together, 'list' is adjusted so that no multibyte character is split

−**s**   Suppresses lines with no delimiter characters in the case of the −f option

Command Arguments:

'file'   Pathname of an input file; if no 'file' operands are specified or if a 'file' operand is −, the standard input will be used

Example(s):   List on stdout the fields username and real name from the /etc/passwd file:
                cut −d: -f1,5 /etc/passwd

---

date–Write the date and time to stdout

Syntax: **date** [−**u**] [+'format']
                date [−**a** [−]'sss.fff']
                date [−**u**] [['mmdd']'HHMM' | 'mmddHHMM'['cc']'yy']['SS']

Purpose: Display or set clock time and calendar date

Output: Date and time on stdout

Options and Option Arguments:

−**a**[−]'sss.fff'   Slowly adjust time by 'sss.fff' seconds ('fff' represents fractions of a second). This adjustment can be positive or negative. The system's clock will speed up or slow down until it has drifted by the number of seconds specified.

−**u**   Display (or set) the date in Greenwich Mean Time (GMT–universal time), bypassing the normal conversion to (or from) local time

Command Arguments:

'mm'   Month number

'dd'   Day number in month

'HH'   Hour number (24-hour system)

'MM'   Minute number

'SS'   Second number

'cc'   Century minus 1

'yy'   Last two digits of year number

Example(s): Show the date:
            date
            Thu Dec 18 21:59:29 GMT 2004

---

dbx–Source-level debugger

Syntax: **dbx** [**-f** 'fcount'] [**-i**] [**-I**'dir'] [**-k**] [**-kbd**] [**-P** 'fd'] [**-r**] [**-s** 'startup']
               [**-sr** 'tstartup'] ['objfile'['corefile' | 'process-id']]

Purpose: Debug and execute at source level programs written in C or other supported languages,
               such as Pascal and FORTRAN 77

Output: dbx-controlled execution of a program

Options and Option Arguments:

-f'fcount'   Alter initial estimate of the number functions in the program being debugged;
                 initial setting is 500

-i   Force dbx to act as though stdin were a terminal or terminal emulator

-I'dir'   Add 'dir' to the list of directories in which to search for a source file

-k   Kernel debugging

-kbd   Debug a program that sets the keyboard to up–down translation mode; this flag is
                 necessary if a program uses up–down decoding

-P'fd'   Create a pipeline to a dbxtool process; 'fd' is the file descriptor through which
                 to pipe output to the front-end process

-r   Execute 'objfile' immediately

-s'startup' Read initialization commands from the file named 'startup'

-sr'tstartup' Read initialization commands from the temporary file named 'tstartup' and then
                   remove that file

Command Arguments:

'objfile'   An object file produced by cc or another compiler, with the -g option to include
             a symbol table

'corefile'   Use dbx to examine the state of the program when the core file was produced

Example(s): Run the dbx debugger on the program short, reading dbx initialization commands
                 from fileinit: **dbx –s fileinit short**

---

dd–Convert and copy a file

Syntax: **dd** ['operand'='value'...]

Purpose: Copy files between devices

Output: File copied to the specified device in the format specified

Options: None

Command Arguments:

if='file'   Specify input path; stdin is the default

of='file'   Specify output path; stdout is the default

ibs='n'   Specify input block size in 'n' bytes (default is 512)

obs='n'   Specify output block size in 'n' bytes (default is 512)

bs='n'   Set both input and output block sizes to 'n' bytes, superseding ibs= and obs=

cbs='n'   Specify conversion block size for block and unblock in bytes by 'n' (default is 0)

files='n'   Copy and concatenate 'n' input files before terminating (for tapes)

skip='n'   Skip 'n' input blocks (using specified input block size) before starting to copy

iseek='n'   Seek 'n' blocks from beginning of input file before copying

oseek='n'   Seek 'n' blocks from beginning of output file before copying

seek='n'   Skip 'n' blocks (using specified outputblock size) from beginning of output file before copying

count='n'   Copy only 'n' input blocks

conv='value'[,'value'...]   Where 'value's are comma-separated symbols from the following list:

    ascii   Convert EBCDIC to ASCII

    ebcdic   Convert ASCII to EBCDIC, if converting fixed-length ASCII records

    ibm   Slightly different map of ASCII to EBCDIC

    block   Treat input as a sequence of newline-terminated or eof-terminated variable-length records independent of input block boundaries

    unblock   Convert fixed-length records to variable length

    lcase   Map uppercase characters specified by the LC_CTYPE keyword to the corresponding lowercase character

    ucase   Map lowercase characters specified by the LC_CTYPE keyword to the corresponding uppercase character

    swap   Swap every pair of input bytes

    noerror   Do not stop processing on an input error

    notrunc   Do not truncate output file

All operands will be processed before any input is read.

Example(s):   Convert a file bigletters to all lowercase, and display on stdout:
```
dd if=bigletters conv=lcase
```

---

delta–Make a delta to an SCCS file

Syntax: **delta** [-nps] [-g 'sid-list' | -g'sid-list'] [-m 'mr-list' | -m'mr-list']
[-r 'sid' | -r'sid'][-y['comment']] 's.file'...

Purpose: Check in a record of line-by-line differences made to a checked-out version of a file under SCCS control

Output: Depending on the options specified and the flags that are set in the s.filename, `delta` may issue prompts on stdout; the SID of the delta is not echoed to stdout

Options and Option Arguments:

-n   Retain the edited g-file, which is normally removed upon completion of processing

-p   Display line-by-line differences on stdout

-s   Silent; do not display warning or confirmation messages

-g'sid-list' | −g'sid-list'   Specify a list of deltas to omit when file is accessed at the SCCS version ID (SID) created by this delta; 'sid-list' is a comma-separated list of SIDs

-m'mr-list' | −m'mr-list'   If the SCCS file has the v flag set, user must supply one or more modification request (MR) numbers for the new delta

-r'sid' | −r'sid'   When two or more versions are checked out, specify the version to check in

-y['comment']   Supply a comment for the delta table (version log); a null comment is accepted and produces an empty commentary in the log

Command Arguments:

d.'file'   Temporary file of differences

p.'file'   Lock file for a checked-out version

q.'file'   Temporary file

s.'file'   SCCS history file

x.'file'   Temporary copy of s.file

z.'file'   Temporary file

Example(s):   Create a new version of the SCCS file short.c: `delta s.short.c`

---

df–Report number of free disk blocks and files

Syntax: `df [-F 'FSType'][-abegklntV][-o 'FSType-specific options'][`'directory' 'block device' 'resource'...]

Purpose: Display available disk space

Output: Amount of free disk space, in blocks, for a mounted device on stdout

Options and Option Arguments:

-a   Report on all file systems, including those whose entries have the ignore option set

-b   Print total number of kilobytes free

-e   Print only the number of files free

-F 'FSType'   Specify the 'FSType' on which to operate

-g   Print entire statvfs(2) structure

-k   Print allocation in kilobytes

-l   Report on local file systems only

-n   Print only the 'FSType' name

-o 'FSType-specific options'   Specify 'FSType-specific' options

-P	Same as –k, except in 512-byte units
-t	Print full lists with totals
-V	Echo complete set of file system specific command lines but do not execute them

Command Arguments:

'directory'	Represents a valid directory name
'block device'	Represents a block special device (e.g., /dev/dsk/c1d0s7); the corresponding file system need not be mounted
'resource'	Represents an NFS resource name

Example(s):   Display information on all mounted NFS filesystems: df –t nfs

---

diff–Display line-by-line differences between pairs of text files

Syntax:	diff [–**bitw**] [–**c** | –**e** | –**f** | –**h** | –**n**] 'file1' 'file2'
	diff [–**bitw**] [–**C** 'number'] 'file1' 'file2'
	diff [–**bitw**] [–**D** 'string'] 'file1' 'file2'
	diff [–**bitw**] [–**c**| –**e** | –**f** | –**h** | –**n**] [–**l**] [–**r**] [-s] [–**S** 'name'] 'directory1' 'directory2'
Purpose:	Display differences on lines of two files
Output:	The diff command compares the contents of 'file1' and 'file2' and writes to stdout a list of changes necessary to convert 'file1' to 'file2'

Options and Option Arguments:

-b	Ignore trailing blanks (spaces and <Tabs>)and treat other strings of blanks as equivalent
-i	Ignore the case of letters (e.g., 'A' equals 'a')
-t	Expands <Tab> characters in output lines
-w	Ignores all blanks

The following options are mutually exclusive:

-c	Produce a listing of differences with three lines of context
-C 'number'	Produce a listing of differences identical to that produced by –c with 'number' lines of context
-e	Produce a script of only a, c, and d commands for the editor ed, which will re-create 'file2' from 'file1'
-f	Produce a similar script, not useful with ed, in the opposite order
-h	Expedient
-n	Produce a script similar to that produced by –e, but in the opposite order and with a count of changed lines on each insert or delete command
-D 'string'	Create a merged version of 'file1' and 'file2' with C preprocessor controls included

The following options are used for comparing directories:

-l	Produce output in long format

-r	Apply diff recursively to common subdirectories encountered
-s	Report files that are identical, which otherwise would not be mentioned
-S 'name'	Start a directory diff in the middle, beginning with the file 'name'

Command Arguments:

'file1' 'file2'   Pathname of a file or directory to be compared; if either file1 or file2 is -, stdin will be used in its place

'directory1' 'directory2'   Pathname of a directory to be compared. Note: if only one of 'file1' and 'file2' is a directory, diff will be applied to the nondirectory file and the file contained in the directory file with a filename that is the same as the last component of the nondirectory file

Example(s):   Compare two text files a and b: diff a b

---

du–Summarize disk usage

Syntax: **du** [**-ador**] ['file'...]

Purpose: Display information on disk usage of files and directories

Output: The du command writes to stdout the size of the file space allocated to the file hierarchy rooted in each of the specified files and the size of the file space allocated to each of its subdirectories

Options:

-a	In addition to the default output, report the size of each file not of type directory in the file hierarchy rooted in the specified file
-d	Do not cross filesystem boundaries
-o	Do not add child directories' usage to a parent's total
-r	Generate messages about directories and files that cannot be read

Command Arguments:

'file'   Pathname of a file whose size is to be written; if no 'file' is specified, the current directory is used

Example(s):   List disk usage in 1024 byte blocks of all ordinary files in the directory/usr1.b/bobk, including the default disk usage: du –a /usr1.b/bobk

---

dump–Display the values of all variables in the current or named function
(a dbx debug command)

Syntax: **dump** ['func'] [**>** 'file']

Purpose: Prints values of variables

Output: Local variable(s) value(s) of the current function at stdout

Options and Option Arguments:

'func'   A named function

Command Arguments:

'file'   Output to named file

Example(s):   Shows the value of the all variables in the current function: `dump`

---

echo–Echo arguments

Syntax:	**echo** ['string'...]
Purpose:	Display a message on stdout
Output:	Strings, file references, and shell variables at stdout

Options and Option Arguments: None

Command Arguments:

'string'   String to be written to stdout. If any operand is –n, it will be treated as a string, not an option. The following character sequences will be recognized within any of the arguments.

\a   Alert character

\b   Backspace

    \c   Print line without newline

    \f   Formfeed

    \n   Newline

    \r   Carriage return

    \t   Tab

    \v   Vertical tab

    \\   Backslash

    \0'n'   Where 'n' is the 8-bit character whose ASCII code is the 1-, 2-, or 3-digit octal number representing that character

Example(s):   Print a message "This is it" on stdout and suppress the NEWLINE at the end of the message (the $ is the shell prompt):
```
$echo This is it\\c $
```

---

emacs–Full-screen text editor

Syntax:	**emacs** ['command-line switches'] ['files'...]
Purpose:	Provide a full-screen text editor with word-processing and program development capabilities
Output:	New or revised text files

Options and Option Arguments:

+'number'   Go to the line specified by 'number' (do not insert a space between + and the number)

–**q**   Do not load an init file

–**u**'user'   Load 'user's init file

−t'file'   Use specified 'file' as the terminal instead of stdin/stdout; must be the first argument specified in the command line

−f'function'   Execute the lisp function 'function'

−l'file'   Load the lisp code in the file 'file'

−batch   'commandfile'

−kill   Exit 'Emacs' while in batch mode

X Window Options and Option Arguments:

−rn'name'   Specifies program name that the user should use when looking up defaults in the user's X resources; must be the first option specified in the command line

−name'name'   Specifies name that should be assigned to the 'Emacs' window

−r   Display 'Emacs' window in reverse video

−i   Use "kitchen sink" bitmap icon when iconifying 'Emacs' window

−font'font'   Set 'Emacs' window's font to that specified by 'font'

−b'pixels'   Set 'Emacs' window's border width to the number of pixels specified by 'pixels'

−ib'pixels'   Set window's internal border width to the number of pixels specified by 'pixels'

−geometry'geometry'   Set 'Emacs' window's width, height, and position as specified. The geometry specification is in the standard X format. The width and height are specified in characters; the default is 80×24.

−fg'color'   On color displays, sets text color

−bg'color'   On color displays, sets window's background color

−bd'color'   On color displays, sets window's border color

−cr'color'   On color displays, sets window's text cursor color

−ms'color'   On color displays, sets window's mouse cursor color

−d'displayname'   Create 'Emacs' window on the display specified by 'displayname'; must be the first option specified in the command line

−nw   Tells 'Emacs' not to use its special interface to X; if user uses this switch when invoking 'Emacs' from an 'xterm' window, display is done in that window; must be the first option specified in the command line

Command Arguments:

'files'...   Files the user wants to edit

Example(s):   Run emacs in the same terminal window you type the command in (i.e., without opening a new X Window window), on the file named `crisp.c`:
`emacs −nw crisp.c`

---

expr–Evaluate arguments as an expression

Syntax: **expr** 'arguments'

Purpose: Takes character strings and evaluates them as expressions

Output: Based on special procedures for expression evaluation

Options and Option Arguments: None

Command Arguments:

'arguments' Terms of the expression, separated by blanks. Characters special to the shell must be escaped. Strings containing blanks or other special characters should be quoted.

Operators and keywords are listed below. The list is in order of increasing precedence, with equal precedence operators grouped within braces, { }.

'expr' \| 'expr'   returns the first 'expr' if it is neither null or 0; otherwise, returns the second 'expr'

'expr' \& 'expr'   returns the first 'expr' if neither 'expr' is null or 0; otherwise, returns 0

'expr' { =, \>, \>=, \<, \<=, != } 'expr' returns the result of an integer comparison if both arguments are integers; otherwise, returns the result of a lexical comparison

'expr' { +, - } 'expr'   addition or subtraction of integer-valued arguments

'expr' { *, /, % } 'expr'   multiplication, division, or remainder of the integer-valued arguments

'expr' : 'expr'   The matching operator: compares the first argument with the second argument, which must be a regular expression

('expr')   pattern symbols; can be used to return a portion of the first argument

'integer'   An argument consisting only of an (optional) unary minus followed by digits

'string'   A string argument that cannot be identified as an 'integer' argument or as one of the expression operator symbols

Example(s):   Multiplication with the multiplication operator (*) quoted with the backslash character: `expr 6 \* 5`

---

file–Determine file type

Syntax: `file [-h] [-m 'mfile'] [-f 'ffile'] 'file'`
`file [-h] [-m 'mfile'] -f 'ffile'`
`file -c [-m 'mfile']`

Purpose: Classify 'file' according to data type content

Output: Designation of 'file'

Options and Option Arguments:

-c   Check magic file for format errors

-h   Do not follow symbolic links

-f'ffile'   'ffile' contains a list of files to be examined

-m'mfile'   Use 'mfile' as an alternate magic file instead of /etc/magic

Command Arguments:

'file'   Pathname of a file to be tested

Example(s):   Run file on the filenames in list and out to a file named classify:
`file -f list > classify`

find–Find files

Syntax:	**find** 'path...' 'expression'
Purpose:	Display files along 'path...' that are specified in 'expression'
Output:	Names of files that match 'expression' at stdout

Options and Option Arguments: None

Command Arguments:

'path...'   Pathname of a starting point in the directory hierarchy

'expression' Valid expressions are as follows.

–atime 'n'	True if file was accessed 'n' days ago
–cpio 'device'	Always true; write the current file on 'dev'
–ctime 'n'	True if file's status was changed 'n' days ago
–depth	Always true; causes descent of the directory hierarchy
–exec 'command'	True if the executed 'command' returns a 0
–follow	Always true; causes symbolic links to be followed
–fstype 'type'	True if the file system to which the file belongs is of type 'type'
–group 'gname'	True if the file belongs to the group 'gname'
–inum 'n'	True if the file has inode number 'n'
–links 'n'	True if the file has 'n' links
–local	True if the file system type is not a remote file system type
–s	Always true; prints current pathname
–mount	Always true; restricts the search to the file system containing the directory specified
–mtime'n'	True if the file's data was modified 'n' days ago
–name 'pattern'	True if 'pattern' matches the current file name
–ncpio 'device'	Always true; write the current file on 'device' in cpio –c format
–newer 'file'	True if the current file has been modified more recently than the argument 'file'
–nogroup	True if the file belongs to a group not in the /etc/group file
–nouser	True if the file belongs to a user not in the /etc/passwd file
–ok 'command'	Like -exec, except that the generated command line is printed with a question mark first and is executed only if the user responds by typing y
–perm [-] 'mode'	Used to represent file mode bits
–print	Always true; causes current pathname to be printed
–prune	Always yields true; do not examine any directories or files in the directory structure below the 'pattern' just matched
–user'uname'`	True if the file belongs to the user 'uname'

-xdev   Same as the -mount primary

Example(s):   Find all files in the present working directory that begin with b:
find . —name 'b*.*'

---

finger–Display information about local or remote users

Syntax: **finger** [**-bfhilmpqsw**] ['username'...] '[username@hostname]'

Purpose: Display information about users

Output: Displays in multicolumn format at stdout the following information about each logged-on user: username, user's full name, terminal name, idle time, login time, and host name, if logged on remotely

Options:

-b   Suppress printing user's home directory and shell in a long format

-f   Suppress printing header that is normally printed in a non-long format

-h   Suppress printing of .project file in a long format

-i   Force "idle" output format, which is similar to short format

-l   Force long output format

-m   Match arguments only on username (not first or last name)

-p   Suppress printing of the .plan file in a long format

-q   Force quick output format, which is similar to short format

-s   Force short output format

-w   Suppress printing full name in a short format

Command Arguments:

'username'   A local user; may be a first or last name or an account name

'[username@hostname]'   Remote user at remote host

Example(s):   Lists information about user with login name tfife: finger tfife

---

fmt–Simple text formatter

Syntax: **fmt** [**-c**] [**-s**] [**-w** 'width' | –'width'] ['inputfile'...]

Purpose: Format text using simple designations

Output: A file containing filled and joined output lines of (up to) the number of characters specified in the -w 'width' option. The default 'width' is 72. The command fmt concatenates the 'inputfile's listed as arguments; if none are given, fmt formats text from stdin.

Options and Option Arguments:

-c   Crown margin mode; preserve indentation of the first two lines within a paragraph and align the left margin of each subsequent line with that of the second line

-s   Split lines only; do not join short lines to form longer ones

-w'width' | -'width'   Fill output lines up to 'width' columns

Command Arguments:

'inputfile'... Input file names; if omitted, the stdin

Example(s):   Format to 30 characters wide and print at stdout the file smythe: `fmt -30 smythe`

---

ftp–File transfer program

Syntax:	`ftp [-dgintv]` ['hostname']
Purpose:	Transfer files over a network
Output:	Interactively transferred files, usually from the Internet
Options:	

-d   Enable debugging

-g   Disable filename "globbing"

-i   Turn off interactive prompting during multiple file transfers

-n   Do not attempt "auto-login" upon initial connection

-t   Enable packet tracing

-v   Show all responses from the remote server and report on data transfer statistics

Interactive commands at the `ftp>` *prompt:*

! ['command']   Run 'command' as a shell command on the local machine

$'macro-name' ['args']   Execute the macro 'macro-name' that was defined with the `macdef` command

account['passwd']   Supply a supplemental password required by a remote system for access to resources once a logon has been successfully completed

append 'local-file' ['remote-file']   Append a local file to a file on the remote machine

ascii   Set the "representation type" to "network" ASCII

binary   Set the "representation type" to "image"

bye   Terminate the FTP session with the remote server and exit ftp

case   Toggle remote computer file name case mapping during `mget` commands

cd'remote-directory'   Change the working directory on the remote machine to 'remote-directory'

cdup   Change the remote machine working directory to the parent of the current remote machine working directory

close   Terminate the FTP session with the remote server and return to the command interpreter

delete'remote-file'   Delete the file 'remote-file' on the remote machine

debug   Toggle debugging mode

dir['remote-directory'] ['local-file']   Print a listing of the directory contents in the directory, 'remote-directory', and, optionally, place output in 'local-file'

disconnect   Same as `close`

form['format-name']   Set the carriage control format subtype of the "representation type" to 'format-name'

get'remote-file' ['local-file']   Retrieve 'remote-file' and store it on the local machine

glob   Toggle filename expansion, or "globbing," for `mdelete`, `mget`, and `mput`

hash   Toggle hash-sign (`#`) printing for each data block transferred

help['command']   Print an informative message about the meaning of 'com- mand'; if no argument is given, `ftp` prints a list of the known commands

lcd['directory']   Change the working directory on the local machine

ls['remote-directory' | -al] ['local-file']   Print an abbreviated listing of the contents of a directory on the remote machine

macdef'macro-name'   Define a macro

mdelete'remote-files'   Delete 'remote-files' from the remote machine

mdir'remote-files' 'local-file'   Like `dir`, except multiple remote files may be specified

mget'remote-files'   Expand 'remote-files' on the remote machine and do a `get` for each file name thus produced

mkdir'directory-name'   Make a directory on the remote machine

mls'remote-files' 'local-file'   Like `ls`, except multiple remote files may be specified

mode['mode-name']   Set "transfer mode" to 'mode-name'

mput'local-files'   Expand wild cards in the list of local files given as arguments

nmap['inpattern' 'outpattern']   Set or unset the filename mapping mechanism

ntrans['inchars' ['outchars']]   Set or unset the filename character translation mechanism

open'host' ['port']   Establish a connection to the specified 'host' FTP server

prompt   Toggle interactive prompting

proxy'ftp-command'   Execute an FTP command on a secondary control connection

put'local file' ['remote-file']   Store 'local-file' on the remote machine with the same name, unless 'remote-file' name is specified

quit   Same as `bye`

quote'arg1' 'arg2'...   Send the arguments specified, verbatim, to the remote server

recv'remote-file' ['local-file']   Same as `get`

remotehelp ['command-name']   Request help from the remote FTP server

rename'from' 'to'   Rename the file 'from' on the remote machine to have the name 'to'

reset   Clear reply queue

runique   Toggle storing of files on the local system with unique filenames

send'local-file' ['remote-file']   Same as `put`

sendport   Toggle the use of PORT commands

status   Show the current status of `ftp`

struct['struct-name']   Set file structure to 'struct-name'

sunique   Toggle storing of files on remote machine under unique file names

trace   Toggle packet tracing (unimplemented)

type['type-name']   Set "representation type" to 'type-name'

user'user-name' ['password'] ['account']   Identify yourself to the remote FTP server

verbose   Toggle verbose mode. In verbose mode, all responses from the FTP server are displayed to the user

?   ['command'] Same as help

Command Arguments:

'hostname'   A remote computer using Domain Name System ftp establishes a connection to a remote computer using the Domain Name System

Example(s):   Establish an ftp session in verbose mode with the remote host lhotse.up.edu, and transfer the file records from the present working directory on the local host to the default directory that you logged in to on the remote host:

```
ftp -v lhotse.up.edu
>put records
```

---

get–Retrieve a version of an SCCS file

Syntax: **get** [**-begkmnpst**] [**-l[p]**] [**-a**'sequence'] [**-c** 'date-time' | **-c**'date-time'] [**-G**'g-file'] [**-i** 'sid-list' | **-i**'sid-list'] [**-r** 'sid' | -r'sid'] [**-x** 'sid-list' | **-x**'sid-list'] 's.filename'...

Purpose: Retrieve a working copy from the SCCS history file, according to the specified options; for each 's.filename' argument, get displays the SCCS delta ID (SID) and number of lines retrieved

Output: The SID being accessed and the number of lines retrieved from the s.file at stdout

Options and Option Arguments:

-b   Create a new branch

-e   Retrieve a version for editing; with this option, get places a lock on the s.file so that no one else can check in changes to the version that the user has checked out

-g   Get the SCCS version ID, without retrieving the version itself

-k   Suppress expansion of ID keywords

-m   Precede each retrieved line with the SID of the delta in which it was added to the file

-n   Precede each line with the %M% ID keyword and a <Tab>

-p   Write the text of the retrieved version to stdout; all messages that normally go to stdout are written to stderr instead

-s   Suppress all output normally written to stdout

-t   Retrieve the most recently created (top) delta in a given release

-l[p]   Retrieve a summary of the delta table (version log) and write it to a listing file

-a'sequence'   Retrieve the version corresponding to the indicated delta sequence number

-c'date-time'   Retrieve the latest version checked in prior to the date and time indicated by the 'date-time' argument; 'date-time' takes the form 'yy'['mm'['dd'['hh'['mm'['ss']]]]]

-**G**'newname'   Use 'newname' as the name of the retrieved version

-**i**'sid-list'   Specify a list of deltas to include in the retrieved version

-**r**['sid']   Retrieve the version corresponding to the indicated SID (delta)

-**x**'sid-list'   Exclude the indicated deltas from the retrieved version

Command Arguments:

g-file   Version retrieved by get

l.'file'   File containing extracted delta table info

p.'file'   Permissions (lock) file

z.'file'   Temporary copy of s.'file'

Example(s):   Display the contents of the file s.short.c: `get –p s.short.c`

---

grep–Search a file for a pattern

Syntax: `grep [-bchilnsvw]` 'regular-expression' ['filename'...]

Purpose: Search in file(s) for a pattern that matches a regular expression

Output: Each line found is copied to standard output; the file name is printed before each line found if there is more than one input file

Options:

-**b**   Precede each line by the block number on which it was found

-**c**   Print only a count of the lines that contain the pattern

-**h**   Prevent the name of the file containing the matching line from being appended to that line

-**i**   Ignore uppercase/lowercase distinction during comparisons

-**l**   Print only the names of files with matching lines, separated by newline characters

-**n**   Precede each line by its line number in the file (first line is 1)

-**s**   Suppress error messages about nonexistent or unreadable files

-**v**   Print all lines except those that contain the pattern

-**w**   Search for the expression as a word as if it were surrounded by \< and \>

Command Arguments:

'filename...'   Pathname of a file to be searched for the patterns; if no 'file' operands are specified, stdin will be used

'regular-expression'   Regular expression

Example(s):   Display the header files that have at least one directive:
```
grep –l '#include' /usr/include/*
```

head–Display first few lines of files

Syntax:	**head** [–'number' | **–n** 'number'] ['filename'...]
Purpose:	Display beginning of a file
Output:	Copies the first 'number' of lines of each 'filename' to stdout; if no 'filename' is given, head copies lines from stdin. Default value of 'number' is 10 lines.

Options and Option Arguments:

–n'number' The first 'number' lines of each input file will be copied to stdout; the 'number' option argument must be a positive decimal integer

–'number' The 'number' argument is a positive decimal integer with the same effect as the –n 'number' option

Command Arguments:

'filename'... Pathname of an input file; if no 'file' operands are specified, stdin will be used

Example(s): Display the first 15 lines of the file named records: `head -15 records`

---

help–Ask for help regarding SCCS error or warning messages

Syntax:	**help** ['argument'] ...
Purpose:	Retrieve information to explain error messages from SCCS commands
Output:	Help on SCSS commands and errors at stdout

Options and Option Arguments: None

Command Arguments:

'argument' ... SCSS command or error message

Example(s): Display help on the SCCS error message when a code is generated: `help code`

---

ident–Identify RCS keyword strings in files

Syntax:	**ident** [**–q**] [**–v**] ['file'...]
Purpose:	Search for all instances of the pattern $'keyword': 'text' $ in the named files or, if no files are named, stdin
Output:	Strings identified in 'file'... on stdout

Options and Option Arguments:

–q Suppress warning if there are no patterns in 'file'...

–v Print ident version number at stdout

Command Arguments:

file ... file(s) to be searched

Example(s):   Show keywords for all RCS files, and suppress warnings:
```
co -p RCS/),v | ident -q
```

---

indent–Change the appearance of a C program by inserting or deleting white space

Syntax: **indent** [**-bad**] [**-bap**] [**-bbb**] [**-bc**] [**-bl**] [**-bliN**] [**-br**] [**-cN**] [**-cdN**] [**-cdb**]
[**-ce**] [**-ciN**] [**-cliN**] [**-cpN**] [**-cs**] [**-bs**] [**-dN**] [**-diN**] [**-fc1**] [**-fca**] [**-iN**]
[**-ipN**] [**-kr**] [**-lN**] [**-lp**] [**-nbad**] [**-nbap**] [**-nbbb**] [**-nbc**] [**-ncdb**] [**-nce**]
[**-ncs**] [**-nfc1**] [**-nfca**] [**-nip**] [**-nlp**] [**-npcs**] [**-nsc**] [**-nsob**] [**-nss**] [**-nv**]
[**-orig**] [**-npro**] [**-pcs**] [**-psl**] [**-sc**] [**-sob**] [**-ss**] [**-st**] [**-T**] [**-tsN**] [**-v**]
[**-version**] ['file']

Purpose: Used to "beautify" or make code easier to read; it can also convert from one style of writing C to another

Output: Input files are specified, indent makes a backup copy of each file, and the original file is replaced with its indented version

Options and Option Arguments:

'**-bad**'   Force blank lines after declarations

'**-bap**'   Force blank lines after procedure bodies

'**-bbb**'   Force blank lines after block comments

'**-bc**'   Force newline after comma in declaration

'**-bl**'   Put braces on line after '`if`', etc.

'**-bliN**'   Indent braces N spaces

'**-br**'   Put braces on line with '`if`', etc.

'**-cN**'   Put comments to the right of code in column N

'**-cdN**'   Put comments to the right of the declarations in column N

'**-cdb**'   Put comment delimiters on blank lines

'**-ce**'   Cuddle `else` and preceding '`}`'

'**-ciN**'   Continuation indent of N spaces

'**-cliN**'   Case label indent of N spaces

'**-cpN**'   Put comments to the right of '`#else`' and '`#endif`' statements in column N

'**-cs**'   Put a space after a cast operator

'**-bs**'   Put a space between '`sizeof`' and its argument

'**-dN**'   Set indentation of comments not to the right of code to N spaces

'**-diN**'   Put variables in column N

'**-fc1**'   Format comments in first column

'**-fca**'   Do not disable all formatting of comments

'**-iN**'   Set indentation level to N spaces

'**-ipN**'   Indent parameter types in old-style function definitions by N spaces

`'-kr'`	Use Kernighan and Ritchie coding style
`'-lN'`	Set maximum line length to N
`'-lp'`	Line up continued lines at parentheses
`'-nbad'`	Do not force blank lines after declarations
`'-nbap'`	Do not force blank lines after procedure bodies
`'-nbbb'`	Do not force blank lines after block comments
`'-nbc'`	Do not force newlines after commas in declarations
`'-ncdb'`	Do not put comment delimiters on blank lines
`'-nce'`	Do not cuddle `'}'` and `'else'`
`'-ncs'`	Do not put a space after cast operators
`'-nfc1'`	Do not format comments in first column as normal
`'-nfca'`	Do not format any comments
`'-nip'`	Zero width indentation for parameters
`'-nlp'`	Do not line up parentheses
`'-npcs'`	Do not put space after the function in function calls
`'-npsl'`	Put the type of a procedure on the same line as its name
`'-nsc'`	Do not put the `'*'` character to the left of comments
`'-nsob'`	Do not swallow optional blank lines
`'-nss'`	Do not force a space before the semicolon after certain statements
`'-nv'`	No verbosity
`'-orig'`	Use the original Berkeley coding style
`'-npro'`	Do not read '.indent.pro' files
`'-pcs'`	Insert a space between the name of the procedure being called and the `'('`
`'-psl'`	Put the type of a procedure on the line before its name
`'-sc'`	Put the `'*'` character to the left of comments
`'-sob'`	Swallow optional blank lines
`'-ss'`	On one-line `'for'` and `'while'` statements, force a blank before the semicolon
`'-st'`	Write to standard output
`'-T'`	Tell `'indent'` the name of typenames
`'-tsN'`	Set tab size to N spaces
`'-v'`	Enable verbose mode
`'-version'`	Output the version number of `'indent'`

Command Arguments:

'file'   File the user wants to beautify

Example(s):   Use standard K&R formatting to format a file named second.c, and output the formatted source to second1.c:

```
indent second.c second1.c -br
```

kill–Send a signal to a process

Syntax:	`kill` [–'signum'] 'pid', 'signum'
Purpose:	Terminate one or more process IDs
Output:	Sends a message to kill one or more processes; the returned value will be 0 if successful; an error code is generated if unsuccessful

Options:

    –'signum'   Signal number or name of a process preceding pid

Command Arguments:

    'pid'   Process ID number of one or more processes user wants to terminate

    'signum'   Signal number; 9 kill, 15 software terminate, and 18 stop are numbers commonly used

Example(s):   Send the kill signal to the process with ID#2345: `kill -9 2345`

less–Display one screenful of a file at a time

Syntax:	`less` [-[+]aBcCdeEfgGiImMnNqQrsSuUVwX] [**-b** 'bufs'] [**-h** 'lines'] [**-j** 'line'] [**-k** 'keyfile'] [**-{oO}** 'logfile'] [**-p** 'pattern'] [**-P** 'prompt'] [**-t** 'tag'] [**-T** 'tagsfile'] [**-x** 'tab'] [**-y** 'lines'] [**-[z]** 'lines'] [+[+]'cmd'] [**--**] ['filename']...
Purpose:	Similar to more; allow backward movement in the file, as well as forward movement
Output:	While the user is viewing a file, less displays a prompt that lets the user move forward or backward in the file by using certain commands; a brief list of these commands follows (^ represents holding down <Ctrl>)

h or **H** Help: Display a summary of these commands

<space> or **^V** or **f** or **^F**   Scroll forward N lines; default is one window (*see* option **-z**)

z   Like <space>, but if N is specified, it becomes the new window size

<Esc-space>   Like <space>, but it scrolls a full screenful, even if it reaches eof in the process

<Return> or **^N** or **e** or **^E** or **j** or **^J**   Scroll forward N lines: default is 1

d or **^D**   Scroll forward N lines; default is one-half the screen size

b or **^B** or <Esc>**-v**   Scroll backward N lines; default is one window

w   Like <Esc>**-v**, but if N is specified, it becomes the new window size

y or **^Y** or **^P** or **k** or **^K**   Scroll backward N lines, default is 1

u or **^U**   Scroll backward N lines, default is one-half the screen size

<Esc>**-)** or <right arrow>   Scroll horizontally to the right N characters; default is 8

<Esc>**-(** or <left arrow>   Scroll horizontally to the left N characters; default is 8

r or **^R** or **^L**   Repaint screen

R   Repaint screen, discarding any buffered input

F   Scroll forward and keep trying to read when eof is reached

g or **<** or <Esc>**-<**   Go to line N in the file; default is 1 (beginning of file)

Options and Option Arguments:

-?	Display a summary of the commands
-- help	Same as -?
-a	Causes searches to start after the last line displayed on the screen, thus skipping all lines displayed on the screen
-b'n'	Specify the number of buffers that n less will use for each file
-B	Disable automatic allocation of buffers for pipes
-c	Cause full screen repaints to be painted from the top line down
-C	Like -c, but screen is cleared before it is repainted
-d	Suppress error message normally displayed if terminal is dumb
-e	Cause 'less' to exit automatically the second time it reaches eof
-E	Cause 'less' to exit automatically the first time it reaches eof
-f	Force nonregular files to be opened (a nonregular file is a directory or a device special file)
-g	Highlight only the particular string found by the last search command
-G	Suppress all highlighting of strings found by search commands
-h'n'	Specify a maximum number of lines 'n' to scroll backward
-i	Cause searches to ignore case; that is, uppercase and lowercase are considered identical
-I	Like -i, but searches ignore case even if pattern contains uppercase letters
-j'n'	Specifies a line 'n' on the screen where the "target" line is to be positioned
-k'filename'	Cause 'less' to open and interpret the named file as a key file
-m	Cause 'less' to prompt verbosely (like 'more'); by default, 'less' prompts with a colon
-M	Cause 'less' to prompt even more verbosely than 'more'
-n	Suppress line numbers
-N	Cause a line number to be displayed at the beginning of each line in the display
-o'filename'	Cause 'less' to copy its input to the named file as it is being viewed
-O'filename'	Like -o, but will overwrite an existing file without confirmation
-p'pattern'	Equivalent to specifying +/'pattern'; that is, it tells less to start at the first occurrence of 'pattern' in the file
-P'prompt'	Provide a way to tailor the three prompt styles to the user's preference
-q	Cause "quiet" operation
-Q	Cause totally "quiet" operation (e.g., the terminal bell is never rung)
-r	Cause "raw" control characters to be displayed
-s	Cause consecutive blank lines to be squeezed into a single blank line
-S	Cause lines longer than the screen width to be chopped rather than folded
-t'tag'	Edit the file containing 'tag'
-T'tagsfile'	Specify a tags file to be used instead of "tags"
-u	Cause backspaces and carriage returns to be treated as printable characters

-U	Cause backspaces, tabs, and carriage returns to be treated as control characters
-V	Display the version number of less
--version	Same as -V
-w	Cause blank lines to be used to represent lines past eof; by default, a tilde character (~) is used
-x'n'	Set tab stops every 'n' positions; the default for 'n' is 8
-X	Disable sending the termcap initialization and deinitialization strings
-y'n'	Specify a maximum number of lines to scroll forward
-[z]'n'	Change the default scrolling window size to 'n' lines
-"	Change the file name quoting character
-	A command line argument of "--" marks the end of option arguments
+	If a command line option begins with +, the remainder of that option is taken to be an initial command to less

Command Arguments:

['filename']...   A list of files that less operates on; if not specified, less takes input from stdin

Example(s):   Scrolls through the file named tests one screenful at a time, with the prompt "Press space bar" to inform the user:

```
less -P "Press space bar" tests
```

---

lint–C program verifier

Syntax: lint ['options'] ['file'...]

Purpose: Allow checking for features that can be bugs, nonportable code, or wasteful of system resources

Output: Advisories on stdout about execution of a C program

Options and Option Arguments:

-a	Ignore long values assigned to variables that are not long
-b	Ignore unreachable break statements
-c	No second pass of linet; save output in .ln files
-F	Output filenames with complete pathname
-h	No test for bugs, improper style, or extra info
-k	Reenable warnings suppressed by /* LINTED [message] */
-L'dir'	Search for lint libraries in 'dir' before standard search path
-lx	Use library llib-lx.ln
-m	Ignore extern declarations that could be static
-n	No compatibility checking
-o'lib'	Create a lint library llib-l, lib.ln after first pass
-p	Check for portability to different C

-R'file'	Place .ln output in 'file'
-u	Ignore undefined or unused functions or external vars
-v	Ignore unused arguments within functions
-V	Print version and release number on stdout
-W'file'	Same as **-R**, except that 'file' is cflow-ready
-x	Ignore unused variables referred to by an extern declaration
-y	Same as **-vx**

Command Arguments:

'file'...   C program file(s)

Example(s):   Checks the type casts in the file test.c: `lint -c test.c`

---

ln–Make hard or symbolic links to files

Syntax: `ln [-fns] 'source file' ['target']`
    `ln [-fns] 'source file'... 'target'`

Purpose: Create a hard link to a file

Output: An entry in the specified directory that points to another file

Options:

-f	Link files without questioning the user, even if the mode of 'target' forbids writing
-n	If link is an existing file, do not overwrite the contents of the file
-s	Create a symbolic link

Command Arguments:

'source file' Pathname of a file to be linked, which can be either a regular or special file; if the s option is specified, 'source file' can also be a directory

'target'   Pathname of the new directory entry to be created or of an existing directory in which the new directory entries are to be created

Example(s):   Create a hard link between the file small and the directory /usr1/b/bobk:
    `ln /usr1.b/bobk small`

    Create a symbolic link between the directory /usr/contrib/bobk and the all the files in directory /usr1.b/bobk : `ln -s usr/contrib/bobk /usr1.b/bobk/*.*`

---

lpq–Show printer queue status

Syntax: `lpq[-E] [-Pprinter] [-a] [-l] [+interval]`

Purpose: Show the current print queue status on the named printer; jobs queued on the default destination will be shown if no printer or class is specified on the command line

Output: Queue status at the specified printer

Options and Option Arguments:

    -a   Display jobs numbers queued on all printers

    -E   Force encrypted connection to the server

    +'interval' Continuously report the jobs in the queue until the queue is empty; the list of jobs is shown once every 'interval' in seconds

    -l   Give a more verbose reporting format

    -P'printer' Display job numbers on queue for 'printer'

Command Arguments: None

Example(s):   View the print queue at the printer named qpr: `lpq  -Pqpr`

---

lpr–Send a job to printer

Syntax: `lpr [-P 'printer'] [-# 'copies'] [-C 'class']`
                    `[-J 'job'] [-T 'title'] [-i ['indent']] [-w 'cols']`
                    `[-m] [-h] [-s] ['filename'...]`

Purpose: Send files to printer

Output: Files sent to the print queue as print jobs

Options and Option Arguments:

    -P'printer' Send output to the named 'printer'

    -#'copies' Produce the number of 'copies' indicated for each named file

    -C'class'   Print 'class' as the job classification on the burst page

    -J'job'   Print 'job' as the job name on the burst page

    -T'title'   Use 'title' instead of the file name for the title

    -i['indent'] Indent output 'indent' <space> characters. Eight <space> characters is the default

    -w'cols'   Use 'cols' as the page width for pr

    -m   Send mail upon completion

    -h   Suppress printing the burst page

    -s   Use full pathnames (not symbolic links) of the files to be printed rather than trying to copy them

Command Arguments:

    ['filename'...] Files to be submitted to print queue and printed

Example(s):   Send the file grades.eps to the PostScript printer named qpr:
                 `lpr —Pqpr grades.eps`

---

lprm–Cancel print jobs

Syntax: `lprm[-E][-][-Pprinter][jobID(s)]`

Purpose: Cancel print jobs that have been queued for printing; the **-P** option specifies the destination printer or class

If no arguments are supplied, the current job on the default destination is cancelled; once you use the `lpq` command to find out jobID(s) numbers, you can specify one or more job ID numbers to cancel those jobs, or use the – option to cancel all jobs

This command is part of the Common UNIX Printing System (CUPS)

Output: Cancelled print jobs on designated printers

Options and Option Arguments:

-E	Force encrypted connection to the server
-P'printer'	The default printer or designated 'printer'
-	Delete all jobs in the print spool

Command Arguments:

jobID(s) Job ID number(s) for jobs you want to dequeue

Example(s): Dequeue Job Number 3991 from the print queue at qpr: `lprm –Pqpr 3991`

---

ls—List contents of directory

Syntax: `ls [-aAbcCdfFgilLmnopqrRstux1]` ['file'...]

Purpose: For each 'file' that is a directory, list the contents of the directory; for each 'file' that is an ordinary file, repeat its name and any other information requested

Output: The output is sorted alphabetically by default. When no argument is given, the current directory is listed. When several arguments are given, the arguments are first sorted appropriately, but file arguments appear before directories and their contents.

Options:

-a	List all entries, including those that begin with a dot (.), which are normally not listed
-A	List all entries, including those that begin with a dot (.), with the exception of the working directory (.) and the parent directory (..)
-b	Force printing of nonprintable characters to be in the octal \'ddd' notation
-c	Use time of last modification of the i-node (file created, mode changed, and so on) for sorting (-t) or printing (-l or –n)
-C	Multicolumn output with entries sorted down the columns
-d	If an argument is a directory, list only its name (not its contents)
-f	Force each argument to be interpreted as a directory; list the name found in each slot
-F	Put a slash (/) after each filename if the file is a directory, an asterisk (*) if the file is an executable, and an at-sign (@) if the file is a symbolic link
-g	Same as –l, except that the owner is not printed
-i	For each file, print the i-node number in the first column of the report
-l	List in long format, giving mode, ACL indication, number of links, owner, group, size in bytes, and time of last modification for each file
-L	If an argument is a symbolic link, list the file or directory the link references rather than the link itself
-m	Stream output format; files are listed across the page, separated by commas

-n	Same as **-l**, except that the owner's UID and group's GID numbers are printed, rather than the associated character strings
-o	The same as **-l**, except that the group is not printed
-p	Put a slash (/) after each filename if the file is a directory
-q	Force printing of nonprintable characters in file names as the question mark (?)
-r	Reverse the order of sort to get reverse alphabetic or oldest first, as appropriate
-R	Recursively list subdirectories encountered
-s	Give size in blocks, including indirect blocks, for each entry
-t	Sort by time stamp (latest first) instead of by name
-u	Use time of last access instead of last modification for sorting (with the **-t** option) or printing (with the **-l** option)
-x	Multicolumn output with entries sorted across, rather than down, the page
-1	Print one entry per line of output

Command Arguments:

'file'	Pathname of a file to be written; if the file specified is not found, a diagnostic message will be output to stderr

Example(s):	List only the names of all files in the present working directory that have the file extension .pdf: `ls *.pdf`
	Display a long listing of all hidden and regular files in the present working directory: `ls -la`

---

mail–Read mail or send mail to users

Syntax:	*Sending mail*
	`mail [-tw] [-m 'message type'] 'recipient'...`
	Reading mail
	`mail [-ehpPqr] [-f 'file']`
Purpose:	Send or read e-mail to/from other users
Output:	When sending e-mail, the user is allowed to compose a message with a header; while reading e-mail, the user is prompted for appropriate commands to view and dispose of messages. The `mail` command, unless otherwise influenced by command line arguments, prints a user's mail messages in last-in, first-out (LIFO) order.

Options and Option Arguments:

The following affect sending mail:

-m'message type'	Add a Message-Type: line to the message header with the value 'message type'
-t	Add a To: line to the message header for each 'recipient'
-w	Send a letter to a remote recipient without waiting for completion of the remote transfer program

The following affect reading mail:

-e	Do not print mail

-h	Display a window of headers initially, rather than the latest message
-p	Print all messages without prompting for disposition
-P	Print all messages with 'all' header lines displayed, rather than the default selective header line display
-q	Mail terminates after interrupts
-r	Print messages in first-in, first-out (FIFO) order
-f'file'	Use 'file' (e.g., mbox) instead of the default 'mailfile'

For each message, the user is prompted with a ? and a line is read from the standard input. The following commands are available to determine the disposition of the message:

#	Print the number of the current message
-	Print previous message
<new-line>, +, or **n**	Print next message
!'command'	Escape to shell to do 'command'
a	Print message that arrived during mail session
d or **dp**	Delete current message and print next message
d'n'	Delete message number 'n'; do not go on to next message
dq	Delete message and quit mail
h	Display a window of headers around current message
h'n'	Display a window of headers around message number 'n'
ha	Display headers of all messages in user's 'mailfile'
hd	Display headers of messages scheduled for deletion
m['persons']	Mail (and delete) the current message to named 'persons'
n	Print message number 'n'
p	Print current message again, overriding any indications of binary (i.e., unprintable) content
P	Override default brief mode and print current message again, displaying all header lines
q or **<Ctrl-D>**	Put undeleted mail back in 'mailfile' and quit mail
r['users']	Reply to sender and other 'user's; then delete message
s['files']	Save message in the named 'file's (mbox is default) and delete message
u['n']	Undelete message number 'n' (default is last read)
w['files']	Save message contents, without any header lines, in the named 'files' (mbox is default) and delete message
x	Put all mail back in 'mailfile' unchanged and exit mail
y['files']	Same as -w option
?	Print a command summary

Command Arguments:

'recipient'... A 'recipient' is usually a valid username or Internet e-mail address. When 'recipients' are named, mail assumes that a message is being sent. It reads from stdin to eof (<Ctrl-D>) or, if reading from a terminal device, until it reads a line consisting of just a period. When either of those indicators is received, `mail` adds the letter to the mailfile for each 'recipient'.

Example(s):   Run `mail` and display a list of message headers rather than the default message: `mail —h`

---

make–Maintain, update, and regenerate related programs and files

Syntax: **make** [**-d** dd D DD e] [**-f** 'makefile'] ...] ['target'] ['macro=value']

Purpose: Maintain the most current versions of executable program modules

Output: List of shell commands associated with each target, typically to create or update a file of the same name

Options and Option Arguments:

-d   Display the reasons why `make` chooses to rebuild a target

-dd   Display the dependency check and processing in detail

-D   Display the text of the 'makefiles' read

-DD   Display the text of the 'makefiles', make.rules file, the statefile, and all hidden dependency reports

-e   Environment variables override assignments within 'makefiles'

-f'makefile'   Use the description file makefile. A '-' as the 'makefile' argument denotes stdin; contents of 'makefile', when present, override the standard set of implicit rules and predefined macros

Command Arguments:

'target'   Target names, which are the executable modules

'macro=value'   Macro definition; this definition overrides any regular definition for the specified macro within the makefile itself or in the environment

Example(s):   Print a test session using the makefile on stdout instead of executing the instructions in the makefile: `make —n source.c`

---

man–Find and display reference manual pages

Syntax: **man** [-] [**-adFlrt**] [**-M** 'path'] [**-T** 'macro-package'] [**-s** 'section'] 'name'...
            man [**-M** 'path'] **-k** 'keyword'...
            man [**-M** 'path'] **-f** 'file'...

Purpose: Display the UNIX online reference manual pages

Output: Complete manual pages that the user selects by 'name' or one-line summaries selected either by 'keyword' **(k)**, or by the name of an associated file **(-f)**

Options and Option Arguments:

-a   Show all manual pages matching 'name' within the manpath search path

-d   Debug; display what a section specifier evaluates to, method used for searching, and paths searched by man

-f'file'...   Attempt to locate manual pages related to any of the given 'file's

-F   Force man to search all directories specified by manpath or the man.cf file, rather than using the windex lookup database

-k'keyword'... Print out one-line summaries from the windex database (table of contents) that contain any of the given 'keyword's

-l   List all manual pages found within the search path matching 'name'

-M'path'   Specify an alternative search path for manual pages

-r   Reformat man page but do not display it

-s'section'... Specify sections of the manual for man to search

-t   Arrange for the specified man pages to be formatted for a troff display

-T'macro-package'   Format man pages, by using 'macro-package', rather than the standard man macros

Command Arguments:

'name'   A keyword or the name of a standard utility

Example(s):   Output the man command content for ssh in a file named sshdoc.txt in the present working directory: `man ssh > sshdoc.txt`

---

mesg–Permit or deny messages

Syntax: `mesg [-n | -y | n | y]`

Purpose: Allow other users to send write, talk, or other utility messages to your console window

Output: With no arguments, report the current state without changing it

Options:

-n | n   Deny permission to other users to send message to the terminal

-y | y   Grant permission to other users to send messages to the terminal

Command Arguments: None

Example(s):   Deny message writing to your terminal: `mesg n`

---

mkdir–Make directories

Syntax: `mkdir [-m 'mode'] [-p] 'dir'...`

Purpose: Create one or more directories under a parent directory

Output: Specified directories under a parent directory for which user has write permission

Options and Option Arguments:

-m'mode'   Allow users to specify mode to be used for new directories; choices for modes are listed under the chmod command

-p   Creates 'dir' by creating all the nonexisting parent directories first. The mode given to intermediate directories will be the difference between 777 and the bits set in the file mode creation mask. The difference, however, must be at least 300 (write and execute permission for the user).

Command Arguments:

'dir'   Pathname of a directory to be created

Example(s):   Create a directory below the present working directory named fall03:
```
mkdir fall03
```

---

more–Browse or page through a text file

Syntax: **more** [**-cdflrsuw**] [–'lines'] [**+**'linenumber'] [**+**/'pattern'] ['filename'...]

Purpose: Display file(s) one screenful at a time on the console window

Output: If stdout is not a terminal, more acts like cat(1), except that a header is printed before each file in a series

Options and Option Arguments:

  -c   Clear before displaying; redraw the screen instead of scrolling (for faster displays)

  -d   Display error messages rather than ringing the terminal bell if an unrecognized command is used

  -s   Squeeze; replace multiple blank lines with a single blank line

  -f   Do not fold long lines

  -l   Do not treat formfeed characters (**<Ctrl-L>**) as page breaks

  -r   Cause more to interpret control characters from input

  -u   Suppress generation of underlining escape sequences

  -w   Normally, more exits at end of its input, but with **-w**, prompts and waits for any key to be struck before exiting

  –'lines'   Display the indicated number of 'lines' in each screenful, rather than the default (the number of lines in the terminal screen less 2)

  +'linenumber'   Start up at 'linenumber'

  +/'pattern'   Start up two lines above the line containing the regular expression 'pattern'

Command Arguments:

'filename'... Files to be scrolled through

Example(s):   Page through the file named sshdoc.txt, showing the control characters as <Ctrl-x>:
```
more -r sshdoc.txt
```

---

mv–Move or rename files

Syntax: **mv** [**-fi**] 'source' 'target file'
               mv [**-fi**] 'source...' 'target dir'

Purpose: Move files and directories and rename them

Output:	In the first syntactic form, mv moves the file named by the 'source' argument to the destination specified by the 'target file'; 'source' and 'target file' may not have the same name. If 'target file' does not exist, mv creates a file named 'target file'. If 'target file' exists, its contents are overwritten. This first syntactic form is recognized when the final argument does not name an existing directory.
	In the second syntactic form, mv moves each file named by a 'source' argument to a destination file in the existing directory named by the 'target dir' argument. The destination path for each 'source' is the concatenation of the target directory, a single slash character (/), and the last pathname component of the 'source'. This second form is recognized when the final argument names an existing directory.

Options:

-f	Move the file(s) without prompting even if writing over an existing 'target'
-i	Prompt for confirmation whenever the move would overwrite an existing 'target'. A y answer means that the move should proceed. Any other answer prevents mv from over-writing 'target'.

Command Arguments:

'source'	Pathname of a file or directory to be moved
'target file'	New pathname for the file or directory being moved
'target dir'	Pathname of an existing directory into which the input files are to be moved

Example(s):	Rename the file named file1 in the present working directory to file2: `mv file1 file2`
	Push or move the file named file2 up to the parent of the present working directory: `mv file2 ..`
	Move the file named filex down into the subdirectory named junk: `mv filex junk`

---

nice–Change scheduling priority of a command

Syntax:	**nice** [–'increment' | **-n** 'increment'] 'command' ['argument'...]
Purpose:	Execute a command line at a lower priority than it ordinarily has
Output:	Commands run at a lower scheduling priority

Options and Option Arguments:

–'increment' | -n 'increment'	An 'increment' must be in the range 1–19; if not specified, an 'increment' of 10 is used. An 'increment' greater than 19 is equivalent to 19.

Command Arguments:

'command'	Name of a command to be invoked
'argument'	Any string to be supplied as an argument when 'command' is invoked

Example(s):	Run the lpr command on the file bank.eps with the lowest possible priority: `nice -n 19 lpr -Pqpr bank.eps`

nm–Print name list of an object file

Syntax:	**nm** [**-AChlnPprRsuVv**] [**-ox**] [**-g** | **-u**] [**-t** 'format'] 'file'...
Purpose:	Display the symbol table of each ELF object file specified by 'file'
Output:	Symbol table on stdout

Options and Option Arguments:

-A	Write full pathname or library name of an object on each line
-C	Clarify C++ symbol names before printing them
-g	Write only external (global) symbol information
-h	Do not display output heading data
-l	Distinguish between weak and global symbols by appending a * to the key letter for weak symbols
-n	Sort external symbols by name before they are printed
-o	Print the value and size of a symbol in octal instead of decimal (equivalent to -t o)
-p	Produce easy-to-parse, terse output; each symbol name is preceded by its value (blanks if undefined) and one of the following letters:

	A	Absolute symbol
	B	bss (uninitialized data space) symbol
	D	Data object symbol
	F	File symbol
	N	Symbol has no type
	S	Section symbol
	T	Text symbol
	U	Undefined

-P	Write information in a portable output format, as specified in stdout
-r	Prepend name of the object file or archive to each output line
-R	Print archive name (if present), followed by object file and symbol name
-s	Print section name instead of section index
-t'format'	Write each numeric value in the specified format; the format depends on a single character used as the 'format' option argument

	d	Write offset in decimal (default)
	o	Write offset in octal
	x	Write offset in hexadecimal

-u	Print undefined symbols only
-v	Sort external symbols by value before they are printed
-V	Print the version of the nm command executing on stderr
-x	Print the value and size of a symbol in hexadecimal instead of decimal

Command Arguments:

'file' Pathname of an object file, executable file, or object-file library

Example(s): Display the version of the nm command: nm −V
Run nm on the object library mathlib.o: nm mathlib.o

---

nohup–Run a command immune to hangups

Syntax: **nohup** 'command' ['arguments']

Purpose: Execute the named command and arguments after user has logged off

Output: All stopped, running, and background jobs will ignore hangup signal and continue running, if their invocations are preceded by the nohup command or if the process programmatically has chosen to ignore the hangup signal

Options and Option Arguments: None

Command Arguments:

'command' Command to be invoked; if the 'command' operand names any special utilities, the results are undefined

'arguments' Any string to be supplied as an argument when invoking the 'command' operand

Example(s): Run the lpr command even after you've logged out:
nohup lpr −Pqpr bank.eps

---

od–Octal dump

Syntax: **od** [**−bcCDdFfOoSsvXx**] [−] ['file'] ['offset string']
od [**−bcCDdFfOoSsvXx**] [**−A** 'address base'] [**−j** 'skip'] [**−N** 'count']
[**−t** 'type string'] ...[−] ['file']

Purpose: Display the octal representation of a file, including nonprinting characters

Output: Copies sequentially each input file to stdout and transforms input data according to the output types specified by the options

Options and Option Arguments:

−A 'address base' Specify the input offset base. The address base option argument must be a character. The characters d, o, and x specify that the offset base will be written in decimal, octal, or hexadecimal, respectively.

−b Interpret bytes in octal

−c Display single-byte characters

−C Interpret bytes as single-byte or multibyte characters, according to the current setting of the lc_ctype locale category

−d Interpret words in unsigned decimal

−D Interpret long words in unsigned decimal

-f	Interpret long words in floating point
-F	Interpret double long words in extended precision
-j 'skip'	Jump over skip bytes from the beginning of the input
-N 'count'	Format no more than count bytes of input
-o	Interpret words in octal
-O	Interpret long words in unsigned octal
-s	Interpret words in signed decimal
-S	Interpret long words in signed decimal
-t 'type string' Specify one or more output types	
-v	Show all input data (verbose); without the **-v** option, all groups of output lines identical to the immediately preceding output line (except for byte offsets) will be replaced with a line containing only an asterisk (*)
-x	Interpret words in hex
-X	Interpret long words in hex

Command Arguments:

–	Use stdin in addition to any files specified; when this operand is not given, stdin is used only if no 'file' operands are specified
'file'	Pathname of a file to be read; if no 'file' operands are specified, stdin will be used

Example(s):   Dump the file sshdoc.txt to stdout showing named characters:
```
od -t a sshdoc.txt
```

---

paste–Merge corresponding or subsequent lines of files

Syntax: **paste** [**-s**] [**-d** 'list'] 'file'...

Purpose: Merge corresponding lines of files into vertical columns

Output: The **paste** command concatenates the corresponding lines of the given input files and writes the resulting lines to stdout. The default operation of **paste** will concatenate the corresponding lines of the input files. The newline character of every line except the line from the last input file will be replaced with a <Tab> character.

Options and Option Arguments:

-d 'list'	Unless a backslash character (\ ) appears in 'list', each character in 'list' is an element specifying a delimiter character. If a backslash character appears in 'list', the backslash character and one or more characters following it are an element specifying a delimiter character.
-s	Concatenate all the lines of each separate input file in command line order; the newline character of every line except the last line in each input file will be replaced with the <Tab> character, unless otherwise specified by the **-d** option.

Command Arguments:

'file'	Pathname of an input file. If - is specified for one or more of the 'file's, the standard input will be used; the standard input will be read one line at a time, circularly, for each instance of **-**.

Example(s):   Constructs a table of people's names and addresses in a single file named addbook from two files named name and address: `paste name address > addbook`

---

pine–A program for Internet news and e-mail

Syntax: `pine` ['options'] ['address'...]

Purpose: To provide a full-screen display e-mail system

Output: Send and receive e-mail, archive e-mail, and dispose of sent messages

Options and Option Arguments:

-c 'context-number'   Number corresponding to folder collection to which **-f** should be applied; by default, **-f** is applied to the first defined folder collection

-d'debug-level'   Output diagnostic information at 'debug-level' (0–9) to the current .'pine-debug' file; a value of 0 turns debugging off and suppresses the '.pine debug' file

-f'folder'   Open 'folder' (in first defined folder collection) instead of Inbox

-F'file'   Open named text file and view with Pine's browser

-h   Help: list valid command line options

-i   Start up in the Folder Index screen

-I'keystrokes'   Initial (comma separated list of) keystrokes that `pine` should execute upon startup

-k   Use function keys for commands

-l   Expand all collections in Folder List display

-n'number'   Start up with current message number set to 'number'

-o   Open first folder read-only

-p'config-file'   Use 'config-file' instead of default '.pinerc' as the personal configuration file

-P'config-file'   Use 'config-file' instead of default systemwide configuration file 'pine.conf' as the configuration file

-z   Enable <Ctrl-Z> and sigtstp so that `pine` may be suspended

-conf   Produce a sample/fresh copy of the systemwide configuration file, 'pine.conf', on stdout; this file is distinct from the per-user '.pinerc' file

-create_lu 'addrbook' 'sort-order'   Create auxiliary index (look-up) file for 'addrbook' and sort 'addrbook' in 'sort-order', which may be 'dont-sort', 'nickname', 'fullname', 'nickname-with-lists-last', 'or fullname-with-lists-last'

-pinerc'file'   Output fresh pinerc configuration to 'file'

-sort'order'   Sort the Folder Index display in one of the following orders: 'arrival', 'subject', 'from', 'date', 'size', 'orderedsubj' or 'reverse; 'arrival' order is the default

-'option'='value'   Assign 'value' to the config option 'option' (e.g., –signature-file=sig1or –featurelist=signature-at-bottom)

Command Arguments:

'address...'   Send mail to 'address'..., which will cause Pine to go directly into the message composer

Example(s):   Runs pine and starts with the Folder Index Screen instead of the Main Menu, then sorts the entries by sender: `pine -i -sort from`

---

ping–Send packets to network hosts and receive replies

Syntax: `ping[-dfLnqRrv][-ccount][-Iifaddr][-iwait][-lpreload]` `[-ppattern][-Sifaddr][-spacketsize][-tttl][-wmaxwait]`host

Purpose: Uses the ICMP protocol's mandatory ECHO_REQUEST datagram to elicit an ICMP ECHO_RESPONSE from a host or gateway. ECHO_REQUEST datagrams ("pings") have an IP and ICMP header, followed by a "struct timeval" and then an arbitrary number of "pad" bytes used to fill out the packet.

This program is intended for use in network testing, measurement, and management.

Output: Datagrams from "pinged" host

Options and Option Arguments:

-c'count'   Stop after sending (and receiving) count ECHO_RESPONSE packets

-D   Set the Don't Fragment bit

-d   Set the SO_DEBUG option on the socket being used

-f   Flood ping. Output packets as fast as they come back or one hundred times per second, whichever is more. For every ECHO_REQUEST sent, a period "." is printed, while for every ECHO_REPLY received, a backspace is printed. This provides a rapid display of how many packets are being dropped. Only the super-user may use this option. This can be very hard on a network and should be used with caution. Only root can do a flood ping.

-I'ifaddr'   Specify the interface to transmit from on machines with multiple interfaces; for unicast and multicast pings

-i'wait'   Wait seconds between sending each packet. The default is to wait for one second between each packet. This option is incompatible with the **-f** option.

-l'preload'   If preload is specified, `ping` sends that many packets as fast as possible before falling into its normal mode of behavior; only root may set a preload value

-L   For multicast pings, disable the loopback so the transmitting host doesn't see the ICMP requests

-n   Numeric output only; no attempt will be made to look up symbolic names for host addresses

-p'pattern'   You may specify up to 16 "pad" bytes to fill out the packet you send. This is useful for diagnosing data-dependent problems in a network. For example, "**-p** ff" will cause the sent packet to be filled with all ones.

-q   Quiet output; nothing is displayed except the summary lines at startup time and when finished

-R   Record route. Includes the RECORD_ROUTE option in the ECHO_REQUEST packet and displays the route buffer on returned packets. Note that the IP header is only large enough for nine such routes. Many hosts ignore or discard this option.

-r	Bypass the normal routing tables and send directly to a host on an attached network. If the host is not on a directly attached network, an error is returned. This option can be used to ping a local host through an interface that has no route through it (e.g., after the interface was dropped by **routed**).
-s'packetsize'	Specifies the number of data bytes to be sent. The default is 56, which translates into 64 ICMP data bytes when combined with the 8 bytes of ICMP header data. If the **-D** or **-T** options are specified, or the **-t** option to a unicast destination, a raw socket will be used and the 8 bytes of header data are included in packet size.
-T'tos'	Use the specified type of service
-t'ttl'	Use the specified time-to-live
-v	Verbose output; ICMP packets other than ECHO_RESPONSE that are received are listed
-w'maxwait'	Specifies the number of seconds to wait for a response to a packet before transmitting the next one; the default is 10

Command Arguments:

host	Hostname for the host you want to ping

Example(s):	Ping the host egr.up.edu:
	`ping egr.up.edu`
	Ping the host egr.up.edu with 3 datagram packets, of byte size 2040:
	`ping -c 3 -s 2040 egr.up.edu`

---

pr–Paginate and print files

Syntax:	**pr** [+'page'] [-'column'] [**-adFmrt**] [**-e**['char']['gap']] [**-h** 'header'] [**-i**['char']['gap']] [**-l** 'lines'] [**-n**['char']['width']] [**-o** 'offset'] [**-s**['char']] [**-w** 'width'] [**-fp**] ['file'...]
Purpose:	Format files in pages, according to options, and display on standard output
Output:	Each page contains a heading of page number, filename, date, and time

Options and Option Arguments:

+'page'	Begin output at page number 'page' of formatted input
-'column'	Produce multicolumn output arranged in 'column' columns (default is 1) and write down each column in the order in which the text is received from the input file
-a	Modify effect of the -'column' option so that the columns are filled across the page in a round-robin order
-d	Produce double-spaced output
-e['char']['gap']	Expand each input <Tab> character to the next greater column position specified by the formula 'n' *'gap'+'1', where 'n' is an integer > 0; if any nondigit character, 'char', is specified, it will be used as the input tab character
-f	Use a formfeed character for new pages
-h'header'	Use the string 'header' to replace the contents of the 'file' operand in the page header

-l'lines'   Override the 66-line default and reset the page length to 'lines'

-m   Merge files; format stdout so that pr writes one line from each file specified by 'file', side by side, into text columns of equal fixed widths according to the number of column positions

-n['char']['width']   Provide 'width'-digit line numbering (default for 'width' is 5); if 'char' (any nondigit character) is given, it will be appended to the line number to separate it from whatever follows (default for 'char' is a <Tab> character)

-o 'offset'   Precede each line of output by offset <space>s

-p   Pause before beginning each page if stdout is directed to a terminal

-r   Write no diagnostic reports on failure to open files

-s['char']   Separate text columns by the single character 'char' instead of by the appropriate number of <space> characters (default for 'char' is the <Tab> character)

-t   Write neither the five-line identifying header nor the five-line trailer usually supplied for each page; quit writing after the last line of each file without spacing to the end of the page

-w'width'   Set the width of the line to 'width' column positions for multiple text-column output only

-F   Fold the lines of the input file. When used in multicolumn mode (with the -a or -m options), lines will be folded to fit the current column's width; otherwise, they will be folded to fit the current line width (80 columns).

-i['char']['gap']   In output, replace <space> characters with <Tab> characters wherever one or more adjacent <space> characters reach column positions 'gap+1', '2*gap+1', '3*gap+1', and so on. If 'gap' is 0 or is omitted, default <Tab> settings at every eighth column position are used. If any nondigit character, 'char', is specified, it will be used as the output <Tab> character.

Command Arguments:

'file'   Pathname of a file to be written; if no 'file' operands are specified or if a 'file' operand is -, stdin will be used

Example(s):   Constructs a three-column list from three input files, f1, f2, and f3, in the file listc:

```
pr —m f1 f2 f3 > listc
```

---

prs–Display selected portions of an SCCS history

Syntax: **prs** [**-ael**] [**-c**'date-time'] [**-d**'dataspec'] [**-r**'sid'] 's.filename'...

Purpose: Display part or all the SCCS file in a user-supplied format

Output: Part or all of an SCCS file at stdout; in the absence of options, prs displays the delta table (version log)

Options and Option Arguments:

-a   Include all deltas, including those marked as removed

-e   Request information for all deltas created earlier than, and including, the delta indicated with -r or -c

-l   Request information for all deltas created later than, and including, the delta indicated with -r or -c

-c'date-time'   Display information on the latest delta checked in prior to the date and time indicated by the 'date-time' argument; the 'date-time' argument takes the form 'yy'['mm'['dd'['hh'['mm'['ss']]]]]

-d'dataspec' Produce a report according to the indicated data specification

-r'sid'   Specify the SCCS ID (SID) of the delta for which information is desired

Command Arguments:

's.filename'...   SCCS file(s) to be examined

Example(s):   Display the delta table for specified file s.source.c: `prs s.source.c`

---

ps–Report process status

Syntax: `ps [-aAcdefjl] [-g 'grplist'] [-n 'namelist'] [[-o 'format'] ...]`
`[-p 'proclist'] [-s 'sidlist'] [-t 'term'] [-u 'uidlist'] [-U 'uidlist']`
`[-G 'gidlist']`

Purpose: Display information on active processes

Output: A five-column display of process identification number (pid), terminal on which displayed (tt), state (e.g., sleeping, idle, running or static), amount of time running (time), and command name with which the process was started (command), all shown on stdout

Options and Option Arguments:

-a   Print information about processes most frequently requested

-A   Write information for all processes

-c   Print information in a format that reflects scheduler properties

-d   Print information about all processes except session leaders

-e   Print information about every process now running

-f   Generate a full list

-g'grplist'   List only process data whose group leader's ID number(s) appears in 'grplist' (A group leader is a process whose process ID number is identical to its process group ID number.)

-G'gidlist'   Write information for processes whose real group ID numbers are given in 'gidlist'; the 'gidlist' must be a single argument in the form of a blank-separated or comma-separated list

-j   Print session ID and process group ID

-l   Generate a five-column-wide listing of process information

-n'namelist' Specify the name of an alternative system 'namelist' file in place of the default

-o'format'   Write information according to the format specification given in 'format'

-p'proclist'   List only process data whose process ID numbers are given in 'proclist'

-s'sidlist'   List information on all session leaders whose IDs appear in 'sidlist'

-t'term'   List only process data associated with 'term'

-u'uidlist'   List only process data whose effective user ID number or login name is given in 'uidlist'

-u'uidlist'   Write information for processes whose real user ID numbers or login names are given in 'uidlist'

Command Arguments: None

Example(s):   Display a verbose listing of information about current processes running: `ps –l`

---

ranlib–Convert archives to random libraries

Syntax: **ranlib** 'archive'

Purpose: Add a table of contents to archive libraries, which converts each archive to a form that can be linked more rapidly

Output: Archived library

Options and Option Arguments: None

Command Arguments:

'archive'   Archive library

Example(s):   Add a table of contents to the object file library mathlib.a: `ranlib mathlib.a`

---

rcp–Remote file copy

Syntax: **rcp** [**-p**] 'filename1' 'filename2'
                   rcp [**-pr**] 'filename...' 'directory'

Purpose: Copy files between one or more machines connected in a network

Output: Copied files

Options:

-p   Attempt to give each copy the same modification times, access times, modes, and ACLs, if applicable, as the original file

-r   Copy each subdirectory rooted at 'filename'; destination must be a directory

Command Arguments:

Each 'filename' or 'directory' argument is either a remote file name of the form 'hostname':'path' or a local file name (containing no ":" (colon) characters, or "/" (backslash) before any ":" (colon) characters). If a 'filename' is not a full pathname, it is interpreted relative to your home directory on 'hostname'. Hostnames can also take the form 'username'@'hostname':'filename' to use 'username' rather than the current local user's name as the username on the remote host. Internet domain addressing of the remote host takes the form 'username'@'host.domain': 'filename' that specifies the username to be used, the hostname, and the domain in which that host resides. Filenames that are not full pathnames will be interpreted relative to the home directory of the user named 'username' on the remote host.

Example(s):   Copy all PDF files in the present working directory to the directory lhotse.up.edu/koretsky/acrobat, retaining the same file permissions:
                   `rcp –p *.pdf lhotse.up.edu:/koretsky/acrobat`

rcs–Change RCS file attributes

Syntax:	**rcs** 'options' 'file'...
Purpose:	Create new RCS files or change attributes of existing files; an RCS file contains multiple revisions of text, an access list, a change log, descriptive text, and some control attributes
Output:	New or modified RCS file(s)

Options and Option Arguments:

-i	Create and initialize a new RCS file, but do not make any revision
-a'logins'	Append the login names appearing in the comma-separated list 'logins' to the access list of the RCS file
-A'oldfile'	Append the access list of 'oldfile' to the access list of the RCS file
-e['logins']	Erase the login names appearing in the comma-separated list 'logins' from the access list of the RCS file
-b['rev']	Set the default branch to 'rev'
-k'subst'	Set the default keyword substitution to 'subst'
-l['rev']	Lock the revision with number 'rev'
-u['rev']	Unlock the revision with number 'rev'
-L	Set locking to 'strict'
-U	Set locking to 'nonstrict'
-m'rev':'msg'	Replace revision 'rev's log message with 'msg'
-M	Do not send mail when doing so would break somebody else's lock
-n'name'[:['rev']]	Associate the symbolic name 'name' with the branch or revision 'rev'
-N'name'[:['rev']]	Act like **-n**, except override any previous assignment of 'name'
-o'range'	Delete ("outdate") the revisions given by 'range'
-q	Run quietly; do not print diagnostics
-I	Run interactively, even if the standard input is not a terminal
-s'state'[:'rev']	Set the state attribute of the revision 'rev' to 'state'
-t['file']	Write descriptive text from the contents of the named 'file' into the RCS file, deleting the existing text
-t–'string'	Write descriptive text from the 'string' into the RCS file, deleting the existing text
-T	Preserve the modification time on the RCS file unless a revision is removed
-V	Print RCS's version number
-V'n'	Emulate RCS version 'n'; see co(1) for details
-x'suffixes'	Use 'suffixes' to characterize RCS files
-z'zone'	Use 'zone' as the default time zone

Command Arguments:

file ...	RCS file(s) to be modified
Example(s):	Create a new RCS-encoded file named RCS/options1: rcs –I options1
	Remove revision 2.0 from the RCS file options1: rcs –o2.0 options1

rcsdiff–Compare versions of an RCS file with `diff`

Syntax:	`rcsdiff` ['options'] ['diffoptions'] 'file'...
Purpose:	Compare revision versions of an RCS file
Output:	Differences in revisions between two files at stdout

Options and Option Arguments:

-kc	Expand keywords using style c
-q[R]	Quiet mode; don't show diagnostics; R is a file revision
-rR1	Use Revision 1 in comparison
-rR2	Use Revision 2 in comparison; **-r**R1 must be specified
-Vn	Emulate version 'n' of RCS
-xsuf	Specify an alternative list of suffixes suf
'diffoptions'	Any valid `diff` options (*see* `diff`)

Command Arguments:

'file'...	RCS file revisions to compare

Example(s):   Compare RCS revisions in files source1 and source2: `rcsdiff source1 source2`

---

rcsmerge–Merge RCS revisions

Syntax:	`rcsmerge` ['options'] 'file'...
Purpose:	Incorporate changes between two revisions of an RCS file into the corresponding working file
Output:	Merged RCS file at stdout if **-p** option is specified

Options and Option Arguments:

-A	Merge all changes leading from 'file2' to 'file3' into 'file1' and generate the most verbose output
-E, -e	Specify conflict styles that generate less information than **-A**
-k'subst'	Use 'subst' style keyword substitution
-p['rev']	Send the result to stdout instead of overwriting the working file
-q['rev']	Run quietly; do not print diagnostics
-r['rev']	Merge with respect to revision 'rev'; here an empty 'rev' stands for the latest revision on the default branch, normally the head
-V	Print RCS's version number
-V'n'	Emulate RCS version 'n'
-x'suffixes'	Use 'suffixes' to characterize RCS files
-z'zone'	Use 'zone' as the time zone for keyword substitution

Command Arguments:

'file'...	Up to three different RCS versions of a file

Example(s):   Combine the currently checked-out version and version (1.1.1.2) of the input.cfile, and save it in merged_input.c: `rcsmerge —r1.1.1.2 —p input.c > merged_input.c`

---

rlog–Print log messages and other information about RCS files

Syntax: `rlog` ['options'] 'file'...

Purpose: Print the following complete information for each RCS file: RCS pathname, working pathname, head (i.e., the number of the latest revision on the trunk), default branch, access list, locks, symbolic names, suffix, total number of revisions, number of revisions selected for printing, and descriptive text

Output: Without options, `rlog` prints complete information at stdout

Options and Option Arguments:

-L   Ignore RCS files that have no locks set

-R   Print only the name of the RCS file

-h   Print only the RCS pathname, working pathname, head, default branch, access list, locks, symbolic names, and suffix

-t   Print the same as –h, plus the descriptive text

-N   Do not print the symbolic names

-b   Print information about the revisions on the default branch, normally the highest branch on the trunk

-d'dates'   Print information about revisions with a check-in date/time in the ranges given by the semicolon-separated list of 'dates'

-l['lockers']   Print information about locked revisions only

-r['revisions']   Print information about revisions given in the comma-separated list 'revisions' of revisions and ranges

-s'states'   Print information about revisions whose state attributes match one of the states given in the comma-separated list 'states'

-w['logins']   Print information about revisions checked in by users with login names appearing in the comma-separated list 'logins'

-V   Print RCS's version number

-V'n'   Emulate RCS version 'n' when generating logs

-x'suffixes'   Use 'suffixes' to characterize RCS files

-z'zone'   Specify the date output format and the default time zone for 'date' in the –d'dates' option

Command Arguments:

'file'...   RCS file(s) about which the user wants information

Example(s):   Display files that have been checked out by user sarwar for editing:
`rlog —L —R —lsarwar RCS/*`

rlogin–Remote login

Syntax:	`rlogin` [`-L`] [`-8`] [`-e`'c'] [`-l` 'username'] 'hostname'
Purpose:	Connect via network connection to a remote host
Output:	After the user supplies a password, a new login session begins in the console window

Options and Option Arguments:

`-L`	Allow the session to be run in "litout" mode
`-8`	Pass 8-bit data instead of 7-bit data across the network
`-e`'c'	Specify a different escape character, 'c', for the line used to disconnect from the remote host
`-l`'username'	Specify a different 'username' for the remote login; if this option is not used, the remote username used is the same as the user's local username

Command Arguments:

'hostname'	Listed in the 'hosts' database, which may be contained in the /etc/hosts file, the Network Information Service (NIS) hosts map, the Internet domain name server, or a combination of these locations. Each host has one official name (the first name in the database entry) and, optionally, one or more nicknames. Either official hostnames or nicknames may be specified in 'hostname'.

Example(s):	Remote login user bobk on host upsun25: `rlogin −l bobk upsun25`

rm–Remove files (unlink)

Syntax:	`rm` [`-fir`] 'file'...
Purpose:	Remove the directory entry specified by each 'file' argument
Output:	If 'file' is a symbolic link, the link will be removed, but the file or directory to which it refers will not be deleted. Users need not write permission to remove a symbolic link, provided that they have write permissions in the directory. If multiple 'file's are specified and removal of a 'file' fails for any reason, `rm` will write a diagnostic message to stderr, do nothing more to the current 'file', and go on to any remaining 'file's.

Options:

`-f`	Remove all files (whether write-protected or not) in a directory without prompting the user. In a write-protected directory, however, files are never removed (whatever their permissions are), but no messages are displayed. If the removal of a write-protected directory is attempted, this option will not suppress an error message.
`-i`	Prompt for confirmation before removing any files; it overrides the `-f` option and remains in effect even if stdin is not a terminal
`-r`	Recursively remove directories and subdirectories in the argument list. The directory will be emptied of files and removed. The user is normally prompted for removal of any write-protected files that the directory contains. The write-protected files are removed without prompting, however, if the `-f` option is used or if the standard input is not a terminal and the `-i` option is not used. Symbolic links encountered with this option will not be traversed. If the removal of a nonempty, write-protected

directory is attempted, the command will always fail (even if the **-f** option is used), resulting in an error message.

Command Arguments:

'file'   Pathname of file to be removed

Example(s):   Delete all files in directory /usr/local/help that end in the extension .pdf:
`rm/usr/local/help/*.pdf`

From the present working directory, delete all files contained in as well as the non-empty directory named fish, plus all subdirectories below fish, and all files in those subdirectories:
`rm-r fish`

Do the same thing as the previous example, but prompt the user before deletion of each file and directory:
`rm -ir fish`

---

rmdir–Remove directories

Syntax: **rmdir** [**-ps**] 'dirname'...

Purpose: Delete the empty directories specified from the parent directory; to delete nonempty directories, see the **rm -r** command

Output: With no options set, the mdir command removes empty directories with no confirmation. If 'dirname' does not exist, an error message is generated. Directories will be processed in the order specified. If a directory and a subdirectory of that directory are specified in a single invocation of **rmdir**, the subdirectory must be specified before the parent directory so that the parent directory will be empty when **rmdir** tries to remove it.

Options:

-p   Allow user to remove the directory 'dirname' and its parent directories that become empty. A message is printed on stderr about whether the whole path is removed or part of the path remains for some reason.

-s   Suppress the message printed on stderr when **-p** is in effect

Command Arguments:

'dirname'   Pathname of an empty directory to be removed

Example(s):   Delete all files in the directory /usr/local/help that end in the extension .pdf:
`rm /usr/local/help/*.pdf`

From the present working directory, delete all files contained in as well as the non-empty directory named fish, plus all subdirectories below fish, and all files in those subdirectories: `rm —r fish`

Do the same thing as the previous example, but prompt the user before deletion of each file and directory: `rm —ir fish`

Delete the empty directory catfish: `rmdir catfish`

rsh–Remote shell

Syntax:	**rsh** [**-n**] [**-l** 'username'] 'hostname' 'command' **rsh** 'hostname' [**-n**] [**-l** 'username'] 'command'
Purpose:	Execute a command on a remote host computer
Output:	The rsh command connects to the specified 'hostname' and executes the specified 'command'; rsh copies its stdin to the remote command, stdout of the remote command to its standard output, and stderr of the remote command to its stderr. Interrupt, quit, and terminate signals are propagated to the remote command; rsh normally terminates when the remote command does. If the local user omits 'command', instead of executing a single command, rsh logs the user on to the remote host, using rlogin.

Options and Option Arguments:

-l'username'	Use 'username' as the remote username instead of the user's local username; in the absence of this option, the remoteuser name is the same as the local username
-n	Redirect the input of rsh to /dev/null; needed to avoid conflicts between rsh and the shell that invokes it

Command Arguments:

'username'	The local user's username
'hostname'	Name of the remote host computer the local user wants to execute 'command' on
'command'	Command the local user wants to execute
Example(s):	Remote login to the computer lhotse.up.edu with the login name koretsky: rsh −l bobk upsun25

---

ruptime–Show host status of local machines

Syntax:	**ruptime** [**-alrtu**]
Purpose:	Give a status line display, showing each machine on the local network; formed from packets broadcast by each host on the network once a minute
Output:	Machines for which no status report has been received for 5 min are shown as being down; normally, the listing is sorted by host name, but this order can be changed by specifying one of the options

Options:

-a	Count even those users who have been idle for 1 hr or more
-l	Sort display by load average
-r	Reverse sorting order
-t	Sort display by up time
-u	Sort display by number of users

Command Arguments: None

Example(s):	Display the uptime status of local area network machines sorted by number of users: ruptime −u

rwho–Who is logged on to local machines

Syntax:	**rwho** [**-a**]
Purpose:	Produce output similar to who, but for all machines on the network. If no report has been received from a machine for 5 min, rwho considers the machine to be down and does not report users last known to be logged on to that machine.
Output:	If a user has not typed to the system for 1 min or more, rwho reports this idle time; if a user has not typed to the system for 1 hr or more, the user is omitted from the output of rwho unless the -a flag is given

Options:

-a	Report all users, regardless of whether they have typed to the system during the past hour

Command Arguments: None

Example(s):   Display usernames logged on to the local area network machines: rwho

sccs–Front end for the Source Code Control System (SCCS)

Syntax:	**sccs** [**-r**] [**-d**'rootprefix'] [**-p**'subdir'] 'subcommand' ['option'...] ['operands'] ['file'...]
Purpose:	Apply the indicated 'subcommand' to the history file associated with each indicated file
Output:	SCCS history file

Options and Option Arguments:

-d'rootprefix'	Define the root portion of the pathname for SCCS history files
-p'subdir'	Define the (sub)directory within which a history file is expected to reside
-r	Run sccs with the real user ID, rather than set to the effective user ID
'subcommand'	An SCCS utility name or the name of one of the pseudo-utilities
'option'	An option or option argument to be passed to 'subcommand'
'operands'	Operands to be passed to 'subcommand'

Command Arguments:

file ...	Source file(s)

Example(s):   Create an SCCS history file named s.input.c by executing the subcommand admin: sccs admin –iinput.c s.input.c

---

scp–Secure copy (remote file copy program)

Syntax:	**scp** [**-pqrvBC46**][**-F** ssh_config][**-S** program][**-P** port] [**-c** cipher] [**-i** identity_file][**-o** ssh_option] [[user@]host1:]file1[...] [[user@]host2:]file2[...]]
Purpose:	Copy files between hosts on a network. It uses ssh for data transfer, and uses the same authentication and provides the same security as ssh. Unlike rcp, scp will ask for passwords or passphrases if they are needed for authentication. Any filename may contain a host and user specification to indicate that the file is to be copied to/from that host. Copies between two remote hosts are permitted.

Output: Copied files on a remote host

Option and Option Arguments:

  -ccipher   Select the cipher to use for encrypting the data transfer; this option is directly passed to
              ssh

  -iidentity_file   Select the file from which the identity (private key) for RSA authentication
              is read; this option is directly passed to ssh

  -p   Preserve modification times, access times, and modes from the original file

  -r   Recursively copy entire directories

  -v   Verbose mode. Cause scp and ssh to print debugging messages about their progress.
              This is helpful in debugging connection, authentication, and configuration problems.

  -B   Selects batch mode (prevents asking for passwords or passphrases)

  -q   Disable the progress meter

  -C   Compression enable; pass the -C flag to ssh to enable compression

  -Fssh_config   Specify an alternative per-user configuration file for ssh; this option is directly passed
              to ssh

  -Pport   Specify the port to connect to on the remote host. Note that this option is written with
              a capital 'P', because -p is already reserved for preserving the times and modes of the
              file in rcp.

  -Sprogram   Name of program to use for the encrypted connection; the program must understand
              ssh options

  -ossh_option   Can be used to pass options to ssh in the format used in ssh_config. This is use-
              ful for specifying options for which there is no separate scp command-line flag. For
              example, forcing the use of protocol version 1 is specified using scp -o Protocol=1.

  -4   Forces scp to use IPv4 addresses only

  -6   Forces scp to use IPv6 addresses only

Command Arguments:

              file1[…],file2[…]   Source and destination file(s) on local and remote machines

Example(s):   Copies a local file named forwarding to the remote host lhotse.up.edu as forward, in
              verbose mode: scp -v forwarding lhotse.up.edu forward

---

sed–Stream editor

Syntax: **sed** [**-n**] [**-e** 'script'] … [**-f** 'script file'] … ['script'] ['file'…]

Purpose: Read one or more text files and make editing changes according to a script of editing
              commands; the script is obtained from either the 'script' option argument string or a
              combination of the option arguments from the e 'script' and -f 'script file' options

Output: Write editing changes to stdout

Options and Option Arguments:

  -e'script'   The 'script' argument is an edit command for sed; if there is just one -e option and
              no -f option, the flag -e may be omitted

  -f'script file'   Take the script from 'script file', which consists of editing commands, one per line

| **-n** | Suppress the default output |

Command Arguments:

| 'file' | Pathname of a file whose contents will be read and edited. If multiple 'file' operands are specified, named files will be read in the order specified and the concatenation will be edited. If no 'file' operands are specified, stdin will be used. |
| 'script' | A string to be used as the script of editing commands. The application must not present a 'script' that violates the restrictions of a text file except that the final character need not be a newline character. |

Example(s):   Read script file named dos, and apply it to edit the file windows.txt:
sed –f dos windows.txt

Display on stdout using the p command all lines in a file named book that contain the word "UNIX": sed '/UNIX/ p' book

---

sftp–Secure shell file transfer program

Syntax: **sftp**[**-v** C1][**-b** batchfile][**-o** ssh_option][**-s** subsystem of sftp_server][**-B** buffer_size]
[**-F** ssh_config][**-P** sftp_server path][**-R** num_requests][**-S** program]host
sftp [[user@]host[:file [file]]]
sftp [[user@]host[:dir[/]]]

Purpose: Interactive file transfer program, similar to ftp, performs all operations over an encrypted ssh transport. It can also use many features of ssh, such as public key authentication and compression. sftp connects and logs in to the specified host, then enters an interactive command mode.

The second usage format will retrieve files automatically if a noninteractive authentication method is used; otherwise, it will do so after successful interactive authentication.

The third usage format allows the sftp client to start in a remote directory.

Output: Files transferred between local and remote machine

Options and Option Arguments:

-bbatchfile	Batch mode reads a series of commands from an input batchfile instead of stdin. Since it lacks user interaction, it should be used in conjunction with noninteractive authentication. sftp will abort if any of the following commands fail: get, put, rename, ln, rm, mkdir, chdir, lchdir and lmkdir.
-ossh_option	Can be used to pass options to ssh in the format used in ssh_config. This is useful for specifying options for which there is no separate sftp command-line flag. For example, to specify an alternate port use: sftp -oPort=24.
-ssubsystem | sftp_server	Specifies the SSH2 subsystem or the path for an sftp server on the remote host; a path is useful for using sftp over protocol version 1, or when the remote sshd does not have an sftp subsystem configured
-v	Raise logging level; this option is also passed to ssh
-Bbuffer_size	Specify the size of the buffer that sftp uses when transferring files. Larger buffers require fewer round trips at the cost of higher memory consumption. The default is 32768 bytes.
-C	Enables compression (via ssh's -C flag)

-Fssh_config   Specifies an alternative per-user configuration file for ssh; this option is directly passed to ssh

-Psftp_server path   Connect directly to a local sftp server (rather than via ssh); this option may be useful in debugging the client and server

-Rnum_requests   Specify how many requests may be outstanding at any one time. Increasing this may slightly improve file transfer speed but will increase memory usage. The default is 16 outstanding requests.

-Sprogram   Name of the program to use for the encrypted connection; the program must understand ssh options

-1   Specify the use of protocol version 1

Interactive Commands:

Once in interactive mode, sftp understands a set of commands similar to those of `ftp`. Commands are case insensitive and pathnames may be enclosed in quotes if they contain spaces.

bye   Quit sftp

lcd path   Change local directory to path

chgrp grp path   Change group of file path to grp; grp must be a numeric GID

chmod mode path   Change permissions of file path to mode

chown own path   Change owner of file path to own; own must be a numeric UID

exit   Quit sftp

get [flags] remote-path [local-path]-   Retrieve the remote-path and store it on the local machine. If the local pathname is not specified, it is given the same name it has on the remote machine. If the -P flag is specified, then the file's full permission and access time are copied, too.

help   Display help text

lls[ls-options [path]]   Display local directory listing of either path or current directory if path is not specified

lmkdir path   Create local directory specified by path

ln oldpath newpath   Create a symbolic link from oldpath to newpath

lpwd   Print local working directory

ls[path]   Display remote directory listing of either path or current directory if path is not specified

lumask umask   Set local umask to umask

mkdir path   Create remote directory specified by path

put [flags] local-path [local-path]   Upload local-path and store it on the remote machine. If the remote pathname is not specified, it is given the same name it has on the local machine. If the -P flag is specified, then the file's full permission and access time are copied, too.

pwd   Display remote working directory

quit   Quit sftp

`rename oldpath`

`newpath`   Rename remote file from oldpath to newpath

`rmdir path`   Remove remote directory specified by path

`rm path`   Delete remote file specified by path

`symlink oldpath`

`newpath`   Create a symbolic link from oldpath to newpath

`!command`   Execute command in local shell

`!`   Escape to local shell

`?`   Synonym for help

Command Arguments:

host   Hostname of the computer you want to establish an ftp connection with

user@host   Username and hostname of the computer you want to establish an ftp connection with

Example(s): Start an interactive sftp session with the host lhotse.up.edu, and then retrieve the file guest from that host into the current working directory on your local host:
`sftp lhotse.up.edu`
`> get guest`

Sends a file named list from the present working directory to the remote host lhotse.up.edu:
`sftp list lhotse.up.edu`

---

sleep–Create a process that waits a specified time

Syntax: `sleep` 'time'

Purpose: Suspend the process that executes sleep for the 'time' specified

Output: Used in shell scripts, process is in the wait state for specified time

Options: None

Command Arguments:

'time'   Interval specified in seconds

Example(s): Create a process running in the background that reminds you to wake up in 10 minutes (600 seconds): `(sleep 600; echo "Wake UP") &`

---

sort–Sort, merge, or sequence check text files

Syntax: `sort` [`-cmu`] [`-o` 'output'] [`-T` 'directory'] [`-y` ['kmem']] [`-dfiMnr`] [`-b`] [`t` 'char'] [`-k` 'keydef'] ['file'...]

Purpose: Sort the lines in 'file', usually in alphabetical order. Comparisons are based on one or more sort keys extracted from each line of input. By default, there is one sort key: the entire input line. Lines are ordered according to a collating sequence.

Output: Files are sorted and merged; then sort writes the result to stdout

Options and Option Arguments:

-c   Check that the single input file is ordered as specified by the arguments and the collating sequence in effect

-m   Merge only; the input files are considered to be already sorted

-u   Unique; suppress all but one in each set of lines having equal keys

-o'output'   Specify name of an output file to be used instead of stdout

-T'directory'   Place temporary files in 'directory'

-y'kmem'   Amount of main memory initially used by sort; if 'kmem' is present, sort will start using that number of kilobytes of memory

The following options override the default ordering rules. When ordering options appear independently of any key field specifications, the requested field ordering rules are applied globally to all sort keys.

-d   "Dictionary" order: only letters, digits, and blanks (<spaces> and <Tabs>) are significant in comparisons

-f   Fold lowercase letters into uppercase letters

-i   Ignore nonprintable characters

-M   Compare as months; the first three nonblank characters of the field are folded to uppercase and compared

-n   Restrict the sort key to an initial numeric string, consisting of optional blank characters, optional minus sign, and zero or more digits with an optional radix character and thousands separators (as defined in the current locale), which will be sorted by arithmetic value

-r   Reverse the sense of comparisons

The treatment of field separators can be altered by using the following options:

-b   Ignore leading blank characters when determining the starting and ending positions of a restricted sort key

-t'char'   Use 'char' as the field separator character

Sort keys can be specified by using the following options:

-k'keydef'   Restricted sort key field definition with format defined as: **-k** 'field start' ['type'] ['field end' ['type']]

Command Arguments:

'file'   Pathname of a file to be sorted, merged, or checked; if no 'file' operands are specified or if a 'file' operand is -, stdin will be used

Example(s):   Alphabetize a file of words named "words", remove duplicate instances, and print the frequency of each on stdout: `sort -fd words | uniq -c`

---

spell—Report spelling errors

Syntax: `spell [-bilvx] [+'local file'] ['file']...`

Purpose: Collect words from the named 'file's and look them up in a spelling list; words that neither occur among nor are derivable (by applying certain inflections, prefixes, or suffixes) from words in the spelling list are written to stdout

Output: Misspelled words at stdout

Options and Option Arguments:

-b	Check British spelling
-i	Cause deroff to ignore .so and .nx commands
-l	Follow the chains of 'all' included files
-v	Print all words not literally in the spelling list, as well as plausible derivations from the words in the spelling list
-x	Print every plausible stem, one per line, with = preceding each word
+'local file'	Specify a set of words that are correct spellings (in addition to spell's own spelling list) for each job; a user-provided file, 'local file', contains a sorted list of words, one per line

Command Arguments:

'file'	Pathname of a text file to check for spelling errors; if no files are named, words are collected from stdin

Example(s):   Check the spelling of words in a file named quotes.txt and output the misspellings into a file named missed: `spell quotes.txt > missed`

---

ssh–Open SSH client (secure shell, remote login program)

Syntax: `ssh[-l` login_name]hostname or user@hostname [command]
`ssh[-afgknqstvxACNPTX1246][-b` bind_address][`-c` cipher_spec]
[`-e` escape_char][`-i` identity_file][`-l` login_name][`-m` mac_spec]
[`-o` option][`-p` port][`-F` configfile][`-L` port:host:hostport]
[`-R` port:host:hostport] [`-D` port] hostname or user@hostname
[command]

Purpose: ssh (SSH client) is a program for logging in to a remote machine and for executing commands on a remote machine. It is intended to replace rlogin and rsh, and provide secure encrypted communications between two untrusted hosts over an insecure network. X11 connections and arbitrary TCP/IP ports can also be forwarded over the secure channel.

ssh connects and logs in to the specified hostname. The user must prove his/her identity to the remote machine using one of several methods depending on the protocol version used.

Output: Secure shell connection between local and remote hosts.

SSH protocol version 1   First, if the machine the user logs in from is listed in /etc/hosts.equiv or /etc/shosts.equiv on the remote machine and the usernames are the same on both sides, the user is immediately permitted to log in. Second, if .rhosts or .shosts exists in the user's home directory on the remote machine and contains a line containing the name of the client machine and the name of the user on that machine, the user is permitted to log in. This form of authentication alone is normally not allowed by the server because it is not secure.

The second authentication method is the rhosts or hosts.equiv method combined with RSA-based host authentication. It means that if the login would be permitted by $HOME/.rhosts, $HOME/.shosts, /etc/hosts.equiv, or /etc/shosts.equiv, and if additionally the server can verify the client's host key (*see* /etc/**ssh**_known_hosts and $HOME/.ssh/known_hosts in the FILES section), only then is login permitted. This authentication method closes security holes due to IP spoofing, DNS spoofing, and routing spoofing. [*Note to the administrator:* /etc/hosts.equiv, $HOME/.rhosts, and the rlogin/rsh protocol in general are inherently insecure and should be disabled if security is desired.]

As a third authentication method, **ssh** supports RSA-based authentication. The scheme is based on public-key cryptography. There are cryptosystems where encryption and decryption are done using separate keys, and it is not possible to derive the decryption key from the encryption key. RSA is one such system. The idea is that each user creates a public/private key pair for authentication purposes. The server knows the public key, and only the user knows the private key. The file $HOME/**.ssh**/authorized_keys lists the public keys that are permitted for logging in. When the user logs in, the **ssh** program tells the server which key pair it would like to use for authentication. The server checks if this key is permitted, and if so, sends the user (actually the **ssh** program running on behalf of the user) a challenge, a random number, encrypted by the user's public key. The challenge can only be decrypted using the proper private key. The user's client then decrypts the challenge using the private key, proving that he/she knows the private key but without disclosing it to the server.

ssh implements the RSA authentication protocol automatically. The user creates his/her RSA key pair by running **ssh**-keygen(1). This stores the private key in $HOME/.ssh/ identity and the public key in $HOME/**.ssh**/identity.pub in the user's home directory. The user should then copy the identity.pub to $HOME/**.ssh**/authorized_keys in his/her home directory on the remote machine (the authorized_keys file corresponds to the conventional $HOME/.rhosts file and has one key per line, though the lines can be very long). After this, the user can log in without giving the password. RSA authentication is much more secure than rhosts authentication.

The most convenient way to use RSA authentication may be with an authentication agent.

If other authentication methods fail, **ssh** prompts the user for a password. The password is sent to the remote host for checking; however, since all communications are encrypted, the password cannot be seen by someone listening on the network.

SSH protocol version 2   When a user connects using protocol version 2, similar authentication methods are available. Using the default values for Preferred Authentications, the client will try to authenticate first using the hostbased method; if this method fails public key authentication is attempted, and; finally, if this method fails, keyboard-interactive and password authentication are tried.

The public key method is similar to RSA authentication described in the previous section and allows the RSA or DSA algorithm to be used: The client uses his private key,

$HOME/.ssh/id_dsa or $HOME/.ssh/id_rsa, to sign the session identifier and sends the result to the server. The server checks whether the matching public key is listed in $HOME/.ssh/authorized_keys and grants access if the key is found and the signature is correct. The session identifier is derived from a shared Diffie-Hellman value and is only known to the client and the server.

If public key authentication fails or is not available, a password can be sent encrypted to the remote host for proving the user's identity.

Additionally, **ssh** supports host-based or challenge-response authentication.

Protocol 2 provides additional mechanisms for confidentiality (the traffic is encrypted using 3DES, Blowfish, CAST128 or Arcfour) and integrity (hmac-md5, hmac-sha1). Note that protocol 1 lacks a strong mechanism for ensuring the integrity of the connection.

Login Session and Remote Execution   When the user's identity is accepted by the server, the server either executes the `given` command or logs in to the machine and gives the user a normal shell on the remote machine. All communication with the remote command or shell will be automatically encrypted.

If a pseudo-terminal is allocated (normal login session), the user can use the escape characters noted below.

If no pseudo tty is allocated, the session is transparent and can be used to reliably transfer binary data. On most systems, setting the escape character to "none" will also make the session transparent even if a tty is used.

The session terminates when the command or shell on the remote machine exits and all X11 and TCP/IP connections are closed. The exit status of the remote program is returned as the exit status of **ssh**.

Escape Characters   When a pseudo terminal is requested, **ssh** supports a number of functions through the use of an escape character.

A single tilde character can be sent as ~~ or by following the tilde by a character other than those described below. The escape character must always follow a newline to be interpreted as special. The escape character can be changed in configuration files using the EscapeChar configuration directive or on the command line by the -e option.

The supported escapes (assuming the default '~') are:

~.	Disconnect
~^Z	Background **ssh**
~#	List forwarded connections
~&	Background **ssh** at logout when waiting for forwarded connection / X11 sessions to terminate
~?	Display a list of escape characters
~C	Open command line (only useful for adding port forwardings using the -L and -R options)
~R	Request rekeying of the connection (only useful for **SSH** protocol version 2 and if the peer supports it)

X11 and TCP Forwarding   If the ForwardX11 variable is set to "yes" (or, see the description of the **-X** and **-x** options described later) and the user is using X11 (the DISPLAY environment variable is set), the connection to the X11 display is automatically forwarded to the remote side in such a way that any X11 programs started from the shell (or command) will go through the encrypted channel, and the connection to the real X server will be made from the local machine. The user should not manually set DISPLAY. Forwarding of X11 connections can be configured on the command line or in configuration files.

The DISPLAY value set by **ssh** will point to the server machine, but with a display number greater than zero. This is normal, and it happens because **ssh** creates a "proxy" X server on the server machine for forwarding the connections over the encrypted channel.

ssh will also automatically set up Xauthority data on the server machine. For this purpose, it will generate a random authorization cookie, store it in Xauthority on the server, and verify that any forwarded connections carry this cookie and replace it by the real cookie when the connection is opened. The real authentication cookie is never sent to the server machine (and no cookies are sent).

If the user is using an authentication agent, the connection to the agent is automatically forwarded to the remote side unless disabled on the command line or in a configuration file.

Forwarding of arbitrary TCP/IP connections over the secure channel can be specified either on the command line or in a configuration file. One possible application of TCP/IP forwarding is a secure connection to an electronic purse; another is going through firewalls.

Server Authentication ssh   automatically maintains and checks a database containing identifications for all hosts it has ever been used with. Host keys are stored in $HOME/**.ssh**/ known_hosts in the user's home directory. Additionally, the file /etc/**ssh_known_hosts** is automatically checked for known hosts. Any new hosts are automatically added to the user's file. If a host's identification ever changes, **ssh** warns about this and disables password authentication to prevent a Trojan horse from getting the user's password. Another purpose of this mechanism is to prevent man-in-the-middle attacks which could otherwise be used to circumvent the encryption. The StrictHostKeyChecking option can be used to prevent logins to machines whose host key is not known or has changed.

Options and Option Arguments:

-a   Disables forwarding of the authentication agent connection

-A   Enables forwarding of the authentication agent connection; this can also be specified on a per-host basis in a configuration file

-b bind_address   Specify the interface to transmit from on machines with multiple interfaces or aliased addresses

-c blowfish|3des|des   Selects the cipher to use for encrypting the session. 3des is used by default. It is believed to be secure. 3des (triple-des) is an encrypt-decrypt-encrypt triple with three different keys. blowfish is a fast-block cipher; it appears very secure and is much faster than 3des. des is only supported in the ssh client for interoperability with legacy protocol 1 implementations that do not support the 3des cipher. Its use is strongly discouraged due to cryptographic weaknesses.

-c cipher_spec   Additionally, for protocol version 2, a comma-separated list of ciphers can be specified in order of preference.

-e ch|^ch|none   Sets the escape character for sessions with a pty (default: '~'). The escape character is only recognized at the beginning of a line. The escape character followed by a dot ('.') closes the connection, followed by <Ctrl-Z> suspends the connection, and followed by itself sends the escape character once. Setting the character to "none" disables any escapes and makes the session fully transparent.

-f   Requests **ssh** to go to background just before command execution. This is useful if **ssh** is going to ask for passwords or passphrases, but the user wants it in the background. This implies –n. The recommended way to start X11 programs at a remote site is with something like ssh -f host xterm.

-g   Allows remote hosts to connect to local forwarded ports

-i identity_file   Selects a file from which the identity (private key) for RSA or DSA authentication is read. The default is $HOME/**.ssh**/identity for protocol version 1, and $HOME/**.ssh**/id_rsa and $HOME/**.ssh**/id_dsa for protocol version 2. Identity files may also be specified on a per-host basis in the configuration file. It is possible to have multiple –i options (and multiple identities specified in configuration files).

-I smartcard_device   Specifies which smartcard device to use; the argument is the device ssh should use to communicate with a smartcard used for storing the user's private RSA key

-k   Disables forwarding of Kerberos tickets and AFS tokens; this may also be specified on a per-host basis in the configuration file

-l login_name   Specifies the user to log in as on the remote machine; this also may be specified on a per-host basis in the configuration file

-m mac_spec   Additionally, for protocol version 2, a comma-separated list of MAC (message authentication code) algorithms can be specified in order of preference

-n   Redirects stdin from /dev/null (actually, prevents reading from stdin). This must be used when ssh is run in the background. A common trick is to use this to run X11 programs on a remote machine. For example, **ssh** –n shadows.cs.hut.fi emacs & will start an emacs on shadows.cs.hut.fi, and the X11 connection will be automatically forwarded over an encrypted channel. The **ssh** program will be put in the background. (This does not work if **ssh** needs to ask for a password or passphrase; *see* also the –f option.)

-N   Do not execute a remote command; this is useful for just forwarding ports (protocol version 2 only)

-o option   Can be used to give options in the format used in the configuration file; this is useful for specifying options for which there is no separate command-line flag

-p port   Port to connect to on the remote host; this can be specified on a per-host basis in the configuration file

-P   Use a nonprivileged port for outgoing connections. This can be used if a firewall does not permit connections from privileged ports. Note that this option turns off RhostsAuthentication and RhostsRSAAuthentication for older servers.

-q   Quiet mode; causes all warning and diagnostic messages to be suppressed

-s   May be used to request invocation of a subsystem on the remote system. Subsystems are a feature of the **SSH2** protocol that facilitate the use of **SSH** as a secure transport for other applications (e.g., **sftp**). The subsystem is specified as the remote command.

-t	Force pseudo-tty allocation. This can be used to execute arbitrary screen-based programs on a remote machine, which can be very useful, e.g., when implementing menu services. Multiple **-t** options force tty allocation, even if **ssh** has no local tty.
-T	Disable pseudo-tty allocation.
-v	Verbose mode. Causes **ssh** to print debugging messages about its progress. This is helpful in debugging connection, authentication, and configuration problems. Multiple **-v** options increases the verbosity. Maximum is 3.
-x	Disables X11 forwarding
-X	Enables X11 forwarding; this can also be specified on a per-host basis in a configuration file
-C	Requests compression of all data (including stdin, stdout, stderr, and data for forwarded X11 and TCP/IP connections). The compression algorithm is the same used by **gzip**, and the "level" can be controlled by the CompressionLevel option. Compression is desirable on modem lines and other slow connections, but it will only slow down things on fast networks. The default value can be set on a host-by-host basis in the configuration files.
-F configfile	Specifies an alternative per-user configuration file. If a configuration file is given on the command line, the system-wide configuration file (/etc/**ssh**_config) will be ignored. The default for the per-user configuration file is $HOME/.**ssh**/config.
-L port:host: hostport	Specifies that the given port on the local (client) host is to be forwarded to the given host and port on the remote side. This works by allocating a socket to listen to port on the local side, and whenever a connection is made to this port, the connection is forwarded over the secure channel, and a connection is made to host port hostport from the remote machine. Port forwardings can also be specified in the configuration file. Only root can forward privileged ports. IPv6 addresses can be specified with an alternative syntax: port/host/hostport
-R port:host:hostport	Specifies that the given port on the remote (server) host is to be forwarded to the given host and port on the local side. This works by allocating a socket to listen to port on the remote side, and whenever a connection is made to this port, the connection is forwarded over the secure channel, and a connection is made to host port hostport from the local machine. Port forwardings can also be specified in the configuration file. Privileged ports can be forwarded only when logging in as root on the remote machine. IPv6 addresses can be specified with an alternative syntax: port/host/hostport
-D port	Specifies a local "dynamic" application-level port forwarding. This works by allocating a socket to listen to port on the local side, and whenever a connection is made to this port, the connection is forwarded over the secure channel, and the application protocol is then used to determine where to connect to from the remote machine. Currently, the SOCKS4 protocol is supported, and **ssh** will act as a SOCKS4 server. Only root can forward privileged ports. Dynamic port forwardings can also be specified in the configuration file.

-1	Force **ssh** to try protocol version 1 only
-2	Force **ssh** to try protocol version 2 only
-4	Force **ssh** to use IPv4 addresses only
-6	Force **ssh** to use IPv6 addresses only

Configuration Files: **ssh** may additionally obtain configuration data from a per-user configuration file and a system-wide configuration file. The file format and configuration options are described in **ssh_config**.

Environment: **ssh** will normally set the following environment variables:

DISPLAY The DISPLAY variable indicates the location of the X11 server. It is automatically set by **ssh** to point to a value of the form "hostname:n" where hostname indicates the host where the shell runs, and n is an integer $>= 1$. ssh uses this special value to forward X11 connections over the secure channel. The user should normally not set DISPLAY explicitly, as that will render the X11 connection insecure (and will require the user to manually copy any required authorization cookies).

HOME Set to the path of the user's home directory

LOGNAME Synonym for USER; set for compatibility with systems that use this variable

MAIL Set to the path of the user's mailbox

PATH Set to the default PATH, as specified when compiling ssh

SSH_ASKPASS If **ssh** needs a passphrase, it will read the passphrase from the current terminal if it was run from a terminal. If **ssh** does not have a terminal associated with it but DISPLAY and **SSH_ASKPASS** are set, it will execute the program specified by **SSH_ASKPASS** and open an X11 window to read the passphrase. This is particularly useful when calling **ssh** from a .Xsession or related script. (Note that on some machines it may be necessary to redirect the input from /dev/null to make this work.)

SSH_AUTH_SOCK Identifies the path of a UNIX-domain socket used to communicate with the agent

SSH_CLIENT Identifies the client end of the connection; the variable contains three space-separated values: client ip-address, client port number, and server port number

SSH_ORIGINAL_COMMAND The variable contains the original command line if a forced command is executed; it can be used to extract the original arguments

SSH_TTY This is set to the name of the tty (path to the device) associated with the current shell or command; if the current session has no tty, this variable is not set

TZ The time zone variable is set to indicate the present time zone if it was set when the daemon was started (i.e., the daemon passes the value on to new connections)

USER Set to the name of the user logging in

ssh reads $HOME/**.ssh**/environment and adds lines of the format "VARNAME=value" to the environment

Files:

$HOME/**.ssh**/known_hosts Records host keys for all hosts the user has logged in to that are not in /etc/**ssh_known_hosts**.

$HOME/**.ssh**/identity, $HOME/**.ssh**/id_dsa, $HOME/**.ssh**/id_rsa Contains the authentication identity of the user. They are for protocol 1 RSA, protocol 2 DSA, and protocol 2 RSA, respectively. These files contain sensitive data and should be readable by the user but not accessible by others (read/write/execute). Note that **ssh** ignores a private key file if it is accessible by others. It is possible to specify a passphrase when generating the key; the passphrase will be used to encrypt the sensitive part of this file using 3DES.

$HOME/**.ssh**/identity.pub, $HOME/**.ssh**/id_dsa.pub, $HOME/**.ssh**/id_rsa.pub Contains the public key for authentication (public part of the identity file in human-readable form).

The contents of the $HOME/.ssh/identity.pub file should be added to $HOME/**.ssh/**authorized_keys on all machines where the user wishes to log in using protocol version 1 RSA authentication. The contents of the $HOME/**.ssh**/id_dsa.pub and $HOME/**.ssh**/id_rsa.pub file should be added to $HOME/**.ssh**/authorized_keys on all machines where the user wishes to log in using protocol version 2 DSA/RSA authentication. These files are not sensitive and can (but need not) be readable by anyone. These files are never used automatically and are not necessary; they are only provided for the convenience of the user.

$HOME/**.ssh**/config   This is the per-user configuration file; the file format and configuration options are described in **ssh**_config(5).

$HOME/**.ssh**/authorized_keys   Lists the public keys (RSA/DSA) that can be used for logging in as this user. The format of this file is described in the **sshd** manual page. In the simplest form, the format is the same as the .pub identity files. This file is not highly sensitive, but the recommended permissions are read/write for the user and are not accessible by others.

/etc/**ssh**_known_hosts   Systemwide list of known host keys. This file should be prepared by the system administrator to contain the public host keys of all machines in the organization. This file should be world-readable. This file contains public keys, one per line, in the following format (fields separated by spaces): system name, public key and optional comment field. When different names are used for the same machine, all such names should be listed, separated by commas. The format is described on the **sshd** manualpage.

The canonical system name (as returned by name servers) is used by **sshd** to verify the client host when logging in; other names are needed because **ssh** does not convert the user-supplied name to a canonical name before checking the key, because someone with access to the name servers would then be able to fool host authentication.

/etc/**ssh**_config   Systemwide configuration file. The file format and configuration options are described in ssh_config(5).

/etc/**ssh**_host_key, /etc/**ssh**_host_dsa_key, /etc/**ssh**_host_rsa_key   These three files contain the private parts of the host keys and are used for RhostsRSAAuthentication and Hostbased Authentication. If the protocol version 1 RhostsRSAAuthentication method is used, **ssh** must be setuid root, since the host key is readable only by root. For protocol version 2, **ssh** uses **ssh**-keysign to access the host keys for HostbasedAuthentication. This eliminates the requirement that **ssh** be setuid root when that authentication method is used. By default, **ssh** is not setuid root.

$HOME/.rhosts   This file is used in .rhosts authentication to list the host/user pairs that are permitted to log in. (Note that this file is also used by rlogin and rsh, which makes using this file insecure.) Each line of the file contains a hostname (in the canonical form returned by name servers), and then a username on that host, separated by a space. On some machines, this file may need to be world-readable if the user's home directory is on an NFS partition, because **sshd**(8) reads it as root. Additionally, this file must be owned by the user and must not have write permissions for anyone else. The recommended permission for most machines is read/write for the user and not accessible by others.

Note that by default, **sshd**(8) will be installed so that it requires successful RSA host authentication before permitting .rhosts authentication. If the server machine does not

have the client's host key in /etc/**ssh**_known_hosts, it can be stored in $HOME/
.ssh/known_hosts. The easiest way to do this is to connect back to the client from the
server machine using ssh; this will automatically add the host key to
$HOME/**.ssh**/known_hosts.

$HOME/.shosts   This file is used exactly the same way as .rhosts; the purpose for having this file is
to be able to use rhosts authentication without permitting login with rlogin or rsh

/etc/hosts.equiv   This file is used during .rhosts authentication. It contains canonical hosts names,
one per line (the full format is described on the sshd manual page). If the client host is
found in this file, login is automatically permitted provided client and server usernames
are the same. Additionally, successful RSA host authentication is normally required.
This file should only be writable by root.

/etc/shosts.equiv   This file is processed exactly as /etc/hosts.equiv; this file may be useful to permit
logins using **ssh** but not using rsh/rlogin

/etc/**sshrc**   Commands in this file are executed by ssh when the user logs in just before the user's
shell (or command) is started; *see* the **sshd** manual page for more information

$HOME/**.ssh**/rc   Commands in this file are executed by ssh when the user logs in just before the
user's shell (or command) is started; *see* the **sshd** manual page for more information

$HOME/**.ssh**/environment   Contains additional definitions for environment variables; *see* section
ENVIRONMENT above

Command Arguments:

    hostname   Remote host

    user@hostname   Username at remote host

Example(s):   Start up an ssh session using the username koretsky on the remote host lhotse.up.edu:
```
ssh –l koretsky lhotse.up.edu
```

---

strip–Strip symbol table and debugging and line number information from an object file

Syntax: `strip [-lVx]` 'file'...

Purpose: Remove the symbol table, debugging information, and line number information from
elf object files

Output: Object file(s) with specified information removed

Options:

    `-l`   Strip line number information only; do not strip the symbol table or debugging
information

    `-V`   Print, on stderr, the version number of `strip`

    `-x`   Do not strip the symbol table; debugging and line number information may be stripped

Command Arguments:

    'file'   Pathname referring to an executable file

Example(s):   Remove the line numbers only from an elf object file named sorted.o:
```
strip –l sorted.o
```

stty—Set the options for a terminal

Syntax:	**stty** [**-a**] [**-g**] ['modes']
Purpose:	Set certain terminal I/O options for the device that is the current stdin; without arguments, it reports the settings of certain options
Output:	Terminal characteristics changed

Options:

-a	Write to stdout all the option settings for the terminal
-g	Report current settings in a form that can be used as an argument to another **stty** command. Emits termios-type output if the underlying driver supports it; otherwise, it emits termio-type output.

Control Modes:

parenb (-parenb)	Enable (disable) parity generation and detection
parext (-parext)	Enable (disable) extended parity generation and detection for mark and space parity
parodd (-parodd)	Select odd (even) parity or mark (space) parity if parext is enabled
cs5 cs6 cs7 cs8	Select character size
0	Hang up line immediately
110 - 460800	Set terminal baud rate to the number given, if possible (All speeds are not supported by all hardware interfaces.)
ispeed 0 - 460800	Set terminal input baud rate to the number given, if possible
ospeed 0 - 460800	Set terminal output baud rate to the number given, if possible
hupcl (-hupcl)	Hang up (do not hang up) connection on last close
hup (-hup)	Same as hupcl (-hupcl)
cstopb (-cstopb)	Use two (one) stop bits per character
cread (-cread)	Enable (disable) receiver
crtscts (-crtscts)	Enable output hardware flow control
crtsxoff (-crtsxoff)	Enable input hardware flow control
clocal (-clocal)	Assume a line without (with) modem control
loblk (-loblk)	Block (do not block) output from a noncurrent layer
defeucw	Set the widths of multibyte Extended UNIX Code (EUC) characters

Input Modes:

ignbrk (-ignbrk)	Ignore (do not ignore) break on input
brkint (-brkint)	Signal (do not signal) INTR on break
ignpar (-ignpar)	Ignore (do not ignore) parity errors
parmrk (-parmrk)	Mark (do not mark) parity errors
inpck (-inpck)	Enable (disable) input parity checking
istrip (-istrip)	Strip (do not strip) input characters to 7 bits
inlcr (-inlcr)	Map (do not map) NL to CR on input

igncr (-igncr)	Ignore (do not ignore) CR on input
icrnl (-icrnl)	Map (do not map) CR to NL on input
iuclc (-iuclc)	Map (do not map) uppercase alphabetics to lowercase on input
ixon (-ixon)	Enable (disable) Start/Stop output control
ixany (-ixany)	Allow any character (only DC1) to restart output
ixoff (-ixoff)	Request that the system send (not send) Start/Stop characters when the input queue is nearly empty/full
imaxbel (-imaxbel)	Echo (do not echo) BEL when input line is too long

Output Modes:

opost (- opost)	Postprocess output (do not postprocess output; ignore all other output modes)
olcuc (-olcuc)	Map (do not map) lowercase alphabetics to uppercase on output
onlcr (-onlcr)	Map (do not map) NL to CR-NL on output
ocrnl (-ocrnl)	Map (do not map) CR to NL on output
onocr (-onocr)	Do not (do) output CRs at column zero
onlret (-onlret)	On the terminal NL to perform (not to perform) CR function
ofill (-ofill)	Use fill characters (use timing) for delays
ofdel (-ofdel)	Fill characters are DELs (NULs)
cr0 cr1 cr2 cr3	Select style of delay for carriage returns
nl0 nl1	Select style of delay for linefeeds
tab0 tab1 tab2 tab3	Select style of delay for horizontal tabs
bs0 bs1	Select style of delay for backspaces
ff0 ff1	Select style of delay for formfeeds
vt0 vt1	Select style of delay for vertical tabs

Local Modes:

isig (-isig)	Enable (disable) checking of characters against the special control characters INTR, QUIT, SWTCH, and SUSP
icanon (-icanon)	Enable (disable) canonical input (ERASE and KILL processing)
xcase (- xcase)	Canonical (unprocessed) uppercase/lowercase presentation
echo (-echo)	Echo back (do not echo back) every character typed
echoe (-echoe)	Echo (do not echo) ERASE character as a backspace-space-backspace string
echok (-echok)	Echo (do not echo) NL after KILL character
lfkc (-lfkc)	The same as echok (-echok); obsolete
echonl (-echonl)	Echo (do not echo) NL
noflsh (- noflsh)	Disable (enable) flush after INTR, QUIT, or SUSP
stwrap (-stwrap)	Disable (enable) truncation of lines longer than 79 characters on a synchronous line
tostop (-tostop)	Send (do not send) SIGTTOU when background processes write to the terminal

echoctl (-echoctl)	Echo (do not echo) control characters as ^'char', delete as ^?
echoprt (-echoprt)	Echo (do not echo) erase character as character is "erased"
echoke (-echoke)	BS-SP-BS erase (do not BS-SP-BS erase) entire line on line kill
flusho (-flusho)	Flush (do not) output
pendin (-pendin)	Retype (do not retype) pending input at next read or input character
iexten (-iexten)	Enable (disable) special control characters
stflush (-stflush)	Enable (disable) flush on a synchronous line after every write
stappl (-stappl)	Use application mode (use line mode) on a synchronous line

Hardware Flow Control Modes:

rtsxoff (-rtsxoff)	Enable (disable) RTS hardware flow control on input
ctsxon (-ctsxon)	Enable (disable) CTS hardware flow control on output
dtrxoff (-dtrxoff)	Enable (disable) DTR hardware flow control on input
cdxon (-cdxon)	Enable (disable) CD hardware flow control on output
isxoff (-isxoff)	Enable (disable) isochronous hardware flow control on input

Clock Modes:

xcibrg	Get transmit clock from internal baud rate generator
xctset	Get the transmit clock from transmitter signal element timing (DCE source) lead, CCITT V.24 circuit 114, and EIA-232-D pin 15
xcrset	Get transmit clock from receiver signal element timing (DCE source) lead, CCITT V.24 circuit 115, and EIA-232-D pin 17
rcibrg	Get receive clock from internal baud rate generator
rctset	Get receive clock from transmitter signal element timing (DCE source) lead, CCITT V.24 circuit 114, and EIA-232-D pin 15
rcrset	Get receive clock from receiver signal element timing (DCE source) lead, CCITT V.24 circuit 115, and EIA-232-D pin 17
tsetcoff	Transmitter signal element timing clock not provided
tsetcrbrg	Output receive baud rate generator on transmitter signal element timing (DTE source) lead, CCITT V.24 circuit 113, EIA-232-D pin 24.
tsetctbrg	Output transmit baud rate generator on transmitter signal element timing (DTE source) lead, CCITT V.24 circuit 113, and EIA-232-D pin 24
tsetctset	Output transmitter signal element timing (DCE source) on transmitter signal element timing (DTE source) lead, CCITT V.24 circuit 113, and EIA-232-D pin 24
tsetcrset	Output receiver signal element timing (DCE source) on transmitter signal element timing (DTE source) lead, CCITT V.24 circuit 113, and EIA-232-D pin 24
rsetcoff	Receiver signal element timing clock not provided
rsetcrbrg	Output receive baud rate generator on receiver signal element timing (DTE source) lead, CCITT V.24 circuit 128, and no EIA-232-D pin
rsetctbrg	Output transmit baud rate generator on receiver signal element timing (DTE source) lead, CCITT V.24 circuit 128, and no EIA-232-D pin

| rsetctset | Output transmitter signal element timing (DCE source) on receiver signal element timing (DTE source) lead, CCITT V.24 circuit 128, and no EIA-232-D pin |
| rsetcrset | Output receiver signal element timing (DCE source) on receiver signal element timing (DTE source) lead, CCITT V.24 circuit 128, and no EIA-232-D pin |

Command Arguments: None

Example(s):   Display current terminal settings: `stty`

---

tail–Deliver last part of a file

Syntax:
    tail [**-f** | **-r**] [**-c** 'number' | **-n** 'number'] ['file']
    tail [+ 'number' [**l** | **b** | **c**] [**f**]] ['file']
    tail [+ 'number' [**l**] [**f** | **r**]] ['file']

Purpose: By default, display the last 10 lines of 'file'. Copying begins at a point in the file indicated by the c 'number', -n 'number', or 'number' option (if +'number' is specified, begins at distance number from the beginning; if – 'number' is specified, begins from the end of the input; if 'number' is null, the value 10 is assumed). Hence, 'number' is counted in units of lines or bytes according to the –c or –n options, or lines, blocks, or bytes, according to the appended option l, b, or c. When no units are specified, counting is by lines.

Output: The `tail` command copies the named file to stdout, beginning at a designated place determined by options and option arguments

Options and Option Arguments:

    -b   Units of blocks

    -c'number' The 'number' option argument must be a decimal integer whose sign affects the location in the file, measured in bytes, to begin the copying

           +   Copying starts relative to the beginning of the file

           –   Copying starts relative to the end of the file

    none   Copying starts relative to the end of the file

The origin for counting is 1; that is, –c +1 represents the first byte of the file and –c –1 the last

    -c   Units of bytes

    -f   Follow; if the input file is not a pipe, the program will not terminate after the line of the input file has been copied but will enter an endless loop. Useful for monitoring growth of a file.

    -l   Units of lines

    -n'number' Equivalent to –c 'number', except the starting location in the file is measured in lines instead of bytes. The origin for counting is 1; that is, –n +1 represents the first line of the file and –n –1 the last.

    -r   Reverse. Copies lines from the specified starting point in the file in reverse order. The default for r is to print the entire file in reverse order.

Command Arguments:

    'file'   Pathname of an input file; if no 'file' operands are specified, stdin will be used

Example(s):   Display the last 20 lines of the file named source.c: `tail -20 source.c`

---

talk–Talk to another user

Syntax: `talk` 'address' ['terminal']

Purpose: Provide a two-way, screen-oriented communication program

Output: When first invoked, `talk` sends a message similar to

`Message from TalkDaemon@ 'her machine' at 'time' ...`
`talk:  connection requested by 'your address'`

`talk:` respond with: `talk` ['your address'] to the specified 'address'. At this point, the recipient of the message can reply by typing: `talk` ['your address'].

Once communication has been established, the two parties can type simultaneously, with their output displayed in separate regions of the screen.

Options: None

Command Arguments:

'address'   Recipient of the talk session; one form of 'address' is the 'username', as returned by who. Other address formats and how they are handled are unspecified.

'terminal'   If recipient is logged on more than once, 'terminal' can be used to indicate the appropriate terminal name. If 'terminal' is not specified, the `talk` message will be displayed on one or more accessible terminals in use by recipient. The format of 'terminal' will be the same as that returned by who.

Example(s):   Talk to the user named sarwar on the local machine upsun25 at ttyp2:
`talk sarwar@upsun25 ttyp2`

---

tar–Create archives and add or extract files

Syntax: `tar c` [**bBefFhiloPvwX**] ['block'] ['tarfile'] ['exclude-file']{ `-I` 'include-file'
`-C` 'directory file' | 'file' }...
`tar r` [**bBefFhilvw**] ['block']{ `-I` 'include-file' | `-C` 'directory file' | 'file' }...
`tar t` [**BefFhilvX**] ['tarfile']['exclude-file'] { `-I` 'include-file' | 'file' }...
`tar u` [**bBefFhilvw**] ['block'] ['tarfile'] 'file'...
`tar x` [**BefFhilmopvwX**] ['tarfile'] ['exclude-file'] ['file'...]

Purpose: Archive and extract files to and from a single file called a 'tarfile'. Actions are controlled by the 'key' option and its arguments. The 'key' is a string of characters containing a single function letter (c, r, t , u, or x) and zero or more function modifiers (letters or digits), depending on the function letter used. The 'key' string contains no <space> characters. Function modifier arguments are listed on the command line in the same order as their corresponding function modifiers appear in the 'key' string. Use of a hyphen (`-`) in front of the 'key' option is not required.

The `-I` 'include-file', `-C` 'directory file', and 'file' command arguments specify which files or directories are to be archived or extracted. In all cases, appearance of a directory name refers to the files and (recursively) subdirectories of that directory. Arguments appearing within braces, { }, indicate that one of the arguments must be specified.

Output: Archived file(s)

Options and Option Arguments:

-I'include-file' Open include-file containing a list of files, one per line, and treat as if each file appeared separately on the command line; if a file is specified in both the exclude-file and the include-file (or on the commandline), it will be excluded

-C'directory file' Perform a `chdir` operation on directory and perform the c (create) or r (replace) operation on file; this option enables archiving files from multiple directories not related by a close common parent

'key' *Function Letters*

c Create; writing begins at the beginning of tarfile, instead of at the end

r Replace; named 'file's are written at the end of tarfile

t Table of contents; names of the specified files are listed each time they occur in tarfile

u Update; named 'file's are written at the end of tarfile if they are not already in the tarfile or if they have been modified since last written to that tarfile

x Extract or restore; named 'file's are extracted from tarfile and written to the directory specified in tarfile, relative to the current directory

'key' *Function Modifiers*

b Blocking factor; use when reading or writing to raw archives. The 'block' argument specifies the number of 512-byte blocks to be included in each read or write operation performed on tarfile; minimum is 1, and the default is 20.

B Block; force `tar` to perform multiple reads (if necessary) to read exactly enough bytes to fill a block. This function modifier enables `tar` to work across the Ethernet because pipes and sockets return partial blocks even when more data are coming.

e Error; exit immediately with a positive exit status if any unexpected errors occur

f File; use the 'tarfile' argument as the name of tarfile

F With one F argument, `tar` excludes all directories named SCCS and RCS from tarfile

h Follow symbolic links as if they were normal files or directories; normally, `tar` does not follow symbolic links

i Ignore directory checksum errors

l Link; output error message if unable to resolve all links to the files being archived; if l is not specified, no error messages are printed

m Modify; modification time of the file is the time of extraction; this function modifier is valid only with the x function

o Ownership; assign to extracted files the user and group identifiers of the user running the program, rather than those on tarfile, for users other than root

p Restore named files to their original modes and ACLs, if applicable, ignoring the present umask

P Suppress the addition of a trailing "/" on directory entries in the archive

v	Verbose; output the name of each file preceded by the function letter. With the t function, v provides additional information about tarfile entries.
w	What; output action to be taken and name of the file; then await the user's confirmation. If the first keystroke is y, the action is performed; otherwise, the action is not performed.
x	Exclude; use the 'exclude-file' argument as a file containing a list of the relative path (or directories) to be excluded from the tarfile when using the functions c, x, or t.

Command Arguments:

'file'	Pathname of a regular file or directory to be archived (when the c, r, or u function is specified), extracted (x), or listed (t). When 'file' is the pathname of a directory, the action applies to all the files and (recursively) to the subdirectories of that directory.

Example(s): Create an archive of /usr1.b/bobk, display the progress of the command on stdout in verbose mode, and save the archive on the device /dev/hd0/bobk:
`tar cvf /dev/hdo /usr1.b/bobk`
Extract or restore the files from device /dev/hd0/bobk into the present working directory:
`tar xvf /dev/hd0/bobk .`

tee–Duplicate the standard input

Syntax: **tee** [**-ai**] ['file'...]

Purpose: Duplicate stdin, one copy to stdout and the other copy to a file

Output: The tee command will copy stdin to stdout, making a copy in zero or more files; the options determine whether the specified files are overwritten or appended to

Options and Option Arguments:

-a	Append output to the files rather than overwriting them
-i	Ignore interrupts

Command Arguments:

'file'	Pathname of an output file

Example(s): Display on stdout the cat of a file source.c and then save it in two files named source1.c and source2.c: `cat source.c | tee source1.c source2.c`

---

telnet–User interface to a remote system

Syntax: **telnet** [**-8ELcdr**] [**-e** 'escape char'] [**-l** 'user'] [**-n** 'tracefile'] ['host' ['port']]

Purpose: Allow communication with another host. If telnet is invoked without arguments, it enters command mode, indicated by its prompt telnet>. In this mode, it accepts and executes its associated commands. If it is invoked with arguments, it performs an open command with those arguments.

Output: Operations in telnet command mode

Options and Option Arguments:

-8	Specify an 8-bit data path
-E	Stop any character from being recognized as an escape character

-L	Specify an 8-bit data path on output, which causes the binary option to be negotiated on output
-c	Disable reading of the user's .telnetrc file
-d	Set initial value of the debug toggle to true
-e'escape char'	Set initial escape character to 'escape char'
-l'user'	When connecting to a remote system that understands the environ option, send user to the remote system as the value for the variable *user*
-n'tracefile'	Open tracefile for recording trace information
-r	Specify a user interface similar to `rlogin`

Command Arguments:

'host'	DNS hostname of remote computer to connect to
'port'	Standard or nonstandard virtual connection on the telnet server

Example(s):   Connect to the remote computer lhotse.up.edu with login name koretsky:
```
telnet -l koretsky lhotse.up.edu
```

---

test–Evaluate condition(s) or make execution of actions dependent on the evaluation of condition(s)

Syntax:	**test** ['condition'] ['condition']
Purpose:	In a shell script, evaluate the 'condition' and indicate result of the evaluation by its exit status; an exit status of 0 indicates that the condition evaluated as true, and an exit status of 1 indicates that the condition evaluated as false
Output:	Exit status of 0 or 1

Options and Option Arguments: None

Command Arguments:

'condition'	An expression that contains one or more criteria

Example(s):   In a shell script, test the value of the variable string1 to see if it is equal to 1:
```
test -n string1
```

---

touch–Change file access and modification times

Syntax:	**touch** [**-acm**] [**-r** 'ref file'] 'file'...
	touch [**-acm**] [**-t** 'time'] 'file'...
	touch [**-acm**] ['date time'] 'file'...
Purpose:	Set access and modification times of each file; 'file' is created if it does not already exist
Output:	Changed access and modification time

Options and Option Arguments:

-a	Change access time of 'file'; do not change modification time unless -m is also specified
-c	Do not create a specified 'file' if it does not exist

-m | Change modification time of 'file'; do not change access time unless -a is also specified

-r'ref file' | Use the corresponding times of the file named by 'ref file' instead of the current time

-t'time' | Use the specified 'time' instead of the current time; 'time' will be a decimal number of the form [['CC']'YY']'MMDDhhmm'['SS'], where each two digits represent the following.

'MM'	Month of the year [01–12]
'DD'	Day of the month [01–31]
'hh'	Hour of the day [00–23]
'mm'	Minute of the hour [00–59]
'CC'	First two digits of the year
'YY'	Second two digits of the year
'SS'	Second of the minute [00–59]

Command Arguments:

'file' | Pathname of a file whose times are to be modified

'date time' | Use specified 'date time' instead of current time; 'date time' is a decimal number of the form 'MMDDhhmm'['YY'], where each two digits represent the following.

'MM'	Month of the year [01–12]
'DD'	Day of the month [01–31]
'hh'	Hour of the day [00–23]
'mm'	Minute of the hour [00–59]
'YY'	(Optional) second two digits of the year

Example(s): | Modifies the date and time of the files source1.c and source2.c:

```
touch -a -d "4:00 Pm Dec 15" source1.c source2.c
```

---

tr–Translate characters

Syntax:
```
tr [-cs] 'string1' 'string2'
tr -s|-d [-c] 'string1'
tr -ds [-c] 'string1' 'string2'
```

Purpose: | Copy stdin to stdout with substitution or deletion of selected characters; the options specified and the 'string1' and 'string2' command arguments control translations that occur while characters and single-character collating elements are being copied

Output: | With no arguments, stdin is copied to stdout

Options:

-c | Complement the set of characters specified by 'string1'

-d | Delete all occurrences of input characters specified by 'string1'

-s | Replace instances of repeated characters with a single character

Command Arguments:

'string1' 'string2'   Translation control strings; each string represents a set of characters to be converted to an array of characters used for the translation

Example(s):   Modifies string UWNIXDOWS to UNIX:
```
echo UWNIXDOWS | tr -d 'WDOWS'
```

---

trace–A dbx command to provide tracing information as a program executes

Syntax: **trace** [restriction options] [if cond]

Purpose: Allow user to monitor execution of a program for debugging purposes

Output: With no options specified, all source lines are printed at stdout before being executed

Options and Option Arguments:

in func   Output while executing function func

inclass class   Output name of function that called any member of class

infunction func   Output name of function that called any top level C++ func

inmethod member   Output name of function that called member of class

expr at n   Output value of expr each time line *n* is reached

func   Output name of function that called func

n   Print source line *n* before executing it

var   Output value of var each time it changes

var [in func]   Output value of var as it changes, but only while executing func

if cond   Any of the above may be followed by this option, which executes the option based on condition cond

Command Arguments: None

Example(s):   Place a "watch point" in a program to monitor the value of variable s_val:
```
trace s_val in main
```

---

tty–Return user's terminal name

Syntax: **tty** [-l] [-s]

Purpose: Write to stdout name of open terminal as stdin

Output: Terminal name connected to stdin; the following exit values are returned:
0 = stdin is a terminal, 1 = stdin is not a terminal, and >1 = an error occurred

Options:

-l   Print synchronous line number to which user's terminal is connected

-s   Inhibit printing of terminal pathname, allowing user to test just the exit status

Command Arguments: None

Example(s): Display the pathname of the current terminal:
```
tty
```

---

umask–Get or set the file mode creation mask

Syntax: **umask** [**-S**] ['mask']

Purpose: Set file mode creation mask of current shell execution environment to value specified by the 'mask' operand; this mask affects the initial value of the file permission bits of subsequently created files

Output: Initial value of file permission bits

Options:

-S Produce symbolic output; the default output style is unspecified but will be recognized on a subsequent invocation of umask on the same system as a 'mask' operand to restore the previous file mode creation mask

Command Arguments:

'mask' A string specifying the new file mode creation mask; the string is treated in the same way as the 'mode' operand described in chmod

Example(s): Under tsch or csh, if the file permissions mask is set to 077, set the permissions on newly created files to be g+rwx,o+rwx:
```
umask 077
```

Under bash, if the file permission mask is set to 077,
set the permissions on newly created files to be g+r,o+r:
```
umask g+r,o+r
```

---

unget–Undo a previous get of an SCCS file

Syntax: **unget** [**-ns**] [**-r**'sid'] 's.filename'...

Purpose: Undo effect of a get -e done prior to creation of the pending delta

Output: Modified SCCS file(s)

Options and Option Arguments:

-n Retain retrieved version, which otherwise is removed

-s Suppress display of the SCCS delta ID (SID)

-r'sid' When multiple versions are checked out, specify which pending delta to abort; a diagnostic results if the specified SID is ambiguous, or if it is necessary but omitted from the command line

Command Arguments:

s.filename ... Target SCCS file(s)

Example(s): Return or check in the SCCS file s.input.c: unget s.input.c

uniq–Report or filter out repeated lines in a file

Syntax: **uniq** [**-c**|**-d**|**-u**] [**-f** 'fields'] [**-s** 'char'] ['input file' ['output file']]
               uniq [**-c**|**-d**|**-u**] [-'n'] [**+**'m'] ['input file' ['output file']]

Purpose: Read an input file comparing adjacent lines and write one copy of each input line on
               the output. The second and succeeding copies of repeated adjacent input lines will not
               be written. Repeated lines in the input will not be detected if they are not adjacent.

Output: If 'output file' is not specified, stdout will be used

Options and Option Arguments:

  -c   Precede each output line with a count of the number of times the line occurred in input

  -d   Suppress writing of lines not repeated in input

  -f'fields' Ignore the first 'fields' fields on each input line when doing comparisons, where
               'fields' is a positive decimal integer; a field is the maximal string matched by the
               basic regular expression: [[:blank:]]*[^[:blank:]]*

  -s'chars'   Ignore first 'chars' characters when doing comparisons, where 'chars' is a positive
               decimal integer

  -u   Suppress writing of lines repeated in input

  -'n'   Equivalent to **-f** 'fields' with 'fields' set to 'n'

  +'m'   Equivalent to **-s** 'chars' with 'chars' set to 'm'

Command Arguments:

  'input file' Pathname of input file; if 'input file' is not specified or if the 'input file' is **-**,
               stdin will be used

  'output file' Pathname of output file. If 'output file' is not specified, stdout will be used.
               The results are unspecified if the file named by 'output 'file' is the file named by
               'input file'.

Example(s):   Display the unique lines UNIX WINDOWS and "UNIX" from the file named OS
               that contains the three lines
               "UNIX WINDOWS"
               "UNIX WINDOWS"
               "UNIX": uniq OS

---

w–Display information about currently logged-on users

Syntax: **w** [**-hlsuw**] ['user']

Purpose: Display a summary of current activity on the system, including what each user is doing

Output: On stdout, a heading line shows current time, length of time system has been up,
               number of users logged on to system, and average number of jobs in run queue over
               the last 1, 5, and 15 min.

               The fields displayed for each user are user's login name; name of the tty user is on;
               time of day user logged on (in 'hours':'minutes'); idle time–that is, number of minutes
               since user last typed anything (in 'hours':'minutes'); CPU time used by all processes

and their children on that terminal (in 'minutes': 'seconds'); CPU time used by currently active processes (in 'minutes':'seconds'); and name and arguments of current process.

Options:

-h	Suppress heading
-l	Produce a long form of output, which is the default
-s	Produce a short form of output; in the short form, the tty is abbreviated and the login time and CPU times are left off, as are the arguments to commands
-u	Produce heading line that shows current time, length of time system has been up, number of users logged on to system, and average number of jobs in run queue over the last 1, 5, and 15 min.
-w	Produce a long form of output, which is also the same as the default

Command Arguments:

'user'	Name of a particular user for whom login information is displayed; if specified, output is restricted to that user

Example(s): Display a short listing of the users on the system: w −s

---

wc–Display a count of lines, words and characters in a file

Syntax: wc [−c | −m | −C] [−lw] ['file'...]

Purpose: Read one or more input files and, by default, write the number of newline characters, words and bytes, contained in each input file to stdout

Output: Writes a total count for all named files, if more than one input file is specified

Options:

-c	Count bytes
-m	Count characters
-C	Same as −m
-l	Count lines
-w	Count words delimited by white space characters or newline characters; if no option is specified, the default is −lwc (count lines, words, and bytes)

Command Arguments:

'file'	Pathname of an input file; if no 'file' operands are specified, stdin will be used

Example(s):   Display the number of lines, words, and characters in the file named OS:
wc −lcw OS

---

whereis–Locate the binary, source, and man page files for a command

Syntax: **whereis [−bmsu] [−BMS** 'directory'... -f] 'filename'...

Purpose: Locate source/binary and manual sections for specified files

Output:	The supplied names are first stripped of leading pathname components and any (single) trailing extension of the form .'ext'—for example, .c; prefixes of s. resulting from use of source code control are also dealt with.

Options:

−b	Search only for binaries
−m	Search only for manual sections
−s	Search only for sources
−u	Search for unusual entries; a file is said to be unusual if it does not have one entry of each requested type
−B	Change or otherwise limit the places where whereis searches for binaries
−M	Change or otherwise limit the places where whereis searches for manual sections
−S	Change or otherwise limit the places where whereis searches for sources
−f	Terminate the last directory list and signal the start of filenames; *must* be used when any of the B, −M, or −S options are used

Command Arguments:

'filename'	Binary, source, and man page files

Example(s):	Search for the C Shell: whereis csh

---

which–Locate a command; display its pathname or alias

Syntax:	which ['filename']...
Purpose:	Take a list of names and look for the files that would be executed if these names were typed as commands. Each argument is expanded if it is aliased and is searched for along the user's path. Both aliases and path are taken from the user's shell resource file.
Output:	Lists paths of commands that are in 'filename'

Options and Option Arguments: None

Command Arguments:

'filename'	A file containing a list of names that are commands

Example(s):	Displays the paths to the commands cat, more, and ls on your system: which cat more ls

---

who–Who is on the system

Syntax:	who [-abdHlmpqrstTu] ['file']
	who −q [−n 'x'] ['file']
	who 'am i'
Purpose:	List user's name, terminal line, login time, elapsed time since activity occurred on the line, and the process-ID of the command interpreter (shell) for each current UNIX system user

Output: The general format for output is

'name' ['state'] 'line time' ['idle'] ['pid'] ['comment'] ['exit']

where:

'name'	is user's login name
'state'	is capability of writing to the terminal
'line'	is name of the line found in /dev
'time'	is time since user's login
'idle'	is time elapsed since user's last activity
'pid'	is user's process id
'comment'	is comment line in `inittab(4)`
'exit'	is exit status for dead processes

Options and Option Arguments:

-a	Process /var/adm/utmp or the named 'file' with -b, -d, -l, -p, -r, -t, -T, and -u options turned on
-b	Indicate time and date of last reboot
-d	Display all processes that have expired and not been respawned by `init`
-H	Output column headings above regular output
-l	List only those lines on which system is waiting for someone to log on
-m	Output only information about current terminal
-n'x'	Take a numeric argument, 'x', which specifies the number of users to display per line; 'x' must be at least 1
-p	List any other process that is currently active and has been previously spawned by `init`
-q	(Quick who) display only names and number of users currently logged on; when this option is used, all other options are ignored
-r	Indicate current 'run-level' of the `init` process
-s	(Default) list only 'name', 'line', and 'time' fields
-T	Same as the -s option, except that the 'state idle', 'pid', and 'comment' fields are also written
-t	Indicate last change to system clock (via the `date` command) by root
-u	List only those users who are currently logged on

Command Arguments:

'am i'	In the "C" locale, limit output to describing invoking user, equivalent to the -m option; the am and i or I must be separate arguments
'file'	Specify pathname of a file to substitute for database of logged-on users that who uses by default

Example(s):   Display who is on your system: who

Displays who you are on your system: who am i

write–Write to another user

Syntax:	**write** 'user' ['terminal']

Purpose: Read lines from user's stdin and write them to the terminal of another user. When first invoked, it writes the message

```
Message from ['sender-login-id'] ['sending-terminal'] ['date']...
```

to 'user'. When it has successfully completed the connection, sender's terminal will be alerted twice to indicate that what the sender is typing is being written to the recipient's terminal.

Output: Message on another user's console window

Options and Option Arguments: None

Command Arguments:

'user'   User (login) name of person to whom message will be written; this argument must be of the form returned by who

'terminal'   Terminal identification in same format provided by who.

Example(s):   Write a message to user bobk on terminal ttyC2:
```
write bobk ttyC2
```

---

xterm–Start an xterm terminal emulator window

Syntax: **xterm** [-'toolkitoption'...] [**-option...**]

Purpose: Open an xterminal terminal emulator window in which UNIX commands can be typed; usually this window provides VT100/102 or Tektronix display capability

Output: An xterm window with display and operating characteristics set by 'toolkitoption' and option

Options and Option Arguments (as of X11 Rel 6.3): 'xtoolkitoptions'

-bg'color'   Specify color to use for background of window; default is "white"

-bd'color'   Specify color to use for border of window; default is "black"

-bw'number'   Specify width in pixels of border surrounding window

-fg'color'   Specify color to use for displaying text. default is "black"

-fn'font'   Specify font to be used for displaying normal text; default is 'fixed'

-name'name'   Specify application name under which resources are to be obtained, rather than the default executable filename; 'name' should not contain "." or "*" characters

-title'string'   Specify window title string, which may be displayed by window managers if user so chooses. Default title is command line specified after the **-e** option, if any; otherwise, it is application name.

-rv   Indicate that reverse video be simulated by swapping foreground and background colors

-geometry'geometry'   Specify preferred size and position of window

-display'display'   Specify X server to contact

-xrm'resourcestring'   Specify a resource string to be used; this option is especially useful for setting resources that do not have separate command line options

-iconic   Indicates that 'xterm' should ask window manager to start it as an icon rather than as the normal window

-dc   Disable escape sequence to change vt100 foreground and background colors, text cursor color, mouse cursor foreground and background colors, and Tektronix emulator foreground and background colors

+dc   Enable escape sequence to change vt100 foreground and background colors, text cursor color, mouse cursor foreground and background colors, and Tektronix emulator foreground and background

options

-help   Cause xterm to print out a verbose message describing its options

-132   Normally, the vt102 deccolm escape sequence that switches between 80 and 132 column mode is ignored; this option causes the deccolm escape sequence to be recognized and the 'xterm' window to resize appropriately

-ah   Indicate that xterm is always to highlight the text cursor; by default, xterm will display a hollow text cursor whenever the focus is lost or the pointer leaves the window

+ah   Indicate that xterm do text cursor highlighting based on focus

-ai   Disable active icon support if that feature was compiled into xterm

+ai   Enable active icon support if that feature was compiled into xterm

-aw   Indicate that auto-wraparound be allowed; cursor automatically wraps to the beginning of the next line when it is at the right-most position of a line and text is output

+aw   Indicate that auto-wraparound not be allowed

-b'number'   Specify size of inner border (distance between outer edge of characters and window border) in pixels; the default is 2

-bdc   Disable display of characters with bold attribute as color rather than bold

+bdc   Enable display of characters with bold attribute as color rather than bold

-cb   Set 'vt100' resource cutToBeginningOfLine to false

+cb   Set 'vt100' resource cutToBeginningOfLine to true

-cc'characterclassrange':'value'[,...]   Set classes indicated by given ranges for use in selecting by words

-cm   Disable recognition of ANSI color change escape sequences

+cm   Enable recognition of ANSI color change escape sequences

-cn   Indicate that newlines not be cut in line-mode selections

+cn   Indicate that newlines be cut in line-mode selections

-cr'color'   Specifies color to use for text cursor; the default is to use the same foreground color used for text

-cu   Indicate that xterm work around a bug in the **more** program that causes it to incorrectly display lines that are exactly the width of the window and are followed by a line beginning with a <Tab> (leading tabs are not displayed)

+cu	Indicate that xterm not work around the **more** bug
-dc	Disable recognition of color change escape sequences
+dc	Enable recognition of color change escape sequences
-e'program' ['arguments' ...]	Specify the program (and its command line arguments) to be run in the xterm window; it also sets the window title and icon name to be the base name of the program being executed if neither **-T** nor **-n** are given on the command line *This must be the last option on the command line.*
-fb'font'	Specify font to be used when displaying bold text. Font must be the same height and width as the normal font. If only one of the normal or bold fonts is specified, it will be used as the normal font and the bold font will be produced by overstriking this font. The default is to do overstriking of the normal font.
-fi	Set font for active icons if that feature was compiled in xterm
-im	Turn on useInsertMode resource
+im	Turn off useInsertMode resource
-j	Indicates that xterm do jump scrolling. Normally, text is scrolled one line at a time; this option allows xterm to move multiple lines at a time so that it does not fall as far behind. Its use is strongly recommended because it makes xterm much faster when the user is scanning large amounts of text. The vt100 escape sequences for enabling and disabling smooth scroll as well as the VT Options menu can be used to turn this feature on or off.
+j	Indicate that xterm not do jump scrolling
-ls	Indicate that the shell started in the xterm window will be a login shell
+ls	Indicate that the shell started should not be a login shell (i.e., it will be a normal subshell)
-mb	Indicate that xterm should ring a margin bell when the user types near the right-hand end of a line; this option can be turned on and off from the VT Options menu
+mb	Indicate that margin bell not be rung
-mcmilliseconds	Specify maximum time between multiclick selections
-ms'color'	Specify color to be used for pointer cursor; the default is to use the foreground color
-nb'number'	Specify number of characters from the right-hand end of a line at which the margin bell, if enabled, will ring; the default is 10
-nul	Enable display of underlining
+nul	Disable display of underlining
-rw	Indicate that reverse wraparound be allowed. This option allows the cursor to back up from the left-most column of one line to the right-most column of the previous line. This option is very useful for editing long shell command lines, and its use is encouraged. This option can be turned on and off from the VT Options menu.
+rw	Indicate that reverse wraparound not be allowed
-s	Indicate that xterm may scroll asynchronously, meaning that the screen does not have to be kept completely up-to-date while scrolling is being done

+s	Indicate that xterm scroll synchronously
-sb	Indicate that some number of lines that are scrolled off the top of the window be saved and that a scrollbar be displayed so that those lines can be viewed; this option may be turned on and off from the VT Options menu
+sb	Indicate that a scrollbar not be displayed
-sf	Indicate that Sun Function Key escape codes be generated for function keys
+sf	Indicate that standard escape codes be generated for function keys
-si	Indicate that output to a window not automatically reposition the screen to the bottom of the scrolling region; this option can be turned on and off from the VT Options menu
+si	Indicate that output to a window is to cause it to scroll to the bottom
-sk	Indicate that pressing a key while using the scrollbar to review previous lines of text is to cause the window to be repositioned automatically in the normal position at the bottom of the scroll region
+sk	Indicate that pressing a key while using the scrollbar is not to cause the window to be repositioned
-sl 'number'	Specify number of lines to save that have been scrolled off the top of the screen; the default is 64
-t	Indicate that xterm is to start in Tektronix mode, rather than in vt102 mode; switching between the two windows is done with the Options menus
+t	Indicate that xterm is to start in vt102 mode
-tm 'string'	Specify a series of terminal setting keywords followed by characters that should be bound to those functions, similar to stty. Allowable keywords include intr, quit, erase, kill, eof, eol, swtch, start, stop, brk, susp, dsusp, rprnt, flush, weras, and lnext. Control characters may be specified as ^char (e.g., ^C or ^U) and ^? can be used to indicate delete.
-tn 'name'	Specify name of the terminal type to be set in the *term* environment variable
-ulc	Disable display of characters with underline attribute as color rather than with underlining
+ulc	Enable display of characters with underline attribute as color rather than with underlining
-ut	Indicate that xterm not write a record into the system log file '/etc/utmp'
+ut	Indicate that xterm is to write a record into the system log file, '/etc/utmp'
-vb	Indicate that a visual bell is preferred over an audible one; instead of ringing the terminal bell whenever a <Ctrl-G> is received, the window will be flashed
+vb	Indicate that a visual bell not be used
-wf	Indicate that xterm wait for window to be mapped the first time before starting the subprocess so that initial terminal size settings and environment variables are correct; it is the application's responsibility to catch subsequent terminal size changes

+wf   Indicate that xterm not wait before starting the subprocess

-c   Indicate that this window should receive console output (not supported on all systems). To obtain console output, user must be the owner of the console device and must have read and write permission for it. If user is running X under xdm on the console screen, user may need to have the session start-up and reset programs explicitly change owner-ship of the console device in order to get this option to work.

-s'ccn'   Specify last two letters of a pseudo-terminal name to use in slave mode, plus the number of the inherited file descriptor; this option is parsed "%c%c%d", which allows xterm to be used as an input and output channel for an existing program

Command Arguments: None

Example(s):   Start an xterm with the login shell: xterm –ls &
Start an xterm with an ordinary shell: xterm +ls &
Start an xterm with a scroll bar in it: xterm –sb &

Glossary

A

Absolute Pathname A pathname that starts with the root directory.

Access Privileges The type of operations that a user can perform on a file. In UNIX, access rights for a file can be read, write, and execute.

Access Time The time taken to access a main memory location for reading or writing.

Adaptive Lempel-Ziv Coding The most widely used lossless compression scheme for encoding variable-length block of characters into a fixed-length block of bits. In this compression scheme we assume that characters occur independently and with known probabilities, and that the probabilities are the same for all positions.

Address Bus A set of parallel wires that are used to carry the address of a storage location in the main memory that is to be read or written.

Address Space *See* Process Address Space.

Alias *See* Pseudonym.

Apple Menu In OS X, a pull-down menu bar activated by clicking on the Apple icon in the upper-left corner of the screen.

Application Programmer's Interface (API) The language libraries and system call layer form the application programmer's interface.

Application Software Programs that we use to perform various tasks on the computer system, such as word processing, graphing, picture processing, and Web browsing.

Application User's Interface (AUI) The application software that a user can use forms the application user's interface.

Archive A collection of files contained in a single file in a certain format.

Array A named collection of items of the same type stored in contiguous memory locations.

Array Indexing The method used to refer to an array item by using its number. The items in an array are numbered, with the first item numbered 1 (in some languages such as C the first item is numbered 0).

Assembler A program that takes a program in assembly language and translates it into object code.

Assembly Language *See* Low-Level Programming language.

Assignment Statement A shell command that is used to assign values to one or more shell variables.

Attributes The characteristics of a process (or file) such as the name of the owner of the process and process size.

B

Background Process When a process executes such that its standard input is not connected to the keyboard, it is said to execute in background. The shell prompt is returned to the user before a background process starts execution, thus allowing the user to use the system (i.e., run commands) while the background processes execute.

Bash The abbreviation for Bourne again shell.

Batch Operating System An operating system that does not allow you to interact with your processes is known as a batch operating system. The VMS system has a batch interface. UNIX and LINUX also allow programs to be executed in the batch mode, with programs executing in the background.

Bistate Devices Devices, such as transistors, that operate in "on" or "off" mode.

Bit Stands for binary digit, which can be 0 or 1. It is also the smallest unit of storage and transmission.

Bit Mask A sequence of bits (usually a byte or multiple bytes) used to retain values of certain bits in another byte (or multiple bytes), or to set them to 0s or 1s, by using a logical operation such as AND or OR.

Blind Carbon Copying E-Mail Sending a copy of an e-mail message composed by you to someone other than the intended recipient. Who received the carbon copy of a message is not known to the receiver because this information does not appear in the e-mail header.

Block-Oriented Devices Devices, such as a disk drive, that perform I/O in terms of blocks of data (e.g., in 512-byte chunks).

Blocks *See* Disk Blocks.

Block Special Files UNIX files that correspond to block-oriented devices (*see* Block-Oriented Devices). These files are located in the /dev directory.

Break Point A program statement where the execution of the program stops while using a symbolic debugger.

Byte In contemporary literature, a byte refers to 8 bits. For example, 10101100 is a byte. In not so recent literature, the term byte also used to be referred to as 9 bits. Because of this, a byte is also called an octet. A storage location that can store 8 bits is also known as a byte.

C

Carbon Copying E-Mail Sending a copy of an e-mail message composed by you to someone other than the intended recipient. Who received the carbon copy of a message is known to the receiver because this information appears in the e-mail header.

Central Processing Unit (CPU) Also known as the brain of a computer system, the CPU executes a program by reading the program instruction from the main memory. It also interacts with the I/O devices in the computer system.

Character-Oriented Devices Devices, such as a keyboard, that perform I/O in terms of one byte at a time.

Character Special Files UNIX files that correspond to character-oriented devices. These files are located in the /dev directory.

Character User Interface (CUI) *See* Command-line User Interface (CUI).

Child Process A process created on behalf of another process. In UNIX, the fork system call has to be used to create a child process. The child process is an exact copy of the process executing fork (*see* Parent Process).

Client Software In the client-server software model, the client software, when executed, takes the user commands and sends them as requests to the server process. The server process computes the responses for requests and sends them to the client, who handles them according to the semantics of the command. All Internet applications are based on the client-server model of computing.

Clock Tick A clock in a computer system ticks as frequently as dictated by the frequency of the clock (ticks per second). For system clocks that are dependent on the frequency of the power line signals (50 or 60 per second), it ticks every 1/50 (or 1/60) of a second.

Cluster The minimum unit of disk storage, which is one or more sectors.

Coding Rules A set of rules used by programmers for writing programs. Such rules are usually designed to enhance the readability of programs and to keep consistency in the "look" of the source programs produced by an organization or a coding team. The use of coding rules helps a great deal during the maintenance phase of a software product.

Colon Hexadecimal Notation A notation used to write 128-bit IPv6 addresses in a compact notation in which 16-bit chunks are represented in hexadecimal separated by colons, as in 76F4:9D5F:FFFF:FFFF:0:3276:70BD:FFFF.

Command Grouping Specifying two or more commands in such a manner that the shell executes them all as one process.

Command Interpreter A program that starts running after you log on to allow you to type commands that it tries to interpret and run. In UNIX, the command interpreter is also known as a shell.

Command Line A line that comprises a command with its arguments and is typed at a shell prompt. You must hit the `<Enter>` key before the command is executed by a shell.

Command Line Arguments The arguments that a command needs for its proper execution, which are specified in the command line. For example, in the command `cp f1 f2`, `f1` and `f2` are command line arguments. Within a shell script, you can refer to these arguments by using positional parameters `$1` through `$9`.

Commandline User Interface (CUI) If you use a keyboard to issue commands to a computer's operating system, the computer is said to have a commandline user interface.

Command Mode Operation Operation that consists of key sequences that are commands to a text editor to take a certain action.

Command Substitution A shell feature that allows the substitution of a command by its output. To do so, you enclose a command in back quotes (grave accents). Thus, in the echo \`date\` command, the output of the date command substitutes for the date command, which is then displayed on the display screen.

Comments Short notes placed in program's source code that explain segments of the code. Comments must be distinguished so they are not executed as program commands (statements). For shell scripts, a comment line must start with the # sign.

Communication Channel *See* Physical Communication Medium.

Compatibility Release A release/version of a software program that is meant to provide uniformity between any particular implementation and its perceived competitors.

Compiler A program that takes software written in a high-level language and translates it into the corresponding assembly program. Almost all C and C++ compilers also perform the tasks of preprocessing, assembly, and linking.

Computer Network An interconnection of two or more computing devices. A device on a network is commonly called a host.

Configuration File A file that contains the definitions of various environment variables to set up your environment while you use a shell. Every shell has a start-up configuration file for every shell in your home directory that is executed when that shell starts running (e.g., .cshrc for C shell).

Control Bus A set of parallel wires that carry control information from the CPU to the main memory or an I/O device. For example, it carries the "read" or "write" instruction from the CPU to the main memory.

Controller The electronic part of an I/O device, which communicates with the CPU or other devices.

Control Unit The part of a CPU that interacts with the devices in a computer system (memory, disk, display screen, etc.) via controllers (*see* Controllers) in these devices. It also fetches a program instruction from the main memory, decodes it to determine whether the instruction is valid, and then passes it on to the execution unit (*see* Execution Unit) for its execution.

C Preprocessor A program that takes a C program as input and processes all the statements that start with the # sign. It produces output that is taken by the C compiler as input to produce the assembly code. A typical C compiler performs all the tasks necessary to produce the executable code for a C program. These tasks are preprocessing, compilation, assembly, and linking.

CPU Scheduling A mechanism used to multiplex the CPU among several processes. This results in all processes making progress in a fair manner and increases utilization of hardware resources in the computer system.

CPU Usage The percentage of the time the CPU in a computer system has been used since the system has been up.

Cryptography The science of transforming information so that it is unintelligible to the inexperienced and understandable to those who have some special knowledge, known as the decryption key.

Csh The abbreviation of C shell.

Current Directory The directory that you are in at a given time while using a computer system. In UNIX, the pwd command can be used to display the absolute pathname of your current directory.

Current Job The job (process) that is presently being executed by the CPU.

Cursor The point that tells you at which part of the screen you are located at a given time.

D

Daemon A system process executing in the background to provide a service such as printing. For example, in a typical UNIX system the lpd daemon offers the printing service and fingerd offers the finger service.

Data Bus A set of parallel wires that carry data from the CPU to a subsystem (memory or I/O device), and vice versa.

Decryption The process of converting an encrypted file (*see* Encryption) to its original version.

Desktop Manager A software system that provides a graphical method of interacting with the operating system.

Disk Blocks The unit of disk I/O. It is one or more sectors (512 bytes).

Disk Scheduling In a time-sharing system, several requests can come to the operating system for reading or writing files on a disk. The disk scheduling code in the operating system decides which request should be served first.

Dispatcher Operating system code that takes the CPU away from the current process and gives it to the newly scheduled process (i.e., it saves the state of the current process and loads the state of the newly scheduled process).

Dock, The In OS X, a menu bar found along the bottom of the screen display, that contains a set of buttons that accomplish common tasks in the Aqua GUI.

Domain Name System (DNS) A distributed database that can be used to convert the domain name of a host to its IP address.

Dosunix In OS X, a utility program that converts DOS-formatted text to UNIX-formatted text, and vice versa, by the substitution of Carriage Return and Linefeed characters.

Dot File *See* Hidden File.

Dotted Decimal Notation (DDN) The 32-bit (4-byte) IP addresses are difficult to remember. This notation is used to express every byte of an IP address in equivalent decimal and place dots between them. Thus, the IP address 11000000100011000000101000000001 (in binary) is 192.140.10.1 in the dotted decimal notation.

Dynamic Analysis The analysis of a program as it executes. The analysis comprises debugging, tracing, and performance monitoring of the program, including testing it against product requirements.

E

Editor Buffer While editing a file, the part of the file that is displayed on the screen is stored in an area in the memory called the editor buffer. If your file is larger than what can be displayed on one screen, the buffer contents change as you move the cursor through the file.

Encrypted File A file that contains a file's contents after it has gone through the encryption process (*see* Encryption).

Encryption The process of converting a file's contents to a completely different form by using a process that is reversible, thereby allowing recovery of the original file.

End-of-File (EOF) Marker Every operating system puts a marker at the end of a file, called the end-of-file (EOF) marker.

Environment Variables The shell variables (*see* Shell Variable) whose values control your environment while you use the system. For example, it dictates which shell process starts running and what directory you are put into when you log on.

Ethernet The most famous protocol for physically connecting hosts on local area networks.

Execute Permission A UNIX access privilege that must be set for a file to be executed by using the file name as a command. When set for a directory, it allows the directory to be searched.

Execution Unit Also called the arithmetic and logic unit (ALU), it executes instructions in a program delivered to it by the control unit.

Exit Status A value returned by a process, indicating whether it exited successfully or unsuccessfully. In UNIX, a process returns a status of 0 on success and a non-0 value on failure.

External Command A shell command for which the service code is in a file and not part of the shell process. When a user runs an external command, the code in a corresponding file must be executed by the shell. The file may contain binary code or a shell script.

External Signal A signal whose source is not the CPU. For example, pressing `<Ctrl-C>` on the keyboard sends an external signal, also called keyboard interrupt, to the process running in the foreground.

F

FCFS *See* First-Come, First-Serve Mechanism.

Fibonacci Series A series of positive integers with the first two numbers being 0 and 1, and the next number in the series calculated by adding the previous two numbers. Thus, the series is 0, 1, 1, 2, 3, 5, 8, 13, 21.

FIFO First-in-first-out order.

File Compression The process of shrinking the size of a file.

File Descriptor A small positive integer associated with every open file in UNIX. It is used by the kernel to access the inode for an open file and determine its attributes, such as the file's location on the disk.

File Descriptor Table A per-process table maintained by the UNIX system that is indexed by using a file descriptor to access the file's inode.

File Maintenance The operation of organizing your files according to some logical scheme is known as file maintenace.

File System A file system is a directory hierarchy with its own root stored on a disk or disk partition, mounted under (glued to) a directory. The files and directories in the file system are accessed through the directory under which they are mounted.

File System Structure The structure that shows how files and directories in a computer system are organized. On most contemporary systems, the files and directories are organized in a hierarchical (tree-like) fashion.

File Table A table maintained by the UNIX operating system to keep track of all open files in the system.

File Transfer Protocol An application level protocol in the TCP/IP protocol suite that allows you to transfer file(s) from a remote host to your host, or vice versa. The UNIX `ftp` command can be used to access this Internet service.

Filter A UNIX term for a command that reads input from standard input, processes it in some fashion, and sends it to standard output. Examples of UNIX filters are `sort`, `pr`, and `tr`.

Fink Package Manager In OS X, a Package Management System which allows you to install new and improved packages to the underlying UNIX system.

First-Come, First-Serve Mechanism A scheme that allows print requests (or any other kinds) on the basis of their arrival time, serving the first request first.

Focus Policy In the X Window System and XFree86, the way in which the current position of the cursor is made to appear in the current open window, or the relationship of the current position of the cursor and the current active window.

Folder Also known as a directory, it is a place on the disk that contains files and other folders arranged in some organized and logical fashion.

Foreground Process A process that keeps control of the keyboard when it executes, i.e., the process whose standard input is attached to the keyboard. Only one foreground process can run on a system at a given time.

Forwarding E-Mail Sending a copy of an e-mail message received from someone to another e-mail address.

FTP *See* File Transfer Protocol.

Full Screen Display Editor An editor that displays a portion of the file being edited in the console window or terminal screen.

Full Screen E-Mail Display Systems E-mail systems that allow you to edit any text you see on a single screen display, as you would on a word processor.

Fully Parameterized Client Client software that has the flexibility of allowing identification of a particular port number where a server runs. Telnet is an example of a fully parameterized client, because, although the telnet server normally runs on the well-known port 23, you can run a telnet server on another port and connect to it by specifying the port number as a command line parameter with the `telnet` command. For example, in the `telnet foo.foobar.org 5045` command, the telnet client will try to connect to the server running on port 5045.

Fully Qualified Domain Name (FQDN) The name of a host that includes the host name and the network domain on which it is connected. For example, www.up.edu is FQDN for the host whose name is www.

Function A series of commands that are given a name. The commands in a function are executed when the function is invoked (called).

Function Body The series of commands in a function.

G

Gateway *See* Router.

General Purpose Buffer An area in the main memory maintained by an editor, it contains your most recent cut/copied text.

Getty Process At system bootup time, UNIX starts running a process on each working terminal attached to the system. This process runs in the superuser mode and sets terminal attributes such as baud rate as specified in the /etc/termcap file. Finally, it displays the login: prompt and waits for a user to log on.

Global Variable A variable that can be accessed by children of the process (executing shell script) in which it is defined.

Graphical User Interface (GUI) If you use a point-and-click device, such as a mouse, to issue commands to its operating system, a computer is said to have a graphical user interface.

Group In UNIX, every user of the computer system belongs to a collection of users known as the user's group.

H

Hard Coding Making a value part of a program as opposed to taking it from an outside source such as the keyboard or a file.

Hard Link A mechanism that allows file-sharing by creating a directory entry in a directory to allow access to a file (or directory) via the directory. Loosely applied, it is a "pointer" to the inode of a file to be accessed via multiple pathnames. The `ln` command is used to create a hard link to a file.

Header *See* Program Header.

Header File A file that contains definitions and/or declarations of various items (e.g., constants, variables, and function prototypes) to be used in the program in the C, C++, or Java programming language.

Here Document A Bourne and C shell feature that allows you to redirect standard input of a command in a script and attach it to data in the script.

Hidden File A file whose name starts with a dot (`.`) is known as a hidden file. Such files are not listed in the output of the `ls` command unless you use the `ls –a` command. Examples of hidden files are ~/.bashrc, ~/.cshrc, ~/.login, and ~/.profile.

High-Level Programming Languages Programming languages such as C, C++, Java, FORTRAN, and LISP that are closer to spoken languages and are independent of the CPU used in the computer system.

Home Directory *See* Login Directory.

Home Page The contents of a file displayed on the screen (the actual contents can be multiple screens long) for an Internet site.

Host A hardware resource, usually a computer system, on a network.

Huffman Coding A lossless compression scheme for encoding fixed-length blocks of characters into a variable-length blocks of bits. In this compression scheme we assume that characters occur independently and with known probabilities, and that the probabilities are the same for all positions. If statistics about fixed blocks of characters are known *a priori*, Huffman coding results in optimal codes.

I

I-list A list (array) of inodes on the disk in a UNIX system. *See* Inode.

Indexed Buffer A buffer used by a text editor that allows you to store more than one temporary string.

Index Number *See* Inode Number.

Index Screen The user interface in full-screen-display e-mail systems. It usually consists of three areas: one that contains the message number, sender's e-mail address, date received, size of the message in bytes, and subject line; a second that contains a list of possible commands; and third, a command area where your typed commands are displayed. These screens vary from one system to another.

Infinite Loop *See* Nonterminating Loop.

Information Hiding A technique used to implement software when the internal structure of a data item is not important. What is important is the type of operations that can be performed on the data and the input/output characteristics of the operations.

Init Process The first user process that is created when you boot up the UNIX system. It is the granddaddy of all user processes.

Inode An element of an array on disk (called i-list) allocated to every unique file at the time it is created. It contains file attributes such as file size (in bytes). When a file is opened for an operation (i.e., read), the file's inode is copied from disk to a slot in a table kept in the main memory, called the inode table (*see* Inode Table), so that the file's attributes can be accessed quickly.

Inode Number A 2-byte index value for the i-list (or inode table) used to access the inode for a file.

Inode Table A table (array) of inodes in the main memory that keeps inodes for all open files. The inode number for a file is used to index this array in order to access the attributes of an open file.

Insert Mode of Operation Mode that allows you to input text to be inserted in the document being edited.

Instruction Set The language that a CPU understands. A CPU can understand instructions only in its own instruction set, which is usually a superset of its predecessors made by the same company.

Interactive Operating System An operating system that allows you to interact with your processes. Almost all contemporary operating systems, such as LINUX, UNIX, and Windows, are interactive.

Internal (Built-In) Command A shell command for which the service code is part of the shell process.

Internal Signal (Trap) An interrupt generated by the CPU. This may be caused, for example, when a process tries to access a memory location that it is not allowed to access. (*See* Process Address Space.)

Internet *See* Internetwork.

Internet Domain Name System A distributed database of domain name and IP address mappings. It is maintained by hosts called name servers. Every site on the Internet must have at least one computer that acts as a name server.

Internet Domain Socket An interprocess communication endpoint in BSD-compliant UNIX systems that can be used for communication between processes on the same computer or between different computers on a network or an internet.

Internet Message Access Protocol (IMAP) A method of accessing e-mail or bulletin-board messages at a mail server by using client software, without transferring any files or messages between the two computers.

Internet Service Provider (ISP) A company that offers Internet services such as e-mail and Web browsing through dialup or cable connections.

Internet Login Logging on to a computer on the Internet.

Internet Protocol (IP) The network layer protocol in the TCP/IP protocol suite that routes packets (known as datagrams in TCP/IP terminology) from the source host to the destination host.

Internetwork A network of computer networks. The ubiquitous internet is called the Internet.

Internetworking Making a network of networks. In terms of software, the term internetworking is usually used to refer to writing client-server programs that allow processes on various hosts on the Internet to communicate with each other.

Interpreted Program A program that is executed one command (statement) at a time by the interpreter.

Interpreter A program that executes statements (or commands) in a program one by one. An example of an interpreter is a UNIX shell that reads commands from a keyboard or a shell script.

Interprocess Communication (IPC) Mechanisms Facilities (channels and operations on them) provided by an operating system that allow processes to communicate with each other. UNIX has several channels for IPC including pipes, FIFOs, and BSD sockets. These channels are created by using UNIX systems called pipe, mkfifo (mknod in older systems), and socket.

Interrupt-Driven Interaction A mechanism used in modern computer systems in which applications wait for a signal from a particular input device and then take an appropriate action.

Intranet A network of computer networks in an organization that is accessible to people in the organization only.

Intranet Login Logging on to a computer on an intranet.

I/O Bound Process A process that spends most of its time performing I/O operations, as opposed to performing calculations by using the CPU.

IP Address A 32-bit positive integer (on IPv4) to uniquely identify a host on the Internet. On IPv6, it is a 128-bit positive integer.

Iteration A single execution of a piece of code in a loop. (*See* Loop.)

J

Job A print request or a process running in the background.

Job ID A number assigned to a print job. On some systems, it is preceded by the name of the printer.

Job Number A small integer number assigned to a background process.

K

K Menu The main K Desktop menu, activated from the K Desktop Panel, which contains several useful menu choices, such as launching applications and logging out.

Kernel That part of an operating system software where the real work is done. It performs all those tasks that deal with input and output devices, such as a disk drive.

Keyboard Interrupt An event generated when you press <Ctrl-C> that causes the termination of the foreground process.

Keyboard Macro A collection of keystrokes that can be recorded and then accessed at any time. This capability allows you to define repetitive multiple keystroke operations as a single command and then execute that command at any time—as many times as you want.

Keystroke Command A command executed buy pressing one or more keys.

Kicker Another name for the K Desktop Panel. (*See* Panel.)

Kill Ring Text held in a buffer by killing it and then restored to the document at the desired position by yanking it.

Ksh The abbreviation of Korn shell.

KWM The default Window Manager for the K Desktop Management System.

L

Language Libraries A set of prewritten and tested functions for various languages that can be used by application programmers instead of having to write their own.

Latency Time The time taken by a disk to spin in order to bring the right sector under the read/write head is called the latency time for the disk. It is dictated by the rotation speed of the disk.

Lazy Locking In version control systems that allow multiple users to check out a file for editing, lazy locking does not lock the file until the file contents are changed by a user.

Legacy Code Program written long ago that has no written documentation describing the purpose of various parts of the program.

Library *See* Language Libraries.

Librarian A nickname commonly used for the UNIX `ar` utility that allows you to archive your object files into a single library file and manipulate the archive file in various ways.

Line Display E-Mail System E-mail systems that allow you to edit one line at a time when you are composing an e-mail message. The UNIX `mail` utility is a prime example.

Link A link is a way to connect a file (or directory) to a directory so that the file can be accessed as a child of the directory. The actual file may be in another directory.

Link File A file in UNIX that contains the pathname for a file (or directory). A link file, therefore, "points to" another file. The type of such a file is link (denoted by `l` in the output of the `ls -l` command). (*See* Symbolic Link.)

Literal Constants Constant values such as digits, letters, and strings. For example 103, 'A', 'x', and "Hello".

Loader Program An operating system program that reads an application from the disk, loads it into the main memory, and sets the CPU state so that it knows the location, in the main memory, of the first program instruction.

Local Area Network (LAN) Multiple computing devices interconnected form a LAN if the distance between these devices is small, usually less than 1km.

Local Client A client process that runs on the host that you are sitting in front of.

Local File System File system used for organizing files and directories of a single computer system. By using a local file system on a computer system, you can access files and directories on that system only. (A remote file system allows you to access files on the remote computers on a local network.)

Local Host Computer System The computer system that you are logged on to.

Local Variable A variable that is not accessible outside the executing shell script in which it is defined.

Lock File Under the SCCS utility, the term is used for a file that is created when an SCCS file has been checked out for editing.

Login Directory The directory that you are placed in when you log on.

Login Name *See* Username.

Login Process A process created by the getty process that accepts your password, checks its validity, and allows you to log on by running your login shell process.

Login Prompt A character or a character string displayed by an operating system to inform you that you need to enter your login name and password in order to use the system. In a UNIX system, the getty process displays the login prompt.

Login Shell The shell process that starts execution when you log on.

Loop A piece of code that is executed repeatedly.

Low-Level Programming Language A computer programming language that is closer to the language that a CPU speaks, called the CPU's instruction set. When written in English-like words called mnemonics, this language is called the assembly language for the CPU.

Lpd Short for line printer daemon. (*See* Printer Daemon.)

M

Machine Code *See* Machine Programs.

Machine Cycle A CPU continuously fetches the next program instruction from the main memory, decodes it to verify if the instruction is valid, and then executes it. This process of fetching, decoding, and executing instructions is known as the CPU cycle.

Machine Language The instruction set of a CPU denoted in the form of 0s and 1s.

Machine Programs Programs written in the instruction set of a CPU and expressed in 0s and 1s.

Main Buffer Also known as the editing buffer, or the work buffer, it is the main repository for the body of text that you are trying to create or modify from some previous permanently archived file on disk.

Mainframe *See* Mainframe Computer.

Mainframe Computer A computer system that has powerful processing and input/output capabilities and allows hundreds of users to use the system simultaneously.

Make Rules The rules used by the UNIX make utility to compile and link various modules of a software product.

Menu Bar A collection of menu choices, arranged in either a horizontal or vertical format, that appears on-screen either permanently or when activated using a mouse button.

Message Body The message text of an e-mail message.

Message Header An important structural part of an e-mail message that usually appears at the top of the message text. It normally contains information such as sender's and receiver's e-mail addresses, subject, date and time the message was sent, attachments, and e-mail addresses of the people who received carbon copies of the mail message.

Metacharacters *See* Shell Metacharacters.

Millisecond One thousandth (10^{-3}) of a second.

Minicomputer A mid-range computer that is more powerful than a PC but less powerful than mainframe computers. Like mainframe computers, the minicomputer also allows multiple users to access the system at the same time.

Mode Control Word A string of characters used with the chmod command to specify file privileges.

Multimedia Internet Mail Standard (MIME) An e-mail standard that defines various multimedia content types and subtypes for attachments. In particular, digital images, audio clips, and movie files can be transported via e-mail at-tachments, even on dissimilar e-mail systems, if the systems are MIME-compliant.

Multi-Port Router A router that can interconnect more than two networks.

Multiprogramming In a computer system, the mechanism that allows the execution of multiple processes by multiplexing the CPU. Under multiprogramming, when the process currently using the CPU needs to perform some I/O operation, the CPU is assigned to another process that is ready to execute.

N

Named Pipes Communication channels that can be used by unrelated UNIX processes on the same computer to communicate with each other. The UNIX system call mkfifo (mknod in older systems) is used to create a named pipe.

Name Server A computer system on an Internet site that helps in mapping a domain name to an IP address, or vice versa. Name servers implement the DNS.

Nanosecond One billionth (10^{-9}) of a second.

Network File System (NFS) Client-server software, commonly used on networked UNIX machines, that allows you to access your files and directories from any computer transparently.

Network Interface Card A circuit board in a computer system that has a link level protocol implemented in it. For example, a network card with the Ethernet protocol implemented in it (also referred to as the Ethernet card).

Network Protocol *See* Protocol.

NIC *See* Network Interface Card.

Nice Value A positive integer value used in calculating the priority number of a UNIX process. The greater the nice value for a process, the higher its priority number, resulting in a lower priority.

Noclobber Option A feature in the C and Bash shells that forces the shell to ask you to have the shell prompt you before deleting a file when you execute the rm command.

Nonterminating Loop A loop that does not have a proper termination condition, and therefore does not terminate. This is usually caused by bad programming, but there are certain applications, such as Internet servers (e.g., Web servers), that must use infinite loops to offer the intended service.

Null Command The Bourne shell command:. It does not do anything except for returning true. When used in a C shell script, this command causes the C shell to execute the remaining script under the Bourne shell.

Null String String that contains no value. When displayed on the screen, it results in a blank line.

O

Object Code A program generated by the assembler program. It is in the machine language of the CPU in the computer, but the library calls have not yet been resolved. The task of resolving library calls is performed by another program called linker (or linkage editor).

Open Software System Software whose source code is freely available to the community of users so they can modify it as they wish. An example is the LINUX operating system.

Others In UNIX, when we talk about a user's access permissions for a file, others refers to everyone except the owner of the file and the users in the owner's group.

P

Packages A collection of program components for an application that can be installed on your UNIX system via a Package Management System.

Package Management System A program that installs new or improved applications or utilities on your UNIX system, usually by compiling and linking program modules from packages.

Packet A term used for a fixed-size message (containing data and control information) in networking terminology. A TCP packet is called a segment, and a UDP or IP packet is called a datagram.

Panel In the K Desktop Management System, a menu bar, found by default at the bottom of the screen display, which contains a set of buttons that accomplish common tasks on the K Desktop.

Parallel Execution Simultaneous execution of multiple commands with the help of CPU scheduling. The processes corresponding to all the commands in the command line are executed in the background.

Parent Process A process that creates one or more child processes.

Password A sequence of characters (letters, digits, punctuation marks, etc.) that every user of a time-sharing computer system must have in order to use the system. (*See* Username.)

Pathname The specification of the location of a file (or directory) with a hierarchical file system.

Personal Computer (PC) A computer system that, typically, allows a single user to use the system at any one time, although some of the newer PCs allow multiple users to use the system simultaneously. Examples of such systems are Macintosh and home computers running under DOS, Windows 9X, and LINUX.

Physical Communication Medium The medium used to connect the hardware resources (computers, printers, etc.) on a network. It includes telephone lines, coaxial cable, glass fiber, a microwave link, and a satellite link.

Pipe Character (|) The symbol used to connect the standard output of a command to the standard input of another command in a shell script or while using a shell interactively.

Point-and-Click Device Under a graphical user interface, a device is needed to point to an icon, button, window, or any other part of a window and press (click) a button on the device to perform an operation such as executing a program. Joysticks and mice are examples of point-and-click devices.

Portability The ability to move the source code (*see* Source Code) for a system easily and without major modifications from one hardware platform to another.

Port Number A 16-bit integer number associated with every Internet service, such as telnet. Port numbers are maintained by TCP and UDP. Well-known services such as ftp, http, and telnet have well-known ports associated with them. The port numbers for some well-known services are: 21 for ftp, 80 for http, and 23 for telnet.

Positional Parameters Shell environment variables $1 through $9 that can be used to refer to the command line arguments with which a shell script is executed.

Post Office Protocol (POP) Method of accessing e-mail messages at a mail server by using client software to "download" the messages to the client machine for off-line reading.

Present Working Directory Also known as the current directory, it is the directory that you are in at a given time. You can use the pwd command to display the full pathname of this directory.

Print Queue A queue associated with every printer where incoming print requests are queued if the printer is busy printing, and printed one by one as the printer becomes available.

Printer Daemon *See* Printer Spooler.

Printer Spooler A system process running in the background that receives print requests and sends them to the appropriate printer for printing. If the printer is busy, its request is put in printer's print queue.

Process An executing program.

Process Address Space The main memory space allocated to a process for its execution. When a process tries to access (read or write) any location outside its address space, the operating system takes over, terminates the process, and displays an error message that informs the user of the problem.

Processor Scheduler A piece of code in an operating system that implements a CPU scheduling algorithm.

Program Control Flow Commands *See* Program Control Flow Statements.

Program Control Flow Statements Shell commands (statements) that allow control of a shell script to go from one place in the program to another. Examples of these statements are if-then-else-fi and case.

Program Generation Tools Software tools and utilities that can be used by application programmers to generate program and executable files. Examples of such tools are editors and compilers.

Program Header Important notes at the top of a program file that include information like file name, date the program was written and last modified, author's name, purpose of the program, and a very brief description of the main algorithm used in the program.

Protocol A set of rules used by computers–network protocols in operating system software or network applications–to communicate with each other. Some commonly used protocols in the networking world are ATM, Ethernet, FTP, HTTP, IP, SMTP, TCP, Telnet, and UDP.

Pseudo Devices Special devices in the /dev directory that simulate physical devices.

Pseudonym Also known as an alias, a nickname given to a command or e-mail address.

Public-key Cryptography An encryption technique that uses two keys: a public key and a private key. The private key is kept on your computer and is used to decode encrypted messages. The public key is made available to anyone who wants to decrypt your messages.

Q

Quantum *See* Time Slice.

Queue An arrangement of items/requests/messages for serving them on first-come-first-serve (FCFS) basis.

R

Random Access Memory (RAM) A storage place inside a computer system that is divided into fixed size locations where each location is identified by a unique integer address and any location can be accessed by specifying its address. Although there are RAMs in various I/O devices, RAM is normally used for the main memory in a computer system, which is also a read-write memory.

RCS *See* Revision Control System.

Read Permission The read permission on a UNIX file allows a user to read the file. The read permission on a directory allows us to read the names of files and directories in the directory.

Real-Time Computer System A real-time computer system is one that must generate output for a command within a specified interval of time, or else the output is useless.

Redirection Operator An operator used in a UNIX shell for attaching standard input, standard output, and standard error of a process to a desired file. (*See* Standard Files.)

Registers Temporary storage locations inside a CPU that are used by it as scratch pads.

Regular Expression A set of rules that can be used to specify one or more items in a single character string (sequence of characters). Many UNIX tools such as `awk`, `egrep`, `fgrep`, `grep`, `sed`, and `vi` support regular expressions.

Remote Client A client process running on a host connected to your server via a network connection.

Request For Comments (RFCs) Technical documents describing the Internet architecture, TCP/IP protocol suite, new protocols, revised protocols, and other Internet-related information items are known as Request For Comments (RFCs). Initial versions of RFCs are called Internet Drafts.

Resource Manager The operating system is also known as the resource manager because it allocates and deallocates computer resources in an efficient, fair, orderly, and secure manner.

Resource Utilization The resource utilization of a resource (usually a hardware resource, such as the CPU) is the percentage of the time it has been in use since the computer system has been running.

Revision Control System A UNIX tool for version control.

Rlogin A UNIX network protocol that allows you to log on to another host on a local area network.

Root The login name of the superuser (*see* Superuser) in a UNIX system.

Root Directory The directory under which hang all the files and directories in a computer system in a hierarchical file system. Thus, it is the granddaddy of all the files and directories.

Root Window The window under which all other windows are opened as its children.

Round Robin Scheduling Algorithm A CPU scheduling algorithm in which a process gets to use the CPU for one quantum and then the CPU is given to another process. This algorithm is commonly used in time-sharing systems like UNIX and LINUX for scheduling multiple processes on a single CPU.

Route The sequence of routers that a packet goes through before it reaches its destination.

Router A special host on an internet that interconnects two or more networks and performs routing of packets (called datagrams in the TCP/IP terminology) from the sender host to the receiver host. Routers are also called gateways.

Rsh A UNIX network protocol that allows you to execute a command on another computer on a local area network.

Run-Time Performance The time and space taken by a program to finish its execution.

S

SCCS *See* Source Code Control System.

Search Path A list of directories that your shell searches to find the location of the executable file (binary or shell script) to be executed when you type an external command at the shell prompt and hit the `<Enter>` key.

Sector Disks are read and written in terms of blocks of data, known as sectors. Typical sector size is 512 bytes.

Seek Time The time taken by the read/write disk head to move laterally to the desired track (cylinder) before a read or write operation can take place.

Sequential Execution One-by-one execution of commands; one command finishes its execution and only then does the execution of the second command start.

Server Software In the client-server software model, the server process computes the response for a client request and sends it to the client, who handles it according to the semantics of the command. All Internet services are implemented on the basis of a client-server software model. An example of a server software is a Web server.

Session Leader The login shell process.

Set-Group-ID (SGID) Bit A special file protection bit which, when set for an executable file, allows you to execute the file on behalf of the file's group. Thus, you execute the file with group privileges.

Set-User-ID (SUID) Bit A special file protection bit which, when set for an executable file, allows you to execute the file on behalf of the file's owner. Thus, you execute the file with the owner's privileges.

Sh The abbreviation of Bourne shell.

Shell A computer program that starts execution when the computer system is turned on or a user logs on. Its purpose is to capture user commands (via the keyboard under a CUI and via a point-and-click device under a GUI) and execute them.

Shell Environment Variables Shell variables used to customize the environment in which your shell runs and for proper execution of shell commands.

Shell Metacharacters Most of the characters other than letters and digits have special meaning to a shell and are known as shell metacharacters. They are treated specially, and therefore cannot be used in shell commands as literal characters without specifying them in a particular way.

Shell Prompt A character or character string displayed by a shell process to inform you that it is ready to accept your command. The default shell prompt for Bourne shell is $ and for C it is %. You can change a shell prompt to any character or character string.

Shell Script A program consisting of shell commands.

Shell Variable A memory location that is given a name which can then be used to read or write the memory location.

Signal *See* Software Interrupt.

Simple Mail Transfer Protocol *See* SMTP.

Single Stepping A feature in symbolic debuggers that allows you to stop program execution after every instruction execution. The next instruction is executed by using a command. This is also sometimes called tracing program execution.

SMTP Simple Mail Transfer Protocol, the protocol used in all e-mail systems (e.g., elm, mail, and pine) running on the Internet.

Sniffing Also known as "packet sniffing," it is the equivalent of wire tapping a telephone conversation for Internet traffic.

Soft Link *See* Symbolic Link.

Software Cost Model A model used to estimate the cost of a software product.

Software Interrupt A mechanism used in UNIX to inform a process of some event, such as the user pressing <Ctrl-C> or logging out.

Software Life Cycle A sequence of phases used to develop a software product. These phases normally consist of analysis of the problem, specification of the product, design of the product, coding of the product, testing of the software, installation of the product, and maintenance of the product.

Sorting Arranging a set of items in ascending or descending order by using some sort key.

Sort Key A field, or a portion of an item, used to arrange items in sorted order (*see* Sorting). For example, the social security number can be used as the sort key for sorting employee records in an organization.

Source Code A computer program written in a programming language to implement the solution for a problem.

Source Code Control System A UNIX tool for version control.

Special Character A character that when used in a command is not treated literally by the command. An example of such a character is \c in the System V compliant echo command that forces the command to keep the cursor on the same line.

Special File UNIX files that correspond to devices (*see* Block Special Files and Character Special Files). These files are located in the /dev directory.

Spoofing Creating TCP/IP packets using some other machine's IP address. Also known as "IP Spoofing." The term "Web Spoofing" is used to describe a situation where an attacker creates a shadow "copy" of the entire World-Wide Web.

Standard Error *See* Standard Files.

Standard Files The files where the input of a process comes from and its output and error messages go to. The standard file where a process reads its input is called standard input. The process output goes to standard output, and the error messages generated by a process go to standard error. By default, the standard input comes from your keyboard, and standard output and standard error are sent to the display screen.

Standard Input *See* Standard Files.

Standard Output *See* Standard Files.

Start-up File A file that is executed when you log on or when you start a new shell process. These files belong to a class of files, called dot or hidden files, as their names start with a dot (`.`) and are not listed when you list the contents of a directory by using the `ls` command. Some commonly used start-up files are `.bashrc` (start-up file for Bash), `.cshrc` (start-up file for C shell), `.profile` (executed when you log on to a System V compliant UNIX system), and `.login` (executed when you log on to a BSD compliant system). All of these files reside in your home directory.

States Conditions a process can be in, such as running, waiting, ready, and swapped.

Static Analysis Analyzing the structure and properties of a program without executing it.

Sticky Bit When an executable file with sticky bit on is executed, the UNIX kernel keeps it in the memory for as long as it can so that the time taken to load it from the disk can be saved when the file is executed the next time. When such a file has to be taken out of the main memory, it is saved on the swap space (*see* Swap Space), thus resulting in less time to load it into the memory again.

Subshell A child shell executed under another shell.

Strong Cryptography An encryption method that cannot be penetrated by anyone except those who have the decryption key.

Supercomputer The name used for most powerful computers that typically have many CPUs in them and are used to solve scientific problems that would take a long time to complete on smaller computers. Supercomputers are used in organizations such as NASA and various U.S. national laboratories.

Superuser A special user in every UNIX system who can access any file (or directory) on the system. This user is the system administrator.

Sure Kill Sending signal number 9 to a process. This signal cannot be intercepted by the process receiving the signal and the process is terminated for sure.

Swap Space An area set aside on the disk at the system boot time where processes can be saved temporarily in order to be reloaded into the memory at a later time. The activity of saving processes on the swap space is called swap out, and of bringing them back into the main memory is known as swap in. The time taken to load a process from the swap space into main memory is less than the time taken to load a file from the disk when it is stored in the normal fashion.

Swapper Process A process that swaps in a process from the swap space into the main memory, or swaps out a process from the main memory to the swap space. *See* Swap Space.

Symbolic Constant A constant value that is given to a name so that the name can be used to refer to the value.

Symbolic Debugger A software tool that allows you to debug your program as the program runs.

Symbolic Link When a symbolic link to a shared file (or directory) is created in a directory, a link file is created that contains the pathname of the shared file. The link file, therefore, "points to" the shared file. The `ln -s` command is used to create a symbolic link.

System Bus A set of parallel wires used to take bits from the CPU to a device, or vice versa.

System Call An entry point into the operating system kernel code. System calls can be used by application programmers to have the kernel perform the tasks that need access to a hardware resource, such as reading a file on a hard disk.

System Mailbox File A file that contains all of the e-mail messages that the system has received for you. It is usually under the /usr/spool/mail directory, in a file with your login name.

T

TCP/IP *See* TCP/IP Protocol Suite.

TCP/IP Protocol Suite *See* Transport Control Protocol/Internet Protocol.

Telnet An application level Internet protocol that allows you to log on to a remote host on the Internet.

Text-Driven Operating System An operating system that takes commands to be executed from the keyboard.

Text Editor A text editor allows you to view and edit (add or delete text in) text files. In spite of all that jazz created by word processors and desktop publishing systems, text files remain the most critical part of computing. They are needed to store source programs written in any type of language (e.g., C, C++, Java, Assembly, and Perl), e-mail messages, test data, and program outputs.

Theme In a Window Manager, the style and appearance of windows and their accompanying components.

Threshold Priority A positive integer number used in the expression for calculating the priority number of a process in the UNIX scheduler. It is the smallest priority number for a user-level process. All system processes have priority numbers less than the threshold priority.

Throughput The number of processes finished in a computer system in unit time.

Tiled Display A technique to arrange windows on the display screen so that they are opened next to each other, just like the tiles on a floor.

Time-Sharing System A multiuser, multiprocess, and interactive operating system is known as a time-sharing system. UNIX and LINUX are the prime examples.

Time Slice In a time-sharing system, a time slice, also known as a quantum, is the amount of time a process uses the CPU before it is given to another process.

Topology The physical arrangement of hosts in a network. Some commonly used topologies are bus, ring, mesh, and general graph.

Transport Control Protocol/Internet Protocol The suite of communication and routing protocols that are the basis of the Internet. They include many protocols such as FTP, ICMP, IP, TCP, Telnet, and UDP.

Transport Layer Interface (TLI) Equivalent of BSD sockets in System V-compliant UNIX systems, it allows processes on the Internet to communicate with each other.

Trap *See* Internal Signal.

Trusted Host Some remote login protocols allow login from a set of hosts without verifying passwords. Such hosts are known as trusted hosts.

U

Universal Resource Locator Protocol://IP_address/pathname or protocol://FQDN/pathname. The "protocol" field is usually http, but can be ftp or telnet as well. The "pathname" field is used to identify the location of a file on the host. URLs are commonly used to identify the location of a Web page to be displayed on your screen. An example of a URL is http://www.up.edu/index.html. In this example, the protocol is http, the FQDN is www.up.edu, and the pathname is ~/index.html.

URL *See* Universal Resource Locator.

UNIX Domain Socket An interprocess communication endpoint in BSD-compliant UNIX systems that can be used for communication between processes on the same computer system.

User In UNIX jargon, this term is used for the owner of a file when we talk about file access privileges.

User-Defined Macro A collection of keystrokes that can be recorded and then accessed at any time. This capability allows you to define repetitive multiple keystroke operations as a single command and then execute that command at any time—as many times as you want.

User-Defined Variables These shell variables are used within shell scripts as temporary storage places whose values can be changed when the script executes.

UserID Every user in a time-sharing system, such as UNIX, is assigned an integer number called his/her userid.

Username A name by which a user of a multi-user computer system is known to it. Before you can use the computer system, you must enter your username at the login prompt and hit the <Enter> key, followed by entering your password and hitting the <Enter> key.

V

Version Control In general, the task of managing revisions to any soft product such as documentation for a product; in particular, to manage revisions to a software product.

Virtual Connection A virtual connection is said to be established between client and server processes when the two have made an initial contact to exchange each other's location (usually IP address and protocol port number). The connection request is almost always initiated by the client process. After the virtual connection has been established, the server process understands that it will receive service requests(s) from the client process. The virtual connection is broken when the client process has received the response to its last request and initiates a request for closing the virtual connection.

Virtual Machine The operating system software isolates you from the complications of the hardware resources, such as a disk drive, and is said to provide you a virtual machine that is much easier to use than the real machine.

W

Web Browser An Internet application that allows you to surf the Web by allowing users to, among other things, view Web pages.

Wide Area Network (WAN) Also known as a long haul network, it is a network that connects computing resources that are thousands of kilometer apart, typically spanning several states, countries, or continents.

Window Manager A particular implementation of the functionality provided by a window system.

Window System A graphical system that provides the generic features of a GUI.

Write Permission The write permission on a UNIX file allows a user to write to the file, thus allowing the insertion or deletion of its contents and its removal from the system. The write permission on a directory allows us to create a new file (or directory) under it.

X

X Window System A graphical intermediary between you and the UNIX operating system. It was developed at MIT in 1983 as part of the Athena Project. It is the de facto GUI for UNIX systems that comes as part of the operating system package.

Y

Yank Marking/saving one or more lines of text in a file under the vi editor to be pasted elsewhere in the file.

Z

Zombie *See* Zombie Process.

Zombie Process A UNIX process that has terminated but still has some system resources allocated to it. Thus, a zombie process results in wastage of system resources. It is usually created when its parent process terminates before it finishes execution.

Index

Symbols

* , 16, 21, 76, 173, 179

! , 77, 325

+ , 196

/ , 16, 173, 179

- , 196

, 76

' , 76

% , 77

? , 77

" , 15, 76

$, 2–4, 62, 76

~ , 20, 65, 77

@ , 179

= , 196

: , 94, 99, 102

>& , 321

; , 352

>> , 229, 314

< , 76, 305–306

> , 12, 76, 230, 306–307

| , 28, 76, 325, 560

& , 76, 324–325, 346, 352, 353

` (accent grave), 428–429, 503–504

A

.a files, 589

Access privileges, 188, 193–201, *See also* File security; File sharing

Access speed and memory, 55

Ada, 567, *See also* Programming languages

Address bus, 56

-admin command, 597–599, 612–614, 731

Advanced Research Projects Agency (ARPA), 368

AF_INET, 167

AF_UNIX, 167

AIX systems, 24, 25, 41

Aliases
  -alias command, 31–32, 33
  -emacs, DOS aliases example, 105–106, 118–119

ALU (arithmetic and logic unit), 55

API (application programmer's interface), 38, 57, 59, 680

Appending to files, 228–230, 314–315

Application software, 38, 57, 60

ar command, 589–593, 656, 732

Archives, *See also* Libraries
  building object files into libraries, 589–592
  creating, 552–556, 590
  deleting, 590–591
  extracting modules from, 591–592
  ordering, 593
  table of contents, 590

ARPA (Advanced Research Projects Agency), 366

Array processing, 536–541

Assembler, 566, 568–569

@ command, 501–503, 534–536

at command, 733

AT&T, 47–49

AUI (application user's interface), 38, 57, 60

-awk command, 734